Métis in Canada

Métis in Canada

HISTORY, IDENTITY, LAW & POLITICS

Edited by
Christopher Adams,
Gregg Dahl & Ian Peach

THE UNIVERSITY OF ALBERTA PRESS

Published by

The University of Alberta Press
Ring House 2
Edmonton, Alberta, Canada T6G 2E1
www.uap.ualberta.ca

LIBRARY AND ARCHIVES CANADA
CATALOGUING IN PUBLICATION

Métis in Canada : history, identity, law and
politics / Christopher Adams, Gregg Dahl, and Ian
Peach, editors.

Includes bibliographical references and index.
Issued also in electronic formats.
ISBN 978-0-88864-640-8

1. Métis—History. 2. Métis—Legal status, laws,
etc. 3. Métis—Politics and government. 4. Métis—
Ethnic identity. I. Adams, Christopher, 1960–
II. Dahl, Gregg III. Peach, Ian, 1965–

FC109.M492 2013   971.004′97   C2013-901841-7

First edition, second printing, 2014.
Printed and bound in Canada by Houghton Boston
Printers, Saskatoon, Saskatchewan.
Copyediting and proofreading by Brendan Wild.
Indexing by Judy Dunlop.

The University of Alberta Press is committed to
protecting our natural environment. As part of our
efforts, this book is printed on Enviro Paper: it
contains 100% post-consumer recycled fibres and
is acid- and chlorine-free.

The University of Alberta Press gratefully acknowledges the support received for its publishing
program from The Canada Council for the Arts. The
University of Alberta Press also gratefully acknowledges the financial support of the Government of
Canada through the Canada Book Fund (CBF) and
the Government of Alberta through the Alberta
Multimedia Development Fund (AMDF) for its publishing activities.

This book has been published with the help of
a grant from the Canadian Federation for the
Humanities and Social Sciences, through the
Awards to Scholarly Publications Program,
using funds provided by the Social Sciences and
Humanities Research Council of Canada.

Canada   Canada Council   Conseil des Arts
          for the Arts   du Canada

Alberta
Government

To my wife Sue and my parents Paul and Louise Adams for their kindness, love and support; and numerous professors who helped guide me, sometimes with success, through days of intellectual darkness. — CHRISTOPHER

To my parents, for distilling my curious mind and always pointing out to me when the Emperor was naked. And, to the memory of my friend Dr. Jerry Hanham, for his willingness to listen tirelessly to my thoughts and offer encouragement nevertheless. — GREGG

To those who engaged my interest in constitutional law, equality, diversity and justice, most notably John D. Whyte; to my Métis friends, who taught me so much about the diversity of identities that exist within the community labelled "Métis"; and to the memory of our late friend Jerry Hanham, as loyal and generous a friend and colleague as one could ever ask for. — IAN

Contents

Introduction

THE IDEA behind having a collection of essays devoted to Métis in Canada began developing at the 2009 Aboriginal Policy Research Conference in Ottawa, at which the three of us were in attendance and presenting papers. Over dinner one evening, possibly inspired by the breadth of research presented at the conference, we began to discuss the challenges involved in understanding the complexity that is the Métis reality in Canada, particularly after the 2003 *Powley* decision.[1] Out of this discussion came our two-year journey toward the completion of *Métis in Canada: History, Identity, Law and Politics*, which included a call for contributors across multiple disciplines and regions, the usual editing, and follow-up discussions with each of the worthy contributors you will meet in this volume, all of whom have been a joy to work with.

As indicated, our initial discussions revolved around the change to the Métis conceptual landscape that was the outcome of the 2003 *Powley* decision from the Supreme Court of Canada. One interesting aspect of the written decision was that the Court referred to a scholarly paper from a 1985 collection of essays on the Métis. This paper was "Many Roads to Red River: Métis Genesis in the Great Lakes Region, 1680–1815" in *The New*

Peoples: Being and Becoming Métis in North America, edited by Jennifer Brown and Jacqueline Peterson.[2] This seminal collection contains several papers that were the most advanced scholarly writing on the Métis at the time. Over 20 years later, we wanted to bring together a collection of papers written after the *Powley* decision; a collection in which all the papers were written a sufficient amount of time after the decision that the implications of the conceptual change it produced had had time to seep into the thinking of people engaged with Métis issues. We also wanted to bring together a collection that provided a forum for some relative new-comers to Métis scholarship and policy because their novel and innovative approaches to the developing understanding of the Métis reality provide us the opportunity to make a unique contribution to the body of literature on the Métis in Canada.

One of the preoccupations of Métis studies prior to the *Powley* decision was a keen attention to terminology. Writers invented terms to clarify the concepts they used to identify the people they were talking about. We want to take notice of this issue and preoccupation, since it was the focus of much discussion in Métis studies.[3] In this collection, the reader should rely on the explicit intentions of the authors, should any distinctions in spelling or word use be needed in order to bring clarity to the specific chapter. The general issue seems, ultimately, to have been anchored in a desire to distinguish the Red River Métis from other Métis populations, a consequence of an emerging nationalism and sense of distinct identity that the Red River Métis are widely acknowledged to have developed in the 1980s and 1990s. It is also important to point out that there has been an aversion to the use of the term "half-breed," which resulted in the invention of terms for the Half-breeds from the English-speaking parishes of the Red River Settlement, including "country-born" and "mixed-blood." As well, a mixture of capitalization and italics in the term Métis was used primarily to avoid the use of the word "half-breed."

For its part, the Supreme Court of Canada was far less concerned about terminology than it was about the historical realities of Métis communities—and certainly far less concerned about terminology than the scholarly and activist communities—when confronted with the need to make a decision in *Powley*. According to the Supreme Court, if a Métis group is to be considered a rights-bearing community, the historical dynamic of an ethnogenesis as a distinct community is a necessary condition. The Supreme Court did not, however, bother with any worries about terminology; whatever this distinct community decided to label itself, it was a Métis community, in the Court's sense of the term, if the substantive conditions had been met. It is the substantive aspects that were important to the Court that provided the following definition in the *Powley* decision: "A Métis community is a group of Métis with a distinctive collective identity, living together in the same geographic area and sharing a common way of life."[4] Thus, according to the Supreme Court, a Métis community could conceivably exist anywhere in Canada.

After the *Powley* decision, the Métis were no longer bound to Rupert's Land. The Supreme Court conceptually set the Métis peoples free from the historical boundaries of the fur trade in Canada. And, for the first time, the possibility was raised in the *Powley* decision that the miscegenation of Inuit and Europeans could be Métis. Such changes were profound and completely undermined government policy on Métis issues, as well as the exclusiveness of Red River Métis nationalism. The changes also went beyond the issues debated in the earlier works of John Foster, Jacqueline Peterson and Jennifer Brown.[5] Whereas these authors looked to the theoretical work of anthropologist Fredrik Barth when considering a theory of the roots of a Métis population, the Court looked more to the expertise of historians to provide documentary evidence to support factual findings that could then be used to support judgments. And finally, whereas the Métis scholars tried to distinguish community within diversity, the Court sought to allow greater diversity within community.

The use of expert historical witnesses and texts in trials has brought an interesting dynamic to Métis scholarship. In the recently published *Contours of a People: Métis Family, Mobility, and History*, Jacqueline Peterson expressed concern about the use of her paper "Many Roads to Red River: Métis Genesis in the Great Lakes Region, 1680–1815" in the *Powley* decision. In her chapter entitled "Red River Redux: Métis Ethonogenesis and the Great Lakes Region,"[6] which was written almost a decade after the decision, Peterson has opined that the court missed the point of her earlier scholarship, which posited the potential formation of a rights-bearing community in the region. According to her, the necessary awakening did not actually occur in the region. The failure of the court to distinguish properly between "Métis" and "metis" erroneously resulted in the court recognizing a Métis community at Sault Ste. Marie. "Red River Redux" contains the idea that the term "Métis" should only be applied to the French-speaking Red River people and by extension should not be a term applied to any other communities, unless they also underwent a similar awakening of national consciousness.

Arthur Ray described exactly the same dynamic in his book *Telling It to the Judge*.[7] An expert witness for many Aboriginal rights cases in Canada, including those related to the Métis, Professor Ray was an expert witness at the *Powley* trial. In relation to that particular case, Ray wrote: "I found that the government records pertaining to the preparation of the negotiation of the Robinson Treaties also affirmed the existence of the Métis as an Aboriginal People by the eve of the treaty and acknowledged that their concerns had to be addressed."[8] It is clear here that Ray's use of the term "Métis" is related to the concept of a rights-bearing Aboriginal people as written in the Constitution of Canada, rather than the sense of the term "Métis" as used by Peterson. The conflation of these two different meanings for the term "Métis" blends the rights of an Aboriginal people in Canada with the rights of a people with a nationalist consciousness that also happens to be Aboriginal. The rights of the Métis in the vicinity of Sault Ste. Marie could arguably be rooted in a self-consciousness about rights to land, rather than being rooted in a consciousness about rights to land that is also nationalistic in nature. Such a distinction is rather nuanced and would not likely be found in a judgment about Aboriginal rights. Scholars might proceed to embrace this rather subtle distinction in future work about the Métis. The resulting scholarship might be interesting. It might also produce greater worries for scholars who serve as expert witnesses, or whose works are referred to in Métis Aboriginal rights cases in Canada; they may find that judges necessarily gloss over their scholarly distinctions in favour of pragmatic and enforceable judgments.

Obviously, questions of terminology have not disappeared because of the *Powley* decision. In fact, the decision has resulted in further debate. In order to give the reader a sense of our approach in this collection of essays, we want to be as clear as possible about our use of the term "Métis." It is more akin to a signifier of a mode of being, a particular mode of humanity, peoples of a particular type, rather than the signifier of a particular population situated in a specific time or place. Our use of the term is perhaps most similar to the use of "Métis" by the Supreme Court of Canada in the *Powley* decision. Each chapter here may contain ideas that apply to a subset of the peoples we call "Métis," but this collection does not exhaust the possible applications of the term. For example, we do not have a chapter here on the Métis people of eastern Canada, nor the Métis in the territories of northern Canada, although we fully recognize the possibility that there are Métis people in these geographic areas. We have attempted to ensure clarity about which people an author addresses within each chapter, rather than attempt to craft a theoretical terminological framework into which all the contributions would fit. We do not believe such a framework exists and that it would be a fruitless exercise to attempt to create one. Hopefully, this idea should become evident once the reader has read the entire collection. The Métis are not a singularity; they are a distinct, but also diverse, group of Aboriginal peoples in Canada.

Given their diversity and uniqueness, the issues surrounding the Métis in Canada are actively considered today in academia and by courts and governments across the country. It is not just professors and students of Aboriginal issues that seize upon the idea of what it means to be Métis in Canada. While theories of Métis identity and rights may arise

in an academic setting, governments across Canada continue to grap-
ple with the practical implications of court decisions such as *Powley* that
have changed the understanding of Métis rights, community and identity.
In addition, Métis political organizations struggle to defend the interests
of their constituents in light of these conceptual developments and their
implications for people on the ground.

To illustrate our point that the issues contained in this collection are
alive and occupy an element of the public discourse on Aboriginal issues
in Canada, the reader should consider the following situation. As this
book goes to print, the Supreme Court of Canada is considering the legal
aspects of the promises made to the children of the Half-breeds and Métis
people of the Red River Settlement at the time Canada created the province of Manitoba. The Métis of Manitoba, as represented by the Manitoba
Metis Federation, and several Métis individuals in Manitoba are appeal-
ing the two decisions that went against them in both the trial and appeal
courts of Manitoba.[9]

The legal strategy of the appellants was clearly stated at the Supreme
Court of Canada hearing by their lawyer, Thomas Berger, on December
13, 2011. After obtaining a declaration from the Court that aspects of the
promises, which became entrenched in sections 31 and 32 of the *Manitoba
Act*, were not carried out properly, the appellants would then seek to begin
negotiations with Canada and Manitoba on how to redress the failure of
the Crown to completely fulfill those obligations. Most of the Court hearing focussed on the issues related to section 31. However, the facta of each
of the parties give a more balanced approach to all of the issues argued in
the case. These documents should be considered required reading for any
students of the legal issues related to the Métis of Manitoba.

As one would expect, at the Supreme Court hearing several judges
asked pointed questions, with many relating to several of the issues
raised in our collection (i.e., identity, legal, political). As we indicated
above, some of these issues have been alive in Manitoba and elsewhere
for the past 140 years and continue to be debated in the courts of Canada.

Such debates will evolve as the courts in Canada continue to rule on the Aboriginal rights of the Métis and render decisions that shift the legal debates between anthropological and historical influences. In the Manitoba case, Madam Justice Rosalie Abella asked the fundamental question about who would be the beneficiaries of any eventual land claim that the appellants wish to create from the declaration they seek. Thomas Berger, the lawyer for the Manitoba Métis, responded that the class of beneficiaries would be determined through initial negotiations between Canada, Manitoba, and the Métis.

Madam Justice Marie Deschamps also approached the issue of who would represent the beneficiaries of a modern land claim with the Métis of Manitoba and was told that the Manitoba Metis Federation (MMF) would be the body to speak on behalf of the Métis of Manitoba. However, any negotiations between Canada, Manitoba, and the Métis would be difficult and they may not result in the outcome described in Court. One difficulty relates to the membership rules of the MMF. If the beneficiaries of a modern claim would be the ancestors of the children who are described in section 31 of the *Manitoba Act* (who are the people logic would seem to imply), then the class of beneficiaries would not be congruent with the membership of the MMF; it may be both narrower and broader than the MMF membership. It is clear that not all the members of the MMF are ancestors of the children named in the *Manitoba Act*. Equally, it is possible that the negotiated class of beneficiaries may result in the formulation of a class of people that has very little relationship with the present-day MMF. Berger, however, maintained that any initial discussion between Canada, Manitoba, and the Métis should begin with the MMF. The parties named may be the most pragmatic start to such a conversation but the outcome is not a foregone conclusion. If the appellants win the declaration they are seeking, the result may be a close examination of the idea of *who* is a living descendant of the people named in the *Manitoba Act, who* would be included in the class of beneficiaries of any land claim negotiation with Canada, and *who* would represent such a class of beneficiaries. The difficulties that animated the judges' questions at the hearing are reflected in the themes we have chosen to examine in this volume. Being Métis in Canada cannot be captured by a homogenous set of rules and descriptions. Being Métis in Canada, we think, is a unique modality of being that is accompanied by diverse histories, identities, laws and political dynamics.

Census data and the Métis

Census data say very little about a person who is Métis in Canada. So much more can and needs to be known about the context within which Métis identification occurs. To understand this point it is useful to consider a few possible examples. If considering a group of Métis from a legal perspective, other information—in addition to self-reported identity— needs to be known. If the context is political, the details that need to be known are different again; if historical, still other information is important. The structure of our collection therefore includes four major sections containing chapters that are devoted to particular issue domains: identity, history, law and politics.

Some readers may be surprised to learn it is not at all clear that the set of people who self-identify as Métis are exactly the same set of people who are affected by the issues raised and considered in these chapters. As well, the authors may not agree with each other on the issues raised. This lack of clarity and consensus is just one aspect of the interest and curiosity that surrounds the idea of being Métis in Canada. Examples that illustrate this complexity are numerous. A person can identify as Métis and not be legally entitled to exercise the Métis Aboriginal right to hunt for food as set out in the *Powley* decision of the Supreme Court of Canada. Self-identification is only one aspect of the determination of which persons can legally hunt for food as Métis under the protection of a right embedded in the Constitution of Canada. Furthermore, being legally entitled to exercise the Métis right to hunt for food does not necessarily indicate that such a person is also a member of a Métis political organization. The Métis political organizations do not accept members simply on the basis of self-identification as a Métis person. As well, a Métis person does not need to be a member of a political organization in order to exercise his or her right to hunt for food.

Clearly, self-identification is just one of the many facets of being Métis. To say "I am Métis" definitely says something about the speaker, but more needs to be known before it can also be said how the speaker is involved in the issues contained in this collection of essays. At this point, however, let us begin with the basic Government of Canada–endorsed snapshot of the Métis based on the most recent Census data; as the reader moves through this collection of chapters it will (hopefully) become apparent that, as with the other Aboriginal populations, there is much more to being Métis in Canada.

The following table is based on the 2006 Canadian Census and provides an overview of the number of individuals in Canada who identified themselves (along with those in their household) as being Métis. The first column of figures shows the number of individuals who reported being Métis. Over one-third of a million (389,785) Canadians reported being Métis, with Alberta having the largest Métis population (85,500), followed by Ontario (73,605), Manitoba (71,805), British Columbia (59,445) and Saskatchewan (48,115). By adding up the relevant figures in the middle column ("Percentage Distribution"), one can see that a majority (52%) of self-reported Métis people in 2006 resided in the Prairie Provinces, and no less than 86% resided in provinces west of the Ontario–Quebec boundary.

The right hand column reveals that the number of Canadians who identify themselves as Métis grew significantly in the ten years between the 1996 and 2006 Census. According to Statistics Canada, Métis population growth outpaced "the growth of the other Aboriginal groups, as well as that of the non-Aboriginal population, over the past decade. Of the 1,172,790 people who identified themselves as an Aboriginal person in the 2006 Census, 389,785 reported that they were Métis. This population has almost doubled (increasing by 91%) since 1996. This rate of growth was more than 11 times that of the 8% in the non-Aboriginal population during

TABLE 0.1 *Population profile (self-identification)*

	Population	Percentage Distribution (of total Canada)	Percentage Change from 1996 to 2006
British Columbia	59,445	15%	+132
Alberta	85,500	22%	+73
Saskatchewan	48,115	12%	+34
Manitoba	71,805	18%	+58
Ontario	73,605	19%	+242
Quebec	27,980	7%	+80
Atlantic Region	18,805	5%	+192
Territories	4,515	1%	+5
Canada	389,785	100%	+91

Source: Statistics Canada, 2006 Census.

the same period. In comparison, since 1996 the First Nations population increased by 29% and the Inuit population by 26%."[10] This growth is attributed to a number of factors, most notably rising fertility rates, a growing sense of pride among Métis, and the benefits that are available to Métis, which include affirmative action hiring practices, social programs and hunting rights, among others.

Identity

The data, and particularly the trends in the data, are interesting, but what do they really tell us about Métis identity? In Part One of this collection there are three chapters that address the complex topic of Métis identity. While the issues are diverse, collectively they pertain to Métis identity and how it is essentially intertwined with the history of the Métis people. Their depiction in art and literature, produced contemporaneously with the emergence of the Métis in the Great Lakes region, is the focus of the chapter written by Gloria Bell; reconstructing feminine Métis identity through the use of narratives produced by Métis women occupies the thoughts of Laura-Lee Kearns; and finally, Gregg Dahl examines the change from the use of the term "Half-breed" to "Métis" for purposes of identity.

In "Oscillating Identities: Re-presentations of Métis in the Great Lakes Area in the Nineteenth Century," Gloria Bell argues that analyzing the written and visual documentation of the Métis in the Great Lakes region in the nineteenth century reveals much about both the observed (the Métis) and the observer (the European chroniclers). Asserting that the Métis have existed in the Great Lakes region for several centuries, the record of their presence depends on who is telling the story or creating the image. Nineteenth-century writers and artists, including Frances Anne Hopkins, Anna Jameson, Paul Kane, William Keating, Henry Rowe Schoolcraft, George Winter and others, described and depicted mixed-heritage peoples in order to entertain European audiences and to create government reports, primarily for the benefit of non-Aboriginal audiences. Describing how the Métis dressed and lived contributes to our understanding of what their clothing communicated to European audiences. It is true that literary and visual depictions were mediated through lenses of European superiority, colonization and racism, yet they provide insight into how the Métis were understood within frontier society. Bell suggests that the varied descriptions and images reflect a multiplicity of identities that the Métis in Canada had, and that they continue to have.

The next chapter in this first section draws upon the Indigenous practice of listening and sharing stories to increase understanding and knowledge. Laura-Lee Kearns explores the silence around Métis identities. She shares part of her own story, that of her mother, and that of two Métis Elders, to inform the reader about her response to understanding Métis identities. By recognizing that the legacies of colonialism and state-sanctioned assimilation policies have resulted in the raising of many people without their Aboriginal cultures, Kearns seeks to understand the everyday forces that contributed to the silence surrounding Métis identity. In recognizing that the many different stories of Métis people need to enter the public realm in order to enable us to begin learning about the past, the author presents her findings as poems to remind herself—and the reader—of the complexity of Métis people and their personal histories. She therefore invites and encourages multiple interpretations of the narratives—and endeavours to acknowledge, support, and affirm Métis identity construction, diversity, fluidity, resilience and silence—through these and other Métis narratives.

The section's third and final chapter was written by one of the editors of *Métis in Canada*, Gregg Dahl, who is a descendant of a Half-breed family that lived in St. Paul's parish in the Red River Settlement, which is now located in downtown Winnipeg, Manitoba. He clearly, and quite comfortably, identifies himself as a "Half-breed." In his chapter, Dahl examines the following questions: Is the term "Half-breed" in the Constitution of Canada? Are the terms "Half-breed" and "Métis "just a matter of English and French translation? Is the same set of people referred to by either term? When did the Half-breeds become the Métis? Could a Half-breed pass the *Powley* test? If yes, would a Half-breed then have a Métis Aboriginal right to hunt for food or engage in other culturally important activities; or, could there be such a thing as a Half-breed Aboriginal right? The answers to these questions are a stark reminder that history is an essential element of the identity of the Métis in Canada, and should neither be ignored nor revised in accordance with the vagaries of language or political preferences.

History

The history of the Métis is quite often characterized as that of a "forgotten people." While understandable, this characterization is not entirely accurate. The amount of information and the written record generated contemporaneously with the ethnogenesis of the Métis in Canada is enormous. The archival records of the fur trade companies (i.e., those of the Hudson's Bay Company and the North West Company), the scrip records, and a wide range of the legal records all undermine the claim that the

Métis are a "forgotten people." It may be more accurate to characterize the history of the Métis as the history of an "ignored people." After all, the extensive written record was nearly completely ignored until 1945, when an academic from France, Marcel Giraud, in *The Métis in the Canadian West*, spawned a focussed interest in the Métis.

Today, the Métis in Canada are the subject of extensive historical analyses using a variety of analytic approaches. The three chapters in this second section of the book help us to understand their history as a political rather than a purely social or anthropological phenomenon; these chapters also provide us with insights through the lens of economic history, political history and, lastly, through the newly discovered writings of Louis Riel.

In the first chapter of Part Two, Darren O'Toole argues that a particular brand of social history analysis has contributed to a better understanding of the ethnogenesis of the Métis in Canada. However, the author argues that there is a need to recall the nuances of the findings concerning Métis identity formation. The research produced, using what he claims is social history with a revisionist slant, does not support the claim made by Gloria Bell in an earlier chapter that a Métis identity crystallized in the Great Lakes region before it did on the Western Plains. He argues that the occupational niche of mixed-bloods was a factor in the leap from entity to identity, but it was not the only factor. Further, if there is no singular mixed-blood identity—as the distinction between the Half-Breeds and the Métis in Red River articulated by Dahl clearly illustrates—then the key factors in identity formation are institutional structures and practices. O'Toole concludes that a more robust understanding of the Métis in Canada must have recourse to political history, and in particular to historical institutionalism and social movement theory.

In the second chapter of Part Two, Liam J. Haggarty challenges the traditional economic history of the Métis in Canada that is often told as the story of the fur trade. That story begins with the emergence of "mixed-bloods," the offspring of European male traders and Indigenous women, a result that, as a social phenomenon, was perfectly suited to economic patterns of trade between the two races. Working as translators, guides, freighters, trappers, middlemen and provisioners, the Métis prospered as the fur trade boomed. They raised families, built communities, and contributed significantly to the spread of mercantilism in North America and the building of a country. But this prosperity would not last. Over time the hunting and trapping economy declined as settlers and agents of the newly minted Dominion of Canada pushed farther west in increasing numbers. Lands that once were commercially valued only for the animals that lived on them became highly valued as potential sites for settlement, railways, and speculation. As told often, the Métis opposed encroachments onto their lands, yet, in the end, resistance appeared to be largely futile. The fur industry faded and the Métis in Canada were exiled to economic marginality. In fact, Haggarty argues the story of Métis economics actually begins before the fur trade and the arrival of non-indigenous peoples. Although seemingly illogical, Haggarty deftly argues that the experiences of Métis people are far more diverse and varied than the fur trade narrative allows. The author is therefore seeking to address the silences in the traditional narrative, and the reader will find that he posits admirably an alternative story of Métis economic history.

The writings by Louis Riel are presented by Glen Campbell and Tom Flanagan in their chapter, "Newly Discovered Writings of Louis Riel." Both Campbell and Flanagan were involved with others who in 1985 published *The Collected Writings of Louis Riel/Les Écrits complets de Louis Riel*.[11] This historically significant five-volume collection contains all of Riel's writings that had been discovered up to that point. The chapter put forward here in Part Two presents a few more materials that have recently come to light: a letter by Louis Riel to his patron Sophie Masson, written on December 30, 1858; a letter by Riel to his former schoolmate, the poet Eustache Prud'homme, on December 14, 1869; and a set of short English poems that Riel composed while imprisoned in Regina in 1885 just prior to his hanging. No doubt this new contribution by Campbell and Flanagan will further our understanding of this Métis leader.

Law

With the constitutional recognition of the Métis as one of the Aboriginal peoples of Canada in 1982, Métis identity is as much a matter of legal categorization as it is a matter of cultural, historical and sociological reality. The access to economic opportunities and political power that recognition as a Métis rights-bearer brings to individuals makes the appropriate determination of who is Métis all the more important, but it also creates incentives for the state to establish all-encompassing identity categories that are too abstract to reflect the complex reality of being Métis. The two essays in Part Three, which in many ways complement the chapters in Part One of this collection, address how the judicial system has defined Métis and the problematic aspects of converting identity questions into exercises in legal categorization.

The first chapter in this section, by co-editor Ian Peach, reviews the history of Métis Aboriginal rights jurisprudence in Canada. His essay shows that the approach used by the courts to determine Métis identity has changed radically in the last decade. He sees the positive in this change, in that the courts now recognize that the Métis are a distinct community, with a distinct history and culture, rather than merely a sort of not-quite-First Nations community. In contrast, the other essay in this section serves to reveal the problems inherent in turning identities into tools of legal categorization, an issue that Peach does not dispute.

Jeremy Patzer's essay challenges the conventional view of the Supreme Court of Canada's *Powley* decision, which affirmed the Métis' constitutional right to hunt, as an important accomplishment for Métis. He notes the risk that, in the search by the courts for a guide to understanding Métis identity, the courts have treated that identity as being determined by a few essential characteristics, ignoring much of the complexity of

Métis identity as irrelevant to legal categorization. As such, the courts may have created new divisions and new exclusions among groups previously united by their shared history and social solidarity, even as they have recognized the group they label "Métis" as being a community bearing Aboriginal rights. Such criticisms pose serious normative challenges to the very exercise of legal categorization.

Politics

The fourth and final section of *Métis in Canada* contains four chapters that explore a number of political dimensions of the Métis people and their representative organizations. Two of these essays contribute to the existing literature by providing an overview of how Métis organizations have developed in response to historical circumstances, cultural survival and political necessity. In the first of these two chapters, Kelly Saunders shows how the Métis people and their leaders have developed their own governing institutions and organizations in the face of what she describes as "constraints imposed by the Crown." Building on the works of those such as Joe Sawchuk (1978), who writes about the circumstances of twentieth-century Aboriginal organizations and their developments, Saunders examines the early arrangements of Métis governance, as well as the evolution of such modern organizations as the Métis National Council and provincial Métis Nation entities, such as the Manitoba Metis Federation.

Siomonn P. Pulla also builds on the work of Sawchuk (among others) and provides us with a historical overview of organizational developments among the Métis people. He places these developments within the contexts both of the efforts of Métis people to achieve self-determination and to exercise a voice in democratic politics, as well as the broader context of the politics of Aboriginal representation in Canada.

The third chapter in Part Four, authored by Janique Dubois, focusses on the particular history of the efforts by Métis in Saskatchewan to create institutions of self-government. She places recent developments in the context of the history of Métis self-government initiatives in the nineteenth and early twentieth centuries. With this history as background, Dubois explores how the adoption of a constitution by the Métis Nation-Saskatchewan in 1993 and the subsequent passage by the Saskatchewan Legislature of *The Métis Act* in 2002 has put the Métis of Saskatchewan on a path that leads away from being organizational service providers and toward being decision makers, with their own institutions of government and an intergovernmental relationship with the provincial government. She also notes, however, the challenges that still confront the Métis of Saskatchewan in making this conversion to a self-governing people, providing a thorough and honest discussion of the evolution of Métis institutions in Saskatchewan.

The fourth and final chapter in Part Four is written by the third co-editor of this collection, Christopher Adams. Here, Adams shifts the focus from the historical development of Métis governing organizations to an examination of the tools that Métis leaders and their organizations are currently using to influence their provincial government counterparts, as well as public opinion, on key issues. Using an interest group theoretical approach, Adams provides results based on his in-depth interviews with the leaders of Métis Nations and organizations across Canada.

The three editors take great pride in presenting to you this collection of essays. We hope that it furthers our understanding, as members of the multinational political community and society called Canada, of what it means to be Métis in Canada.

Notes

1. R. v. Powley, [2003] SCR 207, 2003 SCC 43 (hereafter *Powley*).

2. *Powley*, at paras 39, 41–42, which contain the references to Peterson's paper. It is contained in full in *The New Peoples: Being and Becoming Métis in North America*, ed. Jacqueline Peterson and Jennifer S.H. Brown (Winnipeg: University of Manitoba Press, 1985). The book is a collection of papers presented at a 1981 conference on the Métis in North America that focussed on understanding the Métis as an Aboriginal people emerging from post-European contact.

3. John Foster calls the debate over terminology unprofitable and refers his reader to Jennifer Brown's paper, "Linguistic Solitudes and Changing Social Categories" in *Old Trails and New Directions: Papers of the Third North American Fur Trade Conference*, ed. C.M. Judd and A.J. Ray (Toronto: University of Toronto Press, 1980), 150–58; John E. Foster, "Some Questions and Perspectives on the Problem of métis Roots," in *The New Peoples: Being and Becoming Métis in North America*, ed. Jacqueline Peterson and Jennifer S.H. Brown (Winnipeg: University of Manitoba Press, 1985), 73–91. The debate settles around the use of "mixed-blood" and "metis" to indicate English- and French-speaking people respectively. The term "Métis" is reserved for the nationalist people. We want to acknowledge these debates, which have, hopefully, been overcome here by explicit explanation in the chapters of this volume.

4. *Powley, supra* note 1, at para 12.

5. See Foster, "Some Questions and Perspectives," 73–91. Also, see both Peterson's and Brown's papers in the same collection.

6. See Jacqueline Peterson, "Red River Redux: Métis Ethnogenesis and the Great Lakes Region," in *Contours of a People: Metis Family, Mobility, and History*, ed. Nicole St-Onge, Carolyn Podruchny and Brenda Macdougall (Norman: University of Oklahoma Press, 2012), 22–58.

7. Arthur J. Ray, *Telling it to the Judge: Taking Native History to Court* (Montreal: McGill-Queen's University Press, 2011).

8. Ray, *Telling it to the Judge*, 96.

9. At the time of writing, the decision was expected to be delivered in the first half of 2013.

10. Statistics Canada, "2006 Census: Aboriginal Peoples in Canada in 2006," www12.statcan.gc.ca/census-recensement/2006/as-sa/97-558/tables-tableaux-notes-eng.cfm.

11. George F.G. Stanley, Raymond Huel, Gilles Martel, Thomas Flanagan and Glen Campbell, eds., *The Collected Writings of Louis Riel/Les Écrits complets de Louis Riel*, 5 vols. (Edmonton: University of Alberta Press, 1985).

PART ONE **Identity**

Oscillating Identities | 1

Re-presentations of Métis in the Great Lakes Area
in the Nineteenth Century

GLORIA JANE BELL

PEOPLE OF Indian (Cree, Iroquois, Ojibwa) and European (English, French, Irish, Scottish) heritage, métis, have existed in the Great Lakes region for several centuries, yet their identities have oscillated over time.[1] The record of their presence varies depending on who is telling the story or creating the image. Nineteenth-century travellers and artists including Frances Anne Hopkins, Anna Jameson, William Keating, Henry Rowe Schoolcraft, George Winter and others described and depicted métis peoples in order to entertain non-Native audiences, to create government reports, and to legitimize colonial expansion. Analyzing this written and visual documentation will shed light on how métis, who were conceived of as "other" for their combination of races and their threats to Eurocentric notions of racial and cultural superiority, were perceived by a broad public audience. Descriptions of how métis dressed will be useful in understanding what their clothing communicated to Euro-Canadian, American and British audiences and also how they understood their own cultural identities. Because these literary and visual depictions are not merely reflective of ideas, but "participate in the production of meaning, in the dynamic construction of identities," they provide a particularly rich lens through which to explore how métis were understood in frontier society by non-Natives.[2] How did métis people negotiate these images and depictions? While there are no existing written records by métis within the Great Lakes area, their material culture (sashes, beadwork and quillwork on coats, bags, leggings) evidences how their identities shifted depending on employment, kin networks and trade relations.

As I will argue, identities in the nineteenth century for métis within the Great Lakes area were not conceived of on a nationalistic scale. For this reason then, I will refer to historical configurations of métis identity within the Great Lakes using a lower-case "m," as scholars such as John E. Foster have done.[3] When referring to Métis from the Red River Settlement, Manitoba, I will use an upper-case "M" to highlight their collective efforts to form a Métis consciousness.[4]

Historiography

Most curators and scholars argue that the development of the Métis nation occurred at the Red River Settlement and that Métis families dispersed from there to other regions. As will be discussed, both Ted Brasser, a former curator at the Canadian Museum of Civilization, and Sherry Farrell Racette, a Native Studies scholar and artist, acknowledge the presence of métis in the Great Lakes area but do not describe them as having a distinct nation similar to the Métis of the Red River Settlement.[5] Historian Susan Sleeper Smith has argued that within the Great Lakes region ties of kinship established through relationships with Aboriginal women (female kinship ties) were essential to fur trade routes, expansion and trading itself, and she cites the community of St. Joseph, Michigan, as a prime example. However, she also notes that the Métis did not identify themselves as unique. She argues, "nor were the residents of eighteenth century St. Joseph a distinct Métis people. Identity was embedded in kin networks. People defined themselves by their relatives, while outsiders identified them as either French or Indian."[6] Sleeper Smith's argument is useful for thinking about métis families in the Great Lakes area, and her argument raises a question that is critical to my research. At what point in the mingling between First Nations and Europeans would a family identify as métis? For example, if a Cree woman and a European man had a family, how would they identify their children? Would the children identify with the culture of the Cree mother or the European father, or was this co-mingling the first instance of métis culture?

There is also disagreement among historians about the stability of métis identity in the Great Lakes area in the nineteenth century. Scholar Jacqueline Peterson argues that métis did not exist within the Great Lakes region; rather, they were organized networks of individuals. She states, "the very diffuseness of fur trade communities whose members had married among and were related to more than a dozen tribes—Algonkian, Siouan, and Iroquoian speakers—made group solidarity and combined action difficult to sustain under pressure. In the end, the identity of the Great Lakes Métis, like the transitional economy, which gave it life, was to prove a fragile construction. Between 1815 and 1850, years which witnessed the sudden fluorescence of a distinctive Métis population and culture radiating outward from the junction of the Assinboine and Red Rivers, present-day Winnipeg, the old fur trade communities of the Great Lakes region collapsed, drowned in the flood of American settlement and capitalist expansion."[7] Peterson's argument is generally acknowledged as accurate, as evidenced by the many curators and scholars who have followed in her train of thought, acknowledging the presence of métis culture in the Great Lakes region. Because she does not see them as developing a long-term identity, they would not, by implication, have developed a distinctive artistic production comparable to that of the Métis in western Canada. Was the identity of the métis in the Great Lakes a "fragile construction" as Peterson argues?[8]

One could argue that over time métis identities were unstable, rather than fragile. Scholars such as Karen J. Travers argue that the métis in the Great Lakes area developed along an alternate trajectory. She discusses the migration of métis from Drummond Island to support her argument.

Travers notes, "Great Lakes Métis are continually compared to Red River but they never quite measure up; they are the 'beginning,' the 'prelude,' the 'genesis,' and 'in the process of becoming,' but they always fall short. As a result, histories tend to focus on the 'real' Métis, where the identity was focused in the resistance led by Riel at Red River. Great Lakes Métis villages, of which Drummond Island is one of many, had an entirely different evolution and came before those settlements at Red River. They hunted, fished, gathered all kinds of vegetables, and other products. Both women and men intermarried with Anishinaabe, Iroquois, and Cree in a much earlier period. Thus, the history of the Great Lakes Métis cannot be told solely within this context."[9] Travers's research shows that the métis who are now based in Penetanguishine, Ontario, originally migrated from Drummond Island. She makes her case based on a census from 1901 and discusses the population, religion and living patterns of the community. Travers implies and I argue that métis communities in Ontario should be considered primarily within their own historical context and not necessarily in conjunction with the development of Métis nationalism in western Canada. Travers's research is important in that she establishes that there were métis communities in the Great Lakes region. Indeed, the *Powley* case, a significant legal victory for the Métis of Ontario, was based on a similar argument that a distinct métis community had existed in Sault Ste. Marie. The case was won in 2003 and allows Métis in Ontario and other provinces their harvesting rights.[10] Significantly, there is a rapidly growing number of individuals registering as Métis Citizens with the Métis Nation of Ontario (MNO) and across Canada.[11]

More research needs to be done to investigate communities within Ontario although it presents many challenges, primarily in the identification of métis in the historical record. Further, I agree with scholars such as Peterson who note that caution should be advised in consideration of the historical evidence and reading "Métis" identities back into nineteenth-century documents. Peterson argues, "thus, when contemporary scholars embrace terms such as the Ontario Métis Nation and consciously translate nineteenth-century English-language terms like Half-breeds or mixed-bloods from the documentary record into the politicized French-language term Métis (as in Métis Nation), they change the intended meanings of the original writers and of the terms themselves. Whatever the intent, the use of Métis in this context has implanted Métis communities, Métis identity, and Métis political consciousness into regions and times where they did not exist before."[12] Understanding the complexities of identifying métis in the historical record, remains important to re-examine literary and visual descriptions to grasp how identities may have developed in a more dynamic and fluid fashion.

Julia Harrison, an anthropologist and former curator of Glenbow Museum's ethnology department, supports the view that the Métis are still a strong and distinct nation within Canada. Harrison's book *Metis: People Between Two Worlds* was based on her exhibition of the same title, which examined the Métis from their early inception to present day. However, Harrison focusses predominantly on the Métis in western Canada, at the Red River Settlement and in the Northwest Territories, thereby excluding consideration that there were communities of métis in the Ontario region.

Harrison offers a crucial explanation of why Métis have struggled within western Canada, which could also apply to many other Métis in Canada. She explains the difficulties they have faced in integrating with society. She argues, "Because scrip had denied the Metis any of their privileges of the ward status of the Treaty Indian population, they were often poverty stricken and unable to have access to schooling, health care, and, most critically, land. Some managed to become members of the community, but this was often at the price of denying their ancestry. At the same time, the differences in status between Indians and Metis drove a rift between them that still exists today."[13] Harrison also reported on a major 1956 study of Metis in Manitoba, directed by Jean Lagasse for the Social and Economic Research Office. Legasse found that many people who technically qualified as Metis did not self-identify because they felt humiliated. Harrison states, "Many of those who qualified denied being

Metis because they had been taught to be ashamed of their heritage, and as a result, identification was sometimes made by another individual."[14] According to Harrison, Metis suffered prejudice and were isolated and excluded from both the "white" way of life, and Aboriginal communities.[15] Harrison's proposal that we look at who the Metis and (Métis) are on an individual basis is very relevant, even though her argument is based predominantly on the Metis in western Canada. She makes this assertion: "Who the Metis were in a cultural sense could only be understood by looking at the individual lives of people in the general Metis population. Native heritage is only part of Metis identity. Legal status and social pressures, combined with independence and individuality, have defined the Metis as both Native and white."[16] While I agree with Harrison's suggestion that we can understand Metis and Métis identity by contemplating individual and family histories, we can also consider how material culture might have been used as a source of expression. In this context, I will discuss the prominent Schoolcraft family of Sault Ste. Marie, looking briefly at their identity as a mixed-race family and at the role the material and literary arts played in their development.

Kate Duncan and Barbara Hail contributed another important discussion of the identity of the Métis and their cultural production in their exhibition catalogue *Out of the North: the Subarctic Collection of the Haffenreffer Museum of Anthropology*. Their work was based on an examination of hundreds of beadwork samples from across the Subarctic. Although they focus on the presence of the Métis in the Northwest Territories from the nineteenth century onwards, it is useful to understand how they identify the Métis. They make the following note: "In the southern Subarctic, descendants of French-Canadian workers in the fur trade and their Cree or Ojibwa wives emerged in the early nineteenth century as a distinctive ethnic group at Red River and later on the Saskatchewan River, and were largely Roman Catholic and bilingual in French and Cree. Those living north and west of Fort Simpson in the Mackenzie District, the Yukon, and Alaska, generally known as Northern

Métis, are descendants of more recent unions (post-1850) and northern European (especially Scottish) paternal descent, and are generally Protestant in religion and bilingual in English and an Athapaskan language. The métis played a major role in the development of the Subarctic fur trade, have served as cultural intermediaries, and have contributed significantly to Subarctic cultural life and arts."[17] Hail and Duncan, like Harrison and Brasser, attribute the development of Métis nationhood to the métis at the Red River Settlement. Their use of terms like "Chippewa-Métis" and "Cree/Cree-Métis type" acknowledges the influences of both Aboriginal and European heritage on people's work. They use the term "métis" to address other groups who have mixed Aboriginal and European heritage but do not necessarily come from the Red River.

I would argue that for women in the Northwest Territories in the twentieth and twenty-first century, the specific terms used in the categorization of their work as Aboriginal are not as important as the general impact of the beadwork and floral embroidery that they create. As Duncan and Hail note, "present-day craftswomen maintain that both native and métis women deserve credit for the floral embroidery arts of the Subarctic. As Maria Houle of Fort Chipewyan said, 'It's the same—Cree, Chip, half-breed—the same.' Agnes Mecredi Williams, Chipewyan-Métis, agreed: 'Everybody did it. If there was a difference, perhaps the métis took a little more pains, because they were usually living in more comfortable places, where they were warm.'"[18] This suggests that artwork should be considered within the artist's community context and that categories imposed by governmental institutions may not accurately describe the identities held by Aboriginal peoples. A similar approach could be applied to understanding material culture collections from the Great Lakes and, when possible, family histories should be used to understand artistic development and community influence.

An examination of literature by curators and academics based on museum collections of Métis material culture is critical to understanding previous ideas about Métis cultural identity and development through art. Ted Brasser, Julia Harrison, Kate Duncan, Barbara Hail, and Sherry Farrell Racette have conducted important studies on the material culture of the Métis based on museum collections. The formal analysis of the aesthetic and stylistic qualities of Métis material culture developed by these curators and scholars is essential to the evaluation of whether or not there may be specific métis styles within the Great Lakes area. Farrell Racette's stylistic analysis of collections of material culture identified as Métis and her theory of Métis identity as a fluid and shifting entity are especially influential on my work.[19]

Material Culture and Art

Scholarship on Métis art and identity has shifted over the past 25 years for a number of reasons. For the majority of the twentieth century, many anthropologists and curators espoused a predominantly Indian evolutionism perspective of Métis culture. This perspective posited that Aboriginal people were genetically inferior to the white race and would eventually die out. According to the golden age paradigm, the most prosperous time for Métis artistic development was from the 1820s to the 1870s. Ted Brasser, who wrote several articles on Métis art, published between 1985 and 1987, created this paradigm of a mythical golden era. However, Brasser also verified Métis art, beadwork and embroidery, as distinctive art forms and brought them into academic consciousness. Importantly, he identified the Métis as the "flower beadwork people" and credited them with having influenced the entire artistic production of northwestern Canada in the late nineteenth century. Brasser's identification of material in several institutions is an important stepping point for scholars studying Métis material culture.

Brasser's essay "In Search of métis Art" discusses the development of Métis artistic style, starting with a history of the métis in the Great Lakes, but he credits the Métis of the Red River Settlement, Manitoba, as spreading the floral beadwork style throughout the Northwest Territories. While he mentions the early influences of métis from central Canada, his focus on western Métis suggests he believes Métis identity and cultural production was a significant occurrence only in western Canada. He states, "When, in the early nineteenth century, the métis concentrated on the Red River, they were what sociologists call marginal people, originating from earlier fur-trade frontiers primarily around and north of the Great Lakes where they were referred to as 'French Indians' or 'Homeguard Indians,' depending on their trade affiliations....We may assume that the arts and crafts of these métis were derived indeed from Swampy Cree and Ojibwa traditions, but were modified by a considerable influence from the French mission stations during the eighteenth century."[20] Brasser also argues that, "the métis art style put its stamp on the art of practically every tribal group of the northern plains and the North West Territories. Indian statements from various parts of these regions confirm the effect upon tribal arts exercised by the 'flower beadwork people,' as the métis were referred to by the Sioux."[21] Brasser understands identity as inherently linked to cultural production and notes that the emergence of the floral beadwork style parallels the development of the Métis nation at the Red River Settlement. [22] Brasser also argues that the Roman Catholic missions were the crucial catalyst for introducing the floral beadwork style to the Métis. He notes, "small and stylized floral designs become noticeable on métis products by the 1830s, shortly after the establishment of Roman Catholic mission schools at Pembina, St. Boniface, and Baie St. Paul in the Red River country."[23] Brasser takes a crucial step in recognizing and promoting the work of the Métis, although he subscribes to a paradigm of cultural evolution and decline, and to the idea that the Métis had a distinct golden age and have now disappeared. He identifies métis in the Great Lakes area, but does not credit them as having developed a nation and a cultural iconography similar to the Métis at the Red River Settlement.

While the level of organized political consciousness may not have been the same among people of mixed heritage in the Great Lakes region in the nineteenth century as in western Canada, written and visual descriptions remain important in this dialogue and allow for a rereading and consideration of a multiplicity of identities. This essay presents various ways the métis were perceived culturally, and advises caution against understanding identity and art production as a uniform process.

Although the term "half-breed" may have had derogatory implications when used in previous centuries, Farrell Racette has reclaimed it and proposes a reintegration to convey the vibrant identity of the Métis. In her dissertation, "Sewing Ourselves Together: Clothing, Decorative arts and the Expression of Metis and Half Breed Identity," Farrell Racette focusses largely on the Métis and half-breeds in western Canada. She challenges the narrative forwarded by scholars such as Brasser, and argues that the golden age thesis denies the existence of Métis today. While building on the important work that Brasser and Harrison have done in identifying Métis artistic style in western Canada, Farrell Racette proposes that Métis and half-breed identity is fluid and should be understood on a group and individual basis, within a community context and not in a linear fashion. She argues, "the notion of fluid cultural spaces which are simultaneously marginalized and dynamic has potential for a more accurate understanding of the evolution and persistence of Métis identity."[24]

For Farrell Racette, identity is expressed through the construction and wearing of particular clothing, moccasins, bags, hair adornment and other objects. She notes, "Clothing can be instrumental in the active construction of group identity and not merely reflective of it, communicating underlying histories and current social realities. The clothing worn by Métis and Half Breed people reflects the historic events that have impacted them over time: the fur trade, changing economies, resistance and displacement."[25] Material culture, according to Farrell Racette, is like a contact point; these objects reflect the intricate relationship of the wearer, the maker and their community.[26] Farrell Racette states, "the development of Métis consciousness grew among the individuals, families and entire communities who moved from one location to another, from one *métis* space to another."[27] For Farrell Racette, then, material culture has a serious and powerful role in the expression of Métis and half breed identity: "the consistency of the clothing choices made by Métis and Half Breed people throughout the nineteenth century, particularly between 1820 and 1870, indicates the widespread existence of a stable and visually recognizable identity."[28] ·

A brief study of the representations of the métis in the Great Lakes area in the nineteenth century was undertaken by Farrell Racette in her thesis, "Sewing Ourselves Together." Farrell Racette contrasts the images of "half-castes" by artist Paul Kane with depictions of the Potawatomi and Miami by artist George Winter and argues that there were similarities in dress among Métis at the Red River Settlement and the Great Lakes area. She notes, "both the cut and colour of the knee-length, close-fitting coats worn in the Great Lakes and Red River regions were similar. The sash or *ceinture* was an important accessory, worn around the waist in the Red River, across the chest in the Great Lakes. Men in both areas wore full-length leggings. Indigo and red were the colours of choice in both regions. In addition to the general adoption of cloth, the most identifiable trend observed and represented in visual documents that linked people of mixed ancestry in the Great Lakes and Red River regions was the extensive use of decorative ribbon work. The Rindisbacher and Winter subjects, both male and female, adopted elements of European fashion and combined the innovative application of trade goods and the elaboration of indigenous garment forms to create visually distinctive dress."[29] Farrell Racette's observations on the material culture of the Métis as depicted by Kane and Winter are an important stepping stone for further study. She argues that material culture is a signpost of a shared identity throughout Canada. Farrell Racette's analysis raises several questions that are relevant to this study. To what degree was their (Métis and Half-breed) identity stable? Was there a recognizable métis dress throughout the Great Lakes region that might indicate a shared identity? The descriptions and interactions with métis people, as recorded predominantly by non-Natives, suggest that their clothing was not standardized across this region and depended on personal choice, trade influences and other factors, although there were general fashion trends worn by métis and other Indian peoples such as the sash, beaded leggings and quillworked bandolier (shoulder) bags. In contrast to Farrell Racette's argument, the evidence I present reveals that the fashions that métis wore indicates they did not necessarily have a distinct or stable identity; in fact, many Indian communities shared elements of style across these regions—the use of trade silver, beads and quillwork, for example.

According to Farrell Racette, Métis communicated identity on several levels: in the way they dressed, how they made their clothing, and the meanings this clothing conveyed to other people. She based her research on extensive visual examinations of Métis clothing in museum collections and other sources and traced the family histories of Métis makers and wearers through records held at various archives across Canada and the United States. Farrell Racette's research uncovered many family histories and identified many items in museum collections across North America and Europe as stylistically Métis. In a departure from Farrell Racette's model, I will question the degree of stability that can be identified among the métis in the Great Lakes region, as presented through travel literature and explorer artwork.

Farrell Racette's work builds on the feminist studies of Métis women's relationships and their craft production as analyzed by several scholars. Sylvia Van Kirk's *Many Tender Ties: Women in Fur-Trade Society, 1670–1870* examines the roles of Indian and mixed-race women and their vital position in the fur trade; this work is important for understanding Métis relationships and family dynamics in the eighteenth and nineteenth centuries. Her discussion focusses on Rupert's Land. Using a feminist framework to argue that women are "active agents" rather than passive participants in history, Van Kirk traces the various roles that Indian, mixed-blood and white women had in fur trade society. Van Kirk, writing in the 1980s, provided a strong base for feminist writers such as Sharon Blady. Also presenting women as autonomous subjects, Blady's article "Les Metisses: Towards a Feminist History of Red River" links the agency of

Métis women to the activism of the suffragettes because both played critical roles in shaping Canadian identity. Blady too, however, adopts the golden age paradigm: she focusses on artistic development from the 1820s through the 1870s at the Red River Settlement and neglects to acknowledge that Métis women are still producing artwork today.

My research aims to expand understanding of the relationship between visual culture and the identity of métis in Ontario and, more generally, knowledge about Ontario Native histories. Ideally, this research will add to a critical understanding of historical conceptions of métis in the Great Lakes, current resurgences (such as that of the Métis Nation of Ontario), and how identities manifest through travel descriptions, art and clothing. If we can reread European perceptions (written descriptions and images) as sites and sights of métis presence, scholars can take a more nuanced approach to understanding how métis may have understood and invented themselves through the clothing they wore. The variety of descriptions and images in existing archives indicate a wide array of métis individuals living in diverse communities.

Explorer and Travel Literature Descriptions

Among the earliest to describe métis in the Great Lakes was Alexander Henry, a British explorer and fur trader of the late eighteenth century. He dressed up as a "Canadian" in order to avoid attacks by Native groups who had disagreements with the English. Henry wrote, "I laid aside my English clothes, and covered myself only with a cloth, passed about the middle; a shirt, hanging loose; a molton, or blanket coat; and a large, red, milled worsted cap. The next thing was to smear my face and hands, with dirt and grease; and, this done, I took the place of one of my men."[30] The darkening of his skin probably indicates that these "Canadians" were understood by the British public to be a people of mixed race with a copper skin tone. Henry describes the clothing that became the outfit *de rigueur* for many métis traders and voyageurs during the nineteenth century; in addition, métis people often added to the outfit a sash and more decorative elements like beadwork, feathers and tinkling cones.[31] As Gwen Reimer and Jean-Philippe Chartrand argue, Henry's description may indicate the beginnings of a visually distinctive identity based on material culture. Although the terms used vary from "Canadian" to "half-breed," to identify métis in fur trade records and traveller's descriptions, the use of these terms indicates an attempt to articulate a difference between métis and Indian groups, an effort that began in the late eighteenth century and continued through the nineteenth.[32]

British officer Jasper Grant was stationed in British North America from 1800 to 1809 and was able to observe mixed-race relationships in his daily interactions and amass a large collection of Native art and artifacts. He was employed at various posts including Fort George, but his last post, from 1806 to 1809, was Fort Malden at Amherstburg, near Detroit.[33] While at Amherstburg, he wrote a letter to his brother Alexander about the identities of the people who dined at his table. He notes, "no odium here is attached to Bastardism. I have often at my table several families born of the same fathers but of different mothers, some in wedlock, others not, some copper colored, others white. The same respect is equally shown to all, and illegitimacy given no shame."[34] As art historian Ruth Phillips notes, Grant and his family seemed to have adjusted to these cross-culture relationships; his wife formed a friendship with a Pawnee woman, Mrs. Madeline Askin Richardson, who was married to surgeon Robert Richardson at Amherstburg.[35] Grant's observation of "copper colored" children indicates his awareness of métis relationships. His European ethnocentricity could have led him to condemn these unions; however, his wife's companionship with Mrs. Askin indicates their flexible attitude toward these relationships between Indian women and European men.[36] As Phillips astutely points out, these close ties with Native families in the area were probably vital to the formation of Grant's Native art collection.

Thomas Nuttall, a botanist who travelled along the Arkansas River in 1819, made some observations on the appearance of metif families. For Nuttall, his term "metif" implied people of mixed heritage. His notes on

Indian peoples' physical appearance suggest that distinct elements of clothing were worn by Native peoples, but that there were not necessarily distinctions between "metif," meaning "mixed race," and other Indian groups. He notes the similarities in dress between the Native peoples in Arkansas and British North America, and described them as "blanket capeaus, moccasins, and overalls of the same materials, are here, as in Canada, the prevailing dress; and men and women commonly wear a handkerchief on the head in place of hats and bonnets."[37] Nuttall adds this further description:

> It is hardly necessary to detail the dress of the Arkansas, which scarcely, to my view, in any respect, differs from that of the Delawares, Shawnees, or Chipeways. Its component parts are, as usual, moccasins for the feet; leggings which cover the leg and thigh; a breech cloth; an overall or hunting shirt, seamed up, and slipped over the head; all of which articles are made of leather, softly dressed by means of fat and oily substances, and often rendered more durable by the smoke with which they are purposely imbued. The ears and nose are adorned with pendants, and the men, as among many other Indian tribes, and after the manner of the Chinese, carefully cut away the hair of the head, except a lock on the crown, which is plaited and ornamented with rings, wampum and feathers. Many of them, in imitation of the Canadian French, wear handkerchiefs around their heads, but in the manner of a turban. Some have also acquired the habit of wearing printed calicoe shirts next to the skin.[38]

To Nuttall, a British scientist from England, the material culture of the metif, along with those of other Indian groups such as the Delaware or Lenape, differed little, suggesting that there were great similarities in dress among Native groups. It seems also there was a standard format for men's dress, which included moccasins, leggings, a tunic and sometimes a handkerchief. Metif or métis who worked as traders and interpreters along the Arkansas River, wore clothing similar to that of the other Native groups with whom they associated. Nuttall notes another interesting observation about fashion choice: "They (The Osage women) as well as the Cherokees and others, frequently take the pains to unravel old blankets and cloths, and re-weave the yarn into belts and garters. This weaving is no modern invention of the Indians. Nearly all those whom DeSoto found inhabiting Florida and Louisiana, on either side of the Mississipi, and who were, in a great measure, an agricultural people, dressed themselves in woven garments made of the lint of the mulberry, the papaw, or the elm; and, in the colder seasons of the year, they wore coverings of feathers, chiefly those of the turkey."[39] Finger weaving was also used among the métis and the Iroquois of the Great Lakes to create sashes. Nuttall made this note on a "metif" family: "Mr. Drope remained at the Bluff, trading the remainder of the day with the two or three metif families settled here, who are very little removed in their habits from the savages, with whose language and manners they are quite familiar."[40] Thus, Nuttall understood métis to be similar to other Indians in their dress and other cultural traditions.

William Keating, trained as a professor of Chemistry and Mineralogy at the University of Pennsylvania, was part of Stephen Long's staff on the expedition to the Great Lakes region in 1823. Keating's account of his voyage was published in 1824 and titled *A Journal of Travels into the Arkansas Territory*. Throughout his journal, he expresses fascination with métis women as objects of curiosity. He uses the terms "bois-brulé" and "halfbreed" frequently and wrote this description of the Métis at the Red River Settlement: "Those that are partly of Indian extraction, are nick-named *Bois Brulé* (Burnt wood,) from their dark complexion. Their dress is singular, but not deficient in beauty; it is a mixture of the European and Indian habits. All of them have a blue capote with a hood, which they use only in bad weather; the capote is secured round their waist by a military sash; they wear a shirt of calico or painted muslin, moccasins and leather leggings fastened round the leg by garters ornamented with beads, &c. The *Bois Brulés* often dispense with a hat; when they have one, it is generally variegated in the Indian manner, with feathers, gilt lace and other tawdry ornaments."[41] Keating's notes were based on the Métis in western Rupert's Land, but are still useful in understanding material culture trends because they travelled along the fur trade routes into the Great Lakes, often employed as interpreters, traders and voyageurs.[42] Nuttall and Keating both note the use of personal ornamentation to decorate the body, with either jewellery and, or, hats. Both describe the dress of métis people as non-static, a "mixture of the European and Indian habits" influenced by trade, fashion and practical concerns such as warmth and durability. Within the Great Lakes region, métis were integrated with other Native and non-Native communities, and their fashion choices reflected these relationships.

To Keating and Nuttall, people of mixed heritage—*bois brulé* and metif—were interesting and exotic. They were discussed as objects of fascination and one could argue their presence was also unsettling because of their cultural identity, which was part white and part Indian. Furthermore the geography of their communities bridged white and native cultures; some existed on the edges of white communities and merged with Indian communities. In the nineteenth century, racial paradigms created by white European elite men generally positioned Europeans as the most advanced form of man culturally, physically and mentally, and people of mixed Indian and European heritage were viewed as falling far below the white man's state of development. "Pure blood" Indians were lower still. These racial theories shifted as the century progressed, resulting in the condemnation of—and the passing of legislation against—marriages between different races, which lasted well into the twentieth century.[43]

According to Catharine Parr Traill, a settler who lived in southern Ontario and wrote letters to her sisters and mother, Indian women largely emulated the fashions of European women. She notes in a letter written May 9, 1833, "The women imitate the dresses of the whites, and are rather skilful in converting their purchases. Many of the young girls can sew very neatly. I often give them bits of silk and velvet, and braid, for which they appear thankful."[44] In another of her letters she notes the desire Indian women have to imitate European fashion:

> These Indians appear less addicted to gay and tinselly adornments than for-
> merly, and rather affect a European style in their dress; it is no unusual sight
> to see an Indian habited in a fine cloth coat and trousers, though I must say
> the blanket-coats provided for them by Government, and which form part of
> their annual presents, are far more suitable and becoming. The squaws, too,
> prefer cotton or stuff gowns, aprons and handkerchiefs, and such useful arti-
> cles, to any sort of finery, though they like well enough to look at and admire
> them; they delight nevertheless in decking out the little ones, embroidering
> their cradle wrappings with silk and beads, and tacking the wings of birds to
> their shoulders. I was a little amused by the appearance of one of these Indian
> Cupids, adorned with the wings of the rose-breasted grosbeak; a very beautiful
> creature, something like our British bullfinch.[45]

As this description suggests, Indian and métis women emulated European fashions but made them their own by means of decoration with beadwork, embroidery, featherwork, quillwork and the artistic use of jewellery and ornaments. Throughout her journal, Parr Traill avoids use of the term "half-breed" or anything that suggests people with combined Indian and European heritage, perhaps because she was unaware of the existence of a unique identity for métis in southern Ontario or perhaps there was no distinct identity for this group in this area.

Although travel literature is valuable for understanding British and Euro-American attitudes toward people of mixed heritage, métis iden-tity is difficult to conceive of without looking at specific family instances. Historian Sleeper Smith has argued that within the Great Lakes region, ties of kinship established through relationships with Indian women were essential to fur trade routes, expansion and trading itself, and she cites the community of St. Joseph, Michigan as an example. However, she also notes that the métis did not identify themselves as unique. She argues, "nor were the residents of eighteenth century St. Joseph a distinct Métis people. Identity was embedded in kin networks. People defined themselves by their relatives, while outsiders identified them as either French or Indian."[46] Sleeper Smith's argument suggests, and I propose, that one can understand identity by tracing family links to both Indian and European heritage. One example of a mixed-race family from the nineteenth century in this region, specifically Sault Ste. Marie, is the Schoolcraft family. They illuminate a reality of métis identity in this time period through the personal and public literature they produced about the Indian peoples in the area.

Henry Rowe Schoolcraft, an explorer and government Indian agent, made notes on Natives occupying the Great Lakes region, specifically Lake Superior, beginning with his participation in the Lewis Cass expedition of 1820 and the book he published in 1821, titled *Narrative Journals of Travels Through the Northwestern Regions of the United States*. The Cass expedition was made to survey the land and peoples of Michigan. On the self-ornamentation of Native peoples he notes, "There are no bands of the northern Indians who go entirely without clothes, even in the hottest summer weather; and like all other savages they possess a great fondness for grotesque ornaments of feathers, skins, bones, and claws of animals. They have also an unconquerable passion for silver bands, beads, rings, and all light, showy, and fantastic articles of European manufacture. When silver cannot be procured they use copper."[47] His use of the words "savages" and "grotesque" convey his Eurocentric position as a superior, civilized male and it does not differ much from the language or perspective of other European writers at this time. This passage, however, is useful for establishing that the use of silver jewellery and decoration with natural bone, feathers and other animal parts was prevalent among métis in the Great Lakes area. Nuttall also noted that Indians along the Arkansas River used silver jewellery, which suggests that this trend for ornamentation ran along routes of trade and was not a distinctive marker for métis but, rather, was used by many Indian communities to convey an individual's wealth and style.

Schoolcraft's interpretation of mixed-race relationships can illuminate our understanding of the racial mores of the time, and it foreshadows his marriage to a mixed-race woman. Schoolcraft makes these comments regarding the métis residents of Prairie du Chien, Wisconsin, in 1820:

> The early settlers, according to the principles adopted by the French colonists in the Canadas, intermarried with Indian women, and the present population is the result of this connexion. In it, we behold the only instance which our country presents, of the complete and permanent civilization of the aborigines; and it may be doubted, after all that has been said upon the subject, whether this race can ever be reclaimed from the savage state, by any other method. The result, in the present instance, is such as to equal the most sanguine expectations of the philanthropist, in regard to a mixed species. They are said to exhibit evidences of enterprise, industry, and a regard to order and the laws, at the same time, that we perceive the natural taciturnity of the savage, happily counterpoised by the vivacity and suavity of the French character, producing manners which are sprightly without frivolity, and serious without becoming morose.[48]

Schoolcraft implies that only through the union of Indian and European peoples can the former become "civilized," indicating his acceptance of the Eurocentric values of the time that positioned Europeans as the most highly civilized of men and Indians as less physically, mentally and socially developed. Shortly after the Cass expedition, Schoolcraft moved to Sault Ste. Marie and served as the first Indian agent for the government of the United States. He met and married Jane Johnston, of Ojibwa, Irish and Scottish descent. As a member of the prominent Johnston family, Jane Johnston's social position, education and wealth impressed Schoolcraft despite her racial identity.[49] In light of the remarks just quoted, he may have thought he was advancing civilization by marrying

Johnston while simultaneously using this marriage to advance his career. Although Schoolcraft's marriage was acceptable at the time, racial dogma hardened soon after, and marriages between métis and Europeans were denounced.[50] For example, Governor George Simpson of the Hudson's Bay Company (HBC) left his first wife, who was Native, at the Red River Settlement and married his cousin Frances Simpson in the 1830s. This act set a precedent for other employees of the HBC, who then rejected their métis and Indian wives and thereafter only married white women.[51]

The Schoolcrafts were one of many mixed-heritage families living in the Great Lakes region in the first quarter of the nineteenth century, but it is debatable whether or not they would have self-identified as métis. Mr. Schoolcraft was well aware of his wife's Indian heritage, and capitalized on the Ojibwa legends she told to him by writing many books about them.[52] He was also very active in fighting for land claims on behalf of half-breeds, specifically in the writing of the treaty of Fond du Lac. The Johnston family was set to receive a prime land grant on Sugar Island.[53] His son was of mixed heritage, and Schoolcraft fought to ensure that the son would also receive land title. Ultimately, his son died at a young age, and the treaty fell through. Although Schoolcraft did not explicitly identify his family as a mixed-race family, his actions indicate that he was keenly aware of the fact and tried to use their Native heritage to the best advantage of his family, although he continued to struggle with how to understand Jane's mixed-race status. In the Sault Ste. Marie area, there were, in fact, about 900 people of mixed-race and Canadian descent, according to a census done in 1829, indicating a significant métis presence.[54] However, Mr. and Mrs. Schoolcraft never described themselves as being métis, and one should thus be wary of ascribing identities to them.

Additional important documentation of métis life in the Great Lakes region is provided by British writer Anna Brownell Jameson. She made a voyage by canoe from York (Toronto) to Sault Ste. Marie in 1837 and wrote of her experiences with Indian peoples, including her interaction with the Schoolcraft family and other mixed-race Indians. She praised the conversion of Indian peoples to Christianity and, in general, had high regard for Native peoples. Her descriptions also expressed her fascination with their costume and beauty. She noted the clothing of two Indian boys whom she spotted along the river, past Chatham, in southern Ontario: "they wore cotton shirts, with a crimson belt round the waist ornamented with beads, such as is commonly worn by the Canadian Indians; one had a gay handkerchief knotted round his head, from beneath which his long, black hair hung in matted elf locks on his shoulders."[55] This sketch suggests that the dress of the Native boys and likely that of métis, differed little (if at all) from that of the men's in that period. This account is important because in accounts by Nuttall and Keating, few descriptions of women's or children's dress are provided, arguably because Nuttall and Keating thought this information was of little importance.

Jameson, an early feminist, was interested in the rights and living conditions of women and children and also had a particular interest in the way they chose to adorn themselves.[56] Jameson observed women on the island of Mackinac and documented their dress. She noted, "the dress of the women was more uniform; a cotton shirt, cloth leggings and moccasins, and a dark blue blanket. Necklaces, silver armlets, silver ear-rings, and circular plates of silver fastened on the breast, were the usual ornaments of both sexes."[57] Jameson's observation was made when many women and men from different Indian communities, including the Ottawas and Potawatomis (now generally referred to as Anishinaabe), were travelling to Manitoulin Island in order to collect their annual gifts from the British government, in return for their support in the war of independence.[58] One could argue then that neighbouring European and Indian communities influenced the fashion, culture and lifestyle of métis through trade and annual gatherings.

There are several references in Jameson's accounts to métis and half-caste women, who were well established in their communities. For example, Jameson noted that on her visit to the island of Mackinac, "we were...conducted to a little inn kept by a very fat half-caste Indian woman who spoke Indian, bad French, and worse English, and who was addressed as *Madame*."[59] This métis woman did not move seasonally like the Ottawa or Potawatomis that Jameson mentioned, but rather, as an inn-keeper, had a permanent residence. Jameson also met Mrs. McMurray, a métis woman whose physical appearance and demeanour impressed her greatly. Jameson recounts, "I was introduced to Mrs. McMurray, otherwise O-ge-ne-bu-go-quay, (the wild rose). I must confess that the specimens of Indian squaws and half-caste women I had met with, had in no ways pre-pared me for what I found in Mrs. McMurray. The first glance, the first sound of her voice, struck me with a pleased surprise. Her figure is tall—at least it is rather above than below the middle size, with that indescribable grace and undulation of movement which speaks perfection of form. Her features are distinctly Indian, but softened and refined, and their expres-sion at once bright and kindly."[60] This positive observation reflects other interactions Mrs. Jameson had with métis peoples throughout her voyage. She seemed to have made friends with several of the métis she encoun-tered, indicating her open frame of mind. Throughout her accounts, she made notes on the half-castes and half-breeds at missionary establish-ments and other venues.

Jameson developed a friendship with Mr. and Mrs. Schoolcraft and stayed several days with them at Sault Ste. Marie in the summer of 1837. She was aware of Mrs. Schoolcraft's Native heritage and noted that her mother was a fountain of knowledge about Indian peoples. She wrote, "Her...mother is also celebrated for her stock of traditional lore, and her poetical and inventive faculties, which she inherited from her father, Waub-Ojeeg, who was the greatest poet and story-teller, as well as the greatest warrior of his tribe."[61]

Jameson's respect for the Schoolcrafts indicates, I would argue, her high opinion of their respective heritages and their relationship within the context of settler exploration. Jameson's writings are valuable because she was a unique author: she not only observed people, she interacted with them and had friends who were métis. Consequently, she was not just an outsider observing from a distance and with a "scientific pur-pose," like William Keating. Indeed her friendships were not casual. She was given an Ojibwa name to signify her bravery for going over a set of rapids at the suggestion of George Johnston, Mrs. Schoolcraft's brother.[62] Jameson notes, "I was declared duly initiated, and adopted into the fam-ily by the name of Wah-sah-ge-wah-no-qua. They had already called me among themselves, in reference to my complexion and my travelling pro-pensities, O, daw, yaun, gee, *the fair changing moon*, or rather, *the fair moon which changes her place*: but now, in complement to my successful achieve-ment, Mrs. Johnston bestowed this new appellation, which I much prefer. It signifies…'the woman of the bright foam'; and by this name I am hence-forth to be known among the Chippewas."[63] Although there have been other writers who have claimed to have been inducted into certain Indian societies, Jameson's friendships with several métis, her respect for their traditions, and their acceptance of her indicates that her claims were not just farfetched imaginings produced for the benefit of European audiences.

Throughout her account, Jameson frequently uses the words "pictur-esque" and "grotesque," which convey her attitude toward the dress of Native people, which was one that was shared by many Europeans at that time. As Frances Connelly notes, terms like "picturesque" and "grotesque" were used by western artists and explorers to categorize Indian peo-ples and their artwork as existing at the end of a spectrum opposite the European, who was considered refined and was knowledgeable of classi-cal arts.[64] These ideologies in turn, were used to justify colonial expansion since Indians were noble savages who could exist in nature but could not withstand progress, or so many colonialists believed. Jameson visited the Schoolcraft family and knew that they were literate and educated, which surely went against many European and Euro-American imaginings of Indians as illiterate and culturally undeveloped, yet she wrote of many of them with a fascination that suggests she viewed them as other. Jameson's travel account was very popular among British readers and must have influenced many people to think of métis as curious subjects for their combination of European and Native races and cultures.

Although there were some positive opinions of métis, there was also a significant amount of distrust and hatred manifest in the attitudes of settlers, officials, non-Natives and Natives toward them. For example, the métis people of Potawatomi origin who inhabited the southerly regions around Lake Michigan were denounced by the American settlers as devilish. There was much hostility toward them in the region, they were thought of as unintelligent because they did not speak English, and they were despised because they adopted elements of Potawatomi and Miami spiritual beliefs into their customs.[65] Settlers felt threatened by these métis, who were perceived as uncivilized because their modes of subsistence did not focus on farming, a key marker of civilization for the settlers. As scholar R. David Edmunds notes, "unquestionably, most Americans subscribed to the popular stereotype that 'half-breeds,' at best, were a shifty lot, a people caught between two cultures. According to Baptist missionary and Indian Agent Issac McCoy, the Potawatomi mixed-bloods near South Bend were lazy, possessed and exalted a 'mistaken sense of honor,' and posed a 'formidable obstacle' to the 'improvement' of the other Indians."[66] Throughout the Great Lakes, then, mixed-race families were perceived differently. Some, like the Schoolcrafts, held respected positions of authority but were also despised for their mixed heritage, which threatened notions that civilization belonged solely to the settler population of Euro-Canadians and Americans. Most métis were illiterate and thus there is no written record of whether they self-identified as métis. Further, it could be dangerous to identify as métis and was often a survival method to identify with one's European heritage rather than as "Indian." Considering that métis people were embedded in kinship ties, they did not have need to identify collectively.

Nineteenth-century Images

Another way of understanding attitudes toward people of mixed heritage and how métis presented themselves is by analyzing visual images, though such images are necessarily mediated by Europeans and non-métis. Some artists, like Peter Rindisbacher and George Winter, included the term "half breed" and other terms connoting mixed heritage in the titles of their works. Like written descriptions, these images were created by non-Natives to document their travels and to legitimize their colonial presence while often designating métis as "other" in a distant romanticized past, their "exotic" regalia compounded this distancing created by the viewer's reading of travel books and looking at paintings in galleries, journals and newspapers. These artists created images that were used in newspapers, in collector's books and shown in galleries to advance agendas of white progress and settlement by legitimizing settler takeover of Aboriginal lands. The production and dissemination of these images within Europe and throughout North America legitimized colonial expansion and is an area that needs to be further researched and is beyond the scope of this essay. Yet the material culture of these Native subjects highlights the agency of its creators, who were continuing their cultural traditions through creating clothing and in the pride of the wearers' personal fashion choices.

Peter Rindisbacher was a Swiss-born artist who moved to the Red River Settlement in the early nineteenth century and depicted scenes and people from the area, including métis. His images should, though, be carefully regarded as highly detailed constructions that privileged a "noble savage" rendering. His images were based on first-hand observation, but he was also influenced by images made by early travellers and artists such as Jonathan Carver, who illustrated his travel books with images based on Indians in the Great Lakes region. Laura Peers made an interesting discovery that this image created by Peter Rindisbacher of an Indian family was a near-exact copy of an image created by Jonathan Carver, who explored the Great Lakes region in the late eighteenth century. Thus, Rindisbacher's work represented Indian material culture and trends not only from the Red River Settlement but also from the Great Lakes (through reproducing Carver's works) and they therefore serve as is a source of early images of métis in the Great Lakes region. Peer's work explores the migration of the Ojibwa from the Great Lakes to the Red River Settlement and their cultural interactions with métis and other groups; she does this by examining material culture and colonial paintings by artists such as Rindisbacher. She notes that Rindisbacher used one subject and material culture objects repeatedly in his depictions of various Indian groups, which prompts one to question about how specific and accurate his images of different Native peoples are. Peers asserts, "the tradition of using studio props and lifting sketches of actual objects from one image to another, combined with an artistic tradition of portraying Aboriginal peoples in garments and accoutrements which were widely read by European/settler audiences as signalling 'Noble Savage,' as well as the fact that Rindisbacher was working as a commercial artist from the start of his voyage to Red River and during his entire sojourn there, should make us extremely cautious when using Rindisbacher's work as visual evidence."[67] When looking at these historical images—the representational accuracy of which is rarely questioned—one must consider how they operated within colonial imaginations to portray métis as ignoble savages and how these served to justify colonial settlement. At the same time, there is a general consensus that the clothing Rindisbacher depicted was accurate for the time period and thus is a reference for understanding Native fashion choices.[68] There was extensive travel and exchange of clothing and other goods along the fur trade routes from the Great Lakes through to western Canada. Rindisbacher's images, therefore, should be evaluated for their representation and portrayal of the mobile, shifting context in which métis worked and lived.

The image *A Halfcast with his Wife and Child* by Rindisbacher (circa 1825) is a vividly coloured painting of a métis family. The man stands smoking a short pipe while his wife sits on a rock, smoking a much longer pipe. The family is in the foreground of the image while a grassy land-scape extends behind them, perhaps indicating the flatness of the prairies. The child appears to be wearing a miniature version of the military-style, three-quarter length, dark blue coat the father wears. The man has a red sash tightly knotted around his waist, a style prevalent throughout the Great Lakes, and a top hat decorated with a feather. He appears also to be wearing a porcupine quill–embroidered pouch with a geometric design over his chest, attached to which is a black horn pipe. His leggings are tan with a fringe on the sides and his moccasins have minimal decoration. His starched high collar is visible and he appears to be wearing a scarf over it, which puffs out slightly. He is a métis dandy who confidently holds a hunting gun. The strap dress of his wife has a long, blue, floor-length skirt and her sleeves create a "cape-like" form around her body, edged with green ribbon.[69] She wears earrings and her hair neatly slicked back behind her head with one curl beside her ear. She also sports moccasins and holds a blanket over her knee. This clothing indicates that a skilled maker, possibly the woman depicted, was fluent in cultural aesthetics of quillwork, ribbon work and the creation of tailored garments for her family. Métis women took great pride in decorating clothing for their fam-ilies; Peers notes, "beaded and embroidered clothing worn by métis and European people within fur-trade society had layered meanings derived from diverse heritages. For Native people who participated in the trade, clothing made from trade goods signified the competence of the trapper in obtaining furs and his female kin in dressing them."[70] Thus this image may be read as displaying a métis agency, that of the creators of the cloth-ing and its wearers who took pride in their appearance and non-native viewers would likely delight in the "exotic" apparel displayed. Further, the expressions of the two adults seem blank and posed and their eyes do not engage, allowing the viewer to imagine them in a romanticized and static past, rather than recognize that the identities of métis, like those of many people, were oscillating: some were thriving while others were struggling to survive.

FIGURE 1.1 *Peter Rindisbacher, Canadian (born in Switzerland), 1806–1834, A Halfcast with his Wife and Child (c. 1825), watercolour, ink on paper. Paper: 21.5 x 26 cm, image: 16.5 x 21.7 cm. Collection of the Winnipeg Art Gallery, acquired with financial assistance from the National Museums of Canada, G-82-215. Photo by Ernest Mayer, Winnipeg Art Gallery.*

George Winter, an English artist who travelled through the lands of the Potawatomi and Miami in the southerly regions of Lake Michigan in 1837, created many telling images of the fashions of people with Creole, Potawatomi, and Miami heritage. They generally absorbed different elements of Indian and Creole culture and created a visual style that was elegant, dapper and expressed their wealth. Like their neighbours to the north, however, they were treated with disdain and were despised for being mixed-race.

The drawing by Winter entitled *Noah-Quet, Known as Rice the Interpreter A Half Breed Indian Sketched* (1837), is an image of a young man wearing a European-style coat and vest with a scarf around his neck. His gaze meets the viewer's eyes. Rice was an educated man and served as a liaison interpreting documents that passed between the Potawatomis and the court system of America.[71] Only Rice's upper body is shown in the sketch, which presents the man in European garb; there are no traces of Indian influence in his fashion. Another métis interpreter who spoke English was depicted by Winter, whom he identified as *Bourassa, an Educated Halfbreed*, (1837). In the drawing of Bourassa, the viewer sees a three-quarter view of his face; his head is tilted upright, giving him an air of intelligence and perhaps hinting at his diplomatic abilities. He wears a European-lapelled jacket, ruffled shirt, and what appears to be a silk tie around his neck. His shirt has a high collar. His hair is cut short and close to his face. These images depict respected people of mixed-race who wore unique combinations of Indian and European fashions to convey their status as negotiators between two worldviews: the Potawatomis' and white Americans'.

Another image, labelled *Bouriette—Indian Interpreter* (1837), was also a subject who had mixed heritage. Standing, he wears an elegant, three-quarter length coat and leggings with wide-ribbon decoration that runs down the seam. He wears a vest over a long chemise and he appears to be wearing a tie around his neck. His hair is wrapped in a turban and he has long, tinkling-cone earrings, his visual appearance mirroring the verbal descriptions recorded by Nuttall. Bouriette looks out at the viewer; his legs are slightly crossed in a manner perhaps indicating his comfortable stance in society and ease in the moment. He also wears moccasins. Unlike Rindisbacher's composite images that use the same type of model, face and pose, these images reveal Winter's interest in showing the personality of the sitter, rather than depicting stereotypes of Indian representation.

As R. David Edmunds notes, the clothing that mixed-race people wore in the states around southern Lake Michigan, indicates their considerable wealth and "acculturation."[72] Indeed, these mixed-race peoples combined European and Indian traditions in clothing to create their own

Noah. quet. Known as Rice the Interpreter.
a Half breed Indian
Noah-quet. an educated Indian - a half breed
Sketched - 1837;
Known by the name of Rice, the interpreter.

FIGURE 1.2 *George Winter,* Noah-Quet, Known as Rice the Interpreter A Half Breed Indian
Sketched *(1837), pencil on paper, illustration from Christian F. Feest and R. David Edmunds in*
Indians and a Changing Frontier: The Art of George Winter *(Indianapolis: Indiana Historical*
Society, 1993*). Courtesy of Tippecanoe County Historical Association, Lafayette, Indiana.*

Bourassa   Indian Interpreter

1837 —

FIGURE 1.3 *George Winter*, Bourassa, an Educated Half breed *(1837)*, *Pencil on paper,*
illustration from Christian F. Feest and R. David Edmunds in Indians and a Changing Frontier:
The Art of George Winter *(Indianapolis: Indiana Historical Society, 1993)*. *Courtesy of Tippecanoe*
County Historical Association, Lafayette, Indiana.

Bouriette—Indian Interpreter

no.6 George Winter

FIGURE 1.4 *George Winter,* Bouriette—Indian Interpreter *(1837), watercolour, illustration from Christian F. Feest and R. David Edmunds in* Indians and a Changing Frontier: The Art of George Winter, *(Indianapolis: Indiana Historical Society, 1993). Courtesy of Tippecanoe County Historical Association, Lafayette, Indiana.*

unique designs and trends. Edmunds notes in Winter's paintings that the majority of the men "are dressed in frock coats similar to those worn by prosperous white settlers on the Indiana frontier. The coats are well tailored, with wide, fashionable lapels and natural, unpadded shoulders. Most are sewn from wool or broadcloth and fashioned in black, gray or other conservative colours."[73] The men wore their chemises untucked in their clothing, and most wore the breechcloth as well. Extensive and elaborate ribbon work was used on the leggings, which all the men wore. Decorative turbans and jewellery reflected the broad influence of Indian and European styles on mixed-heritage peoples in the southern Great Lakes. Edmunds notes, "Many of the Potawatomis and Miamis wore brightly colored scarves wrapped around their heads to form turbans. Turbans were common among the Ohio and Indiana tribes and were widely utilized by the Creeks, Cherokees, and some of the other southern Indians."[74]

Women's outfits, like the clothing of the men, were also showy and elaborate, reflecting their fortune and adoption of both European and Indian trends. The women wore modest clothing that almost fully covered the body. As Edmunds notes, "most of the Miami and Potawatomi painted by Winter wore dark, full, broadcloth skirts that fell almost to their ankles, loose-fitting, brightly colored blouses (often sewn of 'the finest silk'), and an embroidered or highly decorated shawl which also could serve as a headscarf."[75] The women also wore large amounts of silver jewellery in the form of earrings and brooches that they placed on their shawls or blankets. Indeed, a painting entitled *Daughter of Mas-saw, Maurie,* (1837) depicts a well-dressed woman who wears a long ribbon appliquéd skirt, moccasins, and a floral shawl over her shoulders, under which she has on a long strap dress, with sleeves. She also wears rings on her fingers, necklaces and silver earrings. She wears a cape over her shoulders like the women depicted in Kane's images, yet with the addition of many silver brooches. Her gaze looks out to the side of the viewer. Her

FIGURE 1.5 *George Winter*, Daughter of Mas-saw, Maurie *(1837), watercolour, illustration from Christian F. Feest and R. David Edmunds in* Indians and a Changing Frontier: The Art of George Winter *(Indianapolis: Indiana Historical Society, 1993). Courtesy of Tippecanoe County Historical Association, Lafayette, Indiana.*

high stature and status is displayed in the elaborate combination of silks, ribbon work and silver jewellery.

The métis (Potawatomi, Creole and Miami) people in the southern states were quite wealthy as a result of trade and resource management and displayed this through their sophisticated combination of native and imported materials including silk, ribbon work, and silver on their clothing and in their jewellery.[76] They worked as interpreters, traders and general labourers for the fur trade companies and thus would travel across borders and imported their style with them to the various forts and posts. The material culture of métis was highly influenced by the Indian groups with whom they were trading and in whose communities some of them were living. Around Lake Michigan, many of the métis had intermarried with other communities and were thus integrated to some degree with the various peoples who lived there, including Ojibwas, Potawatomis and Miamis. Like the métis of the northern Great Lakes, their identities were connected through family networks rather than a greater collective.

Frances Anne Hopkins, was an elite British artist and wife to a Hudson's Bay Company chief trader Edward Hopkins. She sketched voyageurs in the 1860s during a series of pleasure trips through the Great Lakes to legitimize colonial expansion and also to assert her own identity as a woman artist. She created a series of large oil paintings that illustrated her expedition by canoe in the Great Lakes area. The high degree of realism in the paintings in detailing clothing and activity, and the attempt to create picturesque scenes parallel the efforts and images created by Winter. Like previous colonial artists, Hopkins created images that served a documentary function yet were also romanticized. I will discuss three paintings by Hopkins: *Canoes in a Fog, Lake Superior* (1869); *Canoe Manned by Voyageurs Passing a Waterfall* (1869); and *Shooting the Rapids* (1879).

Canoes in a Fog, Lake Superior, images voyageurs paddling into the mist. It is highly detailed and innovative. In the left foreground, seven men paddle a canoe. Hopkins, reading a book, sits beside her husband. In the middle ground and far distance, two more canoes move into the mist. The

FIGURE 1.6 *Frances Anne Hopkins*, Canoes in a Fog, Lake Superior, 1869 *(1869), oil on canvas, Collection of Glenbow Museum, Calgary, Canada, 55.8.1.*

FIGURE 1.7 *Frances Anne Hopkins*, Canoe Manned by Voyageurs Passing A Waterfall, *(1869), oil on canvas, illustration from Janet E. Clark*, Frances Anne Hopkins 1838–1919 *(Thunder Bay: Thunder Bay Art Gallery, 1990). Collection of Library and Archives Canada, c-002771.*

FIGURE 1.8 *Frances Anne Hopkins,* Shooting the Rapids, *(1879), oil on canvas, illustration from Janet E. Clark,* Frances Anne Hopkins 1838–1919 *(Thunder Bay: Thunder Bay Art Gallery, 1990). Collection of Library and Archives Canada, C-002774.*

stem of the canoe in the foreground is painted white with a floral shaped circle, perhaps a symbolic image of the artist, as art historian Kristina Huneault has suggested.[77] In the canoe closest to the viewer's space, a man wearing a purple chemise and grey pants with a sash wrapped tightly around his waist guides the canoe. His hair is shoulder length and he wears a silver earring. Hanging from his yellow cotton or wool sash, he wears a knife, wrapped in what appears to be a quill-wrapped sheath, with a red band and also a fringe along the edge of the pouch. This item was most likely modelled on one of the items from her husband's collection, since he had collected a wide variety of Native artifacts. Another possibility is that Hopkins voyageur was originally wearing this piece, as an earlier sketch shows the voyageur carrying a knife, although not in the pouch. The other men sitting in the canoe wear similar outfits of coloured chemises, sashes, trousers and earrings. Two of the men wear small hats on their heads. The men have dark skin, probably indicating their Native heritage. It is perhaps also significant that during the time that Hopkins created these images of voyageur men, modelling their full-bodied figures, women artists were not permitted by social standards to paint historical scenes or nude men, both considered measures of the true artist.[78] Thus the painting could be seen as innovative on this level, in the depiction of many men in a historical action painting and her participation in this active lifestyle.

The canoe's passengers are reflected in the water indicating a calm and serene moment. The grey mist seems to dissolve the men in the distance as the artist and her canoe pass into the fog, creating a picturesque moment for the viewer. One of the main aesthetic aims of the picturesque was that viewers be transported into a liminal state by the beauty of nature: this scene conveys a dissolution of that beauty, an evaporation of time. This might induce a sense of the vanishing nature of the voyageur labour practice, the métis and other Natives. In *Canoes in a Fog*, the canoe depicted is a much smaller *canot du nord*, manned only by seven voyageurs. Three earlier sketches of this work indicate Hopkins was working on this composition from 1867 to 1869. It was shown at the Royal Academy in London on May 3, 1869. [79] The diagonal line created by the three canoes remains constant in all these compositions, the position of the steersman in the last watercolour sketch departs from the other sketches: his body faces toward the viewer, he has taken his oar out of the water, he wears a red *ceinture fléchée* or sash around his waist, a red scarf around his neck and a yellow cap overtop the voyageur outfit of pants and tunic. Hopkins uses goache to highlight the water and the details on the men's clothing in these earlier sketches. In the final composition, Hopkins alters the angle of the canoe and the position of the steersman so that he pushes it through the water at a sharper angle, away from the viewer, creating a more dynamic diagonal line in the composition.

Also adding to this sense of dissolution of time and space is the skill-ful modelling and blending of colours to achieve perspective in this image. The light source falls from the left foreground, perhaps indicat-ing the rising of the sun on their canoe, the white bow with the floral, possibly Ojibwa motif is highlighted with white. This floral design dif-fers from the motif presented on the larger canoe in *Shooting the Rapids*. The colours used in the other image are predominantly green, yellow and red in a swirling propeller-like design; its execution appears as though it were painted quickly, as it appears sloppily executed. In contrast, the exe-cution of this floral pattern perhaps recalls earlier quillwork designs on jackets and pouches made by métis and Ojibwa women. Along the edge of the canoe, there appears to be a bark-wrapped design, varying from red to white and black, recalling earlier fashion technologies such as the beadwork of Natives within the Great Lakes that also adorns the canoe in *Shooting the Rapids*. The texture of the birch bark and the black pitch used for repairs on the canoe are visible to the eye, as well as the sail support that pokes out from the side of the canoe, showing Hopkins's informed position and knowledge of canoe life and construction. Pastel colours of mauve, pink, yellow and grey are used for the men's clothing. The silhou-ettes of the two canoes in the distance are painted in a grey-mauve tone, blurring with the grey morning sky. Hopkins wears a blue grey mantle coat and a straw hat with a white ribbon wrapped around it. A blanket wrapped around her body suggests the cold temperatures of dawn before sunrise, which contrasts with the unswaddled bodies of the voyageurs indicating the divisions between labourers and travellers, clothed and blanketed, civilized and "primitive."

In Hopkin's *Canoe Manned by Voyageurs Passing a Waterfall*, the canoe passes directly in front of the viewer, and the scene is lit up by bright day-light, revealing the individualized figures clearly. The canoe passes by a large rock face against which the voyageur men's colourful chemises in yellow, white, red, pink, grey and blue stand out. They wear grey trousers, sashes and some wear red scarves about their necks. The second man from the right wears a red toque and one can see the tin water cup attached to his red, woven sash. The man at the bow wears a blue shirt and a white chemise underneath; he also wears a scarf around his neck and a grey hat with a red feather on it. The choices of hats and scarves vary considerably among the men, giving each a distinct personality. As curator Janet Clark notes, "Hopkins has also introduced the element of portraiture, providing each voyageur with a separate 'identity'; each is individualized with earrings, pipes, or hats, in addition to facial features and expressions, reminiscent of Krieghoff's characterizations."[80] This individualization of the voyageurs indicates perhaps an interest in representing their character in a manner similar to Winter's work and that contrasts with Rindisbacher's repeated use of the same face and body type.

There is controversy among academics over the identities of the voyageur men in this series of paintings. Art historian Kristina Huneault asserts that the men presented in this image were Iroquois from Caughna Wauga (today known as Kahnawake), who also made the canoes at Lachine, Montreal, Quebec.[81] Robert Stacey, a historian who wrote an essay for the exhibition presented by the Thunder Bay Art Gallery on Frances Anne Hopkins in 1990 argues that these men are Métis.[82] These men could be *both* Iroquois and métis (although with a small "m"), since at this time in the Great Lakes area métis identities were unstable and they did not necessarily identify as a collective, unlike their fellows in western Canada. Furthermore, focussing on whether or not these men were mixed-blood, Iroquois and, or, métis can be limiting and echoes previous essentialist arguments about race. Instead, as Native Studies professor Brenda Macdougall notes, "we need to move past this preoccupation with whether the Métis were more European than Indian or more French than British because it undermines the authenticity of their identity as Aboriginal people who established a culture intrinsically linked to their homeland."[83] While Macdougall's work focusses on the development of Métis, Cree and Dene communities within Northern Saskatchewan and uses the Cree term *Wahkootowin* (a term used to convey how family ties are the basis for community expressions of identity); her argument is valuable for its insistence on considering métis development on a holistic level.[84] Macdougall's argument also suggests that we be wary of categorizing identities too neatly, when in reality they developed through complex social and cultural relational webs.

Shooting the Rapids (Hopkins did not title many of her works—this was a title given to the work later on) conveys a moment of rearrangement: both for the voyageurs and the HBC. These hale and hearty voyageurs were transporting Governor of Rupert's Land Alexander Grant Dallas, Frances Anne Hopkins, Edward Hopkins and Edward Watkin across the Lachine Rapids on July 26, 1863, as part of an official reorganization of the HBC. The International Finance Society, with its new role as part of the company, implemented shifts in the power relations, causing alarm among employees.[85] The canoe presented is Governor Simpson's *canot du maître*, reserved for special dignitaries and trips around Rupert's Land, was made by métis and Iroquois people in the area of Lachine. This party was surveying the landscape of Canada, which was still a colony of the British crown at this point. Hopkins was asserting an imperial presence through representing herself in the image while at the same time, by presenting the voyageur men with realistic details, she presented their livelihoods.

Iroquois voyageurs from the Lachine district had been employed by the HBC since the early nineteenth century for their canoe and trapping skills. Their livelihoods, like those of the métis, were greatly affected by fur trade activities; they were sent to western Canada throughout the century to obtain furs. Jan Grabowski and Nicole St-Onge note, "the fate of the western Iroquois in these changing times was similar to that of the metis and non-aboriginal free trappers. Some men became guides for government explorers, emigrant wagon trains, and foreign sportsmen....Others followed the fur trade frontier farther and farther northwest and continued as trappers in the Mackenzie district. Finally some Iroquois accepted the closing of the frontier and settled down, often on independent ranches or small farms."[86] Certainly in this time and space, Iroquois had been employed as voyageurs since the beginning of the nineteenth century and often were hired to escort voyages such as the one depicted by Hopkins. In fact, in a later work entitled *The Red River Expedition at Kakabeka Falls* (1877), commissioned by Colonel Garnet Wolseley to commemorate the Red River expedition that sent out military troops to put down the Red River Resistance of Métis, most of the men hired to steer the canoes were of Iroquois descent.[87]

Like the identities of the men in this series of voyageur paintings, the material culture that Hopkins depicted was worn by métis, Europeans, and Iroquois, revealing the large overlaps that existed in the fashion choices of voyageur men. The outfits of voyageurs in this image and in several other images by Hopkins generally consist of a tunic, a woven sash (likely from L'Assomption, Quebec, which was a headquarters for the production of these sashes), as well as a red woolen cap (or fedora with a feather) and scarf. Many voyageurs, be they métis, Iroquois or from another Native group, wore similar outfits. The oarsman in the prow, closest to the viewer, wears a sash wrapped and knotted around his waist. The sash was a very popular item not only for voyageurs at this time; it was also *à la mode* for young women. Sashes were used to tie winter coats together and were also used by the French (habitants), worn over their Hudson's Bay blanket coats. Several images of a fashionable young woman, painted by Hopkins (perhaps a self-portrait) indicate that sashes were the utmost of fashion in Canada at this point. While this Euro-Canadian woman wears a sash around her waist, métis women at the time did not wear the sash, perhaps because few métis women were employed as voyageurs and did not have the same need for it.

In all three images, the artist positions herself in the centre of the canoe, as an adventurous female traveller and artist who recorded the finale of this kind or labour that was so essential to colonial expansion and to the life ways of many Métis. As Janet Clark notes, "the Hudson's Bay Company's role in Canada had diminished both economically and politically, especially after 1869, when Rupert's Land was transferred to the Dominion of Canada, so that Frances Anne Hopkins was documenting in the 1870s what was essentially the end of both the fur-trade era and its principal means of transportation, canoe."[88] Although Hopkins painted these images at the end of the fur trade, they are valuable because she attentively records the material culture of these voyageurs. The material culture of these men reflects the descriptions of métis men from earlier in the century, while their outfits may have changed little, their livelihoods were shifting from voyageur labour to other pursuits, such as farming.[89]

Together, the written descriptions and the images I have discussed present a consistent repertoire of material culture. Métis men wore frock coats, an untucked shirt, leggings, moccasins, usually a sash and sometimes a bandolier bag. On the head, men might have worn a toque or kerchief in the French-Canadian style, a top hat or turban. These items were decorated with quills, beads and, or, lace ribbon work. Women would decorate their families' outfits with quillwork, ribbon decoration and other embellishment they received through trade relations. Women wore leggings, strap dress, moccasins, earrings, and sometimes a blanket or shawl. Both men and women wore silver trade jewellery. Children were dressed like their parents. The combination of European and Indian designs had a dynamic quality. I would argue that rather than there being distinctive looks for different métis communities, fashions varied according to the diverse interpretations and combinations of European and Indian styles that *individuals* wore. Peterson notes that "members of Great Lakes fur trade society served as guides, interpreters, negotiators, mail carriers, portage and ferry tenders, barge and oar men, and officers and spies in the Indian service, as well as tribal business agents and teachers and employees of missions and Indian agencies. In each case, they functioned not as members of a separate ethnic group but as individual carriers, linking Indians and Euro-Americans, and as buffers behind which the ethnic boundaries of antagonistic Indian and Euro-Canadian and Anglo-American cultures resisted transformation."[90] The Indian groups métis traded with and their interaction at fur trade posts with Americans, the British, and Euro-Canadians also influenced their choices.

Were métis individuals indicating a stable identity through their clothing choices as Farrell Racette argues? Farrell Racette's position suggests that métis consciously used clothing and decoration to indicate their identity. However, this argument can be challenged by the fact that they dressed themselves with reference to a wide variety of factors; family ties, community, access to trade goods, and personal preference all played a role in their material culture decisions, in western Canada as well as Ontario. In the Great Lakes region in the nineteenth century, métis were dependent on kin ties and fur trade links and thus did not necessarily want or need to portray a distinct identity that was different from their established family ties to both Indian and European communities. Throughout the century, attitudes toward mixed-race families shifted and it could therefore be dangerous and even deadly to identify oneself as Indian. Many métis were proud of their many heritages and did not necessarily seek to part from any of them. Scholar Harriet Gorham states the following: "Throughout the period of their dependence upon the fur trade, from approximately 1680 to 1830, individuals of mixed Indian and White ancestry in the Great Lakes region appear to have functioned more as a disparate collection of individuals...than as a cohesive group. They lived in small widely scattered settlements such as Sault Ste. Marie, St. Joseph, La Baie, Michilimackinac, and Prairie du Chien, or they maintained their own small trading establishments along the water routes between such centres....As individuals, most mixed-bloods demonstrated a greater awareness of the uniqueness of their way of life as fur traders and their attachment to their homeland in the Great Lakes region, than to any clear sense of distinctiveness created by their mixed ancestry."[91] Perhaps it is impossible to know whether identity was consciously constructed through dress to reflect métis heritage, especially because there were many variations of decoration among the people that lived in the Great Lakes area in the nineteenth century. While uniform food, language and music patterns were widespread throughout this region, one visual marker that métis people had in common across this area was that they dressed predominantly using a combination of European and Indian fashions. Personality, trade items and family ties dictated the details—whether one wore a toque or turban, silver earrings, necklaces, beaded bags or leggings.

Images and descriptions externalized outsider perspectives of métis in the Great Lakes and also presented their identities—although often romanticized as "devilish," "exotic"—as existing in a noble past rather than the present. People of European and Indian descent (métis) and their clothing, and other items of bodily ornamentation, challenged European and Euro-American ideals of civilization. Significantly, these images and descriptions are re-read in this essay for alternative understandings of identity. This evidence presents métis with elaborately decorated clothing, often among their families, indicating their flourishing and dynamic cultural traditions. Thus the identities of métis oscillated for the reader and viewer of these works, but they also shifted for themselves throughout the century, depending on how they identified and were accepted and rejected as individuals, families and communities by a broader non-Native and Native audience. Today, as in the past, understandings of Native identities are fluid and changing, and analyzing the historical record of images and descriptions remains a central component of this dialogue.

Notes

1.   I will also use the terms *Indian*, *Iroquois* and *Ojibwa*, which were terms used to create the historical record in the nineteenth century. I use the term *Indian* to focus my study on the métis and other Indian peoples of the Great Lakes, rather than *Aboriginal* which includes the Inuit. The term *Indian* is problematic because it does not convey the varied experiences of many Native peoples across Canada, yet it is necessary because the term *Aboriginal* is too broad in the context I examine.

    It is important to briefly discuss the Native peoples that were involved in the fur trade in the nineteenth century within the Great Lakes area. Ojibwa and

Iroquois peoples played a key role in the fur trade since the seventeenth century, acting as voyageurs, guides, canoe builders and cultural interpreters while working and travelling throughout North America. People referred to as Ojibwa, Ojibwe and Chippewa in nineteenth-century documents are now referred to collectively as the Anishinaabe. Their territories extend across Canada from Quebec to Saskatchewan. Within the USA, their land extends from Michigan to Montana. Helen Hornbeck Tanner notes, "Ojibwa people have never formed a single organization, but the overlapping of regional groups forms a chain that ultimately links them together. Personal connections through kinship were extended by membership in patrilineal clans. Although there were originally only five or six Ojibwa clans, twenty-one were identified in the mid-nineteenth century with some geographic variations. Sault Ste. Marie has always been associated with the high-ranking Crane clan. The Marten and Loon totems have been well known around Chequamegon Bay, whereas the later-created Wolf clan was prominent in the former Sioux head-quarters at Mille Lacs, Minnesota, where the Ojibwa community incorporated captive Sioux" (*Encyclopedia of North American Indians*, ed. Frederick Hoxie (Boston: Houghton Mifflin, 1996), s.v., "Ojibwa"), 468. Iroquois peoples, today collectively known as the Haudenosaunee, "people of the longhouse," have territories primarily in Ontario, Quebec and New York State. Mohawk, Oneida, Onondaga, Cayuga, Seneca and Tuscarora form the Six Nations Confederacy of the Haudenosaunee.

2. Beth Fowkes Tobin, *Picturing Imperial Power: Colonial Subjects in Eighteenth-Century British Painting* (Durham, NC: Duke University Press, 1999), 2.

3. John E. Foster, "Some Questions and Perspectives on the Problem of métis Roots," in *The New Peoples: Being and Becoming Métis in North America*, ed. Jacqueline Peterson and Jennifer S.H. Brown (Winnipeg: University of Manitoba Press, 1985), 73.

4. The discussion of "Métis consciousness" has been the subject of many studies. Some of the most influential scholarship has been done by Jennifer Brown and Sherry Farrell Racette.

5. Ted J. Brasser, "In Search of métis Art," in Peterson and Brown, *The New Peoples*; Sherry Farrell Racette, "Sewing Ourselves Together: Clothing, Decorative Arts and the Expression of Metis and Half Breed Identity" (PHD diss., University of Manitoba, 2004).

6. Susan Sleeper Smith, "Furs and Female Kin Networks," in *New Faces of the Fur Trade: Selected Papers of the Seventh North American Fur Trade Conference, Halifax,*

Nova Scotia, 1995, ed. Jo-Anne Fiske, Susan Sleeper Smith, and William Wicken (East Lansing: Michigan State University Press, 1998), 62.

7. Jacqueline Peterson, "Many Roads to Red River: Métis Genesis in the Great Lakes Region, 1680–1815," in Peterson and Brown, *The New Peoples*, 64.

8. Peterson, "Many Roads to Red River," 64.

9. Karen J. Travers, "The Drummond Island Voyageurs and the Search for Great Lakes Métis Identity," in *The Long Journey of a Forgotten People: Métis Identities and Family Histories*, ed. Ute Lischke and David T. McNab (Waterloo, ON: Wilfrid Laurier University Press, 2007), 221.

10. Métis Nation of Ontario, "The Powley Story," www.metisnation.org/harvesting/the-powley-story.

11. Based on the 2006 Census, 389,780 Canadians self-identified as Métis. In Ontario, the highest growth was reported, with 73,605 identifying as Métis. Métis Nation of Ontario Annual Report 2008/2009, "Métis Population," 8.

12. Jacqueline Peterson, "Red River Redux: Métis Ethnogenesis and the Great Lakes Region," in *Contours of a People: Metis Family, Mobility, and History*, ed. Nicole St-Onge, Carolyn Podruchny and Brenda Macdougall (Norman: University of Oklahoma Press, 2012), 28.

13. Julia Harrison, *Metis: People between Two Worlds* (Vancouver: Douglas & McIntyre, 1985), 79.

14. Harrison, *Metis: People between Two Worlds*, 123.

15. Harrison, *Metis: People between Two Worlds*, 124.

16. Harrison, *Metis: People between Two Worlds*, 135. Please note: Harrison does not add the French accent to the word "Métis."

17. Barbara A. Hail and Kate C. Duncan, *Out of the North: the Subarctic Collection of the Haffenreffer Museum of Anthropology* (Bristol, RI: The Museum, 1989), 22.

18. Hail and Duncan, *Out of the North*, 33.

19. Farrell Racette, "Sewing Ourselves Together," 185.

20. Brasser, "In Search of métis Art," 222.

21. Brasser, "In Search of métis Art," 225. Please note: Brasser does not capitalize Métis, but does add the French accent.

22. Brasser, "In Search of métis Art," 223.

23. Brasser, "In Search of métis Art," 225.

24. Farrell Racette, "Sewing Ourselves Together," 185.

25. Farrell Racette, "Sewing Ourselves Together," 1.

26. Farrell Racette, "Sewing Ourselves Together," 15.

27. Farrell Racette, "Sewing Ourselves Together," 62.

28. Farrell Racette, "Sewing Ourselves Together," 123.

29. Farrell Racette, "Sewing Ourselves Together," 92.

30. Alexander Henry, *Travels and Adventures in Canada and the Indian Territories Between the Years 1760 and 1776: in Two Parts* (New York: I. Riley, 1809), 34. Available at http://eco.canadiana.ca/view/oocihm.35677/3?r=0&s=1.

31. Gwen Reimer and Jean-Philippe Chartrand, "Documenting Historic Métis in Ontario," *Ethnohistory* 51, no. 3 (2004): 571.

32. As Reimer and Chartrand note, "the term Half-breed was first used by North West Company (NWC) Canadians, who apparently recognized mixed-bloods as members of a distinct social and racial category in the first decades of the 1800s." The use of this term is rare. Further, they note these terms can be jumbled: "Victor Lytwyn's analysis of HBC records at Fort William indicates that the distinction between freeman, Half-breed, Métis and Indian was often blurred; for example, Louis Ross was variously referred to as a half breed, as an Indian, and as belonging to a group of freemen." Reimer and Chartrand, "Documenting Historic Métis in Ontario," 572.

33. Ruth Phillips, *Patterns of Power: The Jasper Grant Collection and Great Lakes Indian Art of the Early Nineteenth Century* (Kleinburg, ON: The McMichael Canadian Art Collection, 1984), 14.

34. Phillips, *Patterns of Power*, 16.

35. Phillips, *Patterns of Power*, 10, 20.

36. Phillips, *Patterns of Power*, 16.

37. Thomas Nuttall, *A Journal of Travels into the Arkansas Territory*, (Ann Arbor, MI: University Microfilms, 1966), 75.

38. Nuttall, *Journal of Travels*, 89.

39. Nuttall, *Journal of Travels*, 193.

40. Nuttall, *Journal of Travels*, 99.

41. William H. Keating, *Narrative of an Expedition to the Source of St. Peter's River, Lake Winnepeek, Lake the Woods, &c. performed in the year 1823, by order of the Hon. J.C. Calhoun, secretary of war, under the command of Stephen H. Long, major U.S.T.E.* (Philadelphia: H.C. Carey & I. Lea, 1824), 41.

42. Reimer and Chartrand, "Documenting Historic Métis," 569.

43. Legislation against mixed-race marriages lasted well into the twentieth century. Robert Young, *Colonial Desire: Hybridity in Theory, Culture and Race* (London: Routledge, 1995 [1836]), 148.

44. Catharine Parr Traill, *The Backwoods of Canada* (Ottawa: Carleton University Press, 1997), 122.

45. Parr Traill, *The Backwoods of Canada*, 209.

46. Sleeper Smith, "Furs and Female Kin Networks," 62.

47. Henry Rowe Schoolcraft, *Narrative Journals of Travels Through the Northwestern Regions of the United States...* (Ann Arbor, MI: University Microfilms, 1966), 228.

48. Schoolcraft, *Narrative Journals of Travels*, 338.

49. Jeremy Mumford, "Mixed-Race Identity in a Nineteenth-Century Family: The Schoolcrafts of Sault Ste. Marie, 1824–27," *The Michigan Historical Review* 25, no. 1 (Spring 1999), 1–23.

50. See Jennifer Brown's *Strangers in Blood: Fur Trade Company Families in Indian Country* (Vancouver: University of British Columbia Press, 1980) for information on marriages in the custom of the country and changing policies of the fur trade companies in relation to marriage to mixed-race women.

51. Demelza Champagne, "Anxiety and Control: Gender and Intermarriage in Nineteenth Century Canada," (master's thesis, San Francisco State University, 2006), 36.

52. Schoolcraft's wife was proud of both her European and Indian heritage and she expressed this through her poetry. Ultimately, Henry's attitude shifted from admiration to disdain for Jane's Indian heritage due to several factors. He converted to Presbyterianism and his wife—who celebrated Native history and therefore "heathen" principles—challenged some of his Christian beliefs. Also, as more whites arrived in Ontario, racial dogma continued to harden and Jane, because she was "half breed," was not welcome among white "civilized" company. Henry did little to ameliorate this situation. Mumford, "Mixed-Race Identity," 13.

53. Mumford, "Mixed-Race Identity," 14.

54. "In 1828, Major Anderson, our Indian agent, computed the number of Canadians and mixed breeds married to Indian women, and residing on the north shores of Lake Huron, and in the neighbourhood of Michilimackinac, at nine hundred. This he called the lowest estimate." Anna Jameson, *Winter Studies and Summer Rambles in Canada*, Sabin Americana 69 (London: Saunders and Otley, 1838), vol. 3, 59.

55. Jameson, *Winter Studies*, vol. 2, 281.

56. Jameson, *Winter Studies*, vol. 3, 29.

57. Jameson, *Winter Studies*, vol. 3, 29.

58. Jameson, *Winter Studies*, vol. 3, 30.

59. Jameson, *Winter Studies*, vol. 3, 26.

60. Jameson, *Winter Studies*, vol. 2, 33. According to Jameson's footnote, "Mrs. McMurray was Charlotte Johnston, the daughter of Col. John Johnston of Michilmackinac."

61. Jameson, *Winter Studies*, vol. 3, 87.

62. Jameson, *Winter Studies*, vol. 3, 200.

63. Jameson, *Winter Studies*, vol. 3, 200.

64. Frances Connelly, *The Sleep of Reason: Primitivism in Modern European Art and Aesthetics, 1725–1907* (University Park: Pennsylvania State University Press, 1995), 19.

65. Lucy Eldersveld Murphy, "To Live among Us: Accommodation, Gender, and Conflict in the Western Great Lakes Region, 1760–1832," in *Contact Points: American Frontiers from the Mohawk Valley to the Mississippi, 1750–1830*, ed. Andrew R.L. Cayton and Fredrika J. Teute (Chapel Hill: University of North Carolina Press, 1998), 281.

66. R. David Edmunds, "George Winter: Mirror of Acculturation," in *Indians and a Changing Frontier: The Art of George Winter*, ed. Sarah E. Cooke and Rachel B. Ramadhyani (Indianapolis: Indiana Historical Society), 26.

67. Laura Peers, "Almost True: Peter Rindisbacher's Early Images of Rupert's Land, 1821–26," in *Association of Art Historians* (Oxford: Blackwell Publishing, 2009), 532.

68. The term "fashion" is a complex one, because it encompasses historical, personal, social desires and human needs. Historian Anne Holander describes fashion as "a design art consummated by the consumer[;] fashion is chiefly identified with the second half of the nineteenth century and the twentieth century." (*Encyclopedia of Aesthetics*, ed. Michael Kelly, (New York: Oxford University Press, 1998), s.v., "fashion").

69. As Frances Densmore notes in *Chippewa Customs*, "This garment (dress) was held in place by strips over the shoulders and confined at the waist by a belt or sash. Arm coverings were usually provided and could be worn or laid aside as desired. These consisted of two strips of cloth, each fastened at the wrist after the manner of a cuff, and the two attached at the back of the neck, forming a capelike protection to the shoulders. When calico was brought by the traders a loose calico sacque was frequently worn by the women over the above-described broadcloth dress without the arm coverings." Frances Densmore, *Chippewa Customs*, (New York: Johnson Reprint Corp., 1970), 32.

70. Laura Peers, "'Many Tender Ties': The Shifting Contexts and Meanings of the S Black Bag," *World Archaeology* 31 (1999): 292.

71. Edmunds, "George Winter," 52.

72. Edmunds, "George Winter," 27.

73. Edmunds, "George Winter," 27.

74. Edmunds, "George Winter," 28.

75. Edmunds, "George Winter," 28.

76. Edmunds, "George Winter," 25. Indeed, R. Edmunds notes that a métis man was reputedly the wealthiest man in Indiana during the nineteenth century. Historian Andrew Jolivétte writes of the Creole population in Louisiana that, "despite the scant attention paid to American Indian populations in the state of Louisiana, there is a long history of Indian–Creole, Indian–French, Indian–Spanish, and Indian–African relations throughout the state that have been virtually ignored. American Indian communities such as the AtakapaIshaks (also known as the Opelousa or Blackleg/Blackfoot), the Clifton-Choctaw, the United Houma Nation, and the Redbones living along the Sabine and Red rivers are but four of the communities that have intermarried with European (primarily French and Spanish) and African populations (mainly from the Senegambia, Senegal, and Gambia areas before 1743) to form the Creole population." See Andrew Jolivétte, *Louisiana Creoles: Cultural Recovery and Mixed-Race Native American Identity* (Lanham, MD: Lexington Books, 2007), 7.

77. Kristina Huneault, "Placing Frances Anne Hopkins: A British-Born Artist in Colonial Canada," in *Local/Global: Women Artists in the Nineteenth Century*, ed. Deborah Cherry and Janice Helland (Aldershot: Ashgate, 2006), 187.

78. Rozsika Parker and Griselda Pollock, *Old Mistresses: Women, Art and Ideology* (Pantheon Books, New York, 1991), 87.

79. "Frances had shown her work between 1860 and 1891 eleven times at the Royal Academy (where one condition of acceptance was that pictures should not have been previously publicly exhibited in London), four times at Suffolk Street (Royal Society of British Artists) and seventy 'Various Exhibitions.'" Alice M. Johnson, "Edward and Frances Hopkins of Montreal," *The Beaver* 302, no. 2 (Autumn 1971): 10.

80. Janet Clark, "Frances Anne Hopkins (1838–1919): Canadian Scenery," in *Frances Anne Hopkins 1838–1919: Canadian Scenery* (Thunder Bay, ON: Thunder Bay Art Gallery, 1990), 27.

81. I use the term "Iroquois" as it was used in the nineteenth century to convey a sense of the historical conceptions of this distinct group of people who are today generally known as Haudenosaunee.

82. Janet Clark and Robert Stacey, "Frances Anne Hopkins and the Canoe-Eye-View," in *Frances Anne Hopkins 1838-1919: Canadian Scenery* (Thunder Bay, ON: Thunder Bay Art Gallery, 1990), 63.

83. Brenda Macdougall, *One of the Family: Metis Culture in Nineteenth-Century Northwestern Saskatchewan* (University of British Columbia Press, Vancouver, 2010), 14.

84. Macdougall notes, "strictly translated, *wahkootowin* can be defined as 'relation-ship' or 'relative,' but this belies much of the meaning and sentiment that the term and its derivatives actually express. The significance ascribed to famil-ial relationships or the concept of relatedness was an idealized social value by which Metis people attempted to order their society." Brenda Macdougall, "Wahkootowin: Family and Cultural Identity in Northwestern Saskatchewan Metis Communities," *The Canadian Historical Review* 87, no. 3 (2006): 433.

85. Johnson, "Edward and Frances Hopkins of Montreal," 10.

86. Jan Grabowski and Nicole St-Onge, "Montreal Iroquois *éngages* in the Western Fur Trade, 1800-1821," in *From Rupert's Land to Canada*, ed. Theodore Binnema, Gerhard J. Ens and R.C. Macleod (University of Alberta Press, Edmonton, 2001), 45.

87. Grabowski and St-Onge, "Montreal Iroquois," 49.

88. Clark, "Frances Anne Hopkins," 27.

89. Significantly, the Métis Nation of Ontario now uses Hopkin's *Shooting the Rapids* for various promotions of their organization. For example, it is featured at the Annual General Assembly, on the website and together with other images and scenes in order to represent the MNO. The contemporary usage suggests that the MNO views the image of the voyageur as representing a central component of Métis identity. Furthermore, the title of a bi-monthly publication, *Métis Voyageur*, highlights the important role that the ideology of the voyageur plays in identity making. The voyageur is used as a symbol for the Métis in Ontario, while the buf-falo is used by the Manitoba Metis Federation and the Red River cart is used by the Métis Nation of Alberta. The voyageur is an interesting symbol because it is not only representative of the Métis, it is also used by French Canadians.

90. Peterson, "Red River Redux," 32.

91. Harriet Gorham, "Families of Mixed Descent in the Western Great Lakes Region," in *Native People, Native Lands: Canadian Indians, Inuit and Métis*, ed. Bruce Alden Cox (Ottawa: Carleton University Press, 1987), 38.

Bibliography

Brasser, Ted J. "In Search of métis Art." In Peterson and Brown, *The New Peoples*, 221–29.

Brown, Jennifer S.H. *Strangers in Blood: Fur Trade Company Families in Indian Country*. Vancouver: University of British Columbia Press, 1980.

Clark, Janet, and Robert Stacey. *Frances Anne Hopkins 1838–1919: Canadian Scenery*. Thunder Bay, ON: Thunder Bay Art Gallery, 1999.

Connelly, Frances S. *The Sleep of Reason: Primitivism in Modern European Art and Aesthetics, 1725–1907*. University Park: Pennsylvania State University Press, 1995.

Densmore, Frances. *Chippewa Customs*. New York: Johnson, 1970.

Edmunds, R. David. "George Winter: Mirror of Acculturation." In *Indians and a Changing Frontier: The Art of George Winter*, edited by Sarah E. Cooke and Rachel B. Ramadhyani, 23–40. Indianapolis: Indiana Historical Society, 1993.

Farrell Racette, Sherry. "Sewing Ourselves Together: Clothing, Decorative Arts and the Expression of Metis and Half Breed Identity." PHD diss., University of Manitoba, 2004.

Feest, Christian F., and R. David Edmunds. *Indians and a Changing Frontier: The Art of George Winter*. Indianapolis: Indiana Historical Society, 1993.

Foster, John E. "Some Questions and Perspectives on the Problem of métis Roots." In Peterson and Brown, *The New Peoples*, 73–91.

Gorham, Harriet. "Families of Mixed Descent in the Western Great Lakes Region." In *Native People, Native Lands: Canadian Indians, Inuit and Métis*, edited by Bruce Alden Cox, 37–55. Ottawa: Carleton University Press, 1987.

Grabowski, Jan, and Nicole St-Onge. "Montreal Iroquois *engagés* in the Western Fur Trade, 1800–1821." In *From Rupert's Land to Canada*, edited by Theodore Binnema, Gerhard J. Ens, and R.C. Macleod, 23–58. University of Alberta Press, Edmonton, 2001.

Harrison, Julia. *Metis: People between Two Worlds*. Vancouver: Douglas & McIntyre, 1985.

Henry, Alexander. *Travels and Adventures in Canada and the Indian Territories, Between the Years 1760 and 1776: in Two Parts*. New York: I. Riley, 1809.

Hoxie, Frederick. ed., *Encyclopedia of North American Indians*. Boston: Houghton Mifflin, 1996.

Huneault, Kristina. "Placing Frances Anne Hopkins: a British-born Artist in Colonial Canada." In *Local/Global: Women Artists in the Nineteenth Century*, edited by Deborah Cherry and Janice Helland, 179-200. Aldershot: Ashgate, 2006.

Jameson, Anna Brownell. *Winter Studies and Summer Rambles in Canada*. London: Saunders and Otley, 1838.

Jasen, Patricia. *Wild Things: Nature, Culture, and Tourism in Ontario, 1790-1914*. Toronto: University of Toronto Press, 1995.

Johnson, Alice M. "Edward and Frances Hopkins of Montreal." *The Beaver* 302, no. 2 (Autumn 1971): 4-19.

Jolivétte, Andrew. *Louisiana Creoles: Cultural Recovery and Mixed-Race Native American Identity*. Lanham, MD: Lexington Books, 2007.

Keating, William H. *Narrative of an expedition to the source of St. Peter's River, Lake Winnepeek, Lake of the Woods, &c., performed in the year 1823, by order of the Hon. J.C. Calhoun, Secretary of War, under the command of Stephen H. Long, Major U.S.T.E.* Philadelphia: H.C. Carey & I. Lea, 1824.

Macdougall, Brenda. *One of the Family: Metis Culture in Nineteenth-Century Northwestern Saskatchewan*. Vancouver: University of British Columbia Press, 2010.

———. "Wahkootowin: Family and Cultural Identity in Northwestern Saskatchewan Metis Communities." *The Canadian Historical Review* 87, no. 3 (2006): 431-62.

Mumford, Jeremy. "Mixed-Race Identity in a Nineteenth-Century Family: The Schoolcrafts of Sault Ste. Marie, 1824-27." *The Michigan Historical Review* 25, no. 1 (1999): 1-23.

Murphy, Lucy Eldersveld. "To Live among Us: Accommodation, Gender, and Conflict in the Western Great Lakes Region, 1760-1832." In *Contact Points: American Frontiers from the Mohawk Valley to the Mississippi, 1750-1830*, edited by Andrew R.L. Cayton and Fredrika J. Teute, 270-303. Chapel Hill: University of North Carolina Press, 1998.

Nuttall, Thomas. *A Journal of Travels into the Arkansas Territory: During the year 1819*. Ann Arbor, MI: University Microfilms, 1966.

Parker, Rozsika, and Griselda Pollock. *Old Mistresses: Women, Art and Ideology*. New York: Pantheon Books, 1991.

Parr Traill, Catharine. *The Backwoods of Canada*. Ottawa: Carleton University Press, 1997 [1836].

Peers, Laura. "'Almost True': Peter Rindisbacher's Early Images of Rupert's Land, 1821–26." *Association of Art Historians* 32, no. 3 (2009): 516–44.

———. "'Many Tender Ties': The Shifting Contexts and Meanings of the S Black Bag." *World Archaeology* 31, no. 2 (1999): 288–302.

Peterson, Jacqueline. "Many Roads to Red River: Métis Genesis in the Great Lakes Region, 1680-1815." In Peterson and Brown, *The New Peoples*, 37–71.

———. "Red River Redux: Métis Ethnogenesis and the Great Lakes Region." In *Contours of a People: Metis Family Mobility, and History*, edited by Nicole St-Onge, Carolyn Podruchny and Brenda Macdougall, 22–58. Norman: University of Oklahoma Press, 2012.

Peterson, Jacqueline, and Jennifer S.H. Brown, eds. *The New Peoples: Being and Becoming Métis in North America*. Winnipeg: University of Manitoba Press, 1985.

Phillips, Ruth. *Patterns of Power: the Jasper Grant Collection and Great Lakes Indian Art of the Early Nineteenth Century*. Kleinburg, ON: McMichael Canadian Collection, 1984.

Reimer, Gwen, and Jean-Philippe Chartrand, "Documenting Historic Metis in Ontario." *Ethnohistory* 51, no. 3 (2004): 567–607.

Schoolcraft, Henry Rowe. *Narrative Journals of Travels through the Northwestern Regions of the United States....* Ann Arbor, MI: University Microfilms, 1966.

Schoolcraft, Jane Johnston. *The Sound the Stars Make Rushing Through the Sky: The Writings of Jane Johnston Schoolcraft*, edited by Robert Dale Parker. University Park: University of Pennsylvania Press, 2007.

Sleeper Smith, Susan. "Furs and Female Kin Networks: The World of Marie Madeleine Réaume L'Archevêque Chevalier." In *New Faces of the Fur Trade: Selected Papers of the Seventh North American Fur Trade Conference, Halifax, Nova Scotia, 1995*, edited by Jo-Anne Fiske, Susan Sleeper Smith and William Wicken. East Lansing: Michigan State University Press, 1998.

Tobin, Beth Fowkes. *Picturing Imperial Power: Colonial Subjects in Eighteenth-Century British Painting*. Durham, NC: Duke University Press, 1999.

Young, Robert. *Colonial Desire: Hybridity in Theory, Culture and Race*. London: Routledge, 1995.

(Re)claiming | 2
Métis Women Identities

Three Stories and the Storyteller

LAURA-LEE KEARNS

*Listen to the story. You'll take from it what you need, what you are ready
to hear.*

— RAVEN MURPHY, *Oral Storyteller*[1]

HANNAH ARENDT SAID that we have the opportunity for an "enlarged
mentality" when we visit others and listen to and share stories.[2] This is
something that Indigenous[3] people have known since the beginning. Stories
are shared between and among families, friends, communities and the
public. As Lischke and McNab write, Métis people attest to being Métis
"as a result of their own knowledge of their identities, family histories,
and communities."[4] Stories are not simply a means of learning about others and history, they can also have deeply personal meanings and can
potentially transform peoples' understanding of one another and
themselves.

Dion affirms that "the understanding of narrative as a source of harmony and balance is a recurring theme within Aboriginal conceptions
of storytelling and history."[5] Lischke also says to "be Métis...to survive,

you need to be a good balancer."[6] I am seeking a balance—to understand what being Métis means to me through listening to stories that begin to help illuminate the complexity and diversity of Métis identities. Part of my interest in finding out more about Métis people and learning from them comes from not being told explicitly that I was Métis when growing up; although, looking back, there were very tangible connections to and a family interest in Indigenous people. Naming oneself or ourselves as "Métis" is like finding a missing piece of a puzzle that brings the picture into clearer view. But some of the mystery still remains because identity is not static and never complete and can be negotiated and renegotiated.

Part of my journey has been to learn about and try to understand the historical silence surrounding Métis identities (and some people still remain silent). I have been honoured by Métis Elders who were willing to share some of their life stories with me. I share some of these stories as part of my political, pedagogical and personal responsibility as a Métis person and an academic to promote understanding of the diversity, fluidity, resilience and silence of Métis identities. Because many Indigenous people adhere to the "practice of contextualizing knowledge,"[7] I also tell you about myself, in my efforts to respect this tradition, as I understand it at this point in my own learning journey. The three Métis women interviewed for the telling of this story include: my mother, Claire (Bellehumeur) Kearns, a Métis woman who has been an acting Métis Senator and is the Women's Representative on the Oshawa and Durham Region Métis Council, and a member of the All Our Relations Métis Circle, a women's hand drum group; Honorary Métis Senator Helen (LePage) Bradley, the senator for the Métis Nation of Ontario and a member of the Georgian Bay Métis Council; and Olivine (Bousquet) Tiedema, an Honorary Métis Senator for the Métis Nation of Ontario and for the Oshawa and Durham Region Métis Council, as well as a Métis Councillor for the latter, and a revered Elder, originally from St. Boniface, Manitoba. The women I present here have shared some knowledge about their own family histories and the communities in which they live and have lived, and they are all part of the larger Métis community.

In trying to understand the silence surrounding some Métis identities, it is important to recognize a number of factors that complicate Indigenous identity formation. The legacy of colonialism and numerous historical assimilationist policies and practices that "encouraged Native people to abandon their heritage"[8] resulted in many people being raised without their Indigenous cultures. The state-sanctioned assimilation policies of residential schools in Canada, for example, that could forcibly remove children from their homes and communities, denied many children love, care, support, language and culture. The effects of residential schooling are described by some as "hell on earth"[9] or "genocide,"[10] and these descriptions attest to the overt and covert ways shame, abuse, silence and the force of assimilation shaped some Indigenous identities.

Further, the Indian Act in 1869 stipulated that a status or treaty "Indian" woman "who married a non-Indian man would have their and their children's status revoked."[11] So, any Aboriginal woman who married a white male, for example, was "now considered to be a bona fide member of Canadian society. She lost her Indian status and every right that came with it."[12] In Canada in the Making—Aboriginals: Treaties and Relations, Bron and Houle explain that as a result of the Indian Act of 1876 "[a]ll 'half-breed' Indians, like the Métis, were not entitled to Indian status."[13] They also note that "Sir John A. Macdonald summed up the government's position nearly a decade later in 1885 when he said: 'If they are half-breed, they are [considered by the government to be] white.'"[14] Fiske reminds us that in its efforts "to assimilate Indians into mainstream society...the state has frequently revised the criteria it uses to assign legal status."[15] Given the state's assimilationist approach to identity and identification, the state's definitions of Indigenous people constrained who could and could not define themselves as Métis or Indigenous, and this impacted differently-located Métis women, men and children in a variety of ways and degrees.[16]

Dion writes that she and her family "are survivors of the government's forced assimilation policy. We have been denied our culture and are struggling to understand how that came to be that we were deprived of the experiences of our ancestors and much of their rich traditional knowledge."[17] I think many Métis, Inuit and First Nations, or "Aboriginal," families share this experience. Many of us were not raised within an overt Aboriginal culture; others were, but may have faced systemic racism as a result of the legacy of colonialism. So, for a number of reasons, many of us did not have the opportunity to learn as much about our ancestors, their stories and knowledge as we would have liked. Many of us find ourselves looking to thread together pieces of our inherited culture and learn more for ourselves and future generations.

In our active search for connection and reconnection, and as part of my own and my mother's learning journeys, we have regularly visited the Elders' conference at Trent University since 1990. It is here that we have learned about "blood memories" and the importance of our connections to all of our ancestors. Similar to being connected to all of our relations, parents, grandparents, great grandparents, human family, and to the whole living planet, blood memories are part of who we are. It is the way—either genetically or through spirit or heart or mind or body—we are interwoven with our ancestors. It is the happiness we feel when we listen to a traditional song that fills us with joy; it is not only our happiness, but the memories of our ancestors imprinted within us that also fill us with joy. It is also the burden we carry for the harm, the silencing and injustice our ancestors experienced. To carry this teaching is a great responsibility that cannot be fully articulated or expressed on paper; I simply signal here that my mother and I have learned that—much like she and I are connected— we share connections to and with our ancestors.

Many Indigenous people have come, or are coming, to terms with who we are. Some of us were raised with Indigenous cultures, some of us were adopted out, some of us came to learn about our ancestry as adults, and it is through opportunities to learn from, with, and alongside Elders in different contexts that we grow and deepen our connections and our understandings. As I continue to visit First Nations and Métis celebrations, and speak with Elders, I am so grateful for the opportunity to share stories emotionally, spiritually and intellectually.

The sharing of Métis stories, family histories, life experiences and knowledge of past community dynamics with Métis and, or, other Indigenous people, presents many pedagogical opportunities for transforming the public realm. It helps contribute to the collective consciousness of Métis peoples, strengthening our pride in our own identities and those of all our relations. I also think the telling and sharing of stories is an invitation for more people to claim their ancestry and begin their own journeys. As other Aboriginal writers have stated, some of us "have questioned the legitimacy of our indigenous identity...[as we learn more] we realize that those feelings were directly related to the government's policy of forced assimilation."[18] Part of my own desire to learn with and from others is to confront the legacy of silence that is a result of colonialism. It is important to me personally and as an educator to put narratives of Métis Elders and their experiences into the public realm in order to help change and transform public consciousness.

Sharing Stories

Over the last year I have had the opportunity to visit and interview several Métis women, men and couples, each of whom have generously shared some of their stories. For me, collecting stories is not only an academic endeavour, it is also part of my quest to get to know my family and myself, and why we (and others) have been silent in naming ourselves "Métis." One of my most cherished childhood memories is visiting family and friends with my mother during the summer. I feel very fortunate that I can continue these visits, sometimes with my mom, and sometimes without, in my academic journey as my and our circle of Métis family, friends and community continues to grow. In this chapter I share some of my memories and recollections of these visits.

There are several approaches I could have taken to present the knowledge gained by visiting three Métis Elders and interviewing them. Instead of using a more standard academic format to report and discuss the findings as a way to disseminate the information collected from the qualitative interviews, I want to present Claire, Helen, and Olive's stories, memories, narratives and history—which are always partial, fluid and incomplete—as found poems. One may create a found poem by taking a traditional prose text and selecting words and sentences from the text and arranging them in a poetic manner—that is, one may transform prose text "into poetry by playing with the space of the page, line lengths, and stanzaic structures."[19] The poems presented here have been created using the Elders' words, drawn from the written transcripts of the oral interviews. This format is a way to respond ethically and honourably to the "voices" of the storytellers, since it is their words that are used to create the poems. Yet, in transforming and selecting their words and arranging them in a poetic form, the very format signals that I have arranged the stories to be interpreted by the reader and it is only a partial representation of the stories shared. Poems in and of themselves are open to multiple interpretations, careful consideration, debate and play, and they invite associations and connections. The found poems I share here are connected to my personal understanding at this time. After listening to and reflecting on the stories of these three Métis women, I present here the parts of their narratives that stood out for me and that I can learn from at this time. If I (re)visit this research, these words, these experiences and these women at a different time, new connections could be awakened, different poems may be written, and my perspective, understanding and questions could change.

I have also presented part of my story as a poem. In inserting my own narrative alongside those of the three Métis women whose stories I share, I am not only contextualizing knowledge, but also showing that these stories are a part of, and are closely interwoven within, my own being: mind, body, heart, spirit.[20] In presenting narratives (re)constructed as poems, I hope to highlight the traces of Indigenous consciousness that were gifted to me and my interviewees, and to show that there are more stories to tell.

Narrating Métis stories in the public realm invites me to question and reflect in different ways, at different times and with different purposes pedagogically, personally and politically. I want to remember and listen to these stories to help transform public consciousness and understanding. I invite the reader to experience these poems ethically and with pedagogic responsibility. Using found poems and poetry not only invites multiple interpretations, but it also alters the ethical relationship between the listener and teller; one is asked to be responsive and responsible. In sharing my own story and those of the three Métis women I interviewed as poems and found poetry, I want to remind myself and the reader of the complexity of the stories and, further, that no story can capture the entire experience of the teller or of all Métis people.

I invite multiple interpretations of the narratives. In Indigenous conceptions of story-telling, one is invited to take from stories what one can, "to find meaning in them."[21] Some Aboriginal Elders and wise Anishnaabe and Métis people have implored me to simply listen to stories with an open heart, mind and spirit, and that by doing so I would take from the story what is necessary and important—what I can grasp and need at this moment. I invite you to do the same.

Me, Laura-Lee (Bellehumeur) Kearns

My mother always said the French and the "Natives" have to stick together
That is what her father told her
"Mémère" (my mom's mom) once told me that I was lucky to have
An English surname
(although three of my grandparents have French names
and my surname is Irish)

My mother always brought us to places with
"Native" art and history,
Our home always had "Aboriginal" art within and on its walls

My mother is a teacher.
Her mother was a teacher.
Her father was a teacher.
Her two sisters and brother are teachers.

My mother was drawn to take courses in
"Native" Studies at Trent University and
Continues to be compelled to learn more.

My mother likes nature.
She taught her five children to respect nature.
She planted a garden at our home and
Planted a few community gardens at her schools.

My mother knows about herbs,
Indigenous wild plants, and
How to use birch bark.
She knows how to call birds.
She takes great care to plant flowers
To attract and support butterflies.
She does not use pesticides.
My mother would stop the car,
Get out on the side of the road and
Carefully dig out a few plants that were naturally occurring
(that were abundant),
Like pussy willows,
To take home.

One day, she stopped the car to help a big
Turtle cross the road,
So that it wouldn't get run over.

One night, she stopped the car to help families of
Frogs cross the road;
She waited patiently and we waited and waited.

My mother is a great collector of rocks.
I think everyone in my family has been
Asked or compelled to go help her
Collect them or lift the heavy ones for her.
When she came to my university office
She brought me rocks from the Ocean and
Made me promise to get a big rock for the door entrance.

My mother always talks about how the Aboriginal
People were treated badly by the government—
That the newcomers would have died without
The gift of cedar tea from the First Nations People
Mother always complained about the
Injustice of building over sacred "Native" burial grounds,
She complained that when my father and herself went shopping for their
First house they were shown several homes that
Were/are over sacred "Indian" burial grounds
(in Toronto and in Oshawa, Ontario)
—of course, she did not choose to live there
—she also supported my camping out at Trent to support
The Mohawks at Oka in 1990.

In school, I remember learning about the Métis in Grade 8.
I thought they were people from the 16th and 17th centuries
—the offspring of the coureurs de bois and "Native" women.
No Indigenous group was ever mentioned again.

Today:

I am grateful that being Métis is an available

Cultural and

Legal identity.

I am grateful that my kids can jig in public.

And we have so much more to learn...

Reflection:

I know that not all families grow up with this kind of consciousness.

I am grateful that I did, even though we didn't always

Name the voices of the ancestors who helped shape that consciousness.

All my relations,

My mother, Claire (Bellehumeur) Kearns

I was born in 1944 in Montreal during the war;

My dad was a Canadian soldier stationed near there.

After the war, we moved back to Penetanguishene

To be near my dad's family.

Mom and dad spoke French

My father always said:

The French and the "Indians" have to stick together.

My grandfather, Edmund Bellehumeur,

was known as an "Indian" Guide on the French River.

He was always proud of his nature ways;

In nature, he could find many things that were good for you.

He knew a lot about plants, fish and furs.

He became a butcher and

could prepare wild game.

He made maple syrup and

I heard that he ate some every day of his life.

One year I bought a lovely fox hat and he said that it wasn't a very good fur;
it should have a good colour, and have a thicker Winter growth.
And I had paid so much for it in Toronto...

My dad's mom died when he was three.
We know that his grandmother was known as a "Métisse"
—it was a very derogatory remark at this time.

The word Métis we didn't hear it...
Not in the community,
Not in school...
Oh. Except in Grade 7
My teacher was a French Catholic nun who thought Louis Riel was a Hero.
In Grade 10, I attended an English Public H.S. and learned that
Louis Riel was considered a rebel and worse.
I was always ashamed by how badly the whites treated "Native" people.

We knew we were related to people who had "Native" blood
Dad never explained this;
We would just visit relatives and friends.
My dad always took us to all the Native places.
He wanted us to know the history,
He brought us to Michlimakenac.
He brought us to Drummond Island.
He told us about where the Drummond Islanders got their land,
across the bay.
He was always friendly with all of their descendants.

When I was 8 years old,
My mom and dad took me to the Martyr's Shrine.
There were beautiful Wendat dancers there,
In full regalia

—I wanted to be a part of that.

Last year, at the Native Friendship Centre in Toronto,

I was invited to participate and learn the women's dance.

I was very deeply moved.

It really meant a lot to me.

I felt at home.

I had really waited a long time for this.

Here, take the talking stick.

Summer Visits

My mother, some of my siblings, myself and my family (husband and two children), as well as my aunt, who is a Métis Senator, and several of my cousins, attended the Métis Heritage Celebration in Oshawa in late June 2010. There was great music (our women's hand drum group, for example) and fiddlers, jiggers, vendors, display tables, tepees, a red river cart and a birch bark canoe. My mom purchased a beautiful "Native" hand drum and beadwork from Métis Senator Helen (LePage) Bradley. As we spoke further, my mom realized that Helen was currently living right beside the house she had grown up in Penetanguishene, in the Georgian Bay area. Helen knew my mom's parents and her grandfather. We spoke briefly about my research and my wanting to interview Métis women about their lives and experiences. She invited us over for the following week. Because Helen had grown up in the same community that my mom had, I was anxious to find out a little more about that time. As we drove, navigating our way down one little side road after another, Mom pointed out where Helen had grown up.

My mother also brought the drum she purchased from Helen. There was a beautiful picture of a bass on the drum, painted and signed by Helen's good friend, but mom wanted Helen to sign the drum; the drum is a work of art and very powerful. As my mother and I spoke with Helen and listened to her, Helen made a better drumstick for my mother's new drum. She asked her niece to go and get leather, and using my mom's original wooden stick, worked the leather (cutting, sewing, feeling, and intuiting with her hands) and made a drumstick. She had many of her beading supplies

all around her, within arm's reach. Later, she asked her niece to get her some bear oil,
which had been gifted to her, so she could work it into the drum. She gifted my mom
with some bear oil to take home with her as well. With much gratitude and thanks,

Métis Senator Helen (LePage) Bradley

I am the 10th child of 13 kids,
Born September 25, 1934
to an Ojibwa-speaking father
from Drummond Island and
a French-speaking mother from Quebec, originally from France,
Mom was married at 13 and
Dad was 9 years older.

Dad was a commercial fisherman
He would travel further north on Georgian Bay
Leave on Saturday and be back on Thursday
Friday we would deliver fish by wagon
To different houses in town
In those days people didn't eat meat on Friday;
They ate fish

Mother would take people's old clothes or torn coats
Cut them into squares
Tie them all up
Made all her own blankets
We never had any that were bought
Mom was very good at using sugar bags,
Dying them white and
Making our clothes.

We only spoke French at our house
Now my father knew how to speak "Indian"
We just laughed 'cause we couldn't make it out

I'm sorry
I didn't learn more earlier

I started school in Grade 1
All I knew was French
I didn't even know there was an English language
I picked it up real fast
Mom learned to understand, but she always answered back in French
Father spoke better English than my mother
He had to 'cause people would buy fish from him,
he had to place orders, he had to deal with the government.

We were not allowed to play with the Protestant kids
We had to play with Catholic kids
I liked the Doctor's daughter
We used to hide to play
We were not allowed to do that.

The Métis were never mentioned in school
No

I went to Grade 11 and then I quit
It wasn't my cup of tea

I was always crafty
In school, I made blankets for poor families
When I married at 17, and had children
I made my own son and daughter's clothes
Now,
I enjoy beading,
Making the drums

Mom would always say she didn't have any native blood

Remember the Indian list?
They couldn't go into hotels,
The Indians were getting bad names because of that
That's why
I think
They didn't want us to let on that we had native blood in us.

My dad taught us how to fish,
To navigate the water.
He said:
Watch the bottom
Don't hit any rocks.

My brother-in-law drowned in 1969
He was in a boat with two others and never made it out
It was a bad night with the wind
We took Mom's Good Friday Bread in the boat
We left the shore,
Put the bread down in the location that some cottagers had
Pointed out to us,
Nothing,
I squeezed the bread out like a sponge,
We went a little further out,
I put the bread down,
Waited
All of a sudden the bread took off,
You would have thought that somebody had it at the end of a fishing line,
The bread circled,
We put the marker down.

On the 9th day he came right up

Where the marker was

The OPP said he must have been trapped under the rocks.

I think that was the most powerful thing that happened to me in my whole life.

In 1993

When the Métis Nation formed

I was a founding member

The 64th to join

I got my family to join

So proud

I am a Senator

I have been verified

We are so proud to be Métis

Now they are fighting to get me out of there

The Ministry of Natural Resources wants to make damn sure that we are Métis

—because of the Powley case and because we now have harvesting rights.

They won't take my card away.

I lived on an Island for 17 years.

I cleaned cottages,

That's how I got pulmonary fibrosis

Oven cleaners

Toilet bowl cleaners

Damaged my lungs,

I didn't wear a mask.

I believe in the Creator and what's going to be

I still follow a lot of the teachings of the Aboriginal people,

Like the healing

And smudging.

I can't go into the sweat lodges anymore.

I'm still Catholic, but not Roman.

I follow Father Tony, who was

Excommunicated for baptizing the children of unwed mothers and

Marrying people who were divorced and wanted to be married

In their religion.

I'm ready.

I don't want a wake.

I want a celebration of life.

I have a 3-year-old granddaughter.

She's very interested in beading.

Here, the drum sounds better.

A Story of Teaching/Learning

My mother and I attended a meeting at the Oshawa Métis Council (now the Oshawa and Durham Region Métis council) in the early 2000s. It was at the very first meeting that my mother and I attended that we met Olivine (Bousquet) Tiedema. Olive is a Métis Elder, originally from Manitoba, whose presence in our lives has enriched our paths and those of our families. Olive is an honoured Elder for many in the Métis community. Thanks for sharing parts of your story with me.

Chi Migwetch,

Olivine (Bousquet) Tiedema

I was born March 29, 1928

Mother was French from Quebec,

My dad was a Métis,

My grandfather, Napoleon Bousquet;

He was really the one who embedded within us kids to be proud of who we are.

Never be ashamed of your ancestors,

I'm part Cree/Salteaux/French/Scotch

We spoke French at home,

But I also heard Michif from my dad and

Salteaux from my grandfather

I grew up in St Boniface, Manitoba,

Which was a French community,

There was about maybe six or seven Métis families living there.

The Métis community was in St Vital,

The Academy St Joseph used to bring all the Métis children by bus from

St Vital to St Boniface.

It was maybe a 15–20 minute bus ride.

Some of the nuns were not very good to us Métis kids,

Some were good, but not too many of them.

My name was Bousquet, which was a Métis, well, a French name,

But Métis mixture, two nations.

They were pretty mean to us at times

Of course, I was a very stubborn child;

I look back now and I think no wonder I got punished so many times [laughter].

I always fought for the rights of the Métis.

I always knew who I was and I was never ashamed of it.

Mom would say we were white, French, Catholic

I went to school with Rita Riel, who was Louis Riel's niece, and of course she was

Métis,

A beautiful young lady, dark skin, dark eyes, pitch black hair.

I had pitch black hair at one time too.

I really looked Métis when I was young.

My two older brothers and two older sisters were very light skin—
I guess they took more on the Scottish side or something.

My dad was the best jigger.
I used to jig when I was young.
On avait la plus grosse cuisine et puis une fois par mois
Ils mettaient tous [toute] leur 5 sous et puis ils achetaient une caisse de bière
Dancing,
Dancing
I used to play guitar.
My cousin had the harmonica.
Et puis mon autre cousin avait l'accordéon and the fiddle.
We had lots of fun.
We used to put all the furniture to the side.
So once a month we had a big party.

We used to have lots of fields to play in.
We used to play cowboys and Indians and we used to make tepees.
I always wanted to be the Indian.
If I found a white man I would torture him [laughter, pretending].
We used to play hide and seek.
A group would go and hide.
There was always a captain.
And then we would make a map to show where they went...
We had a lot of places to hide. A lot of bush.
I feel kind of sorry the kids don't have that today...soccer, baseball, hockey,
not to have competition...
We all made our own fun
—Kick the can
'Cause who could afford their own ball?
It was a nice childhood.

I never remember when the trouble kind of started.

I forget what grade I was in.

But there was the history of the battle of Batoche.

And I said to the Sister at the time...'cause Louis Riel was a traitor

—As far as their history was concerned.

I said to the nun:

Sister, you tell us if we lie God will punish us,

And she said yes,

And I said:

Well everything in this book is a lie.

She said: How do you know?

And I said: My grandfather was there and he told me the truth about the battle of

Batoche.

Consequently,

I never passed French History

Because I refused to write it.

My grandfather, whenever he talked about the battle of Batoche and Louis Riel,

He always had tears in his eyes,

I remember the tears falling on my nose,

He used to sit me on his knees and tell me the story.

He loaded the muskets at the battle.

He told me that Louis Riel was a very religious man

He didn't believe in killing,

It's not like they didn't write petition after petition,

But at that time they had to defend themselves,

And Gabriel Dumont, he was captain of the hunt,

(He was my great uncle and Madeleine Willkie was my great auntie),

They were fighting for the plight of the Métis,

The First Nations too,

Louis was hung and a lot of First Nations too.

Everyone was starving.

They were bringing all the so-called whites and giving away the land
Without any regard for people
They just stole it!
It even happened to the Veterans.
My uncle who was First Nation, and my aunt, who was Métis,
They had all kinds of land, but when he came back, half the land
Was given away without any payment or anyone being aware of it.

I quit school
Soeur Angèle Thérèse said:
Olivine, why are you quitting school?
And I said Sister, I'm 16 years old
(I failed Grade 8 three times, my friends are in grade 10 and 11).
I'll never forget what she told me,
I didn't know what she meant at the time.
She said:
Whatever you have there [pointing to her heart],
—Don't ever lose it.
And she said:
Do you know?
—You are ahead of your time

Louis Riel said:
Our people are going to sleep for 100 years
And they will wake up.
I guess he foresaw...
He was very attuned with his feelings.
He was a very good poet.
He was a smart man.

Eventually we are going to get a monument for Louis Riel.

Why don't we celebrate his birthday instead of his hanging?

Growing up, the nearest Lake is 50 miles away.

All we had was the Assiniboine River, the Seine River and the Red River.

I'd never seen a lake in my life.

I forget what grade I was in, but that year,

The girls were going to go to the lake.

I went to a Catholic school, it was all girls, no boys;

If there had been boys I might have still been in school [laughter],

I was voted the most popular girl in my class,

'Cause I used to be quite a nut;

I used to like to make people laugh.

I'll never forget this;

The school priest,

(who I hated, as far as I was concerned, he was just a damned hypocrite);

Anyway, he came to my dad, and I was so happy,

I thought I must have done something special,

And this has stayed with me my whole life,

He came to my dad and said we can't take your daughter on the field trip to the lake

—she's a bad influence on the other girls.

And my dad said: we know she's outspoken but she's not a bad person.

I know I wasn't a bad person,

I just used to like to make people laugh.

I'm happy now that the schools are opening their ears

And their eyes

To the truth.

It has been long enough.

I went to work

In a sewing factory

And a whole gang of us, we were 16,

We took a train and went to

Winnipeg Beach.

I had never seen a beach in my life.

I was just sitting there

The moon coming over the lake

Nothing so beautiful.

I'll never forget it.

The others said,

Come Olive we are all going dancing.

And I said, non, no,

I just have to sit here.

That was the first time I ever saw the reflection of the moon over the water.

It was so beautiful.

I kept working.

I had quite a few boyfriends,

It was just before Lent and I was going to give up dancing.

And this handsome air man asked me to dance.

And I said, o.k.

We danced and he took me home.

He said: Can I see you tomorrow?

And I said sure. But I never thought he would find his way

I took him through alleyways and back lanes.

So the next day, sure enough, he showed up.

On our third date,

He asked my parents if he could have my hand in marriage

([laughter]—the biggest mistake in my life)

Out of it I have five beautiful children, very good children.

And beautiful grandchildren

And great grandchildren.

When I moved to Toronto
I used to go to Yonge and Queen
To see if I could see anyone who looked Métis...

I joined my husband's culture.
I can still sing in Ukrainian.
I can dance, we used to dance, it was really beautiful.

I think it was...'92
I got a phone call.
Were you Olivine Bousquet from St Boniface Manitoba?
I thought my past had caught up to me.
The voice said: we are starting the Métis Nation of Ontario.
And I said you mean to say there are other Métis here?
So, that's how it all started.
I really started to put my best foot forward and tried to learn more about my culture.
I knew the white culture,
But the Aboriginal culture,
The traditions were not too exposed to us.

When my dad's family used to come and visit
They used to all stand in the corner and speak Michif.
And my sister and I ([made the sign of whispering]
—don't they talk funny, you know how kids are),
I would say, Dad what kind of language is that?
And he'd say:
You don't want to learn...
It's too bad because it would have been nice to learn...

When my mom's family came, my dad always spoke very quietly and slowly in French.
My mom's family were upset that she married a Métis.
My dad's family was upset that he didn't marry a Métis.

So there you go, there was prejudice even in those days,

Even amongst family.

But my mom and dad were married over 50 years before my mom passed away.

In my grandfather's time,

The Whites didn't accept the Métis

And the First Nation didn't accept the Métis.

I'm not saying all, but a lot of them they didn't.

On my 80th birthday,

Robert Pilon, our president, announced a dance group in my name:

The Olivine Bousquet Métis Dancers

Which is an honour.

I'm very appreciative and it's very touching

I make medicine bags,

And whatever I sell, half goes to the dancers,

The other half to buy the leather.

Here, take this medicine bag.

Pedagogical Significance of Memories and the Past

What kind of personal, political or pedagogical response do these stories elicit? These stories have offered me assurance in my (re)claiming Métis ancestry and a contemporary Métis identity. These narratives offer healing; they offer connections to the heartbeat of mother earth and to all my relations. In order to understand the silence and come out of the silence, we need to contextualize our own lives, and those of our ancestors, by learning and recognizing the importance of the past. Roger Simon speaks of the potential of public historical memory to become "transactional," and having the potential "to expand that ensemble of people who count for us, who we encounter, not merely as strangers…but as teachers, people who in telling their stories change our own."[22] Stories ought to provoke questions, consideration, attention and draw out implications, and a response.[23]

My conversations with my mother, a revered Métis Elder in her family hometown community, and a revered Métis Elder within my Métis community, helps broaden my perspective and my understanding about some of the issues and pressures to assimilate that influenced the silence around our Indigenous ancestry. I have more questions about the influence of nature, music, dancing, religion, French and English relations, language, class, historical policies, racism, and societal and cultural norms that helped perpetuate and sustain and complicate the silence and have also left traces of Aboriginal heritage and resistance.

Cathy Richardson, for example, explores how disclosure of Métis identity could be "unsafe and imprudent for many Métis families" and why many families made the tactical decision to become a part of dominant culture for "economic and emotional wellness."[24] Certainly, for many of the relatives of my interviewees, such a decision appears to have been made, especially when passing down Aboriginal languages and practices, and adopting English were concerned. However, denying parts of oneself is not easy and does not protect individuals "from the internal wounds received by witnessing racism towards Métis people."[25] For many Métis, there was a tension between trying to "pass" for white and a "sadness of being excluded in the First Nations world."[26] There may be a full range of emotions—guilt, shame, loss—in witnessing systemic racism and navigating these tensions internally and externally. For me, these stories open up the space for discussion, acceptance and understanding. In acknowledging the past, I find hope for the future and a space to begin to recognize all of the diverse experiences of Métis people and their identities.

The forces that shape and have shaped Métis identities are great: economic, cultural, historical, colonial, gendered, institutional and governmental. One might also consider, for instance, the role schools had and have in shaping the silence surrounding Métis consciousness. A Métis Elder described the rejection of Métis historical perspectives in schools, and the impact of Louis Riel being constructed as an enemy of the state as untenable. Another Elder, who left school early, attests to the complete absence of Métis presence in the curriculum. Certainly, schools were hostile places for some Métis people, whose identities were shaped in limiting and sometimes damaging ways. Schools are public institutions that exist within larger social, political, economic, cultural and historical frameworks that systemically devalue Indigenous languages, stories, people and knowledge.[27] Yet, there was some resistance; the stories told by some Métis people show that Métis people in different times and contexts tried to preserve and even use traditional knowledge to make a living and enrich the lives of others. Outside of school, our Métis Elders have been honoured for their volunteerism, their resilience, their leadership, and they are sometimes asked to share their perspectives. Sharing stories of Métis resistance, resilience, silence, and identities helps open up the public space to legitimize Métis people's diversity, complexity, stories, experiences and understandings. There are so many more aspects to consider from these stories that could help enrich, inform and potentially help to change and shape the public realm.

Imagining the Future

Jo-ann Archibald stipulates that "Indigenous peoples' history of colonization has left many of our peoples and our cultures weak and fragmented. Cultural knowledge, traditions, and healing have lessened the detrimental effects of colonization. Cultural knowledge and traditions have also helped us resist assimilation. I believe that Indigenous stories are at the core of our cultures. They have the power to make us think, feel, and be good human beings."[28] Many historical tensions and ambiguities persist, along with the need for fluid and tactical identities. One Métis Elder, teacher and storyteller, Joseph Paquette, is quick to recall a time when it was unsafe for Indigenous Elders to share their knowledge. He maintains that now is the time to move from shame to pride.[29]

I and the Métis women I interviewed all have a strong commitment to (re)claim our Aboriginal ancestry, to not be complicit in the public erasure of Aboriginal presence, to support the seven generations and all our relations on Turtle Island. We have not disappeared. As long as we share, hear, and listen to stories, we will become stronger. As Richardson says, the sharing of experiences helps Métis people create "a sense of 'home' and has helped connect them to other Métis people."[30] Knowledge of history and stories can only help to create greater awareness and understanding between and among the Métis, different Indigenous people, and all people. Arendt certainly believed that totalitarian forces, and I suggest colonialism is such a force, could be changed by including more stories in the public realm. I am grateful for this historical moment when people's awareness is starting to change. If we cannot recognize the experiences of the Métis in all their complexity and plurality, then we fail to challenge the homogeneity that excludes and silences. It is by revealing and talking about the silenced Aboriginal lives of our ancestors, and (re)claiming our identities as Métis people and as Indigenous people, that a more just public realm will unfold and enable us to live "as distinct and unique beings among equals."[31]

Author's Note

Many, many thanks to my mother Claire, Helen (who passed away shortly after our interview), Olivine, my Elders, and to all my relations. I would also like to thank the members of the Oshawa and Durham Region Métis Council (Rob Pilon, Art Henry, Senator Cécile Wagar, Senator André Bosse, and everyone), and the All Our Relations Métis Circle, some of whom grew up with Métis culture and others whose "spirit" memories and connections to traditional ways of life are very strong; I thank them in particular for their passion for sharing and recognizing that the Métis need a place to share and learn and grow, and for welcoming all Métis with open arms. I would also like to thank Elder Joe Paquette for his encouragement and for sharing his traditional knowledge, heart and spirit with myself and countless others, especially the youth. I have so many people to thank for enriching my life and encouraging me on this path— you are all in my heart, Chi Migwetch.

Notes

1. Raven Murphy spoke quite passionately about the importance of this teaching in her "The Elements and You" conference presentation at the Spirit Calling—Ways of Knowing: Durham Aboriginal Education Symposium, at the Durham District School Board, 5 May 2010, in Whitby, Ontario, Canada.

2. Hannah Arendt, *Between Past and Future* (New York: Penguin, 2006), 241.

3. I use the term "Indigenous" to encompass Métis, First Nation and Inuit people. The term "Aboriginal" is also used to designate Métis, First Nation and Inuit people. I use the term "Indian" or "Native" people when used in reference to legislation or when authors or storytellers use it as well. Different terms have been used at different times in different circles for different reasons. I use these terms with the utmost respect and recognize that there are those who find some of them problematic, even offensive, and I apologize in advance if anyone is hurt by the terms, but I believe the speakers and authors I quote and context signal different historical shifts. Further, who has defined people and who may define themselves in the public realm is part of a larger, ongoing discussion between and among Indigenous people themselves at this time and in larger public spaces.

4. Ute Lischke and David T. McNab, "Introduction," in *The Long Journey of a Forgotten People: Métis Identities and Family Histories*, ed. Ute Lischke and David T. McNab (Waterloo, ON: Wilfrid Laurier University Press, 2007), 1.

5. Susan Dion, *Braiding Histories: Learning from Aboriginal People's Experiences and Perspectives* (Vancouver: University of British Columbia Press, 2009), 48.

6. Ute Lischke, "Reflections on Métis Connections in the Life and Writings of Louise Erdrich," in *The Long Journey of a Forgotten People: Métis Identities and Family Histories*, ed. Ute Lischke and David T. McNab, (Waterloo, ON: Wilfrid Laurier University Press, 2007), 39.

7. Kim Anderson, *A Recognition of Being: Reconstructing Native Womanhood* (Toronto: Sumach Press, 2008), 21.

8. Anderson, *A Recognition of Being*, 23.

9. Agnes Grant, *Finding My Talk: How Fourteen Native Women Reclaimed Their Lives after Residential School* (Calgary: Fifth House, 2004), 9.

10. Melanie J. Murray, *A Very Polite Genocide, or the Girl Who Fell to Earth*. Play performed at Buddies in Bad Times Theatre, 21 December 2008, in Toronto, Ontario, Canada.

11. Jo-Anne Fiske, "Political Status of Native Indian Women: Contradictory Implications of Canadian State Policy," in *The Days of Our Grandmothers: A*

Reader in Aboriginal Women's History in Canada, ed. Mary-Ellen Kelm and Lorna Townsend. (Toronto: University of Toronto Press, 2006), 340.

12. Ian Bron and Zachary Houle, "Canada in the Making—Aboriginals: Treaties and Relations" para. 2. Accessed 28 August 2010, www.canadiana.ca/citm/themes/aboriginals/aboriginals8_e.html.

13. Bron and Houle, "Canada in the Making."

14. Bron and Houle, "Canada in the Making," para. 3.

15. Fiske, "Political Status of Native Indian Women," 340.

16. Given the state-defined legal definitions of Aboriginal or Indigenous identity, many people were no longer able to declare themselves Métis or First Nations. As part of my own and my mother's trajectory of definitions, for example, we know that one of our great grandmothers defined herself as Ojibwa and another as Métis in census data. Then there was no mention of any Indigenous ancestry until we were able to declare our Indigenous identity, as recognized members of the Métis Nation of Ontario. So now we are once again able to "count" as Indigenous. So again, the acts of being named and of naming oneself add to the complexity of connecting with and being connected to Indigenous communities. In our case, a Métis organization is helping to re-establish community, connection and identification. Yet this, too, is not without complications, since some Métis do not have the proper documentation to join some organizations. As a result, a variety of organizations are addressing cultural needs, while other organizations are addressing legal and cultural needs. Many Métis, especially in eastern Canada, are fighting for recognition. Many First Nations also struggled and some are still struggling to name themselves legally as First Nations, that is, treaty rights holders. On December 15, 2010, Bill C-3: *Gender Equity in Indian Registration Act* received Royal Assent; this legislation may help several children and grandchildren of women who lost their Indian status as a result of marrying non-Indian men regain their Indian status and be registered as treaty "Indians" or "Aboriginals." Accessed 17 December 2010, www.ainc-inac.gc.ca/br/is/bll/index-eng.asp. This follows other modifications to the *Indian Act*, such as Bill C-31, in 1985, that revoked the loss of a woman's "Indian" status as a consequence of her marrying a non-Indian man, as Jo-Anne Fiske notes in "Political Status of Native Indian Women," 341.

17. Dion, *Braiding Histories*, 18.

18. Dion, *Braiding Histories*, 19.

19. Carl Leggo, *Teaching to Wonder: Responding to Poetry in the Secondary Classroom* (Vancouver: Pacific Educational Press, 1997), 17.

20. Kim Anderson elaborates on the process of "contextualizing knowledge" as a means to not only show that one's knowledge is "tied closely to one's personal experience," but that it also "challenges the objectification of knowledge" of Indigenous people because it more fully reveals who the storyteller is and how the researcher-interviewer is actively involved in the knowledge production process and is not not positioned neutrally outside it. See Kim Anderson, *A Recognition of Being*, 21–22.

21. Dion, *Braiding Histories*, 16.

22. Roger Simon, "The Touch of the Past: The Pedagogical Significance of a Transactional Sphere of Public Memory," in *Revolutionary Pedagogies: Cultural Politics, Instituting Education, and the Discourse of Theory*, ed. Peter Pericles Trifonas (New York: Routledge, 2000), 63.

23. Simon, "The Touch of the Past," 63–67.

24. Cathy Richardson, "Metis Identity Creation and Tactical Responses to Oppression and Racism," *Variegations* 2 (2006): 61–62.

25. Richardson, "Metis Identity Creation," 61.

26. Richardson, "Metis Identity Creation," 62.

27. See Olive P. Dickason, *The Myth of the Savage and the Beginnings of French Colonialism in the Americas* (Edmonton: University of Alberta Press, 1984); Thomas King, *The Truth about Stories: A Native Narrative* (Toronto: House of Anansi Press, 2003).

28. Jo-ann Archibald, *Indigenous Storywork: Educating the Heart, Mind, Body, and Spirit* (Vancouver: University of British Columbia Press, 2008), 139.

29. Joseph Paquette, "Who me…Métis? No more fear or shame." Conference presentation at the Spirit Calling—Ways of Knowing: Durham Aboriginal Education Symposium, Durham District School Board, 5 May 2010, in Whitby, Ontario, Canada.

30. Richardson, "Metis Identity Creation," 67.

31. Hannah Arendt, *The Human Condition* (Chicago: University of Chicago Press, 1998), 178.

Bibliography

Anderson, Kim. *A Recognition of Being: Reconstructing Native Womanhood*. Toronto: Sumach Press, 2008.

Arendt, Hannah. *Between Past and Future*. New York: Penguin, 2006.

———. *The Human Condition*. Chicago: University of Chicago Press, 1998.

Archibald, Jo-ann. *Indigenous Storywork: Educating the Heart, Mind, Body, and Spirit*. Vancouver: University of British Columbia Press, 2008.

Bron, Ian, and Zachary Houle. "Canada in the Making—Aboriginals: Treaties and Relations." Accessed 28 August 2010. www.canadiana.ca/citm/themes/ aboriginals/aboriginals8_e.html.

Dickason, Olive P. *The Myth of the Savage and the Beginnings of French Colonialism in the Americas*. Edmonton: University of Alberta Press, 1984.

Dion, Susan. *Braiding Histories: Learning from Aboriginal People's Experiences and Perspectives*. Vancouver: University of British Columbia Press, 2009.

Fiske, Jo-Anne. "Political Status of Native Indian Women: Contradictory Implications of Canadian State Policy." In *The Days of Our Grandmothers: A Reader in Aboriginal Women's History in Canada*, edited by Mary-Ellen Kelm and Lorna Townsend, 336–66. Toronto: University of Toronto Press, 2006.

Grant, Agnes. *Finding My Talk: How Fourteen Native Women Reclaimed Their Lives after Residential School*. Calgary: Fifth House, 2004.

Indian and Northern Affairs Canada. Bill C-3: *Gender Equity in Indian Registration Act*. www.ainc-inac.gc.ca/br/is/bll/index-eng.asp.

King, Thomas. *The Truth about Stories: A Native Narrative*. Toronto: House of Anansi Press, 2003.

Lischke, Ute. "Reflections on Métis Connections in the Life and Writings of Louise Erdich." In *The Long Journey of a Forgotten People: Métis Identities and Family Histories*, edited by Ute Lischke and David T. McNab, 39–53. Waterloo, ON: Wilfrid Laurier University Press, 2007.

Lischke, Ute, and David T. McNab. "Introduction." In *Long Journey of a Forgotten People: Métis Identities and Family Histories*, edited by Ute Lischke and David T. McNab, 1–9. Waterloo, ON: Wilfrid Laurier University Press, 2007.

Murphy, Raven. "The Elements and You." Conference presentation at the Spirit Calling—Ways of Knowing: Durham Aboriginal Education Symposium, Durham District School Board, Whitby Ontario, 5 May 2010.

Murray, Melanie J. *A Very Polite Genocide, or the Girl Who Fell to Earth*. Play performed at Buddies in Bad Times Theatre, 21 December 2008, in Toronto, Ontario, Canada.

Paquette, Joseph. "Who me...Métis? No more fear or shame." Conference presentation at the Spirit Calling—Ways of Knowing: Durham Aboriginal Education Symposium, Durham District School Board, Whitby Ontario, 5 May 2010.

Richardson, Cathy. "Metis Identity Creation and Tactical Responses to Oppression and Racism." *Variegations* 2 (2006): 56–71.

Simon, Roger. "The Touch of the Past: The Pedagogical Significance of a Transactional Sphere of Public Memory." In *Revolutionary Pedagogies: Cultural Politics, Instituting Education, and the Discourse of Theory*, edited by Peter Pericles Trifonas, 61–80. New York: Routledge, 2000.

A Half-breed's Perspective | 3
on Being Métis

GREGG DAHL

On reading the will of my great-great-great-grandfather,
David Magnus Cusitar.

...

He could have said:
My wild rose, my sweet prairie crocus,
Name yourself to be âpihtaw-kosisa   half-sons or half-breed
And our children and their children
Lift your sad face from these pages
And set a feast at the table;

Good lass, use me wee mother's linen,
Aye, the silver
Passed down from me gran

...

He could have said:

My wild rose, me sweet prairie crocus,

Tapwe, mistahi ki-sâkihitin!   It is true, I love you very much!

—GREGORY SCOFIELD,

excerpted from "The Will" in Singing Home the Bones *(Vancouver: Polestar, 2005)*

THE IDEA for this chapter germinated in the realization that the word I use most comfortably for my Aboriginal identity can occasionally yield discomfort in some of my interlocutors. Despite my assurances that I do not mind being labelled a "Half-breed," many people do not understand why that is and why, in fact, it is a point of pride for me. Many times, from many non-Aboriginal people, I have heard: "Well, that's OK for you to call yourself *that*, but I can't call you *that*."

My pride in being a Half-breed has several dimensions. One aspect is the affidavits my relations signed to swear they were Half-breeds for the purposes of the land distribution mechanism (the scrip process) used by Canada to live up to the intent of section 31 of the *Manitoba Act*. Thus, my family name and the people from whom I descended had been in the region that became Manitoba for quite some time prior to 1870. Another source of my pride in being a Half-breed is that my relations were willing to accept the label used by the Canadian government to indicate their racial category. Why would I not honour my relations' acceptance of that label, given that they were English-speaking people in the Red River Settlement and would have had some understanding of the term? Another source of my pride is the Constitutional recognition of the Half-breeds.

Moreover, I don't relate all that closely with much of the "Métis mythology" that has developed around the events and experiences of the French-speaking people of the Red River colony, such as the Seven Oaks affair, the Sayer trial, the provisional government of Rupert's Land and,

Jane Cummings (née Monkman), born 1822 in St. Paul's parish, Red River Settlement; daughter of James Monkman and Mary, a Swampy Cree woman; married Robert Cummings.

more recently, the implications of the inclusion of "Métis" in section 35(2) of the Constitution of Canada in 1982. Much of what I hear from the leaders of the political representative organizations of the Métis in Manitoba regarding the "birth of the Métis Nation" and the "Métis Homeland" does not harmoniously resonate with me. However, it does feed a keen historical interest in the life and experiences of my ancestors. Perhaps this is because I descend from a Hudson's Bay Company (HBC) servant and a Selkirk settler, and I know of no familial connection with any North West Company (NWC) employees of the time; that is, the voyageurs and coureurs de bois, from which many of the western Métis descend. As this chapter attempts to demonstrate, the people in the English-speaking parishes of the settlement were rather distinct.

The sense of my Aboriginal identity resonates with the following description from 1896 of the people of the Red River Settlement by historian George Bryce:

The settlement was made up of three principal elements: First, there were the descendants of the early French traders and voyageurs, who had married the Indian women of the country, and left behind them the French half-breeds, or as they were often called the Métis, or at other times the Bois-brulee. These people lived chiefly up the Red River from the mouth of the Assiniboine in the parishes of St. Boniface, St. Vital, St. Norbert and Ste. Agathe, in St. Charles, St. François Xavier, and Baie St. Paul on the Assiniboine, and at two outlying settlements, one on the Seine at Pointe de Chene, and the other at St. Laurent on Lake Manitoba. Though somewhat severely spoken of by Ross in his work on the Red River, the French halfbreeds are kind and obliging to those who treat them as friends, and though deprived of the benefits of education are a chivalrous and well-mannered people.

Second, among the elements of Red River people are the descendants of the older employees of the Hudson's Bay Company, many of them from the Orkney Islands, who also on the mother's side were related to Indians of the country. These were known as the English, i.e., English-speaking halfbreeds. The chief English halfbreed settlements were on the Red River in the parishes of St. Paul, St. Andrews, and St. Clements, with St. James, Headingley, Poplar Point, and Portage la Prairie on the Assiniboine. The English half-breed was more docile than the French, less of a hunter and more of a worker, and hospitable to a fault.

Last of the elements of the Red River people were the Selkirk settlers, and their descendants, who lived north of the present site of the city of Winnipeg, in the parish of Kildonan, or in the parish of St. John's, which included much of the site of the present city of Winnipeg. The Kildonan people were almost entirely of Highland origin, and had features of language and character and a parish life, quite distinctive in this mixture of races.

This tripartite community varied much in religion, manners and customs. The French halfbreeds were Roman Catholics, the English halfbreeds belonged chiefly to the Church of England, and the Selkirk settlers were largely Presbyterians.

As to numbers the census of 1849 given by Ross states that there were in all 5,391 of a population. The population of the settlement in 1870, in the year *when Manitoba was formed, has usually been stated at about 12,000, of whom 5,000 were French halfbreeds, 5,000 English halfbreeds and 2,000 whites. It should be stated that the whites were not all confined to Kildonan and St. John's but were to some extent scattered through the other parishes.*[1]

The one element of the Settlement's population rather ignored in the description above is the maternal ancestry of the Half-breeds. As all mothers have, the country wives of the NWC and HBC employees had an essential influence on their offspring. Sylvia Van Kirk observed in her study of women within fur trade society that the English-speaking descendants of the HBC employees did not seem too interested in their Indian relatives. The Indian mothers and grandmothers of the Half-breeds and Métis had differing relationships with their progeny. The characterization of the relationship between the Métis and their maternal ancestry as *connected* between the Métis and their maternal ancestry is labelled as *distant* between the Half-breeds and their mothers. It is an interesting social aspect of the realities of having a mixed heritage. As Van Kirk observed, "This fact may indeed be a distinguishing characteristic of the English mixed-blood group which serves to differentiate them from their Métis cousins. Captain Palliser, who led an exploring expedition through Rupert's Land in the late 1850s, observed that there was a sharp difference in attitude between what he called the Scotch and the French half-breeds."[2]

Perhaps the distinction between the English-speaking Half-breeds and the French-speaking Métis described in the historiography[3] still exists in the population of descendants of the inhabitants of the Red River Settlement. And it is this distinction that might provide some comfort with, and acceptance of, the epithet "Half-breed."

My paternal great-great-grandparents, John George Dahl and Elizabeth Cummings, were married on January 13, 1870. The ceremony was in St. Paul's parish church in the Red River Settlement. The date of the wedding means they were married during the earliest days of Manitoba's history when the provisional government of Rupert's Land was formulated at Fort Garry in the Red River Settlement. They were married in what is now the oldest church in Manitoba. According to Alexander Begg's journal, the weather that day was very sharp and frosty.[4] The fact that their wedding happened in St. Paul's parish church during the Red River Resistance speaks to the degree of involvement some of the Half-breeds had with the political events at the Forks. In St. Paul's parish, north of the Forks, life for some Half-breeds seems to have continued pretty much as it had prior to the political actions taken by Louis Riel and his supporters.[5]

My point is that I am a descendant of a Half-breed family of St. Paul's parish, making me a Half-breed quite clearly and comfortably in accordance with many descriptions of my ancestors and the time in which they lived.

However, in 2003, I was asked to sign an affirmation of being Métis for the purposes of an Aboriginal employment program of the Department of Indian Affairs and Northern Development. I was accepted as being Métis, which made me curious. One could not identify as Half-breed.[6] As a result of that incident I formulated a few questions: Are the terms "Half-breed" and "Métis" just a matter of English and French translation with the same set of people being referred to by either term? When did the Half-breeds become Métis? Could a Half-breed pass the *Powley* test? If yes, would a Half-breed then have a Métis Aboriginal right to hunt for food; or, could there be such a thing as a Half-breed Aboriginal right to hunt for food in the environs of the former Red River Settlement? Or, if the Half-breeds were more workers than hunters in the settlement, might they have other Aboriginal rights? Is the term "Half-breed" in the Constitution of Canada?

Anyways, my curiosity was piqued and I went in search of information that might provide some answers to these questions. This chapter is the result of my search.

Elizabeth Anne Dahl (née Cummings, daughter of Jane and Robert Cummings) and John George Dahl (son of Elizabeth and Alexander Dahl). Paternal grandparents of Frank Dahl.

Frank Dahl and Helen Dahl (née Bodie). Married 1936 in Bagot, Manitoba, close to Portage la Prairie. Paternal grandparents of Gregg Dahl.

Is "Half-breed" in the Constitution of Canada?

To answer this question, one needs to look at the terms used in the legislation that brought about the addition of Rupert's Land to Canada and the creation of the original province of Manitoba. The constitutional legislation that achieved this geographic expansion, and redrew the map of the Dominion of Canada, was the *British North America Act, 1871*.

In order to trace the inclusion of the terms "Half-breed" and "Métis" in that act, it is helpful to follow the legislative steps taken by both the Canadian and British Parliaments, and the related communications between them, that allowed for and supported the creation of Manitoba out of Rupert's Land.

Canada expanded geographically by admitting other British North American colonies, including Rupert's Land, in accordance with section 146 of the *British North America Act, 1867* (now the *Constitution Act, 1867*). Section 146 required the Houses of the Canadian Parliament to send an address to the Queen to set out the terms of admittance of Rupert's Land and the North-West Territory to Canada.[7] The address sent to Queen Victoria in December 1867 included the following as a commitment from Canada: "And furthermore, that, upon the transference of the territories in question to the Canadian Government, the claims of the Indian tribes to compensation for lands required for purposes of settlement will be considered and settled in conformity with the equitable principles which have uniformly governed the British Crown in its dealing with the aborigines."[8] The principles referred to in this commitment to the Queen would arguably have been those articulated in the Royal Proclamation of 1763.[9]

The Parliament of Canada passed the *Manitoba Act* in early 1870. The word "Half-breed" appears in the English version of the act, and "Métis" appears in the French version. Section 31 of the English version of the act reads as follows: "And whereas, it is expedient, towards the extinguishment of the Indian Title to the lands in the Province, to appropriate a portion of such ungranted lands, to the extent of one million four hundred thousand acres thereof, for the benefit of the families of the half-breed residents, it is hereby enacted, that, under regulations to be from time to time made by the Governor General in Council, the Lieutenant-Governor shall select such lots or tracts in such parts of the Province as he may deem expedient, to the extent aforesaid, and divide the same among the children of the half-breed heads of families residing in the Province at the time of the said transfer to Canada...."[10] One possible inference to be drawn from this text is that the Half-breed residents were to receive land as compensation for their possible Indian title. Canada was not sure if the Half-breeds had Indian title; but if they did, it was intended to be extinguished by section 31. In other words, Canada was not sure whether or not the Half-breeds were aborigines in the territories Canada was acquiring, but Canada was operating under a commitment to Queen Victoria to deal with *any* aborigines on the terms outlined in the address to her setting out the terms of bringing Rupert's Land into the country.

The Queen replied to the address from Canada in the Order of Her Majesty in Council admitting Rupert's Land and the North-Western Territory into the union, dated the 23rd day of June, 1870. Among other things, the reply stated at item 14 that "Any claims of Indians to compensation for lands required for purposes of settlement shall be disposed of by the Canadian Government in communication with the Imperial Government: and the Company [Hudson's Bay Company] shall be relieved of all responsibility in respect of them."[11] Therefore, Canada needed to deal with any land having Indian title attached to it that Canada may wish to open up for settlement. The HBC operated under a Royal Charter and, therefore, was an emanation of the Crown. However, whatever emanation of the Crown infused the HBC, that particular emanation was relieved of all capacity or responsibility for dealing with Indian title, according to Queen Victoria's order. It was now up to Canada to deal with the Indians and, in those dealings, to live up to the equitable principles of the Crown.

As indicated above, the *Manitoba Act, 1870*, was passed by Canada but it became part of the constitutional legislation for Canada upon the passing of the *British North America Act, 1871*, by the UK Parliament. Section 5 of that British act noted: "The following Acts passed by the said Parliament of Canada,….and, 'An Act to amend and continue the Act 32 and 33 Victoria, chapter 3; and to establish and provide for the Government of the Province of Manitoba,' shall be and be deemed to have been valid and effectual for all purposes whatsoever from the date at which they respectively received the assent, in the Queen's name, of the Governor General of the said Dominion of Canada."[12] It may seem rather excessive to trace this legislative and communications trail, but all of the steps taken by the Canadian and UK parliaments combine to indicate an interesting aspect of the contemporary relationship between the Crown and the Half-breeds. The Crown allocated land to the Half-breeds in order to further the desire on the part of Canada to extinguish Indian title in Manitoba. It was not the case that the Half-breeds were legally determined to have possessed Indian title. Canada was not sure. But rather than delay settlement in their newly acquired territory by first determining an answer to the question of whether or not the Half-breeds had Indian title, Canada opted to allocate land for the purpose of extinguishing any possible Indian title the Half-breeds may have had at the time. Thus, political expediency dictated a form of practical resolution to a problematic situation.

The pragmatic solution to Canada's problem resulted in the inclusion of the term "Half-breed" in section 31 of the *Manitoba Act, 1870*. Canada was erring on the side of caution. It anticipated and wanted an influx of settlers to the area and it wanted to live up to its commitments in its address to Queen Victoria and the instructions they received from her in response. And so, in order to uphold both, Canada treated the Half-breeds as aborigines for the sake of not impeding settlement into the North West. As a result, "Half-breed" and "Métis" are constitutional labels for an Aboriginal people located in the area of Canada that included the original province of Manitoba as of May 12, 1870. The people were named as a result of a cautionary approach taken by Canada to address whether or not the people in Rupert's Land were "aborigines" and the possibility, therefore, that they may have had Indian title.

Obviously getting a deal was a fundamental consideration, but it would have also been the case that satisfying the promises to the Crown was an element of securing that deal. If the people were aborigines of some type, then the Half-breeds may have had an interest in the land that was to be compensated and addressed by the entitlement created by section 31 of the *Manitoba Act*. The only Aboriginal title of concern to the Crown in 1870 was Indian title. And so Canada decided that land was to be given in exchange for the possible Indian title, thereby extinguishing it. Canada could then invite settlers to move into the territory, enticed by various land transfer schemes, without having to worry about whether the land deals could be undone. Land offers that could fall apart would not have been good for attracting settlers to the new province. Settlement needed to be supported by clear land title.

We will return to the idea of a Half-breed or Métis interest in the land a little later. First we should recall the idea that Aboriginal title (or Indian title as it was called at the time) is not created by legislation. The *Manitoba Act* did not create the possible Indian title that the Half-breeds may have possessed. Aboriginal title is manifested in the fact of exclusive prior occupation and usage of the land by Aboriginal people in what now makes up Canada.[13][14] The Aboriginal title that the Half-breeds may have had was extinguished by legislation, but did the entitlement to 1.4 million acres in the act extinguish any and all of their interests in the land? This idea will be pursued further below, but I want to foreshadow it here.

Clearly the answer to the question above is "yes." The term "Half-breed" is in the Constitution of Canada, as formulated in 1871. It is important to remember that once a term is embedded in the Constitution, explicit removal of it, a substitution for it, or a change in terms would require a constitutional amendment. In other words, constitutional legislation is required to achieve any of the above. To date, no constitutional legislation has removed, substituted, changed, or replaced the term "Half-breed." However, in addition to the use of the term "Métis" in the French version of the *Manitoba Act*, the term "Métis" is included in Part II of the *Constitution Act, 1982*. What does this additional inclusion mean?[15]

"Métis" in Part II of the *Constitution Act, 1982*

First, let us be clear about the terminology for the Aboriginal people referred to in the *Constitution Act, 1982*. In addition, let us begin by being clear about the elements of the most recent and repatriated incarnation of the Constitution of Canada. Those elements are defined in Part VII of the *Constitution Act, 1982*, which reads:

> *52. (2) The Constitution of Canada includes*
>
> *(a) the Canada Act 1982, including this Act;*
>
> *(b) the Acts and orders referred to in the schedule; and*
>
> *(c) any amendment to any Act or order referred to in paragraph (a) or (b).*[16]

The "schedule" in section 52(2)(b) includes the *Manitoba Act, 1870*, and the Rupert's Land and North-Western Territory Order.

Section 56 of the *Constitution Act, 1982*, is also relevant to purposes of this chapter. It reads: "Where any portion of the Constitution of Canada has been or is enacted in English and French..., the English and French versions of that portion of the Constitution are equally authoritative."[17] Given that the *Manitoba Act, 1870*, was enacted by Canada in both English and French, and the act is part of the "schedule" referred to in section 52, then it must be concluded, in accordance with section 56, that the terms "Métis" and "Half-breed" are included by reference in the *Constitution Act, 1982*. And so, again, let me reiterate the point I made above: "Half-breed" is a term included in the Constitution of Canada. Moreover, according to section 56, "Métis" and "Half-breed" are of equal constitutional authority. And by further inference, it would seem that either of the terms refer to the same set of people. The main point is that the two terms are referentially equivalent when it comes to the set of people referenced in section 31 of the *Manitoba Act*, and that both terms are included in the *Constitution Act, 1982*.

However, "Métis" is included in another section of the Constitution in 1982, outside of the *Manitoba Act*. It is this second inclusion of the term

"Métis" that is given such reverential importance by some purveyors of what I have called the "Métis mythology." It may be quite familiar to the reader, but for the sake of thoroughness and argument, here is the second passage in the Constitution of Canada where the term "Métis" appears:

PART II

RIGHTS OF THE ABORIGINAL PEOPLES OF CANADA

35. (1) The existing aboriginal and treaty rights of the aboriginal peoples of Canada are hereby recognized and affirmed.

(2) In this Act, "aboriginal peoples of Canada" includes the Indian, Inuit and Métis peoples of Canada.[18]

As most people who are members of western Métis political organizations know, the reason for the inclusion of "Métis" in section 35(2) of the Constitution Act, 1982, is that the term was included as a result of the lobbying efforts of Harry Daniels, then leader of the Native Council of Canada. As a result of those efforts, Jean Chrétien, then Minister of Justice and Attorney General of Canada, requested the word be added. The inclusion of "Métis" was a last minute addition to the legislation and very little thought went into what or who the word referenced. What was thought at the time was that the terms employed in section 35(1) did not actually "recognize or affirm" anything for the Métis, since they had no existing treaty or Aboriginal rights. Moreover, any rights they may have had were extinguished through the scrip system that was used to implement the land entitlements of the Manitoba Act and the Dominion Lands Act. The Métis were not being given constitutional protection of their rights, since it was thought they had no treaty or Aboriginal rights. Their rights had been extinguished, if they ever had any. The term "Half-breed" did not come up during the drafting of section 35(2). It was not considered.

The drafters of section 35 felt that the inclusion of the Métis, in relation to Aboriginal and treaty rights, was anomalous and confusing.[19] This notion was reflected in the policy and legal positions of the federal government up to the time of the *Powley* decision; that is, the Métis had no treaty rights and they could not prove Aboriginal rights. The federal position was changed in light of the *Powley* decision, which described a Métis Aboriginal right to hunt for food in the environs of Sault Ste. Marie, Ontario, and provided a test for determining if Métis Aboriginal rights could exist in other areas of Canada.[20]

So, what is the meaning of the use of "Métis" in section 35(2) of the *Constitution Act, 1982*? I have argued that it does not mean that "Métis" replaces "Half-breed" constitutionally, or in English legal language. It does not mean that "Half-breed" is substituted by "Métis" in any fashion. I think what it does mean is that the second use of the term "Métis" in the *Constitution Act, 1982*, is the result of some significant lobbying efforts and is reflective of prevailing linguistic preferences at the time. In addition, I want to point out that any replacement, or substitution, of the term "Half-breed" may have the unintended consequence of being viewed as an attempt to deny an Aboriginal people their self-determination and their Aboriginal identity. Surely such a perception should be avoided.

Notwithstanding such considerations, the truth is that the term "Métis" is predominant in popular, academic, and legal narratives, as well as government policy and English historical texts. This fact cannot be denied. It may, perhaps, be understood as a result of the inclusion of the term "Métis" in section 35(2) of the *Constitution Act, 1982*. This is a plausible explanation, given the attention that section 35 received in media coverage at the time of the constitutional negotiations and the academic attention it has acquired since.

An additional fact may also help explain the preponderance in English texts of the term "Métis," which is the judicial usage of "Métis." This fact may also give credence to the notion of a change in legal terminology. The importance of the judicial finding of the Métis right to hunt for food in the *Powley* case is undeniable. It is a significant point in the history of the determination of the Métis rights in Canada. The next section of this essay examines this preference for the term "Métis" over the constitutional (and historically accurate) term "Half-breed" in the English language; in other words, why and when did "Half-breed" become "Métis"?

However, before considering that question, let us return to the above foreshadowed issue of a potential Half-breed or Métis interest in land, which Canada was grappling with in 1870. In a case that originated in the courts of Manitoba, both a trial court judge and appeal court judges have written extensively in their decisions about section 31 of the *Manitoba Act*. At trial, the claimants argued that the interest in the land that the Half-breeds and Métis possessed was Aboriginal title, and they also argued that the Aboriginal title had been extinguished by the legislation at section 31.[21] The trial judge decided that the provision was simply a tool to get the deal done with the local people, to satisfy the opposition in the House of Commons, to bring Manitoba into the country, and to make way for settlers. But the puzzle Canada faced at the time continues to draw attention.

Shin Imai stated in his commentary on the *Indian Act* in 2002 that "section 31 provides constitutional recognition that there existed a 'half-breed' interest in the land."[22] After the decision in the Manitoba Court of Queen's Bench in the case, Imai changed his comments in the 2010 edition of the same book to read that "the judge explained that the opening words in section 31 were merely a 'political expediency' and that therefore, they could be ignored."[23] On this point, the trial court judge wrote that it was not the intention of the Canadian Parliament to recognize the Indian title of the people in section 31: "Rather it was a political expedient used successfully by (John A.) Macdonald and his government to satisfy the delegates (representatives of the Red River Settlement sent to Ottawa) and make palatable to the opposition in Parliament the grant of land to the children of the half-breeds and to thereby ensure passage of the Act."[24] Given this determination, the trial judge came to the following conclusion: "In light of my findings I conclude there was no *sui generis* relationship in respect of the subject land as between the Métis and the Crown prior to the enactment of section 31. And, what section 31 did was nothing more than to create a grant to a certain class of people, in this case, the Métis children. But that interest or entitlement to land did not derive from an interest independent of the Crown. Rather, it was an interest that was created by the Crown by legislation. Accordingly, the Crown's duty here was a public law duty and no fiduciary relationship was thereby created nor did any fiduciary duty or obligation arise between the Crown and the Métis children as a result."[25] The trial judge clearly dismisses the claimants' argument that there was the recognition of Aboriginal title by Canada and also rejects the notion that a fiduciary duty regarding the transfer of the land was owed to the beneficiaries named in section 31 of the *Manitoba Act*, since there was no Aboriginal title in the land held by the Half-breeds or the Métis. On appeal, the entire decision of the trial court was upheld; that is, it was decided that the claimants were making this claim too late. Limitations blocked the claim, according to both the trial and appeal court judges.

However, the appeal court judge delved into the issue of a fiduciary duty in obiter comments. He outlined a legal analysis of "fiduciary duty" that may be claimed in the absence of Aboriginal title. Then the judge proceeded to contemplate "whether an interest in land short of Aboriginal title is a sufficient basis for a cognizable Aboriginal interest therein."[26] This entire line of analysis, the judge conceded, was quite vexing in the case before him and, more generally, in the case of the Métis and their interest in the section 31 lands. But, unlike the trial judge, he decided that "the Métis of Red River had an interest of some kind sufficient to be recognized, at least for political purposes, as having been extinguished through the (*Manitoba*) *Act*."[27] After concluding that it is possible that the Métis had an interest in land that would have been a "cognizable Aboriginal interest" sufficient to satisfy the first element of the test he outlined in his decision for the existence of a fiduciary duty, the judge backs away from concluding that the Métis actually had such a "cognizable Aboriginal interest." He concluded the theoretical possibility of a cognizable Métis interest, but not an actual one, and further concluded that

It is to be expected that the approach to a cognizable Métis interest could well differ from that with respect to Indians. The Supreme Court of Canada in Powley modified the pre-contact Aboriginal rights test in a manner that made it possible for the Métis, as a people with post-contact origins, to assert rights protected by section 35 of the Constitution Act, 1982. Modification of the other components of the Aboriginal rights test was not addressed, but would surely have to be in the circumstances before this court. For example, the test for a cognizable Métis interest, if there is one, by definition would not require that a reserve be involved.

The question of exactly what does constitute a cognizable Métis interest, and whether one exists in this truly unique case I leave for another day...all the more so since focussed argument on whether or not this critical component of a fiduciary obligation existed has not taken place.[28]

The Supreme Court of Canada demonstrated in the *Powley* decision a willingness to modify the test for Aboriginal rights in order to accommodate the reality of the post-contact existence of the Métis. And so the concepts of "ethnogenesis" and "effective European control" entered into the test for Aboriginal rights in the context of the Métis. Could the Aboriginal rights landscape be changed again by the Supreme Court of Canada to include the concept of a "cognizable Métis interest" in land? The possibility is raised that the test for a cognizable Aboriginal interest may need to be modified in order to allow for the actuality of a cognizable Métis interest in the land that became Manitoba and was intended to be addressed by section 31 of the *Manitoba Act*.

If the possibility of a "cognizable Métis interest in land" is realized, the following paragraph in the trial decision needs to be remembered. The trial judge wrote, "I note that at the material time, those of mixed English and Indian ancestry were called 'half-breeds' and those of mixed French and Indian ancestry were called 'Métis.' The Act (*Manitoba Act*) called both 'half-breeds.' Today however, both are called 'Métis.' In this judgment, my use of the phrase 'English half-breeds' will refer to those of the English and Indian ancestry, and my use of the phrase 'French Métis' will refer to those of French and Indian ancestry at the material time. My use of the word 'Métis' will refer to both the English half-breeds and the French Métis, then and now."[29] It is readily apparent that the term "Half-breed" refers to a people having had the same interest in the land now called Manitoba that the "Métis" had. The question remains whether this theoretic possibility will find a judicial characterization at the Supreme Court of Canada. It is also clear from the definition in the trial court decision that the use of the term "Métis" is a matter of preference, rather than a legal requirement. When it comes to legal matters addressing the Aboriginal rights of the mixed-heritage people of the Red River Settlement, "Half-breed" refers to a particular people whose rights would be protected by section 35 of the Constitution just as Métis rights are protected. The only difference is that Métis rights are possible across Canada since the *Powley* decision, whereas Half-breed rights would be located in the former postage-stamp province of Manitoba.

To conclude, whatever the reasoning may have been at the time of drafting the *Manitoba Act*, the fact remains that the terms "Half-breed" and "Métis" are constitutional terms since the enactment of the *British North America Act, 1871*, which is part of the Constitution of Canada as of 1982. Although the Half-breeds are not listed in section 35(2) as one of the Aboriginal peoples of Canada, we have seen that this absence does not mean that the term is replaced by "Métis." Nor does the inclusion of the Métis in section 35(2) add anything extra to the "constitutional weight" of the term "Métis." What has happened to the term "Métis" is that the geographic area where the Métis may exist has expanded due to judicial findings in cases that originated in geographic areas where Métis have existed but may have no connection whatsoever to the people referred to as "Métis" in the French-language version of the *Manitoba Act, 1870*. By contrast, where the Half-breeds existed and originated remains legally limited to the geographic area upon which the original province of Manitoba was created. The *Powley* decision resulted in a legal test for finding a Métis community that could have arisen and continues to exist anywhere in Canada. It is a rather odd result of the case, but our interest here is focussed on the terminological implications. A conceptual change occurred on the legal landscape of Métis rights, but Métis terminology can be confusing.

An understanding of why the terminology is rather confusing might be alleviated by examining some of the historical usages in Canada of "Half-breed" and "Métis." The definitional contortions some modern historians and commentators have performed for the sake of historical accuracy and sensitivity to the preferences of the people they are striving to describe can be both curious and puzzling. A person can sometimes feel as if standing on their left leg when using a particular term signifies one subset of the Red River people, but standing on their right leg and using the exact same term signifies a different subset of people. The following examples should suffice to demonstrate my point:

As all students of North-American mixed-blood people know, it is hard to find satisfactory terms to describe them. Conferences on mixed-blood history always produce wrangling over terminology. I have adopted the following policy. When I refer to people of mixed Indian-white ancestry in the context of twentieth-century Canada, I write "Métis"...When I refer generally to mixed bloods in the nineteenth century, whether English or French, I write "half-breed," the prevailing term in the English language at that time, although I realize the word is today offensive to many people, especially white liberals who sympathize with native aspirations. (Interestingly, contemporary Métis spokesmen often are proud to be called half-breed.)...When I refer specifically to the French-speaking half-breeds in Manitoba or the North-West, I write, "Métis," italicized to show that it is a French word...It is important to have a precise designation for the French half-breeds, for they constituted a cohesive social group. They often called themselves "the new nation," showing consciousness of a distinct identity which did not include the English half-breeds, whose racial ancestry was equally mixed but did not participate in the same community.[30]

And the following,

Another problem arose over the word "Metis" itself, since, unlike Anglophone writers, Giraud uses it to describe all persons of mixed blood in the West. Since to continue this usage would have led frequently to confusion, I have adopted the practice of restricting it to the people of partly French descent—the "Metis canadien" of Giraud's title. In describing in a general way people of partly Indian descent I have favoured the term "mixed blood." And in describing those of partly Scottish or English descent, who lived apart from Metis society as described in this book, I have had recourse to the term "half-breed." I am aware that in certain circles this usage has fallen into disfavour. On the other hand, it is hallowed by the practice of historians and it is the translation of "Metis" favoured by the definitive bilingual Dictionnaire Canadien/Canadian Dictionary *(1962) prepared by the Lexicographic Research Centre of the Université de Montréal.*[31]

In a third example, there are the terms used by the editor W.L. Morton of a journal—kept throughout the Red River uprising—by Alexander Begg. Morton uses the following configuration and style of letters— "*métis*"—to indicate "the population of mixed blood in Red River which was French by speech and Roman Catholic by faith."[32] He does not define "half-breed," but he uses the word liberally throughout the extensive introduction to the journal and collection of papers. Deeper into Morton's introduction to the journal there is the same puzzling use of the two terms, even within an apparent determination to be precise. Morton writes that the North West Company "had encouraged the *métis* to claim title to the lands of the North-West as a birthright from their Indian mothers, and to think of themselves as a 'new nation.' The nation metisse had never lost this original sense of identity; and even after being reconciled to the colony of which it had been the scourge, and to the Company that its old bourgeois had fought, the 'new nation' of the half-breeds remained a community apart in the larger community of Red River."[33]

The *métis* (using Morton's style) are quite clearly a separate and large portion of the French component of the Red River colony. Morton uses "half-breeds" as his racial indicator and separates a subset of the race as being "*métis*" which is the French, Catholic portion that has the additional feature of having a perception of being a nation unto themselves. What of the English speaking "Half-breeds"? Morton is quite clear that the progeny of the HBC servants and officers were more agricultural in trade and more monarchist in outlook, more aligned with the Crown. And yet, "both *métis* and English half-breeds claimed a share of (Indian title) through their Indian mothers."[34] But the North West Company progeny clung to the idea of nationhood as inculcated by their fathers' employer and the Hudson's Bay Company progeny recognized the HBC as essentially another emanation of the Imperial Crown. The distinction that Morton makes between the "Half-breeds" and, what he calls "the *métis*," certainly is evident through many historical descriptions of the inhabitants of the Red River Settlement, and is evident in the political efforts of the settlement to appear somewhat united during the negotiations with Canada (see endnote 3).

What is clear from the Morton material is that the requirement for a label to indicate the new and distinct people of Red River arose from the fact of the miscegenation of Indians and Europeans. Rupert's Land, and specifically the Red River Settlement, grew to be the first multicultural area in what became Canada and was emblematic of the future of the country. Even though it was not the only region of Canada where biological mixing between Europeans and Indians occurred, the progeny of that particular geographic area were, and continue to be, labelled in various ways. The same labels began to be self-applied relatively recently—that is, the Métis people and Half-breed people self-identifying as such. "Métis" is predominately used as the preferred label of self-identification. In fact, self-identification as "Métis" is required as a condition of membership by most representative political organizations of the Métis.

Far more prominent in the historical descriptions of the Red River Settlement people is the application of the labels by others. Self-identification is not abundantly evident in the documentary history, although there are some instances. People descended from the inhabitants of the Red River Settlement use the "Métis" label more than "Half-breed." There are quite a number of self-identifying Half-breeds in Canada and they do not mean to indicate the sense of identity in which "everyone is a Half-breed, really." Yes, it is true; *all* people are a mix of their parents. But the use of "Half-breed" described above is intended to indicate that the person is a descendant of a particular group of people that inhabited Rupert's Land, and the Red River Settlement in particular, prior to Canada acquiring and governing that same land. Members of that particular population form a part of the ancestry of many families in Canada today, and they were labelled "Half-breed" by the Canadian Government, as well as by contemporary and present-day English speakers.

I have collected samples of the usage of the labels from various times in the history of the Red River people and provided some commentary on them. One of the earliest uses I could find is in the evidence and final report of Coltman[35] during his investigations held under an Imperial Commission of Inquiry into the disturbances in the Indian Country, as it was called, and in the records of the Council of Assiniboia.[36] The Coltman inquiry was the investigation by the Imperial Crown into the deaths at Seven Oaks in the Red River Settlement.[37] The Métis, generally and popularly, consider this incident to be the moment at which the "Métis Nation" is born and becomes self-conscious.

In January 1814, the governor of the District of Assiniboia (the name of the land containing the Red River Settlement and a large surrounding area deeded to Lord Selkirk by the HBC) issued a proclamation that banned the export of pemmican and other provisions, except by licence from him. The reaction to this proclamation was swift and included the upheaval of the Selkirk settlers, several clashes between the NWC and the HBC employees, and resulted in the following agreement between the local representatives of the HBC and the "Half-breed Indians" in 1815, led by Cuthbert Grant and others, which was intended to end the hostilities:

Articles of Agreement entered into between the Half-Breed Indians of the Indian Territory, on the one part, and the Honorable Hudson's Bay Company on other, viz.

1. *All settlers to retire immediately from this river and no appearance of a colony to remain.*

2. *Peace and amity to subsist between all parties, traders, Indians, and freemen in future throughout these two rivers, and on no account any person to be molested in his lawful pursuits.*

3. *The Honorable Hudson's Bay Company will, as customary, enter this river with, if they think proper, three to four of their former trading boats and with four to five men per boat as usual.*

4. *Whatever former disturbance has taken place between both parties, that is to say, the honorable Hudson's Bay Company and the Half-breeds of the Indian Territory, to be totally forgotten, and not to be recalled by either party.*

5. *Every person retiring peaceable from this river immediately shall not be molested in their passage out.*

6. *No people passing the summer for the Hudson's Bay Company, shall remain in the buildings of the colony, but shall retire to some other spot where they will establish for the purpose of trade.*

Chiefs of the Half-Breeds.
Cuthbert Grant,

Bostonais Pangman

Wm. Shaw

Bonhomme Montour

And for the Hudson's Bay Company.
James Sutherland, *Chief Factor*

James White, *Surgeon*

25 June, 1815[38]

Whoever drafted this agreement did not use "Métis" as the label for the group of chiefs. This particular use of "Half-breed" is more indicative of who may have drafted it than it is of how the so-called "chiefs" might have self-identified. If the NWC was trying to appear not to be directly involved in the protection of its interests, then having the sons of their employees and contract employees defend them can be seen as a tactical manoeuvre in order to appear uninvolved. But, while the agreement stated that the disturbances, resulting from the "pemmican proclamation," were to be totally forgotten and never recalled, the ill-feelings between the parties (both direct and indirect) certainly seemed to have persisted. The Seven Oaks incident was to follow approximately one year later. It is likely that the 1815 agreement was drafted by someone working on behalf of the HBC or Selkirk. In any case, it was drafted in English and so "Half-breed" was used to identify the representatives of the non-HBC party in the agreement. This is one of the earliest examples of the use of "Half-Breed" in an English document to refer to the people that are now understood to be more properly and popularly labelled "Métis."

Seven Oaks happened on June 19, 1816, and has been extensively treated in the historiography of Manitoba.[39] The incident itself, as indicated, did not happen without preceding skirmishes and occasions that may have led up to the unfortunate loss of life. But, regardless of which version of the histories is correct, it is fair to say that the creation of Assiniboia by Selkirk was perceived by the NWC as a possible threat to its profits. When corporate profits are perceived to be threatened, the owners of corporations, or their representatives, tend to act to protect those profits. In this case the protection of profits led to a serious incident causing the unnecessary deaths of a few men.

The Imperial government struck a commission into the clash at Seven Oaks, led by William Coltman. The genesis for the inquiry may have rested with Lady Selkirk, but the characterization of the clash as a "massacre" was by Lord Selkirk himself.[40] In his final report, submitted in May 1818 to Lord Bathurst in the British government, Coltman placed blame for the violence on everyone involved; the HBC, the NWC, the fur trade, Lord Selkirk's agents at Red River, the pemmican proclamation—all were responsible and contributing factors to what Coltman characterized as "an inadvertent explosion rather than a deliberate action."[41]

In the beginning of his report, Coltman provides a brief background on two of the main characters and uses the labels for the people of interest in this chapter. But he uses these terms to describe the offspring of the former NWC employees: "Alexander MacDonnell, who was in charge of the North-West company's post, near which Miles MacDonnell wintered, appeared for some time to live with him on the most friendly and intimate footing, as was natural, from their being both cousins and brothers-in-law: the freemen also and their children by Indian women who form the bulk of the population called 'Half-breeds or Metiss and sometimes Bois Brule' finding that no practical exercise of their exclusive rights was attempted and experiencing the advantages to be derived from an amicable intercourse with the settlers, appear to have become well disposed towards the colony."[42] This is the first example of a French term being used in an English text as an equivalent to "Half-breed," and used to refer to the offspring of the NWC employees who would have most likely been French-speaking. It is a matter of speculation as to whether or not the equivalency, as expressed by Coltman, would have been the result of his picking up the words from the people who provided him evidence and depositions to assist in the formulation of the inquiry's final report; alternatively, he may have picked up the terms from other sources. Most likely, he employed the various terms used by the people with whom he spoke and that they were a mix of French and English speakers.

The presence of both "Half-breed" and "Métis" in English texts in the early 1800s speaks to the usage of the terms by people trying to label those people who are neither Indian nor European. The Europeans were trying to come up with words to apply to types of people. Predominately in English texts, the word used for the people of mixed heritage was "Half-breed." But the presence of the term "Métis" speaks to the multilingual nature of the Red River Settlement, rather than to the use of the reference as a term of self-identity used by the people asked to comment on events at Seven Oaks at the time. It is safe to say the term "Half-breed" was the term used in the English language to describe the people of Red River, and that French speakers would have referred to the same people as "Métis." The finer distinctions between the two populations do not seem to be apparent in the usage of the terms in the early 1800s. But this situation eventually evolved into the use of "Métis" in the English language by the mid-1900s. The interesting point of inquiry for this chapter, and let us return to it now, is the reason for the change and when it happened.

Why and when did "Half-breed" become "Métis"?

Thus far we have seen that "Métis" has become the term of choice for mixed-heritage Aboriginal peoples across Canada partly due to its explicit inclusion in section 35(2) of the *Constitution Act, 1982*, and partly due to judicial findings over the last decade and a half in which "Métis" is always the term used for the people seeking to have their rights recognized. After *Powley*, according to the judicial description in that decision, Métis people can potentially be found anywhere in Canada. But we also have seen that "Half-breed" refers to the English-speaking mixed-heritage Aboriginal people of the Red River Settlement and their descendants, and that "Half-breed" has equal constitutional status as "Métis." However, the predominance of "Métis" as the term of identification, both self-identification and identification by others, is evident in the historical literature, policy documentation, and the publications of the Métis political organizations. When did this happen? An answer to this question is far from definitive and is best left in general terms. Nevertheless, it can be traced from examples in the records and reports related to the Red River Settlement and some modern examples of terminology. It is difficult to pinpoint a precise moment when the preference for the term "Métis" proliferated, but one can find writers who claim to justify why the terminology should be, and was, changed.

In a paper two decades ago, Paul Chartrand went to some effort to separate the historic populations within the Red River Settlement and went so far as to conclude that the "Half-breeds" did not achieve the requisite apprehension of nationalism to be recognized as a people. So, while both terms were used to denote populations having European and Indian parentage, the term used to indicate Francophone-Indian ancestry came to have additional signification: "The point is that by 1870 the Metis of the Red River region had acquired a distinct national identity as a new 'people,' distinct from both their European and 'Indian' forebears. That distinct identity had been forged, it is said by historians, from common experiences that emphasized the national consciousness of the 'new nation.'"[43] Although it is clear that the Half-breeds and the Métis did not exactly see eye-to-eye on the course of events leading to the creation of Manitoba, the idea that the Half-breeds did not view themselves as distinct from their ancestors is a stretch (another research project would be needed to examine thoroughly the question of whether or not the Half-breeds were a distinct Aboriginal people of Canada). Chartrand points to the difference in attitudes toward the Red River Resistance as simply a matter of attachment to causes and human alliances, a condition no different than one in modern times: "It seems undeniable, that people form alliances, both personal and collective, in response to their particular, temporal needs. It should cause no surprise to find strains and stresses among the forebears of today's Métis, which comprise descendants of both groups [Half-breeds and Métis] or at least no more surprise than is occasioned by the contemporary strains and stresses in Canadian society."[44]

Disagreement about the course of action taken by the Métis during the Red River and Northwest rebellions certainly led to divisions between the Half-breeds and the Métis. The implication is that those divisions would have led to further distancing from the Métis by the Half-breeds. This distance would have been supported by a desire on both sides to be labelled by distinct terms, in order not to appear unified. But Chartrand suggests that "such evidence of disunity is not, of course, to be emphasized today in the Métis surge towards nationalism because national movements—the rise of peoples—are not predicated upon a scientific examination of historical minutiae, but upon the glorification of an idealized antiquity."[45]

It is this general notion of an idealized antiquity that I refer to as the Métis mythology in the particular context of the people of Red River. Chartrand correctly points to the same basis for today's Métis nationalism. But faithfully identifying with the glorification of the past can be difficult and sometimes requires an uncomfortable leap of logic, especially when the glorification brings with it an expansion of the set of people referred to by the label used to identify the people who are claimed to have risen in resistance to the Canadian government. So, while perhaps obsessively resorting to historical minutiae, it is still possible to stop short of wanting to be identified as Métis when one is a descendant of the Half-breeds.

Nevertheless, Chartrand offers an interesting contributing factor to an explanation of why "Métis" took over "Half-breed" as the prevailing term for the self- and other-identification of people having European and Aboriginal ancestry. The contributing factor is his suggestion that nationalistic aspirations are not always conducive to historical accuracy.

He is also clear on how he feels about the latter word: "The definitely pejorative term 'Half-breed' is now rarely used in the Canadian literature although the usage of the term persists, even among members of the designated group."[46] Chartrand finds the term distasteful and insulting.

Joseph Hargrave captured this same point in 1869, while writing about the Red River Rebellion from the vantage point of an immigrant to the Settlement: "Unfortunately for Canadians coming to this country, they are impressed with the idea that half-breeds are a sort of half and half specimen of humanity, hardly entitled to the privilege of being called rational beings. This idea of the people of this country is not only unfortunate but uncalled for, as those who come here to judge for themselves soon see. The word half-breed merely signifies where there is a tinge more or less of Indian blood—but whoever started the term Breed ought to have been choked before he had time to apply it to human beings."[47] Both writers make similar points, but they are separated by over 100 years in time. Chartrand wrote in the early 1980s when "Métis" was the prevalent and preferred term—Hargrave when "Half-breed" prevailed. So neither writer offers much to the question of *when* the term became pejorative, but they do indicate a discomfort and resistance to the zoological connotations they feel are attached to the term and so contribute to *why*. Similar connotations are experienced by others who find the term distasteful. Several of these people conjure up horses as an example of an animal that is a "breed," but humans are not. The people who find "Half-breed" distasteful accept the fact that humans are animals, but our reproductive realities are accepted reluctantly, and as somewhat unfortunate. The term "breed" may be too literal, or too similar to what humans have used to construct typologies of other animals, but it is nonetheless true and applicable to the human animal, however unfortunate this fact may be.

Other people simply resent the suggestion that they are "half" anything. It is possible to find this perception in the writings of Louis Riel:

> The Metis have as paternal ancestors the former employees of the Hudson's Bay and North-West Companies and as maternal ancestors Indian women belonging to various tribes. The French word Metis is derived from the Latin participle mixtus which means "mixed"; it expresses well the idea it represents.

Quite appropriate also, was the corresponding English term "Half-Breed" in the first generation of blood mixing, but now that European blood and Indian blood are mingled to varying degrees, it is no longer generally applicable.

The French word Metis expresses the idea of this mixture in as satisfactory a way as possible and becomes, by that fact, a suitable name for our race.[48]

Some commentators have suggested that Riel rejected the term. However, there is evidence that even Louis Riel did not entirely reject the word "Half-breed." When writing poetry, when it is arguable that the writer pays very careful attention to diction, Louis Riel used "Half-breed" in a number of his English poems:

And when my dear Halfbreeds
Will have receiv'd, in three
Or four years, scrips and deeds,
Happy, honour'd and free;

When they will sell their lands,
If I live, I will know
The good hearts, the good hands
Who sav'd me from sorrow.[49]

And while in Montana, he wrote:

You have tried, last fall, to buy cash,
Through me, fourty half-breed voters.
Wholesale affairs of such a dash
Might throw you behind some shutters.

You have tried to purchase my vote.
You have tried intimidation
You hate that I didn't turn my coat
Gentlemen, to your fashion.

You have disfranchis'd the Half-breeds
In fact, because they voted free.
If the fifteenth amendment reads
Freedom, you will never hold me.[50]

One can easily demonstrate the fact that "half" is not to be taken too literally by asking: "Would the child of two 'Half-breeds' be a 'Quarter-breed'?" Clearly, no. The arithmetic of racial terminology is not to be taken too seriously, since blood quantum can be argued to be entirely irrelevant to identity.

Both of these sorts of objections to the term "Half-breed," although undoubtedly heart-felt, are rather off the point and create unnecessary obfuscation. The point seems to be rooted in the fact, especially if the objector is Métis, that there is a pride and comfort felt in relation to their term of choice. It is seemingly without negative connotations. The conclusion should be for the Métis that they insist on being called "Métis," when that is what they are correctly and comfortably identified as being. But this conclusion is sometimes extended to a demand that it is correct for all people with roots in the Red River. That they should all be called "Métis" is a sentiment often expressed. But it is that extension and demand that is unwarranted. Be it for the sake of historical accuracy or personal preference, to insist that all mixed-heritage people ancestrally connected to the Red River Settlement be properly labelled "Métis" fails to respect the identity of a distinct people. The preference of the Métis should not be ignored, but it is rather ironic that a purportedly nationalistic people should act to provide rules of self-identification for the Half-breeds or any other people.

"Half-breed" may have been rejected by most Métis as a term applicable to themselves, but this does not mean it is no longer applicable in law or rejected by all to whom the label might apply and by whom it may be used for self-identification. To reject "Half-breed" is fine. But to suggest that no one should self-identify as or be called "Half-breed" goes too far. Such a declaration ignores the fact, not only, that both terms apply equally to the same class of persons in the *Manitoba Act*, but it also ignores histor-ically evident distinctions. Chartrand correctly suggests that nationalistic aspirations override historical accuracy, but the imposition of a term sometimes denies an identity.

The preference for the term "Métis" can, therefore, be characterized as an instance of remediation by exaggeration. In order to rid themselves of the English label, the Métis insist that *all* mixed-heritage people use the French label. The result is a situation that is not historically accurate. If one were to seek an "Aristotelian mean" to attenuate the exaggeration, then the Métis should encourage the descendants of the Red River people to self-identify in accordance with their wishes. And, avocation for a sin-gle identifier would be challenged as too extreme. If only we lived in an Aristotelian world. The social dynamics in the modern age seem rather more rigid in these circumstances. However, the use of "Half-breed" as a self-identifier today can be seen as reclamation of the historic recognition afforded to the people of the English-speaking parishes of the Red River Settlement. It was recognition by not only their contemporary observers, including Riel and his followers, but also modern historians and commentators.[51]

Gerald Friesen and Sylvia Van Kirk provide some insight on the social dynamic in existence between the Half-breeds and the population of immigrants to Manitoba in the last half of the 1800s. Friesen observes that "the English-speaking Protestants [Half-breeds] of the parish [St. Andrew's] had been made to feel subordinate to the incoming settlers from Ontario. They were treated as survivors from a by-gone age, interesting remnants of a fur-trade civilization that no longer represented a new majority in the district. During the next generation, their children integrated into the larger community as if a distinctive English-speaking community of mixed European and Aboriginal heritage had never existed."[52] And, Sylvia Van Kirk notes that "the fur-trade society of Rupert's Land was justified in feeling suspicious of the attitudes of the 'Canadian' newcomers from Ontario. This small group which began to be a vocal presence in Red River in the 1860s made no secret of the fact that they considered themselves to be a vanguard of civilization in the West. Again there is evidence that the air of racial superiority by the few white women in this group caused social conflict within the colony."[53] The subsequent silence from the Half-breeds about their community identification may be partially explained by their desire to blend into their surroundings—a desire not exclusive to the Half-breeds. The Métis were also generally unseen for periods of time, a sociological factor identified in the *Powley* decision.[54]

The earliest use of "Métis" in English legislation occurs in 1938 in Alberta. *An Act Respecting the Metis Population of the Province* is the provincial legislature's response to a recommendation made in a report from Mr. Freeman Ewing. The former judge of the Supreme Court of Alberta was commissioned to inquire "into the condition of the half-breed population of the Province of Alberta, keeping particularly in mind the health, education, relief and general welfare of such population."[55] The act drafted in response to the commission defines "Métis" as "a person of mixed white and Indian blood but does not include either an Indian or a non-treaty Indian as defined in The Indian Act...."[56] In reference to the Ewing Commission Report, the act states that "the ways and means of giving effect to such recommendations should be arrived at by the means of conferences and negotiations between the Government of the Province and representatives of the metis population of the Province."[57]

In the history of the political representative organizations of the Métis population in Alberta, it is at the first meeting of the earliest organization that a motion is made to use the term "Métis" in the name of that organization, rather than the term "Half-breed." The motion was passed by those assembled. The Ewing Commission Report was submitted on February 15, 1936. The distaste for the term "Half-breed" had resulted in it being rejected as a term in the name of the political representative organization for the population studied by the Ewing Commission. The reasons for the term being regarded as pejorative are not articulated, but the term is rejected in Alberta by the members of the Métis political organization in the province.

An element of the explanation for this particular rejection of "Half-breed" can be found in the migration of the Métis population from Manitoba to Saskatchewan, and, finally, into Alberta. Combined with the ever westward migration of the Métis was a rapidly growing settler population, predominately English-speaking.[58] No doubt a significant majority of the population of English-speaking settlers came with prejudicial attitudes toward the mixed-heritage population, probably for reasons of race and rebellions. In this context, it is little wonder the term "Half-breed" acquired and sustained negative connotations.

Finally, an objection to "Half-breed" that is heard occasionally is that it is the same as the "N-word." This idea reflects a grave misunderstanding of the history of the "N-word" as a pernicious racist label.[59] The history of that term is far more lengthy, severe, and bears little similarity to that of Half-breed. Try, for example, to find the N-word in the constitution of any country. In fact, the one sliver of similarity the two terms have is their use as insults. The use of "Half-breed" as an insult should neither be ignored nor forgotten. But, if it is true that ethnicity and race are social constructs and that the labels used to indicate those constructs are simply descriptions of what is,[60] then it should not come as a surprise that humans can take those descriptions or labels and fling them at each other as insults. Any label that is applied to a human racial distinction or ethnicity can be cast as an insult with the right tone of voice, inflection, or emphasis. It is all part of dealing with humans and their foibles. "Half-breed" may still be an insult in some circles, but that insult may exist only in the way it is said and the intent attached to its utterance. The same can be said of many racial terms.

Conclusion

Canadians are free to label their identity any way they choose. Hopefully, they are not self-delusional in so choosing. The ancestors of the French-speaking parishes of the Red River decided that they did not like the English term historically applied to them. They decided that the descendants of the "Half-breeds" should also use the French term and would prefer that they too use the term "Métis."[61] It is a decision that reflects a desire on the part of the Métis political organizations that extends too far and drips with irony. It is a position that denies that Half-breeds should have the ability to choose freely the term they use for self-identification, even though the term is historically accurate and used with utter respect for their ancestry. It is interesting to note that it is not only the Métis that appear to want Half-breeds to join up with them, as the following argument demonstrates: "It is difficult to say when a half-breed ceases to become a half-breed, and is looked upon as white; the manner of life and associations has much to do with it. Colloquially speak-ing, those who are known to have Indian blood in them, not necessarily half, but possibly a quarter or an eighth, and show traces of it physically, combining with that trait any characteristics of the Indian in their man-ner of life, are called, loosely, half-breeds; but at the same time there are many cases where two people might have exactly the same amount of Indian blood and be so different in appearance and mode of life, that while the one would readily be spoken of as a half-breed, the other would readily be accepted as a white man."[62] Such is the unique conundrum that a Half-breed faces: officially, one has to be white or Métis.

Meaning is a fluid aspect of words, especially those words used as typo-logical labels for people. Because they are used to sort people into different types, the words can change according to the social categories of the era in which they are used. Time is wonderfully adept at bringing about change in almost everything, including the meaning of words used to label people. At this moment in time, the term "Métis" has been judicially found to be applicable to a person of European and Indian or Inuit ancestry across Canada (with some other conditions to be satisfied with respect to the exercise of section 35 rights). The term "Métis" also seems to be used by almost any person who has discovered there is an Indian ancestor some-where in the family tree. It is reasonable to suggest, therefore, that use of the term "Half-breed" as a self-identifier has the potential to function as a very specific reference to an Aboriginal person who claims an ancestral connection to a particular class of people who were instrumental in the first expansion of the Canadian confederation and who represent an Aboriginal people distinct from the Métis—a people constitutionally recognized.

In other words, the declaration—I am a Half-breed—quite sensibly indicates an ancestral connection to the Aboriginal people of the English-speaking parishes of the Red River Settlement and distinguishes the person making the declaration from the Métis, including those Métis whose ancestry lay within the French-speaking parishes of the Red River Settlement. Aspects of this idea are not overly burdensome to grasp.[63] And perhaps most importantly, in legal and historical contexts, it reflects accurately the life and experiences of many who inhabited the Red River Settlement.

Notes

1. George Bryce, "Worthies of Old Red River," Manitoba Historical Society Transactions, 1st ser., no. 48. Read 11 February 1896, www.mhs.mb.ca/docs/transactions/1/redriverworthies.shtml.

2. Sylvia Van Kirk, *Many Tender Ties: Women in Fur-Trade Society, 1670–1870* (Winnipeg: Watson & Dwyer, 1980), 201.

3. See Marcel Giraud, *The Métis in the Canadian West*, trans. George Woodcock (Edmonton and Lincoln: University of Alberta Press and University of Nebraska Press, 1986); George Stanley, *The Birth of Western Canada: A History of the Riel Rebellions* (Toronto: University of Toronto Press, 1960); Alexander Begg, *The Creation of Manitoba, or A History of the Red River Troubles* (Toronto: A.H. Hovery, 1871); W.L. Morton, ed., *Alexander Begg's Red River Journal and Other Papers Relative to the Red River Resistance of 1869–1870* (Toronto: The Champlain Society, 1956); Alexander Ross, *The Red River Settlement: Its Rise Progress and Present State, with some account of The Native Races and its General History, to the present day* (London: Smith, Elder and Co., 1856); Joseph James Hargrave, *Red River* (Montreal: John Lovell, 1871); E.E. Rich, *The Fur Trade and the NorthWest to 1857* (Toronto: McClelland & Stewart, 1967); Gerhard Ens, "Métis Lands in Manitoba,"

Manitoba History 5 (Spring 1983); Tom Flanagan, *Riel and the Rebellion: 1885 Reconsidered* (Saskatoon: Western Producer Prairie Books, 1983); Frits Pannekoek, "The Anglican Church and the Disintegration of Red River Society, 1818-1870," in *Interpreting Canada's Past*, vol. 1, *Before Confederation*, ed. J.M. Bumsted (Toronto: Oxford University Press, 1986); John E. Foster, "The Métis: The People and the Term," *Prairie Forum* 3, no. 1 (Spring 1978), 79-90; Paul Chartrand, "Aboriginal Rights: The Dispossession of the Métis," *Osgoode Hall Law Journal* (Fall 1991); Alexander Morris, *The Treaties of Canada with the Indians of Manitoba and the North-West Territories, including the negotiations on which they were based, and other information relating thereto* (Toronto: Belfords, Clarke & Co., 1880); A.S. Morton, introduction, *London Correspondence Inward from Eden Colvile, 1849-1852*, ed. E.E. Rich (London: The Hudson's Bay Record Society, 1956).

To my mind, the clearest example of the difference and similarity is found in Stanley's *The Birth of Western Canada*, page 9: "As a rule the English-speaking half-breeds formed a contrast to the French....But to say that the English half-breeds cultivated more land, were better educated and possessed more of the world's goods, is not to speak slightingly of the French, nor to say that they were more honest or loyal. Each possessed distinct characteristics and each played a part in the history of the half-breed race." And, "In spite of these differences there was a common bond between the English and the French half-breeds. Both sprang for a common race; both claimed territorial rights to the North-West through their Indian ancestry; both, in a large measure, spoke their mother tongue in addition to French or English. The half-breeds as a race never considered themselves as humble hangers-on to the white population, but were proud of their blood and deeds."

4. W.L. Morton, ed., *Alexander Begg's Red River Journal and Other Papers Relative to the Red River Resistance of 1869-1870* (Toronto: The Champlain Society, 1956), 259.

5. One aspect of the settlement at the time of John and Elizabeth's wedding that would have been rather unique to that time would have been the flying of the American flag at the Emerling Hotel near the Forks. This would have been due to the owner Alfred Scott, who was an annexationist at the time and an American. Also, one can imagine that the solicitations of a representative of the Provisional Government to join the cause of the Métis may have happened at a wedding, given that people would have been gathered and showing up where people were gathered would have made the appeal to join the Provisional Government more efficiently carried out. Very sharp and frosty weather can make people very

efficient at seeing people with whom they wish to speak. See Morton, *Alexander Begg's Red River Journal*, 255–60. John's father, Alexander Dahl, was nominated as a delegate from St. Paul's parish on December 7, 1869, to go see Col. Stoughton Dennis, the Canadian surveyor, with a couple of other delegates from Kildonan and St. John's, to investigate what could be done, after Riel had stopped the surveyor. The nomination took place at a meeting at Frog Plain schoolhouse, called by John Sutherland, amongst several men from the English-speaking parishes, including James Ross, Colin Inkster, Don Matheson, Alexander Polson, and others, to discuss the situation with the surveyor and the French having asked Sutherland to convey the message that they wanted to speak to English parish delegates and had declared that the English parishes had agreed to the French demands. See Morton, *Alexander Begg's Red River Journal*, 441.

6. As of January 1, 2010, the Aboriginal declaration process has been taken on by the Public Service Commission (PSC) which produced a form to be signed that seems to be very closely based on the form that was used by Indian and Northern Affairs Canada before 2010. See the PSC form at www.psc-cfp.gc.ca/plcy-pltq/ eead-eeed/dg-gd/docs/aaa-frm-eng.rtf.

7. *British North America Act and Amendments: 1867-1948* (Ottawa: King's Printer and Controller of Stationery, 1948), 91.

8. The sections of the proclamation relating to Indians remain a primary aspect of the Crown–Aboriginal legal landscape. The proclamation is part of the *Constitution Act, 1982*, since it settles disputes between the French and English concerning their colonial land holdings in North America and sets out the principles for land transactions with the Indians. It is somewhat difficult to read, but it is a foundational part of the legal and policy relationship between Canada and the Indians. The King of the day was George III, who declared, generally speaking, among other things, that only the Crown can purchase lands from the Indians. Full text of the proclamation can be found at avalon.law.yale.edu/18th_ century/proc1763.asp.

9. *British North America Act and Amendments: 1867-1948*, 139.

10. *The Manitoba Act, 1870, Title—An Act to amend and continue the Act 32 and 33 Victoria, chapter 3; and to establish and provide for the Government of the Province of Manitoba*, in *British North America Act and Amendments: 1867-1948*, 182.

11. *The Manitoba Act, 1870*, in *British North America Act and Amendments: 1867-1948*, 137. See also J. Timothy S. McCabe, *The Law of Treaties Between the Crown and Aboriginal Peoples* (Markham, ON: LexisNexis Canada, 2010), 9.

12. *British North America Act and Amendments: 1867–1948*, 96.

13. *British North America Act and Amendments: 1867–1948*, 182.

14. For an understanding of the concept of Aboriginal rights and their constitutional protection in Canada since 1982, see Peter Hogg, *Constitutional Law of Canada* (Toronto: Thomson Carswell, 2006), section 28 and in particular 28-28 to 28-30. Also, Patrick J. Monahan, *Constitutional Law* (Toronto: Irwin Law, 2006), 439–75.

15. Jean Teillet, in her paper "Métis Law Summary 2009," which can be accessed at www.metisnation.ca, makes the following claim: "The constitutional use of the term 'Métis' in 1982, replaces the previous term 'Half-breeds' in English legal language." (See page 2 of her Summary and the footnote to her claim). It is difficult to understand such a claim. It leads one to think that there exists a legislative amendment to achieve such a replacement of terms and, therefore, support her claim. But no such legislative amendment exists, which makes her claim false. Her footnote to the claim simply refers to the *Manitoba Act, 1870*, and the *Dominion Lands Act*, neither of which amended terminology and therefore do not actually relate in the way she implies by referencing them as support to her claim. In addition, the use of the term "Métis" in the *Constitution Act, 1982*, does not, by itself, achieve the replacement of "Half-breed" in English legal language. It could be said that the judicial usage of "Métis," in place of "Half-breed," is supportive of her claim that a replacement of the one term by the other has occurred; but even this claim is not the same as the one she makes in her 2009 law summary.

16. http://laws.justice.gc.ca/en/const/9.html#anchorsc:7-bo-ga:1_II. Accessed 26 August 2010.

17. http://laws.justice.gc.ca/en/const/9.html#anchorsc:7-bo-ga:1_II. Accessed 26 August 2010.

18. http://laws.justice.gc.ca/en/const/9.html#anchorsc:7-bo-ga:1_II. Accessed 26 August 2010.

19. A conversation on August 6, 2010, with Ms. Mary Dawson who drafted section 35 under the general instruction of Jean Chrétien. According to Ms. Dawson, she was not aware of any discussion about who the people were that are referenced by the term "Métis" before it was included in section 35(2).

20. *R. v. Powley*, [2003] 2 SCR 207, 2003 SCC 43. http://scc.lexum.umontreal.ca.

21. The trial case is Manitoba Metis Federation Inc. v. Canada (Attorney General) et al., [2007] MBQB 293 and the appeal decision is Manitoba Metis Federation Inc. v. Canada (Attorney General) et al., [2010] MBCA 71. The appeal decision has

been appealed to the Supreme Court of Canada. The complainants have filed their leave to appeal to the s c c as of September 30, 2010. The hearing at the s c c occurred on December 13, 2012. Judgment was reserved at the hearing.

22. Shin Imai, *The 2002 Annotated Indian Act and Aboriginal Constitutional Provisions* (Toronto: Carswell, Thomson Reuters Canada, 2001), 386. See also Thomas Isaac, *Aboriginal Law*, 3rd ed. (Saskatoon: Purich Publishing, 2004), where he writes: "The Manitoba Act, 1870 conferred certain rights to the 'half-breeds.'[32] These rights are codified in section 31 of the *Manitoba Act, 1870*. *The Dominion Lands Act* provided that 'any claims existing in connection with the extinguishment of the Indian title, preferred by half-breeds resident in the North-West Territories outside of the limits of Manitoba' be satisfied. Both Acts recognise a degree of Métis interest in the land." 281. Footnote 32 says: "Although it is a term that many find objectionable, it is used here only in the interests of historical accuracy."

23. Shin Imai, *The 2010 Annotated Indian Act and Aboriginal Constitutional Provisions* (Toronto: Carswell, Thomson Reuters Canada, 2009), 533.

24. Manitoba Metis Federation Inc. v. Canada (Attorney General) et al., [2007] M B Q B 293, para. 656.

25. Manitoba Metis Federation Inc. v. Canada (Attorney General) et al., [2007] M B Q B 293, para. 661.

26. Manitoba Metis Federation Inc. v. Canada (Attorney General) et al., [2007] M B Q B 293, para. 507.

27. Manitoba Metis Federation Inc. v. Canada (Attorney General) et al., [2007] M B Q B 293, para. 505.

28. Manitoba Metis Federation Inc. v. Canada (Attorney General) et al., [2007] M B Q B 293, paras. 508–09.

29. Manitoba Metis Federation Inc. v. Canada (Attorney General) et al., [2007] M B Q B 293, para. 32.

30. Tom Flanagan, *Riel and the Rebellion: 1885 Reconsidered* (Saskatoon: Western Producer Prairie Books, 1983), viii–ix.

31. George Woodcock, writing in the translator's introduction to Marcel Giraud, *The Métis in the Canadian West*, trans. George Woodcock (Edmonton and Lincoln: University of Alberta Press and University of Nebraska Press, 1986), xv.

32. W.L. Morton, ed., *Alexander Begg's Red River Journal and Other Papers Relative to the Red River Resistance of 1869–1870* (Toronto: The Champlain Society, 1956), 1.

33. Morton, *Alexander Begg's Red River Journal*, 15.

34. Morton, *Alexander Begg's Red River Journal*, 15

35. National Archives of Canada, RG 4, A1, vol. 620, 1852-2148. *The Coltman Report*. Other early uses of the term "Métis" in English are found in the journal written by Edward Chappell, published in 1817, and in a letter from Colin Robertson to Andrew Colvile, written at Eastmain on Hudson's Bay on November 12, 1816. Chappell, in a note on page 220 of his journal, wrote the following: "Disputes with the *Metiffs* of the Country, a race between *Canadians* and *Indians*, inflamed the natural jealousy which the latter have always felt, relative to the agricultural encroachments on their hunting-grounds in the interior, and, we understand, compelled his Lordship's Governor to abandon the establishment which had been made." In his letter to Colvile, Robertson wrote: "Your European Servants and Metiss are in many places deserting over to the North West company. What is the cause of all this?" See E.E. Rich, editor, *Robertson's Correspondence Book, September 1817 to September 1822* (Toronto: The Champlain Society, 1939), 248. It is difficult to discern whether or not Coltman's report may have been known and discussed at the time of these references. It is possible that the term "Métis" was starting to be used in English around the time of all these references.

36. E. Oliver, editor, *Publications of the Canadian Archives, No. 9—The Canadian North-West—Its Early Development and Legislative Records—Minutes of the Councils of the Red River Colony and the Northern Department of Rupert's Land* (Ottawa: Secretary of State, Government Printing Bureau, 1914).

37. For an excellent account of the incident at Seven Oaks and subsequent events surrounding the establishment of the Red River Settlement see J.M. Bumsted, *Selkirk: A Life* (Winnipeg: University of Manitoba Press, 2009); see also Ross, *The Red River Settlement*.

38. Oliver, *The Canadian North-West*, 196-97.

39. For understanding the debate that went on between the North West Company and the Hudson's Bay Company over the incident at Seven Oaks see: *Statement Respecting the Earl of Selkirk's Settlement upon the Red River in North America; Its Destruction in 1815 and 1816; and the massacre of Governor Semple and his Party, with Observations upon a recent publication, entitled "A Narrative of Occurrences in the Indian Countries," &c*, John Murray, Albemarle Street, London, 1817, reprinted by Coles Publishing Company (Toronto: 1970). For the NWC version of events, see the narrative referred to in the HBC version, the full name of which is: *A Narrative of Occurrences in the Indian Countries of North America, since the Connexion of the Right Honourable the Earl of Selkirk with the Hudson's Bay Company, and his Attempt to establish a Colony on the Red River; with a detailed Account of his Lordships Military*

Expedition to, and subsequent Proceedings at Fort William in Upper Canada, which can be found at http://eco.canadiana.ca. See also Ross, *The Red River Settlement*, and Bumsted, *Selkirk: A Life*.

40. Bumsted, *Selkirk: A Life*, 314.

41. Bumsted, *Selkirk: A Life*, 314.

42. National Archives of Canada, RG 4, A1, vol. 620, *The Coltman Report*, 1853. This may also be one of the first uses of the term "Metiss" in written English.

43. Paul L.A.H. Chartrand, "Aboriginal Rights: The Dispossession of the Metis," *Osgoode Hall Law Journal* (Fall, 1991), 459.

44. Chartrand, "Aboriginal Rights," 461.

45. Chartrand, "Aboriginal Rights," 462.

46. Chartrand, "Aboriginal Rights," 461.

47. Joseph Hargrave in an 1869 letter, reproduced in, J.M. Bumsted, *Reporting the Resistance: Alexander Begg and Joseph Hargrave on the Red River Resistance*, (Winnipeg: University of Manitoba Press, 2003), 4.

48. "The Metis: Louis Riel's Last Memoir," in A.-H. de Tremaudan, *Hold High Your Heads*, trans. E. Maguet (Winnipeg: Pemmican Publications, 1982), 200.

49. Excerpt from 4-135, "Psalmic form of Prayer to Jesus," Regina, 85/06/19, in *The Collected Writings of Louis Riel/Les Écrits complets de Louis Riel*, ed. Glen Campbell (Edmonton: University of Alberta Press, 1985), 412.

50. Excerpt from 4-112, "Last fall, I had a vote to give...," Fort Benton, 83/05/11, in *The Collected Writings of Louis Riel/Les Écrits complets de Louis Riel*, ed. Glen Campbell (Edmonton: University of Alberta Press, 1985), 412.

51. For an interesting survey of terminology for "Métis" and "Half-breed" see: "Sewing Ourselves Together: Clothing, Decorative Arts and the Expression of Metis and Half Breed Identity," by Sherry Farrell Racette, an unpublished PHD dissertation in the Interdisciplinary Doctoral Program (Winnipeg: University of Manitoba, 2004). The reader is also encouraged to read Jennifer Brown's "Linguistic Solitudes in the Fur Trade," in *Old Trails and New Directions: Papers of the Third North American Fur Trade Conference*, ed. Carol Judd and Arthur Ray (Toronto: University of Toronto Press, 1980), 147.

52. Gerald Friesen, *River Road: Essays on Manitoba and Prairie History* (Winnipeg: University of Manitoba Press, 1996), 8–9. A fascinating example of the degree to which the next generation or two of the Half-breed denied their heritage and the label attached to it is described by Friesen on page 11: "By the 1940s, the racial stereotypes of the "white" Commonwealth prompted a different reaction [denial of

Aboriginal ancestry] among the [English] grandchildren of old Red River....One illustration of the difference occurred in 1947–48, when a plaque commemorating the career of John Norquay, to that time the only Manitoba-born citizen to hold the position of Premier, was unveiled in the Legislature. Though there had never before been any question about Norquay's mixed-race family background, and though he had declared in the Legislature in the 1870s that he was proud of every drop of Aboriginal blood that flowed in his veins, his descendants refused to accept the wording of the plaque that described him as a "Half-breed" and provoked a minor scene, and then a continuing agitation, despite the drafting of a genealogical report that demonstrated fairly clearly the identity of Norquay's partly Aboriginal foremothers."

In the Dahl family, the generation of children born in the 1940s and 1950s have very little knowledge of their Half-breed heritage. It was not talked about or discussed, and certainly not with any pride. A lack of interest, silence, denial, uncomfortable joking or teasing were some of the indications of how the family heritage was viewed. But open exploration and discussion of the heritage is now sometimes pursued, in absence of any of those silly racial prejudices that imbued the worldview of previous generations.

53. Sylvia Van Kirk, *Many Tender Ties: Women in Fur-Trade Society, 1670–1870* (Winnipeg: Watson & Dwyer, 1980), 201.

54. R. v. Powley, [2003] 2 SCR 207, 2003 SCC 43, paras. 24–26.

55. For a general description of the creation of the Métis representative organization in Alberta see: www.albertametis.com/MNAHome/MNA-Culture2.aspx. For the Ewing Commission Report see: www.albertasource.ca/metis/eng/people_and_communities/issues_ewing_commission.html. 1. See also, Fred V. Martin, "Alberta's Métis Settlements: A Brief History," in *Forging Alberta's Constitutional Framework*, ed. Richard Connors and John M. Law (Edmonton: University of Alberta Press, 2005), 345.

56. See http://historyonline.msgc.ca/1935-1944/Gift-Lake/Land-Acquisition for a PDF downloadable copy of *An Act Respecting the Metis Population of the Province*, which was passed in November 1938 by the Province of Alberta in follow-up to the Ewing Commission Report, 1.

57. *An Act Respecting*, 1.

58. The population of Manitoba was 12,228 in 1871, and 65,954 in 1881. A large majority of the growth was in the English-speaking portion of the population. The 1881 census states that the vast majority of the population was English-speaking

and born in the province. See John Macoun, *Manitoba and the Great North West* (Guelph, ON: World Publishing, 1882), 679–87. Immigrants who came and stayed arrived primarily from Ontario. The same pattern was repeated across Saskatchewan and Alberta. Other commentators also noticed and wrote about the migration westward: "Mr. Sifton was about eight years in Sir Wilfrid Laurier's Cabinet, and during that time immigration steadily increased until at the present the population from the Eastern Boundary of Manitoba to the Rocky Mountains has nearly doubled and business is in a very healthy state." See John H. O'Donnell, *Manitoba as I Saw It* (Toronto: Musson Book Company, 1909), 122.

59. For an excellent and sensitive history of this troubling word, see Randall Kennedy, *Nigger: The Strange Career of a Troublesome Word* (New York: Pantheon Books, 2002).

60. For a good analysis of identity, and how it operates within the context of the law in particular, see Sébastien Grammond, *Identity Captured by Law: Membership in Canada's Indigenous Peoples and Linguistic Minorities* (Montreal: McGill-Queen's University Press, 2009). The following quotations capture the ideas resulting from his analysis: "The concept of ethnicity was developed by social scientists to analyse human diversity. It is a descriptive concept: it aims at describing how things *are*, by figuring out categories into which the social reality, with its irreducible complexity, can be sorted," 3–4. Grammond also writes, "Most scientists today believe that the concept of race is seriously flawed and should be abandoned. They now see race as a socially constructed category. Yet ordinary people who employ the concept of race think that it refers to an objective reality, although they would be hard-pressed to define it," 6.

61. For evidence of the extent to which the Métis political organizations prefer the use of "Métis," regardless of historical accuracy, consider the following passage located on the website of Library and Archives Canada: "The terms 'Métis' and 'Half-Breed' are used synonymously throughout this database to refer to those people in western Canada who trace their roots to a shared Native and European ancestry—an ancestry which at some point would have been enumerated by a commission with the authority to issue land or money scrip. The term 'Half-Breed' was used almost exclusively by the federal government throughout the late nineteenth and early twentieth centuries when referring to these people. The term completely pervades departmental memoranda, reports, registers, federal statutes, orders-in-council, and official publications. Indeed, it is possible for researchers to use the federal record of this period without ever

encountering the term 'Métis.' Consequently, 'Half-Breed' has been retained in this guide when referring to archival records where the term has been used exclusively. In keeping with the preferences of the Métis National Council, however, the term 'Métis' is used when making a general reference to these people as a separate cultural group." Accessed 31 August 2010, www.collectionscanada. gc.ca/archivianet/0201200112_e.html.

The one exception to the explanation expressed above is the expression "Métis Scrip," which I don't think is a combination of words to be found in any legal document from the period when scrip was issued. However, none of the references made by Library and Archives Canada to the land distribution scheme use the word "Half-breed."

62. Archer Martin, *The Hudson's Bay Company's Land Tenures* (London: William Clowes and Sons, 1898), 100.

63. Not only is the idea not difficult to grasp, it carries with it several practical implications. One is the proposal to include "Half-breed" as an Aboriginal identifier on surveys. There may be problems with effectively communicating the finer points of the historical support for Half-breed as an identifier. This would be rather difficult and might result is some skewed data. Many an individual might think he or she is a Half-breed, so clear communications would be vital for preventing erroneous reporting. But the ability to statistically separate Half-breeds from Manitoba from Métis could more accurately reflect the populations and the socio-economic conditions of each of these Aboriginal populations. In addition, the representative political organizations of Manitoba could target the population that identifies as Half-breed in order to expand its membership.

Bibliography

Begg, Alexander. *The Creation of Manitoba, or A History of the Red River Troubles*. Toronto: A.H. Hovery, 1871.

Bryce, George. "Worthies of Old Red River." *Manitoba Historical Society Transactions*, Series 1, no. 48, read 11 February 1896, www.mhs.mb.ca/docs/transactions/1/redriverworthies.shtml.

British North America Act and Amendments: 1867–1948. Ottawa: King's Printer and Controller of Stationery, 1948.

Bumsted, J.M. *Reporting the Resistance: Alexander Begg and Joseph Hargrave on the Red River Resistance*. Winnipeg: University of Manitoba Press, 2003.

———. *Selkirk: A Life*. Winnipeg: University of Manitoba Press, 2009.

Campbell, Maria. *Halfbreed*. Toronto: McClelland & Stewart, 1973.

Chappell, Edward. *Narrative of a Voyage to Hudson's Bay in His Majesty's ship Rosamond*. Toronto: Coles Publishing, 1970.

Chartrand, Paul L.A.H. "Aboriginal Rights: The Dispossession of the Métis." *Osgoode Hall Law Journal* 457 (Fall 1991): 163–94.

Ens, Gerhard. "Métis Lands in Manitoba." *Manitoba History* 5 (Spring, 1983): 363–87.

Flanagan, Tom. *Riel and the Rebellion: 1885 Reconsidered*. Saskatoon: Western Producer Prairie Books, 1983.

Foster, John. "The Métis: The People and the Term." *Prairie Forum* 3, no. 1 (1978): 19–27.

Friesen, Gerald. *River Road: Essays on Manitoba and Prairie History*. Winnipeg: University of Manitoba Press, 1996.

Giraud, Marcel. *The Métis in the Canadian West*. Translated by George Woodcock. 2 vols. Edmonton and Lincoln: University of Alberta Press and University of Nebraska Press, 1986.

Goulet, George, and Terry Goulet. *The Métis: Memorable Events and Memorable Personalities*. Calgary: FabJob, 2006.

Grammond, Sébastien. *Identity Captured by Law: Membership in Canada's Indigenous Peoples and Linguistic Minorities*. Montreal and Kingston: McGill-Queen's University Press, 2009.

Hargrave, Joseph James. *Red River*. Printed for the author by John Lovell, Montreal, 1871.

Hogg, Peter. *Constitutional Law of Canada*. Toronto: Thomson Carswell, 2006.

Imai, Shin. *The 2010 Annotated Indian Act and Aboriginal Constitutional Provisions*. Toronto: Carswell, Thomson Reuters, 2009.

———. *The 2002 Annotated Indian Act and Aboriginal Constitutional Provisions*. Toronto: Carswell, Thomson Reuters, 2001.

Isaac, Thomas. *Aboriginal Law*, 3rd ed. Saskatoon: Purich Publishing, 2004.

Kennedy, Randall. *Nigger: The Strange Career of a Troublesome Word*. New York: Pantheon Books, 2002.

Macoun, John. *Manitoba and the Great North West*. Guelph, ON: World Publishing, 1882.

Martin, Archer. *The Hudson's Bay Company's Land Tenures*. London: William Clowes and Sons, 1898.

Martin, Chester. "Red River Settlement: Papers in the Canadian Archives relating to the Pioneers." Ottawa: Archives Branch, 1910.

McCabe, J. Timothy S. *The Law of Treaties Between the Crown and Aboriginal Peoples.* Markham, ON: LexisNexis Canada, 2010.

Monahan, Patrick J. *Constitutional Law.* Toronto: Irwin Law, 2006.

Morris, Alexander. *The Treaties of Canada with the Indians of Manitoba and the North-West Territories, including the negotiations on which they were based, and other information relating thereto.* Toronto: Belfords, Clarke, 1880.

Morton, W.L. Introduction. In *London Correspondence Inward from Eden Colvile, 1849–1852*, edited by E.E. Rich. London: The Hudson's Bay Record Society, 1956.

———. *Manitoba: A History.* Toronto: University of Toronto Press, 1967.

———, ed. *Alexander Begg's Red River Journal and Other Papers Relative to the Red River Resistance of 1869–1870.* Toronto: The Champlain Society, 1956.

National Archives of Canada. RG 4, A1, vol. 620, no. 138, Summary of evidence respecting the transactions at Red River, 1815.

O'Donnell, John H. *Manitoba as I Saw It.* Toronto: The Musson Book Company, 1909.

Oliver, E., ed. *Publications of the Canadian Archives, No. 9 — The Canadian North-West — Its Early Development and Legislative Records — Minutes of the Councils of the Red River Colony and the Northern Department of Rupert's Land.* Ottawa: Secretary of State, Government Printing Bureau, 1914.

Pannekoek, Fritz. "The Anglican Church and the Disintegration of Red River Society, 1818–1870." In *Interpreting Canada's Past.* Vol. 1, *Before Confederation*, edited by J.M. Bumsted, 273–87. Toronto: Oxford University Press, 1986.

Rich, E.E. *The Fur Trade and the NorthWest to 1857.* Toronto: McClelland & Stewart, 1967.

Robertson, Colin. *Robertson's Correspondence Book, September 1817 to September 1822*, edited by E.E. Rich. Toronto: The Champlain Society, 1939.

Ross, Alexander. *The Red River Settlement: Its Rise Progress and Present State, with some account of The Native Races and its General History, to the present day.* London: Smith, Elder and Co., 1856.

Stanley, George. *The Birth of Western Canada: A History of the Riel Rebellions.* Toronto: University of Toronto Press, 1960.

de Trémaudan, A.-H. "The Metis: Louis Riel's Last Memoir." In *Hold High Your Heads: History of the Metis Nation in Western Canada*, translated by Elizabeth Maguet, 200–10. Winnipeg: Pemmican Publications, 1982 [1885].

Van Kirk, Sylvia. *Many Tender Ties: Women in Fur-Trade Society, 1670–1870.* Winnipeg: Watson & Dwyer, 1980.

PART TWO **History**

Overleaf: Carol James, 2008. Chénier Pattern. *Beads decorated many finger-woven sashes of the 1800s. The weight of the beads made these sashes less practical for a fur trader and more appropriate to ceremonial wear. Dr. Jean-Olivier Chénier died defending the town of Saint-Eustache, Quebec, wearing a sash of this pattern which features white glass beads. Huron chiefs also have been depicted wearing sashes of this pattern.*

From Entity to Identity to Nation | 4

The Ethnogenesis of the Wiisakodewininiwag
(Bois-Brûlé) Reconsidered

DARREN O'TOOLE

Qui a composé la chanson
Pierre Falcon, poète du canton.
Elle a été faite et composée
Sur la victoire que nous avons gagnée.
Elle a été faite et composée
Chantons la gloire de tous les Bois-Brûlés.

—La bataille de la Grenouillère, 1816

IN 1811, the Hudson's Bay Company (HBC) granted 116,000 acres to Thomas Douglas, fifth Earl of Selkirk, to establish a settlement in Red River.[1] Between 1812 and 1815, Selkirk brought four contingents of mostly Scottish settlers to the colony.[2] The North West Company (NWC) interpreted this as a move on the HBC's part to cut off their supply lines and interrupt the flow of furs west of Red River.[3] The fierce competition degraded into a veritable feud, or "private hostilities" as Commissioner William B. Coltman would call it.[4] It was at this point that the NWC is said to have convinced the Métis "to claim title to the lands of the North-West as a birthright from their Indian mothers, and to think of themselves as a 'new nation.'"[5] The confrontation between the two companies culminated on June 19, 1816, in the *Bataille de la Grenouillère*, or the Battle of Seven Oaks, which left Governor Semple and 20 of his men dead.[6] The incident was subsequently celebrated as the founding moment of the "New Nation."[7]

According to Pannekoek, the Battle of Seven Oaks "is often cited as the single event that acted as the catalyst that shaped the Métis identity."[8] A classical example of this narrative can be found in the works of historian George Stanley, when he claimed it was at "the door of the North West Company [that] must be laid the responsibility for rousing the racial consciousness of the métis."[9] In effect, the narrative that represents the Métis as empty vessels instilled with a sense of national self-awareness by unscrupulous NWC men in order to turn them against the Selkirk Settlement has arguably crystallized into a sort of orthodox account.[10]

However, this "orthodox account" of the role of the NWC and of the Battle of Seven Oaks in Métis identity formation has since been called into question by what might be termed "heretical" narratives. In this regard, Michael Payne has spoken of the "revisionist tenor" or "revisionist slant" of the latest research in the fur trade historiography due to the fact that the "urge to particularize fur trade experience has led to the proliferation of genealogical, particularly of Métis families, and demographic studies."[11] To be sure, Payne observed that "this interest in history from other perspectives than the national and political is scarcely unique to fur trade or even Canadian history."[12] By way of illustration, Payne underlined the clear "connection between their work and what Maurice Careless has defined as the idea of 'limited identities,' organizing history around ethnicity, gender, class, and/or region."[13] If the current tendency in Métis studies is to stress ethnogenesis and identity formation,[14] it also increasingly emphasizes identities that are either geographically or economically limited and often does so at the expense of nationhood.[15]

However, as Samuel W. Corrigan pointed out, in "one sense all history, like the common law of Canada, is revisionist."[16] If Payne has branded these "heretical" accounts as being "revisionist," the question I will explore in this chapter is that of what specific aspects of previous narratives they are revising and to what degree such revisions are justified both from a theoretical and empirical standpoint. To do so, it is first necessary to distinguish the findings of a more recent "second revisionist wave" of orthodox accounts concerning the origins of Métis identity from the studies of a "first revisionist wave," notably those of Jennifer Brown, Jacqueline Peterson, John Foster and Harriet Gorham.[17] The research of the latter is often cited in support of claims that would have us believe, for example, that the Red River sense of identity can be traced back to the Great Lakes "métis." The contours of the Great Lakes métis identity is said in turn to be largely determined by occupational niches and therefore to originate in class structures rather than in other poles of identity, such as "race," ethnicity, language or religion. It is precisely this "heretical" account of the ethnogenesis of the métis in the Great Lakes region that has led some to not only displace the narrative that accords the Battle of Seven Oaks a pivotal role as a catalyst in Métis identity formation, but to question the initial emergence of a Métis identity in Red River.

One of the problems with the findings of the scholars of this second revisionist wave is that they often fail to take into account the conceptual distinction between the leap from "entity to identity" and the further leap of identity to national consciousness that is present in the first revisionist wave's works on Métis ethnogenesis.[18] Furthermore, the research of the first wave is extremely cautious about concluding that the Great Lakes mixed-ancestry communities *preceded* Red River in Métis identity formation, simply because they may not have made the leap from entity to identity. While noting the origin of Métis identity in occupational niches of the fur trade, first-wave scholars never limited it to any single variable, but insisted on multiple factors. Indeed, in order to explain the emergence of two distinct peoples of mixed ancestry within Red River itself—the Métis and the Scots or English Half-Breeds—early revisionists sought to understand and explain identity formation in such a way so as to emphasize the dialectic between institutions and occupational niches, rather than simply insisting on "class" as *the* explicative variable.

In addition, while Brown, Peterson, Foster and Gorham's research questioned the role of the NWC in general, or that of the Battle of Seven Oaks specifically, in Métis *identity formation*, they never denied their respective roles in the development of Métis *national consciousness*. Furthermore, if they viewed the fur trade war as insufficient in itself to explain Métis identity formation, it was not because it failed to take into account the class factor, but because it portrayed the organizational capacity of the Red River Métis as exogenous rather than endogenous. Ultimately, it is this organizational capacity of the Métis that is seen not only as playing a vital role in the group cohesion and solidarity of the Red River Métis, but also as the key factor that distinguished them from both the Half-Breeds and the mixed-ancestry communities of the Great Lakes. Finally, none of them denied the importance of political history, but saw social and political history as complementary. In this regard, it may be of interest to take into account both historical institutionalism and social movement theory in order to account for the ethnogenesis of Métis identities.

Historiographical Overview

To be sure, first-wave scholars have questioned the orthodox account of the role of the NWC in Métis identity formation. For example, Joe Sawchuk found that it "is not entirely convincing."[19] According to Duke Redbird, "the Métis existence is a result of human relationships and not political machinations [...]. The birth of the Métis came about as a 'participation mystique,' a desire of people wanting to get together. It had no intentional political function [...]."[20] Interestingly, Redbird also referred to the antecedents of Métis identity in eastern Canada.[21] It is precisely the research of Peterson, Dickason and Foster that made an initial contribution to a better understanding of Métis identity formation and unearthing potential links between the Red River Métis and the Great Lakes mixed-bloods.[22]

In terms of a pre-existing Métis identity, James R. Miller claimed that "Peterson [1985] found that the communities she examined so thoroughly had evinced *a sense of* Metis *nationalism long before* the tensions between rival fur-trading companies in Rupert's Land supposedly engendered that feeling of ethnic pride and aspiration."[23] Métis legal scholar Larry Chartrand has also asserted that recent "historical scholarship has, however, raised doubts about the traditionally held views regarding the birth of *Métis self-consciousness as a separate and distinct community* arising in the northwest."[24] It is striking that Chartrand quotes John Foster[25] and Heather Devine[26] to support his claim. In actual fact, while the research does support the claim that "a separate Métis *identity* was well established before the events of 1812–1814,"[27] it does not contend that Métis *national consciousness* was well established "long before" the fur trade war and it is inconclusive regarding the extent to which those of mixed ancestry in the Great Lakes possessed a distinct "self-conscious" identity in contrast to simply forming separate ephemeral communities and an uncertain, fluid sense of identity. I will elaborate more on this latter point further on.

For his part, political scientist Thomas Flanagan has queried "whether 'nation' is the correct term for scholars to apply to the Métis."[28] While Flanagan argued that the *contemporary* "Métis are an economically marginal, incohesive assortment of heterogeneous groups, widely dispersed across Canada,"[29] scholars have since operationalized what were arguably derogatory and polemical remarks into a research agenda for studying *historical* Métis communities. For Nicks and Morgan, as "an extant Alberta métis population which developed independently of Red River, Grande Cache may prove to be a typical rather than an exceptional case."[30] Nicks and Morgan also cite articles by Peterson, Dickason, Long and Brown in the same volume, as proof that "métis studies are already on the way to overcoming the 'Red River myopia' which has been characteristic in the past."[31] Similarly, after referring to Peterson and Brown's *The New Peoples: Being and Becoming Métis in North America*,[32] Miller asserted that what "the intensive study of specific communities has shown thus far is that many of our generalizations are flimsy, and that the Métis experience is an extremely diverse one."[33] He also agreed that during "the past fifteen years the study of mixed-blood communities has made rapid progress. It has broken free of its old fixation with the Great Man, and it has been partially cured of 'Red River myopia.'"[34] In Pannekoek's view, the "new dynamic" of what Payne termed the "revisionist trend" is "forcing Metis historiography out of the bog of Red River in which some argue it has been mired for too long."[35] As Payne remarked, some of these studies "focusing on the Métis have shown that Métis identities and experiences do not all arise from Red River."[36] Métis geographer Brenda Macdougall specifically bemoaned that the role of "Seven Oaks in 1817 [sic] is still widely accepted without question," notably because it perpetuates the "notion that a singular Metis consciousness and national identity emerged."[37] In her study of the community of St. Laurent, Manitoba, Nicole St-Onge "goes further and argues that even in the traditional areas of Métis studies a historical interpretation is required."[38] As we shall see, if "orthodox" accounts have tended to perpetuate the notion of a singular Métis nation, they rarely ever presumed the existence of a single nation *of mixed ancestry* and have for the most part always distinguished Scots Half-Breeds from the *Métis canadien*.

In terms of the question of the emergence of a specific Métis identity, the "second revisionist wave" arguably tends to adopt a reductionist view of identity formation that places undue weight on the single variable of a shared occupational background in the fur trade. It consequently places economic subordination at the centre of its analysis, to the exclusion of other variables such as ethnicity, "race," religion or language. In itself, there is nothing particularly new or original about the role of occupational niches in Métis identity formation. While Giraud insisted on factors such as "race," or Aboriginal ancestry,[39] and language as the "principle of cohesion and solidarity" among the Métis,[40] he also claimed that economic niches of the *voyageurs canadiens* were transmitted to their mixed-blood offspring.[41] Similarly, W.L. Morton advanced that the *Canadien* free-men "transmitted to their progeny of mixed-blood...the organized buffalo hunt."[42] But whereas these "orthodox" scholars also grounded Métis identity in other sources, such as religion and language, Nicole St-Onge found that by the late 1860s, a petty bourgeois trader and merchant elite had emerged among the Métis in Red River, and concluded that their "mixed-blood ancestry was secondary to the reality of their class position."[43] On this basis, St-Onge asserted that the Métis were a "people-class."[44] More recently, she has followed Miller's cue and accepted that it is only when research is "sensitive to the reality of class structures within mixed-blood populations and to class-based links between the Métis and the larger world" that "the histories of dual-descent populations [can] be truly understood and appreciated."[45] Historian Gerhard Ens found completely inadmissible Pannekoek's thesis[46] concerning the role of "sectarian and racial conflict" in Red River. In Ens's view, "Metis identity was not defined by biology, blood, or religion, but rather by the economic and social niche they carved out for themselves in the fur trade."[47] Similarly, Brenda Macdougall claims that "Foster's work furthered the notion of Metis diversity, concluding that class, rather than culture, was its source" and cites with approval Ens's "compelling study on the nature of class in Metis society."[48]

These conclusions would appear to be based on the findings of the early research on the Great Lakes mixed-bloods. To be sure, one can find passages that, if read in isolation, seem to even reduce "outside naming" to the analytical category of *class* despite the obvious zoological references.[49] For example, Jacqueline Peterson wrote that mixed-ancestry designations such as *chicot*, *bois-brûlé* and *gens libre* all "pointed to either occupational or mobility patterns characteristic of Métis, rather than to race."[50] In her view, if the "Great Lakes Métis were able to construct a separate identity" it was due to their "monopolization of the middle occupational rungs of the fur trading system."[51] Harriet Gorham also noted that when the "terms 'half-breed' and 'half-Indian' came into currency" they were "used most often to describe members of the labouring class who lived on the edge of settlements or Indian reserves."[52] Later, Peterson specified that the Great Lakes mixed-bloods had "a personal and group identity which was less place-specific than regionally and occupationally defined."[53] In Jennifer Brown's view, Red River Métis identity found its origin among the mixed-bloods of the NWC who "tended to constitute the lower classes of the fur trade," although she also insisted that they "joined a common cause that emphasized their maternal descent."[54] Olive Dickason agreed that the fur trade "put a premium on the services of the métis, who had grown up in the trade and who were uniquely qualified to carry it on."[55] In refuting Pannekoek's thesis concerning religious divisions in the Red River Settlement, Irene Spry asserted the divisions were between "the well educated and well-to-do gentry" and "the mass of unlettered, unpropertied natives of the country," as well as between "the professional farmer and the hunter and plains trader."[56] Again, we shall see that on further examination these scholars were in fact much more nuanced in their findings. As James Miller noted of Diane Payment's study of Batoche between 1870 and 1910, she "emphasized the differences between the Métis bourgeoisie, who had tended to cosy up to authority in 1885 and afterwards, and the rest of the population that had been much more volatile politically."[57] Despite these studies, Miller still felt the need to insist that "We must, in short, study class as a factor among the Métis."[58]

Entity, Identity and Nationhood

The definition of *nation*, both as an analytical category and a historically existing collective actor, is notoriously difficult and it is of little interest here to attempt a quixotic ontological quest to find the essence of what is signified by the expression "Métis nation." For the purpose of this chapter, let us simply put forward the following working definitions. An *entity* is a group that is defined as such by outsiders based on objective criteria, but lacks the subjective perception of itself as a distinct group or the desire to collectively maintain such objective distinctions. Due to the lack of evidence of self-ascription, I will use the expression "mixed-ancestry" (or "mixed-blood") to designate mere separateness. An *identity* involves the group moving toward a subjective perception and self-ascription of itself as a distinct group, but it remains *social* or pre-political in that it does not necessarily entail a strong desire or capacity to maintain such distinctions, either individually or collectively. To designate such mixed-ancestry communities, I will use the lower-case "métis."

For its part, a nation implies not only self-ascription, but a *political* consciousness that is shaped by a dialectical movement where political action is both motivated by a strong desire and capacity to maintain the objective and subjective aspects that distinguish it from other groups and shapes the very subjectivity and agency that nourishes that desire. It is uniquely for this group that I will use the upper-case "Métis." It should be noted, however, that by using the terms "mixed-ancestry" or "métis" I am not insinuating in any way that it is inappropriate to use the term "Métis" to ascribe such groups whether it be in the past or as a reformulation of identity in the present. I am merely indicating that the proof that scholars of the first revisionist wave initially put forward did not *at that time* allow them to go any further than using the lower-case "métis" to designate such groups, although enough evidence may have since accumulated that we may presently revise their initial findings.

The Leap from Entity to Identity

While historians like Peterson, Brown, Foster and Gorham have contributed to our understanding of how agglomerations of mixed-ancestry families may have formed, it is not entirely clear that this was in itself sufficient to develop an awareness of a shared sense of collective identity. For example, Brown was careful to stress her study's "upper class" bias since it focussed primarily on the traders who "were predominantly officers, or at least men who attained a clerkly or higher rank at some point in their careers."[59] Brown pointed out that "very few Scottish North Westers had made their homes in Red River" and suggests that they "preserved no communal existence; patrifocality led to their mobility, dispersal, and assimilation in larger white communities."[60] In other words, Brown concluded that no distinct ethno-cultural identity developed among the mixed-ancestry descendants of Scottish officers of the NWC fur trade system. Of course, some lower rung Scottish employees and some officers, such as Cuthbert Grant, did make their homes in Red River.[61] However, in the case of Grant, he converted to Catholicism, married a Catholic, French-speaking *Métisse* and spent the last 30 years of his life in (what later became) Saint-François-Xavier conversing, eating, hunting, sleeping, dancing and drinking with French Catholic Métis and was about as assimilated as anyone who had not actually been born into a Métis community could possibly be.[62] While his personal trajectory is an illustration of the fact that at the boundaries of collective identities there exists a "zone of indistinction" and that such boundaries are in no way impermeable, the old adage that the exception does not the rule make certainly applies here.

As for the hypothesis that the origin of the Métis identity in Red River finds its roots among the mixed-ancestry descendants of *Canadien* voyageurs in the Great Lakes region, Harriet Gorham claimed the French "mixed-blood people of the Great Lakes region *never developed a sense of shared ethnic identity*," despite the fact that they appeared "to conform to the theoretical definitions of an ethnic group on the basis of sharing certain *objective* criteria such as common language, religion, style of dress, housing construction, and some forms of artistic expression."[63] In addition, she acknowledged that the "group under study included [...] descendants of the old French bourgeoisie that controlled the fur trade before 1760."[64] Much like Brown's mixed-ancestry descendants of the Scottish *bourgeois* of the NWC who did not develop a distinct identity, this group "was a more 'élite' group than the mixed-blood voyageurs of the Great Lakes region, or many of the Métis of Red River. In many respects, we have been tracing the career and marital choices of *a very different socio-economic group* than the Red River Métis."[65] While there certainly is an emphasis here on occupational niches, we shall see that it is in itself insufficient to account for the ethnogenesis of the Métis. What I wish to emphasize here is that these particular mixed-bloods never seemed to have made the leap to "métis," or "from entity to identity."[66]

As we have seen, Miller claimed that Peterson, in her article "Many Roads to Red River," had asserted the Great Lakes mixed-bloods had not only evinced a sense of identity as "Métis," but a sense of nationalism, and that they did so *long before* the Red River Métis.[67] Similarly, Ens claimed to "borrow heavily"[68] from Peterson in order to conclude that there was a "crystallization of a Métis identity in the various communities along the Great Lakes [that] occurred after the British Conquest of New France and the fall of Michilimackinac to the British in 1763."[69] However, Peterson was careful to specify that the finding of mere separateness was "*not* to suggest that the Peoples and communities we are about to describe *were* [...] *self-consciously Métis*, but rather that they were a people in the process of becoming, whose distinctiveness was fully apparent to outsiders, *if not themselves*."[70] In other words, if the empirical evidence allows us to conclude the "objective" existence of a collective mixed-ancestry *entity*, it was insufficient to allow us say anything about their subjective sense of *identity*. Indeed, Peterson has recently claimed that "there is no evidence that prior to, or even subsequent to 1815, mixed-descent residents of Great Lakes fur-trading communities had developed a separate ethnic group identity or political consciousness [...]."[71] For his part, Foster found that such research gave the impression it was more a matter of "*Canadien* communities that happened to have mixed-blood components but do not consider themselves as distinct from *Canadien*."[72] Both Peterson and Foster were therefore circumspect about concluding that the mixed-ancestry communities formed around the Great Lakes self-ascribed themselves as "métis," much less "Métis."

Occupational Niches and Identity Formation

As we have seen, the second revisionist trend relies on the first wave's research on the role of occupational niches in identity formation to stress the social belonging of the Métis chiefly in terms of socio-economic class. There are several problems with attributing an occupationally determined identity to the research of this earlier generation. First of all, none of the works of the first revisionist wave suggest that the occupational factor was sufficient in itself for ethnogenesis.[73] Dickason attributed the emergence of a distinct identity to the Anglo-French rivalry in the Old Northwest, where "the forces influencing the métis to identify with either French or Amerindian were much weaker" than elsewhere in New France, and they consequently "began to look upon themselves as representing a distinctive blend of the two cultures."[74] For his part, Foster speculated that what may have contributed to a sense of distinct identity was the shift in focus from Montreal to the Great Lakes as a result of the Seven Years' War, when "Montréal, in myth and in fact, could no longer occupy a central position in their sense of themselves."[75] Later, when Foster emphasized that the *Canadiens* became the *gens libres* in order to fill a provisioning niche, he attributed this to "a deep-rooted Euro-Canadian ethos" and concluded that "a significant dimension in the heritage of the Metis is an ethos that heavily influenced the lives of adult males whose cultural founts were pre-industrial France and Britain."[76] It is noteworthy that he never deployed the analytical category of "class" in doing so. As Peterson has recently remarked, these occupational niches "ensured the survival of individuals but did not of themselves stimulate the emergence of a 'new people' within fur trade society."[77]

The second difficulty is that even if mixed-ancestry designations such as *chicot*, *bois-brûlé* and *gens libre* (or *otipemisiwak* to use the Cree equivalent) can be said to be occupational rather than racial in nature,[78] terms like "métis" and "half-breed" were already imbued with racist undertones from the outset and did not simply refer to occupational niches. The use of the terms "métis" and "half-breed" only appeared in the Red

River area in the second decade of the nineteenth century[79] and in the third decade in the case of the Great Lakes region.[80] Aside from the fact that this means outside naming only occurred in the Great Lakes *after* it appeared in Red River, Peterson commented that it was only after the War of 1812 that "terms such as *half-breed*, *métis* and *métif* began to appear with increasingly frequency in the travel literature, carrying with them the pejorative baggage of social inferiority or degeneracy."[81] It was precisely in this period that "racial prejudices were expressed more openly."[82] Foster maintained that the term "métis," like "half-breed" "could suggest 'mongrel' rather than mixed" and that the term "half-breed" "was taking on racial and cultural connotations of a negative nature."[83] When the term "half-breed" was initially applied to the mixed-blood offspring of the HBC trading system, attributes "of race or blood were linked with cultural and behavioural traits."[84]

Whatever the terms used, Foster questioned the pertinence of the regional identity of the Great Lakes métis for the Métis of the plains.[85] Although he recognized that those who supported Jean-Louis Riel in 1849 "appear to have had roots in the Great Lakes métis experience," he nevertheless noted a "few examples of what could be an inventory of distinctions between the métis populations of each area," including 1) the duration of the presence of the French, 2) the particular Amerindian tribes in each region, and 3) the connections with the Missouri River trade. In other words, it "was the establishment of a separate geographical, economic and cultural space, rather than biological *métissage* itself, that led to the creation of a distinctive ethnic consciousness that came to be identified as Métis."[86] For her part, Peterson claimed that the "geographic mobility of Great Lakes Métis [...] ultimately proved a liability. [...] In the end, the Great Lakes Métis identity, like the transitional economy which gave it life, was to prove a fragile construction."[87] In any event, to the extent that these scholars applied a historical materialist framework whereby occupational niches (infrastructure) underpin identity (superstructure), they were consequent in finding that, with the collapse of the very economy in which such niches were located, so, too, disappeared any sense of métis identity.[88]

Métis and Half-Breeds

In his study of the "Social Origins of the Riel Resistance," Pannekoek felt the need to remind readers that "the mixed bloods of Red River should not be seen as a monolith, but rather as two communities with two separate identities."[89] Certainly, as Métis legal scholar Paul Chartrand and Joe Sawchuk have observed, there is a tendency in contemporary popular culture and Métis political organizations to anachronistically confound the two groups.[90] A superficial reading of a few professional historians may give the impression that it was their common Aboriginal ancestry that united the Métis and the Half-Breeds as a single people. For Stanley, "there was a common bond between the English and French half-breeds. Both sprang from a common race."[91] Similarly, Giraud also placed heavy emphasis on common Aboriginal ancestry as the source of group cohesion and solidarity.[92] As we have seen, Brown, too, claimed that the two groups "joined a common cause that emphasized their maternal descent."[93]

But a more detailed analysis leaves one wondering whether Pannekoek's remarks are a textbook case of attacking the proverbial straw man. If Stanley opined that "there was a common bond between the English and French half-breeds. Both sprang from a common race" and applied the term "New Nation" to the two groups indistinctly, he also commented that, as "a rule the English-speaking half-breeds formed a contrast to the French."[94] While Pannekoek was of the opinion that Giraud failed "to distinguish adequately between Halfbreed and Métis,"[95] Giraud could not have been any clearer about the scope of his study when he specified that it was "essentiellement circonscrite aux métis d'ascendance franco-indienne" and that "le métis écossais n'intervient que lorsqu'il nous permet de mieux dégager, par voie de comparaison, la personalité du métis canadien, et d'opposer les conceptions et les habitudes de vie des deux groupes."[96]

Furthermore, if there was a tendency among early amateur historians and contemporaneous commentators to obscure distinctions between different groups in Red River, it was not so much between the Métis and the Half-Breeds as between the latter and the Scottish settlers.[97] A typical example can be found in the work of Rev. R.G. MacBeth, which divided the Settlement into two groups—the French half-breeds and the Selkirk settlers.[98] MacBeth included among the latter "those of their class (who composed one part of it)."[99] Further on, he again mentioned the "Selkirk settlers and other people of that class."[100] The closest he came to mentioning Scots Half-Breeds is when he referred to a new arrival who "wrote to eastern papers [...] and made reference to the dark-skinned people under the somewhat contemptuous name of 'breeds,'" and when he wrote of the "Selkirk settlers and men of that class" who were "of less nomadic habits."[101] Afterward, MacBeth simply referred to the "English speaking settlers."

There was also a tendency to ignore the English or Scots Half-Breeds during debates of the House of Commons over the Manitoba bill. For example, contemporaneous federal MPs made several references to "half-breeds," "Catholics" and "French," but it is often difficult to tell whether they perceived these as various qualities of the same group or as distinct groups. The term "half-breed" is most often used alone, although some comments add epithets that suggest it applies solely to those of French extraction.[102] If the MPs did tend to presume that "half-breeds" were essentially francophone and Catholic, it may explain the opposition to the land grant and the opposition's accusations that the government was trying to reserve Manitoba to the French and Catholics.[103] That being said, on February 21, 1870, well before the tabling of the bill, Cartier did explicitly refer to the "Scotch and English half-breeds" and the "French-Canadian half-breed."[104]

Even so, other contemporaneous commentators hardly ignored the linguistic, religious and lifestyle distinctions between the two groups. Individuals who were closely associated with the Resistance, notably Oscar Malmros as well as reverends Ritchot and Giroux, clearly distinguished the two groups,[105] as did an anonymous writer.[106] Similarly, contemporaneous amateur historians such as Ross, Hargrave, Begg and Cowie all noted such distinctions.[107] Even early scholarly works in English not particularly sympathetic to the Métis noted the difference.[108] A.G. Morice specifically cited the 1870 census that enumerated "4,063 English half-breeds" and compared the characteristics of the two groups.[109] That being said, many of these same authors often restricted the term "half-breed" to the Métis, although at times they also used the more specific term "French half-breed," often shortened simply to "the French."[110]

Despite his emphasis on "the common bond of Indian ancestry," Stanley also wrote that, as "a rule the English-speaking half-breeds form a contrast to the French" and cited contemporaneous sources that accentuated a difference in lifestyle—farming as opposed to "the chase."[111] Auguste-Henri de Trémaudan[112] used the expression "nation métisse" inclusively, but nevertheless specified that it included "deux groupes assez distincts, les Métis français ou Bois-Brûlés, dont la langue paternelle était le français, et les métis anglais dont la langue paternelle était l'anglais."[113] A.S. Morton also maintained the distinction throughout his chapter on the Resistance, restricting the militia based on the bison hunt and the term "New Nation" to the "French half-breeds."[114] Similarly, W.L. Morton restricted his use of the term "métis" to "the population of mixed blood in Red River which was French by speech and Roman Catholic by faith"[115] and restricted not only the term "New Nation" to the "métis,"[116] but also the bison hunt formation.[117]

Among contemporary scholars, Flanagan in particular was insistent that "Riel's people" only extended to "the French-speaking element of the Western half-breeds."[118] Brown agreed that *The Collected Writings of Louis Riel* "as a whole, lend support to de Trémaudan's [1984] thesis that the Metisism of Riel was resolutely Catholic and French in orientation."[119] Furthermore, as Pannekoek admitted, Sprague and Frye[120] "pointed out that there were serious economic and social differences between mixed-blood language groups and that these differences lasted until after the Riel

Resistance."[121] To be sure, this does not take away from the originality of Pannekoek's attempt to tackle the great divide from a viewpoint that is all too often overlooked. In this regard, Gregg Dahl's chapter in this volume, as the title "A Half-Breed's Perspective on Being Métis" suggests, further explores the specificity of Half-Breed identity.

Nevertheless, if one is tempted to conclude that the Métis/Half-Breed distinction is so commonplace among contemporary scholars that it seems like a classic case of overstating the painfully obvious to belabour the point,[122] there are those who contest such boundaries of identity. For example, Brenda Macdougall has recently admonished "scholars of all intellectual bends" for their "continued reliance on terms and categories such as French-speaking, English-speaking, mixed-blood, Métis, Halfbreed, country born, Catholic Métis, or Protestant Halfbreeds" and proposes in their stead the constructed vocabulary of 'Metis' (without an acute accent over the "e").[123] To support her argument, Macdougall claims that Irene Spry "refuted the existence of racial and/or cultural divisions along French and British lines."[124] In fact Spry did no such thing. The context of Spry's comments was a critique of Pannekoek's claim that there was "hatred" between Half-Breeds and Métis that was caused by "sectarian and racial conflict."[125] First of all, she agreed with Pannekoek on the score of religious divisions. In her view, if such "antagonism as there may have been between French- and English-speaking communities [...] does not seem to have been racial in origin," but that it "was, indeed, sectarian."[126] As this quotation suggests, she also agreed with Pannekoek on the score of a French and English divide between the two peoples. Indeed, Spry constantly used the terms "métis" in reference to the former and "mixed-blood" in reference to the latter.[127] What Spry claimed was that the rapport between the Half-Breeds and Métis was "far from being mutually hostile." As proof of this, she notably mentioned "mixed ventures" where the Métis accepted the leadership of Half-Breeds like James Sinclair.[128] Interestingly, in the most in-depth biographical account of Sinclair written to date, D. Geneva Lent restricted her use of the term "Métis" to the

French Catholics of mixed ancestry. She noted that the "Citizens of the New Nation" were "to be recognized [by] the striking differences in personality between the *Métis* and the English or Scotch half-breeds."[129]

Furthermore, while Macdougall relied on Spry to assert that mixed marriages between Catholics and Protestants were "fairly widespread,"[130] Spry was careful to point out the "fragmentary nature of the documentary record" and provided a series of reasons to be circumspect about her findings.[131] Indeed, Macdougall's own references to mixed marriages, wherein Protestant men had to convert to Catholicism to marry Catholic women, illustrate both that religion was one of the principal boundaries between the two groups and, somewhat paradoxically, that such boundaries were porous. It is curious in this regard that Macdougall ends up using the very terms that she disapproved of when penned by her colleagues: "Saulteaux French Metis from Red River," "Halfbreeds from Red River," "a Halfbreed from St. Peter's Parish at Red River," "an English-speaking Halfbreed from Red River" and "an English Halfbreed from Red River."[132] In doing so, she not only illustrates the difficulty of avoiding contemporaneous self-ascriptions, but also inadvertently confirms that the Métis and Half-Breeds were indeed divided along linguistic and sectarian lines.

Moreover, insofar as *wahkootowin* signifies a worldview that is "rooted in family relationships begun on the land, where the marriage of two individuals spread outward to encompass all their relatives,"[133] these "many tender ties" between English River Catholic Métis and Red River Protestant Half-Breeds call into question Macdougall's claim that "Île à la Crosse is an ideal place to begin addressing the development of Metis culture and identity *far beyond the Plains experience*, thereby establishing new paradigms for Metis ethnogenesis."[134] In fact, as Andersen has remarked, many "enthnohistorians have highlighted the fundamental importance of relational and geographically expansive networks of kinship to the operation and facilitation of the subarctic fur trade" and that we should not be surprised to find "commonalities and affiliative connections in the circulation of people, goods, cultural meanings and identities in locales as historically distant as Red River and the Upper Great Lakes"[135]—or the English River District in this case. For Andersen, a "peoplehood-based framework, attentive to a core/periphery dynamic" encourages an analysis that takes into account such "geographically dispersed and contextually crosscutting nature of allegiances and alliances and into the magnitude or significance of Métis identity at the far reaches of its gravitational pull—none of which can be conceived of, let alone analyzed, in ethnohistorical accounts that remain obsessed with [...] isolationist/localized logics."[136]

In terms of language, while Macdougall refers to "*so-called* English- and French-speaking families at Red River,"[137] she relates that when religious services were first offered in French on October 31, 1824 in Île à la Crosse, the people "were pleased to attend and hear the services in French."[138] While she cites one occasion where mass was delivered in Cree and Dene as well as French,[139] she acknowledges that "as the records make evident, it had become commonplace for services to be held in French."[140] Furthermore, the use of Indigenous languages was apparently done exceptionally to respond to "a rumour that Catholic missionaries might be responsible for a number of deaths in *Indian communities*"[141] and therefore may not have been at all intended to address *Métis communities*. Given that when this took place—on September 17, 1865—mass had been delivered in French for some 40 years, it would be a little hasty to take this anecdote as sufficient evidence that the "dominant language" of the Métis was Cree or Dene as opposed to French. Suffice to say, we can more or less take for granted in scholarly works that the Métis and Half-Breeds formed two distinct peoples. The focus of inquiry shifts, then, to how the first revisionist wave explained the emergence of two distinct mixed-ancestry identities.

The Role of the NWC and Seven Oaks in the "Birth of a Nation"
In his study on the reformulation of Métis identity, Sawchuk relied on Abner Cohen's studies of the Hausa of Ibadan in Nigeria to advance the hypothesis that "an ethnic group only becomes clearly defined when it

has something to defend."[142] Relying on concepts in the field of anthropology, Sawchuk further maintained that "attraction among individuals was increased with the realization that: 1) there is a common threat stemming from an external source; and 2) there exists the possibility that co-operative behaviour may reduce or eliminate the threat."[143] In other words, it is a basic *political* function of a shared sense of ethnicity, no matter how real or imagined, that explains the extent to which a group can be mobilized to effectuate a collective response to an external threat. As German jurist Carl Schmitt put it, the "substance of the political is contained in the context of a concrete antagonism."[144] For this reason, a more encompassing account of the ethnogenesis of the Métis must take into consideration not only their *perception* of a common threat, but also the specific, concrete antagonisms and their "cultural mechanisms [that] already exist for organizing" a collective reaction to that antagonism.[145] To be sure, Giraud insisted on the role of common Aboriginal origins and language in the formation of a national identity among the Red River Métis.[146] Nevertheless, he also argued that even territorial claims were insufficient to create and maintain the national idea among the Métis. In his view, this could only have taken shape under the *organization* of the NWC.[147] While Giraud's portrayal of the Métis *being organized under* the NWC is questionable—as if Métis were incapable of the effective collective co-ordination to paddle a *jiimaan* in the same direction—he nevertheless recognized the importance of institutionalized organization in maintaining national consciousness. As Flanagan has pointed out, one of the telltale signs of the existence of a *nation* is that "there must be a widespread consciousness of national identity and a degree of cohesion and commitment sufficient to permit collective action."[148]

What the occupational niche factor seems unable to account for is the fact that one of the most significant distinctions between the Red River Métis and their Great Lakes métis cousins was the former's endogenous organizational capacity, despite the fact that both were raised in the French regime/NWC fur trade system. Dickason held that the "métis of the

'Old Northwest' were a short step from the 'New Nation.' But *it was a step that was never taken*, as it was forestalled by the rush of settlement."[149] For Peterson, "the very diffuseness of fur trade communities [...] made *group solidarity and combined action almost impossible to sustain*."[150] Likewise, when Gorham looked "for fairly obvious examples of collective action and of shared attitudes,"[151] she found that the métis in the Great Lakes region "were never able [...] *to take significant collective action to protect their shared interests*" and that they "appear to have functioned more as *a disparate collection of individuals* rather than as *a cohesive group*."[152] Aside from a shared sense of identity, one of the clues to the Métis' capacity to form a collective political actor is the cultural practice of a ritually repeated discourse that constantly reaffirms a political representation of themselves as a *nouvelle nation*. It is precisely traces of this type of cultural practice that the early research failed to find among the Great Lakes mixed-bloods.

As we have seen, the "plots of the North West Company are what most historians feel formed the basis of half-breed *nationalism* [...] implying that the Metis were 'created' as an *ethnic group* by the intrigues of a few fur traders in the Northwest."[153] The first and second revisionist waves agree that this orthodox explanation "is not entirely convincing," as Sawchuk put it.[154] However, what the first wave of revisionists questioned is not so much the role the NWC's intrigues played in the birth of Métis nationalism—that is, in their *political* self-awareness—but rather the assertion that it *created* the Métis *as an ethnic group*. For example, Peterson argued that "the debate over the role of the NWC and the connection between métis *political consciousness* and the HBC and NWC war for control over the interior fur trade begs the question of métis *group identity*."[155] For Peterson, the Battle of Seven Oaks "did not mark the beginnings of *a distinctive Métis culture*," since the latter "was a culmination of nearly two centuries of ethnic formation rooted along the St. Lawrence and in the Upper Great Lakes and transplanted, of necessity, in the northern Red River Valley."[156] Initially, Foster seemed to agree with other scholars that "the Métis as such did not exist at the time" (that is, the second decade of the nineteenth century), and that at "best one may use the term proto-Métis."[157] Later, however, Foster came to think that the awareness of a particular identity "predated by a number of years the Battle of Seven Oaks in Red River in 1816, the incident usually associated with the Red River métis' sense of themselves as the 'New Nation.'"[158]

There is certainly evidence to support the claim that the Métis of Red River demonstrated a self-awareness of a distinct "ethnic" identity by the 1810s at the very latest. According to Pierre Pambrun's testimony at the Coltman inquiry in 1818: "I do not think they [the Bois-Brûlés] consider themselves as white man, or that they are so considered by the white men, nor do they consider themselves as only on a footing with the Indians."[159] On March 14, 1818, William McGillivray, a NWC partner whose wife was Cree, wrote to William B. Coltman, the commissioner who inquired into the causes of the fur trade war, that "the half-breeds under the denominations of bois-brûlés and métifs have formed a separate and distinct tribe of Indians *for a considerable time back*, has been proven to you by various depositions."[160] In terms of "outside naming," McGillivray's deposition confirms that the term *half-breed* was initially applied to the mixed-ancestry offspring associated with the NWC fur trade system.[161] It also confirms that the occurrence of these specific terms of "other ascription" in Red River are contemporaneous with rather than subsequent to the same phenomenon in the Great Lakes, which also seems to have only begun in the early decades of the 1800s.[162]

However, these scholars neither denied the intrigues of the NWC nor their attempts to manipulate the Métis and sometimes even recognized the success of such attempts. For Sawchuk, "these tactics undoubtedly contributed to Metis unity."[163] Initially, Foster asserted that it was "with little difficulty [that] the officers of the North West Company instilled in the minds of the Métis the view 'that the land was theirs and that the English company was taking it away from them.'"[164] Furthermore, it was the NWC that "assisted the Métis in organizing themselves to take purposeful action against the settlers."[165] Later, Foster added that it "was natural that the North West Company officers would encourage these people, the 'Métis,' to see themselves as the 'New Nation' whose interests were threatened by the arrival of the Selkirk Settlers and the policies of the Hudson's Bay Company."[166] Dickason agreed that there "is no doubt, however, that the North West Company encouraged the situation for its own ends."[167] When Sawchuk expressed the view that these "intrigues of the North West Company would have met with little success had there not been a solid basis for the concept of national unity,"[168] he suggests that the attempt to instil the Métis with a sense of *national* consciousness was ultimately successful precisely because it was built on a solid basis—an already existing *ethnic identity*.

In this regard, Peterson thought that rather "than imputing métis nationalism to the designs of outsiders, it may be more fruitful to treat it as a paradigmatic reformulation of a set of symbols, however inchoate and unarticulated, which had formerly joined those who, after 1815, wore the new identity."[169] Although Peterson remained silent about how this paradigmatic reformulation of an already existing métis identity came about, she nevertheless implied that Métis political consciousness was a reformulation of a previous identity. Agreeing with orthodox accounts, Peterson did not hesitate to speak of Red River as "the birthplace of Métis national consciousness" and of "the flowering of a Métis national consciousness at Red River after 1815."[170] Peterson also maintained that the "wide and persistent appeal" of Métis nationalism "throughout the nineteenth century suggests that it stood for a type of social cohesion which was much older"[171] and even went so far as to recognize that "there is no question that Louis Riel's proclamation signalled the political maturity of the Manitoba Métis."[172] She recently asserted that "it is important to recall the sheer force of Métis numbers and ethnic and political consciousness [that] manifested at Red River after 1815. *In contrast to what can be seen elsewhere*, the reality of the Métis Nation on the northeastern plains is both incontrovertible and stunning."[173] Brown likewise followed orthodox accounts when she asserted that it "was in Manitoba that the Métis became conspicuous as a socio-political entity in Canadian history."[174]

To be sure, Dickason advanced that "the process was actually much more profound and complex" than "the machinations of the North West Company."[175] Noting the leap from social identity to political consciousness, Dickason concluded that when "settlers finally arrived at Red River in 1812, they were too few to overwhelm this spirit; instead, their presence was the catalyst which transformed mild awareness into conviction."[176] Similarly, for Foster it was the *"events of the decade*, focussing on the Battle of Seven Oaks, June 16, 1815 [sic], [that] caused the Métis to emerge as a self-conscious entity with a particular past and a particular destiny."[177] In other words, even if we accept that the N W C attempted to convince the Métis that they were a nation, and thereby played a role in bringing about Métis national self-awareness, the simple diffusion of a nationalist discourse is insufficient in itself to bring about a shift in self-perception. It is the receptivity of the actors and their practical political experiences—in this case, a conflict that lasted several years and culminated in the Battle of Seven Oaks—that would have lent credence to such discourse.

From a sociological perspective, Métis lifestyle and culture was a fertile ground in which the seeds of a nationalist discourse, regardless of its ultimate source, could easily take root, while concrete conflict was the catalyst that made it sprout. My own inclination is to agree with Gwyneth Jones, who opined as an expert witness in *R. v. Goodon* that the Métis "had an agenda of their own, that they had interests of their own that they would be willing to defend but they would not be put out of their way to defend somebody else's interests if they didn't really see the purpose of it."[178] Whatever the actual role of the N W C in the emergence of a Métis national consciousness, it would nevertheless be correct to say that "group identities are not mere fabrications. [...] They must depend upon a core of characteristics held, even if not yet fully recognized, in common."[179]

Furthermore, what seems to confirm Sawchuk's and Peterson's claim that the Métis had a solid basis for the concept of national unity is Giraud's remark that, if the North West Company partners and Cuthbert

Grant had wished that the idea of a Métis nation included "les métis du Nord-Ouest, sans acception d'ascendance," it was "réduite en fait à la fraction métis canadien." In other words, "à l'exception des chefs qui avaient assumé direction, la nation des Bois-Brûlés comprenait essentiellement des métis canadiens."[180] Here, we detect what is perhaps the main distinction between the Red River Métis and the Great Lakes métis: in the former case, there existed "the possibility that co-operative behaviour may reduce or eliminate the threat." In Brown's eyes, it was the efforts of the Métis "to seek and protect their rights in the Red River region [that] helped to lead to their survival as an entity in Western Canada."[181]

The Role of Institutions in Identity Formation

To better understand the differences in identity formation between the Great Lakes métis and the Red River Métis, it is necessary to come back to the question of what factors allow us to account for the difference between the Métis and Half-Breeds. As has been suggested, while occupational niche is a factor in identity formation, it is in itself neither sufficient nor necessary. In his seminal work on the *Métis canadien*, French ethnologist Marcel Giraud contrasted the development of the southern (*meridonial*) and northern (*septentrional*) centres of ethnogenesis of mixed-bloods, which respectively correspond to the NWC and the HBC trading systems.[182] Similarly, Foster suggested institutional factors when he asserted that over time "the particular nature of influences emanating from specific metropolitan centres left distinctive cultural legacies. As these legacies were incorporated in the various ways of life of the participants in each of the two trading systems, they created two distinct fur trade traditions."[183]

Brown's study also followed Giraud's lead by focussing on "institutionalisation as a major phenomenon."[184] Brown argued that the HBC was characterized by vertical integration and applied the concept of *frame* to describe the "binding of heterogeneous individuals into one institution."[185] The notion of a vertical integration model provides at least a partial explanation as to why the glass ceiling for mixed-bloods in the HBC was set between the London Committee on one hand and the governors, masters, factors and traders in Rupert's Land on the other. Brown asserted that it was due to this vertical integration that the "HBC offspring lacked the distinct community and economic base upon which to build a separate identity."[186]

Brown saw the NWC, for its part, as being "characterised by internal horizontal homogeneity" and applied the concept of *attribute*, which refers to "the classification of individuals into horizontally extended occupations, status, or kin groups."[187] For this reason, the glass ceiling for mixed-bloods in the case of the NWC was situated between the clerks, bourgeois and partners—who tended to be of Scottish descent, along with a few token *Canadiens*—and the voyageurs, guides and interpreters—who tended to be *Canadiens* and Métis along with a few Scottish and Iroquois.[188] As the Métis largely emerged out of this latter group, we can see that, while this confirms the hypothesis that Métis identity owes something to particular occupational niches, it also introduces the variable of institutional practices and ethnicity to explain why the Métis were in fact confined to such positions in the first place. Similarly, Peterson's description of the NWC trading system also points to the role of institutional structures in the ethnogenesis of the Métis.[189]

One of the institutional factors that might explain the politics of outside naming, was not only the lack of vertical mobility in the NWC, but that the NWC practice of wintering provided an institutional incentive for intermarriage whereas the HBC practice of "sleeping by the sea" allowed enforcement of official prohibition.[190] This may explain why the HBC documents refer to mixed-blood offspring simply as "English," at least to the extent they lived a European lifestyle.[191] As Sawchuk noted, in the early 1800s the term "métis" "referred specifically to the French-speaking half-breeds of the Red River Settlement."[192] If the term "half-breed" was initially used in the NWC as an English translation of "métis" and later become a form of outside naming used by men like Governor George

Simpson to designate certain mixed-ancestry employees of the HBC, by the end of the 1840s the latter "no longer saw themselves as English" and when "acting in concert with the Métis they used the term 'Halfbreed' to refer to their collective interest."[193] Citing Collins and Raven, who defined *group cohesiveness* as "those forces which act to keep a person in a group and prevent him from leaving,"[194] Sawchuk asserted that "group cohesiveness is enhanced when people in low status groups cannot, as individuals, achieve mobility" while, conversely, it "suffers if individuals are able to achieve mobility as a result of individual effort."[195] Surely, it is no mere coincidence that "Half-Breed" became a self-ascription precisely in the period when those who identified themselves as such saw their social mobility increasingly limited within the HBC (Van Kirk, 1980: 150–51). On the other hand, one can see how the internal horizontal homogeneity of the NWC, or the concept of *attribute*, partially accounts for the group cohesiveness of the Métis.

In terms of institutions, whether or not Brown "might have been more cautious in borrowing [...] Nakane's 'vertical society' model" is beside the point,[196] since her emphasis was arguably not so much on structure itself as on "the formal or informal procedures, routines, norms and conventions embedded in the organizational structure" that "provide moral or cognitive templates for interpretation and action."[197] Brown's study is in fact a classical example of historical institutionalism, where the "individual is seen as an entity deeply embedded in a world of institutions, composed of symbols, scripts and routines, which provide the filters of interpretation, of both the situation and oneself, out of which a course of action is constructed."[198]

Apart from the fur trade companies, another important institution that can be seen as a variable in the formation and crystallization of a distinct Métis identity is that of the church. For example, while Purich agreed with Redbird concerning the role of the NWC and the Great Lakes antecedents of Métis identity, he nevertheless thought "the influence of the Catholic Church was also critical."[199] Pannekoek remarked that an interesting "extension of Brown's landmark research would have been to see if these distinctions could be traced through the actions of each group in the Riel Resistance."[200] Further on, Pannekoek speculated that whereas "before the two companies provided focus, after their union in 1821 there was one company which accommodated neither tradition in its entirety. The Church of England can be argued to have reinforced the Hudson's Bay Company's Protestant heritage, and the Church of Rome the French Canadian one."[201] While I share Spry's reserve about the level of animosity between Half-Breeds and Métis, Pannekoek's assertion that religion "reinforced past experiences, memories and kinship,"[202] and thereby reinforced distinct identities, should not be peremptorily dismissed. Indeed, as we have seen, Spry herself recognized that such "antagonism as there may have been between French- and English-speaking communities [...] was, indeed, sectarian."[203] Devine concurred that the "presence of these missions, both Roman Catholic and Protestant, was instrumental in the development of distinct and separate corporate identities for the biracial people of Red River, whose social, economic and political activities and interests evolved further and further away from those of their aboriginal relations in Native bands."[204] While Ens criticized Pannekoek's claim that Métis and Half-Breeds were divided along racial and religious lines in Red River,[205] Karl Hele has suggested that "Catholicism served to bind [Métis] communities across the Great Lakes" and that religious "bigotry on the part of evangelically minded Protestant ministers, in the form of sectarianism, only reinforced the Catholic identity of the Métis."[206] Likewise, Macdougall has noted that the sacramental registries in Île à la Crosse "suggest the mission had a high degree of involvement in the lives of its parishioners" and that the "Church's role in setting social parameters and establishing who was a member of the community cannot be underestimated."[207] Macdougall notably points out that "in order for non-Catholic outsider males to become socially acceptable as spouses and join the local community through marriage, they were required to undergo the lengthy conversion process,"[208] thereby confirming that religious divisions did indeed exist between Catholics and Protestants. Furthermore, Macdougall found that "the daily or weekly religious observances of the Catholic Church, which were a regularized means of *supporting and nourishing social cohesion* in the northwest, becoming, in turn, *a large part of the Metis cultural identity*."[209] Again, this is a classical example of sociological institutionalism, whereby individuals, "when they act as a social convention specifies, [...] simultaneously constitute themselves and reinforce the convention to which they are adhering."[210]

Social Movement Analysis

This emphasis on institutions reveals what seems to underlie the main concern regarding the "orthodox" accounts that would have us believe the NWC instilled the Métis with a sense that they were a "New Nation." In Giraud's narrative, the Métis "give way to the directives that the influence of a strong will exerts over them with a docility that proceeds from their natural passivity." This portrayal of them as having an "absence of will power" leaves them "destined to be docile instruments of execution."[211] As Ania Loomba recognized, questions concerning the capacity of subalterns to answer back "are not unique to the study of colonialism but are also crucial for any scholarship concerned with recovering the histories and perspectives of marginalized people—be they women, non-whites, non-Europeans, the lower classes and oppressed castes."[212] Social history shares with postcolonial analysis the emphasis on the subaltern's capacity to answer back by "recognizing the agency and trying to understand the motivations of people who had often been treated as passive victims."[213]

In this regard, Arthur Ray has shown how Amerindians were active agents in the fur trade rather than simply passive dupes of Europeans.[214] Similarly, Foster asserted that the Métis were "entrepreneurial native hunters and traders [...] who had responded quickly and effectively to market opportunity."[215] Somewhat paradoxically, it is precisely in occupational niches, and therefore on the inferior social, political and economic status of the subaltern, that the agency of the Métis is to be located. Noting that the term "subaltern" is derived from Gramsci's writings, the historian of ideas John Pocock observed that it is used "to denote the culturally subordinate and, in particular, those having no identity except that which they can derive from the fact of their subordination."[216] What the cultural practice of repeated representation of the foundational violence of the Battle of Seven Oaks reveals is that the Métis did not attribute their national consciousness or sense of self to any such feeling, much less "fact," of subordination in occupational niches, but rather grounded it in a triumphant political moment that they ascribe to their superior military capacity.

The problem with this obsession of the Métis as active agents is that it risks blinding us to the fact that passivity can be one of many possible strategies that an agent may consciously choose in certain situations: "switching strategies, Nal'anal'mot [...] became very quiet. There were different ways to challenge conflict. He saw other choices he could make. [...] He knew that opposition didn't always require a defiant stance. Stealth and patience could also be effective."[217] More to the point, an account that represents agency and victimization as mutually exclusive can easily be turned on its head in order to construct a narrative of "blaming the victim." For a case in point, Flanagan has argued that in "portraying the Metis as hapless victims of others' evil plans, their contemporary spokesmen [...] degrade the dignity of individual Metis human beings."[218] But to argue that the Métis were victims *of a system* of land distribution because there was an unequal distribution of power that rendered their agency ineffective in no way implies that they were "hapless." Payne has remarked in this regard that Frank Tough's *As Their Natural Resources Fail*[219] has duly refocussed attention on the political economy of the fur trade, and suggested "a much less benign legacy of three centuries of trade than other historians allow."[220] As Loomba queries, "if we suggest that the colonial subjects can 'speak' and question colonial authority, are we romanticising such resistant subjects and underplaying colonial violence?"[221]

Besides, a narrative that involves manipulation, far from denying agency, is paradoxically a recognition of agency. Devine fully acknowledged that because the freemen could not be physically coerced, the fur trade companies "were compelled instead to use persuasion, deception, and bribery to manipulate the behaviour of the freemen."[222] Furthermore, Devine had no difficulty with the idea that "a freemen such as Tullibii could enhance his stature and extend his influence amongst the regional hunting population simply by acquiring and manipulating these symbols of supernatural power," or that freemen "manipulated their kin connections to foment discontent amongst the local natives."[223] In Devine's account, the agency of Tullibii and the freemen necessarily implies a potential capacity to manipulate others and to be manipulated. Similarly, Adrian Tanner, who "has in the past been critical of the way [Indians] are seen as passive people whose lives are determined by others" and looked at "the active creative responses of Indians to the influx of Europeans,"[224] nevertheless recognized that the hunting territory system offered "traders some *potential for influencing* the activities of Indians *for their own purposes*" and claimed to "have observed this kind of *manipulation* in recent times."[225] In other words, both Devine and Tanner show the extreme complexity of human relations, where persuasion and manipulation are only possible due to, and therefore necessarily postulate, the existence of agency.

If it is necessary to further comfort those concerned with properly portraying the agency of "subalterns," the capacity of the Métis for collective action points to the relevance of social movement theory. For example, Ens has made some attempt to harness social movement theory to analyze the Métis when he suggested "the Resistance of 1869–70 can be better understood in light of 'interest group' and 'class' politics than as a 'national' rising."[226] Of course, Ens's representation of social movements and national movements as being somehow mutually exclusive calls to mind Kiera Ladner's critique of Jane Jenson's remarks on Indigenous peoples movements.[227] According to Kiera, Jenson's study implies that Indigenous peoples organizations are mere social movements that use national-ist rhetoric.[228] In Ladner's view, such an approach diminishes the status of Indigenous peoples as nations. If there is some risk of this, it does not necessarily have to be the case, as both Jo-Anne Fiske's and David Long's analyses of contemporary Indigenous peoples' organizations demon-strate.[229] If social movement analysis *may* explain the effective political behaviour of Indigenous peoples, it does not have to deny their status as a people. As Sawchuk observed, "most pressure groups become replica-tions of the political structures around them, and Native pressure groups are no exception."[230] Given the institutional structure in which they oper-ate, they may have little choice but to use the available social movement tools in order to exploit the existing channels that allow them voice in a colonial State. To be sure, one should be cautious when applying such a theoretical framework to colonized peoples. As Leanne Simpson points out, when "resistance is defined solely as large-scale political mobili-zation," there is a risk that "the lens of colonial thought and cognitive imperialism" will prevent us from being able to see the strategies of mobilization of our ancestors.[231] Nevertheless, social movement models arguably allow us to account for the dialectical dynamic whereby national identity underpins collective political action, while collective political action reaffirms national identity.

Conclusion

It could certainly be said that the first wave of revisionist scholars pos-tulated that objectively identifiable mixed-ancestry communities in the Great Lakes region existed prior to those in Red River. However, despite claims to the contrary, they carefully avoided concluding that a subjec-tive *métis* identity crystallized in the Great Lakes region *before* it did so in Red River. While they emphasized the role that occupational niches played in the leap from mixed-blood entity to *métis* identity, none of them relied on this factor alone to explain the process of becoming *métis*. On the con-trary, they also postulated that institutional structures and practices were key factors in *métis* identity formation and that the two distinct fur trade traditions produced two distinct mixed-ancestry peoples, the Half-Breeds and the Métis, in the Red River Settlement. If there is a consensus among them that a distinct Red River Métis identity had already crystallized prior to the fur trade war, they also agreed that it was nevertheless due to events during this feud that a Métis national consciousness emerged in Red River. In other words, it is impossible to account for the emergence of the national consciousness of the Red River Métis solely in terms of social history and class. Recourse to political history and other identity factors, such as ethnicity, language, religion, institutions and organizational capacity is required in order to explain the phenomenon.

One of the problems with the second revisionist wave is arguably that, as Pocock remarked of social history in general, it has tended to exclude so-called classic or traditional history, which is seen as emphasizing political and military events, and therefore consists of aristocratic, bourgeois and male-dominated narratives, in favour of "an infinite series of micro-narratives, micro-moments and micro-managements."[232] For her part, Sandy Grande dismisses this "preoccupation with parochial questions of identity and authenticity" because it has "obscured the social-political and economic realities facing indigenous communities, substituting a politics of representation for one of social transformation."[233] On the one hand, social history may constitute an act of subversion in that it records the lives of those who have been excluded from, or simply subjected to, colonial narratives. On the other hand, as Chris Andersen has argued, "in presenting mere separateness as a basis for Métis identity, ethnohistory marginalizes an otherwise obvious hallmark of Métis 'groupness'—political self-consciousness as Métis and attachment to a self-ascribing Métis people."[234]

In terms of the relevance of such biographical micro-narratives, Bruce Trigger remarked that the unit of analysis in anthropology ranged from "society" as a whole, on one end of the scale, to the biography on the other. In his view, however, a biographical narrative "*at its best* is a perceptive examination *of the social forces at work in a particular situation* as these can be related to the life of a well-documented individual."[235] A classical example of this can be found in Devine's study of the Desjarlais clan. If she did not mention the specific incident of the Battle of Seven Oaks nor its effects on them, she nevertheless concluded with the remark that "it was inevitable that these separate biracial groups would coalesce into a corporate entity that could mobilize to protect the economic, cultural and political interests they shared."[236] She thereby suggested that "economic and political policies, hostile to the very survival of these fledgling mixed-race communities," played a fundamental role in the development of a national consciousness.[237]

To be sure, the first "revisionist turn" of social historians was and is a much-needed corrective to the previous hegemony of classical political history. That being said, these scholars arguably sought to complement rather than outright displace political history. For example, Miller noted that Diane Payment's *Batoche, 1870–1910*[238] was "a significant example of the social history that was becoming increasingly important" relative to political history, it nevertheless "provided a link between the newer social history concerns and the older political and military preoccupations."[239] Similarly, Brown mentioned that "Métis" could be understood in "social *or* political terms."[240] In other words, they neither suggested that political history had become entirely obsolete, nor did they see political and social history as mutually exclusive. More recently, Nathalie Kermoal has successfully woven social history with an emphasis on gender and ethnicity into the political history of the Resistance of 1869–1870 and the Rebellion of 1885.[241]

It should be added that if the early research of Brown, Foster and Peterson would seem to suggest that the Great Lakes mixed-bloods did not have the necessary organizational capacity for collective action to survive as communities, we should be careful about drawing any definitive conclusions on the matter. Peterson has recently concluded that "we now know, after more than three decades of cumulative research and publication [...] that the Great Lakes was the birthing ground of neither the Red River Métis nor a separate ethnic group of mixed ancestry and culture like the Red River Métis."[242] But if "a new generation of scholars strains to locate the occasional reference to métis individuals and even less frequently to métis communities,"[243] the problem may be, as Gloria Bell's chapter in this volume on the *visual* representations of Great Lakes métis suggests, that we rely too heavily on the *written* record. In terms of my own insistence on political history, when Reimer and Chartrand suggested four indicators to identify Métis communities in Ontario, they notably included "political identity evident in expressions of collective goals and rights."[244] Interestingly, there seem to be links between Sault Ste. Marie and Red River during the three major political moments of the Battle of Seven Oaks in 1816, the Sayer trial in 1849 and the Resistance in 1869–70. The Battle of Seven Oaks apparently "sent shock waves throughout the Upper Great Lakes community" and "a group of Ojibwe and métis warriors [travelled] from Sault to Rainy and Red River to attack Selkirk's supporters."[245] The central figure in the 1849 standoff in Red River, Pierre Guillaume Sayer, was originally from Sault Ste. Marie. Perhaps it is no coincidence that the Mica Bay incident was contemporaneous to the Sayer trial in Red River. Several métis from Sault Ste. Marie were involved in the "Michipicoten War" in 1849 at Mica Bay,[246] an incident that bears some evidence of both political consciousness and organizational capacity. It was none other than William McTavish, future governor of Assiniboia, who warned George Simpson that "the latest news is that 2,000 Red River half breeds are to be down in spring to act as allies of Shinkgwaukonse, having sent him a wampum belt with a message to that effect this autumn."[247] Reimer and Chartrand pointed out that the communication of fur traders between Fort Frances and Red River "may have heightened the political consciousness of the Fort Frances Métis."[248] According to McNab, the Métis of Rainy Lake managed to take advantage of the Red River Resistance as leverage to force the federal government to include them in Treaty No. 3.[249] However, as Andersen noted, "though ethnohistorians have only scratched the surface of such connections between these regions, the little research that has been undertaken reveals tantalizing connections."[250]

To be sure, the question of genealogical connections between the Great Lakes métis and the Red River Métis remains largely unexplored. As Pannekoek pointed out, "a comparative examination of Métis surnames in American settlements with those in Red River has not been conclusive and much work needs to be done to confirm what is at this moment only an interesting hypothesis."[251] For his part, Ens indicated that "Métis surnames in M[ichilim]ackinac birth and marriage registers of that time later appear in the parish registers of St. François Xavier."[252] Knight and Chute have also shown a genealogical connection of the Sayers and the Nolins in Sault Ste. Marie and Red River.[253] However, it is still unfortunately the case that "detailed published accounts of the formation and ethnogenesis of Métis communities in Ontario are lacking."[254]

Of particular interest is the suggestion that relations with surrounding Indigenous peoples are central to Métis identity formation.[255] Foster is one of the few to have observed that the emergence of the Red River Métis was a continuation of the relations between the Saulteux (Anishinaabeg) and the traders as both moved westward from the Great Lakes.[256] In this regard, Brian Gallagher attempted to sidestep the cultural distinctions between the Cree and Saulteux, by claiming "the Pembina Chippewa were not generally thought of as Saulteaux and were known to be acculturating towards the Cree culture of the majority of the Metis."[257] However, in a much more detailed analysis of the Plains Ojibwe, Laura Peers found that when they moved out onto the plain from the woodlands, they "retained their older, central core of identity."[258] As Sylvie Berbaum observed, the distinction between the Woodlands and Plains Ojibwe "has minimal meaning in the eyes of the Ojibwa themselves."[259] In the case of the Red River Métis and the Great Lakes mixed-bloods, they not only shared the common heritage of the NWC fur trade tradition, they were also *inawendi-wag*—related to each other—through a common cultural, linguistic and religious heritage on *both sides* of their mixed ancestry. This raises the question of the extent to which the specific institutions and culture of the Anishinaabeg played a role in the development of a common national identity in both the Red River Métis and the Great Lakes Region.

When Alexis de Tocqueville travelled in the Old Northwest in 1831, he remarked that Saginaw, Michigan, was made up of four groups that were separately huddled together—the English, the French (that is, *Canadiens*), the "Indians" and the "métis."[260] The spatial separation as much from the *Canadiens* as the Anishinaabeg is an indication that, at least in 1831, the Great Lakes métis had some sense of a collective identity. Indeed, on his way to Saginaw, Tocqueville ran into the son of a *Canadien* and an Indian who ascribed himself, not as a *métis*, but as a *bois-brûlé*. In other words, he used the very same term that the Red River Métis used as a self-ascription at the time of the Battle of Seven Oaks—the French translation of the Anishinaabemowin word *Wiisakodewininiwag*, meaning the "partly burnt wood men." From this point of view, Andersen's proposal to "reposition the upper Great Lakes region and its settlements in light of a peoplehood analytic" where the forks of the Red and Assiniboine Rivers constitute a power centre or the core of Métis national consciousness and the Great Lakes region a periphery[261] is particularly interesting. First of all, it shows that the disparaging references to the "Red River bog" or "Red River myopia" are themselves mired in a narrow view that reduces the political economy of "Red River" to the District of Assiniboia. More importantly, it raises the question of a vast *Wiisakodewininiwag* nation that emerged out of an *Anishinaabeg-Canadien métissage* and the institutional framework of a fur trade system that stretched from the Ottawa River to southern Saskatchewan. In effect, when Pierre Falcon sang "à la gloire de tous les *Bois-Brûlés*," what were the psychological and geographical boundaries of the *Wiisakodewininiwag* to which he was referring?

Author's Note

I would like to thank the anonymous reviewers for their helpful comments. This chapter was undertaken while a SSHRC post-doctoral fellow.

Notes

1. Arthur S. Morton, *A History of the Canadian West to 1870–1871* (Toronto: University of Toronto Press, 1973 [1939]), 534.

2. A.S. Morton, *A History of the Canadian West*, 539, 550, 566 and 573.

3. John Perry Pritchett, *The Red River Valley, 1811–1849: A Regional Study* (Toronto: The Ryerson Press, 1942), 41.

4. John M. Bumsted, *Fur Trade Wars: The Founding of Western Canada* (Winnipeg: Great Plains Publications, 1999), 190.

5. William L. Morton, ed., *Alexander Begg's Red River Journal and Other Papers Relative to the Red River Resistance of 1869–1870* (New York: Greenwood Press, 1969 [1956]), 15; see also A.S. Morton, *History of the Canadian West*, 806; Marcel Giraud, *Le Métis canadien* (Saint-Boniface, MB: Éditions du Blé, 1984 [1945]), 533–99.

6. Arthur S. Morton, "The New Nation, The Métis," in *The Other Natives: The–Les Métis*, vol. 1, *1700–1885*. ed. Antoine S. Lussier and D. Bruce Sealey (Winnipeg: Manitoba Metis Federation Press and Éditions Bois-Brûlés, 1978 [1939]), 30; George F.G. Stanley, *The Birth of Western Canada: A History of the Riel Rebellions* (Toronto: University of Toronto Press, 1961), 12; Margaret Arnett MacLeod and William Lewis Morton, *Cuthbert Grant of Grantown: Warden of the Plains of Red River* (Toronto: McClelland & Stewart, 1974 [1963]), 38–52.

7. MacLeod and Morton, *Cuthbert Grant*, 51.

8. Frits Pannekoek, "Métis Studies: The Development of a Field and New Directions," in *From Rupert's Land to Canada*, ed. Theodore Binnema, Gerhard J. Ens and R.C. Macleod (Edmonton: University of Alberta Press, 2001), 113.

9. Stanley, *The Birth of Western Canada*, 11.

10. See A.S. Morton, "The New Nation," 29–30; Giraud, *Le Métis canadien*, 502, 508–11, 533–34; W.L. Morton, ed., *Alexander Begg's Red River Journal*, 15; MacLeod and Morton, *Cuthbert Grant*, 23.

11. Michael Payne, "Fur Trade Historiography: Past Conditions, Present Circumstances and a Hint of Future Prospects," in Binnema, Ens and Macleod, *From Rupert's Land to Canada*, 8, 10 and 6.

12. Payne, "Fur Trade Historiography," 7.

13. Payne, "Fur Trade Historiography," 7.

14. Pannekoek, "Métis Studies," 123.

15. There are of course exceptions to this. See Joe Sawchuk, *The Dynamics of Native Politics: The Alberta Métis Experience* (Saskatoon: Purich Publishing, 1998); Paul Chartrand, "Introduction," in *Who Are Canada's Aboriginal Peoples? Recognition, Definition and Jurisdiction*, ed. Paul Chartrand (Saskatoon: Purich Publishing, 2002); and Chris Andersen, "Moya 'Tipimsook' ("The People Who Aren't Their Own Bosses"): Racialization and the Misrecognition of 'Métis' in Upper Great Lakes," *Ethnohistory* 58, no. 1 (2011): 37-63. Also see Paul Chartrand and John Giokas, "Defining 'The Métis People': The Hard Case of Canadian Aboriginal Law," in *Who Are Canada's Aboriginal Peoples? Recognition, Definition and Jurisdiction*, ed. Paul Chartrand (Saskatoon: Purich Publishing, 2002); and Albert Peeling and Paul Chartrand, "Sovereignty, Liberty, and the Legal Order of the 'Freemen' (Otipahemsu'uk): Towards a Constitutional Theory of Métis Self-Government," *Saskatchewan Law Review* 67, no. 1 (2004): 339-57.

16. Samuel W. Corrigan, "Some Implications of the Current Métis Case," in *The Struggle for Recognition: Canadian Justice and the Métis Nation*, ed. Samuel W. Corrigan and Lawrence J. Barkwell (Winnipeg: Pemmican Publications, 1991), 195.

17. I use the terms "first" and "second revisionist wave," as well as "orthodox" and "heretical," somewhat facetiously here. While providing convenient categories, they are somewhat awkward because the idea of a "wave" suggests a generational gap. Some of those whom I have classed in the "second wave" are contemporaries of, rather than successors to, the "first wave." In addition, so-called "orthodox accounts," like that of Stanley's, was in fact "revisionist" at the time it was written.

18. While there is obviously a temporal element, the emphasis here is on structure: a collective identity can only emerge from a pre-existing entity, and a sense of identity necessarily undergirds a national consciousness. But there is nothing linear, progressive or necessary about the "leap" from one phase to another.

19. Joe Sawchuk, *The Métis of Manitoba: Reformulation of an Ethnic Identity* (Toronto: Peter Martin Associates, 1978), 24.

20. Duke Redbird, *We Are Metis: A Metis View of the Development of a Native Canadian People* (Ontario Métis and Non-Status Indian Association, 1980), 3.

21. Redbird, *We Are Metis*, 2.

22. Jacqueline Peterson, "Prelude to Red River: A Social Portrait of the Great Lakes Metis," *Ethnohistory* 25 (1978): 46; Jacqueline Peterson, "Many Roads to Red River: Metis Genesis in the Great Lakes Region, 1680-1815," in *The New Peoples: Being*

and *Becoming Métis in North America*, ed. Jacqueline Peterson and Jennifer S.H. Brown (Winnipeg: University of Manitoba Press, 1985), 38; Olive P. Dickason, "From 'One Nation' in the Northeast to 'New Nation' in the Northwest: A Look at the Emergence of the Métis," in Peterson and Brown, *The New Peoples*, 31; John E. Foster, "Some Questions and Perspectives on the Problem of métis Roots," in Peterson and Brown, *The New Peoples*, 81.

23. James R. Miller "From Riel to the Métis," *Canadian Historical Review* 69, no. 1 (1988): 14. Emphasis added.

24. Larry Chartrand, "The Definition of Métis Peoples in Section 35(2) of the *Constitution Act, 1982*," *Saskatchewan Law Review* 67, no. 1 (2004): 218. Emphasis added.

25. John E. Foster, "Wintering, the Outsider Male and the Ethnogenesis of the Western Plains Métis," in Binnema, Ens and Macleod, *From Rupert's Land to Canada*, 179–92.

26. Heather Devine, *The People Who Own Themselves: Aboriginal Ethnogenesis in a Canadian Family, 1660-1900* (Calgary: University of Calgary Press, 2004).

27. Larry Chartrand, "The Definition of Métis Peoples," 218. Emphasis added.

28. Thomas Flanagan, review of *The Genealogy of the First Métis Nation* by Douglas N. Sprague and R.P. Frye, *Canadian Ethnic Studies Journal* 17, no. 2 (1985): 149.

29. Thomas Flanagan, "Métis Aboriginal Rights: Some Historical and Contemporary Problems," in *The Quest for Justice: Aboriginal Peoples and Aboriginal Rights*, ed. Menno Boldt and J. Anthony Long (Toronto: University of Toronto Press, 1985), 245.

30. Trudy Nicks and Kenneth Morgan, "Grande Cache: The Historic Development of an Indigenous Alberta métis Population," in Peterson and Brown, *The New Peoples*, 173.

31. Nicks and Morgan, "Grande Cache," 173.

32. Peterson and Brown, *The New Peoples*.

33. Miller, "From Riel to the Métis," 15.

34. Miller, "From Riel to the Métis," 20.

35. Pannekoek, "Métis Studies," 111.

36. Payne, "Fur Trade Historiography," 6.

37. Brenda Macdougall, "Wahkootowin: Family and Cultural Identity in Northwestern Saskatchewan Metis Communities," *The Canadian Historical Review* 87, no. 3 (2006): 434.

38. Nicole St-Onge, *Saint-Laurent, Manitoba: Evolving Métis Identities, 1850–1914* (Regina: Canadian Plains Research Center, 2004), 2.

39. Giraud, *Le Métis canadien*, 550.

40. Giraud, *Le Métis canadien*, 551. My translation.

41. Giraud, *Le Métis canadien*, 370.

42. William L. Morton, *Manitoba: A History* (Toronto: University of Toronto Press, 1967 [1957]), 41.

43. Nicole St-Onge, "The Dissolution of a Métis Community: Pointe à Grouette, 1860–1885," *Studies in Political Economy* 18 (1985), 164.

44. St-Onge, "The Dissolution of a Métis Community," 163–64.

45. St-Onge, *Evolving Métis Identities*, 2.

46. Frits Pannekoek, *A Snug Little Flock: The Social Origins of the Riel Resistance of 1869–1870* (Winnipeg: Watson & Dwyer, 1991).

47. Gerhard Ens, *Homeland to Hinterland: The Changing World of the Red River Métis in the Nineteenth Century* (Toronto: University of Toronto Press, 1996), 4.

48. Macdougall, "Wahkootowin," 435, 435 note 9. Oddly enough, Macdougall later accused Canadian scholars of having "been overly occupied with race at the expense of culture." Brenda Macdougall, *One of the Family: Metis Culture in Nineteenth-century Northwestern Saskatchewan* (Vancouver: University of British Columbia Press, 2010), 14.

49. Paul Chartrand, "'Terms of Division.' Problems of 'Outside Naming' for Aboriginal People in Canada," *Journal of Indigenous Studies* 2, no. 2 (1991): 12.

50. Peterson, "Prelude to Red River," 54.

51. Peterson, "Prelude to Red River," 54.

52. Harriet Gorham, "Families of Mixed Descent in the Western Great Lakes Region," in *Native People, Native Lands: Canadian Indians, Inuit and Métis*, ed. Bruce Alden Cox (Ottawa: Carleton University Press, 1987), 42.

53. Peterson, "Many Roads to Red River," 63.

54. Jennifer Brown, *Strangers in Blood: Fur Trade Families in Indian Country* (Vancouver: University of British Columbia Press, 1980), 219.

55. Dickason, "A Look at the Emergence of the Métis," 30.

56. Irene M. Spry, "The Métis and Mixed-Bloods of Rupert's Land before 1870," in Peterson and Brown, *The New Peoples*, 112–13.

57. Miller, "From Riel to the Métis," 17. See Diane Payment, *Batoche (1870–1910)* (Saint-Boniface, MB: Éditions du Blé, 1983).

58. Miller, "From Riel to the Métis," 17.

59. Brown, *Strangers in Blood*, xxi.

60. Brown, *Strangers in Blood*, 219, 220.

61. One of my ancestors, Alexander Bremner, is an example of this.

62. See MacLeod and Morton, *Cuthbert Grant*.

63. Gorham, "Families of Mixed-Blood Descent," 38–39. Emphasis added.

64. Gorham, "Families of Mixed-Blood Descent," 50.

65. Gorham, "Families of Mixed-Blood Descent," 50. Emphasis added.

66. Gérard Bouchard, *Genèse des nations et cultures du Nouveau Monde* (Montréal: Les éditions du Boréal, 2001), 13.

67. Miller, "From Riel to the Métis," 14.

68. Ens, *Homeland to Hinterland*, 194 note 8. Citing Peterson, "Prelude to Red River," and "Settlement and Growth of a 'New People.'"

69. Ens, *Homeland to Hinterland*, 15.

70. Peterson, "Settlement and Growth of a 'New People,'" 24–25. Emphasis added. Andersen picked up on this very same quotation in "Moya 'Tipimsook,'" 41. I thank the anonymous reviewer who brought his article to my attention.

71. Jacqueline Peterson, "Red River Redux: Métis Ethnogenesis and the Great Lakes Region," in *Contours of a People: Metis Family, Mobility, and History*, ed. Nicole St-Onge, Carolyn Podruchny and Brenda Macdougall (Norman: University of Oklahoma Press, 2012), 40.

72. Foster, "Some Questions and Perspectives," 80.

73. The buffalo hunt was not simply an "economic niche," but a way of life that potentially involved warfare with the Dakota, and therefore added a militaristic and patriotic dimension to Métis identity.

74. Dickason, "A Look at the Emergence of the Métis," 30.

75. Foster, "Some Questions and Perspectives," 80–81.

76. John E. Foster, "The Plains Metis," in *Native Peoples: The Canadian Experience*, ed. R. Bruce Morrison and C. Roderick Wilson (Don Mills, ON: Oxford University Press, 2004), 301–02.

77. Peterson, "Red River Redux," 31.

78. I doubt this is true in the case of *bois-brûlé*. It is a literal translation of *Wiisakodewininiwag* or "half-burnt wood people." The Anishinabek term clearly designates that it is the people themselves who are "half-burnt" and does not simply mean people who half-burn wood.

79. John E. Foster, "The Métis: The People and the Term," in *The Western Métis: Profile of a People*, ed. Patrick C. Douaud (Regina: Canadian Plains Research Center, 2007 [1978]), 26.

80. Gorham, "Families of Mixed-Blood Descent," 40.

81. Peterson, "Many Roads to Red River," 39.

82. Gorham, "Families of Mixed-Blood Descent," 42.

83. Foster, "The Métis: The People and the Term," 26, 29.

84. Jennifer Brown, "The Métis: Genesis and Rebirth," in *Native People, Native Lands: Canadian Indians, Inuit and Métis*, ed. Bruce Alden Cox (Ottawa: Carleton University Press, 1987), 141.

85. Foster, "Some Questions and Perspectives," 78.

86. Devine, *The People Who Own Themselves*, 202.

87. Jacqueline Peterson, "Ethnogenesis: The Settlement and Growth of a 'New People' in the Great Lakes Region." *American Indian Culture and Research Journal* 6, no. 2 (1982): 56.

88. One sees here the deductive conclusion inherent in historical materialism: if material life underpins identity, the latter necessarily disappears with the former. Of course, there are Métis communities that did survive in the Great Lakes region, as the Supreme Court of Canada's decision in R. v. Powley, [2003] 2 SCR 207 brought to our attention.

89. Pannekoek, *A Snug Little Flock*, 114.

90. Paul Chartrand, *Manitoba Métis Settlement Scheme of 1870* (Saskatoon: Native Law Centre, 1991), 29. Sawchuk, *The Métis of Manitoba*, 34.

91. Stanley, *The Birth of Western Canada*, 10.

92. Giraud, *Le Métis canadien*, 550–51.

93. Brown, *Strangers in Blood*, 219.

94. Stanley, *The Birth of Western Canada*, 10 and 9.

95. Pannekoek, *A Snug Little Flock*, 13. Pannekoek postulated that Giraud's "discomfort with English may also have led him to inadvertently concentrate on the Métis." He further speculated that Giraud "tended to translate all of his research notes into French which may have caused some problems in later focus." Pannekoek, *A Snug Little Flock*, 14. Similarly, Bumsted found it regrettable that "Giraud's 'Métis' increasingly became associated with the Francophone Roman Catholic population, and the Anglophone mixed-bloods were in later sections virtually ignored." Bumsted, *Fur Trade Wars*, 26. Giraud chose quite consciously, not "inadvertently" as Pannekoek claims, to limit the scope of his object of research to the Métis

canadien, as the title clearly indicates. Given that his study consists of almost 1,300 pages, it was a perfectly justifiable decision by any scientific standard.

96. Giraud, *Le Métis canadien,* vii.

97. Alexander Ross, *The Red River Settlement: Its Rise, Progress and Present State* (Minneapolis: Ross and Haines, 1957 [1856]), 81, 335; Joseph James Hargrave, *Red River* (Altona, MB: Friesen Printers, 1977 [1871]), 92; John M. Bumsted, ed., *Reporting the Resistance: Alexander Begg and Joseph Hargrave on the Red River Resistance* (Winnipeg: University of Manitoba Press, 2003), 122; Georges Dugas, *Histoire véridique des faits qui ont préparé le mouvement des Métis à la Rivière-Rouge en 1869* (Montréal: Librairie Beauchemin, 1905).

98. R.G. MacBeth, *The Making of the Canadian West: Being the Reminiscences of an Eyewitness* (Toronto: William Briggs, 1898), 14–16.

99. MacBeth, *The Making of the Canadian West,* 15.

100. MacBeth, *The Making of the Canadian West,* 30.

101. MacBeth, *The Making of the Canadian West,* 27 and 38. The reference is to the Charles Mair incident. In his letter, Mair made abundant use of the term "half-breed." Although MacBeth found the term "breed" to be "contemptuous" in this context, this did not prevent him from constantly referring to the Métis as "French half-breeds."

102. Canada, *House of Commons Debates,* 3rd Session, 1st Parliament, 1870: 1315, 1431, 1469 and 1483.

103. Canada, *House of Commons Debates,* 3rd Session, 1st Parliament, 1870: 1356, 1435.

104. Canada, *House of Commons Debates,* 3rd Session, 1st Parliament, 1870: 118.

105. See respectively Hartwell Bowsfield, ed., *The James Wickes Taylor Correspondence, 1859–1870* (Altona, MB: D.W. Friesen & Sons, 1968), 81; Noël-Joseph Ritchot, "Le journal de l'abbé N.J. Ritchot—1870," George Stanley, ed., *Revue d'histoire de l'Amérique française* 17, no. 4 (1964): 557; English translation in William L. Morton, ed., *Manitoba: The Birth of a Province* (Winnipeg: Manitoba Record Society Publications, 1965), 91; Gilles Martel, *Le messianisme de Louis Riel* (Waterloo, ON: Wilfrid Laurier University Press, 1984), 62.

106. Bumsted, *Reporting the Resistance,* 71.

107. Ross, *The Red River Settlement,* 121, 232, 238, 248; Hargrave, *Red River,* 174; Begg, *The Creation of Manitoba;* Isaac Cowie, *The Company of Adventurers: A Narrative of Seven Years in the Service of the Hudson's Bay Company During 1867–1874* (Lincoln: University of Nebraska Press, 1993 [1913]), 64–66; For Hargrave and Begg, see also Bumsted, *Reporting the Resistance,* 33, 126–27.

108. George Bryce, *The Romantic Settlement of Lord Selkirk's Colonists* (Charleston, SC: Bibliobazaar, 2007 [1909]).

109. A.G. Morice, *A Critical History of the Red River Insurrection After Official Records and Non-Catholic Sources* (Winnipeg: Canadian Publishers, 1935), 34 note 1, and 36–37.

110. Ross, *Red River Settlement*, 24, 232; Hargrave, *Red River*, 89; Bryce, *The Romantic Settlement of Lord Selkirk's Colonists*, 120, 127, etc.; MacBeth, *The Making of the Canadian West*, 30; Bumsted, *Reporting the Resistance*, 41, 62, 68, 73, 75, 76, etc.

111. Stanley, *The Birth of Western Canada*, 9.

112. Pannekoek asserts that de Trémaudan was "French-Canadian." Pannekoek, *A Snug Little Flock*, 217. Although de Trémaudan was born in Saint-Chrysostome, Quebec, in 1874, his parents were both French immigrants who arrived in Canada in 1871. They returned to France between 1881 and 1893, when they again emigrated to Montmarte, Saskatchewan.

113. Auguste-Henri de Trémaudan, *Histoire de la nation métisse dans l'Ouest canadien* (Saint-Boniface, MB: Éditions des plaines, 1984 [1936]), 47. Note that it is only in the case of the *Métis français* that de Trémaudan used a capital "M." That he excluded the Half-Breeds from the ambit of his study is hardly surprising; it was, after all, the Union nationale métisse Saint-Joseph du Manitoba that commissioned his work with two objectives: 1) "[écrire] un récit simple, aussi complet que possible, des faits et des gestes de *la race métisse canadienne-française* dans l'Ouest canadien"; 2) "établir [...] que depuis deux siècles, le français a droit de cité dans l'Ouest." de Trémaudan, *Histoire de la nation métisse*, 20. Emphasis added.

114. A.S. Morton, *A History of the Canadian West*, 803, 872.

115. W.L. Morton, ed., *Alexander Begg's Red River Journal*, 1, note 3.

116. W.L. Morton, ed., *Alexander Begg's Red River Journal*, 3.

117. W.L. Morton, *Manitoba: A History*, 124.

118. Thomas Flanagan, "The Political Thought of Louis Riel," in *Riel and the Métis*, ed. Antoine S. Lussier (Winnipeg: Manitoba Metis Federation Press, 1979), 137.

119. Jennifer Brown, "People of Myth, People of History: A Look at Recent Writings on the Metis," *Acadiensis* 17 (1987): 152. See *The Collected Writings of Louis Riel/Les Écrits complets de Louis Riel*, 5 vols. (Edmonton: University of Alberta Press, 1985).

120. Douglas N. Sprague and R.P. Frye, *The Genealogy of the First Métis Nation: The Development and Dispersal of the Red River Settlement, 1820–1900* (Winnipeg: Pemmican Publications, 1983).

121. Pannekoek, *A Snug Little Flock*, 11.

122. See for example George Woodcock, *Gabriel Dumont: The Métis Chief and His Lost World* (Edmonton: Hurtig Publishers, 1976), 50; Sawchuk, *The Métis of Manitoba*; Flanagan, "The Political Thought of Louis Riel," in *Métis Lands in Manitoba* (Calgary: University of Calgary Press, 1991); Foster, "The Métis: The People and the Term"; Brown, *Strangers in Blood*; Peterson, "Many Roads to Red River"; Sylvia Van Kirk, *Many Tender Ties: Women in Fur-Trade Society, 1670–1870* (Winnipeg: Watson & Dwyer, 1980); "'What if Mama is an Indian?': The Cultural Ambivalence of the Alexander Ross Family," in Peterson and Brown, *The New Peoples*; P. Chartrand, *Manitoba Métis Settlement Scheme*; John Giokas and Paul Chartrand, "Who Are the Métis in Section 35?" in *Who Are Canada's Aboriginal Peoples? Recognition, Definition and Jurisdiction*, ed. Paul Chartrand (Saskatoon: Purich Publishing, 2002), 85–86; Ens, *Homeland to Hinterland*.

123. Macdougall, One *of the Family*, 14. To paraphrase Chris Andersen, the use of the term "Metis" may be an acceptable contemporary self-ascription, but one may query as to whether such anachronistic terminology is appropriate for "ethnohistorians as well." Andersen, "Moya 'Tipimsook,'" 51.

124. Macdougall, One *of the Family*, 14.

125. Spry, "The Métis and Mixed-Bloods of Rupert's Land," 97. See Pannekoek's reply in *A Snug Little Flock*, 10–11.

126. Spry, "The Métis and Mixed-Bloods of Rupert's Land," 97.

127. Spry, "The Métis and Mixed-Bloods of Rupert's Land," 97.

128. Spry, "The Métis and Mixed-Bloods of Rupert's Land," 108.

129. D. Geneva Lent, *West of the Mountains: James Sinclair and the Hudson's Bay Company* (Seattle: University of Washington Press, 1963), 72. It is important to note that Lent's account of Sinclair's role during the Sayer crisis in 1849 completely evacuates any mention of the role of the Métis council, and notably of Jean-Louis Riel's leadership. See William L. Morton, "Introduction," in *London Correspondence Inward From Eden Colville, 1849–1852*, ed. E.E. Rich (London: The Hudson's Bay Record Society, 1956), lxxxiii.

130. Macdougall, One *of the Family*, 14.

131. Spry, "The Métis and Mixed-Bloods of Rupert's Land," 99–103.

132. Macdougall, One *of the Family*, 145.

133. Macdougall, One *of the Family*, 3. I question the premise that merely mapping out genealogy is a sufficient indication of the *type* and *quality* of relations between immediate family, extended family and in-laws. Macdougall's use of the term *wahkootowin* would seem to imply that family relations are necessarily

harmonious relations. In Anishinabek thought, harmonious relations must constantly and endlessly be strived for in a world of conflicting forces, as exemplified by the eternal struggle between *Biboon* and *Niibin*, or *Animikii* and *Mishi Bizhiw*. See for example Basil Johnston, *Ojibway Heritage* (Toronto: McClelland & Stewart, 1976) and Theresa S. Smith, *The Island of the Anishinaabeg: Thunderers and Water Monsters in the Traditional Ojibwe Life-World* (Moscow, ID: University of Idaho Press, 1995). From a Western view, claiming that the use of terms like "Half-Breed" and "Métis," as I do here, "fosters a notion that pulls the community apart rather than binds it together" (Macdougall, *One of the Family*, 14) takes the *historical* existence of a *single* community to be an axiom rather than a hypothesis subject to falsification. From an Anishinaabe view, it is an attempt to deal with potential conflict that inevitably exists within a homogenous community as well as between heterogeneous communities by denying it exists rather than managing it through sharing, prayer, deliberation, festivities, ceremony and ritual.

134. Macdougall, "Wahkootowin," 339, 440. Emphasis added.

135. Andersen, "Moya 'Tipimsook,'" 53.

136. Andersen, "Moya 'Tipimsook,'" 55. I have omitted Andersen's reference to "cataloguing collectivity according to mixed/racialized [...] logics" because it does not apply to Macdougall's work. She has also called on scholars to move beyond the "racial paradigm." Macdougall, "Wahkootowin," 14.

137. Macdougall, "Wahkootowin," 14. Emphasis added.

138. Macdougall, "Wahkootowin," 148.

139. Macdougall, "Wahkootowin," 148.

140. Macdougall, "Wahkootowin," 148.

141. Macdougall, "Wahkootowin," 148. Emphasis added.

142. Sawchuk, *The Métis of Manitoba*, 12.

143. Sawchuk, *The Métis of Manitoba*, 73.

144. Carl Schmitt, *The Concept of the Political* (Chicago: University of Chicago Press, 2007), 30.

145. Sawchuk, *The Métis of Manitoba*, 12.

146. Giraud, *Le Métis canadien*, 550.

147. Giraud, *Le Métis canadien*, 551.

148. Tom Flanagan, *First Nations? Second Thoughts* (Montreal: McGill-Queen's University Press, 2000), 86.

149. Dickason, "A Look at the Emergence of the Métis," 30. Emphasis added.

150. Peterson, "Settlement and Growth of a 'New People,'" 56. Emphasis added.

151. Gorham, "Families of Mixed-Blood Descent," 49.

152. Gorham, "Families of Mixed-Blood Descent," 38. Emphasis added.

153. Sawchuk, *The Métis of Manitoba*, 24. Emphasis added.

154. Sawchuk, *The Métis of Manitoba*, 24.

155. Peterson, "Many Roads to Red River," 38. Emphasis added.

156. Peterson, "Prelude to Red River," 46. Emphasis added. Peterson actually stated this in the context of "Riel's proclamation," but it can be inferred by what follows that she probably meant to refer to the events at Seven Oaks as the "birth of a national consciousness" and to the Resistance as a sign of political maturity.

157. John E. Foster, "Saulteaux and Numbered Treaties—An Aboriginal Rights Position?" in *The Spirit of the Alberta Indian Treaties*, ed. Richard Price (Montreal: Institute for Research on Public Policy, 1980), 174.

158. Foster, "Some Questions and Perspectives," 81.

159. Jennifer Brown, "Woman as Centre and Symbol in the Emergence of Métis Communities," *The Canadian Journal of Native Studies* 3, no. 1 (1983): 43.

160. Brown, "Woman as Centre and Symbol," 44; "Genesis and Rebirth," 140. Emphasis added.

161. Foster, "The Métis: The People and the Term," 26, 28.

162. Gwen Reimer and Jean-Philippe Chartrand, "Documenting Historic Métis in Ontario," *Ethnohistory* 51, no. 3 (2004): 570–77.

163. Sawchuk, *The Métis of Manitoba*, 24.

164. Foster, "Saulteaux and Numbered Treaties," 176.

165. Foster, "Saulteaux and Numbered Treaties," 176.

166. Foster, "The Métis: The People and the Term," 27.

167. Dickason, "A Look at the Emergence of the Métis," 31.

168. Sawchuk, *The Métis of Manitoba*, 24. Unfortunately, the events that solidified Métis nationalism cited by Sawchuk occurred for the most part *after* the Fur Trade War. For example, Sawchuk mentioned "other factors contributing to the ethnic solidarity of the Métis," such as the bison hunt and the "recurring conflicts with the Sioux." Sawchuk, *The Métis of Manitoba*, 26. These conflicts were arguably a result of the bison hunt, during which the Métis made incursions into Dakota territory. The former was not formally organized until the 1820s. The one factor he points to that was pre-1815 was the close association of the Métis with the fur companies, but this suggests a historical institutionalist explanation of identity formation.

169. Peterson, "Many Roads to Red River," 38.

170. Peterson, "Settlement and Growth of a 'New People,'" 28, 24.

171. Peterson, "Many Roads to Red River," 38.

172. Peterson, "Prelude to Red River," 46.

173. Peterson, "Red River Redux," 30.

174. Brown, "Genesis and Rebirth," 139. More recently, Flanagan maintained that the "idea of a 'Métis Nation' goes back to 1815, when officials of the North West Company, caught up in their fur trade war against the Hudson's Bay Company, encouraged the Red River Métis to attack the Selkirk settlers." Flanagan, *First Nations? Second Thoughts*, 81. In an earlier article, Flanagan had also asserted that at "least since the clash with the Hudson's Bay Company and the Battle of Seven Oaks (1816), many Métis thought of themselves as in some sense the owners of the land which they inhabited." Thomas Flanagan, "The Case Against Métis Aboriginal Rights," *Canadian Public Policy* 9, no. 3 (1983): 316. However, Flanagan hinted at a distinction between collective identity and national consciousness when he maintained that the "Metis of Rupert's Land did not become a distinct social group until the end of the eighteenth century or the beginning of the nineteenth century. They dramatically signalled their existence to the outside world in 1816 in the battle of Seven Oaks." Flanagan, "Métis Aboriginal Rights," 236.

175. Dickason, "A Look at the Emergence of the Métis," 31.

176. Dickason, "A Look at the Emergence of the Métis," 31.

177. Foster, "The Métis: The People and the Term," 27. Emphasis added.

178. R. v. Goodon, [2008] MBPC 59 (Man Prov Ct), para. 26.

179. Peterson, "Settlement and Growth of a 'New People,'" 24.

180. Giraud, *Le Métis canadien*, 617–18.

181. Brown, *Strangers in Blood*, 220.

182. Giraud, *Le Métis canadien*, 291–428.

183. Foster, "The Métis: The People and the Term," 23.

184. Brown, *Strangers in Blood*, xix.

185. Brown, *Strangers in Blood*, 47.

186. Brown, *Strangers in Blood*, 139.

187. Brown, *Strangers in Blood*, 47.

188. Brown, *Strangers in Blood*, 45–47.

189. Peterson, "Settlement and Growth of a 'New People,'" 26; "Many Roads to Red River," 40.

190. This statement is of course overly simplistic. In 1806, the NWC partners created regulations in an attempt to prevent their employees from marrying Indigenous women. The policies and practice of the HBC also shifted quite a bit over time.

191. Foster, "The Métis: The People and the Term," 28.

192. Sawchuk, *The Métis of Manitoba*, 34.

193. Foster, "The Métis: The People and the Term," 28-29.

194. B.E. Collins and B.H. Raven, "Group Structure, Attraction, Coalitions, Communications and Power," in *The Handbook of Social Psychology*, ed. Gardner Lindzay and E. Aronsen (Reading, MA: Addison-Wesley, 1969), 120.

195. Sawchuk, *The Métis of Manitoba*, 73-74.

196. Miller, "From Riel to the Métis," 12-13. Miller doubted that Chie Nakane's "vertical society" model—because it was developed to explain certain aspects of Japanese society—could "work as well for links between British entrepreneurs" or that partnerships were "structured like Japanese families, even the extended families of the business and industrial world."

197. Peter Hall and Rosemary Taylor, "Political Science and the Three New Institutionalisms," *Political Studies* 44, no. 5 (1996): 938-39.

198. Hall and Taylor, "Political Science and the Three New Institutionalisms," 939.

199. Donald Purich, *The Metis* (Toronto: James Lorimer & Company, 1988), 26.

200. Pannekoek, *A Snug Little Flock*, 8.

201. Pannekoek, *A Snug Little Flock*, 41.

202. Pannekoek, *A Snug Little Flock*, 41.

203. Spry, "The Métis and Mixed-Bloods of Rupert's Land," 97.

204. Devine, *The People that Own Themselves*, 7.

205. Ens, *Homeland to Hinterland*, 4.

206. Karl S. Hele, "Manipulating Identity: The Sault Borderlands Métis and Colonial Intervention," in *The Long Journey of a Forgotten People: Métis Identities and Family Histories*, ed. Ute Lischke and David T. McNab (Waterloo, ON: Wilfrid Laurier University Press, 2007), 170.

207. Macdougall, *One of the Family*, 144 and 157.

208. Macdougall, *One of the Family*, 144.

209. Macdougall, *One of the Family*, 147. Emphasis added.

210. Hall and Taylor, "Political Science and the Three New Institutionalisms," 948.

211. Giraud, *Le Métis canadien*, 511, 510, 509. My translation.

212. Ania Loomba, *Colonialism/Postcolonialism* (New York: Routledge, 2005 [1998]), 193.

213. Payne, "Fur Trade Historiography," 8.

214. Arthur J. Ray, *Indians in the Fur Trade: Their Role as Hunters, Trappers and Middlemen in the Lands Southwest of Hudson's Bay, 1660-1870* (Toronto: University of Toronto Press, 1974).

215. John E. Foster, "The Métis and the End of the Plains Buffalo in Alberta," in *Buffalo*, ed. John E. Foster, Dick Harrison and I.S. MacLaren (Edmonton: University of Alberta Press, 1992), 66.

216. John G.A. Pocock, *Political Thought and History: Essays on Theory and Method* (Cambridge: Cambridge University Press, 2009), 246.

217. John Borrows, *Drawing Out Law: A Spirit's Guide* (Toronto: University of Toronto Press, 2010), 110.

218. Flanagan, *Métis Lands in Manitoba*, 232.

219. Frank Tough, *As Their Natural Resources Fail: Native Peoples and the Economic History of Northern Manitoba, 1870-1930* (Vancouver: University of British Columbia Press, 1996).

220. Payne, "Fur Trade Historiography," 11.

221. Loomba, *Colonialism/Postcolonialism*, 192-93.

222. Heather Devine, "Les Desjarlais: The Development and Dispersion of a Proto-Métis Hunting Band, 1785-1870," in Binnema, Ens and Macleod, *From Rupert's Land to Canada*, 134.

223. Devine, "Les Desjarlais," 151.

224. Adrian Tanner, "Algonquian Land Tenure and State Structures in the North," *The Canadian Journal of Native Studies* 3, no. 2 (1983): 312.

225. Tanner, "Algonquian Land Tenure and State Structures in the North," 313. Emphasis added.

226. Ens, *Homeland to Hinterland*, 175.

227. Jane Jenson, "Naming Nations: Making Nationalist Claims in Canadian Public Discourse," *Canadian Review of Sociology and Anthropology* 30, no. 3 (1993): 337-58.

228. Kiera Ladner, "Women and Blackfoot Nationalism," *Journal of Canadian Studies* 35, no. 2 (2000): 35-60. I'm not entirely sure I agree with Ladner's interpretation of Jenson's article, but for the sake of argument let us accept that it is an accurate one.

229. Jo-Anne Fiske, "The Womb is to the Nation as the Heart is to the Body: Ethnopolitical Discourses of the Canadian Indigenous Women's Movement," *Studies in Political Economy* 51 (1996): 65-96; David Long, "Culture, Ideology and Militancy: The Movement of Native Indians in Canada, 1969-1991," in *Organizing*

Dissent: Contemporary Social Movements in Theory and Practice, ed. William D. Carroll (Toronto: Garamond Press, 1992).

230. Sawchuk, *The Dynamics of Native Politics*, 31.

231. Leanne Simpson, *Dancing on Our Turtle's Back: Stories of Nishnaabeg Re-Creation, Resurgence and a New Emergence* (Winnipeg: Arbeiter Ring Publishing, 2011), 15–16. It is interesting to note that the Anishinabek post-secondary institution Shingwauk Kinoomaage Gamig offers a course entitled ANIS 2007: *Anishinaabe Social Movements*. http://shingwauku.com/courses (consulted 8 January 2012).

232. Pocock, *Political Thought and History*, 244–45.

233. Sandy Grande, *Red Pedagogy: Native American Social and Political Thought* (Lanham, MD: Rowman & Littlefield, 2004), 1.

234. Chris Andersen, "From Nation to Population: The Racialisation of 'Métis' in the Canadian Census," *Nations and Nationalism* 14, no. 2 (2008): 39. It may also serve the political objective of reinforcing the perception that we Métis are a mere *social* problem to be dealt with as a *population* rather than a *political* problem to be dealt with as a *people*. As Andersen has astutely observed, the notion of 'populations' and "the census which produces them thus do not merely *reflect* social reality, they *produce* it through the political rationalities that animate them, the categories and questions used to formulate them, who they include, how they include them and the ways in which such quintessentially political documents are disseminated to broader society as neutral, scientific 'facts.'" Ibid., 357. "More conceptually," Andersen adds, "the construction of this population estimate clearly requires a certain level of discursive violence which shears 'Métis' of any national or even historical political roots." Ibid., 359. In other words, we are to be to be to be managed and administered under ss. 15(2) of the *Charter* as a disadvantaged *population* requiring special selective and provisional training and education programmes aimed at *individual* members in order to facilitate our *economic* integration into 'whitestream' society rather than an Indigenous *people* to be negotiated with *collectively* to redistribute *political* power under the terms of s. 35 of the *Constitution Act, 1982*. (The term "whitestream" is used here to indicate that "Canadian society, while principally structured on the basis of the European, 'white,' experience, is far from being simply 'white' in socio-demographic, economic and cultural terms." Claude Denis, *We Are Not You* (Peterborough, ON: Broadview Press, 1997), 13 note 5.

235. Bruce Trigger, "Brecht and Ethnohistory," *Ethnohistory* 22, no. 1 (1975): 51. Emphasis added.

236. Devine, "Les Desjarlais," 152.

237. Devine, "Les Desjarlais," 152.

238. Payment, *Batoche.*

239. Miller, "From Riel to the Métis," 9.

240. Brown, "People of Myth, People of History," 150.

241. Nathalie Kermoal, « Les rôles et les souffrances des femmes métisses lors de la Résistance de 1870 et de la Rébellion de 1885 », *Prairie Forum* 19, no. 2 (1993): 153–68.

242. Peterson, "Red River Redux," 30.

243. Peterson, "Red River Redux," 30.

244. Reimer and Chartrand, "Documenting Historic Métis in Ontario," 582.

245. Alan Knight and Janet E. Chute, "In the Shadow of the Thumping Drum: The Sault Métis—The People In-Between," in *Lines Drawn Upon the Water: First Nations and the Great Lakes Borders and Borderlands*, ed. Karl S. Hele (Waterloo, ON: Wilfrid Laurier University Press, 2008), 262 note 54, 267 note 81.

246. David T. McNab, "Free and Full Possession of Their Lands," in *Circles of Time: Aboriginal Land Rights and Resistance in Ontario* (Waterloo, ON: Wilfrid Laurier University Press, 1999), 25.

247. Victor Lytwyn, "Echo of the Crane: Tracing Anishinawbek and Métis Title to Bawating (Sault Ste. Marie)," in *New Histories for Old: Changing Perspectives on Canada's Native Pasts*, ed. Ted Binnema and Susan Neylan (Vancouver: University of British Columbia Press, 2008), 57.

248. Reimer and Chartrand, "Documenting Historic Métis in Ontario," 596.

249. McNab, "Free and Full Possession of Their Lands," 27–30.

250. Andersen, "Moya 'Tipimsook,'" 53.

251. Pannekoek, *A Snug Little Flock*, 2.

252. Ens, *Homeland to Hinterland*, 15.

253. Knight and Chute, "In the Shadow of the Thumping Drum," 259–60 note 41.

254. Reimer and Chartrand, "Documenting Historic Métis in Ontario," 568.

255. Olive P. Dickason and David T. McNab, *Canada's First Nations: A History of Founding Peoples from Earliest Times*, 4th ed. (Oxford: Oxford University Press, 2008).

256. Foster, "Saulteaux and Numbered Treaties," 176.

257. Brian Gallagher, "The Whig Interpretation of the History of Red River" (unpublished master's thesis, University of Manitoba, 1986), 19.

258. Laura Peers, *The Ojibwa of Western Canada, 1780–1870* (Winnipeg: University of Manitoba Press, 1994), xi.

259. Sylvie Berbaum, *Ojibwa Powwow World* (Thunder Bay, ON: Lakehead University Centre for Northern Studies, 2000), 1.

260. Alexis de Tocqueville, « Quinze jours dans le désert », in *Regards sur le Bas Canada*, ed. Claude Corbo (Montréal: Éditions Typo, 2003), 115.

261. Andersen, "Moya 'Tipimsook,'" 53.

Bibliography

Andersen, Chris. "Moya 'Tipimsook' ("The People Who Aren't Their Own Bosses"): Racialization and the Misrecognition of 'Métis' in Upper Great Lakes." *Ethnohistory* 58, no. 1 (2011): 37–63.

———. "From Nation to Population: the Racialisation of 'Métis' in the Canadian Census." *Nations and Nationalism* 14, no. 2 (2008): 347–68.

Berbaum, Sylvie. *Ojibwa Powwow World*. Thunder Bay, ON: Lakehead University Centre for Northern Studies, 2000.

Binnema, Theodore, Gerhard J. Ens and R.C. Macleod, eds. *From Rupert's Land to Canada*. Edmonton: University of Alberta Press, 2001.

Boreskie, Thomas G. "Corbett, Griffith Owen." *Dictionary of Canadian Biography Online*, www.biographi.ca/009004-119.01-e.php?BioId=40766.

Borrows, John. *Drawing Out Law: A Spirit's Guide*. Toronto: University of Toronto Press, 2010.

Bouchard, Gérard. *Genèse des nations et cultures du Nouveau Monde*. Montréal: Les éditions du Boréal, 2001.

Brown, Jennifer. "Métis." In *Canadian Encyclopedia*, vol. 2. Edmonton: Hurtig Publishers, 1985.

———. "People of Myth, People of History: A Look at Recent Writing on the Metis." *Acadiensis* 17 (1987): 150–62.

———. "The Métis: Genesis and Rebirth." In *Native People, Native Lands: Canadian Indians, Inuit and Métis*, edited by Bruce Alden Cox. Ottawa: Carleton University Press, 1987.

———. *Strangers in Blood: Fur Trade Families in Indian Country*. Vancouver: University of British Columbia Press, 1980.

———. "Woman as Centre and Symbol in the Emergence of Métis Communities." *The Canadian Journal of Native Studies* 3, no. 1 (1983): 39–46.

Bryce, George. *The Romantic Settlement of Lord Selkirk's Colonists*. Charleston, SC: Bibliobazaar, 2007.

Bumsted, John M., ed. *Reporting the Resistance: Alexander Begg and Joseph Hargrave on the Red River Resistance*. Winnipeg: University of Manitoba Press, 2003.

———. *Fur Trade Wars: The Founding of Western Canada*. Winnipeg: Great Plains Publications, 1999.

Chartrand, Larry. "The Definition of Métis Peoples in Section 35(2) of the *Constitution Act, 1982*." *Saskatchewan Law Review* 67, no. 1 (2004): 209–33.

Chartrand, Paul. *Manitoba Métis Settlement Scheme of 1870*. Saskatoon: Native Law Centre, 1991.

———. *Who Are Canada's Aboriginal Peoples? Recognition, Definition and Jurisdiction*. Saskatoon: Purich Publishing, 2002.

———, with John Giokas. "Defining 'The Métis People': The Hard Case of Canadian Aboriginal Law." In *Who Are Canada's Aboriginal Peoples? Recognition, Definition and Jurisdiction*, edited by Paul Chartrand, 268–303. Saskatoon: Purich Publishing, 2002.

Corrigan, Samuel W. "Some Implications of the Current Métis Case." In *The Struggle for Recognition: Canadian Justice and the Métis Nation*, edited by Samuel W. Corrigan and Lawrence J. Barkwell, 195–206. Winnipeg: Pemmican Publications, 1991.

Denis, Claude. *We Are Not You*. Peterborough, ON: Broadview Press, 1997.

Devine, Heather. *The People that Own Themselves: Aboriginal Ethnogenesis in a Canadian Family, 1660–1900*. Calgary: University of Calgary Press, 2004.

Dickason, Olive P. "From 'One Nation' in the Northeast to 'New Nation' in the Northwest: A Look at the Emergence of the Métis." In Peterson and Brown, *The New Peoples*, 19–36.

Dickason, Olive P., and David T. McNab. *Canada's First Nations: A History of Founding Peoples from Earliest Times*. Oxford: Oxford University Press, 2008.

Dugas, Georges. *Histoire de l'Ouest canadien de 1822 à 1869, époque des troubles*. Montréal: Librairie Beauchemin, 1906.

———. *Histoire véridique des faits qui ont préparé le mouvement des Métis à la Rivière-Rouge en 1869*. Montréal: Librairie Beauchemin, 1905.

Ens, Gerhard J. *Homeland to Hinterland: The Changing World of the Red River Métis in the Nineteenth Century*. Toronto: University of Toronto Press, 1996.

Fiske, Jo-Anne. "The Womb is to the Nation as the Heart is to the Body: Ethnopolitical Discourses of the Canadian Indigenous Women's Movement." *Studies in Political Economy* 51 (1996): 65–95.

Flanagan, Thomas. "The Case Against Métis Aboriginal Rights." *Canadian Public Policy* 9, no. 3 (1983): 314-25.

———. "F.A. Hayek on Property and Justice." In *Theories of Property: Aristotle to the Present*, edited by Anthony Pare, 335-54. Waterloo, ON: Wilfrid Laurier University Press, 1979.

———. *First Nations? Second Thoughts*. Montreal and Kingston: McGill-Queen's University Press, 2000.

———. "Métis Aboriginal Rights: Some Historical and Contemporary Problems." In *The Quest for Justice: Aboriginal Peoples and Aboriginal Rights*, edited by Menno Boldt and J. Anthony Long, 230-46. Toronto: University of Toronto Press, 1985.

———. *Métis Lands in Manitoba*. Calgary: University of Calgary Press, 1991.

———. "The Political Thought of Louis Riel." In *Riel and the Métis*, edited by Antoine S. Lussier, 131-60. Winnipeg: Manitoba Metis Federation Press, 1979.

———. Review of *The Genealogy of the First Métis Nation*, by Douglas N. Sprague and R.P. Frye. *Canadian Ethnic Studies Journal* 17, no. 2 (1985): 148-50.

Foster, John E. "The Country Born and the Red River Settlement, 1820-1850." PHD diss., University of Alberta, 1973.

———. "The Métis: The People and the Term." In *The Western Métis: Profile of a People*, edited by Patrick C. Douaud, 21-30. Regina: Canadian Plains Research Center, 2007.

———. "The Plains Metis." In *Native Peoples: The Canadian Experience*, edited by R. Bruce Morrison and C. Roderick Wilson, 375-403. Toronto: McClelland & Stewart, 2004.

———. "Saulteaux and Numbered Treaties—An Aboriginal Rights Position?" In *The Spirit of the Alberta Indian Treaties*, edited by Richard Price, 161-80. Montreal: Institute for Research on Public Policy, 1980.

———. "Some Questions and Perspectives on the Problem of métis Roots." In Peterson and Brown, *The New Peoples*, 73-91.

———. "Wintering, the Outsider Male and the Ethnogenesis of the Western Plains Métis." In Binnema, Ens and Macleod, *From Rupert's Land to Canada*, 179-94.

Foster, Martha Harroun. *We Know Who We Are: Métis Identity in a Montana Community*. Norman: University of Oklahoma Press, 2006.

———. "The Spring Creek (Lewistown) Métis: Métis Identity in Montana." In *Métis Legacy: A Métis Historiography and Annotated Bibliography*, edited by Lawrence J. Barkwell, Leah Dorion, and Darren R. Préfontaine, 99-104. Winnipeg: Pemmican Publications, 2001.

Gallagher, Brian. "The Whig Interpretation of the History of Red River." Master's thesis, University of Manitoba, 1986.

Giraud, Marcel. *Le Métis canadien*. Saint-Boniface, MB: Éditions du Blé, 1984 [1945].

Gorham, Harriet. "Families of Mixed Descent in the Western Great Lakes Region." In *Native People, Native Lands: Canadian Indians, Inuit and Métis*, edited by Bruce Alden Cox, 37–55. Ottawa: Carleton University Press, 1987.

Grande, Sandy. *Red Pedagogy: Native American Social and Political Thought*. Lanham, MD: Rowman & Littlefield, 2004.

Hall, Peter, and Rosemary Taylor. "Political Science and the Three New Institutionalisms." *Political Studies*, 44 (1996): 936–57.

Hargrave, Joseph James. *Red River*. Altona, MB: Friesen Printers, 1977 [1871].

Havard, Valery. "The French Half-breeds of the Northwest." In *Annual Report of the Smithsonian Institution*. Washington, DC: Government Printing Office, 1880.

Hele, Karl S. "Manipulating Identity: The Sault Borderlands Métis and Colonial Intervention." In *The Long Journey of a Forgotten People: Métis Identities and Family Histories*, edited by Ute Lischke and David T. McNab, 163–96. Waterloo, ON: Wilfrid Laurier University Press, 2007.

House of Commons Debates, 1st Parliament, 3rd Session, 1870.

Jenson, Jane. "Naming Nations: Making Nationalist Claims in Canadian Public Discourse." *Canadian Review of Sociology and Anthropology* 30, no. 3 (1993): 337–58.

Kermoal, Nathalie. « Les rôles et les souffrances des femmes métisses lors de la Résistance de 1870 et de la Rébellion de 1885 ». *Prairie Forum* 19, no. 2 (1993): 153–68.

Knight, Alan, and Janet E. Chute. "In the Shadow of the Thumping Drum: The Sault Métis—The People In-Between." In *Lines Drawn Upon the Water: First Nations and the Great Lakes Borders and Borderlands*, edited by Karl S. Hele, 85–113. Waterloo, ON: Wilfrid Laurier University Press, 2008.

Ladner, Kiera. "Women and Blackfoot Nationalism." *Journal of Canadian Studies* 35, no. 2 (2000): 35–60.

Lent, D. Geneva. *West of the Mountains: James Sinclair and the Hudson's Bay Company*. Seattle: University of Washington Press, 1963.

Long, David. "Culture, Ideology and Militancy: The Movement of Native Indians in Canada, 1969–1991." In *Organizing Dissent: Contemporary Social Movements in Theory and Practice*, edited by William D. Carroll, 118–34. Toronto: Garamond Press, 1992.

Loomba, Ania. *Colonialism/Postcolonialism*. New York: Routledge, 2005.

Lytwyn, Victor. "Echo of the Crane: Tracing Anishinawbek and Métis Title to Bawating (Sault Ste. Marie)." In *New Histories for Old: Changing Perspectives on Canada's Native Pasts*, edited by Ted Binnema and Susan Neylan, 41–65. Vancouver: University of British Columbia Press, 2007.

MacBeth, R.G. *The Making of the Canadian West: Being the Reminiscences of an Eyewitness*. Toronto: William Briggs, 1898.

MacLeod, Margaret Arnett, and William Lewis Morton. *Cuthbert Grant of Grantown: Warden of the Plains of Red River*. Toronto, McClelland & Stewart, 1974.

Macdougall, Brenda. *One of the Family: Metis Culture in Nineteenth-century Northwestern Saskatchewan*. Vancouver: University of British Columbia Press, 2010.

———. "Wahkootowin: Family and Cultural Identity in Northwestern Saskatchewan Metis Communities." *The Canadian Historical Review* 87, no. 3 (2006): 431–62.

McNab, David T. "Free and Full Possession of Their Lands." In *Circles of Time: Aboriginal Land Rights and Resistance in Ontario*, 21–34. Waterloo, ON: Wilfrid Laurier University Press, 1999.

Miller, James R. "From Riel to the Métis." *Canadian Historical Review* 69, no. 1 (1988): 1–20.

Morton, Arthur S. *A History of the Canadian West to 1870-1871*. Toronto: University of Toronto Press, 1973.

———. "The New Nation, The Métis." In *The Other Natives: The-Les Métis*. Vol. 1, *1700-1885*, edited by Antoine S. Lussier and D. Bruce Sealey, 27–37. Winnipeg: Manitoba Metis Federation Press and Éditions Bois-Brûlés, 1978.

Morton, W.L. *Manitoba: A History*. Toronto: University of Toronto Press, 1967.

———. ed. *Alexander Begg's Red River Journal and Other Papers Relative to the Red River Resistance of 1869-1870*. New York: Greenwood Press, 1969.

———. ed., *Manitoba: The Birth of a Province*. Winnipeg: Manitoba Record Society Publications, 1965.

Pannekoek, Frits. "Métis Studies. The Development of a Field and New Directions." In Binnema, Ens and Macleod, *From Rupert's Land to Canada*, 111–28.

———. "The Rev. Griffiths Owen Corbett and the Red River Civil War of 1869-70." *The Canadian Historical Review* 57, no. 2 (1976): 133–49.

———. *A Snug Little Flock: The Social Origins of the Riel Resistance of 1869-1870*. Winnipeg: Watson & Dwyer, 1991.

Payment, Diane. *Batoche (1870-1910)*. Saint-Boniface, MB: Éditions du Blé, 1983.

Payne, Michael. "Fur Trade Historiography: Past Conditions, Present Circumstances and a Hint of Future Prospects." In Binnema, Ens and Macleod, *From Rupert's Land to Canada*, 3–22.

Peeling, Albert, and Paul Chartrand. "Sovereignty, Liberty, and the Legal Order of the 'Freemen' (Otipahemsu'uk): Towards a Constitutional Theory of Métis Self-Government." *Saskatchewan Law Review* 67, no. 1 (2004): 339–57.

Peterson, Jacqueline. "Ethnogenesis: The Settlement and Growth of a 'New People' in the Great Lakes Region." *American Indian Culture and Research Journal* 6, no. 2 (1982): 23–64.

———. "Many Roads to Red River: Métis Genesis in the Great Lakes Region, 1680–1815." In Peterson and Brown, *The New Peoples*, 37–71.

———. "Prelude to Red River: A Social Portrait of the Great Lakes Metis." *Ethnohistory* 25 (1978): 41–67.

———. "Red River Redux: Métis Ethnogenesis and the Great Lakes Region." In *Contours of a People: Metis Family, Mobility, and History*, edited by Nicole St-Onge, Carolyn Podruchny and Brenda Macdougall, 22–55. Norman: University of Oklahoma Press, 2012.

Peterson, Jacqueline, and Jennifer S.H. Brown, eds. *The New Peoples: Being and Becoming Métis in North America*. Winnipeg: University of Manitoba Press, 1985.

Pocock, John G.A. *Political Thought and History: Essays on Theory and Method*. Cambridge: Cambridge University Press, 2009.

Pritchett, John Perry. *The Red River Valley, 1811–1849: A Regional Study*. Toronto: The Ryerson Press, 1942.

Purich, Donald. *The Metis*. Toronto: James Lorimer & Company, 1988.

R. v. Goodon, [2009] 2 CNLR 278.

Ray, Arthur J. *Indians in the Fur Trade: Their Role as Hunters, Trappers and Middlemen in the Lands Southwest of Hudson's Bay, 1660–1870*. Toronto: University of Toronto Press, 1974.

Redbird, Duke. *We Are Metis: A Metis View of the Development of a Native Canadian People*. Ontario Métis and Non-Status Indian Association, 1980.

Reimer, Gwen, and Jean-Philippe Chartrand. "Documenting Historic Métis in Ontario." *Ethnohistory* 51, no. 3 (2004): 567–607.

Ritchot, Noël-Joseph. « Le journal de l'abbé N.J. Ritchot—1870 ». George F.G. Stanley, ed., *Revue d'histoire de l'Amérique française* 17, no. 4 (1964): 537–64.

Ross, Alexander. *The Red River Settlement: Its Rise, Progress and Present State*. Minneapolis: Ross and Haines, 1957 [1856].

Sawchuk, Joe. *The Dynamics of Native Politics: The Alberta Métis Experience*. Saskatoon: Purich Publishing, 1998.

———. *The Métis of Manitoba: Reformulation of an Ethnic Identity*. Toronto: Peter Martin Associates, 1978.

Schmitt, Carl. *The Concept of the Political*. Chicago: University of Chicago Press, 2007.

Simpson, Leanne. *Dancing on Our Turtle's Back: Stories of Nishnaabeg Re-Creation, Resurgence and a New Emergence*. Winnipeg: Arbeiter Ring Publishing, 2011.

Sprague, Douglas N., and R.P. Frye. *The Genealogy of the First Métis Nation: The Development and Dispersal of the Red River Settlement, 1820–1900*. Winnipeg: Pemmican Publications, 1983.

Spry, Irene M. "The Métis and Mixed-Bloods of Rupert's Land before 1870." In Peterson and Brown, *The New People*, 95–118.

Stanley, George F.G. *The Birth of Western Canada: A History of the Riel Rebellions*. Toronto: University of Toronto Press, 1961.

St-Onge, Nicole. "The Dissolution of a Métis Community: Pointe à Grouette, 1860–1885." *Studies in Political Economy* 18 (1985): 149–72.

———. *Saint-Laurent, Manitoba: Evolving Métis Identities, 1850–1914*. Regina: Canadian Plains Research Center, 2004.

Tanner, Adrian. "Algonquian Land Tenure and State Structures in the North." *The Canadian Journal of Native Studies* 3, no. 2 (1983): 311–20.

Thistle, Paul C. "The Twatt Family, 1780–1840: Amerindian, Ethnic Category, or Ethnic Group Identity?" In *The Western Métis: Profile of a People*, edited by Patrick C. Douaud, 73–89. Regina: Canadian Plains Research Center, 2008.

Thorne, Tanis C. "'Breeds are not a Tribe': Mixed-Bloods and Métissage on the Lower Missouri." In *Métis Legacy: A Métis Historiography and Annotated Bibliography*, edited by Lawrence J. Barkwell, Leah Dorion, and Darren R. Préfontaine, 93–98. Winnipeg: Pemmican Publications, 2001.

———. *The Many Hands of My Relations: French and Indians on the Lower Missouri*. Columbia: University of Missouri Press, 1996.

Tocqueville, Alexis de. « Quinze jours dans le désert ». In *Regards sur le Bas Canada*, edited by Claude Corbo. Montréal: Éditions Typo, 2003.

Tough, Frank. *As Their Natural Resources Fail: Native Peoples and the Economic History of Northern Manitoba, 1870–1930*. Vancouver: University of British Columbia Press, 1996.

de Trémaudan, Auguste-Henri. *Histoire de la nation métisse dans l'Ouest canadien*. Saint-Boniface, MB: Éditions des plaines, 1984.

Trigger, Bruce. "Brecht and Ethnohistory." *Ethnohistory* 22, no. 1 (1975): 51-56.

Van Kirk, Sylvia. "'What if Mama is an Indian?': The Cultural Ambivalence of the Alexander Ross Family." In Peterson and Brown, *The New People*, 207-20.

Métis Economics | 5

Sharing and Exchange in Northwest Saskatchewan

LIAM J. HAGGARTY

THE ECONOMIC HISTORY of Métis people in Canada has often been told as the story of the fur trade. It begins with the emergence of "mixed-bloods," the offspring of male traders and indigenous women, who were well suited to facilitate trade between the two groups. Acting as translators, guides, bison-hunters, freighters, trappers, middlemen and provisioners, Métis peoples prospered as the fur trade boomed. Over time, their numbers increased and a collective identity emerged that was different in subtle but important ways from that of both their indigenous and non-indigenous forebears. In the process, they contributed significantly to the spread of mercantilism in North America and the building of the Canadian nation. But this prosperity would not last. Over time, the international demand for fur declined while settlers and agents of the newly minted Dominion of Canada pushed further west in increasing numbers. Lands that once were valuable only for the animals that lived on them became highly valued as sites for settlement, railways, industrial economic activity and speculation. Métis people for their part opposed exclusionary encroachments onto their lands, but in the end resistance was largely futile. The fur industry faded and Métis people were pushed to the fringes of Canadian geography and imagination as the once prosperous agents of the fur trade were exiled to economic marginality.[1]

Containing many elements of a classic tragedy, the appeal of this fur trade narrative is obvious. Less obvious is the history the narrative hides. Although the fur trade and the other events that dot the storyline are historically significant and meaningful to many of the actors, the narrative obscures as much as it reveals. The fur trade, for example, was only one of a number of economic activities pursued by Métis people. Indigenous subsistence practices and systems of exchange were equally and sometimes more important. The nature and composition of these activities also varied greatly by region and place. In some areas, such as Red River, the fur trade was of great importance, while in areas further away from major fur trade centres subsistence often took precedence. Similarly, the importance of economic activities, including the fur trade itself, shifted over time as new resources and opportunities became available to local populations. Indeed, the roots of Métis economics, predicated on indigenous exchange networks, run deeper than the fur trade and the arrival of non-indigenous peoples. The experiences of Métis people, therefore, are far more diverse and varied than the fur trade narrative allows.

To address the silences in this narrative and posit a fuller story of Métis economic history, new sources and methodologies are required. In some areas of indigenous history this process is already well underway. Historians and other scholars have begun to write counter-narratives that challenge standard interpretations and offer valuable new insights into the history of the Americas. In *Peasant and Nation: The Making of Postcolonial Mexico and Peru*, for example, historian Florencia Mallon "decentres" prevailing understandings of concepts like politics, nationalism and the state to re-imagine the political history of Latin America while her book *Courage Tastes of Blood: The Mapuche Community of Nicolás Ailío and the Chilean State, 1906–2001* adopts a sophisticated community-based analysis of indigenous–state relations and the struggle for control of lands and resources. In North America, Keith Basso's *Wisdom Sits in*

Places: Landscape and Language among the Western Apache thoughtfully engages Apache worldviews through a detailed study of their relationships with land and the natural environment, while Julie Cruikshank's *Do Glaciers Listen? Local Knowledge, Colonial Encounters, and Social Imagination* describes and contrasts place-based indigenous understandings of history and the world with non-indigenous ones informed by imperialism, colonialism and science. The innovative approaches and methods employed by each of these scholars allow them to craft more nuanced and meaningful interpretations of past events and the complex relationships forged between segments of indigenous and non-indigenous populations.[2]

The work of Native Studies scholar Brenda Macdougall has applied aspects of this approach to northwest Saskatchewan directly. Grounded by a genealogical approach to studying the past, her research stresses the importance of family and familial relationships to understanding Métis history and culture, including exchange. Using the Cree term *wahkootowin*, a fluid philosophical concept used to describe familial social networks and "togetherness," her book *One of the Family: Metis Culture in Nineteenth-century Northwestern Saskatchewan* illuminates subtle aspects of Métis identity and culture through the reconstruction of prominent local family lineages. In so doing, she argues that although the fur trade, colonialism and other historical events have certainly shaped Métis life and society, the idea of *wahkootowin* was and remains the single most important part of Métis culture and the foundation of social, economic and political behaviour in northwest Saskatchewan.[3] *Wahkootowin*, from this perspective, not only mediated Cree and Métis people's perceptions of and interactions with non-indigenous others but actually absorbed Euro-Canadian peoples, ideas and practices into an indigenous cultural framework. The history of cultural mixing is therefore a story of perseverance and cultural survival.

This chapter aims to contribute to and build on this emergent historiography by presenting an alternative history of Métis economics in northwest Saskatchewan. Like Macdougall, I stress the significance of familial networks and socio-economic co-operation. But rather than conduct a genealogical analysis, I adopt an economic perspective firmly rooted in ethnohistorical methods. Although I generally agree with Macdougall's argument and use of *wahkootowin*, this chapter suggests that economic considerations were not just a feature of family exchange networks but rather a key determinant thereof and part of a larger pattern previously identified by scholars in other indigenous communities.[4] In so doing, I propose a more complicated and messy interpretation of community and family centred on power and relations of power within kin-based social networks and co-operative communities. My goal is not to challenge the importance of ideas of community and family to the construction of Métis culture and identity but to add greater depth and sophistication to our historical reconstructions of these important socio-economic institutions. Although families and communities certainly engaged in co-operative and sometimes selfless acts of sharing and reciprocity, they were nonetheless products of subtle but complex negotiations of power.

Using historic information and ethnographic observations recorded by anthropologists, missionaries and others, this chapter begins with a thick description of Cree and Dene systems of sharing that they practiced in northwest Saskatchewan circa 1800.[5] In this context I use sharing to encompass the culturally mediated systems and processes involved in redistributing wealth generated from harvesting and managing local resources, both physical and metaphysical. Normally practiced among members of kin-based social networks, this form of sharing, done without the expectation of immediate return or profit-making, affirmed the existing social order and networks that supported it. Unlike some popular definitions of sharing, this usage does not imply that sharing was necessarily altruistic, benevolent or voluntary. In fact, sharing in this context was often mandatory, a product of cultural obligations and an expression of individual and collective power. Most often characterized by reciprocal exchange within and between families connected by ancestry and marriage, the systems of sharing examined here mediated human interaction with each other and the natural and spiritual world; regulated resource use; insulated families and individuals from the unpredictability of environmental variation; and brokered power relations. As such, sharing has and continues to serve as the basis for Métis and other indigenous peoples' most important collective identities and a defining feature of culture.

The chapter's second part examines how these systems of sharing and the collective identities they produced changed in the nineteenth and twentieth centuries to make sense and take advantage of the arrival of non-indigenous peoples, the fur trade, modernization and other historical events. Relying on both written and oral records, it traces the effects of ongoing sedentarization and individualization as wealth, prosperity and poverty all came to be experienced and managed individually rather than collectively. In contrast to analyses of cultural trauma and change, the story presented here is one of adaptation and continuity. Although novel and exotic, these events, and contact with non-indigenous people in general, were perceived and rationalized by local indigenous peoples within existing social, economic and political structures that rendered them knowable and familiar. Moreover, through constant negotiation with new peoples and ideas, a unique expression of cultural hybridity emerged that fused indigenous systems of sharing with Euro-Canadian mercantilist practices. In the process, the nature and structure of family-based networks shifted to accommodate and take advantage of newly available economic opportunities, demonstrating the distinct and dynamic nature of Métis economics in northwest Saskatchewan.

By thus employing a community-based, ethnohistorical approach to the study of Métis peoples and families in northwest Saskatchewan, and by taking seriously oral histories and other non-traditional forms of historical enquiry, this chapter challenges prevailing interpretations of Métis history that portray Métis people as by-products of, and wholly dependent on, the fur trade and reduce Métis economics to a superficial amalgam of the economic activities of two cultures. Instead, I argue for a richer, more complicated history that contextualizes Métis people and society within an ongoing history of economic exchange, hybridization and adaptation. It is the story of a particular form of sharing and the central role it has played in the lives of Métis people across northwest Saskatchewan.

Indigenous Systems of Sharing

The history of sharing in northwest Saskatchewan begins long before the appearance of non-indigenous peoples and their mixed offspring. Within indigenous societies, sharing was one of a number of exchange activities pursued in the area. For example, raiding, practiced almost exclusively on the periphery of a group's social world, targeted people with whom the raiders had no kin ties or other social affiliations. Trading, meanwhile, was characterized by a desire to generate profit through the one-time exchange of goods or services and therefore occurred most often among distant relatives and non-hostile strangers residing between the periphery and centre of the actor's social network. Sharing, on the other hand, was practiced at the core of the social world among close family, relatives, and in-laws who co-operatively redistributed the wealth they accumulated from the natural world. Although raiding, trading and other forms of exchange were therefore important aspects of indigenous economies, sharing was particularly important to daily life and social identity in both the distant and more recent past. Moreover, it was these systems of sharing that formed the basis of the hybrid economic systems and structures generated by the offspring of unions between indigenous and non-indigenous peoples. More than the biological descendants of these indigenous groups, Métis peoples are also their cultural and philosophical heirs, the benefactors of hundreds if not thousands of years of economic innovation and adaptation. Exploring the history of indigenous systems of sharing in northwest Saskatchewan is therefore crucial to understanding more recent changes and events.

The village now known as Île à la Crosse has functioned as an epicentre of this history of sharing in northwest Saskatchewan. Located on a peninsula near the centre of Lac Île à la Crosse, the small northern village serves as a junction between important waterways connecting Hudson's Bay to the western prairies via the Churchill, Beaver and Canoe river systems. Long before Euro-Canadian activity and settlement in the area, it was an important meeting place and harvesting site for local indigenous peoples. In the late eighteenth century, it became a strategic stopping point for traders and explorers travelling westward from British colonies in north-eastern North America. Founded in 1776, the original trading post at Île à la Crosse is the second oldest in what is now inland western Canada, and the site remained a critically important economic and religious centre of colonial and state expansion until its significance began to decline in the twentieth century. Today, the northern village boasts a modest population of 1,600, with most residents identifying as Métis. Although the area remains economically depressed, recent resource extraction projects in northern Saskatchewan have rekindled some of its economic significance.[6]

Prior to appearance of fur traders and explorers, the area was occupied by at least two indigenous groups. From the north, groups of Athapaskan-speaking Dene peoples (formerly known as Chipewyan) travelled through, worked in and occupied areas in and around Ile a la Crosse, including the modern-day communities of Patuanak, Dillon, Buffalo Narrows and La Loche. Over time, regional identities emerged among these more southern Dene who referred to themselves as *thilanottine*, meaning "men of the end of the head" or "those who dwell at the head of the lakes." Those directly involved in the Île à la Crosse trading sphere became known as *kesyehot'ine*, meaning "poplar house people" or "dwellers among the quaking aspen," in reference to the trees and logs used to build early trade forts.[7] Although most Dene populations relied almost exclusively on the northern caribou herds for food and other necessities, the more southern *kesyehot'ine* also hunted moose, deer and other terrestrial animals; trapped fur bearers; gathered berries, roots, eggs and other plants and herbs; and fished for marine and riverine foods. Although their identification with trade posts suggests their southern movements were a result of the fur trade, ethnographic and archaeological evidence suggests that Dene peoples used the waterways and visited these areas at least seasonally long before the beginning of the fur trade.[8]

The Île à la Crosse region has also been a homeland for Algonquian-speaking Rock Cree peoples, sometimes called Woodland Crees, who are related to, but distinct from, the Plains and Swampy Cree. According to Reverend Marius Rossignol, a resident of Île à la Crosse for more than three decades in the early twentieth century, they referred to themselves as *assiniskawidiniwok*, meaning "human beings (of the country where there is) an abundance of rocks," or more generally as *ne᛫hiyawak*, "those who speak the same language."[9] As with the Dene, the historical movement of Crees in and around the area prior to the appearance of Euro-Canadians is difficult to track, though archaeological data seems to date Cree presence to at least "late prehistoric times."[10] Regardless, by the time the Hudson's Bay Company (HBC) erected its first post in the area, the Rock Cree were well established and formed a majority of the indigenous peoples living around Île à la Crosse as well as other modern-day communities, including Pinehouse, Beauval, Green Lake and Meadow Lake. The groups subsisted principally on moose, deer, elk, ducks, as well as rabbits and other small fur-bearing animals and various types of fish and gathered foods. Due in part to their avid involvement in the fur trade and existing tensions with the Dene, the Cree were more likely to form unions with traders than with their Dene neighbours, whose relative populations decreased. As anthropologist Robert Jarvenpa notes, this led to the emergence of a large Cree-Métis population in and around Île à la Crosse and its network of secondary posts.[11]

Despite the emphasis anthropologists and some local people have placed on their cultural differences—and, at times, hostile relationship—Dene and Cree groups in the area practiced similar economic, social and political customs prior to widespread contact with non-indigenous peoples.[12] Of these, systems of sharing, practiced both locally and regionally as well as horizontally (between equals) and vertically (between elites and non-elites), were critically important.[13] At the local level, the most important social units were the family household, often consisting of two brothers and their families, and the hunting group, consisting of several related families that worked together co-operatively. From fall through spring, hunting groups directed economic, social and political activities as families hunted and trapped in relative isolation. Consisting of 10 to 30 people, the hunting group is the basis of what became known as "bands," with each family within the band occupying a separate section of land for hunting, trapping, fishing and gathering. Because kinship was determined bilaterally, band membership was flexible and movement between bands was common where kin ties could be demonstrated. Consequently, political alliances were often temporary and leadership was largely informal and by consensus. As Reverend J.M. Penard noted, historically "there was no chief[,] properly speaking," but Dene groups did recognize a headman, or *denettheritset'in*, noted for his wisdom and experience, and successful hunters were regularly joined by kin who wanted to hunt in his territory. Similarly, Rock Cree people recognized a leader, or *okima·w*, "based on his experience, ability as a hunter and organizer, and possession of spiritual powers."[14]

Sharing within Cree and Dene families and bands was largely horizontal, often taking the form of unbalanced or delayed reciprocity. For example, although animals killed by a hunter were his property, the meat was distributed among the entire group either by the "chief" or by the hunter himself.[15] In times of need, entire bands shared food with one another and gave freely to visitors. Historically, Rossignol reported, "Those who had better luck than the others would, with a real family spirit, then share what they had with the poorer ones." Similarly, when a family was travelling from one place to the next, Cree hunting groups "did their best to aid [the family]," giving it "all the food which they had at their disposal if [the family] happened to be in need. These Indians were naturally very hospitable....The law of hospitality [that is, the willingness to share food and other goods] was everywhere inviolable."[16] Penard concurs, stating that the Dene "were not at all inhospitable to strangers, and if a stranger wished to settle peacefully among them they granted him permission to hunt and fish, provided he observed the Chippewayan usages and customs."[17]

At the regional level, sharing was practiced most often between extended families and kin that did not live or hunt together in winter but were connected through marriage.[18] Normally arranged by fathers in consultation with their wives and brothers, marriages granted new in-laws access to one another's resource base and labour pool and established strict protocols for co-operation and mutual assistance. Ideally, marriages joined together paternal cross-cousins—not considered relatives—or pairs of siblings from two families to create a "double brother-in-law" relationship. So important were these alliances that some families would betroth children even before birth.[19] These in-law relationships formed the core of the larger social unit, or "regional band," called *ellotine* among the Dene and *ntotimuk* or *wahkootowin* among the Cree. Like those of the smaller social units, the boundaries of these larger collectives were flexible and membership often overlapped, allowing families to mobilize a variety of kinship ties according to prevailing environmental and social conditions.[20]

Most regional sharing took place during the summer at large gatherings where vertical exchange was more common. After the snow melted and the spring trapping season ended in late spring, family and hunting groups from across the region converged at a single, predetermined meeting place, usually near a lake or river where fish, game and berries could temporarily sustain a larger, more sedentary population. This regional band, according to anthropologist James Smith, was "the largest cooperative unit" and was led by an informally elected leader or chief: "This was the time of major socializing, reinforcement of social ties, realignment of families and planning for the winter dispersal."[21] Feasting, Rossignol noted, was an important part of these gatherings: "all the groups held a feast together, offered sacrifices, and talked over the events of the year," he remarked. During the feasts, families made "magnificent presents... of pelts, wearing apparel, etc." to demonstrate their abilities and wealth: "Naturally the visitors who took away these presents, had in turn to send invitations and give presents the following year to their hosts of the previous one. This custom was a symbol of friendship but it was also a matter of justice. Certainly the first givers expected a return of the favor and would consider themselves injured if they received nothing in return for their courtesy and generosity."[22] In the process, families effectively became indebted to one another much as they did in coastal indigenous societies during elaborate potlatch ceremonies that demonstrated the hosts' status and prestige, thereby securing their rights to access productive resources sites.[23] As fall approached, the families dispersed, returning to their winter camps with close kin.[24]

Together, these local and regional indigenous systems of sharing formed the basis of Cree, Dene and, later, Métis social, economic and political life. From an ecological perspective, sharing was most important as a mechanism for offsetting regional, seasonal and annual fluctuations in resource availability and for insulating families from potential hardships and starvation.[25] In the words of former Île à la Crosse resident Reverend Lavasseur, "The best ice box for game is in the stomachs of your neighbors—give to receive....The best insurance policy was the good will of one's neighbour."[26] Socially, however, sharing was most often practiced not as an environmental adaptation but as a meaningful part of Cree and Dene worldviews governed by strict cultural protocols. As Lavasseur observed, sharing was the philosophical hub from which everything else radiated: "[It was] a pattern for living, a pattern with a definite focal point with radiating spokes...the most logical response to the pressure of the environment, the surest way of being assured help, food, and shelter in moments when the elements were not favorable....[T]heir philosophy demands that they must share."[27]

Sharing thus created a safety net, a form of social welfare, available to all members of the local and regional group provided they abided by the relevant protocols. Co-operation, assistance and hospitality at the local level, Smith notes, were expected "as a matter of course....[E]very form of assistance is given for the asking—or even without asking," making these groups "the nucleus of the traditional settlements."[28] Those who had the means to share but refused were often labelled "stingy and miserly" and excluded from future distributions of food and goods. Sometimes this "boycotting" was used as a general form of punishment to expel unwanted members of a band.[29] Poor people therefore were not those who lacked material goods or wealth but those without the family connections that made them part of a viable and accessible economic network.[30] In this context, poverty, like prosperity, was experienced and managed collectively.

But sharing was not purely ecological in function, nor was it necessarily altruistic. As a key determinant of status and prestige, sharing, especially vertical sharing, was also a source of power for local and regional leaders or chiefs. "It is an honour to share," Lavasseur remarked: "Those in the community who have the most to share are naturally the best providers, the best hunters, they are also the natural leaders or chiefs in the community. Those who ask him for help feel that they are honouring him. In other words, providing the chief with an opportunity to fulfill his role in the community as a great 'Giver' or 'Sharer.'" The chief is paid for his services by asking him for them. "Asking him for a material favour was payment and, more important, payment with honour to the Chief. It was in effect acknowledging the Chief's reputation as a 'Giver,' the acceptance of his leadership."[31] Sharing in this context was situational. It was a means of acquiring and expressing power, and through the act of receiving, the less powerful implicitly recognized and affirmed the power of elites. As anthropologist Marshall Sahlins notes, the act of giving inevitably produces a reciprocal, though not necessarily balanced, exchange with the giver often receiving in return an intangible benefit, such as enhanced status.[32]

Contrary to idealized notions of community that stress unity and social harmony, these power relations and the dialectic nature of sharing allude to the ongoing internal conflict present in all levels and types of society. Communities are neither static nor singular, argues Mallon. Rather, they are the product of "communal hegemony," the constant and ongoing negotiation of power within a heterogeneous, dynamic social unit at a specific place and time.[33] What we see in the historical record, therefore, are snapshots of processes in motion, momentary reconstructions that necessarily privilege the words and actions of the powerful. Even in the more egalitarian communities of northwest Saskatchewan, our interpretations of the past are mediated by those whose ideas of community became dominant.

Despite the challenges associated with studying past communities, the historical significance of sharing is clear. Combined with its central role in managing natural resources and environmental fluctuation, as well as providing a socio-economic safety net for its members, the power infused in systems of sharing made them the most important aspect of indigenous collective identity in northwest Saskatchewan. Over time, these systems changed as the appearance of fur traders and other members of non-indigenous societies challenged prevailing hegemonies and influenced the creation of new ones. Even when combined with other economic systems, sharing continued to regulate behaviour and provide structure and meaning in the lives of Métis and other indigenous peoples throughout the nineteenth and twentieth centuries. In so doing, it also established the parameters within which leadership, power, prestige and other important aspects of Métis culture and society were performed, affirmed and challenged.

Métis Economics

When fur traders and other "newcomers" first arrived in the Île à la Crosse area, they were viewed as strangers with no perceivable connection to the land, its ancestors or its resources. Lacking kin connections, they could not readily access the sharing networks that permeated Cree and Dene society. Instead, exchange with strangers was usually characterized by trade, which was profit-driven, or raiding, which was only forbidden among family and kin where sharing was the norm. Unlike the more stable access provided by kin-based systems of sharing, traders' access to goods and resources required a supply of items in demand among local groups, and the social safety net that insulated indigenous people from environmental change and starvation did not necessarily apply. Therefore, despite the novelty of exotic trade goods and new trading partners, fur traders, in this important respect at least, were seriously disadvantaged. In a world where survival, prosperity and power depended primarily on family relationships and kin ties, traders were, at least initially, impoverished.

But traders did not remain strangers for long. Although fur companies initially discouraged their employees from forming relationships with indigenous women, they quickly realized the benefits and inevitability of such unions that, by the time the first trading post was established in Île à la Crosse in 1776, had become common practice. As Arthur Ray and others have demonstrated, "social distance had a bearing on the type of exchange that took place and...the flow of goods....Clearly the Europeans had to accommodate themselves to these exchange traditions....[T]his was one of the reasons why European traders took Indian wives. It served to cement ties with Native groups."[34] Unconnected men, men without recourse to *ellotine* and *wahkootowin* social networks, were seriously disadvantaged in the trade.[35] Likewise, Cree and, to a lesser extent, Dene families were eager to formally connect themselves to traders through arranged marriages that guaranteed them access to the goods and resources controlled by the post "family."

What resulted, however, was not a simple insertion of Euro-Canadian men into existing indigenous kin networks or an integration of indigenous families into trading post commercial activity. Rather, a new system emerged that combined indigenous systems of sharing with profit-based mercantilism in a unique and genuinely hybrid economy. As traders and their families, which included the post manager or chief factor as leader and patriarch, became connected to regional *ellotine* and *wahkootowin* networks through marriage, they and their new indigenous in-laws became active participants in the creation of new social and economic protocols that governed family and kin relationships. Within this arrangement, sharing, which continued to dominate exchanges negotiated between family members and close relatives, was balanced with a greater emphasis placed on trade and market exchange, especially wage labour, which was normally restricted to strangers and more distant relations. Through marriage, non-indigenous people connected to a local *wahkootowin* were therefore provided for in times of need. Even the post itself could call on additional aid and provisions—and it often did.[36]

Traders also used marriage ties and family connections to secure access to furs procured by local hunters. Rather than being shared, these furs, as well as labour, provisions and other goods, were traded within an exchange system that allowed members of extended kin networks, both indigenous and non-indigenous, to generate a profit. By marrying into and becoming members of local a *wahkootowin*, traders effectively built a steady and reliable clientele. Similarly, while continuing to share with both indigenous and non-indigenous relations, local Cree and Métis people secured access to trade and the profits derived therefrom through their familial connections with traders and their descendants. In this way, indigenous systems of sharing became, through intercultural negotiation, infused with elements of profit-driven systems of trade channelled through the post. This joining of sharing, normally minimized in market-based economies, and trade, formerly prohibited within both Cree and Dene families, demonstrates both the originality and hybridity of Métis economics in northwest Saskatchewan.

Evidence of this hybrid system of exchange is manifest in the activities of fur traders and Métis people in the mid- to late nineteenth century. Members of the trading post family, for example, reciprocated the aid it received from Métis and other indigenous people by sharing resources and participating in a wide range of exchange activities. On a regular basis they shared food within their immediate families and with close in-laws, especially in times of need. During the summer, the post organized feasts and participated in the reciprocal gift-giving ceremonies that occurred between prominent families, demonstrating in the process the wealth and power of the post family. Similarly, fur trade practices like the gift-giving ceremony, which preceded virtually every exchange involving the HBC during its first two hundred years, and the credit system, which provided indigenous hunters with goods in advance of their hunts on the condition that the furs they acquired would be sold back to the Company, neatly combined fur trade practices with the more intimate forms of sharing required among traders and their in-laws. This "ceremonial exchange of European goods," anthropologist A.D. Fisher notes, "complemented informal means of exchange within the family hunting band" and helped establish respectful, lasting and profitable trading relationships.[37]

The best evidence of Company participation in these hybrid systems of sharing, however, is the direct allocation of relief and other forms of aid. By the 1860s, the same items routinely presented as gifts and on credit were also being given regularly to widows, orphans, "old Indians" and other people not directly involved in the fur trade.[38] Sometimes, recipients were provided with ball and shot that they could then gift to hunters in exchange for a portion of their produce.[39] In 1869, for example, the Company extended these benefits to Île à la Crosse "pensioners," most of whom were either descendants of former Company employees, hunters no longer able to work, and, or, members of powerful families.[40] Unlike Company servants and retired traders, these "freemen" were not eligible for regular HBC pensions. Local officials, however, seemed compelled by the tenets of *wahkootowin* and *ellotine* social organization to provide relief to local Métis people even if it was not approved by Company administrators and, in some cases, justifying freemen pensions as necessary safeguards against competition from rival trading companies.[41] Termed "social overhead costs of production," these practices not only mimicked aspects of indigenous economies, they entrenched employees, or family members, in the very fabric of Cree and Dene systems of sharing.[42]

The Catholic Church also participated in these systems of sharing and other exchange activities. After establishing a mission in Île à la Crosse in 1846, Oblates and other missionaries became connected to local individuals and families through religion and godparentage, an institution that would become an increasingly important form of inter-family connectedness in subsequent decades.[43] The church would also distribute rations of fish and potatoes at the conclusion of the Sunday service to families allied with the post and would host large feasts at weddings, funerals and other community events.[44] In the process, the church "family" effectively reciprocated, at least in the eyes of the recipients, the relief occasionally afforded to it by Métis and other indigenous peoples.

Aspects of longstanding indigenous economies were likewise adapted to accommodate kin-based trade and take advantage of other new exchange opportunities. Seasonal cycles, for example, were modified to include the trading post, which, like trapping grounds and berry patches, was viewed as a resource site. Speaking to anthropologists Robert Jarvenpa and Hetty Jo Brumbach in the 1970s, Dene elder Moise McIntyre detailed the historic movements of his people as recalled in the 1940s by Sarah Bell, an elderly woman he referred to as grandmother. Recited in a narrative style, he described how the trading post was integrated into the winter and summer activities of both the nuclear and extended family:

> The southern nomadic round included Chipewyan who made a traditional summer trading rendezvous at Ile a la Crosse. These people, including Sarah Bell's extended family and other kin, wintered in small multi-family encampments in the vast area between the headwaters of the Foster River and Cree Lake. Prior to spring break-up, they positioned themselves near groves of birch trees where new bark canoes could be assembled. With the disappearance of the ice, families descended the Mudjatik River in canoe caravans and reassembled in late June at Big Island, the primary summer gathering place near the Île à la Crosse post. The aggregation at Big Island lasted about one month and served as a renewal of kinship and friendship bonds for Chipewyan from throughout the

area. It was also the period for exchanging furs at the post for credit and outfits
for the next winter's hunt....[I]n early August the Chipewyan had largely com-
pleted the summer rendezvous at Ile a la Crosse. Small travelling units, usually
composed of four to six closely related families, began moving south and south-
eastward from Île à la Crosse by canoe. In many instances, the canoe travel
parties represented families that wintered in the same locale.[45]

Rather than challenging existing practices or breaking with the past, trade and other post activities became integrated quite seamlessly into existing indigenous economies and systems of sharing.

The trading post figured even more prominently in the activities of Cree and Métis families. Instead of viewing the post as a seasonal meeting place, Cree families, Smith notes, often settled in close proximity to the post and became largely sedentary: "Subsequent to the establishment of a trading monopoly in 1821, there was an increased tendency for the [Cree] bands to be localized and oriented to a specific post, a first stage in the process of sedentarization." Gradually, this "trading post–mission com-plex," Smith argues, became "the focal point of band life and was visited at the end of the main trapping season at Christmas, at Easter, and in the summer for the rituals of treaty payment." The credit system also contrib-uted to this sedentarization of local groups by fixing band membership to the post, thereby limiting the social and physical mobility of individu-als and families and augmenting the status of the post family and factor. In fact, as the H B C and non-indigenous people in general acquired greater control of local resources, the post factor became known among the Cree as *okima·w*, the traditional term for "chief, leader, person of authority or influence," while the Cree chiefs became *okima·hka·n*, literally "surro-gate or substitute chief."[46] By ascribing such terms to post factors, local Métis and other indigenous people were implicitly recognizing the role of these men as controllers of resources, holders of wealth, and providers of aid. This elevation of post officials and demotion of hereditary elites hint at a general shift in Métis and indigenous perceptions and expressions of wealth, as well as wealth redistribution toward more Euro-Canadian models, as mercantile systems of exchange became infused with principles of sharing.

Economic adaptation also facilitated Métis people's involvement in paid labour activities and other forms of profit-driven exchange. Throughout the mid- to late nineteenth century, Métis men and women worked either seasonally or permanently for the HBC as traders, guides, freighters, translators and provisioners. Based on a close analysis of HBC account books for the 1890s, Jarvenpa and Brumbach reconstructed the economic activities of three men: Francis Roy, Magloire Maurice, and Michael Bouvier, all of whom pursued indigenous subsistence techniques alongside paid labour. Of the three men, Maurice, who received "contract wages," appears to be the only one employed full-time by the Company while Bouvier was paid for "temporary labor" and Roy was paid by the job for providing the Company with fish, cutting firewood and building sleds and snow shoes. All three also traded furs to the Company for various goods, but whereas Maurice, who received employee rations, spent virtually all his credit on clothing and textiles, Roy mostly bought imported food, and Bouvier split his credit almost evenly between clothing and food.[47] Despite their access to Company food, however, all three, Jarvenpa and Brumbach argue, obtained between 50 and 85 per cent of their families' annual caloric needs from subsistence activities outside the fur trade.[48] Although the sample size is small, these case studies demonstrate the diversity of individual Métis economic practices and how new economic opportunities and resources were integrated into existing structures, thereby preserving the resilience and adaptiveness that characterized Métis systems of sharing.

Historian John Lutz characterizes this type of economic hybridity as "moditional," a term used to describe the cultural integration of different modes of production into a single, comprehensive economic arrangement. Based on case studies of two First Nations in British Columbia, Lutz argues that throughout the nineteenth and early twentieth centuries, indigenous people combined subsistence activities, wage labour and government transfer payments, such as relief or income assistance, to take full advantage of all the economic opportunities they encountered.[49] In some respects, these moditional economies are similar to mixed economies studied by anthropologists, and economies of makeshifts identified by Europeanists.[50] But whereas these terms most often refer to the simultaneous pursuit of economic activities that derive from outwardly oppositional economic models (usually hunter-gatherer and capitalist or modern and traditional), the term "moditional," due to its ethnohistorical genesis, emphasizes the joining not of activities but of culturally prescribed modes of production not linked to any one economic philosophy or model. By focussing specifically on the intercultural perception of and complex interplay between distinct economic systems, Lutz's approach offers particularly rich and sophisticated insights into economic history and the study of indigenous–non-indigenous relations.

Although Lutz's study is confined to indigenous British Columbians, his ideas shed light on the motivations and processes of exchange in other areas, such as northwest Saskatchewan, where people had access to a considerable number and variety of modes of production. When, for example, the price paid by the H B C for furs declined, Métis people adjusted their moditional economies to emphasize the harvesting of subsistence foods, paid labour at the post or company relief. Alternatively, when fur prices were high, relatively less time would be spent on subsistence activities and other modes of production. By adjusting in this way, Métis people in northwest Saskatchewan crafted distinct economies.[51] Although the individual modes may be classified as either "indigenous" or "Euro-Canadian," the particular way in which they were combined—forming moditional economies—were just as culturally unique as the economic structures espoused by local indigenous and non-indigenous peoples. More than the grafting of one set of economic activities onto another, Métis economic practices from this perspective appear as cultural hybrids, the unique products of ongoing cultural adaptation and negotiation.[52]

These moditional economies were a central feature of the distinct Métis culture developing in northwest Saskatchewan. Although the precise timing of the emergence of a collective Métis identity in the area is difficult to pinpoint and may not have been fully realized until sometime after the 1885 Northwest Resistance and subsequent scrip payments made by the federal government, the process of identity formation was well underway by the mid-nineteenth century.[53] As the first offspring of Cree-Métis and Cree-Dene unions had children of their own, often with other offspring of "mixed" marriages, the number of people living in and around Île à la Crosse who were neither fully indigenous nor fully Euro-Canadian began to increase rapidly. In the process, the region, Macdougall argues, was gradually transformed into "a Metis homeland not only by virtue of the children's occupation of the territory, but also through their relationships with the Cree and Dene women and fur trader men from whom they were descended" and by their participation in reciprocal sharing networks based on respectful behaviour between family members.[54] Although the use of the term *wahkootowin* to describe sharing networks during this period is absent in the written record, Macdougall infers from her genealogical research that the idea and structure represented by *wahkootowin* "contextualize[d] how relationships were intended to work within Métis society by defining and classifying relationships, prescribing patterns of behaviour between relatives and non-relatives, and linking people and communities in a large, complex web of relationships" and economies. Forged though intercultural negotiation, these hybrid systems of exchange contributed to a common cultural identity in the Métis communities of northwest Saskatchewan "based on familial—especially interfamilial—connectedness."[55]

In the closing decades of the nineteenth century, this emergent collective identity continued to provide meaning and structure in a rapidly modernizing world that privileged individualism and a sedentary lifestyle over collectivism and mobility. The importance of Euro-Canadian institutions and services, for example, increased sedentarization around the trading post–mission complex as Métis moditional economies shifted their focus to take advantage of new social and economic opportunities. Similarly, the communal hunting of big game gave way to individual or small-group hunting and the economic significance of trading and commercial trapping and fishing reduced the amount of time spent on subsistence activities.[56] As a result, the nuclear family and close kin became increasingly more important relative to the more expansive social units of the past.

Government intervention in the north also required adaptation. Eager to divest itself of economic responsibility for indigenous peoples, including Métis peoples, and limit its social overhead costs of production, the HBC began transferring power to the federal government with the sale of Rupert's Land in 1869. Although the Company remained active in the Île à la Crosse region for several more decades as settlement progressed further south, the government assumed greater control of the area in 1906 as it attempted to extinguish indigenous land title with Treaty No. 10 and scrip payments prior to the creation of the province of Saskatchewan. Like the gift-giving system on which they were partly based, treaty and scrip payments implicitly connected the government to indigenous economies and systems of sharing in particular. Writing to Company shareholders in June 1871, Prime Minister John A. Macdonald articulated his desire to utilize existing HBC institutions and practices within government: "It would be of advantage to us, & no doubt it would be of advantage to you that we should be allowed to make use of your officers & your posts for the purpose of making those payments to the Indians which will have to be made annually by the Government of Canada in order to satisfy their claims & keep them in good humour."[57]

In the process, members of the North West Mounted Police, conservation officers, Department of Indian Affairs agents and other representatives of the federal and provincial governments replaced HBC officials as the controllers of resources and wealth. But what the HBC justified as the social overhead costs of production, the government saw as tools of pacification crucial to the building of a nation. Rather than a means of developing socio-economic ties between themselves and indigenous peoples, various governments used systems of sharing—and the political power inherent in them—to undermine and assimilate the very societies that had created them. The Catholic Church, meanwhile, maintained and periodically increased its relief allocations in the post–fur trade era to offset shortages resulting from this changeover.[58] As the nineteenth century drew to a close, Métis systems of sharing and the collective identities they informed thus faced unprecedented pressure from a variety of sources.

Sharing in the Twentieth Century

In the twentieth century, Métis economies continued to adapt to changing economic and social circumstances as ongoing missionization, government intervention and technological modernization promoted increased sedentarization and individualism. Shortly after the creation of the new province, for example, Métis and other indigenous peoples were required to purchase individual licences to hunt and fish and to register their traplines. In addition to further eroding the communal nature of historic subsistence practices, these regulations also limited mobility by promoting a sedentary lifestyle. Funded by the federal government, the church-run school in Île à la Crosse exacerbated these changes, especially among families with young children, and the geographical extent of seasonal rounds decreased as more time was spent at or near the school. Technological changes, especially the introduction of the gas engine, the building of the first roads, and refrigeration, which allowed families to transport and store food for long periods of time, further limited the ecological necessity of sharing. As Smith notes, by mid-century, the main village complex, which now included the school, post office and a variety of social services, was "becoming the basis for the modern village...with only men leaving for the traplines and hunting territories in the winter."[59] Welfare and other government transfer payments were also becoming increasingly important to individuals and families unable to access the natural resources and other economic opportunities that once were abundant.[60] Again, Métis moditional economies adapted according to a changed economic landscape to take advantage of new opportunities.

This greater emphasis on blood relatives and most immediate affinal kin changed the way families shared with one another, especially in times of hardship or emergency. According to Smith, although "one may still, within this more limited group, expect gifts or sharing of caribou or moose meat from successful hunters without need for cash payment," the frequency and extent of instances of sharing was declining.[61] At the same time that the frequency of sharing declined, prosperity and poverty came to be experienced individually rather than collectively. Whereas wealth had formerly been measured according to widespread social networks and reciprocal exchange, it gradually came to be associated with the individual or small family and was characterized by hoarding without the expectation of redistribution. Earlier ideas of wealth, economics and sharing that had once been dominant throughout northwest Saskatchewan were being subsumed by a new hegemonic order more heavily informed by Euro-Canadian ideals.

Yet, despite the effects of sedentarization and individualism, sharing has remained critically important to the Métis communities of northwest Saskatchewan and the collective identities of community members.[62] After arriving in Île à la Crosse in the early twentieth century, Rossignol found that the protocols regulating sharing and proper conduct were still very much in effect. In practice, however, they were subtle and inconspicuous to most outsiders: "In asking something from one another, they have many ways of expressing themselves. They very rarely employ direct formulae: "Give me," smacks of discourtesy among them. Instead, they say, "Lend me this," or else, "I should like to borrow this from you." Another still more subtle method is to extol or praise the thing that one wishes. Thus, you should never say to anyone: "You have a beautiful pipe," if you don't wish to possess it, for this would be the same as asking it of the owner. If you did so, he would answer as a matter of course: "Take it, it is yours." As Rossignol learned first-hand, outsiders, especially those living in or having connections to the community, remained subject to these protocols even if their participation was unintentional. While visiting an elderly woman, he was unknowingly "speaking cree" when he complimented her pet dog: "'You have a beautiful little dog, my grandmother,' I said to her, thinking to please her. 'Yes,' she said to me compressing her lips, 'You speak Cree, it is true, but I don't want to give him to you.' I excused myself as best I could, telling her that I would not be able to take him with me even if she gave him to me. But I had committed an indiscretion; by my imprudent remark made without reflection I had asked outright for the little dog as a present. This method of 'asking without asking' is called 'speaking Cree.' The natives sometimes make fun of strangers in the country who, but newly arrived, go into ecstasies over the least thing. 'Oh, you already speak Cree,' they say." Similarly, when people chose to sell an item rather than share it, the price for family and friends was "much lower than to strangers."[63]

Oral histories are rife with examples of sharing and its cultural significance. Jules Daigneault, an elder, former mine worker and semi-retired skiff and sleigh builder in Île à la Crosse, recalls life before families permanently relocated to the village, affirming in the process the importance of sharing to Métis identity: "Everybody used to share. Nobody was stingy, nobody....When people used to go hunting, the whole family went. They all went in the river and they found a certain spot where it's good to set up tents. That's where the family would stay while the men would go further on to go shoot a moose or set nets or something. They had a hunting party, and the party would go on further off the river to look for moose tracks and everything....The women that was at the camp, hunting camp, they did all the work hauling wood, setting the teepee or smokehouse, getting everything ready."[64] After the hunt, the produce was shared widely with friends and relatives. Able-bodied people helped themselves to the meat while deliveries were made to those unable to travel: "So they used to go from house to house, the widows first get meat, and the elders, the old men and the old ladies that can't go hunting, those ones too were fed. It was very important to feed your relatives, your family. And if there's somebody living on the island not related to you, you still go check. Maybe somebody's sick or something, they go check them out....And in return, when the people start to get old, the young ones start to go hunting and they feed the elders....Everybody used to share [ammunition, guns, boats, canoes, fishing nets]. They even shared their kettles, teapots...even the clothes."[65]

Although many instances of sharing were informal and spontaneous, explicit strategies of redistribution also emerged at this time. For example, George Malboeuf, a mine worker and community hunter in Île à la Crosse, recalls witnessing as a child the communal sharing that occurred after a hunt: "When I was growing up, that's what was the importance in my family. Not only in my family but among a lot of elders that used to hunt in their community. When they come in [to town] after they've shot a moose, then the community people used to come in and share with each other. They sat down and had a big cookout where people just—whatever they wanted to eat was available for them. Nothing was expected in return. And that's the tradition I'm trying to keep [the lessons] from what I was taught when I was young. I'm trying to share that."[66] Further north in Buffalo Narrows, Brian MacDonald, a commercial fisher, professional guide and traditional land user, recalls with pride his father's role as a community hunter. After the government introduced a permit system for hunting, elders and other community members were able to obtain a permit to give to a hunter: "My dad would go out and he would hunt and then he would share with different people throughout the community....People that were eligible, they had to hunt for themselves [but elders and other people that weren't able would] go get a permit...and my dad would go out and shoot the moose and we'd get a little bit and they'd get the rest. So my dad never really had to get his own permit 'cause he was always hunting for others. We got all of our meat through that all the time." Sanctions for failing to share were also still in place, MacDonald remembers: "I know one time they were mad at a fellow that shot a moose and never shared it so after that they suffered him by not giving him any."[67]

For MacDonald, sharing is part of a broad philosophy that permeates his relationships with other people, ancestors and the land. "We shared everything," he says. "We'd go hunting ducks in the spring, we'd shoot twenty, thirty ducks and we'd come back and everybody'd be making duck soup." The same was true of moose, fish and other animals that were shared widely with the community, beginning with elders, widows and families with many children. People also shared their labour as a way to reciprocate past acts. When hauling wood for an elderly woman, for example, MacDonald was thanking her father for past aid: "That wood wasn't brought from me, I just delivered it. That wood came from somebody else....Her dad. We used to walk the shoreline trapping [musk]rats. He was an old man, I was a young kid. If there was a rat in my trap, it'd be dead and put away there so nothing'd bother it. And I did the same for him. So when I hauled her the wood, this is why I hauled it. Not for her, it was for that old man I used to know....I told her, 'Your dad is still helping you. You think he's gone but he's not, he's here. That wood came from him, he's still helping.' Just 'cause they pass away and are gone that don't mean they're gone. And you never let them die, through these things. It still relates back to that [relationships]."[68] Sharing thus connected people not only with each other and the natural world but with ancestors and spirits as well.

Inherent in these systems of sharing is a respect for the land and its resources. The act of killing an animal, MacDonald was taught, has significant consequences for both the environment and the hunter: "Whatever eats you, you become that. So when you eat the moose or the fish, that fish's spirit now looks through my eyes, speaks through my voice. His spirit becomes me. Whatever consumes me one day, I become. And the spirit just travels all around like that...the bug crawling there, the tree over there, the owl, the eagle, the bear, the fish—whatever eats you, that's what you become. When you come to understand that, you learn not to go and whack on that tree and chop on it for no reason, because maybe that's your uncle or your grandfather. Maybe that eagle you're gonna shoot coming over there is your aunty. You don't know this stuff. But when you understand all living things are some spirit, you don't damage any of them for no reason other than to eat it...." Although not considered "living," aspects of the natural environment also are part of cyclical systems of sharing that demand respect: "So you have a respect for all living things, but at the same time you're taught you have respect for all dead things.... If you have no respect for the ground right over there, that's where you plant your potatoes, that's where the cherries grow out of the ground. Those things won't grow if they don't have respect for it, and pretty soon you can't eat from it....So you have respect for all living and all dead." This respect, according to MacDonald, is a shared one that is reciprocated to him whenever he is out on the land: "I always told my wife, 'you know, don't worry about me, I'm out there all over and it's sometimes dangerous and that, but you don't worry about me 'cause there's an old lady that looks after me.' And my reference is to Mother Nature, 'cause I treat her well, and when you treat someone well they treat you back the same. I've always been treated well by her."[69] Combined with the other oral histories summarized here, MacDonald's testimony demonstrates both the historic and contemporary significance of sharing as well as its importance as a key marker of Métis identity and northern life today.

Ethnographic evidence recorded by Smith corroborates these oral histories. Writing in the late 1960s and 1970s, he noted that the nuclear family and immediate kin remained "the basis for traditional hunting and trapping partnerships" and in some cases had been extended to commercial fishing and even wage labour at mines or fishing resorts. Among these groups, "one may borrow food or cash, dogs or motors, freely.... Long-term reciprocity is [still] expected, but failure to reciprocate is common and resented, with a consequent decline in expectations."[70] Although the ecological importance of sharing was in decline and its connection to power weakened, the social and culture significance of sharing remains evident in the Métis communities across northwest Saskatchewan. As demonstrated most clearly by excerpts from oral histories, sharing is fundamental to Métis and other indigenous lifeways and a defining feature of individual and collective identities. As a result, these systems of sharing will likely play a central role in future attempts to achieve recognition of Métis status and to secure access to local lands and resources.

Conclusion

The history of Métis economics in northwest Saskatchewan is best told as the story of sharing. Adapted from indigenous systems of reciprocity, co-operation and mutual obligation, it mediated human interaction with the natural environment and provided the flexibility necessary to adapt to regional, seasonal and annual fluctuations in resource availability. Socially, it prescribed proper behaviour between individuals, families, in-laws, bands, regional groups and strangers as well as deceased ancestors, creating in the process a type of social-welfare network that insulated its members from starvation and hardship. As a key determinant of status and prestige, sharing was also a prerequisite of power in Métis society, as well as among Cree and Dene groups. By accepting the produce of natural resources and family labour shared by leaders, Métis individuals and families implicitly recognized the power of these elites and affirmed their control of productive resource sites. Most importantly, it formed— and continues to form—the basis of people's most meaningful collective identities and has become a primary marker of indigeneity not only in northwest Saskatchewan but around the world.

These systems were never static. Long before the appearance of non-indigenous people, they were changing, constantly adapting to new ecological circumstances and power relations. This adaptation continued in the late eighteenth century after the arrival of fur traders and the resources they possessed. Through marriage, some strangers became known and familiar and were gradually integrated into indigenous systems of sharing, becoming in the process active participants in the creation of a unique economic system and examples of genuine hybridity. Justified as social overhead costs of production, trading practices, such as the gift-giving and credit systems, wove traders directly into the social fabric of indigenous life in the area. Initially, these traders, like most non-indigenous people, were heavily dependent on indigenous systems of sharing and the relief they provided to people in need. Indeed, for much of the late eighteenth and nineteenth centuries, non-indigenous people were the recipients of social-welfare provisions allocated by indigenous people connected to them through marriage. Métis and other indigenous peoples, on the other hand, eagerly exploited the new economic opportunities available to them, developing in the process unique moditional economies that combined various modes of production into a comprehensive and remarkably adaptive economic model.

Gradually, traders and the post families they represented became increasingly well connected to prominent local families, thereby augmenting their power and legitimating their access to and control of local resources. Missionaries and other church officials also became part of systems of sharing through godparentage and other social networks based on shared values and spirituality. Over time, this trading post–mission complex, centrally located in the village of Île à la Crosse and other northern communities, became an increasingly important resource site and gathering place for local indigenous groups, especially Métis families who maintained close familial connections to post employees, and their moditional economies. In fact, many of these families abandoned portions of their historic seasonal rounds, choosing instead a largely sedentary life that combined longstanding subsistence activities with increased opportunities for paid work at the fort. In the process, a distinct culture emerged as the children of indigenous–non-indigenous unions married each other and developed their own language, dress, customs and traditions, all of which were heavily informed by the social, economic and political structures that developed from systems of exchange practiced by both their indigenous and non-indigenous ancestors. Rather than a people born of the fur trade and "in between," this emergent Métis population was part of a unique process of hybridity, strategically combining and negotiating fundamental aspects of the economic systems practiced by their forebears.

Over the past century, Métis economics have continued to adapt to social, political, economic and environmental change. Together, these pressures, many of which are external in origin, have compelled Métis families to become increasingly more sedentary and individualistic. Rather than living all or part of the year "in the bush," virtually every family spends the entire year in town near the church, school, hospital and other public buildings. Refrigeration and other technological changes have allowed people to conveniently store meat and other foods for long periods of time, thereby eliminating some of the practical and ecological reasons for sharing produce with family, friends, neighbours and relatives. Government restrictions and licensing programs have further reduced the amount of time spent on land-use activities, such as hunting, trapping, fishing and gathering, while full-time wage labour has become increasingly important. As anthropologist James Waldram argues, scrip, treaty, and other government policies at this time also reified the legal identities ascribed to Métis and other indigenous people and exacerbated cultural divisions not readily apparent in the historical record.[71] As a result, sharing at the regional level, once a critical part of Cree and Dene societies, has largely been replaced by local forms of exchange practiced within the nuclear family and with immediate in-laws. However, as demonstrated by oral historical information, sharing remains a defining feature of Métis identity in northwest Saskatchewan and indigeneity more broadly.

Informed by ethnohistorical methods and anchored by community-based research, this story offers an alternative history of Métis economics in northwest Saskatchewan. Whereas previous interpretations have analyzed historic events and activities from the perspective of non-indigenous peoples and society within a narrative of westward expansion and increasing economic sophistication, this history emphasizes continuity and the contemporary significance of indigenous systems of sharing and other "traditional" structures. Although the fur trade and other events are clearly important to this story, they appear here not as catalysts of change or cultural trauma but as new economic, social and political opportunities that were rather easily integrated into hybrid structures and worldviews. It is, in other words, an economic history of continuity, adaptation and cultural perseverance aimed at producing a more reflexive, balanced and meaningful explanation of the past.

Author's Note

A number of people have been instrumental in the research, writing and over-all production of this chapter. I am indebted to elders and community members of Île à la Crosse, Buffalo Narrows, Beauval and surrounding communities, including George and Norma Malbeouf, Albert Daigneault and family, Jules Daigneault, Brian MacDonald, Jimmy Favel, Don Favel, Pierre Chartier, and Duane Favel, who shared with me not only their history but also meals, their homes, and numerous stories. I would also like to thank Amanda Fehr, Stephanie Danyluk, Katya MacDonald, and Omeasoo Butt for collaborating on shared research projects, and Keith Carlson for his ongoing support and guidance. Earlier versions of this chapter were much improved by comments offered by Keith and a number of graduate students of the University of Saskatchewan as well as the anonymous reviewers who provided valuable feed-back prior to publication. This research was funded in part by the Social Sciences and Humanities Research Council of Canada. I alone am responsible for any errors contained herein.

Notes

1. Aspects of this narrative are most evident in Marcel Giraud, *The Métis in the Canadian West*, trans. George Woodcock, 2 vols. (Edmonton and Lincoln: University of Alberta Press and University of Nebraska Press, 1986); G.F.G. Stanley, *The Birth of Western Canada* (Toronto: University of Toronto Press, 1961); W.L. Morton, *Manitoba: A History* (Toronto: University of Toronto Press, 1967); George Woodcock, *Gabriel Dumont: The Métis Chief and his Lost World* (Edmonton: Hurtig Publishers, 1975); and Thomas Flanagan, *Louis 'David' Riel: Prophet of the*

New World (Toronto: University of Toronto Press, 1979). Although more balanced and nuanced, some more recent publications also implicitly privilege the fur trade and Euro-Canadian actors, thereby producing a narrative of change and instability that obscures evidence of adaptation and continuity. See, for example, D.N. Sprague, *Canada and the Métis, 1869-1885* (Waterloo, ON: Wilfrid Laurier University Press, 1988); and Gerhard Ens, *Homeland to Hinterland: The Changing Worlds of the Red River Metis in the Nineteenth Century* (Toronto: University of Toronto Press, 1996). Aspects of this narrative are also discernible at times in the excellent scholarship that broadened the field, both thematically and geographically, during the 1980s and 1990s. See Jennifer S.H. Brown, *Strangers in Blood: Fur Trade Company Families in Indian Country* (Vancouver: University of British Columbia Press, 1996); Sylvia Van Kirk, *Many Tender Ties: Women in Fur-Trade Society, 1670-1870* (Winnipeg: Watson & Dwyer, 1980); Jacqueline Peterson and Jennifer S.H. Brown, eds., *The New Peoples: Being and Becoming Métis in North America* (Winnipeg: University of Manitoba Press, 1985).

2. Florencia E. Mallon, *Peasant and Nation: The Making of Postcolonial Mexico and Peru* (Berkeley: University of California Press, 1995); Florencia E. Mallon, *Courage Tastes of Blood: The Mapuche Community of Nicolás Ailío and the Chilean State, 1906-2001* (Durham, NC: Duke University Press, 2005); Keith H. Basso, *Wisdom Sits in Places: Landscape and Language among the Western Apache* (Albuquerque: University of New Mexico Press, 1996); and Julie Cruikshank, *Do Glaciers Listen? Local Knowledge, Colonial Encounters, and Social Imagination* (Vancouver: University of British Columbia Press, 2005). See also John Lutz, *Makúk: A New History of Aboriginal-White Relations* (Vancouver: University of British Columbia Press, 2008); and Keith Thor Carlson, *The Power of Place, the Problem of Time: A Study of Aboriginal History and Collective Identity along the Lower Fraser River* (Toronto: University of Toronto Press, 2011).

3. Brenda Macdougall, *One of the Family: Métis Culture in Nineteenth-Century Northwestern Saskatchewan* (Vancouver: University of British Columbia Press, 2010). Note that in order to include both French and English lineages, Macdougall prefers "Metis" rather than "Métis." In this chapter, I use the more conventional spelling, "Métis."

4. See also Winona Stevenson [Wheeler], "'Ethnic' Assimilates 'Indigenous': A Study in Intellectual Neocolonialism," *Wicazo Sa Review* 13, no. 1 (Spring 1998): 33. Studies placing greater emphasis on the economic factors, and which recognize the economic motivations as determinants of social affiliations, include Beatrice

Medicine's study of the Sioux system of the "reciprocity family model" and Keith Thor Carlson's "Stó:lō Exchange Dynamics." See Beatrice Medicine, "American Indian Family: Cultural Change and Adaptive Strategies," *Journal of Ethnic Studies* 18, no. 4 (Winter 1981): 17; and Keith Thor Carlson, "Stó:lō Exchange Dynamics," *Native Studies Review* 11, no. 1 (1997): 5.

5. I borrow this term from anthropologist Clifford Geertz, "Thick Description: Toward an Interpretive Theory of Culture," in *The Interpretation of Cultures* (New York: Basic Books, 1973), 3.

6. See Robert Longpré, *Ile-a-la-Crosse, 1776–1976: Sakitawak Bi-centennial* (Ile-a-la-Crosse, SK: Ile-a-la-Crosse Bi-Centennial Committee, 1977); and Macdougall, *One of the Family.*

7. Robert Jarvenpa and Hetty Jo Brumbach, "The Microeconomics of Southern Chipewyan Fur Trade History," in *The Subarctic Fur Trade: Native Social and Economic Adaptations*, ed. Shepard Krech, III (Vancouver: University of British Columbia Press, 1984), 152; and James G.E. Smith, "Chipewyan," in *Handbook of North American Indians*, vol. 6, *Subarctic*, ed. June Helm (Washington, DC: Smithsonian Institution, 1981), 271. The more northern Dene groups were called *hoteladi* by the southerners but the separation between these regional groups was neither rigid nor inflexible. Throughout the north, southern and more northern Dene groups occupied overlapping wintering ranges, intermarried, and forged close kinship ties between families and communities, thereby allowing for considerable mobility between regional groups.

8. Beryl C. Gillespie, "Changes in the Territory and Technology of the Chipewyan," *Arctic Anthropology* 13, no. 1 (1976): 6.

9. M. Rossignol, "Property Concepts among the Cree of the Rocks," *Primitive Man* 12, no. 3 (July 1939): 61; and James G.E. Smith, "Western Woods Cree," in Helm, *Handbook of North American Indians*, vol. 6, *Subarctic*, 267.

10. Jarvenpa and Brumbach, "The Microeconomics of Southern Chipewyan Fur Trade History," 148; and Smith, "Western Woods Cree," 257.

11. Robert Jarvenpa and Hetty Jo Brumbach, "Occupational Status, Ethnicity, and Ecology: Metis Cree Adaptations in a Canadian Trading Frontier," *Human Ecology* 13, no. 3 (1985): 311. Dene women were more likely to form unions with traders further west. See Richard Slobodin, *Metis of the Mackenzie District* (Ottawa: Canadian Research Centre for Anthropology, Saint-Paul University, 1966).

12. See Gillespie, "Changes in the Territory and Technology of the Chipewyan."

13. Richard White, *The Roots of Dependency: Subsistence, Environment, and Social Change among the Choctaws, Pawnees, and Navajos* (Lincoln: University of Nebraska Press, 1983), 176.

14. Smith, "Western Woods Cree," 259; Smith, "Chipewyan," 276; James G.E. Smith, "The Chipewyan Hunting Group in a Village Context," *The Western Canadian Journal of Anthropology* 2, no. 1 (1970): 62; and James G.E. Smith, "Economic Uncertainty in an 'Original Affluent Society': Caribou and Caribou Eater Chipewyan Adaptive Strategies," *Arctic Anthropology*, 15, no. 1 (1978): 75. See also Regina Flannery, "The Position of Women among the Eastern Cree," *Primitive Man* 8, no. 4 (October 1934): 86; A.D. Fisher, "The Cree of Canada: Some Ecological and Evolutionary Considerations," *The Western Canadian Journal of Anthropology* 1, no. 1 (1969): 14; and J.M. Penard, "Land Ownership and Chieftaincy among the Chippewayan and Caribou-Eaters," *Primitive Man* 2, nos. 1 and 2 (January–April 1929): 21.

15. Rossignol, "Property Concepts," 68; and Penard, "Land Ownership and Chieftaincy," 42.

16. Rossignol, "Property Concepts," 65.

17. Penard, "Land Ownership and Chieftaincy," 23.

18. Adoption and, later, godparentage constituted other ways of establishing kin relationships. See Macdougall, *One of the Family*, 82–83; and Kerry Abel, *Drum Songs: Glimpses of Dene History* (Montreal: McGill-Queen's University Press, 2005), 20. Prisoners of war were also sometimes brought into kin relationships. See J.R. Miller, *Compact, Contract, Covenant: Aboriginal Treaty-Making in Canada* (Toronto: University of Toronto Press, 2009), 8.

19. Smith, "Economic Uncertainty in an 'Original Affluent Society,'" 79; Smith, "Western Woods Cree," 259; and Smith, "Chipewyan," 277.

20. Beyond the *ellotine*, individuals also identified with the larger Chipewyan "nation" that was distinct from other Athapaskan and other indigenous and non-indigenous groups. According to Smith, the Inuit are called *otel'ena*, "enemy of the barrens," the Cree are *ena*, or "enemy," Euro-Canadians are known as Өe'otine, "people of the stone house," and Euro-Americans are called *Bes-cok*, or "big knives." See Smith, "Economic Uncertainty in an 'Original Affluent Society,'" 75–76; and Smith, "Western Woods Cree," 260. See also Abel, *Drum Songs*, 18–19; and Henry Stephen Sharp, "The Kinship System of the Black Lake Chipewyan" (PHD diss., Duke University, 1973).

21. Smith, "Western Woods Cree," 259–60.

22. Rossignol, "Property Concepts," 69. See also Smith, "Western Woods Cree," 260.

23. See Aldona Jonaitis, ed., *Chiefly Feasts: The Enduring Kwakiutl Potlatch* (Vancouver: Douglas & McIntyre, 1991); and Christopher Bracken, *The Potlatch Papers: A Colonial Case History* (Chicago: University of Chicago Press, 1997).

24. Rossignol, "Property Concepts," 63.

25. For an ethnographic discussion of the ecological significance of sharing, see Wayne Suttles, *Coast Salish Essays* (Seattle: University of Washington Press, 1987).

26. Canada, Department of Indian and Northern Affairs, RG10-C-VI, 1956–1959. Social Welfare, Saskatchewan—The 4P File: Policy, Principles, Procedure, Practice. Circular no. 10.1: 1–2.

27. Canada, Department of Indian and Northern Affairs, RG10-C-VI, 1956–1959. Social Welfare, Saskatchewan—The 4P File: Policy, Principles, Procedure, Practice. Circular no. 10.1: 1–2.

28. Smith, "The Chipewyan Hunting Group," 63; and Smith, "Chipewyan," 276.

29. Rossignol, "Property Concepts," 65, 68–69.

30. See Tom Johnson, "Without the Family We Are Nothing," in *Native Heritage: Personal Accounts by American Indians, 1790 to Present*, ed. Arlene Hirschfelder (New York: Macmillan, 1995).

31. Canada, Department of Indian and Northern Affairs, RG10-C-VI, 1956–1959. Social Welfare, Saskatchewan—The 4P File: Policy, Principles, Procedure, Practice. Circular no. 10.1: 2, 4–5.

32. See Marshall Sahlins, *Stone Age Economics* (Chicago: Aldine-Atherton, 1972).

33. Mallon, *Peasant and Nation*, 11–12. See also Carlson, *The Power of Place, the Problem of Time*.

34. Arthur Ray, "Reflections on Fur Trade Social History and Métis History in Canada," *American Indian Culture and Research Journal* 6, no. 2 (1982): 102–03. See also Van Kirk, *Many Tender Ties*; and Brown, *Strangers in Blood*.

35. See Macdougall, *One of the Family*, 177.

36. See Liam Haggarty, "Métis Welfare: A History of Economic Exchange in Northwest Saskatchewan." *Saskatchewan History* 61, no. 2 (Fall 2009): 7–17.

37. Fisher, "The Cree of Canada," 15. See also Arthur Ray, Jim Miller and Frank Tough, *Bounty and Benevolence: A History of the Saskatchewan Treaties* (Montreal: McGill-Queen's University Press, 2000), 92–93; and Miller, *Compact, Contract, Covenant*, 8–10, 286.

38. Hudson's Bay Company Archives, B.89/d/82–162, Île à la Crosse Account Books, 1853–1872; Hudson's Bay Company Archives, B.89/a/4–35, Île à la Crosse Post Journals, 1819–1865.

39. Ray, Miller, and Tough, *Bounty and Benevolence*, 13.

40. Hudson's Bay Company Archives, B.89/d/159–162, Île à la Crosse Account Books, 1869–1872.

41. Macdougall, *One of the Family*, 226–28. Safeguarding against competition suggests that economic pragmatism, as well as a feudal sense of *noblesse oblige*, also contributed to ongoing relief efforts.

42. See Ray, Miller, and Tough, *Bounty and Benevolence*, 92–93; Miller, *Compact, Contract, Covenant*, 8–10, 286; and Fisher, "The Cree of Canada," 15.

43. Macdougall, *One of the Family*, 271–72.

44. Macdougall, *One of the Family*, 140–48. See also Timothy P. Foran, "'Les gens de cette place': Oblates and the Evolving Concept of Métis at Île-à-Crosse, 1845–1898" (PHD diss., University of Ottawa, 2011).

45. Jarvenpa and Brumbach, "The Microeconomics of Southern Chipewyan Fur Trade History," 153–54. The northern cycle reached as far south as Cree Lake, a major gathering site where the two cycles met and people from both were able to socialize, intermarry and affirm kin ties. According to Bell, the cycles acted like a gear with the northern one operating in a clockwise fashion and the southern cycle rotating counter-clockwise. This overlapping system began to break down around the 1870s as increased pressures from religious officials and the emergence of secondary posts interrupted migration patterns and stressed a more sedentary lifestyle.

46. Smith, "Western Woods Cree," 258, 264–65; and Smith, "Chipewyan," 280.

47. In addition to "Imported food" and "Clothing/textiles," the other categories listed by Jarvenpa and Brumbach are "Productive technology," "Domestic technology," "Personal" and "Unknown."

48. Jarvenpa and Brumbach, "Occupational Status, Ethnicity, and Ecology." See also Philip T. Spaulding, "The Metis of Ile-a-la-Crosse" (PHD diss., University of Washington, 1970), 96–98.

49. Lutz, *Makúk*.

50. See, for example, Richard B. Lee and Richard Daly, eds., *The Cambridge Encyclopedia of Hunters and Gatherers* (Cambridge: Cambridge University Press, 1999); and Steven King and Alannah Tomkin, eds., *The Poor in England, 1700–1850: An Economy of Makeshifts* (Manchester: Manchester University Press, 2003).

51. Other examples of indigenous groups balancing the fur trade and other novel economic opportunities with existing pursuits are evident in Daniel Francis and Toby Morantz, *Partners in Fur: A History of the James Bay Fur Trade* (Montreal and Kingston: McGill-Queen's University Press, 1983); Frank Tough, *"As Their Natural Resources Fail": Native Peoples and the Economic History of Northern Manitoba* (Vancouver: University of British Columbia Press, 1996); and Richard Mackie, *Trading Beyond the Mountains: The British Fur Trade in the Pacific, 1793–1843* (Vancouver: University of British Columbia Press, 1997).

52. For a longer discussion of mimicry, and hybridity as well, see Homi Bhabha, *The Location of Culture* (New York: Routledge, 1994).

53. See Foran, "'Les gens de cette place.'"

54. Macdougall, *One of the Family*, 44–45.

55. Macdougall, *One of the Family*, 7–8. In his broader study of subarctic Canadian Métis populations, anthropologist Richard Slobodin also found strong evidence of cultural continuity as well as distinct cultural traits based on kin ties, sharing and reciprocity. Household composition and family structure, for example, were "only marginally different from those of the [Cree and Dene] peoples among whom Métis reside; in some instances, they are not different at all." Marriages also continued to be arranged, and basic social groupings and kinship patterns were largely congruent, though the nuclear family, so important among non-indigenous people, often took precedence over the hunting group. What separates Métis people from other northern groups, Slobodin argues, is their participation in "a distinct communication network" based on kin ties and sharing networks: "In the North, with its small and relatively mobile population, people are linked over great distances by kinship ties, friendship, acquaintance, and shared occupational interests. The dynamic concomitants of these bonds are patterns of communication formed and maintained by travel, visiting, message- and gift-exchange which are fairly distinctive for Indians, western Eskimos, Whites, and Métis. For the Métis of the region, it has been possible to trace a series of communication circuits, analogous to sociometric patterns, which together form an interlinked network extending from the northern prairie provinces well into Alaska. The Métis communication network, owing its existence to common interests and a consciousness of kind, in turn functions to maintain these." So important in fact was this "long distance sociability" that Slobodin considered it a criterion of Métis ethnicity. See Richard Slobodin, "Subarctic Métis," in Helm, *Handbook of North American Indians*, vol. 6, *Subarctic*, 362–64;

and Richard Slobodin, "The Subarctic Métis as Products and Agents of Culture Contact," *Arctic Anthropology* 2, no. 2 (1964): 50.

56. Smith, "Western Woods Cree," 264.

57. Quoted in Ray, *Indians in the Fur Trade*, 4-5.

58. See Foran, "'Les gens de cette place,'" 130-31.

59. Smith, "Western Woods Cree," 259.

60. Fisher, "The Cree of Canada," 64.

61. Smith, "The Chipewyan Hunting Group," 65; and Smith, "Chipewyan," 282.

62. Ray, "Reflections on Fur Trade Social History," 104.

63. Rossignol, "Property Concepts," 69-70.

64. Jules Daigneault, interviewed in Buffalo Narrows by Liam Haggarty and Stephanie Danyluk, 10 June 2010.

65. Jules Daigneault, interviewed in Buffalo Narrows by Liam Haggarty and Stephanie Danyluk, 10 June 2010.

66. George Malboeuf, interviewed in Buffalo Narrows by Liam Haggarty, 23 March 2010.

67. Brian MacDonald, interviewed in Buffalo Narrows by Liam Haggarty, 24 March 2010.

68. Brian MacDonald, interviewed in Buffalo Narrows by Liam Haggarty, 24 March 2010.

69. Brian MacDonald, interviewed in Buffalo Narrows by Liam Haggarty, 24 March 2010.

70. Smith, "The Chipewyan Hunting Group," 65.

71. James Waldram, "The 'Other Side': Ethnostatus Distinctions in Western Subarctic Native Communities," in *1885 and After: Native Society in Transition*, ed. F. Laurie Barron and James Waldram (Regina: Canadian Plains Research Center, 1986), 280.

Bibliography

Interviews

Daigneault, Jules. Interviewed in Buffalo Narrows by Liam Haggarty and Stephanie Danyluk, 10 June 2010.

MacDonald, Brian. Interviewed in Buffalo Narrows by Liam Haggarty, 24 March 2010.

Malboeuf, George. Interviewed in Buffalo Narrows by Liam Haggarty, 23 March 2010.

Archival Sources

Canada, Department of Indian and Northern Affairs, RG10-C-VI, 1956–1959. Social
Welfare, Saskatchewan—The 4P File: Policy, Principles, Procedure, Practice.
Circular no. 10.1: 1–2.

Hudson's Bay Company Archives, B.89/d/82–162, Île à la Crosse Account Books,
1853–1872.

Hudson's Bay Company Archives, B.89/d/159–162, Île à la Crosse Account Books,
1869–1872.

Hudson's Bay Company Archives, B.89/a/4–35, Île à la Crosse Post Journals, 1819–1865.

Secondary Sources

Abel, Kerry. *Drum Songs: Glimpses of Dene History*. Montreal: McGill-Queen's University
Press, 2005.

Basso, Keith. *Wisdom Sits in Places: Landscape and Language among the Western Apache*.
Albuquerque: University of New Mexico Press, 1996.

Bhabha, Homi. *The Location of Culture*. New York: Routledge, 1994.

Bracken, Christopher. *The Potlatch Papers: A Colonial Case History*. Chicago: University
of Chicago Press, 1997.

Brown, Jennifer. *Strangers in Blood: Fur Trade Company Families in Indian Country*.
Vancouver: University of British Columbia Press, 1980.

Carlson, Keith Thor. *The Power of Place, the Problem of Time: A Study of Aboriginal History
and Collective Identity along the Lower Fraser River*. Toronto: University of Toronto
Press, 2011.

———. "Stó:lō Exchange Dynamics." *Native Studies Review* 11, no. 1 (1997): 5–48.

Cruikshank, Julie. *Do Glaciers Listen? Local Knowledge, Colonial Encounters, and Social
Imagination*. Vancouver: University of British Columbia Press, 2005.

Geertz, Clifford. "Thick Description: Toward an Interpretive Theory of Culture." In *The
Interpretation of Cultures*. New York: Basic Books, 1973.

Gillespie, Beryl. "Changes in the Territory and Technology of the Chipewyan." *Arctic
Anthropology* 13, no. 1 (1976): 6–11.

Giraud, Marcel. *The Métis in the Canadian West*. Translated by George Woodcock. 2 vols.
Edmonton and Lincoln: University of Alberta Press and University of Nebraska
Press, 1986.

Ens, Gerhard. *Homeland to Hinterland: The Changing Worlds of the Red River Metis in the
Nineteenth Century*. Toronto: University of Toronto Press, 1996.

Fisher, A.D. "The Cree of Canada: Some Ecological and Evolutionary Considerations." *The Western Canadian Journal of Anthropology* 1, no. 1 (1969): 7–17.

Flanagan, Thomas. *Louis 'David' Riel: Prophet of the New World*. Toronto: University of Toronto Press, 1979.

Flannery, Regina. "The Position of Women among the Eastern Cree." *Primitive Man* 8, no. 4 (October 1934): 81–86.

Foran, Timothy P. "'Les gens de cette place': Oblates and the Evolving Concept of Métis at Île-à-Crosse, 1845–1898." PHD diss., University of Ottawa, 2011.

Francis, Daniel, and Toby Morantz. *Partners in Fur: A History of the James Bay Fur Trade*. Montreal and Kingston: McGill-Queen's University Press, 1983.

Gillespie, Beryl C. "Changes in the Territory and Technology of the Chipewyan." *Arctic Anthropology* 13, no. 1 (1976): 6–11.

Haggarty, Liam. "Métis Welfare: A History of Economic Exchange in Northwest Saskatchewan." *Saskatchewan History* 61, no. 2 (Fall 2009): 7–17.

Helm, June, ed. *Handbook of North American Indians*. Vol. 6, *Subarctic*. Washington, DC: Smithsonian Institution, 1981.

Jarvenpa, Robert, and Hetty Jo Brumbach. "The Microeconomics of Southern Chipewyan Fur Trade History." In *The Subarctic Fur Trade: Native Social and Economic Adaptations*, edited by Shepard Krech, III, 147–83. Vancouver: University of British Columbia Press, 1984.

———. "Occupational Status, Ethnicity, and Ecology: Metis Cree Adaptations in a Canadian Trading Frontier." *Human Ecology* 13, no. 3 (1985): 309–29.

Johnson, Tom. "Without the Family We Are Nothing." In *Native Heritage: Personal Accounts by American Indians, 1790 to Present*, edited by Arlene Hirschfelder, 7–29. New York: Macmillan, 1995.

Jonaitis, Aldona, ed. *Chiefly Feasts: The Enduring Kwakiutl Potlatch*. Vancouver: Douglas & McIntyre, 1991.

King, Steven, and Alannah Tomkin, eds., *The Poor in England, 1700–1850: An Economy of Makeshifts*. Manchester: Manchester University Press, 2003.

Lee, Richard B., and Richard Daly, eds. *The Cambridge Encyclopedia of Hunters and Gatherers*. Cambridge: Cambridge University Press, 1999.

Longpré, Robert. *Ile-a-la-Crosse, 1776–1976: Sakitawak Bi-centennial*. Ile-a-la-Crosse, SK: Ile-a-la-Crosse Bi-Centennial Committee, 1977.

Lutz, John. *Makúk: A New History of Aboriginal-White Relations*. Vancouver: University of British Columbia Press, 2008.

Macdougall, Brenda. *One of the Family: Métis Culture in Nineteenth-Century Northwestern Saskatchewan*. Vancouver: University of British Columbia Press, 2010.

Mackie, Richard. *Trading Beyond the Mountains: The British Fur Trade in the Pacific, 1793–1843*. Vancouver: University of British Columbia Press, 1997.

Mallon, Florencia E. *Courage Tastes of Blood: The Mapuche Community of Nicolás Ailío and the Chilean State, 1906–2001*. Durham, NC: Duke University Press, 2005.

———. *Peasant and Nation: The Making of Postcolonial Mexico and Peru*. Berkeley: University of California Press, 1995.

Medicine, Beatrice. "American Indian Family." *Journal of Ethnic Studies* 18, no. 4 (Winter 1981): 13–23.

Miller, J.R. *Compact, Contract, Covenant: Aboriginal Treaty-Making in Canada*. Toronto: University of Toronto Press, 2009.

Morton, W.L. *Manitoba: A History*. Toronto: University of Toronto Press, 1967.

Penard, J.M. "Land Ownership and Chieftaincy among the Chippewayan and Caribou-Eaters." *Primitive Man* 2, nos. 1 and 2 (January–April 1929): 20–24.

Peterson, Jacqueline, and Jennifer S.H. Brown, eds. *The New Peoples: Being and Becoming Métis in North America*. Winnipeg: University of Manitoba Press, 1985.

Ray, Arthur. "Reflections on Fur Trade Social History and Métis History in Canada." *American Indian Culture and Research Journal* 6, no. 2 (1982): 92–107.

Ray, Arthur, Jim Miller and Frank Tough. *Bounty and Benevolence: A History of the Saskatchewan Treaties*. Montreal: McGill-Queen's University Press, 2000.

Rossignol, M. "Property Concepts Among the Cree of the Rocks." *Primitive Man* 12, no. 3 (July 1939): 61–70.

Sahlins, Marshall. *Stone Age Economics*. Chicago: Aldine-Atherton, 1972.

Sharp, Henry Stephen. "The Kinship System of the Black Lake Chipewyan." PHD diss., Duke University, 1973.

Slobodin, Richard. *Metis of the Mackenzie District*. Ottawa: Canadian Research Centre for Anthropology, Saint-Paul University, 1966.

———. "Subarctic Métis." In Helm, *Handbook of North American Indians*, 361–71.

Smith, James G.E. "Chipewyan." In Helm, *Handbook of North American Indians*, 271–84.

———. "The Chipewyan Hunting Group in a Village Context." *The Western Canadian Journal of Anthropology* 2, no. 1 (1970): 60–66.

———. "Economic Uncertainty in an 'Original Affluent Society': Caribou and Caribou Eater Chipewyan Adaptive Strategies." *Arctic Anthropology* 15, no. 1 (1978): 68–88.

———. "Western Woods Cree." In Helm, *Handbook of North American Indians*, 256–70.

Spaulding, Philip T. "The Metis of Ile-a-la-Crosse." PHD diss., University of Washington, 1970.

Sprague, D.N. *Canada and the Métis, 1869–1885*. Waterloo, ON: Wilfrid Laurier University Press, 1988.

Stanley, G.F.G. *The Birth of Western Canada*. Toronto: University of Toronto Press, 1961.

Stevenson [Wheeler], Winona. "'Ethnic' Assimilates 'Indigenous': A Study in Intellectual Colonialism." *Wicazo Sa Review* 13, no. 1 (Spring 1998): 33–51.

Suttles, Wayne. *Coast Salish Essays*. Seattle: University of Washington Press, 1987.

Tough, Frank. *"As Their Natural Resources Fail": Native Peoples and the Economic History of Northern Manitoba*. Vancouver: University of British Columbia Press, 1996.

Van Kirk, Sylvia. *Many Tender Ties: Women in Fur-Trade Society, 1670–1870*. Winnipeg: Watson & Dwyer, 1980.

Waldram, James. "The 'Other Side': Ethnostatus Distinctions in Western Subarctic Native Communities." In *1885 and After: Native Society in Transition*, edited by F. Laurie Barron and James Waldram, 279–95 Regina: Canadian Plains Research Center, 1986.

White, Richard. *The Roots of Dependency: Subsistence, Environment, and Social Change among the Choctaws, Pawnees, and Navajos*. Lincoln: University of Nebraska Press, 1983.

Woodcock, George. *Gabriel Dumont: The Métis Chief and his Lost World*. Edmonton: Hurtig Publishers, 1975.

Newly Discovered Writings of Louis Riel | 6

GLEN CAMPBELL & TOM FLANAGAN

BECAUSE LOUIS RIEL is probably the best-known figure in Canadian history, scholars, students of history and Métis political activists are keenly interested in everything he wrote. Under the leadership of the eminent historian George Stanley, we were part of the team that in 1985 published *The Collected Writings of Louis Riel/Les Écrits complets de Louis Riel*.[1] This five-volume set contained all of Riel's writings that had been discovered up to that point. But time marches on, and scholarship with it, leading to the discovery and publication of several new Riel texts in subsequent years.[2] Now we present a few more manuscripts that have recently come to light: a letter by Louis Riel to his patron Sophie Masson, 30 December 1858; a letter by Riel to John Bruce, president of the Comité National des Métis de la Rivière Rouge, 19 October 1869; a letter by Riel to his former schoolmate, the poet Eustache Prud'homme, 14 December 1869; and a set of short English poems that Riel composed while imprisoned in Regina in 1885.[3]

Louis Riel to Sophie Masson, 30 December 1858
This letter is particularly interesting because it is the earliest production from the hand of Louis Riel; he was barely 14 when he composed this

letter to the woman who was helping to pay his expenses to study at the College of Montreal. The earliest text previously known was a similar letter from Riel to Sophie Masson, written 29 December 1861, when he was 17.[4] Researchers will note that the orthography of the 1861 letter is more polished than that of the 1858 letter, showing the advantage of three years of instruction at the College of Montreal.

When we were doing the research for *The Collected Writings of Louis Riel*, George Stanley arranged for Major Henri Masson to give us photocopies of eight Riel texts in what was then the private collection of the Masson family.[5] For some reason, this body of material did not include the letter to Sophie Masson, 30 December 1858, published here for the first time. That letter was discovered when the Masson family gave its papers to the Société historique de Saint-Boniface in fall 2009. The manuscript can now be viewed online on the Société's website.[6] We print it here but not the other Masson letters, because they were included in *The Collected Writings of Louis Riel*.[7]

A.-A. Taché, Bishop of St. Boniface from 1853 onwards, made great efforts to bring missionaries from Quebec and France to the North-West. He also nourished dreams of ordaining young native men to become Catholic priests. Toward that end, he arranged in 1858 for four young Métis boys—Louis Riel, Daniel McDougall, Louis Schmidt and Joseph Nolin—to attend school in Quebec. Nolin did not go, but the other three travelled east in the summer of 1858, arriving in Montreal on July 5. McDougall was to attend the college at Nicollet, Schmidt would go to St. Hyacinthe, and Riel would study at the Sulpician College of Montreal.[8]

According to George Stanley, the colleges had agreed to educate the boys for free.[9] However, although the details are not clear, Sophie Masson, the Seigneuresse of Terrebonne, was also involved in the equation. She was already helping Riel's father to purchase a textile mill for installation at Red River; indeed, the younger Riel met his father travelling west with the machinery when he was travelling east to Quebec.[10] Starting with the 1858 letter, Riel would repeatedly write to Sophie Masson in highly emotional terms, thanking her for her protection and generosity. He spoke of having visited her, and how she had encouraged him to think of her as a mother because he was so far removed from his natural parents.[11] In another letter he thanked her for the presents she had sent him through her commercial agent, John Atkinson.[12] It is also possible that, either directly or indirectly, she was helping to pay Riel's fees at the College of Montreal, but we have no real evidence on this point.

Riel's name appears in a four-page document listing the College of Montreal students who were recipients of scholarships offered by the Saint-Sulpice Seminary in 1861–1862. Riel's expenses are detailed as follows, in pounds, shillings, and pence:

Room and board	£21/10/0
Clothing	£16/11/1
12 months laundry	£3/0/0
Books and supplies	£1/10/0
Total	£42/11/1

No individual sponsor names are indicated on the document; the Seminary is listed as the sole benefactor.[13]

When Riel wrote this letter to Mme Masson, he was probably staying with his aunt and uncle, Lucie and John Lee, at their home in Mile End, then a suburb of Montreal, now an inner-city neighbourhood. When Riel was not at the College, he sometimes stayed at the convent of the Grey Nuns, but it seems likely he would have been with his relatives for the Christmas and New Year's season.

The letter does not contain any information about historical events, but we can learn quite a bit about Riel by studying it carefully. Remembering that he was only 14 when he wrote it, go to the illustrations to compare the penmanship of this letter with that of his letter to Eustache Prud'homme, written ten and a half years later. This letter shows the still slightly rounded, conventional script of a boy on the verge of adolescence, while the later letter exhibits the forceful, flowing handwriting of a confident, mature man.

Look also at the orthography of the 1858 letter. It contains some errors ("avez fais," "avez daignez") that Riel would never have made later in life. These are phonetic spellings, characteristic of native speakers who have not yet had enough formal education to master all the complexities of French orthography. They help explain why Riel was generally ranked in the lower half of his class during his first year at the College, 1858–1859. But he learned quickly and moved close to the top of his class thereafter.[14] The mature Riel would write almost entirely correct French, marred only by a few archaic spellings that he had assimilated, such as "abyme" (for "abîme") and "plustôt" (for "plutôt"). Though he was a Métis boy from Red River with only a sketchy primary education, his native ability coupled with Sulpician discipline soon made him the equal of anyone in Quebec in his use of the French language.

The reader will also note in this letter a certain exaltation of style, bordering on the grandiloquent. Riel repeatedly refers to Mme Masson as "Noble dame" and himself as "pauvre" and "misérable." This was not just the overreach of a boy trying to write an adult letter. Riel grew up to be an emotional man who expressed himself in strong, sometimes exaggerated language. We can see some of these traits already present in the 14-year-old boy.

Transcription

À Madame Masson.
Montréal 30 Décembre 1858

Très respectable dame.
Excusez s'il vous plait, Noble dame, un pauvre et misérable élève, qui, dans la simplicité de son intelligence, prend la liberté d'addresser · [15] *à une aussi honorable Dame que vous quelques paroles qui puissent vous signifier le respect et*

la reconnaissance dont son esprits · est naturellement sensé d'avoir pour vous.

*Oh! vous Noble Dame, qui, dans votre grandeur d'âme avez fais · tant de bien-
faits à celui qui, après Dieu, est l'objet de mon tendre amour et qui avez même
daignez · en faire à moi-même qui pourrait me suggérer des paroles et des
termes qui puissent vous témoigner ma Reconnaissance? Comme je ne pourrais
jamais vous rendre de tels bienfaits, je vous addresserai · une parole qui comme
vous savez sort de la bouche d'un pauvre misérable. C'est Très honorable dame
que j'addresse · et j'addresserai · tous les jours de ma pauvre vie de ferventes
prières ou du moins tant que je pourrai m'exciter à la ferveur, oui des prières
afin que Dieu veuille bien vous rendre dans l'autre vie les bienfaits dont vous
vous remplissez de votre généreuse main ici-bas.*

*Cela c'est là dans la céleste patrie que nous nous réjouirons tous ensemble
dans le seigneur si nous avons le bonheur d'y parvenir un jour. Toujours en vous
témoignant la plus grande reconnaissance et le plus grand respect. Encore une
fois je ne vous oublirai · jamais dans mes prières.*

Je suis toujours
un des vos plus humbles serviteurs
Louis Riel-fils[16]

Translation

To Madame Masson.
Montreal 30 December 1858

Most Worthy Lady.
*Noble Lady, please excuse a poor and miserable student who, in the naivety of
his understanding, is so bold as to address an Honourable Lady such as you a
few words which might express to you the respect and gratitude that his mind is
naturally supposed to have for you. Oh! You Noble Lady, who in your generosity
of spirit have been so kind to the one who, after God, is the object of my tender
love*[17] *and who has even deigned to do the same for myself, who could suggest*

words and expressions that might express my gratitude? Since I could never

repay such kindness, I will give you my word that as you know comes from the

mouth of a poor wretch. It is, Most Honorable Lady, that I am offering and will

continue to offer my devout prayers every day of my poor life, or at least as long

as I am able to kindle my devotion, yes prayers so that God may give back to

you in the afterlife all the kindness of your earthly generosity.

It is in our heavenly home that we will all rejoice together in our Lord if

we have the good fortune to reach there one day. As always showing you the

greatest gratitude and the greatest respect. Once again I will never forget you

in my prayers.

I am forever
one of your most humble servants
Louis Riel—son

Letter to John Bruce, 19 October 1869

Our second letter was acquired in 2011 by the Société historique de Saint-Boniface from the heirs of Frank Larned Hunt.[18] Hunt was an American lawyer who came to Red River in 1860 and practiced law. When he retired, he moved to Poplar Point, where John Bruce also owned land;[19] perhaps that connection enabled Hunt to acquire this letter from Riel to Bruce. In any case, Hunt and Bruce must have known each other, for Hunt was a lawyer and Bruce was an informal legal advisor to Métis litigants and later was appointed a magistrate.[20]

Riel wrote this letter on October 19, 1869, in the midst of organizing the Métis against the entry into Red River of William McDougall, who had been sent by the government of Canada as the new governor of the colony. Riel put together an informal committee in September 1869, which was transformed into the Comité National des Métis de la Rivière Rouge on October 16. Riel became the secretary of the "National Committee" while nominating John Bruce as president. George Stanley called Bruce "an ill-educated, weak man,"[21] but that may be a little unfair.[22] Bruce did not last long as president, resigned on December 27, 1869, allegedly due to poor health.[23] He later became estranged from Riel, advocating the American annexation of Red River and testifying against Ambroise Lépine at his 1874 trial for the murder of Thomas Scott.[24]

The wording of the letter confirms that there must have been some tension between Riel and Bruce from the very beginning. Although Bruce was supposed to be president, it is Riel the secretary who appears to be calling the meeting.[25] Riel, therefore, reassured Bruce of his importance: "Je vous en donne connaissance pour vous prouver le respect et la déférence que je vous porte comme Président et ami." Whether or not Bruce actually suffered from ill health when he résigned as president in late December 1869, he must have felt from the beginning that he was, in Stanley's words, "a figurehead."[26]

Transcription

Monsieur John Bruce.

Cher Monsieur,
Il est neuf heures du soir. Je pars pour la pointe de chênes · tout de suite. Le Nouveau monde · du 2 octobre annonce le départ de McDougall pour ici.—Voudriez-vous, s'il vous plaît, venir demain soir chez Baptiste Amable afin d'aviser à une certaine organisation. J'envoie le même billet d'invitation à tous les représentants. Je vous en donne connaissance pour vous prouver le respect et la déférence que je vous porte comme Président et ami.

Celui qui vous estime sincèrement
Louis Riel.
St Vital 19 octobre 1869.

Translation

Mr. John Bruce.

Dear Sir,

It is nine o'clock in the evening. I am leaving immediately for La Pointe-des-Chênes.[27] Le Nouveau Monde[28] of October 2 announces McDougall's departure for here. — Would you please come to Baptiste Amable's[29] home tomorrow evening to tend to some organizing. I am sending the same invitation to all the representatives. I am informing you of this to show you the respect and regard which I have for you as President and friend.

One who holds you in sincere esteem
Louis Riel.
St. Vital October 19, 1869.

Louis Riel to Eustache Prud'homme, 14 December 1869

Our third letter, from Riel to the Quebec poet Eustache Prud'homme, was acquired by the University of Alberta Libraries in 2002 from the Montreal collectors Alfred Van Peteghem and David Ewens, who had purchased it at Iegor-Hôtel des Encans in Montreal. The letter is particularly interesting because it dates from the turbulent days of late 1869, and little from Riel's own hand has survived from that period. No report about the provenance of the letter is available, but in the absence of contrary information it is logical to suppose that it came from a descendant of Prud'homme.[30]

Riel wrote this letter on 14 December 1869, less than a week after he had taken control of the Red River Colony. It is worth briefly recalling the chronology of events.[31] On March 8, 1869, Canada had signed an agreement to purchase Rupert's Land, including the Red River Colony, from the Hudson's Bay Company. The residents of the territory were not consulted in the negotiations, and some of them, particularly the

French-speaking Métis, began to worry about their status under the prospective Canadian regime. Starting in August 1869, the young Riel, whose education at the College of Montreal had given him the tools of political leadership, quickly moved to the head of the Métis resistance. Riel ordered William McDougall, the governor sent out by Canada, not to enter Rupert's Land; he also organized meetings to draw up lists of rights that Canada would have to recognize before taking possession of the territory it had purchased.

On December 7 Riel made prisoners of most of the Canadians in the Colony because they wanted to help McDougall assume the reins of government. The next day, Riel declared a Provisional Government, justified by the grandiloquent "Declaration of the People of Rupert's Land and the North-West" (probably drafted by the missionary priest Georges Dugas).[32] Riel's letter to Prud'homme thus came at the height of his power, when he had just seized control and temporarily quelled opposition, and before the more serious conflict arose that led to the execution of Thomas Scott.

These circumstances help explain the ebullient tone of Riel's letter. "Dear friend, everything is going well here, everything!" he writes; "I have seized the right moment. Undoubtedly Heaven is thus offering me the very way to wipe out some unfortunate years. I have succeeded far beyond my dreams." At the same time, however, we detect a note of guilt intertwined with the exultation, when he writes that "pride is banished from my heart. I have already more than felt what its poison can do." He reassures himself that he is not giving in to pride by saying, "The goal of my ambition is to do good." He would use similar language two months later writing to William Dease, one of his rivals for leadership among the Métis: "No, there is no ambition in my heart, and if I can accomplish anything, I do it for everyone."[33]

We see here in Riel, when he is only 25 years old and wielding political power for the first time, an emotional syndrome that would dominate his career: desire for power and excitement in exercising it, a sense of guilt over giving in to the sin of pride, and an attempt to reconcile the two by telling himself that his ambition was only for the common good, not for his own selfish interest. These emotions would manifest themselves six years later in much more extreme form when Riel redefined himself as the "Prophet of the New World," endowed by God with a special mission to lead the Métis, the new Chosen People, in reviving religious fervour in North America.

Another important aspect of this letter is Riel's attempt to persuade his old school classmate, Eustache Prud'homme, to move to Red River: "We need learned, decent people! We lack well-educated people in the French-Canadian Métis population. Come if you want! I am in charge of almost everything here at present, and I will do all that I can for you. And by coming here, you will do the country and Lower Canada's cause a great favour." Riel also asks Prud'homme to encourage another schoolmate of theirs, Joseph Dubuc, to come to Manitoba: "Also, I would like you to share this letter with Dubuque [Dubuc]; I do not know where he is, but you must. He will do so much good here!"

In this effort to promote immigration, Riel was aligned with Archbishop Taché, who helped bring Dubuc, Joseph Royal, and Marc-Amable Girard to Red River in 1870.[34] All would go on to play leading roles in business, politics and cultural life among the French-speaking inhabitants of Manitoba. Another of Riel's mentors among the clergy, Father N.-J. Ritchot, also worked hard to promote francophone immigration to Manitoba, buying up land claims from the Métis who were moving further west and reselling them to immigrants from Quebec and France.[35]

In this connection, it is interesting that Riel portrays himself as French-Canadian, not Métis. "All I know is that above all I am French-Canadian! And that can give insight to my ideas and feelings." This statement was typical of Riel's views in these early years. In 1874, he wrote to the president of the Saint-Jean-Baptiste Society of Montreal: "The French-Canadian Metis of the North[-West] are a branch of the French-Canadian tree. They want to grow like that tree, with that tree; they never want to be separated from it, they want to suffer and rejoice with it."[36]

Later the same year he wrote to Father Ritchot about the necessity of promoting French immigration to Manitoba, to help the Métis adopt "more French-Canadian customs and traditions, so that while we call ourselves the Metis people, we may become in fact assimilated to the province of Quebec through education—without resistance or recalcitrance."[37] It was only with the onset of his prophetic mission at the end of 1875 that Riel moved on from French-Canadian nationalism to Métis nationalism.[38] From then on, he would often be severely critical of the French-Canadian elite in Manitoba, whom Taché, Ritchot and he had worked so hard to recruit.[39]

What of Eustache Prud'homme, to whom the letter is addressed? Prud'homme was born near Montreal in 1845. He began his classical studies with the Sulpician fathers at the College of Montreal in 1857. When Louis Riel arrived from St. Boniface in 1858, he became one of Prud'homme's classmates, and eventually a close friend.

We do not know if Prud'homme responded to the invitation to come to Red River, no such correspondence ever having been found in Riel's papers. However, just over two months after Riel wrote his letter, Prud'homme published, in the Montreal periodical *L'Opinion publique*, an article entitled "Louis Riel."[40] In it, he gives a short biography of his former classmate, commenting on his proud, noble and generous nature, and asserting that he was one of the most talented students in his class. He describes how the young Louis fascinated the College of Montreal students with tales, obviously well embellished, of his years on the prairies, living in the midst of native tribes, wild horses and bold hunters. He then goes on to describe the esteem in which the schoolboys held Riel and his scholarly abilities.

Records from the Saint-Sulpice Archives reveal that the two boys were very good students, and ranked consistently in the upper levels of their class. They were often in contention for prizes. In 1863, for example, Riel won first prize in English-to-French translation while Prud'homme won second prize in Latin-to-French translation. That same year, in the category of Latin discourse, Riel took top honours and Prud'homme came second. Interestingly, their schoolmate Joseph Dubuc, mentioned in Riel's letter, who was several years older than Riel and Prud'homme, also won prizes in many categories.[41]

In the article in *L'Opinion publique*, Prud'homme also speaks of his and Riel's love of poetry and their competitiveness in the "poetic arena," as both began composing verses during their years at the College. Prud'homme includes three poems found in Riel's "calepin de poésie," a notebook containing nearly three dozen poems penned by Louis between January 1864 and June 1866.[42] Although he does not have his friend's permission, declares Prud'homme, he assumes all responsibility for publication of the three poems in his article.[43]

In the holdings of the Saint-Sulpice Archives are two poems written by Prud'homme. They are addressed to "Monsieur le Directeur," Charles-Octave Lenoir, director of the College from 1859 to 1871.[44] Both poems, as one would expect, are full of praise for the director's guidance and devotion over the years. The first is dated 4 November 1862, date of the *fête* of Saint Charles Borromée and name-day of Lenoir, and is written on behalf of the students of the College ("nous" is used when addressing the director):

Amis chantons dans nos accords
Notre père plein de tendresse;
Et répétons dans nos transports
Les chants qu'inspire l'allégresse.[45]

The second, dated June 1865, and composed in the final month of Prud'homme's studies at the College, is more personal and expresses the gratitude and affection of an "élève respectueux." He prefaces his poem with the following: "Daignez recevoir cette petite pièce de poésie, écho bien faible, il est vrai, d'un coeur qui n'emportera que de doux souvenirs du collège, mais dont le retentissement provient d'une âme sincère et pleine de reconnaissance." The poem concludes with the following lines:

Avant de m'engager dans ces déserts terribles
J'emporte la science et les vertus paisibles
Que j'ai pu recueillir dans ce foyer pieux.
Oh! Soyez-en bénis, directeurs pleins de zèle!
Vos souvenirs ainsi qu'une étoile immortelle
Brilleront dans mon coeur comme elle brille aux cieux.[46]

As far as is known, Riel did not publish any of his poems himself; they were, however, often circulated among family and friends, or addressed to particular individuals. Unlike Riel, Prud'homme did publish his poetry. His first major foray in the public domain came in 1867 when he received an Honorable Mention in Laval University's literary competition with his poem "La découverte du Canada." In the same competition in 1868, he won the Silver Medal with his major poetic opus *Les Martyrs de la foi en Canada*, which was published the following year.[47] Although he published some 50 pieces of poetry in various French-Canadian periodicals, literary historians conclude that he never reached the stature of a great poet. These same critics concede nonetheless that he made a valid contribution to the literary renewal of 1860–1880.[48] Prud'homme's poetry deals with diverse themes, with religious and historical subjects, his homeland, and with contrasts between urban and rural life. It reveals his enchantment with nature as well as his fascination with the burgeoning Montreal metropolis.

Prud'homme studied law, and in 1868 became a notary, a profession that he would practice for the rest of his working life. He married in 1874, and lived in Montreal until his death in 1927.

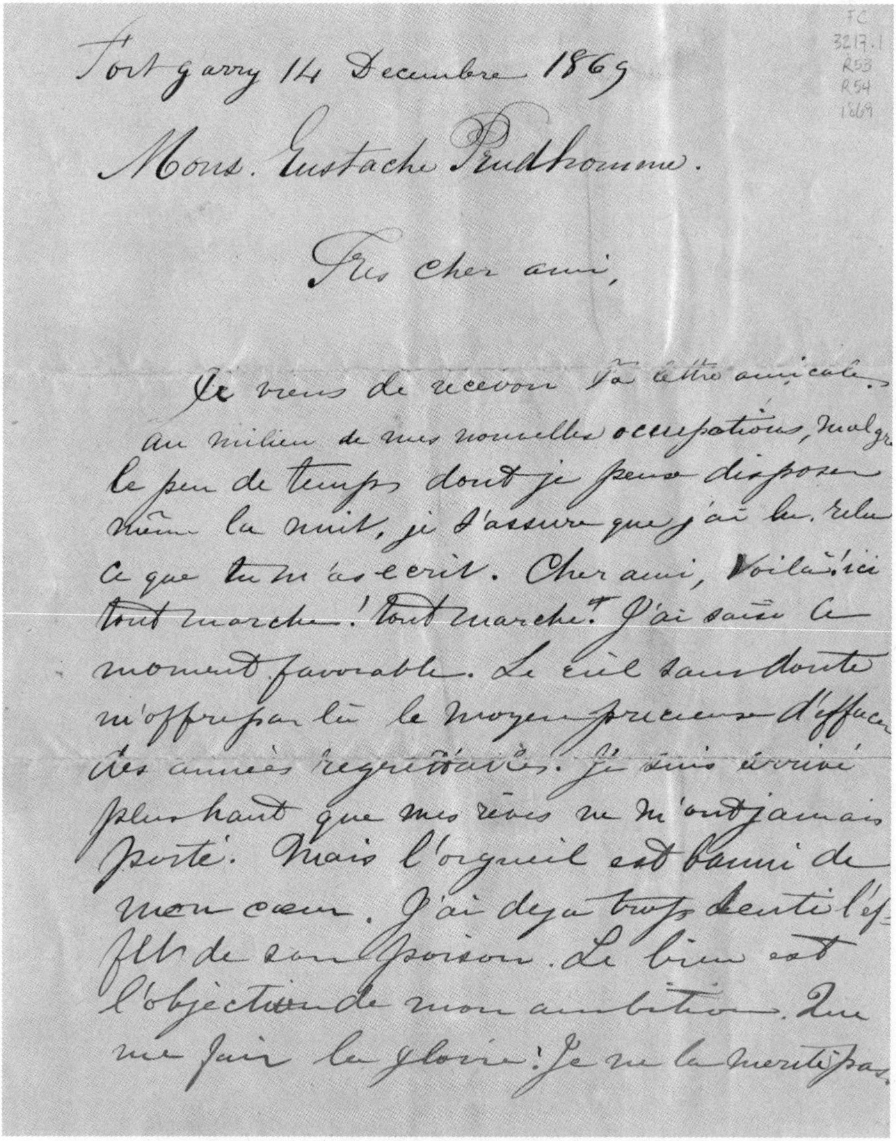

Fort Garry 14 Décembre 1869

Mons. Eustache Prud'homme.

Très cher ami,

Je viens de recevoir ta lettre amicale. Au milieu de mes nouvelles occupations, malgré le peu de temps dont je puis disposer même la nuit, je t'assure que j'ai bu relu ce que tu m'as écrit. Cher ami, Voilà ici tout marche! Tout marche! J'ai saisi le moment favorable. Le ciel sans doute m'offrira par là le moyen précieux d'effacer des années regrettables. Je suis arrivé plus haut que mes rêves ne m'ont jamais porté. Mais l'orgueil est banni de mon cœur. J'ai déjà trop senti l'effet de son poison. Le bien est l'objection de mon ambition. Que me fait la gloire! Je ne la mérite pas.

FIGURE 6.1 *Louis Riel, 1844–1885. [Letter] 14 déc. 1869, Fort Garry [to] Eustache Prud'homme, Montreal. 4 pages on 1 leaf. Courtesy of Bruce Peel Special Collections Library, University of Alberta.*

FC 3217.1 R53 R54 1869

qui me font les honneurs ? J'ai tant
été abreuvé déjà par les humiliations !
Cher ami, tu me parles de la Fortune !
Je n'ai pas un sou. Je suis indépendant, libre comme un oiseau. Et
c'est ce qui fait ma joie aujourd'hui.
Je n'ai que ma vie ! Je l'expose,
je la risque, je la mets partout en
avant ; heureux si je mourais pour
la justice, l'honneur et mon pays.
Je sais bien que Dieu serait aussi
plus disposé à avoir pitié de moi !
Et toi aussi tu as une fortune ! Quelle
fortune ? Presque comme la mienne
peut-être, mais veux-tu que je te
dise ? Avant longtemps il y aura
ici de l'argent en masse.

Je ne puis pas te dire : viens ici tu feras de l'argent. Mais voici : nous avons besoin de gens instruits, d'honnêtes personnes.' Nous manquons de personnes instruites parmi la population Mtis Canadienne Française. Viens si tu veux.' Je conduis à peu près tout ici pour le présent : et je ferai tout ce que je pourrai pour toi. Et toi, en venant ici, tu rendras au pays à la cause du Bas-Canada un grand service. ah! Si Monsieur Cartier eut fait plustôt attention aux insinuations de ma faible voix.'.... Il est peut-être encore temps.'....

Tout ce que je sais, c'est qu'avant tout Je suis Canadien Français.' Et cela peut montrer la direction de mes idées et de

mes sentiments. — Je voudrais aussi que
tu montrasses cette lettre a Dubuque; je
ne sais où il est; mais tu dois le savoir.
Ici, il fera tout debien! Il y aurait
bien quelques petits sacrifices a faire
pour commencer! Sacrifier; c'est a dire
ne pas être récompensé, rémunéré peut
être autant qu'on le mériterait. Mais il
y a ici un grand complot. Et tout ceux
qui y mettront la main passeront à
l'immortalité! Je ne mens pas! La Rivière
Rouge est un vaste theatre. Il s'y passe
des évènements qui feront mémoire dans
l'histoire d'Albion.

Cher ami   je suis et serai pour
                    la vie

Ton tout devoué ami
Louis Riel.

265

Fort garry · 14 Décembre 1869
Mons. Eustache Prudhomme.

Très cher ami,

Je viens de recevoir ta lettre amicale. Au milieu des mes nouvelles occupations,
malgré le peu de temps dont je peux disposer même la nuit, je t'assure que j'ai
lu, relu ce que tu m'as écrit. Cher ami, Voilà! ici tout marche! tout marche! J'ai
saisi le moment favorable. Le ciel sans doute m'offre par là le moyen précieux
d'effacer des années regrettables. Je suis arrivé plus haut que mes rêves ne
m'ont jamais porté. Mais l'orgueil est banni de mon coeur. J'ai déjà trop senti
l'effet de son poison. Le bien est l'objective · de mon ambition. Que me fait la
gloire? Je ne la mérite pas.

Que me font les honneurs? J'ai tant été abreuvé déjà par les humiliations!
Cher ami, tu me parles de la Fortune! Je n'ai pas un sou. Je suis indépendant,
libre comme un oiseau. Et c'est ce qui fait ma force aujourd'hui. Je n'ai que ma
vie! Je l'expose! Je la risque; je la mets partout en avant; heureux si je mourais
pour la justice, l'honneur et mon pays. Je sais bien que Dieu serait ainsi plus
disposé à avoir pitié de moi! Et toi aussi tu as une fortune! Quelle fortune?
Presque comme la mienne peut-être, mais veux-tu que je te dise? Avant long-
temps il y aura ici de l'argent en masse.

Je ne puis pas te dire: viens ici tu feras de l'argent. Mais voici. Nous avons
besoin de gens instruits, d'honnêtes personnes! Nous manquons de personnes
instruites parmi la population Métis Canadienne Française. Viens si tu veux!
Je conduis à peu près tout ici pour le présent; et je ferai tout ce que je pourrai
pour toi. Et toi, en venant ici, tu rendras au pays à la cause du Bas-Canada un
grand service. Ah! Si Monsieur Cartier eut fait plustôt · attention aux insinua-
tions de ma faible voix!...Il est peut-être encore temps!...Tout ce que je sais, c'est
qu'avant tout Je suis Canadien Français! Et cela peut montrer la direction de
mes idées et de mes sentiments.

Je voudrais aussi que tu montrasses cette lettre a Dubuque · [Dubuc]; je
ne sais où il est, mais tu dois le savoir. Ici, il fera tant de bien! Il y aurait bien
quelques petits sacrifices à faire pour commencer! Sacrifices; c'est à dire ne
pas être récompensé, rémunéré peut-être autant qu'on le mériterait. Mais il
y a ici un grand complot. Et tout · ceux qui y mettront la main passeront à
l'immortalité! Je ne mens pas! La Rivière Rouge est un vaste théâtre. Il s'y passe
des évènements qui feront mémoire dans l'histoire d'Albion.[49]

Cher ami je suis et serai pour la vie
Ton tout dévoué ami
Louis Riel.

Translation

Fort Garry 14 December 1869
Monsieur Eustache Prud'homme.

Very dear friend,
I have just received your kind letter. In the midst of my new pursuits, in spite of
the small amount of time I have at my disposal, even at night, I assure you that
I have read and re-read what you have written to me. Dear friend, everything
is going well here, everything! I have seized the right moment. Undoubtedly
Heaven is thus offering me the very way to wipe out some unfortunate years.
I have succeeded far beyond my dreams. Indeed, pride is banished from my
heart. I have already more than felt what its poison can do. The goal of my
ambition is to do good. What do I care about glory? I do not deserve it.

What do I care about honours? I have already been humiliated so much!
Dear friend, you speak to me about Fortune! I do not have a cent. I am inde-
pendent, free as a bird. And that is where my strength lies today. My life is all
I have. I am offering it up! I am risking it; I am exposing it to danger, happy to
die for justice, honour, and my country. I am well aware that God would then

be more willing to have pity on me! And you too have a fortune! What fortune?
Almost like mine perhaps, but do you want me to tell you? Before long, there
will be massive amounts of money here.

I cannot tell you more: come here yourself, you will make money. But here
are the facts. We need learned, decent people! We lack well-educated people
in the French-Canadian Métis population. Come if you want! I am in charge of
almost everything here at present, and I will do all that I can for you. And by
coming here, you will do the country and Lower Canada's cause a great favour.
Oh, if only Monsieur Cartier had paid attention sooner to the innuendos of my
feeble voice!...[50] *Maybe there is still time!...All I know is that above all I am*
French-Canadian! And that can give insight to my ideas and feelings.

Also, I would like you to share this letter with Dubuque [Dubuc]; I do
not know where he is, but you must. He will do so much good here! To begin
with, one might have to make some small sacrifices! Sacrifices, like not being
rewarded, or paid as much as one's worth. But there is a major drama unfold-
ing here. And all those who take part in it will be immortalized! I am not lying!
Red River is a vast theatre. Events taking place here will long be remembered in
Albion's history.

Dear friend, I am and will be for life
Your most devoted friend
Louis Riel.

English Poetry, 1885

During the nearly six months of his incarceration in Regina Jail, 23 May
to 16 November 1885, Riel continued to write extensively. Included in
these writings are poetic compositions addressed to men of the North-
West Mounted Police who were guarding him. Captain Richard Burton
Deane, commander of the jail, received three such poems. In them, Riel
attempts to curry favour with Deane and to sensitize him to his plight, and
to that of his wife and children who were in desperate financial straits.[51]
The prison guards, mainly English-speaking, were also recipients of his

poetry. Riel was obviously on good terms with these young men, and his verses dispense to them snippets of moral and religious advice.[52]

In November 2008, at a Toronto auction organized by Dirk Heinze of the CBC's *Canadian Antiques Roadshow*, the descendants of one of the jailers, Constable Robert Hobbs, put up for sale two notebooks containing poems written by Riel during his imprisonment. The Métis leader is said to have given them to Hobbs as an expression of gratitude for supplying him with writing materials.[53] The Manitoba Metis Federation placed the winning bid at the auction, and made public the contents of the notebooks in Winnipeg on Louis Riel Day 2009.[54] Belonging to the Louis Riel Institute, which is the educational arm of the Manitoba Metis Federation, the poems are currently housed in the Centre du patrimoine de la Société historique de Saint-Boniface.[55]

There appear to be seven poems in total, although divisions in the text are not always clearly delineated. They are all written in English and are similar in nature to the prison poetry discussed above. From a technical point of view, they are little more than doggerel, criticism that can be mitigated somewhat when one takes into account that the poet was not composing in his mother tongue. Thematically, the poems reinforce what we know of Riel's state of mind during his months in prison. He was certainly aware of the possible fate that awaited him: "The rope / Threatens my life," he states, but then adds assuredly that he has nothing to fear due to his belief that higher powers will protect him as they have done in the past: "Mary / The Virgin Immaculate / Has sav'd me up to this date."

Two of the poems deal with Protestants, undoubtedly the denomination of most of the guards. Riel speaks kindly of them and offers the following bit of wisdom:

Happy is the congregation
Which obeys, with true devotion,
The sermons of its Minister...

but adds, with true missionary zeal:

...if you fall in sorrow
You have only to borrow
Beeds · and say the rosary.

Interestingly, the Church of England is singled out for its "very fine perfume / Of truth" since it accepts the concept of the virgin birth of Christ.

Riel had convinced himself earlier that God would side with him and the Métis to overcome any adversity in order to fulfill their destiny. In the final poem, we see that he has not deviated from this belief, and will continue to carry out his mission, stating categorically: "Prophet of the New World, I / Do the work of the Most High." He remains steadfast in his conviction that he, sincere and humble, along with his people, will eventually be rewarded for their efforts.

Transcription

I must
Speak of God in whom
I trust.
In him I have room
To hope.
The rope
Threatens my life; but
Thank God, I fear not.
* * *
My works for all classes
Will soon shine as glasses
Under a bright
Electric light.
—

The love of Jesus
Is all my genius.

—

At home and abroad
My helper is God.

—

* * *

I do not wish to oppose
The creed, the belief of those
Who profess the contrary,
But I assure that Mary
The Virgin Immaculate
Has sav'd me up to this date,
Through her kind intercession.
And Saint Joseph's protection
Is the splendid citadel
Whence the merciful pleasure
Of God helps without measure
Poor Louis "David" Riel.
* * *

Protestants my good brethren!
Allow me to let you know
Whosoever you may be, men,
Boys, girls, women and children,
That, if you fall in sorrow
You have only to borrow
Beeds · and say the rosary
* * *

The morning dew, with silver drops,
Never shines as much as the word
Of the Preacher who developes ·
The blessed teachings of the Lord.

—

ₔ

Happy is the congregation
Which obeys, with true devotion,
The sermons of its Minister,
For the sake of Christ, the Master!
Louis "David" Riel

* * *

There is a very fine perfume
Of truth, in the church of England!
The Blessed Virgin, I presume,
Occupies therein, a great stand.
She is honor'd as the mother
Of Jesus-christ! She is the Queen
Whose sweet prayers have always been
Succesfull · near God the Father.
Louis "David" Riel.

* * *

Prophet of the New World, I
Do the work of the Most High.
I assert it with no pride.
I live in humility.
Is there any one to side
With me? Yes. Sincerity
Will gather up its recruits.
And we will soon taste its fruits.
Louis "David" Riel.

* * *

Notes

1. George F.G. Stanley et al., *The Collected Writings of Louis Riel/Les Écrits complets de Louis Riel*, 5 vols. (Edmonton: University of Alberta Press, 1985). Hereafter cited as CW.

2. Thomas Flanagan and Glen Campbell, "Updating *The Collected Writings of Louis Riel*," in *From Rupert's Land to Canada*, ed. Theodore Binnema, Gerhard J. Ens and R.C. Macleod (Edmonton: University of Alberta Press, 2001), 271–88; David G. McCrady, "Louis Riel and Sitting Bull's Sioux: Three Lost Letters," *Prairie Forum* 32, no. 2 (Fall 2007): 223.

3. We present only previously unknown texts in this chapter. There are other cases in which original manuscripts of texts included in cw, which were based on other printed copies, have since come to light. For example, "Louis Riel," *Le Figaro* (Paris), 10 November 1885, contains a photocopy of the manuscript of cw, 3–102, which we did not have when cw was published, and also a typescript of cw, 3–152. These texts must have been collected by the French travel writer Georges Demanche when he visited Riel in Regina in 1885. As well, the University of Saskatchewan Library has acquired the original copy of cw, 4–147, Riel's poem dedicated to Robert Gordon, one of his jailers in Regina.

4. Louis Riel to Sophie Masson, December 29, 1861, cw, 1–001.

5. cw, 1–001, 1–002, 1–005, 1–006, 1–125, 1–127, 1–129, 1–136.

6. www.shsb.mb.ca/dbtw-wpd/textbase/riel/rlrechw.htm. The archival reference for the letter is as follows: Société historique de Saint-Boniface (shsb), Major Henri Masson Collection, 0592 1813 01a–01c.

7. However, access to the manuscript allows us to clarify some wording that could not be made out in the photocopy of Riel's letter to Sophie Masson, December 12, 1861. In cw, 1–001, we printed the following: "il m'est donné de vous exprimer une fois de plus, combien je suis sensible et confus de me voir l'objet d'une bien-veillance dont je suis si indigne et qui n'a [...] d'autres l[...]tes de la générosité de votre âme." The correct reading is "et qui n'a d'autres limites de la générosité de votre âme."

8. George F.G. Stanley, *Louis Riel* (Toronto: Ryerson Press, 1963), 20–23.

9. Stanley, *Louis Riel*, 24 and 380, 17.

10. Stanley, *Louis Riel*, 22; see also, Raymond J.A. Huel, *Archbishop A.-A. Taché of St. Boniface: The "Good Fight" and the Illusive Vision* (Edmonton: University of Alberta Press, 2003), 56.

11. Louis Riel to Sophie Masson, December 12, 1862, cw, 1–002.

12. Louis Riel to Sophie Masson, December 24, 1864, cw, 1–005.

13. Archives du Séminaire de Saint-Sulpice, Montréal (asssm), Pl: 11.3-120.

14. Stanley, *Louis Riel*, 25.

15. In line with the editorial practices followed in *The Collected Writings of Louis Riel*, we have not changed Riel's spelling and capitalization but have made silent corrections to accents. Instead of using "sic" to indicate Riel's particular orthography or spelling errors, we have chosen to use the symbol · following the erroneous or non-standard word.

16. I.e., Louis Riel, Jr. His father was also named Louis Riel.

17. Young Louis is here referring to his father who was helped financially by Madame Masson, as was mentioned above.

18. SHSB, Frank Larned Hunt Collection, 0621/1813/1. On the envelope containing the letter is the following annotation: "Within is a letter from Riel to John Bruce—it may in the future be not amiss in the Records of some future Historical Society of Manitoba. FL Hunt"; Memorable Manitobans, Frank Larned Hunt (1825–1903), www.mhs.mb.ca/docs/people/hunt_fl.shtml.

19. Poplar Point lot 67, according to D.N. Sprague and R.P. Frye, *The Genealogy of the First Metis Nation* (Winnipeg: Pemmican Publications, 1983), Table 5.

20. N.E. Allen Ronaghan, "John Bruce," *Dictionary of Canadian Biography Online*, www.biographi.ca/009004-119.01-e.php?BioId=40117.

21. Stanley, *Louis Riel*, 61.

22. Ronaghan, "John Bruce."

23. Louis Riel, "L'Amnistie," in Riel, *CW*, 1–188, p. 304; Louis Riel and Louis Schmidt, "Orders of the Provisional Government of Rupert's Land," 8 January 1870, Riel, *CW*, 1–027.

24. Ronagahn, "John Bruce."

25. The 1869 photo of the Métis' provisional government reinforces this view regarding Riel's primacy since it is he who sits in the centre of the group, with Bruce to his right.

26. Stanley, *Louis Riel*, 61.

27. Later renamed Sainte-Anne-des-Chênes. Located 40 kilometres southeast of Winnipeg, the town should not be confused with Oak Point, which is situated near Lake Manitoba.

28. Montreal newspaper established in 1867 by Joseph Royal.

29. Amable is a French personal name, not a family name. Baptiste Amable may be Baptiste Tourond, who was a member of the National Committee and lived in St. Norbert (*CW*, 5–352). Riel says in the letter that he is leaving for La Pointe-des-Chênes, and St. Norbert, being on the way, would have been a convenient place for a meeting.

30. Email from Merrill Distad, University of Alberta Libraries, to Glen Campbell. A photographic image of the letter, together with a transcription and English translation, is available at http://peel.library.ualberta.ca/cocoon/peel/7436.html.

31. J.M. Bumsted, *The Red River Rebellion* (Winnipeg: Watson & Dwyer, 1996).

32. Riel, CW, 1-021.

33. Louis Riel to William Dease, 15 February 1870. CW, 1-031.

34. Louis Riel to Joseph Dubuc, 29 August 1870. CW, 1-066.

35. Philippe Mailhot, *Ritchot's Resistance: Abbé Noël Joseph Ritchot and the Creation and Transformation of Manitoba* (PHD diss., University of Manitoba, 1986), 243-62.

36. Louis Riel to C.-J. Coursol, 24 June 1874. CW, 1-201.

37. Louis Riel to N.-J. Ritchot, 5 October 1874. CW, 1-215.

38. Tom Flanagan, *First Nations? Second Thoughts*, 2nd ed. (Montreal and Kingston: McGill-Queen's University Press, 2008), 81-84.

39. E.g., some of the poetry written while Riel was in asylum at Beauport. CW, 4-059, 4-060.

40. *L'Opinion publique*, 19 February 1870.

41. ASSSM, Palmarès 1863.

42. The notebook was first published in its entirety in Gilles Martel, Glen Campbell and Thomas Flanagan, eds., *Louis Riel: Poésies de jeunesse* (Saint-Boniface, MB: Éditions du Blé, 1977).

43. *L'Opinion publique*, 19 February 1870.

44. See Olivier Maurault, PA, p.s.s., *Le Collège de Montréal, 1767-1967*, second edition, reviewed and updated by Antonio Dansereau, p.s.s. (Montréal: 1967), 158-59.

45. ASSSM, Pl: 11.3-124.

46. ASSSM, Pl: 11.3-124. On November 4, 1865, Riel also addressed a poem of praise to "Honoré Directeur" Lenoir. CW, 4-032.

47. Eustache Prud'homme, *Les Martyrs de la foi en Canada* (Québec: Augustin Coté et Cie, 1869).

48. Jeanne d'Arc Lortie, *La Poésie nationaliste au Canada français (1606-1867)* (Québec: Presses de l'Université Laval, 1975), 381-84; Réginald Hamel, John Hare and Paul Wyczynski, *Dictionnaire des auteurs de langue française en Amérique* (Montréal: Éditions Fides, 1989), 1128-29.

49. Albion is a poetic name for England.

50. Riel apparently refers to the three verse letters he wrote to G.E. Cartier in 1866, asking for a patronage appointment. CW, 4-033, 4-035, 4-036.

51. CW, 4-133, 4-134, 4-135.

52. CW, 4–141, 4–143, 4–144, 4–147, 4–151, 4–155, 4–156, 4–157.

53. www.cbc.ca/canada/manitoba/story/2008/11/14/riel-poems.html?ref=rss.

54. Dawn Walton, "The plain, strong hand of Riel lives on," *The Globe and Mail*, 17 February 2009, A3; www.thestar.com/news/canada/2009/02/16/metis_leaders_welcome_return_of_louis_riel_poems.html.

55. Louis Riel Institute documents, Centre du patrimoine de la Société historique de Saint-Boniface.

PART THREE **Law**

Métis Aboriginal Rights Jurisprudence in Canada

IAN PEACH

MÉTIS WERE RECOGNIZED as an Aboriginal people of Canada in section 35 of the *Constitution Act, 1982*, the section that recognizes and affirms the "existing aboriginal and treaty rights" of the Aboriginal peoples of Canada.[1] They had also been recognized much earlier, in the *Manitoba Act, 1870*, as the beneficiaries of lands to be provided by the government "towards the extinguishment of the Indian Title to the lands in the Province."[2] Yet the effort to give legal meaning to the recognition of the Métis as an Aboriginal people and as the holders of Aboriginal rights has really only just begun. While the development of a modern doctrine of Aboriginal rights and Aboriginal title for First Nations can be considered to have begun with the Supreme Court of Canada's decision in *Calder et al. v. Attorney-General of British Columbia*[3] in 1973, and while litigation to address whether or not Métis had Aboriginal rights goes back to 1976, in the Saskatchewan case of *R. v. Laprise*,[4] the first Supreme Court of Canada decision on Métis rights did not come about until 2003, with *R. v. Powley*.[5] As well, while there have now been nearly 40 cases decided by the Supreme Court of Canada that have addressed the Aboriginal and treaty rights and Aboriginal title of First Nations, the Supreme Court has only addressed the Aboriginal rights of Métis in two cases, *Powley* and *R. v. Blais*.[6]

In looking at the decisions of all levels of court in Métis Aboriginal rights cases, one begins to see some indications of why it has taken so long for the promise of section 35 to be given substance for Métis. At heart, the challenge has been to make the very concept of Métis, as a distinct cultural and political community, cognizable to state actors, who look first for indications of identity and community in the laws of the state. First Nations can point to such indicators of their identity in treaties and, probably most importantly, the *Indian Act*, but the legislative record of recognition of Métis as a distinct people is extremely sparse. In the absence of clear state recognition of a group as a community, with a cognizable definition of membership and clear structures for representation in political and legal discourse, governments are unlikely to accept assertions of collective rights. The state's court system, bound as it is by the incrementalist logic of legal reasoning, is equally unlikely to strike out boldly to establish regimes of collective rights for those unrecognized communities. Only with *Powley* has Canadian jurisprudence turned the corner to recognize Métis as having a history and culture distinct from both First Nations and settlers and capable of being the source of its own, *sui generis* regime of Aboriginal rights. This chaper will seek to demonstrate this point by reviewing the case law on Métis Aboriginal rights with a particular focus on how the problem of cognizability of Métis identity has made the judicial recognition of Métis Aboriginal rights slower and more difficult to achieve than the recognition of Aboriginal rights for First Nations.

The Case Law Prior to *Powley* and *Blais*

A number of lower courts decided Métis Aboriginal rights claims prior to the Supreme Court of Canada's decisions in *Powley* and *Blais* in 2003. In the face of the general view of settler state governments that Métis had no "existing Aboriginal...rights," analysis of Métis claims began by comparing them to the archetypal Aboriginal peoples, "status Indians," and testing the "authenticity" of Métis claims through this comparison. This is not surprising, considering that the legal method in common-law legal systems is to draw legal principles from established precedents (previous court decisions) and, by drawing analogies to those precedents, apply those principles to the new fact situation before the court. The effect of the legal method in these cases, though, is that the courts turned to the conceptually simpler exercise of drawing on what they claimed to know about "Indians" to make Métis cognizable, rather than approaching Métis questions from first principles. Thus, Métis rights decisions, at least in the period prior to *Powley*, inevitably followed First Nations Aboriginal rights claims temporally and turned on the extent to which Métis claimants were like First Nations people (or "followed an Indian mode of life").

This reasoning process also made it impossible for courts to imagine that Métis people could have Aboriginal rights that are more extensive than those of First Nations people or unique to the Métis, because Métis were treated as "less Aboriginal" than First Nations peoples, at least unless they could demonstrate that they, too, lived an "Indian mode of life." In essence, the scope of a group's Aboriginal rights was determined by the degree of genealogical "mixedness" or "purity" of the Aboriginal group. Because Métis were perceived by the settler state as less "pure" than First Nations, their Aboriginal rights were assumed to be less.

The first case, *Laprise*, which predates the *Constitution Act, 1982*, is a prime example of this approach to understanding Aboriginal rights. In that case, the Saskatchewan Court of Queen's Bench decided that the accused, a Métis, was guilty of a Saskatchewan *Game Act* violation because it concluded that the term "Indians" in the *Natural Resources Transfer Agreement* of 1930, which preserved the rights of "Indians" to hunt, trap, and fish, only applied to "treaty Indians" and did not extend to those, such as Métis, who were not the beneficiaries of treaties.[7] This decision was upheld by the Saskatchewan Court of Appeal on appeal.[8] In the opinion of the Saskatchewan judiciary of the late 1970s, "Indianness," and therefore access to Aboriginal rights, was to be determined by one's treaty status.

The 1992 Manitoba case of R. v. McPherson was a challenge to a charge of illegal moose hunting based on the argument that the accused, as a Métis, had a common-law Aboriginal right to hunt.[9] This decision is the first and, in the pre-Powley period, a rare effort to understand Métis as a people. The court looked at the question of whether the Métis were an organized group (taking as a given that they are an Aboriginal people, because of their recognition in section 35 of the Constitution Act, 1982). The court agreed, on the basis of their history, that the Métis of the Red River Settlement constituted an organized, distinct community, but concluded that the ancestors of the accused did not constitute an organized community.[10] The court saw the Scots-Aboriginal Half-breeds of the Big Eddy area, on the other hand, as sometimes part of settler society and sometimes part of First Nation society, but as never having an organized society of their own.[11] Despite coming to the conclusion that the Half-breeds of the area did not have a distinct organized society, the court decided that the accused did have an Aboriginal right to hunt for food because it found an unbroken chain of use of the lands in question by his ancestors for a "reasonable period of time."[12]

The Alberta Provincial Court, Criminal Division was confronted with a Métis Aboriginal rights case not long thereafter, in the 1993 case of R. v. Ferguson.[13] This case, like Laprise, turned on the question of whether or not the accused, a Métis who had been charged with hunting moose without a licence, was an "Indian" for the purposes of the Natural Resources Transfer Agreement. The court determined that the defendant was an "Indian" culturally and "at least one-half Indian racially" and that he followed an "Indian mode of life."[14] As such, the court found that the defendant was a "non-Treaty Indian" and then went on to conclude that "non-treaty Indians" were contemplated as being "Indians" whose Aboriginal hunting rights were protected under the terms of the Natural Resources Transfer Agreement.[15] The court thus acquitted the defendant on the charges. This result was upheld on appeal by the Court of Queen's Bench, which also concluded that the periodic participation of the accused in the wage economy did not mean that he did not lead an "Indian mode of life."[16]

The 1996 Alberta case of *R. v. Desjarlais* focussed entirely on whether the Métis accused lived an "Indian mode of life" and had "sufficient identified Indian blood" to be considered "Indian" for the purpose of claiming Aboriginal hunting rights under the *Natural Resources Transfer Agreement*.[17] The Alberta Provincial Court, quickly concluding that both accused had "sufficient Indian blood," turned its attention to the question of whether they lived an "Indian mode of life," looking at family associations, language, diet, and reliance on hunting.[18] The court was particularly interested in the employment status of the accused (whether they relied on wage employment).[19] In the end, the court concluded that the accused did live an "Indian mode of life" so that they could claim an Aboriginal right to hunt and dismissed the charges.[20] The acquittal against Mr. Desjarlais was upheld by the Alberta Court of Queen's Bench on appeal, that court noting in the course of its decision that the requirement of "Indian blood" under the 1927 version of the *Indian Act* (which was being used to interpret the reference to "Indians" in the *Natural Resources Transfer Agreement*) did not mean that individuals had to have a preponderance of "Indian" ancestry and confirming that there was adequate evidence that Mr. Desjarlais did follow an "Indian mode of life," despite his occasional participation in the wage economy.[21] The court, however, allowed the appeal against the acquittal of the other accused, Mr. Willier, and ordered a new trial, as there was no evidence that Mr. Willier had "Indian blood," since he had been adopted through a custom adoption.[22]

Continuing with this interpretive approach, in the Saskatchewan case of *R. v. Grumbo*, the Court of Queen's Bench concluded that the Métis accused had an Aboriginal right to possess wildlife hunted by an "Indian," but the decision turned entirely on whether Métis were "Indians" as that term was used in the *Natural Resources Transfer Agreement* of 1930, not whether the history of the relationship of the Métis with the Crown had led to the Crown recognizing their traditional activities as Aboriginal rights.[23] The terms of the *Indian Act* in effect at various times up to 1930 had included Métis as "Indians" if they lived among First Nations people or lived "an Indian mode of life" and had not shared in the "distribution of half-breed lands."[24] The court used these definitions to conclude that Mr. Grumbo should not have been convicted of a violation of the Saskatchewan *Wildlife Act* because it is reasonable to conclude that he was an "Indian," and therefore a holder of Aboriginal rights, and any doubt on this question should be resolved in his favour.[25] The Saskatchewan Court of Appeal overturned this decision and ordered a new trial, but on the basis merely that more evidence was required to determine whether Mr. Grumbo was an "Indian" under the terms of the *Natural Resources Transfer Agreement*.[26] In the course of its decision, the Court of Appeal did raise the question of whether the Métis were an Aboriginal people distinct from First Nations and, if so, if Métis, too, had an Aboriginal right to hunt.[27] This would have provided an opening for the court to look, instead, at Métis history and culture and the Crown–Métis relationship to determine the content of Métis Aboriginal rights; unfortunately, the Saskatchewan Court of Appeal, as with other courts confronted with the same issue prior to *Powley*, did not take this opportunity.

In contrast, and in a foreshadowing of what was to come with *Powley*, the decision of the Provincial Court of Saskatchewan in *R. v. Morin and Daigneault* focussed on whether the Métis were well established in the area in which Mr. Morin was fishing prior to the assertion of British sovereignty (which the court determined was 1870) and whether fishing was an important part of the Métis lifestyle and an important source of food for the Métis.[28] By concluding that the Métis were well established in the area by 1870 and that fish were abundant in the area and were, thus, an important food source for the Métis, the court decided that the Métis of the area, including Mr. Morin, had an Aboriginal right to fish; this was decided without the necessity of comparing Métis to First Nations people.[29] Indeed, the court went so far as to review the evidence

distinguishing between those who "took treaty" (now commonly characterized as treaty or Status Indians) and those who took scrip (now
commonly characterized as Métis) and determined that those who took
scrip nonetheless retained their Aboriginal rights to hunt and fish.[30] The
court also went on to state that the division of the Aboriginal people of
northwest Saskatchewan into First Nations and Métis by the agents of
the Crown was an arbitrary and artificial distinction between people who
"lived very much alike."[31] As such, the court concluded that to grant one
group of Aboriginal people benefits denied the other was discriminatory.[32]
On appeal, the Saskatchewan Court of Queen's Bench held that the Crown
was correct to argue that the Aboriginal right of the Métis of the region
should be restricted to a right to fish for food, but the existence of a Métis
Aboriginal right was not questioned.[33]

Given the reasoning process involved in deciding most of these early
cases, it is no surprise that Métis Aboriginal rights claims were only being
decided by the courts after the law on First Nations Aboriginal rights had
become relatively settled and, in many cases, Métis Aboriginal rights were
seen as derivative of First Nations rights. A dramatic break with this analytical paradigm was about to come to Canadian jurisprudence, however,
with the decision of the Supreme Court of Canada in *Powley*.

Powley's Conceptual Breakthrough for Métis Identity and Rights

In 2003, the Supreme Court of Canada first addressed the issue of Métis
Aboriginal rights. Its decision in *R. v. Blais* is a fairly conventional decision,
analyzing whether Métis are included in the term "Indians" in the *Natural
Resources Transfer Agreement*. The Court, however, arrived at a conclusion
contrary to most of the earlier case law, a decision that was ultimately useful for taking Métis out from under the shadow of "Indians," even if it
led to these particular defendants losing their case. The Court noted that
Métis were treated as a different group than "Indians" for the purposes of
identifying their rights and the protections afforded them, in particular
because governments did not treat Métis as wards of the Crown.[34] It thus

concluded that the protection of the hunting rights of "Indians" in the *Natural Resources Transfer Agreement* does not provide a Métis defendant with a defence against charges of unlawfully hunting.[35]

Powley, decided at the same time, represents a significant breakthrough in understanding Métis rights, though, in part because it is focussed on whether Métis have an Aboriginal right to hunt under section 35 of the *Constitution Act, 1982*, rather than under the *Natural Resources Transfer Agreement*. As the Court noted,

> ...the term "Métis" in s. 35 does not encompass all individuals with mixed Indian and European heritage; rather, it refers to distinctive peoples who, in addition to their mixed ancestry, developed their own customs, way of life, and recognizable group identity separate from their Indian or Inuit and European forebears.[36]

The Court then went on to state that "A Métis community can be defined as a group of Métis with a distinctive collective identity, living together in the same geographic area and sharing a common way of life."[37] This led the Court to determine that

> [t]he inclusion of the Métis in s. 35 is based on a commitment to recognizing the Métis and enhancing their survival as distinctive communities. The purpose and the promise of s. 35 is to protect practices that were historically important features of these distinctive communities and that persist in the present day as integral elements of their Métis culture.[38]

By recognizing the Métis as a distinct Aboriginal community with a distinct history and distinct cultural practices, the Court was able to institute such innovations in thinking about Métis Aboriginal rights as establishing the period of "effective European control," rather than European contact, as the key point in time for determining what cultural practices could ground Aboriginal rights, and identifying current rights-bearing communities by looking for indicia of distinct Métis communities prior to effective European control, rather than by tracing the connection of Métis individuals to rights-bearing First Nations communities.[39] Most importantly, though, the Court developed a means to determine whether an individual was a member of a rights-bearing Métis community by looking at whether the individual self-identified as a Métis, had an ancestral connection to a historical Métis community, and was accepted as Métis by a current Métis community, rather than simply looking at whether an individual had First Nations ancestry.[40]

In introducing these indicia, the Court clearly stated that "While determining membership in the Métis community might not be as simple as verifying membership in, for example, an Indian band, this does not detract from the status of Métis people as full-fledged rights-bearers."[41] The Court also commented that "the criteria for Métis identity under s. 35 must reflect the purpose of this constitutional guarantee: to recognize and affirm the rights of the Métis held by virtue of their direct relationship to this country's original inhabitants and by virtue of the continuity between their customs and traditions and those of their Métis predecessors."[42] Later, in discussing at greater length the rationale for setting the period of "effective European control" as the relevant timeframe for determining what practices ground Métis Aboriginal rights, the Court also noted that

> the recognition of Métis rights in s. 35 is not reducible to the Métis' Indian ancestry. The unique status of the Métis as an Aboriginal people with post-contact origins requires an adaptation of the pre-contact approach to meet the distinctive historical circumstances surrounding the evolution of Métis communities.[43]

This conclusion speaks to the Court's commitment to going beyond what was then the mainstream inquiry of lower courts into whether Métis are "Indians" and undertaking the more difficult, but ultimately more legitimate, task of identifying Métis communities as distinct communities and identifying individuals as Métis by virtue of their membership in those distinct communities. In keeping with this approach, the Court concluded that subsistence hunting was a constant in the Métis community in the vicinity of Sault Ste. Marie and that it was an important aspect of Métis life, to the point of declaring it a "defining feature of their special relationship to the land,"[44] such that the practice could ground a Métis Aboriginal right. This emphasis from Canada's highest court on understanding Métis communities as distinct, rights-bearing communities, rather than simply as a watered-down version of rights-bearing First Nations communities, has changed how lower courts have approached the task of defining Métis Aboriginal rights in subsequent cases. Métis are becoming cognizable to the courts as Métis because of the guidance that the Supreme Court of Canada has given them in undertaking this analytical process. It is to the post-*Powley* jurisprudence on Métis Aboriginal rights that we will now turn, to see the effect of *Powley* on legal reasoning about Métis Aboriginal rights.

Post-*Powley* Jurisprudence: Evolution of Cognizability?
There has been quite a bit of Métis Aboriginal rights jurisprudence in the courts since *Powley*, all of which has taken the Supreme Court of Canada's direction seriously.[45] Certainly in the first post-*Powley* case, *R. v. Willison*, the British Columbia Provincial Court carefully applied the *Powley* test, looking at whether there was a distinctive Métis community in the relevant area prior to effective European control, whether there was a current Métis community, whether the accused met the identity indicia set out in *Powley*, and whether hunting was an integral part of the distinctive culture of the Métis community in the area.[46] This analysis led the Provincial Court judge to conclude that Mr. Willison had proven that he had an Aboriginal right to hunt.[47] On appeal, the British Columbia Supreme Court overturned Mr. Willison's acquittal, but on the basis that there was no historical or contemporary Métis community in the relevant region;[48] in its approach to analyzing the question of whether Mr. Willison had an

Aboriginal right, the British Columbia Supreme Court, like the Provincial Court, followed the Supreme Court of Canada's analytical approach in *Powley*.

At almost the same time as the British Columbia Provincial Court decided *Willison*, the Saskatchewan Provincial Court decided *R. v. Norton*.[49] Here again, the Court applied the analytical approach set down in *Powley* but convicted the accused of illegal fishing because the defence did not lead sufficient evidence to establish an ancestral link between the accused and the historical Métis community of the Qu'Appelle valley.[50] Thus, the accused were unable to prove that they were the holders of an Aboriginal right to fish, though the Provincial Court did recognize the existence of a historical Métis community in the Qu'Appelle valley.[51]

In the 2005 case of *R. v. Laviolette*, the Saskatchewan Provincial Court carefully applied the *Powley* criteria once more, this time to determine that the Métis defendant did have an Aboriginal right to fish.[52] Possibly the most interesting aspect of this case is that the Provincial Court also declared that the "community" that possessed an Aboriginal right to fish was the Métis within the region of Green Lake, Ile a la Crosse, and Lac La Biche and including Meadow Lake, rather than a particular community (i.e., city, town, or village).[53] This decision begins the process of expanding the understanding of a Métis "community" in which an Aboriginal right exists to a region in which a group of Métis traditionally lived and in which they engaged in traditional activities.

In early 2006, the Alberta Provincial Court also followed the *Powley* line of analysis in deciding *R. v. Kelley*.[54] In applying this analysis, however, the Provincial Court concluded that there was neither a historic nor a contemporary rights-bearing Métis community in the area around Hinton, Alberta, and convicted Mr. Kelley of hunting without a licence.[55] This conviction was overturned by the Alberta Court of Queen's Bench on appeal but on the basis that Alberta's *Interim Métis Harvesting Agreement* should have protected Mr. Kelley from prosecution for his trapping activities; the Court of Queen's Bench did not overturn the Provincial Court's finding that Mr. Kelley had not proven that he was the holder of an Aboriginal right to trap, as this question was not in issue in the appeal.[56]

A 2006 case from Newfoundland and Labrador, *Labrador Métis Nation v. Newfoundland and Labrador (Minister of Transportation and Works)*, raised the question of the application of *Powley* in the context of government's duty to consult with Aboriginal peoples. The Newfoundland and Labrador Supreme Court noted the degree of certainty with which the Royal Commission on Aboriginal Peoples and the Supreme Court of Canada (in *Powley*) identified the Labrador Métis as a distinct Aboriginal people and that numerous individuals of mixed Inuit and European ancestry identify themselves as Labrador Métis.[57] The Court therefore concluded that a culturally mixed group of people, whose descendants now refer to themselves as Métis, emerged prior to effective European control of southern Labrador and formed a community in that region.[58] The Court also spoke to the issue of the regional nature of Métis communities directly, stating,

> I find that the use of the word "community" by itself is presumptively restrictive and implies perhaps a single group of people in a single place. This use of the word would make it impossible to deal with determining the rights of any large group of aboriginal people and inject legal frustration into the resolution of their circumstance and result in endless applications before the courts.
>
> Unless specified otherwise, the court in the present case, views the community of Labrador Metis people...represented by the Labrador Metis [as those who] originated [on] the south coast of Labrador and who share the same customs, traditions and heritage. [sic][59]

It is also interesting that the Court concluded that the Labrador Métis can have their interests represented by an agent and that the Labrador Métis Nation (LMN) can act as their agent for consultation purposes; this conclusion came in the face of an argument by the provincial government that only recognized "governing bodies" of communities, such as band councils or chiefs but not the Labrador Métis Nation, can represent communities in consultations with government.[60] The Court also drew attention to the fact that the provincial government signed a land claims agreement with the Labrador Inuit Association on behalf of the Labrador Inuit.[61] On the basis of these determinations, the Newfoundland and Labrador Supreme Court concluded that the provincial government did, indeed, have a duty to consult with the Labrador Métis, as represented by the Labrador Métis Nation. On appeal, the Newfoundland and Labrador Court of Appeal decided that it was not necessary that the Labrador Métis Nation members decide whether they are making an Aboriginal rights claim as Métis or Inuit to trigger the duty of the provincial government to consult, stating,

> Whether the present day LMN communities are the result of an ethnogenesis of a new culture of aboriginal peoples, that arose between the period of contact with Europeans and the date of the effective imposition of European control, is not yet established, although it is possible that such an ethnogenesis occurred. If so, the members of the LMN communities could be, in law, constitutional Métis.
>
> However, it is also possible that the LMN communities are simply the present-day manifestation of the historic Inuit communities of south and central Labrador that were present in the area prior to contact with the Europeans.[62]

The Court of Appeal therefore concluded that although the trial judge did not have enough evidence before him to conclude that Métis ethnogenesis occurred, all that the Labrador Métis Nation members were required to do to trigger the Crown's duty to consult was show a credible claim to have Aboriginal rights, whether based on their Inuit or Métis identity.[63] Clearly, the courts in Newfoundland and Labrador, in the aftermath of *Powley*, are taking some care to investigate the distinct cultural contexts of different Indigenous peoples in determining their Aboriginal rights, even though in this case the Court of Appeal concluded that the particular cultural group of which the claimants were members was not relevant to the claim.

In 2007, the Saskatchewan Provincial Court decided *R. v. Belhumeur*, in which the accused claimed a Métis Aboriginal right in defence to an illegal fishing charge. As with the other post-*Powley* cases from lower courts, the Saskatchewan Provincial Court decided this case by the application of the *Powley* criteria to the question of whether the defendants were Métis and whether there was a distinct Métis community in the area (the Qu'Appelle valley) that had an Aboriginal right to fish.[64] By applying this analysis to the evidence in this case, the Provincial Court concluded that the accused were Métis and could claim an Aboriginal right to fish in the Qu'Appelle valley.[65] The Provincial Court also followed the earlier decision in *Laviolette* in defining the rights-bearing community as the Métis of the Qu'Appelle valley region, rather than a particular settlement, though it did not go so far as to declare the community comprised the entire Prairie grasslands area, as had been argued by the defence.[66]

One of the more interesting claims for a Métis right is a 2008 Tax Court of Canada decision, *Janzen v. Canada*.[67] In this case, the appellant claimed he was not subject to taxation because he was a Métis according to the *Powley* indicia.[68] The Court, however, concluded that *Powley* did not stand for the proposition that Métis were exempt from income tax and therefore did not discuss the application of the *Powley* indicia to the appellant.[69]

A major, and to date the only, Métis Aboriginal title case was decided by the Manitoba Court of Queen's Bench in 2008, in *Manitoba Metis Federation v. Canada (Attorney General)*.[70] While the *Powley* analysis of Métis Aboriginal rights is not particularly relevant in this case, at the Court of Queen's Bench level, it is the most extensive review of the history of the Red River Métis community and its relationship with the federal government, which resulted in the establishment of the province of Manitoba and the grant of lands to the Métis of the region, of any decision in any Canadian court. This analysis went into great detail about the circumstances that led to the decision of the federal government to grant lands to the Métis and whether this grant of lands in the nineteenth century could ground a Métis Aboriginal title claim. The Court of Queen's

Bench, however, dismissed the claim, concluding that the grant of lands was a part of a unilateral Act of Parliament rather than a treaty or agreement with the Métis.[71] The Court noted, for example, that neither the Prime Minister nor Sir George-Étienne Cartier referred to the negotiation of a treaty or agreement with the provisional government of Red River in the Parliamentary debates over the *Manitoba Act*.[72] The Court also noted that the delegates chosen by the provisional government to enter into discussions with the Government of Canada were not representatives of an Aboriginal community but of the Red River Settlement, so the legal principles governing the interpretation of agreements with Aboriginal peoples did not apply here.[73]

The Court did, however, apply the *Powley* analysis that the period of "effective European control" was the relevant period for determining Métis Aboriginal rights to the question of Métis Aboriginal title, while stating that the other criteria for a finding of Aboriginal title remained the same in a Métis title claim as in a First Nations title claim.[74] The Court therefore determined that the Métis did not have the necessary exclusivity of occupation to ground Aboriginal title; neither did they hold title communally nor was their title inalienable, as would be required to find Aboriginal title.[75] The Court also agreed with the federal government that the grant of land to the Métis was not intended to create or preserve a Métis land base.[76]

Interestingly, even after coming to these conclusions, the Court of Queen's Bench went on to address the issue of whether Métis were "Indians," in something of a throwback to the pre-*Powley* case law. The Court repeatedly declared that the Métis of Red River were not "Indians," commenting that,

> *Placed in historic context, the evidence in this case is overwhelming that the Métis were not Indians. They did not consider themselves to be Indians. They saw themselves, and wanted to be seen, as civilized and fully enfranchised citizens. So, too, did the entire Settlement see them that way...The evidence clearly*

establishes that the entire Settlement, including the Métis, viewed the Indians as being inferior, being in need of care or guardianship and being incapable or unfit for enfranchisement and the enjoyment of the rights of full citizens.[77]

While the Court connects this conclusion to its conclusion that the federal government did not owe the Métis a fiduciary duty and that the grant of land to the Métis was not designed to establish or preserve a Métis land base,[78] it is not clear what purpose the Court's determination that Métis were not "Indians" in 1870 actually serves. It also seems inconsistent with the rest of the post-*Powley* jurisprudence to even address this question, rather than focus on the particular history of the Métis' relationship with the Crown, in the context of a Métis Aboriginal rights (or title) claim.

The appeal of this decision reached the Manitoba Court of Appeal in 2010. The Court of Appeal dismissed the appeal and upheld the trial decision on the basis that the action was barred because of the limitation period, the doctrine of laches, and the mootness of the issue.[79] It nonetheless went on to address the issue of whether the Crown owed the Métis a fiduciary duty and, if so, whether it was breached. The Court of Appeal, therefore, also extensively reviewed the history of the Red River Settlement. In commenting on the substantive matters decided by the trial judge, the Court of Appeal stated that

With very few exceptions...there was evidence, in many instances overwhelming evidence, to support the trial judge's conclusions with respect to the context and purpose of s. 31 of the [Manitoba] Act [which provided for the grant of land to the Métis], as well as the inferences that he drew from them.[80]

The Court of Appeal also commented, in the course of its review of the trial judge's decision, that "There can be no doubt, as the trial judge found, that the aboriginality of the Métis was (and is) distinctly different than that of the Indians."[81] The Court went on to state that "The important differences between Indians and Métis (in the nineteenth century and today) and the fact that this is not a traditional historic land claim could well be factors when considering the nature and extent of any fiduciary obligation owed to the Métis."[82] Later, the Court reviewed the comments of the Supreme Court of Canada in *Powley* that recognized the Métis as a distinct Aboriginal people whose rights are not merely derivative of the rights of their First Nations ancestors.[83] The Court commented, in this context, that

> [w]hile both the Métis and Indians are Aboriginal peoples, as explained by the
> trial judge, there are differences in their experiences and histories. The facts of
> any given case will reflect these differences to the extent that they are relevant
> in the circumstances. As a result, the law sometimes develops differently with
> respect to different Aboriginal groups, as it has with the interpretation of s. 35.
> The differences between the Métis and Indians are reflected in their experiences
> as they emerge in the evidence in each case, and through the application of the
> same law to the unique fact situations in each case.[84]

These comments reinforce the appropriateness of the post-*Powley* approach of looking at the particulars of Métis identity, rather than seeking to determine their rights by determining whether Métis are "Indians."

Interestingly, the Court of Appeal found that the Métis are the beneficiaries of the fiduciary relationship between the Crown and Aboriginal peoples, though the Court noted that the existence of a fiduciary relationship is not sufficient to determine whether a fiduciary obligation existed in the particular circumstances of any particular case.[85] The Court also noted that during the events surrounding the enactment of the *Manitoba Act* there was uncertainty about the nature and extent of the Métis interests that s. 31 of the *act* purported to extinguish (i.e., whether they held Aboriginal title).[86] In the end, though, the Court concluded that while there was a fiduciary relationship and they could not determine whether there was a cognizable Métis interest in land that could give rise to a fiduciary obligation (but that this was possible, at least under s. 31) and that the Government of Canada exercised complete discretion in the administration of the interests of the Metis, the Métis claimants did not prove a breach of the fiduciary standard of conduct in the administration of s. 31 of the *Manitoba Act*, so the question of the existence of a fiduciary duty did not need to be answered.[87]

One of the rare cases of a Métis Aboriginal rights claim from the Maritimes is the 2004 case of *R. v. Hopper*.[88] In this case, the defendant self-identified as a Métis and showed the conservation officer who confronted him, over his possession of a deer carcass, his Métis membership card.[89] At trial, in the New Brunswick Provincial Court, the Provincial Court judge applied the *Powley* indicia but concluded that there was no evidence the defendant's ancestors belonged to a distinctive Aboriginal group that continued to live as a distinct Aboriginal community.[90] This decision was appealed to the Court of Queen's Bench, where the trial judge's decision was upheld as being reasonable on the evidence.[91] On a further appeal to the New Brunswick Court of Appeal, the defendant argued that proof of descent from a treaty signatory is all that is required to successfully assert treaty rights.[92] In deciding that this was not so, Bell, JA for the Court of Appeal, noted that the *Powley* test has been used in New Brunswick to determine whether "non-status Indians" were rights-bearing Aboriginal people.[93] Bell, JA also concluded that Mr. Hopper did not meet the indicia outlined in *Powley* for determining Métis identity and he therefore could not claim an Aboriginal identity.[94] In the end, the Court of Appeal dismissed the appeal and upheld Mr. Hopper's conviction.[95]

The 2009 Manitoba case of *R. v. Goodon* also applied the *Powley* test to a Métis Aboriginal rights claim.[96] The case is probably most important, however, for its treatment of the questions of what constitutes a Métis community and where the community could exercise its Aboriginal rights. In deciding this case, the Manitoba Provincial Court referred to evidence that, as early as 1815, Métis were recognized as being distinct from First Nations.[97] It also accepted the evidence that Métis were transient and that, therefore, the community was a regional one, commenting that

> [t]he Metis created a large inter-related community that included numerous
> settlements located in present-day southwestern Manitoba, into Saskatchewan
> and including the northern Midwest United States. This area was one com-
> munity as the same people and their families used this entire territory as their
> homes, living off the land, and only periodically settling at a distinct loca-
> tion when it met their purposes. Within the Province of Manitoba this historic
> rights-bearing community includes all of the area within the present boundar-
> ies of southern Manitoba from the present day City of Winnipeg and extending
> south to the United States and northwest to the Province of Saskatchewan
> including the area of present day Russell, Manitoba.[98]

Thus, the court defined the relevant Métis community as the Métis of
southwestern Manitoba.

The 2010 Alberta case of *R. v. Lizotte* is also interesting because, in
applying the *Powley* indicia of Métis identity, the Alberta Provincial Court
had to address the question of whether membership in an Alberta Métis
settlement (a statutory creation of the Government of Alberta) automatically identifies an individual as Métis for the purposes of determining
whether they are the bearers of Aboriginal rights.[99] The Provincial Court
judge commented that there was commonality between the criteria for
membership in the Métis Settlements and the indicia of Métis identity in
Powley and concluded that

> [i]n essence the people of Alberta...recognized that they trusted the Métis
> Settlements to decide for themselves, within the framework provided [by the
> 1990 legislation], who was a "Métis." The Crown wants to create a parallel
> world of unnamed bureaucrats to analyze Métis genealogical records and sec-
> ond-guess the work of the Settlements. This is inconsistent with the Act, and
> with common sense.[100]

Thus, as the Provincial Court judge noted, in Alberta, it is sufficient for an
individual to prove membership in a Métis Settlement to meet the identity
criteria in *Powley*.[101]

The most recent Métis Aboriginal rights case also comes from Alberta. *R. v. Hirsekorn* is another case in which Métis were charged with hunting illegally.[102] While the Alberta Provincial Court decided that the Aboriginal rights defence failed because the accused were not hunting for subsistence purposes,[103] the court did go on to consider the application of the *Powley* decision to Mr. Hirsekorn's and Mr. Jones's situation. One of the court's determinations was that prior to 1874 there was "no consistent pattern of use or occupation of southern Alberta by Métis hunters" as a consequence of the strength of the Blackfoot Confederacy in southern Alberta.[104] Rather, the historical Métis community existed in a region around modern-day Edmonton.[105] The court also found that it was the extension of effective European control to southern Alberta, set at between 1874 and 1878, that allowed Métis to enter the region and eventually establish a distinct Métis community in the region, so that there were no Métis with Aboriginal rights arising from pre-European control practices in the region.[106] Because of this finding, the court found that there was no contemporary rights-bearing Métis community in the region, though there is a contemporary Métis community in the area around Medicine Hat, and that, therefore, the defendants were not members of a contemporary rights-bearing community, even though they self-identified as Métis, had Métis ancestry, and were accepted as members of a contemporary Métis community.[107]

As can be seen from this review, there has been a great deal of Métis Aboriginal rights jurisprudence since the Supreme Court of Canada decided *Powley* in 2003. Virtually all of this jurisprudence has carefully considered and applied the *Powley* analysis of Métis Aboriginal rights claims as claims to a distinct regime of rights held by distinct communities. In all of the decisions but the Manitoba Court of Queen's Bench decision in the *Manitoba Metis Federation* case, the typical pre-*Powley* characterization of Métis Aboriginal rights as arising from the terms of the *Natural Resources Transfer Agreements* and the typical analytical approach of asking if Métis were "Indians" has been abandoned in preference for the application of the *Powley* indicia. While not always resulting in victories for Métis claimants, on the whole this should be seen as a positive development for Métis.

Conclusion

Judicial recognition of Métis identity and the existence of Métis Aboriginal rights has been a long, slow process. Courts in common-law legal systems rely on legal sources such as statutes, legal agreements, or common-law precedents to make claims of legal rights cognizable. While they were recognized by the *Constitution Act, 1982*, as one of the Aboriginal peoples of Canada, Métis, unlike First Nations, were largely invisible in the Canadian legal landscape; this made Métis identity, let alone Métis Aboriginal rights, difficult for the courts to understand and recognize. The first instincts of the courts in responding to Métis Aboriginal rights claims was thus to look to the holders of the Aboriginal rights that they did recognize, First Nations and particularly "status Indians," and ask whether Métis were "like Indians." This inquiry led to questions about the "Indian" genealogy of Métis rights claimants and whether the claimants lived "an Indian mode of life." This approach, however, meant that Métis were only cognizable to the extent that they were "like Indians" and restricted the conception of Métis rights as being something derivative from First Nations' Aboriginal rights. Such an approach did a serious disservice to the distinct cultural identity of Métis, their legal status as a distinct Aboriginal community on par with those of First Nations and Inuit peoples, and their distinct relationship with the Crown.

The Supreme Court of Canada's decision in *Powley* thus represents a significant breakthrough for Métis. By looking not to whether Métis were "like Indians" but to the history of Métis ethnogenesis and the cultural practices of Métis communities, the Supreme Court made Métis identity cognizable to the judiciary and made it possible for Canadian jurisprudence to develop a distinct body of Métis Aboriginal rights. The importance to Canadian Aboriginal law jurisprudence of the *Powley* decision is

demonstrated by how completely the indicia and analytical process articulated in *Powley* has come to dominate Métis Aboriginal rights jurisprudence
in the lower courts, even in the absence of any further Supreme Court of
Canada decisions on Métis Aboriginal rights to reinforce and refine the
Powley approach. As yet, this has not resulted in the identification of any
Métis Aboriginal rights that are distinct to the Métis, but there is no reason that the *Powley* approach to understanding Métis Aboriginal rights
could not result in the protection, as Aboriginal rights, of practices that
are central to Métis identity as a distinct community. Such practices
would not necessarily be integral to the culture of First Nations. Thus,
although a long and slow process, and subject to a decade of jurisprudence
that could best be described as a "false start," the development of a Métis
Aboriginal rights jurisprudence in the first decade of the twenty-first century has been valuable in making Métis cognizable as a distinct Aboriginal
community and giving some substance to the recognition given to Métis
as an Aboriginal people in the *Constitution Act, 1982*.

Author's Note

I would like to thank Aaron Mintz, my research assistant, for his comments on, and
careful footnoting of, this chapter, and my colleagues Gregg Dahl and Chris Adams and
the anonymous reviewers for their valuable comments on an earlier draft of the text.

Notes

1. *Constitution Act, 1982*, s 35 (1).
2. *Manitoba Act, 1870*, s 31.
3. [1973] SCR 313.
4. [1977] 3 WWR 379; 9 CNLC 634 (SKQB).
5. 2003 SCC 43; [2003] 2 SCR 207.
6. 2003 SCC 44; [2003] 2 SCR 236.
7. *R v Laprise*, [1977] 3 WWR 379; 9 CNLC 634 (SKQB).
8. *R v Laprise*, [1978] 6 WWR 85 (SKCA).
9. [1992] 4 CNLR 144 (Man Prov Ct).
10. Ibid at 151–52.

11. Ibid at 152.

12. Nonetheless, the court convicted the accused of breaking Manitoba's hunting regulations, deciding that, though the regulations had to be declared invalid, this declaration of invalidity should temporarily be suspended to allow the Manitoba government to enact new regulations that could be justified as a legitimate infringement of Métis Aboriginal rights. The Crown appealed the declaration of invalidity of the regulations made by the Provincial Court judge and the accused appealed their convictions. The Crown and the accused made a joint recommendation to the Court of Queen's Bench that the accused be acquitted. The court allowed both appeals, acquitting the accused of the charges.

13. [1993] 2 CNLR 148 (Alta Prov Ct (Crim Div)).

14. Ibid at 153.

15. Ibid at 154.

16. *R v Ferguson*, [1994] 1 CNLR 117 at 120 (ABQB).

17. *R v Desjarlais*, [1996] 1 CNLR 148 (Alta Prov Ct) at 149.

18. Ibid at 150–51 (interestingly, the Crown argued that the accused had insufficient "Indian association" (i.e., did not associate with individuals recognized as "Indians" sufficiently) in responding to the Aboriginal rights defence of the defendants. See 151).

19. Ibid at 151–52.

20. Ibid at 152.

21. *R v Desjarlais*, [1996] 3 CNLR 113 (ABQB), at 119–20.

22. Ibid at para 121.

23. [1996] 10 WWR 170; 3 CNLR 122 (Sask QB), at 130.

24. Ibid at 126–27.

25. Ibid at 130.

26. *R v Grumbo*, (1998), 159 DLR (4th) 577; [1999] 1 WWR 9 (Sask CA), at paras 27–28, 36. The charges against Mr. Grumbo were eventually dropped, so there was no new trial.

27. Ibid at paras 33, 35.

28. *R v Morin and Daigneault*, [1996] 3 CNLR 157 (Sask Prov Ct), at 165, 167–68.

29. Ibid at 168.

30. Ibid at 169–73.

31. Ibid at 174.

32. Ibid at 176.

33. *R v Morin*, [1998] 2 WWR 18; [1998] 1 CNLR 182 at 196 (Sask QB).

34. *R v Blais*, at paras 19–20.

35. Ibid at para 42.

36. *R v Powley*, at para 10.

37. Ibid at para 12.

38. Ibid at para 13.

39. Ibid at paras 17–18, 21–23.

40. Ibid at paras 31–33.

41. Ibid at para 29.

42. Ibid at para 29.

43. Ibid at para 36.

44. Ibid at para 41.

45. Interestingly, a number of cases in Atlantic Canada have used the Supreme Court of Canada's criteria for Métis identity laid out in *Powley* to answer the question of who is a "non-status Indian" for the purpose of claiming Aboriginal rights. Prior to *Willison* (see note 47), the New Brunswick Provincial Court and, on appeal, the New Brunswick Court of Queen's Bench in *R v Acker* used the indicia of Métis identity set out in *Powley* to assess whether an individual who claimed to be Mi'kmaq but was not a "status Indian" was an "Indian" under section 35 of the *Constitution Act, 1982*, and therefore had an Aboriginal right to hunt. Both courts concluded that Mr. Acker had not either the necessary self-identification or community acceptance as an "Indian" to be a holder of Aboriginal rights. In *R v Lavigne*, 2005 NBPC 8, 283 NBR (2d) 298; [2005] 3 CNLR 176, the New Brunswick Provincial Court concluded that the defendant was an "Indian" for the purpose of an Aboriginal rights defence to a hunting charge because he self-identified as Aboriginal, was of Aboriginal heritage, and was accepted by the community (in this case, the New Brunswick Aboriginal Peoples Council) as Aboriginal, though the court also connected his self-identification to evidence of an Aboriginal life-style: see para 59. In deciding the appeal of this case, the New Brunswick Court of Queen's Bench specifically addressed the *Powley* decision, commenting that, "In my view, although *Powley* dealt with a Métis case, the three criteria applied in that case are equally applicable to the question of who is an Indian under section 35 of the *Constitution Act, 1982*.": see *R v Lavigne*, 2007 NBQB 171, [2007] 4 CNLR 268, at para 39. It is also worth noting that, in the 2010 case of *R v Bernard*, [2010] NBJ no 277 (QL) (Prov Ct) in which the Crown argued that the Supreme Court of Canada's *Powley* decision should also be applied to determining the Aboriginal rights of "status Indians," the New Brunswick Provincial Court rejected the Crown's argument, noting that, "that case was intended to deal with the issue of

Métis and not Inuit or Indian people" and referred to the conclusion in *Blais* that Métis are a separate and distinct group of people: see para 56.

46. *R v Willison*, 2005 BCPC 131, [2005] 3 CNLR 278, at paras 87, 111, 113–14, 123–24.

47. Ibid at para 142.

48. *R v Willison*, 2006 BCSC, [2006] 4 CNLR 253, 985 at paras 34, 48.

49. 2005 SKPC 46, 263 Sask R 128; [2005] 3 CNLR 268.

50. Ibid at para 32.

51. Ibid at paras 31, 35.

52. 2005 SKPC 70, 267 Sask R 291; [2005] 3 CNLR 202, at para 3.

53. Ibid at paras 26–28.

54. [2006] 3 CNLR 324 (Alta Prov Ct), at para 28.

55. Ibid at paras 32, 34–35, 51.

56. *R v Kelley*, 2007 ABQB 41, 413 AR 269; [2007] 2 CNLR 332, at para 78.

57. *Labrador Métis Nation v. Newfoundland and Labrador (Minister of Transportation and Works)*, 2006 NLTD 119, 258 Nfld & PEIR 257; [2006] 4 CNLR 94, at paras 8–17, 26–34.

58. Ibid at paras 49–50.

59. Ibid at paras 53–54.

60. Ibid at para 60.

61. Ibid at paras 68–70.

62. *Labrador Métis Nation v Newfoundland and Labrador (Minister of Transportation and Works)*, 2007 NLCA 75, 272 Nfld & PEIR 178; 288 DLR (4th) 641, at paras 37–38. (The Court of Appeal also agreed with the Newfoundland and Labrador Supreme Court that an agent can act on behalf of an Aboriginal community to enforce a right to be consulted: see para 46).

63. Ibid at paras 39–40.

64. *R v Belhumeur*, 2007 SKPC 114, [2008] 2 CNLR 311; 301 Sask R 292, at paras 140–42, 169, 174.

65. Ibid at paras 181, 206–07.

66. Ibid at paras 203–04.

67. 2008 TCC 292, [2009] 1 CTC 2151.

68. Ibid at para 4.

69. Ibid at para 31.

70. 2007 MBQB 293, [2008] 2 CNLR 52; [2008] 4 WWR 402.

71. Ibid at paras 464–66.

72. Ibid at para 476.

73. Ibid at paras 531, 533.

74. Ibid at paras 577–78.

75. Ibid at paras 589–93.

76. Ibid at paras 927–28.

77. Ibid at paras 600–01.

78. Ibid at paras 633, 928.

79. *Manitoba Metis Federation Inc. v Canada (Attorney General)*, 2010 MBCA 71, [2010] 12 WWR 599; [2010] 3 CNLR 233, at para 10.

80. Ibid at para 238.

81. Ibid at para 243.

82. Ibid at para 245.

83. Ibid at para 379.

84. Ibid at para 384.

85. Ibid at paras 432–33, 443.

86. Ibid at para 475.

87. Ibid at paras 509, 534.

88. (2004), 275 NBR (2d) 251; 61 WCB (2d) 117 (Prov Ct).

89. Ibid at para 2.

90. Ibid at para 21.

91. See e.g. *R v Hopper*, 2005 NBQB 399, 295 NBR (2d) 21, at paras 23–24.

92. *R v Hopper*, 2008 NBCA 42, 331 NBR (2d) 177, at paras 5, 7.

93. Ibid at para 9.

94. Ibid at paras 14–18.

95. Ibid at para 23.

96. 2008 MBPC 59, [2009] 2 CNLR 278 (Man Prov Ct).

97. Ibid at para 43.

98. Ibid at paras 46–48.

99. [2010] 1 CNLR 326 (Alta Prov Ct).

100. Ibid at para 29.

101. Ibid at para 32.

102. 2010 ABPC 385 (available on QL).

103. Ibid at para 32.

104. Ibid at para 114.

105. Ibid at para 115.

106. Ibid at paras 138–39.

107. Ibid at paras 146, 148, 151.

Bibliography

Calder et al v Attorney-General of British Columbia, [1973] SCR 313.

Constitution Act, 1982, s 35 (1).

Janzen v Canada, 2008 TCC 292, [2009] 1 CTC 2151.

Labrador Métis Nation v Newfoundland and Labrador (Minister of Transportation and Works), 2006 NLTD 119, 258 Nfld & PEIR 257; [2006] 4 CNLR 94.

Labrador Métis Nation v Newfoundland and Labrador (Minister of Transportation and Works), 2007 NLCA 75, 272 Nfld & PEIR 178; 288 DLR (4th) 641.

Manitoba Act, 1870, s 31.

Manitoba Metis Federation v Canada (Attorney General), 2007 MBQB 293, [2008] 2 CNLR 52; [2008] 4 WWR 402.

Manitoba Metis Federation Inc. v Canada (Attorney General), 2010 MBCA 71, [2010] 12 WWR 599; [2010] 3 CNLR 233.

R v Belhumeur, 2007 SKPC 114; [2008] 2 CNLR 311; 301 Sask R 292.

R v Bernard, [2010] NBJ no 277 (QL) (Prov Ct).

R v Blais, 2003 SCC 44; [2003] 2 SCR 236.

R v Desjarlais, [1996] 1 CNLR 148 (Alta Prov Ct).

R v Desjarlais, [1996] 3 CNLR 113 (ABQB).

R v Ferguson, [1993] 2 CNLR 148 (Alta Prov Ct (Crim Div)).

R v Ferguson, [1994] 1 CNLR 117 (ABQB).

R v Goodon, 2008 MBPC 59, [2009] 2 CNLR 278 (Man Prov Ct).

R v Grumbo, [1996] 10 WWR 170; 3 CNLR 122 (Sask QB).

R v Grumbo, (1998) 159 DLR (4th) 577; [1999] 1 WWR 9 (Sask CA).

R v Hirsekorn, 2010 ABPC 385.

R v Hopper, (2004) 275 NBR (2d) 251; 61 WCB (2d) 117(Prov Ct).

R v Hopper, 2005 NBQB 399, 295 NBR (2d) 21.

R v Hopper, 2008 NBCA 42, 331 NBR (2d) 177.

R v Kelley, [2006] 3 CNLR 324 at para 28 (Alta Prov Ct).

R v Kelley, 2007 ABQB 41, 413 AR 269; [2007] 2 CNLR 332.

R v Laprise, [1977] 3 WWR 379; 9 CNLC 634 (SKQB).

R v Laprise, [1978] 6 WWR 85 (SKCA).

R v Lavigne, 2005 NBPC 8, 283 NBR (2d) 298; [2005] 3 CNLR 176.

R v Lavigne, 2007 NBQB 171, [2007] 4 CNLR 268.

R v Laviolette, 2005 SKPC 70, 267 Sask R 291; [2005] 3 CNLR 202.

R v Lizotte, [2010] 1 CNLR 326 (Alta Prov Ct).

R v McPherson, [1992] 4 CNLR 144 (Man Prov Ct).

R v Morin and Daigneault, [1996] 3 CNLR 157 (Sask Prov Ct).

R v Morin, [1998] 2 WWR 18; [1998] 1 CNLR 182 (Sask QB).

R v Norton, 2005 SKPC 46, 263 Sask R 128; [2005] 3 CNLR 268.

R v Powley, 2003 SCC 43; [2003] 2 SCR 207.

R v Willison, 2005 BCPC 131, [2005] 3 CNLR 278.

R v Willison, 2006 BCSC 985, [2006] 4 CNLR 253.

Even When We're Winning, | 8
Are We Losing?

Métis Rights in Canadian Courts

JEREMY PATZER

AFTER A LONG HISTORY of neglect and disregard at the hands of
the Crown, a response to the simple question of what constitutes a turnaround for the Métis in Canada becomes difficult to gauge. Would it be
section 35(1) of the *Constitution Act, 1982*, which brought constitutional
recognition of the Métis after more than a century of little or no formal
recognition? In effect, section 35 affirms the existence and recognition of
the Indian, Inuit, and Métis peoples, as well as their "existing Aboriginal
and treaty rights."[1] Although there was nothing that explained or outlined
what, for the Métis, their *Aboriginal rights* were, the repatriation of the
constitution was sufficient to spur western Métis to leave the pan-Aboriginal Native Council of Canada[2] and form the Métis National Council—a step
taken in their effort to better represent both the nation and the cultural
content that would underlie these rights. Or, rather than in 1982, was the
turnaround in 2003, when after years of failed constitutional wrangling
the Supreme Court of Canada (scc) took a small first step in recognizing
and delineating Métis rights? Indeed, after more than two decades with
no content ascribed to the Aboriginal rights purportedly "recognized and

affirmed" in the *Constitution Act, 1982*,[3] the inclusion of the Métis in section 35 seemed more and more like an empty promise. The year 2003, on the other hand, saw a legal victory sufficiently monumental to cause many Métis to perceive it as the beginning of a tidal shift.

Specifically, the landmark decision of *R. v. Powley*[4] recognized, for Métis in and around Sault Ste. Marie, an Aboriginal right to hunt for food. Jean Teillet, a member of the legal team for Steve and Roddy Powley, was clear and to the point when she asserted their argument was predicated on the Powleys' ancestral connection to a Métis Nation whose territory encompasses "the Prairies and a little bit [of] BC and Ontario."[5] What the 2003 decision meant for members of the Métis Nation outside of Sault Ste. Marie, and for Métis peoples in other regions of Canada, for that matter, was a source of immediate and widespread speculation.

Amidst the excitement, however, I am seeking to introduce a certain amount of circumspection into the debate. Just as many Aboriginal groups—after long histories of political struggle—know all too well, the concept of "the turnaround" must be considered with suspicion. I argue simply that the *Powley* decision may not be the panacea that many hope or claim it to be. But my unease with the *Powley* precedent—and with the Supreme Court of Canada's latest approach to rights and title in general—stems from more than an assessment of the likelihood of Métis peoples "winning" legal recognition of the various rights they wish to assert. (Although such an assessment is still a critical component of a full critique of the courts' approach to Aboriginal rights.) Rather, my unease also stems from the fact that, independent of the balance between wins and losses, there is a lot more than just a decision concerning a right to a practice that is solidified in these legal processes.

The Canadian judiciary's current approach to Aboriginal rights and title—often referred to as the cultural rights approach—both departs from and actively helps create and propagate an Aboriginal subjectivity that is rooted in a quaint, "authentic" past tethered to discrete and tightly delimited practices. It is a romantic, idealized vision of Aboriginality, to be sure, and one that mobilizes a cunning politics of difference in which claimants are apt to be cast as too distant from their own Aboriginality to merit the recognition of their rights. The cultural rights approach makes use of a historico-cultural test that inevitably shapes the Aboriginal rights trial into an evaluation of the "authenticity" of contemporary Aboriginal rights claims, and thus represents a further incursion of colonial power and legal-bureaucratic categorization into the lives, perceptions and self-perceptions of Aboriginal Canadians. This should be of particular concern to Canada's Métis, given that it disallows for them certain idiosyncrasies so common to non-Aboriginal nations, and that are arguably even more vital to the identities of those who spring from miscegenation and ethno-genesis: complexity, variability and adaptability.

Additionally, the current approach to Aboriginal rights and title has the effect of reversing the burden of proof in the wake of the colonial encounter. The cultural rights trial is, from the outset, premised on a per-vasive uncertainty over the existence of a right and requires Aboriginal claimants to establish that the right exists according to the historico-cultural criteria set out by the scc. For historical practices such as hunt-ing and fishing, this essentially revives the extinguishment of rights and title that was supposedly proscribed by the *Constitution Act, 1982*, for Métis claimants may find their long held practices are simply not recognized as a right—despite the obvious importance of these activities to many Aboriginal peoples. The consequences of these deficiencies are all the more acute for Métis claimants, however, given that they are not seeking the simple revision of some aspect of an already existing rights regime. Rather, they are striving to build up a rights regime from a relatively com-plete absence of such recognition. Unfortunately, the finality of juridical discourse is such that once Canadian courts assert that an Aboriginal right does not exist legally, it will be all the more difficult for Métis organiza-tions to convince governments and the rest of Canadian society otherwise.

Aboriginal Rights and Title Jurisprudence

One of the earliest and most important precedents to rule on the nature of Aboriginal rights to land was the 1888 decision for *St. Catherine's Milling and Lumber Company v. The Queen*.[6] The Ojibway group discussed in the decision was not a party in the legal dispute. Rather, determining the nature of the "Indian title" they formerly held over their land, prior to extinguishment of that title by an 1873 treaty, was crucial to helping the courts decide whether the Province of Ontario or the Dominion of Canada had jurisdiction over the land. Thus the essential question before the Judicial Committee of the Privy Council (JCPC) in London, which was Canada's highest court at that time, was "What kind of legal relationship did Aboriginal peoples have to their land?"

The JCPC based its judgment squarely on an interpretation of the *Royal Proclamation of 1763*.[7] The *Royal Proclamation* was an outcome of the Seven Years War, in which the British overcame the French. Following the Treaty of Paris, the *Proclamation* was meant to establish boundaries and administrations for the British Crown's newly expanded possessions in the New World. Having benefited from alliances with Aboriginal groups, King George also sought to offer an assurance in the *Proclamation* that lands that had not been "ceded to, or purchased by Us, are reserved to them, or any of them, as their Hunting Grounds."[8] In the *St. Catherine's Milling* case, Ontario argued that the *Royal Proclamation* established that ultimate title for the lands in question was with the Crown from 1763, and that the Indian title was merely a burden of usage on the Crown's absolute title. The Dominion, for its own purposes, actually argued that Indian title was equivalent to a complete proprietary interest. The JCPC agreed with the Province of Ontario on its characterization of Indian title. The JCPC decision rested on terms of the *Royal Proclamation* that referred to the lands outside of the four 1763 colonies as "Parts of Our Dominions and Territories," reserved and protected for use as Aboriginal hunting grounds "for the present, and until Our further Pleasure be known."[9] Such passages were used to infer that King George had asserted a radical, underlying title to all the lands in his purview, identifying Indian title as a mere usufructuary right dependent on the good will of the Crown.

It is significant that, at that point in jurisprudential history, justice was understood to be synonymous with the will of the sovereign. Having a notion of justice limited in this way helped to smooth over the inconsistencies, caprices and contrivances embedded within the legal history of colonization. The most significant of these contrivances, of course, is how the Crown justly and legitimately acquired—prior to and independent of treaty-making—ultimate title over the entirety of British North America. This is a pertinent question because, in contradistinction to theories based on the concept of *terra nullius*, Aboriginal peoples' occupation of land *was* largely seen as having juridical dimensions. For example, Brian Slattery outlines an early colonial history of papal bulls, royal patents and royal charters during which the British and French Crowns argued with their Spanish and Portuguese counterparts that simple discovery alone does *not* grant one possession of new lands.[10] That this is the case is demonstrated first and foremost, however, by the entire history of treaty-making itself. While the meaning, interpretation and legitimacy of treaty processes are all open to question, such formalized agreements for the cession of Aboriginal territory entail, at a minimum, that Aboriginal peoples were at least implicitly recognized as being in some way in possession of their land. This, however, becomes difficult to square against the British Crown's later colonization of significant stretches of territory without the benefit of treaty. Perhaps the best explanation is that the jurisprudential concept of Aboriginal title—something less than full title, existing at the pleasure of the Crown, and subject to its caprices—offered a post-hoc legal foundation for the moral contradictions of colonization. Much of Canada's jurisprudence up until the late twentieth century thus amounted to two somewhat incongruent conclusions: Aboriginal peoples' occupation of land does have juridical dimensions, yet all of this is for naught should the Crown act otherwise.

Whatever guarantees were expressed in the *Royal Proclamation* were not understood by the judiciary as applicable to Aboriginal peoples across the full breadth of Canada. This was a fact the Nisga'a of British Columbia would sadly discover a century later with the decision in *Calder et al. v. Attorney-General of British Columbia*.[11] Because no treaty existed between the Crown and the Nisga'a by which the latter surrendered title to the former, and because no explicit provincial or federal legislation declared the Nisga'a title extinguished, the Nisga'a felt assured that they still retained title to their lands. They actually lost their case due to a technicality, but the scc justices who wrote the deciding opinion against them also asserted that the *Royal Proclamation* would not have afforded them title. In essence, the estimation of several of the justices was that, given when the *Proclamation* was written, the Nisga'a territory would have existed outside the geographical scope of the King's assurances. However, perhaps in tacit recognition that such legal casuistry would be difficult to justify in the late twentieth century, the *Calder* decision opened a door for the Nisga'a and many other Aboriginal groups by stating that the *Royal Proclamation of 1763* was not the *only* source of Aboriginal title. The other source, in this case, was simply prior occupation. A striking example of why common-law systems are sometimes referred to as "judge-made law," the *Calder* decision essentially created the possibility of sourcing title claims in the fact that the group in question had occupied the land prior to the arrival of Europeans. Of course, the early case law to follow would show there were numerous and significant qualifications to this new source of Aboriginal title recognized at common law. Aboriginal groups would have to prove, as though the matter were still unresolved, that they belonged to an "organized society" at the time of European contact. Aboriginal groups also had to prove they occupied their respective regions exclusive of any other groups, and that their title had not been extinguished by treaty or by the explicit or implicit unilateral intent of colonial governments and their activities.[12] Despite these many qualifications and conditions, *Calder* ushered in an era in which the judiciary sought to find some sort of compromise for Aboriginal groups that were without treaties in the aftermath of the colonial assumption of sovereignty.

The next landmark precedents came with *R. v. Sparrow*[13] and *R. v. Van der Peet*,[14] representing the moment in Canadian common law when the scc made an implicit choice—inspired by the use of the term "rights" in reference to Aboriginal peoples in the *Constitution Act, 1982*—to parse discrete practices, in the form of *specific rights*, from historic jurisprudential discussions of *title*, and, notably, from a larger grammar of sovereignty, self-determination and decolonization most commonly employed by Aboriginal groups. Specific Aboriginal rights can thus be considered legally defined practices to which Aboriginal groups may have a right but that are not sufficiently exclusive that they amount to title over the land on which these practices occur.[15] Among other things, the *Sparrow* decision stated that, as a result of the new constitutional protection, Aboriginal rights and title could no longer be extinguished but, rather, only infringed, with justification and on a provisional basis. It also affirmed that any government's intention to legally extinguish an Aboriginal right prior to 1982 must have been clear and plain and cannot simply be inferred after the fact from a body of policy and practice that was adverse to the maintenance and exercise of the right. It left unanswered, however, the critical question of defining what is and what is not an Aboriginal right. This was left to the *Van der Peet* decision.

The case of *R. v. Van der Peet* sought to determine whether Dorothy Van der Peet, a member of the Stó:lō First Nation, had an Aboriginal right to sell ten fish that she had caught under the authority of an Indian food fish licence. To this end, the Supreme Court of Canada outlined what it referred to as the "integral to a distinctive culture" test, according to which—in order to qualify as an Aboriginal right—"an activity must be an element of a practice, custom or tradition integral to the distinctive culture of the aboriginal group claiming the right."[16] The deciding opinion of the Court also stated that the defining characteristics of Aboriginal societies can only come from their *pre-contact* nature. Thus only those practices, customs and traditions that have *continuity* with those that existed prior to contact with European society can qualify as Aboriginal rights.

Not surprisingly, this pre-contact criterion left the Aboriginal rights of Métis peoples an open question. This, of course, is because the very existence of the Métis is due to a specific history of miscegenation: the intermarriage of mainly European men with Aboriginal women and the ethnogenesis of a distinctive culture and identity that arose from it. The *Van der Peet* decision acknowledges this incongruence but does not attempt to resolve it. It left the issue for another time, when the courts are presented, specifically, with a Métis claim to an Aboriginal right; the decision does, however, emphasize an underlying policy of non-generalizability for the new doctrine of Aboriginal rights. According to the *Van der Peet* decision, rights cannot be bundled together or "piggybacked" one on the other. In this sense, just because historic treaties with First Nations often provided for the recognition of the right to continue hunting, fishing and trapping on all lands where they had a right of access, this did not mean that a legal victory for the Métis would bring a similar rights regime to them. Rather, common-law Aboriginal rights are much more limited and specific: the fact that one Aboriginal group gains recognition of the right to a practice does not necessarily mean a neighbouring group also gains that right. The scc thus asserted that there is no universal package of Aboriginal rights, and that the case of the Métis would have to be heard on its own merits and in relation to a specific practice.

R. v. Powley was decided by the Supreme Court of Canada in 2003. In October 1993, Steve Powley and his son Roddy Powley, both Métis from the Sault Ste. Marie area in Ontario, were charged with hunting a bull moose without the proper licence. Just as with other important Aboriginal rights precedents, however, these facts were not in dispute. Initially, the basic question framed by the courts was whether the licensing requirements of Ontario's *Game and Fish Act* were "of no force or effect with respect to the respondents, being Métis, in the circumstances of this case, by reason of their aboriginal rights under s. 35 of the *Constitution Act, 1982*."[17] The scc decision for *Powley*, however, reformulated the question in more limited, specific terms, asking whether "members of the Métis community in and around Sault Ste. Marie enjoy a constitutionally protected right to hunt for food under s. 35 of the *Constitution Act, 1982*."[18]

The major adjustment to the *Van der Peet* test came with the need to establish the relevant time frame for identifying Métis rights. The argument of the defence was that Métis rights should find their origin in the pre-contact practices of the Métis' Aboriginal ancestors—in other words, the relevant First Nations. Acceptance of this assertion might have provided for a certain degree of equivalence of rights among a number of First Nations and Métis groups, but the Court refused this assertion. Rather, because the Court did not want to "deny to Métis their full status as distinctive rights-bearing peoples whose own integral practices are entitled to constitutional protection under s. 35(1)," the Court decided that Métis history can be accommodated best by employing the *Van der Peet* test but adapting it to focus "on the period after a particular Métis community arose and before it came under the effective control of European laws and customs."[19] With the *Powley* test thus formulated, it was determined that Steve, Roddy and the Métis community with historic roots in and around Sault Ste. Marie did indeed have an Aboriginal right to hunt for food.

Misgivings

These cases, summarized above, represent the most fundamental turns in Aboriginal rights and title jurisprudence. With *St. Catherine's Milling* the legal concept of Aboriginal title was diminished to a mere right of use—a burden on the radical, underlying title of the Crown. A controversial question that remains unexplored by Canadian courts is how the Crown legitimately acquired such title prior to any treaty-making process. Recent case law, however, is more apt to be construed in a positive light. *Calder*, a monumental turning point for Aboriginal rights and title jurisprudence, effectively created a concept of Aboriginal title—still subject to the Crown's paramount title, however—to be claimed at common law by those excluded from historic treaties. While Aboriginal title is considered a form of Aboriginal right, *Sparrow* splintered off discrete practices that could be established as separate, less onerous rights. This development was propitious for those, such as the Métis, who would likely have great difficulty claiming title to land, and it recognized that Aboriginal rights and title now had constitutional protection thanks to section 35 of the *Constitution Act, 1982*. In effect, Aboriginal Canadians seemingly found a new body of law that would offer some opportunities, concessions and protections that earlier jurisprudence would not.

Cultural rights decisions such as *Powley* and *Van der Peet*, however, and their tendency to imprison Aboriginality in the past, have now incited a storm of controversy among anthropologists and critical legal scholars. While the courts maintain that culture and cultural practices can change over time, decisions such as *R. v. Pamajewon*[20] conjure fears that this is not the case. An Ojibway people sought to hold gambling operations according to their own by-law and as a right inherent to a self-determining nation; the claim was rejected, however, because the gaming traditional to Ojibway culture did not occur in the past on the same scale as it would in the twentieth century. Yet, as Borrows replies, "not many activities in any society, prior to this century, took place on a twentieth-century scale," so "what would it be like for Canadians to have their fundamental rights defined by what *was* integral to European people's distinctive culture prior to their arrival in North America?"[21]

If the scc insists that Aboriginal rights are not to be frozen in time, then this forces us to ask why it chose a formula that characterizes the rights and title of colonized groups as somehow being *cultural* rather than *political* issues,[22] and that mobilizes a conception of Aboriginal culture as something that existed *in the past*. There is nothing written in the heavens that necessitates that Aboriginal rights be determined via a historical cultural test. This is an avenue chosen by the Supreme Court of Canada, but the demands and requirements of justice did not make it self-evident and inevitable. Parallel with my discussion of the Supreme Court's choice to fragment rights from larger questions of title and self-determination, Chris Andersen maintains that the scc, just as easily, could have opted to protect Aboriginal autonomy, rather than Aboriginal cultural difference.[23] Commonwealth governments and judiciaries, though, have assumed unquestioningly that Aboriginal claims must be founded on cultural difference. Unfortunately, as John Sharp has observed, the cultural essentialism integral to a politics of difference can create a paralyzing bind for Aboriginal groups:

> It follows that when the leaders of indigenous minorities within these states enter into dialogue with the consciousness, and the consciences, of the general public, they must assert an identity of fundamental cultural difference, of absolute primordial continuity with the precolonial past. If they did not do this, their claims for restoration of their dignity, for social justice, and for restitution for past dispossession would simply not be seen as legitimate. The unspoken rule is that those who make claims and demands on the basis of difference had better be really different. One is looking at a form of cultural relativism that deals, paradoxically, in absolutes: real difference resides in being, and in having always been, essentially different. Real difference is not seen as a precipitate of the divergent experiences that flow from differential positioning in processes of historical change.[24]

The judiciary's foray into cultural issues brings it into a territory traditionally navigated by the social sciences; unfortunately, as Ronald Niezen laments, its perspectives have not kept pace with contemporary anthropological theories that view culture as something unstable, contested, and more process than thing.[25] The Canadian judiciary's views of Aboriginality are reminiscent of the outmoded paradigms Johannes Fabian once criticized in the anthropology of another time.[26] If Aboriginality cannot exist in the here and now, then "the court is in danger of reducing Aboriginality to a package of anthropological curiosities rather than manifestations of an Aboriginal right to occupation, sovereignty and self-government."[27] Kent

McNeil fears that this approach to rights and title issues, if carried to the extreme, could "condemn Aboriginal societies to extinction, as cultures which cannot adapt to changing conditions are bound to disappear."[28]

But if the historical threshold used to define Aboriginal rights hints at the arbitrariness that underlies them, then so does the battery of indeterminate concepts used in their calculation. Justice McLachlin's dissenting opinion in the *Van der Peet* case was quite prescient, stating that "different people may entertain different ideas of what is distinctive, specific or central. To use such concepts as the markers of legal rights is to permit the determination of rights to be coloured by the subjective views of the decision-maker rather than objective norms."[29] Michael Asch thus warns of the development of an arbitrary judicial power over the determination of Aboriginal rights,[30] and Fae Korsmo suggests the possibility that "the more state-like the Aboriginal claim...the less likely the Aboriginal claimants are to convince courts of their claim."[31] As the *Pamajewon* decision suggests, the law's flexibility may be such that justifications for the rejection of a rights claim are always available when desired.

Much in line with these observations, the rights that the Métis are able to pursue in the courts are problematic in their specificity. *Powley* made it clear there would be neither a sweeping recognition of hunting rights for all Métis peoples across Canada, nor even recognition of hunting rights for the Métis Nation throughout the extent of its traditional homeland—to say nothing of other practices Métis people may wish to claim as rights. In the courts, and especially in provincial implementations of *Powley*, the *communal* nature of Aboriginal rights has been conflated, more often than not, with a tightly delimited geography of local *community*. After a providential combination of positive precedents and constitutional change, the judiciary seems to have geared itself to achieve a certain *reining in* of Aboriginal rights such that these rights are rehabilitated as a multiplicity of legal questions that will remain in the courts for some time to come.[32] *Powley* recognizes, for Métis who are living in and around Sault Ste. Marie, and who have an ancestral connection to the historic Métis community in and around Sault Ste. Marie, subsistence hunting rights that can be exercised only within that same area. This ruling leaves open the question of whether a Métis from one rights-bearing community who moves to another rights-bearing community would lose the ability to claim any Aboriginal rights. How such a rights regime, rooted in each individual's historical ancestry within a certain geographical radius, could be regulated is not clear.

To further complicate the issue of mobility, though, one need only consider the extensive mobility of most historic Métis. It is hard to understand why the courts feel justified in according Métis hunting rights to only those contemporary communities that can demonstrate continuous cultural roots that predate effective Crown control of their area, despite the fact that many Métis themselves were extremely mobile—especially those whose seasonal activities obliged them to travel across vast regions. While the Provincial Court of Manitoba did recognize Métis hunting rights across the southwest corner of the province in *R. v. Goodon*,[33] the claimant in *R. v. Hirsekorn*[34] sought unsuccessfully at the trial court level to source his hunting rights in a larger rights-bearing community spanning the entirety of the traditional Métis Nation homeland. Perhaps in reference to the fact that *treaty* hunting rights are often valid in all unoccupied Crown land and any other lands where hunters have a right of access, counsel for the defence emphasized the fact that, if Métis from one historical community cannot hunt in another, then they would be the only Aboriginal people who cannot. The Provincial Court justice presiding over the case is then reported to have responded that accepting this argument would require going outside accepted legal boundaries.[35] In the end, the trial court judge's decision affirmed the Province of Alberta's assertion that there was no historic rights-bearing Métis community in southern Alberta prior to the date of effective European control of the region.[36]

Such a restrictive and piecemeal method of resolving rights disputes makes for an insidious form of justice, particularly in the case of the Métis. The burden of proving continuity of community (itself an elastic concept) from pre-control to the present, let alone continuity of integral practices, may be onerous for many Métis claimants. For the many who trace their roots back to Red River, it is notable that the historical moment of Crown control of the new province of Manitoba coincided with a significant outward migration—due in part to the disappearance of the bison, but it was "also the result of the poisonous atmosphere in Red River itself."[37] The period of history immediately after 1870 has thus been characterized by some historians as one of dispossession, dispersal and a "reign of terror,"[38] only to be followed by more than one hundred years of a policy of silent non-recognition. Thus, for a people who were often itinerant, marginalized and disregarded, the reification of such time thresholds and the localization of historical rights allowed Thomas Rothwell, attorney for Alberta Justice in *R. v. Hirsekorn*, to declare to the media that "you may be Métis but you may not be part of a rights-bearing community."[39] In the Provincial Court of Saskatchewan, with Justice Green's finding that on a "balance of probabilities" the Manitoba Métis community of San Clara did not come into existence until about 20 years after effective Crown control—the settlement is still over a century old, nevertheless—such artificial time thresholds also allow Canadian justice to readily tell Métis communities as a whole: *you may be a Métis community, but you may not necessarily be a rights-bearing Métis community*. The gravity of this is all the more acute given that, of the three Aboriginal peoples recognized in the *Constitution Act, 1982*, the Métis were unique for the degree to which their rights were not recognized prior to the *Powley* decision. They are therefore not building upon a pre-existing rights regime, such as with claimants from other Aboriginal groups that have fought in court to fish with a certain type of net or to sell some of their catch. Rather, the Métis struggle is to achieve basic recognition of the right to carry on practices important to Métis people. The prospect of building a complex checkerboard of varying rights through a patchwork of court decisions—despite the fact that the *Sparrow* judgment specifically identified the need to avoid this—certainly looks like an arduous and never-ending task.

Apart from the casting of Aboriginal rights as a historico-cultural question, however, the other salient feature of recent Aboriginal rights jurisprudence is the determination and management of rights through a *test*. The mechanism of the test introduces a specific dynamic: it entails a sort of modern trial by ordeal for which Aboriginal Canadians must shape and present themselves as claimants who might "qualify" or "pass," and it implies the ever-present possibility of failure. This shapes the Aboriginal rights trial, invariably and undeniably, into a test of Aboriginal *authenticity*. In developed settler states, questions of Aboriginal authenticity currently stand as one of the most insidious forms of subjectification of Aboriginal peoples, or, put another way, one of the most penetrating incursions of power and power relations into the very meaning and being of Aboriginality. While the subjectification of colonized peoples is as old as the colonial relationship itself, the juridical field in Canada has intensified the effects of its subjectifying power with the cultural rights approach, because this foray into culture talk represents a further infiltration of legal-bureaucratic categorization into the lives and self-perceptions of Aboriginal Canadians. Hinging Aboriginal peoples' aspirations to restore lost self-determination on the successful performance of the colonizer's restrictive notions of Aboriginality is contradictory in itself, and it further imperils what remains of an Aboriginal agency and sense of self-assuredness in their own processes of debating and defining what it means to be Métis, First Nations, or Inuit, from the national to the community level. Parallel with Elizabeth Povinelli's observations of Aboriginal claims in Australia, power is exercised over Aboriginal Canadians, and their very sense of who they are, when they are "called on to perform an authentic difference in exchange for the good feelings of the nation and the reparative legislation of the state."[40] This notion of "authentic difference" alludes to the fact that there has been a conceptual reversal in the nature of the Aboriginal subject: rather than being scrutinized for its divergences from Eurocentric standards of civilization, "authentic" Aboriginality is now projected as an idealized, romanticized standard. The Commonwealth judiciary, for its part, has undergone a similar shift. Whereas courts would once typically look for qualities that signalled the "advancement" of a colonized people's prior social organization,[41] now they look for the opposite: "in other words, those qualities that make them 'distinct' from the dominant society."[42] Unfortunately for many "really existing" Aboriginal Canadians, this same discursive framework tends to find them wanting, construing them as "culturally contaminated, corrupted descendants of their putatively spiritual ancestors rather than their spiritual heirs."[43]

The extent to which political, bureaucratic and legal authority seek to shape the contours of Aboriginal identity in Canada is worrisome, not only because of the outmoded conceptions of Aboriginal culture these institutions maintain, but also because these conceptions are increasingly incapable of accommodating any fluidity or variability in manifestations of Aboriginal culture and identity. This creates a situation in which change, adaptation and evolution are apt to be discursively framed as cultural erosion, Europeanization or inauthenticity. It also creates a situation in which complex and variable identities tend to be cemented rigidly into a few prevalent historico-narrative tropes. In the case of the Labrador Métis Nation (LMN), this desire to simplify and reduce to dominant narratives brings the ironic twist of having their story told after the fashion of the western Métis Nation's ethnogenesis, rather than in terms of their strong Inuit identity. In *Newfoundland and Labrador v. Labrador Métis Nation*,[44] a case in which the LMN sought to demonstrate a credible claim to Aboriginal rights in order to enforce the province's duty to consult on potential highway developments, the difficulty juridical discourse had in processing their claims to *an Inuit culture* is telling. The justice in the trial court prior to this appeal heard their submission based on Inuit rights, but found in their favour on the basis of Métis rights.[45] This forces the question: could it not have been possible for European men to have integrated into the fold of Labrador Inuit culture? From the court's perspective, perhaps not. It therefore seems that while Canadian legal discourse is eminently able to conceive of people as having lost their Aboriginality (hence the process for determining whether or not they still have rights to their Aboriginal practices), it has much difficulty conceiving of European settlers integrating and assimilating into an Aboriginal culture. Despite centuries of living as Inuit, the courts can only assume that whiteness must have blotted out some of their Inuit colour.

The fact that the LMN was successful, despite its steadfast insistence on a cultural identity that was discordant with prevailing conceptions, might seem like an exception to my cautionary argument. But it is in fact the exception that proves the rule. In this case, rather than requiring the definitive legal establishment of rights to certain specific practices, enforcing a government's *duty to consult* required a less onerous demonstration of a *credible claim* to the existence of Aboriginal rights of some form or another. Indeed, the Supreme Court of Newfoundland and Labrador Court of Appeal was only able to find in favour of the LMN by bracketing out its own process of determining whether the LMN was in fact Métis or Inuit.

The manifestation of communal identity and history that is required for a typical rights case, however, suggests that translating the political struggles of Aboriginal peoples into formulae based on cultural difference will always encounter the problem of power imbalance. In essence, Aboriginal groups themselves have little or no say in what counts as difference, or in how that difference is mobilized. The result in contemporary settler states seems to be an overriding desire for Aboriginal claimants to demonstrate a collective sense of identity that is singular, undisputed, authentic and essential. The problem is that collective identities do not benefit from such unanimity, for any culture. This is a prime reason why many areas of social science have moved toward conceptions of culture as dynamic, processual and contested, rather than as a static "thing." Jennifer Hamilton discusses the judiciary's demand for Aboriginal singularity in her study of a case involving two Alaskan Tlingit youth in Washington Superior Court. The trial judge, James Allendoerfer, agreed to an experiment whereby the two youths were banished to a remote area in their home state by a traditionalist tribal court. The controversies surrounding the traditional court and its leader in the media, and especially in the Tlingit community itself, were overwhelming, such that the experiment was dismissed as a failure. For Hamilton, the court distanced itself from any questions of colonial relations in order to cast itself as a neutral observer and "benevolent pluralist" in its pursuit of cultural sensitivity to indigenous difference. It "was, however, unprepared to encounter another kind of indigenous difference, one that recognizes the complex and multilayered cultural and political lives of contemporary indigenous communities. Rather, Allendoerfer was looking for a coherent representative-representation of The Tlingit community, one lacking the conflict and contradiction so often reflected in so-called modern societies, but considered antithetical to indigenous ones. This, of course, was a need the involved parties were unable to fulfill."[46]

The particular difficulty that the Canadian penchant for Aboriginal cultural unanimity and fixedness poses for dual-descent peoples is that a relatively high tolerance for fluidity and variability in identity-formation often goes hand in hand with historically significant cases of miscegenation, hybridity and ethnogenesis. In her historical studies of the Métis community of St. Laurent, Manitoba, Nicole St-Onge quickly discovered "that life experience was more diverse, 'Métis' self-identification more nebulous, and class-based structures and relations more complex within the sphere of the Red River colony than has been argued. The variability and distinctions that other researchers into dual ancestry communities have begun to discuss holds true for the Red River region even within the traditionally clearly defined French, Catholic, and Métis population of Red River."[47] In fact, prior to the 1868 immigration of Métis families coming from the south, the Freemen Métis of St. Laurent appear to have had "few direct links or contacts with the older parishes of Red River, the Catholic hierarchy, or with HBC personnel."[48] Largely Cree speakers, with the intermingling of Saulteaux from their close ties to the lakeshore population, "their livelihood came from a mixture of subsistence activities that resembled those of the Saulteaux population, with which they were closely allied, and the production of dried or frozen fish, pelts, and salt (till the late 1860s) for exchange."[49]

If history can be seen as a field defined by the outcome of a complex play of power, politics, and knowledge, then this is also true of our very conception of who we are. From his era and his political vantage point, de Trémaudan's lament for the lost chance at "a French province, a second Quebec," in Manitoba colours his portrait of Métis identity, insisting that "if there is none more Catholic than a Metis there is none more French.... In religion he is Catholic; in nationality he is French from head to toe— in mind, heart, word and deed."[50] Today, though, if we have come a long way in exorcizing the weary and exclusionary bi-national politics of French-English enmity (itself a Eurocentric colonial inheritance) from the question of Métis identity, we still find the workings of a power subtle and persistent enough that it prompts a certain complicity from Aboriginal groups and Aboriginal rights advocates who feel the need to cast claimants within historical narratives of some sort of traditional authenticity and cultural singularity. Indeed, even within the Métis Nation of the northwest of the continent, one of the most difficult issues to address will be the extent to which the suspicious and scrutinizing power of dominant society informs the Métis sense of history, culture and self. In her examination of Métis historiography, Jennifer Brown has already cautioned how susceptible the past is to being made to serve present needs: "In the efforts of scholars to impose order on the past, and in the enthusiasm to have the past serve and strengthen the ethnic needs and solidarities of the present, we create both scholarly and political myths. It is very difficult to return to the people of the past and to greet them on their own terms, as Metis, Halfbreed, Indian, or ethnically neutral, with appreciation for the meanings and implications of whatever designation they may have elected or may have endured from others. 'Metisism' is a fluid concept, the braiding of channels in a river, 'a living and re-creative process,' to borrow again Emma LaRocque's phrase."[51]

Although it may provide for some rights recognition, this judicial grip that the cultural rights approach maintains on the Aboriginal subject is the antithesis of one form of emancipation that Aboriginal nations need—namely, to be afforded the same idiosyncrasies that all nations possess. While Canadians can hold disparate and conflicting views about their nation and what it means to be Canadian, Aboriginal nations are not granted such licence. The judiciary's cultural essentialism can be particularly inauspicious for Métis peoples. Lost in the "neither white, nor Indian" hinterland, their civilizational qualities were under the disdainful scrutiny of colonial elites for years.[52] Now Métis peoples find themselves in an era in which Aboriginality has been romanticized into an idealized standard against which contemporary communities are apt to be found wanting, and in which, as the Crown's arguments in the *Powley* case indicate, variability and fluidity in self-identity are potential obstacles to ensuring rights are recognized.

Synthesis: The Aboriginal Subject as the Site of its own Justice

The jurisprudence of Aboriginal rights and title forms a vast, historical edifice of contestable claims made concerning Aboriginal Canadians and what justice can purportedly afford them. And while the most recent jurisprudence presents itself as a purely positive development for Aboriginal claimants, it nonetheless guards for itself a micromanaging control and hidden elasticity in its practice. Métis leaders and rights claimants would therefore do well to consider the warning offered by Kent McNeil regarding Aboriginal title protections in Australia and Canada, for he provides a pertinent parallel to this discussion:

Regardless of the strengths of legal arguments in favour of Indigenous peoples, there are limits to how far the courts in Australia and Canada are willing to go to correct the injustices caused by colonialism and dispossession. Despite what judges may say about maintaining legal principle, at the end of the day what really seems to determine the outcome in these kinds of cases is the extent to

which Indigenous rights can be reconciled with the history of British settlement
without disturbing the current political and economic power structure. I think
this is a reality that Indigenous peoples need to take into account when decid-
ing whether courts are the best places to obtain redress for historical wrongs
and recognition of present-day rights. It may be advantageous to formulate
strategic approaches that avoid surrendering too much power to the judicial
branch of the Australian and Canadian state.[53]

But beyond the concern that the judiciary benefits from too much flexibility—one that can serve well an antipathy to Métis rights, especially at the
trial court level—I would warn against surrendering such power to the
judiciary precisely because of the losses inherent in these legal processes.

The law is a special case in the subjectification of Aboriginal peoples.
Its peculiar social power proclaims justice with each new decision, and
the principle of *stare decisis*—the respect of precedent, especially precedent set by a higher court—dictates the basis on which future disputes
are obliged to premise themselves. The manner in which these questions
of justice are framed, the limitations placed on their resolution as well
as the notions of Aboriginality contained within them are all established
by the courts. All those things that, for Métis, intuitively fall short of the
epiphanic fulfillment of justice—the specificity of Aboriginal rights, their
contingency on neocolonial cultural formulae, the recharacterization
and depoliticization of claims as they are considered by the courts—form
obligatory passage points that claimants must tacitly accept in order to
pursue the recognition of rights within the juridical field. In this way
the courts effectively limit how we perceive, characterize and pursue
Aboriginal rights.

The most fundamental problem, however, and the one that is the source
of all those enumerated here, is the judiciary's insistence that the solu-
tions to colonial political problems are to be deduced as self-evident
conclusions flowing from the Aboriginal legal subject itself. Contemporary
Aboriginal rights and title jurisprudence is premised on the assumption

that answers to questions concerning Aboriginal rights—their nature, their limits, and whether or not they exist for the claimant—inhere culturally within the Aboriginal claimants themselves. For all the sea change that *Calder*, *Sparrow*, and the *Constitution Act, 1982*, represent, characterizing the legal problem as a riddle to be solved within the claimant has essentially allowed the Crown to continue as it has done for two and a half centuries—that is, failing to face the difficult question of how it justly and legitimately acquired sovereignty and a radical, underlying title over the entirety of Canada.[54] In effect, rather than being the object of question in Aboriginal rights and title case law, the Crown's paramount sovereignty serves as a sort of *grundnorm*—a central assumption from which the rest of the jurisprudence flows.[55] For the courts, questions concerning the legitimacy of Crown sovereignty are not justiciable. Contemporary cases such as *Van der Peet* thus describe Aboriginal rights and title as the means "to reconcile the existence of pre-existing aboriginal societies with the sovereignty of the Crown."[56]

The symptom of this legal neurosis becomes a reversed burden of proof. Kent McNeil thus asks, in relation to a body of case law purportedly justified by the indisputable *prior occupation* of Aboriginal peoples—again, with title serving as a parallel to specific rights—"why the onus is on Aboriginal peoples to prove their own title as against the European colonizers when we all know that they were here occupying lands when the newcomers arrived."[57] The cultural rights test, with its ability to assess Métis claimants with a certain scrutiny, preserves the constant possibility of failure. And, in this sense, with its demonstrated desire to rein in Aboriginal rights, the Supreme Court of Canada has revived in quick order the very concept of extinguishment that it declared dead with the *Constitution Act, 1982*. Indeed, by predicating Aboriginal rights jurisprudence on a pervasive uncertainty over the initial existence of a right, extinguishment has returned through the back door.[58]

There is no doubt that Métis hunters and Métis organizations resorted to legal battles because of the frustrations they encountered through years of unsuccessful constitutional wrangling. The difference between taking recourse to the courts and resorting to other forms of more direct political struggle is that the latter can be renewed more easily. In essence, with non-judicial forms of political struggle, there may be a "drawing board" to which embattled Métis advocates can eventually return.[59] There is an ominous element of finality, however, to judicial declarations. With R. v. Langan,[60] the Provincial Court of Saskatchewan has declared that the Métis community in and around the border town of San Clara, Manitoba—the very province brought into Confederation by the Métis—cannot benefit from Aboriginal rights because they were probably a few years late in settling down. With the recent trial court decision for R. v. Hirsekorn, no Métis community in the entirety of southern Alberta is rights-bearing. Given that it is the law that has the final say in interpreting matters of j ustice, it is unlikely that any amount of political lobbying will now persuade these provinces that Métis rights should exist in those places. Thus, while elevation to constitutional status means that Aboriginal practices submitted successfully to the doctrine of Aboriginal rights will enjoy a more robust protection, it also means that "justice" will be able to tell some groups, with even greater finality, that they do not have rights to their traditional practices.

Author's Note

This research was supported by the Social Sciences and Humanities Research Council of Canada.

Notes

1. Constitution Act, 1982, s. 35, being Schedule B to the *Canada Act 1982* (UK), 1982, c. 11.
2. Now known as the Congress of Aboriginal Peoples.
3. *Constitution Act, 1982*, s. 35.
4. R. v. Powley, SCC 43, [2003] 2 SCR 207, 230 DLR (4th) 1. [*Powley* cited to SCR].

5. Cited in Paul Barnsley, "Monumental win for Métis: Powley determines who can access Section 35 rights," *Windspeaker*, 1 October 2003.

6. St. Catherine's Milling and Lumber Company v. The Queen, [1888] 14 AC 46 (PC).

7. George R., Proclamation, 7 October 1763 (3 Geo. III), reprinted in RSC 1985, App. II, No. 1.

8. George R., Proclamation, 7 October 1763 (3 Geo. III).

9. George R., Proclamation, 7 October 1763 (3 Geo. III).

10. Brian Slattery, "Paper Empires: The Legal Dimensions of French and English Ventures in North America," in *Despotic Dominion: Property Rights in British Settler Societies*, ed. John McLaren, A.R. Buck and Nancy E. Wright (Vancouver: University of British Columbia Press, 2005).

11. Calder et al. v. Attorney-General of British Columbia, [1973] SCR 313, 34 DLR (3rd) 145.

12. See, for instance, Hamlet of Baker Lake et al. v. Minister of Indian Affairs and Northern Development et al., [1980] 1 FC 518, 107 DLR (3rd) 513.

13. R. v. Sparrow, [1990] 1 SCR 1075, 70 DLR (4th) 385.

14. R. v. Van der Peet, [1996] 2 SCR 507, 137 DLR (4th) 289 [*Van der Peet* cited to DLR].

15. There is a legal distinction between Aboriginal rights and treaty rights. Some Aboriginal groups may have a right to hunt, fish and trap guaranteed by treaty — be it a historic treaty regulated by the Indian Act or a modern treaty stemming from a land claim agreement. These are thus rights that stem from codified statutes. Aboriginal rights, on the other hand, stem from a body of case law.

16. *Van der Peet*, at 310.

17. *Powley*, at 233–34.

18. *Powley*, at 212.

19. *Powley*, at 227.

20. R. v. Pamajewon, [1996] 2 SCR 821, 138 DLR (4th) 204.

21. John Borrows, "Frozen Rights in Canada: Constitutional Interpretation and the Trickster," *American Indian Law Review* 22 (1997): 54.

22. See Michael Asch, "The Judicial Conceptualization of Culture after Delgamuukw and Van der Peet," *Review of Constitutional Studies* 5 (2000).

23. Chris Andersen, "Residual Tensions of Empire: Contemporary Métis Communities and the Canadian Judicial Imagination," in *Reconfiguring Aboriginal-state Relations. Canada: The State of the Federation 2003*, ed. Michael Murphy (Montreal and Kingston: McGill-Queen's University Press, 2005).

24. John Sharp, "Ethnogenesis and Ethnic Mobilization: A Comparative Perspective on a South African Dilemma," in *The Politics of Difference: Ethnic Premises in a World of Power*, ed. Edwin N. Wilmsen and Patrick McAllister (Chicago: University of Chicago Press, 1996), 91–92; emphasis in original.

25. Ronald Niezen, "Culture and the Judiciary: The Meaning of the Culture Concept as a Source of Aboriginal Rights in Canada," *Canadian Journal of Law and Society* 18 (2003).

26. Johannes Fabian, *Time and the Other: How Anthropology Makes its Object* (New York: Columbia University Press, 1983).

27. Chilwen Chienhan Cheng, "Touring the Museum: A Comment on *R. v. Van der Peet*," *University of Toronto Faculty of Law Review* 55 (1997): 432.

28. Kent McNeil, "The Meaning of Aboriginal Title," in *Aboriginal and Treaty Rights in Canada: Essays in Law, Equality and Respect for Difference*, ed. Michael Asch (Vancouver: University of British Columbia Press, 1997), 151.

29. *Van der Peet*, at 376.

30. Asch, "The Judicial Conceptualization of Culture."

31. Fae Korsmo, "Claiming Memory in British Columbia: Aboriginal Rights and the State," *American Indian Culture and Research Journal* 20 (1996): 73.

32. Jeremy Patzer, "Legitimate Concerns: Aboriginal Rights and the Limits of Canadian Justice," in *Thinking About Justice: A Book of Readings*, ed. Kelly Gorkoff and Richard Jochelson (Halifax: Fernwood, 2012).

33. R. v. Goodon, [2008] MBPC 59.

34. R. v. Hirsekorn, [2010] ABPC 385, AJ no 1389. Between the writing of this chapter and the publication of this volume, Garry Hirsekorn appealed to the Court of Queen's Bench of Alberta with only partial success and was granted leave to appeal his case to the Court of Appeal of Alberta.

35. Alex McCuaig, "Metis Rights Case in Judge's Hands," *Medicine Hat News*, 24 June 2010.

36. In a new use of traditionality against Aboriginal claimants, Justice Fisher also found against Hirsekorn with a casuistic no-win twist of logic: because Hirsekorn was on a communal protest hunt with the intention of being charged and launching a test case, the hunt was deemed to have occurred for neither ceremonial nor subsistence purposes. According to Justice Fisher's logic, then, Aboriginal rights and civil disobedience do not mix, and no practice of Aboriginal rights related to "traditional" purposes can serve as an intentional legal test case.

37. Gerald Friesen, *The Canadian Prairies: A History* (Toronto: University of Toronto Press, 1987), 196.

38. Fred Shore, "The Emergence of the Metis Nation in Manitoba," in *Metis Legacy: A Metis Historiography and Annotated Bibliography*, ed. Lawrence J. Barkwell, Leah Dorion and Darren R. Préfontaine (Winnipeg: Pemmican Publications, 2001), 75.

39. Cited in Alex McCuaig, "Trial Begins for Three Métis Men Accused of Breaching Hunting Rules," *Medicine Hat News*, 4 May 2009.

40. Elizabeth Povinelli, *The Cunning of Recognition: Indigenous Alterities and the Making of Australian Multiculturalism* (Durham, NC: Duke University Press, 2002), 6.

41. See, for instance, In re Southern Rhodesia, [1919] AC 210 (PC).

42. Niezen, "Culture and the Judiciary," 7.

43. Bruce G. Miller, "Culture as Cultural Defense: An American Indian Sacred Site in Court," *American Indian Quarterly* 22 (1998): 89.

44. Newfoundland and Labrador v. Labrador Métis Nation, 2007 NLCA 75, 272 Nfld & PEIR 178.

45. Labrador Métis Nation v. Newfoundland and Labrador (Minister of Transportation and Works), 2006 NLTD 119, [2006] 4 CNLR 94.

46. Jennifer A. Hamilton, *Indigeneity in the Courtroom: Law, Culture, and the Production of Difference in North American Courts* (New York: Routledge, 2009), 23.

47. Nicole St-Onge, "Variations in Red River: The Traders and Freemen Métis of Saint-Laurent, Manitoba," *Canadian Ethnic Studies* 24 (1992): 1. See also Nicole St-Onge, *Saint-Laurent, Manitoba: Evolving Métis Identities, 1850–1914* (Regina: Canadian Plains Research Center, 2004).

48. St-Onge, "Variations in Red River," 4.

49. St-Onge, "Variations in Red River," 12.

50. Cited in Jennifer Brown, "People of Myth, People of History: A Look at Recent Writings on the Métis," *Acadiensis* 17 (1987): 152.

51. Jennifer Brown, "People of Myth, People of History," 161.

52. Thibault Martin and Jeremy Patzer, "Yvon Dumont ou la renaissance du leadership Métis," *Revue d'éthique et de théologie morale: Le Supplément* 226 (2003).

53. Kent McNeil, "The Vulnerability of Indigenous Land Rights in Australia and Canada," *Osgoode Hall Law Journal* 42 (2004): 300–01.

54. See Asch, "The Judicial Conceptualization of Culture."

55. Patzer, "Legitimate Concerns."

56. *Van der Peet*, at 315. My thanks to Ian Peach for pointing out a potential shift heralded by the *duty to consult* case law, especially Haida Nation v. British Columbia

(Minister of Forests), 2004 SCC 73, [2004] 3 SCR 511 and Taku River Tlingit First Nation v. British Columbia (Project Assessment Director), 2004 SCC 74, [2004] 3 SCR 550. Indeed, in these cases, the extent to which the SCC characterizes Aboriginal rights and title to be less the means to reconcile Aboriginal claims with the sovereignty of the Crown and more a *process of reconciliation* in the wake of the Crown's assertion of sovereignty, there may be a subtle, implicit acknowledgement that the core of the Crown's legitimacy and the (legal) injustice of colonization are one and the same.

57. Kent McNeil, "Aboriginal Rights in Transition: Reassessing Aboriginal Title and Governance," *American Review of Canadian Studies* 31 (2001): 324.

58. Patzer, "Legitimate Concerns."

59. This is not to imply that Métis organizations across Canada have completely abandoned their objectives concerning political advocacy and negotiation. In September 2004 the Métis Nation of Alberta entered into an Interim Métis Harvesting Agreement with the Province of Alberta. In July 2007, however, the new provincial government under Premier Ed Stelmach terminated the agreement. The Métis Nation-Saskatchewan, for its part, has entered into two memorandums of understanding with the Province of Saskatchewan in the hopes of putting in place a process that would arrive at a resolution for Métis harvesting rights. In 2004, the Métis Nation of Ontario (MNO) entered into an interim agreement with the province that recognized the harvesting rights of a small number of hunters. There was subsequent disagreement between the two parties over the geographical scope of the *Interim Enforcement Policy*, and the MNO was successful in its litigation concerning the matter. Most recently, in September 2012, the Manitoba Metis Federation and the Province of Manitoba signed an agreement that recognizes harvesting rights in a number of regions and that lays out a process for considering claims in other regions not recognized by the province.

60. R. v. Langan, [2011] SKPC 125.

Bibliography

Legislation

Constitution Act, 1982, being Schedule B to the *Canada Act 1982* (UK), 1982, c. 11.
George R., Proclamation, 7 October 1763 (3 Geo. III), reprinted in RSC 1985, App. II, No. 1.

Jurisprudence

Calder et al. v. Attorney-General of British Columbia, [1973] SCR 313, 34 DLR (3rd) 145.

Haida Nation v. British Columbia (Minister of Forests), 2004 SCC 73, [2004] 3 SCR 511.

Hamlet of Baker Lake et al. v. Minister of Indian Affairs and Northern Development et al., [1980] 1 FC 518, 107 DLR (3rd) 513.

In re Southern Rhodesia, [1919] AC 210 (PC).

Labrador Métis Nation v. Newfoundland and Labrador (Minister of Transportation and Works), 2006 NLTD 119, [2006] 4 CNLR 94.

Newfoundland and Labrador v. Labrador Métis Nation, 2007 NLCA 75, 272 Nfld & PEIR 178.

R. v. Goodon, 2008 MBPC 59.

R. v. Hirsekorn, 2010 ABPC 385, AJ no 1389.

R. v. Langan, 2011 SKPC 125.

R. v. Pamajewon, [1996] 2 SCR 821, 138 DLR (4th) 204.

R. v. Powley, 2003 SCC 43, [2003] 2 SCR 207, 230 DLR (4th) 1.

R. v. Sparrow, [1990] 1 SCR 1075, 70 DLR (4th) 385.

R. v. Van der Peet, [1996] 2 SCR 507, 137 DLR (4th) 289.

St. Catherine's Milling and Lumber Company v. The Queen, [1888] 14 AC 46 (PC).

Taku River Tlingit First Nation v. British Columbia (Project Assessment Director), 2004 SCC 74, [2004] 3 SCR 550.

Secondary Materials

Andersen, Chris. "Residual Tensions of Empire: Contemporary Métis Communities and the Canadian Judicial Imagination." In *Reconfiguring Aboriginal-state Relations. Canada: The State of the Federation 2003*, edited by Michael Murphy, 295–325. Montreal and Kingston: McGill-Queen's University Press, 2005.

Asch, Michael. "The Judicial Conceptualization of Culture after *Delgamuukw* and *Van der Peet*." *Review of Constitutional Studies* 5, no. 2 (2000): 119–37.

Barnsley, Paul. "Monumental Win for Métis: Powley Determines Who Can Access Section 35 Rights." *Windspeaker*, 1 October 2003.

Borrows, John. "Frozen Rights in Canada: Constitutional Interpretation and the Trickster." *American Indian Law Review* 22, no. 1 (1997): 37–64.

Brown, Jennifer. "People of Myth, People of History: A Look at Recent Writings on the Métis." *Acadiensis* 17, no. 1 (1987): 150–62.

Cheng, Chilwen Chienhan. "Touring the Museum: A Comment on *R. v. Van der Peet*." *University of Toronto Faculty of Law Review* 55, no. 2 (1997): 419–34.

Fabian, Johannes. *Time and the Other: How Anthropology Makes its Object*. New York: Columbia University Press, 1983.

Friesen, Gerald. *The Canadian Prairies: A History*. Toronto: University of Toronto Press, 1987.

Hamilton, Jennifer A. *Indigeneity in the Courtroom: Law, Culture, and the Production of Difference in North American Courts*. New York: Routledge, 2009.

Korsmo, Fae. "Claiming Memory in British Columbia: Aboriginal Rights and the State." *American Indian Culture and Research Journal* 20, no. 4 (1996): 71–90.

Martin, Thibault, and Jeremy Patzer. "Yvon Dumont ou la renaissance du leadership Métis." *Revue d'éthique et de théologie morale: Le Supplément* 226 (2003): 379–404.

McCuaig, Alex. "Metis Rights Case in Judge's Hands." *Medicine Hat News*, 24 June 2010.

McCuaig, Alex. "Trial Begins for Three Métis Men Accused of Breaching Hunting Rules." *Medicine Hat News*, 4 May 2009.

McNeil, Kent. "The Vulnerability of Indigenous Land Rights in Australia and Canada." *Osgoode Hall Law Journal* 42, no. 2 (2004): 271–301.

McNeil, Kent. "Aboriginal Rights in Transition: Reassessing Aboriginal Title and Governance." *American Review of Canadian Studies* 31, no. 1/2 (2001): 317–29.

———. "The Meaning of Aboriginal Title." In *Aboriginal and Treaty Rights in Canada: Essays in Law, Equality and Respect for Difference*, edited by Michael Asch, 135–54. Vancouver: University of British Columbia Press, 1997.

Miller, Bruce G. "Culture as Cultural Defense: An American Indian Sacred Site in Court." *American Indian Quarterly* 22, no. 1/2 (1998): 83–97.

Niezen, Ronald. "Culture and the Judiciary: The Meaning of the Culture Concept as a Source of Aboriginal Rights in Canada." *Canadian Journal of Law and Society* 18, no. 2 (2003): 1–26.

Patzer, Jeremy. "Legitimate Concerns: Aboriginal Rights and the Limits of Canadian Justice." In *Thinking about Justice: A Book of Readings*, edited by Kelly Gorkoff and Richard Jochelson, 83–100. Halifax: Fernwood, 2012.

Povinelli, Elizabeth. *The Cunning of Recognition: Indigenous Alterities and the Making of Australian Multiculturalism*. Durham, NC: Duke University Press, 2002.

Sharp, John. "Ethnogenesis and Ethnic Mobilization: A Comparative Perspective on a South African Dilemma." In *The Politics of Difference: Ethnic Premises in a World of Power*, edited by Edwin N. Wilmsen and Patrick McAllister, 85–103. Chicago: University of Chicago Press, 1996.

Shore, Fred. "The Emergence of the Metis Nation in Manitoba." In *Metis Legacy: A Metis Historiography and Annotated Bibliography*, edited by Lawrence J. Barkwell, Leah

Dorion and Darren R. Préfontaine, 71–78. Winnipeg: Pemmican Publications, 2001.

Slattery, Brian. "Paper Empires: The Legal Dimensions of French and English Ventures in North America." In *Despotic Dominion: Property Rights in British Settler Societies*, edited by John McLaren, A.R. Buck and Nancy E. Wright, 50–78. Vancouver: University of British Columbia Press, 2005.

St-Onge, Nicole. *Saint-Laurent, Manitoba: Evolving Métis Identities, 1850–1914*. Regina: Canadian Plains Research Center, 2004.

———. "Variations in Red River: The Traders and Freemen Métis of Saint-Laurent, Manitoba." *Canadian Ethnic Studies* 24, no. 2 (1992): 1–21.

PART FOUR **Politics**

No Other Weapon | 9

Métis Political Organization and Governance in Canada

KELLY L. SAUNDERS

IN 1940, while commenting on the need for the Métis to take their social, economic and political future into their own hands, Jim Brady declared "the Métis have no other weapon except organization."[1] Given Brady's status as a founder and as a key organizer in the Métis movements in Saskatchewan and Alberta for over three decades, his words are particularly sage. Brady's reference to the salience of political action reflects several key points at the heart of the Métis reality in Canada. To begin with, the Métis have never relinquished their inherent right to self-government.[2] As such, the Métis have long viewed organization as essential to both the maintenance of their identity and the protection of their rights as a distinct Aboriginal people, and the best means by which to force the state's hand to recognize these rights. Indeed, as John Weinstein notes, the central feature common to the continuum of Métis leaders throughout history, from Cuthbert Grant to Louis Riel to current Métis National Council (MNC) President Clément Chartier, has been the desire for self-determination: "Self-government is and has always been the one practice most integral to the survival of the Métis as a distinct Aboriginal people."[3] An examination of political practices from the birth of the Métis

Nation to the contemporary era also reveals a third theme: the willingness of the Métis to use whatever tools are at their disposal to develop the institutions, processes and mechanisms that would enable them to achieve their goal of self-determination, while at the same time they consistently push at the boundaries imposed by the state that seeks to deny and contain this goal.

In spite of the voluminous works that have been written about Louis Riel and his historical prominence in the grand narrative of Canadian nation-building, the concept of Aboriginal self-government is not easily associated with the Métis.[4] As Paul Chartrand articulates, "the emergence of the Métis as an indigenous people distinct from the ancient First Nations peoples is not a well-known story, even though the Métis have featured prominently in the general histories of western Canada."[5] It is for this reason that, in relation to other Aboriginal peoples in the country, the Métis have been described as Canada's "forgotten people."[6] The federal government has long resisted the view that Métis are Indians within section 91(24) of the *Constitution Act, 1867*, and hence that Parliament has either the jurisdiction or the constitutional responsibility to preserve and promote Métis communities.[7] Hence, from an institutional, legal and policy perspective, the Métis have always been treated differently from Canada's two other groups of Aboriginal peoples, the First Nations and Inuit. While the Métis did gain legal recognition in 1982 as a distinct, rights-bearing collective in section 35 of the *Constitution Act, 1982*, the promise of these section 35 rights largely failed to materialize in practice.[8] Crown policy toward the Métis has historically been one of denial: "governments denied that Métis collectivities existed, denied that they were Aboriginal, denied their Aboriginal and treaty rights, and denied that government had any legal obligations towards the Métis."[9]

Traditionally excluded from many of the legal protections and government policies, programs and services that are extended to First Nations and Inuit, the Métis have long been caught in a game of jurisdictional football, with the federal government maintaining obligations to First

Nations and Inuit but leaving matters affecting the Métis to the vagaries of provincial governments.[10] For their part the provinces, with the exception of Alberta, consistently maintain that the Métis are predominantly or exclusively a federal responsibility.[11] As a result, Métis rights in Canada have historically been under-theorized and poorly understood, given little attention by academics and Canadian courts alike.[12] As expressed by Bradford Morse and John Giokas, "Aboriginal constitutional and legal issues are notoriously complex, and none more so than those surrounding the Métis."[13]

Unrestrained from the confines of the Indian Act and other state policies toward Canada's First Nations and Inuit peoples, the Métis have been left to develop their own political organizations and processes.[14] Over the years these entities have steadily evolved from benevolent associations and lobby groups into more meaningful vehicles of self-government and self-determination for Métis citizens across the Métis Nation in Canada.[15] In this endeavour the Métis have been aided, in the years following the 1982 constitutional amendments, by a number of legal victories in provincial courts as well as at the Supreme Court of Canada. These victories, in the area of land claims, harvesting rights and Aboriginal self-government, have had significant political repercussions, and have positioned the Métis and their representative organizations as legitimate actors negotiating the contours of federalism alongside provincial and federal governments. Today, the Métis Nation in Canada is represented at the provincial level by five governing bodies: Métis Nation British Columbia (MNBC), Métis Nation of Alberta (MNA), Métis Nation-Saskatchewan (MN-S), the Manitoba Metis Federation (MMF), and the Métis Nation of Ontario (MNO). Together, these organizations constitute the Métis National Council (MNC), which represents the Métis Nation federally and internationally.

This chapter will explore the evolution of Métis self-government in Canada. It begins by describing how, since the birth of their Nation, the Métis have always seen themselves as a self-governing people, organizing not only the internal affairs of their own communities but also engaging in political action as the most effective way of protecting their identity and way of life from external oppression. From the organization of the buffalo hunts and the provisional governments that dotted the landscape of the Northwest, to the negotiation of the *Manitoba Act, 1870,* and the numerous rights and land petitions initiated by Métis communities scattered throughout the Métis homeland, "as the Métis Nation grew and developed during the 1800s so too would the institutions that would support it."[16] Contemporary Métis governing bodies will then be examined, with particular attention paid to their structure and functions, models of decision making, electoral processes and the culture and values that define them. The chapter will conclude with a consideration of some of the challenges confronting the Métis political leadership in Canada as it moves toward making self-governance a reality. Specifically, issues pertaining to identity and citizenship, accountability and capacity building, as well the relationship between provincial Métis governments and their national umbrella organization, the MNC, remain prominent on the Métis self-government agenda. In advancing this discussion, this chapter asserts the view that while the Métis have had to work within the constraints imposed by the Crown and the attending processes of colonization, domination and assimilation, they have nonetheless remained active agents of resistance against these forces.[17]

The Evolution of Métis Self-Government

Since the birth of their Nation more than 200 years ago, the Métis have managed their own communities and engaged in collective action to protect and fight for their rights, land and continued existence as a distinct Aboriginal people. In many ways the desire for self-determination is rooted in the ethnogenesis of the Métis Nation itself. The nature of the fur trade in the Northwest encouraged the growth of "freemen" fur traders on the plains. Through the wintering practices of these freemen and the social networks that were formed, initially with Indigenous tribes and later with other freemen and their mixed-race offspring, culturally distinct Métis communities emerged.[18] The mixed-race children of the unions between freemen and Aboriginal women "inherited their father's [sic] penchant for freedom, a value that would become a fundamental characteristic of the Métis."[19] Neither European nor First Nation, the Métis were referred to by the Cree as *O-tee-paym-soo-wuk*, the people who own themselves. As the country underwent colonization, the Métis turned to political action as a means to protect their right to govern themselves, to hunt and trade freely and to practice their own distinctive culture. Hence, long before Confederation, "there is a lengthy history of Métis organization and representation in the early years of this territory;...of organized Métis objecting successfully to externally-imposed restrictions upon their freedom."[20] This quest for self-determination has been a constant thread in the saga of the Métis people. As a study prepared for the Royal Commission on Aboriginal Peoples (RCAP) by the Métis Society of Saskatchewan noted, "this enduring theme in our Métis history—that we as a people have struggled against often overwhelming odds to reclaim our traditional Homeland and assert our sense of nationhood—lies behind much of the current drive towards self-government."[21]

The early 1800s marked a period of intense political activity as the Métis in the Red River organized to protest the laws being imposed upon them by the governors of the settlement, which they perceived as illegitimate and a threat to their way of life.[22] Angered by restrictions on their hunting and trading practices and the encroachment of their land by Lord Selkirk's settlers, in 1815 the Métis, led by Cuthbert Grant, declared themselves to be the New Nation and negotiated an agreement with representatives of the Hudson's Bay Company (HBC) that demanded the settlers removal.[23] This agreement constituted the first of its kind, "which asserted the rights of the Métis as a free Aboriginal people."[24] Nonetheless, the peace that it established proved to be short-lived. Tensions erupted between the HBC and the Métis, who were aligned with the North West Company, for control of the fur trade and the cessation of what the Métis considered to be attacks on their homeland.[25] These tensions culminated in the Battle of Seven Oaks; the victory of the Métis and the North West Company in this battle was marked by the hoisting of a flag of the New Nation for the first time in recorded history.[26] As settlement continued throughout the west, the years that followed were marked by other forms of dissent on the part of the Métis. These ranged from letters and petitions to state authorities requesting recognition of their rights to the land and the right to participate in the governing of the territory, to demonstrations over such events as the Sayer trial, where the Métis protested the trade monopoly imposed by the HBC.[27]

Métis Provisional Governments

More commonly known are the provisional governments established by the Métis throughout the Northwest, beginning with the government formed in 1869 under the presidency of Louis Riel to negotiate the terms of Manitoba's entry into Canada. Declaring that it was time for the people of the Red River Settlement to form a provisional government to both protect themselves and to force Canada to grant them "a form of responsible government," Riel purportedly stated "we want to govern ourselves. We will accept no concessions."[28] The Legislative Assembly of Assiniboia that was subsequently constituted under Riel's leadership included a total of 28 elected representatives, 14 from English-speaking parishes and 14 from French-speaking parishes in the Red River area.[29] While dominated by individuals of mixed-blood ancestry (21 out of the 28 elected representatives were Métis or half-breed, along with the President and Chief Justice of the Legislative Assembly, Louis Riel and James Ross respectively), it was important to Riel that the residents of the Red River Settlement be united, with both English and French-speaking individuals equitably represented in a unified council.[30] In her examination of the Legislative Assembly of Assiniboia, Norma Hall comments on its complex and highly developed institutions and processes. "Among Métis members of the community there was awareness of, and sophisticated—even cosmopolitan—familiarity with forms of governance that go well beyond a reliance on traditional ways of organizing for buffalo hunts."[31]

In the spring of 1870, the Legislative Assembly ratified a List of Rights that was then presented to the government of Canada. While undergoing several amendments, the list reflected the three primary areas of concern for the Métis: political status, language and land.[32] It called for the full and fair representation of the people of the Red River Settlement in the Canadian Parliament; the admission of the settlement as a province into Confederation; the recognition of both French and English as the official languages of the new province; and provincial control of public lands.[33] As John Weinstein explains, while the Métis saw themselves as an indigenous people and co-owners of the land with the First Nations, "they also saw themselves as a nation, not a tribe, and as such sought political equality with English Ontario and French Quebec in the form of provincial status and powers."[34]

The onset of settlement and the land policies of the Canadian government, as well as the promise of new economic opportunities in the burgeoning buffalo robe trade, pushed the Métis further west.[35] As at Red River, Métis subsequently established other forms of local self-governance in communities such as the Qu'Appelle district and St. Albert. In the South Saskatchewan River area of St. Laurent, Métis residents elected a council comprising eight councillors under the presidency of Gabriel Dumont. Between 1873 and 1875, the Council of St. Laurent codified a total of 28 laws. Reflecting a highly developed level of political organization, the Laws of St. Laurent covered nearly the entire life of the community, including the responsibilities of the Council, the conduct of the buffalo hunt, the collection of taxes, "theft, inviolability of contracts between employer and employee, prevention and control of prairie fires, and respect of young women."[36] Penalties were established for those in violation of the law, and a commission was created to settle boundary disputes and disagreements regarding ownership of land.[37] Social values and traditions prevalent among the Métis, such as respect and authority of elders, care of the sick and infirm, the adoption of children, and divorce (or the "turning off" of spouses), were also subject to moral persuasion and community control. Métis social organization was both communal and democratic, with all laws (including those that had been passed down orally to subsequent generations) requiring ratification or amendment through public assemblies.

In terms of social control, Lawrence Barkwell maintains that Métis communities in western Canada practiced forms of criminal justice that were far in advance of anything the Canadian state had to offer at the time: "Métis legislation in those days was highly progressive, containing reparative, restitutive measures with minimal reference to the corporal punishments of Upper Canada."[38] Punishments decreed in the Laws of the Buffalo Hunt were notable for their relative mildness. Physical sanctions were regarded as the last resort, to be used only against the habitual offender and against the worst crime that could be committed by a hunter, which was to break order and risk scaring the buffalo herd prematurely.[39]

These ongoing attempts by the Métis to determine their own affairs, however, proved to be no more successful at warding off efforts by the Canadian government to solidify control over the new country than had been the case at Red River. With the Métis denied a voice in the territorial government and incurring resistance from the North West Mounted Police and the territorial administrators for any form of Métis self-government, conflicts and confrontations between the state and the Métis continued throughout much of this period.[40] In 1884 a delegation of French and English Métis from Saskatchewan sent word to Louis Riel (at the time in Montana), requesting his return to Canada to once again petition the Canadian state on their behalf.[41] In March 1885 a provisional government was established at Batoche, Saskatchewan, with Louis Riel as its president and Gabriel Dumont as its military leader. A "Revolutionary Bill of Rights" was prepared that asserted scrip for the Métis, more liberal treatment for the First Nations and responsible government for the European settlers.[42]

Laws of the Buffalo Hunt

The Métis also organized around the buffalo hunt. As a people that lived off the land, hunting was integral to the sustenance of families and communities, and also served as the backbone of the Métis economy. The mechanisms that were designed to oversee such hunting expeditions were developed "to ensure efficiency, protection and discipline."[43] In a larger sense, however, grand events such as the biannual buffalo hunts also provided opportunities for entire Métis communities to come together; as such, they played a seminal role in fostering Métis nationalism and cultural expression, as well as political identity.[44]

The early Métis developed a comprehensive system of laws, processes and controls to not only organize the hunts, but also to oversee the good stewardship of the land and the resources derived from it. Passed down from one generation to the next, the Laws of the Buffalo Hunt stipulated the orderly manner by which hunts were to occur, the rules to be observed during the hunt, as well as punishments for those who violated them.[45] In his first-hand account of the Métis in the Red River Settlement, Alexander Ross describes how, at the commencement of each hunt, all the adults would gather and a council meeting would be called.[46] At these council meetings nominations for the leaders of the hunt, referred to as captains, would be taken and a vote would be held. Ten captains of the hunt would be elected, one of whom would also be chosen as Chief of the Hunt. Below each captain and serving under his command were ten soldiers and ten guides. The Chief of the Hunt, along with his captains, were responsible for ensuring compliance with the customary rules and regulations of the hunt, as well as providing for the safety and security of the camp. Because the captains of the hunt were freely chosen by the people and were required to govern according to the laws established by the community (in this instance, the Métis of the Red River Settlement), the leaders' authority was seen as legitimate and freely accepted.[47]

At the commencement of each new hunt, the community would gather once again to elect their leaders, as well as to reinstate the rules of the previous hunt, with minor changes as necessary. In order to become official, all rules and decisions had to be first ratified and affirmed by the entire community through the council process. As the Métis caravan traversed the Canadian prairies in search of the buffalo, the Chief of the Hunt and the council thus operated as a type of "moving government."[48] As Larry Chartrand explains, "It was the governance traditions of the buffalo hunt that were relied on by Métis communities when they grew and became more permanent as Métis families transitioned from primarily a hunting economy to a farming economy. When these larger, more permanent communities desired a more formal governing authority, they would rely on the tradition of using the Laws of the Buffalo Hunt as the basis for their constitutions."[49]

It is important to note the high degree of politicization among "rank and file" Métis throughout the nineteenth century. As Thomas Pocklington observes, the conventional account of political activity among the Métis tends to concentrate almost exclusively on the singular person of Louis Riel. Pocklington's concern is not that a preoccupation with this extraordinary man is unwarranted, nor the fact that it tends to overshadow other great Métis leaders such as Cuthbert Grant and Gabriel Dumont; rather, the focus on Riel and his political accomplishments leads one to assume that the majority of "average" Métis were politically unsophisticated and passive, pushed into political action that they would otherwise not have taken were it not for the charismatic presence of Riel. As he cogently argues, "neglected in the 'Riel Rebellions' perspective is the fact that 'ordinary' Métis were political forces to be reckoned with prior to and during both uprisings."[50] Pocklington reminds us that Riel was not a member of the tribunal that in 1870 sentenced Thomas Scott to death. At the same time, while Riel was in exile in the United States, the Métis of the St. Laurent area formed their own governing council that repeatedly petitioned the federal government for settlement of their land claims. It was this council that subsequently sent a delegation to Montana urging Riel to return to Canada and join them in their struggle. As Pocklington observes,

"The current political vitality of the Métis is not a birth but a rebirth....
Métis political activism did not begin and end with Riel. Although they lay
dormant for some years, the roots of Métis political energy and skill are
deep and strong."[51]

Métis Organization Post-1885

Hence, while many assume that the Métis quest for self-determination
"ended on the Batoche battlefield or the Regina gallows," the historical
record demonstrates that this is not the case.[52] The devastating legacy of
those events and the persecution that followed did cause many Métis to
go underground; however, they nonetheless continued to practice their
culture and traditions, and worked to preserve these for future generations. Indeed, in 1887, a mere two years after the Resistance at Batoche,
the Union nationale métisse Saint-Joseph du Manitoba was created in
Winnipeg to protect and promote Métis culture and traditions. In 1891, the
Union erected a monument on Riel's tomb in the St. Boniface Cathedral
cemetery.[53] The organization also sought to correct what it believed to be
the state's deliberate distortion of the Métis, and to recast the "official"
version of the events of 1870 and 1885 from a Métis perspective.[54]

In the 1920s, other Métis groups and movements began to emerge
across the Canadian prairies and into British Columbia and Ontario.[55]
Together, these organizations were seen as a means to confront the crush-
ing social and economic conditions that were a reality for far too many
Métis families. Neither "Indian" nor "white" enough, for much of the first
half of the twentieth century the Métis endured a life of deprivation,
shame and social ostracism.[56] While First Nations acquired, at least legally,
a secure land base, this was not the case with the Métis.[57] Dispossessed
of their land through the failings of the scrip process, in the years following 1885 many Métis families found themselves with no legal title to
their land.[58] Soon displaced from their homes in the face of extensive
non-Aboriginal settlement on the prairies, many Métis took up temporary residences in shanty communities, living as squatters along road

allowances. Here they were faced with a vicious cycle: because many Métis did not have title to the land, and hence paid no taxes, the majority of Métis families were denied access to public schooling, medical services or relief. At the same time, because they were not First Nation and therefore not included on Band Registries, Métis could not partake in the services and benefits provided to on-reserve First Nations.[59] On top of this was the prejudice many Métis faced: "the stigma of being called 'rebels' or 'traitors' and being discriminated against for having Aboriginal ancestry forced many Métis to deny their identity."[60]

The organizations that appeared during this time reflected the political re-emergence of the Métis as a significant force in Canada, and the pursuit of what they saw as their rightful place in Canadian society. They also reflected the Métis' desire for "recognition of their inherent right to self-government, and the fair redress of legitimate historical grievances."[61] In turn, the materialization of these political movements led to a resurgence of Métis identity and nationalism. As Joe Sawchuk advances, it was the political actions of the Métis, not solely their existence as a unique cultural group, that delineated the Métis as a distinctive nation: "It is generally an act of political assertion that delineates the group, not the fact that it is a cultural unit."[62] In his examination of the political history of the Métis in Manitoba, Sawchuk notes that organizations such as the Manitoba Metis Federation, while aimed at improving the general economic and political conditions of their members, also act as "a catalyst in the regeneration of ethnic identity, bringing new people into the fold and causing others to restate their ethnicity in new terms."[63]

Métis Organization on the Prairies

The oldest governing member within the Métis National Council, the Métis Nation of Alberta (MNA), traces its roots back to 1929 when a small group of Métis in the Cold Lake area began to meet and organize over the decision of the federal government to transfer responsibilities for natural resources to the provinces. There were concerns over the impact that this decision would have on the Métis that were residing on Crown lands.[64] Originally named L'Association des Métis Alberta et les Territoires du Nord-Ouest, the organization was incorporated in 1932 with the mandate to push for a land base for the Métis. The success of this political mobilization led to the passage of the *Métis Population Betterment Act* by the Province of Alberta in 1938 and the creation of several Métis settlements in the province, making Alberta the only jurisdiction in the country with an established Métis land base.[65]

The Métis in Saskatchewan also began organizing in the 1930s, establishing two associations in 1938: the Métis Society of Saskatchewan (MSS), based in the southern part of the province, and the Métis Association of Saskatchewan (MAS), which represented Métis and Non-Status Indians in the north.[66] Similar to the struggles of the Alberta Métis, these organizations advocated for a just resolution of Métis land claims in Saskatchewan and for federal support of Métis agricultural and industrial enterprises.[67] In 1967, the MSS and the MAS amalgamated under the banner of the Métis Society of Saskatchewan, which became the official Métis organization for the entire province (eventually adopting the name Métis Nation-Saskatchewan in 1993).

While the roots of the Métis political movement in Manitoba run deep, the province's current Métis organization, the Manitoba Metis Federation (MMF), grew out of the annual Indian and Métis conferences that were sponsored by the Community Welfare Planning Council of Winnipeg.[68] These conferences, which began in 1954, served to focus public attention on the needs of Aboriginal people and to provide a forum through which they could meet and discuss ways to overcome their social and economic challenges.[69] At the 1967 Conference, discussions were held on the reorganization of the Manitoba Indian Brotherhood (MIB), an organization that, in various forms, had been in existence since the 1930s. In particular, the debate focussed on whether the Métis would be adequately represented by (or indeed, even invited to join) a revamped MIB, or whether they would be better off forming their own Métis-specific organization.

In the end, the decision was taken by the delegates in attendance to form a separate entity, and in December 1967 the MMF was created as a not-for-profit organization under the province of Manitoba's *Companies* (later *Corporations*) *Act*. The 1960s also marked the emergence of the first organization representing Métis people and Non-Status Indians in British Columbia, which subsequently evolved in 1996 into the Métis Provincial Council of British Columbia (today, Métis Nation British Columbia). In 1971 the Ontario Métis and Non-Status Indian Association was created; in 1993, the contemporary representative body of the Ontario Métis, the Métis Nation of Ontario (MNO), was established.

1960s: The Era of Red Power

As Siomonn P. Pulla discusses in this volume, the 1960s represented a particularly dynamic period for Métis political activity in Canada, not only at the provincial level but nationally as well. During this era of "Red Power," a new set of circumstances led to a revival of Aboriginal consciousness generally, and Métis nationalism and political organization specifically. The civil rights movement, Quebec's Quiet Revolution, and the search for a Canadian identity in light of Canada's centennial led to the reorganization of older Métis associations and the formation of new ones.[70] The policies of the Trudeau Government, notably the White Paper of 1969 and its offer to provide core funding for three national Aboriginal organizations (representing Status Indians, Inuit and Non-Status/Métis respectively), also encouraged Métis mobilization.[71] Three national associations were soon created: the National Indian Brotherhood created by Status Indians, the Inuit Tapirisat of Canada representing the Inuit, and the Native Council of Canada (NCC) comprising Non-Status Indians and Métis.[72] At the time, a marriage of convenience between Non-Status and Métis made sense, given that both were in the same legal position with regard to the federal government. Excluded from the definition of Status Indian under the *Indian Act*, Métis and Non-Status Indians formed a "residual category" of Native peoples in Canada.[73] Suffering a loss of identity and land rights as a result of federal legislation and policy, both groups were "recognized as Aboriginal minorities with special problems rather than special rights."[74]

However, tensions were inherent from the start in the NCC, as it attempted to reconcile the cultural differences between the Métis from western Canada and the largely eastern-based, Non-Status Indians that composed its membership.[75] Nonetheless the NCC, under the inimitable leadership of Harry Daniels, along with the other Aboriginal groups helped usher in a historic achievement with the inclusion of Aboriginal and treaty rights in the Constitution Act, 1982. This was a particular victory for the Métis, who became explicitly recognized as one of Canada's three Aboriginal peoples within section 35(2) of the act. "What may have appeared to be a simple statement of fact represented a monumental triumph for the Métis people."[76] The 1982 amendment was to be followed by a series of four First Ministers Conferences, beginning in 1983, the purpose of which was to give definition and meaning to these rights. Emboldened by their constitutional recognition, however, and the fact that by this time neither the president nor the vice-president of the NCC were Métis (a problem given that the NCC was allotted only two seats at the upcoming First Ministers conferences), Métis leaders from the Prairies began to question whether the NCC could—or should—represent the interests of the Métis Nation, or whether the time had come to form a Métis-specific national representative body.[77] In March 1983, the Métis National Council (MNC) was born.[78]

Contemporary Métis Governing Bodies: Common Themes

Today, the Métis Nation in Canada is represented through democratically elected governance structures from Ontario westward; these include the Métis Nation of Ontario (MNO), the Manitoba Metis Federation (MMF), the Métis Nation-Saskatchewan (MN-S), the Métis Nation of Alberta (MNA) and the Métis Nation British Columbia (MNBC). A national body, the Métis National Council (MNC), serves as the umbrella organization of these five provincial bodies, which are referred to as "governing members." Incorporated under federal corporations law, the MNC is governed by the presidents of the provincial Métis organizations, which collectively form the MNC's board of governors.[79] Along with these five governors sits a national president, elected every three years by the MNC's general assembly. The MNC president is responsible for representing the Métis Nation as a whole in its dealings with the federal government, as well as representing the interests of the Métis internationally. The president is also responsible for appointing Ministers from the board of governors who are assigned portfolio responsibilities in such areas as economic development, health, environment and Métis rights. The focus of the MNC is not program and service delivery; this is the responsibility of the various provincial Métis governments. Instead, the MNC is responsible for achieving consensus among the governing members on policy matters related to the implementation of the inherent right to self-government, as well as other Métis rights and interests.[80]

Examination of Métis governance and political organization in Canada illustrates the degree to which the Métis have sought to combine western-style political structures, which have garnered them increased legitimacy (albeit somewhat reluctantly) in the eyes of the state, with traditional cultural practices and traditions. While these governance structures continue to evolve, they represent "the contemporary expression of the centuries-old struggle of the Métis Nation to be self-determining within the Canadian federation."[81] At the same time, the manner in which Métis governance in Canada has progressed is rooted in the history and evolution of the Métis as a distinct Aboriginal people.[82] Particularly germane was the refusal of nineteenth-century Métis to become "wards (of the state) through the paternalistic and restrictive treaty and reserve system."[83] In doing so the Métis were not renouncing their rights as an Aboriginal people; instead, they rejected the protection of the Crown as the necessary price for retaining their ability to remain self-governing.[84] As a result, the state has been reluctant to recognize the existence of Métis rights; nonetheless, it has been their ability to continually negotiate this path that accounts for the endurance of the Métis as a separate Aboriginal people as well as their political successes to date.

Given that reserves were not set aside for the Métis through the negotiation of treaties, as was the case with the First Nations, Métis governance in Canada has (with the exception of the Métis settlements in Alberta) largely evolved in the absence of a recognized land base.[85] Because the Métis do not fall under the band council system of governance outlined in the *Indian Act*, and were historically ignored by provincial governments who did not perceive the Métis as their responsibility, either as a people or a collectivity, they were left to create their own political entities separate from provincial and federal government dictates. Hence, most Métis political organizations first incorporated under some form of not-for profit or societies legislation, which was the only legal option available to them if they wished to access any kind of state funding.[86]

The Royal Commission on Aboriginal Peoples defined several key principles fundamental to Indigenous political culture; these include the centrality of the land, individual autonomy and responsibility, the rule of law and oral tradition, the role of women and elders, the importance of the family and extended kin networks, and modes of decision making based on consensus and community involvement.[87] Drawing on these ideals, at the heart of Métis governance are the core values of inclusivity, democracy, community and nation-building.[88] Governing institutions, processes, and laws within Métis political organizations are rooted in oral traditions and customary practices that have been passed down from one generation to the next.[89] Reflecting the practices established in the Laws of the Buffalo Hunt and the provisional governments that were formed in Métis communities throughout Manitoba and Saskatchewan, community participation and direct democracy remain important features of contemporary Métis governance structures.[90] Within Métis governments, decision-making processes are based on consensus rather than simple majority rule, with all substantive policy directions requiring ratification and affirmation by the whole community before they become official.[91] As discussed in the

following paragraphs, Métis governing practices also reflect the centrality of families, kinship and local grassroots structures, with leadership
derived from "adherence to common culture, community identity, and the
promotion of collective well-being."[92] Emphasis is placed on the involvement of elders and women, as they are seen as the custodians of Métis
culture, traditions and wisdom.[93] This is reflected in the incorporation of
women's organizations within each Métis provincial government, as well
as the involvement of elders through such bodies as Métis elders councils,
judicial councils and senates.

Each of the governing members that constitute the MNC operates
through a series of internal structures and institutions that support the
overall goal of implementing Métis self-government, as well as within a
legal and accountability framework typically codified in a constitution,
by-laws, electoral codes and a variety of other regulatory instruments.
These framework documents set out the goals, membership requirements and governing mechanisms of each Métis organization, which are
reviewed and amended as necessary by the membership through annual
general assemblies. In Alberta, for example, Article 1 of the by-laws of
the MNA outlines the objectives of the organization as follows: the cultural, economic, educational, political and social development of the Métis
in Alberta and Canada; the re-establishment of Métis land and resource
bases; the promotion, pursuit and defense of Métis and Aboriginal rights;
and the promotion of self-government and self-determination of the Métis
in Alberta and Canada.[94]

These framework documents also stipulate the rules of membership
for each provincial Métis organization. Involvement (in terms of participating in the annual general assemblies and other types of community
meetings, voting in elections and running for political office) is restricted
to members only, with provincial membership lists and registries maintained by each separate Métis government. As shall be explored later, the
issue of Métis identity and citizenship has been a challenging one for the
Métis in Canada, with the definition of Métis undergoing some significant

changes over time. In the past, most Métis organizations tended to have fairly fluid membership requirements, allowing Non-Status Indians and any individuals of mixed white-Aboriginal ancestry to apply for membership.[95] Thus, at the time of its formation in 1967, the MMF in Manitoba granted membership to any "unregistered person of Indian descent who is eighteen years or older," as well as non-Indian spouses of persons of Indian descent.[96]

In the years following the inclusion of the Métis in section 35 of the *Constitution Act, 1982*, the Métis National Council engaged in considerable discussion with its provincial counterparts on the need for a more consistent and tighter definition of Métis.[97] At its 2002 Annual General Assembly the MNC adopted a national definition of Métis, which was agreed to in principle by each of the five governing members. The spirit of the MNC definition was also subsequently endorsed by the Supreme Court of Canada in its 2003 decision in *R. v. Powley*. In this groundbreaking case involving Métis harvesting rights, the Court outlined a process for determining a Métis rights-bearing community that reflected the criteria established by the Métis people themselves.[98] Under these new guidelines individuals that wish to apply for membership in any of the provincial Métis organizations must self-identify as Métis; provide documentation objectively verifying his or her ancestral connection to the historic Métis Nation Homeland (defined as the traditional territory in west central North America that was used and occupied by the Métis); and be accepted by the contemporary Métis community in each province.[99]

Community-Based Structures

In terms of organizational structure, at the heart of contemporary Métis governments from British Columbia to Ontario are local Métis communities.[100] Referred to variously as "community councils" (in the case of Ontario), "communities" (BC) and "locals" in the other provinces, it is these grassroots bodies that comprise the backbone of Métis governance in Canada, providing representation, community-based decision-making authority, and cultural, economic and social program and service delivery to Métis citizens throughout the provinces.[101] Every member of a provincial Métis organization belongs to a local at the community level in their city, town or village. The number of locals varies from province to province, currently ranging from 24 in Ontario, to 67 in Alberta and 133 each in Manitoba and Saskatchewan. The policies and procedures that guide these community structures are outlined in the constitutions of each provincial Métis organization. While there is no limit on the number of locals that can be established in any province, in order for a local to maintain active status, it must typically hold a minimum number of public meetings, call elections at regular intervals and be financially accountable to the membership. The number of locals can vary from year to year, as some existing locals become inactive while new locals emerge in communities that previously had none. Members of the local are responsible for electing their community leaders (usually comprising a chair, a vice-chair and a secretary-treasurer) who serve on a voluntary basis for, on average, a three-year term. Each local sends delegates to regional meetings that are typically held each year, as well as the province-wide annual general assemblies. Locals are involved in a number of activities, from organizing cultural events and festivals to working with regional offices (as discussed below) in the delivery of programs and services.

Collectively, these locals are aggregated into six to twelve regions within each of the various provinces; it is these regions that compose the second level of governance in Métis political organizations. Each region is governed by some type of regional council, consisting of a regional president and vice-president, and/or regional directors. In some provinces, such as Saskatchewan and Alberta, the presidents of the locals that comprise that region also sit on the regional council. In Manitoba, the M M F is divided into seven regions (Winnipeg, Southwest, Southeast, Interlake, Northwest, Thompson, and The Pas), which together cover the entire province, as well as a number of associated subsidiaries and affiliations. Each region is headed up by a regional vice-president, as well as two regional board members, each of whom are elected to four-year terms by the members in that region. Given that the MMF is a federated structure, each region is incorporated separately, and thus exercises a wide measure of autonomy in managing its affairs. Each region maintains a regional office to represent the interests of its locals, and to serve the Métis residents of the area. Regional offices are responsible for delivering a wide array of programs and services in their area, reviewing applications for membership in the MMF, approving harvester cards and representing the views of their locals at the executive level.

At the apex of Métis provincial governing structures are the provincial councils (or board of directors, as it is still referred to in Manitoba and BC, and, in Ontario, the provisional council). Comprising the provincial leadership (president, vice-president, secretary and treasurer) and regional representatives, the provincial councils serve as the executive decision-making body within each of their respective organizations. Most provinces (with the exception of Alberta) also include representatives from their women's organizations on their provincial councils, and in the case of Ontario, BC and Saskatchewan, their youth wings as well.

In Manitoba, each of the 23 members that constitute the MMF board of directors is assigned an area of responsibility by the president, akin to ministers in the Westminster model of governance. These portfolios include such policy areas as finance, natural resources, education, economic development, justice, housing, the Michif language, land claims, and Métis rights. Along with the president, the board of directors "leads, manages and guides the policies, objectives and strategic direction of the Federation and its subsidiaries."[102] Together, the president and board of the MMF oversee two dozen departments serving Métis citizens throughout the province.[103] Like the vice-presidents and the regional board members, the president of the MMF is elected to a four-year term by the membership of the MMF. However, while MMF members vote in their respective regions for their vice-president and two regional board members, the president of the MMF is elected by the entire membership through a province-wide ballot. As with other provincial presidents, the president of the MMF serves as the chief executive officer, leader and spokesperson of the Métis government in Manitoba, and is responsible for overseeing its day-to-day operations.

In addition to the community-based nature of Métis governing bodies, the Métis take pride in the fact that they directly elect their provincial leaders, a claim that no other citizen of Canada can make.[104] In 1984, the MMF became the first Métis organization in Canada to adopt a province-wide ballot box electoral process for its provincial president; prior to this, the president was selected by delegates attending the MMF annual general assemblies.[105] Métis organizations in other provinces subsequently followed Manitoba's lead and adopted a similar electoral process, which is now a requirement under MNC by-laws.[106] Participation in these elections, which are typically held every four years, is based on the principle of "one member, one vote."

Role of Women

An intriguing feature of Métis governing structures is the generally high representation of women in elected executive positions, in addition to their substantial presence at the local level. This could reflect the fact that women's representative structures in each of the provinces are integrated into the overall governance framework of the Métis Nation in Canada. As mentioned previously, each provincial Métis government outside of Alberta has a Métis women's organization whose chairperson sits on the executive body.[107] In turn, these provincial representatives are part of a national organization, Women of the Métis Nation, which represents the collective voice of Métis women on the Métis National Council.[108] Alberta's Métis government, the MNA, has been led by a female president (Audrey Poitras) since 1996; in 2003, she also served as interim president of the MNC. Indeed, of the current 12 regional presidents and vice-presidents that form the provincial council in Alberta, seven are women, while in Manitoba, four of the current seven vice-presidents on the MMF board of directors are women.[109] Analysis of MMF electoral results demonstrates that since ballot box elections began in the early 1980s women have constituted approximately 46 per cent of all elected representatives at the regional and vice-presidential levels.[110] Moreover, the trend since 1984 until the most recent general election in 2010 shows an almost 10 per cent increase in the percentage of women elected, from 43 per cent to 52 per cent. This upward trend of women in provincial and regional elected representation reflects a similar pattern in elected local representation. Since the conception of the MMF in 1967, women have continually made up the majority of locally elected representatives, in addition to their strong presence as regional board members and vice-presidents. Indeed, as stated by the spokesperson for the MMF's women's organization, Métis Women of Manitoba, "women make up the backbone of the MMF."[111] The ongoing and significant involvement of women at the local level may be seen as an entry point for women in subsequent regional and provincial elections.

Electoral Processes

The five provincial Métis organizations that comprise the MNC each hold an annual general assembly.[112] These assemblies, which are open to all provincial members, provide individuals with an opportunity to ask questions directly of their regional and provincial leadership and to raise issues of concern. Assemblies must also approve all by-laws and constitutional amendments, financial and accounting statements, and significant policy decisions. Representatives from each local within the various regions also meet annually to discuss regional programs, services and other activities, as well as to approve audited financial statements. In addition to the annual assemblies, accountability to Métis citizens is manifested through province-wide ballot box elections held at regular intervals, as well as through established electoral procedures that are ratified by the membership and codified in electoral codes, laws and constitutions. Thus, for example, in British Columbia, MNBC's Electoral Act outlines the procedures by which a chief electoral officer, appointed and approved by the general assembly (which constitutes MNBC's executive arm, the board of directors, as well as presidents of each of the community locals) is to oversee MNBC elections at the regional and provincial levels.

In the case of Manitoba, the constitution of the MMF similarly outlines the process for regional and provincial MMF elections.[113] Near the completion of each four-year executive term, the board of directors appoints an individual to serve as chief electoral officer (CEO), who is responsible for administering the subsequent electoral process.[114] In Manitoba, the past few CEOs have been members of the judiciary. Alvin Zivot, QC, a former justice of the Court of Queen's Bench, served as the CEO in the most recent MMF election in June 2010; in the two elections that preceded this the responsibility was carried out by Alvin Hamilton, a retired Chief Justice of Manitoba.[115] The duties of the CEO, as outlined in the MMF constitution, include the following: announcing the date of the election (a maximum 60-day writ period); appointing a deputy chief electoral officer, deputy returning officers and poll clerks; determining the eligibility of candidates for office as well as the eligibility of members to vote in the election; and preparing the list of electors on the basis of the membership lists supplied to it by the MMF home office.[116]

Despite the MMF's ongoing efforts to strengthen its electoral processes (typically the reports prepared by the CEOs at the conclusion of each election include recommendations for further electoral reform), voter turnout remains a problem. In the last election, for example, there were over 52,000 eligible voters in Manitoba; of these, less than 10 per cent cast their ballot.[117] This represents a significant drop over the last few previous elections, in which the voter turnout rate averaged 16 per cent.[118] While this could be due to incumbency factors (the current president of the MMF has served in this position since 1997), it nonetheless remains a matter of concern for the organization. As explained by Will Goodon, advisor to the current president, "We want Métis citizens to see the MMF as their government, as the defender of Métis rights and identity in Manitoba. In order to continue to advance the self-government agenda, it is incumbent that our citizens become more engaged in the electoral process."[119]

Pushing the Boundaries: The Métis Nation-Saskatchewan

Under corporate law in Canada, each of the separate sub-units that comprise Métis political organizations (locals/community councils and regions) must be separately incorporated. This has sometimes made it difficult for Métis governments to speak with a consistent voice and ensure clear accountability and transparency to their members.[120] On a symbolic level, however, the issue of having to resort to provincially dictated corporations or societies law in order to have their inherent right to self-government formally recognized by the state remains an untenable situation for the Métis. Thus some Métis organizations, such as MN-S in Saskatchewan and MNBC in British Columbia, have implemented innovative means of asserting their right to self-government, while at the same time recognizing the constraints imposed by state funding requirements. As Janique Dubois discusses in this volume, the MN-S, which has one of the most evolved governance structures in Canada, adopted a new constitution in 1993 at its annual general assembly. Constitutional reform was seen by the Saskatchewan Métis as an appropriate and necessary step for several reasons.[121] The new constitution split governance responsibilities from administration functions within the MN-S, effectively establishing the MN-S as a self-governing entity outside of the Saskatchewan *Non-Profit Corporations Act*. At the same time, a Secretariat was maintained under the act for the sole purpose of carrying out the administrative duties of the MN-S.[122] With this move, the Métis citizens in Saskatchewan asserted control of their own governance, basing its legitimacy upon the consent of the people rather than the statutory allowances of the state. In 2003, Métis in British Columbia followed suit, revising the constitution of the MNBC to separate the governance and administration functions of its Métis government.[123]

In 2002 the Saskatchewan Legislature formally recognized the MN-S with the passage of *The Métis Act*. This act, while lauding the "contributions of the Métis people to the development and prosperity of Canada," also committed the Government of Saskatchewan to work together with the MN-S "through a bilateral process to address issues that are important to the Métis people."[124] The legislation provides the mechanism through which the MN-S is able to engage in a bilateral process of negotiations with the Saskatchewan government on matters related to capacity building, land and resources, governance and harvesting.[125] Saskatchewan's *Métis Act* rendered the MN-S the first Métis government in Canada to have its governing body legally recognized outside of provincial non-profit corporations legislation.

Elders Councils

Some provincial Métis organizations have also established other innovative institutions such as senates, elders councils and legislative assemblies. Designed in part to improve accountability and create more checks and balances within the system (an ongoing issue of concern, discussed shortly), the creation of senates and elders councils also reflects the significance placed on the role of elders in traditional Métis communities. In 2006, MNBC passed the *Senate Act* that led to the establishment of a new provincial senate in its governing structure. Under the terms of the act, each of the seven regions contained within MNBC appoints a respected individual from its area; collectively, these non-political senators form the judicial arm of the MNBC. Appointed to four-year terms the senators undertake a number of responsibilities, including ceremonial activities; dispute resolution and mediation at the provincial, regional and community levels; citizenship appeals; and appeals arising through the elections process (for example, in terms of candidate/voter disqualification appeals).[126]

Alberta created a similar body, called the Métis Judiciary Council, to serve as its judicial arm. Comprising representatives from each of the province's six regions, the council's powers are itemized in the MNA by-laws. The judicial council reviews and decides upon matters related to membership disputes, conflicts of interest, suspension and/or reinstatement of MNA membership rights, and also reviews local and regional boundaries. MNA also has a Métis Council of Elders, again comprising representatives appointed from its six regions, to promote the history and culture of the Métis Nation in Alberta and to provide advice and wisdom to its executive body, the Métis Provincial Council.[127] Ontario adopted a similar mechanism for its elders, one of whom also sits on the MNO's executive body, the provisional council.

In addition to their annual general assemblies, Métis in Alberta, British Columbia and Saskatchewan have also established legislative assemblies. In Saskatchewan, the Métis Nation Legislative Assembly consists of its executive body (the Provincial Métis Council), presidents of all the locals, representatives from the Métis Women of Saskatchewan, as well as representatives from the MN-S Youth Council. Meeting annually, the legislative assembly is charged with the responsibility of enacting legislation, regulations, rules and resolutions governing the affairs and conduct of the MN-S.[128]

Challenges of Governance

As evidenced in the preceding section, the practical manifestation of Métis self-government has achieved some real successes over the years. Nonetheless, there remain outstanding challenges that will require some degree of resolution if the Métis are to continue to move forward on this front. Issues related to resolving the question of the legislative jurisdiction of the Métis; more effectively communicating the argument for Métis self-government to the public at large; settling outstanding land claims and achieving a Métis land base; strengthening electoral processes (namely, improving voter turnouts in Métis provincial elections); building a Métis public service and enhancing current administrative mechanisms; and better co-ordinating and integrating the growing range of programs, services and activities that are provided to Métis citizens are just some of the challenges that will affect the future success of Métis self-governance in Canada.[129] While these and other matters remain prominent on the agenda, this section will limit its discussion to the following issues: clarifying Métis identity and citizenship, enhancing accountability and checks and balances within Métis governments, and defining more clearly the relationship between provincial Métis governments and their national umbrella organization, the MNC.

Clarifying Métis Identity and Citizenship

Without question, one of the most pressing and divisive issues facing the Métis Nation today involves ongoing debates over identity and citizenship. If the Métis are going to advance their self-government agenda over the next decade, it is crucial that outstanding questions related to identity and membership be clarified by the governing members. In many ways, the lack of movement on Métis rights in Canada has largely been justified by the state in the context of debates over this very issue. As Robert Nichols explains, "Indian Bands have registries, [and] Inuit people have a treaty to which there are a limited number of beneficiaries. Métis people have neither."[130] Although recognized as a distinct Aboriginal people under section 35, over the intervening years there has been little consensus among governments, academics and, most significantly, among the Métis themselves, over who can claim membership in the Métis Nation.[131] Given that section 35 infers group rights on the Métis, a clear understanding of what constitutes membership in that group is not merely an academic exercise. That governments could (and indeed have) used this as an excuse for inaction on Métis issues has been recognized by the courts themselves, as evidenced by the decisions related to the case of *R. v. Powley*.

While progress was made on clarifying who the Métis are at the 2002 MNC annual general assembly, the issue remains far from resolved in a practical sense. As referenced earlier, the definition of "Métis" that was adopted in principle in 2002 includes as one of the criteria proof of an individual's ties to the "Historic Métis Nation Homeland." Yet there still remain questions over what constitutes the specific boundaries of this Homeland. The geographic territory that most assume this term corresponds with includes the Canadian prairies, extending into British Columbia towards the west, the Northwest Territories in the north, and into Ontario to the east.[132] However, this defies the historic reality of the Métis as a highly mobile people, moving within an expansive territory located throughout the Northwest in search of economic opportunities.[133] As a people that lived off the land, the Métis continually traversed the expanse of central North America as they followed the buffalo hunt and the fur trade. This historic feature has rendered the idea of well-defined and objectively verifiable geographic borders exceedingly challenging in the case of the Métis.

In many ways the Supreme Court's decision in R. v. Powley further complicated the problem by outlining the test by which a Métis rights-bearing community could be identified. While this decision specifically concerned harvesting rights, the Court's usage of the word "community," which provincial governments have chosen to interpret in a narrow, geographic sense (typically involving a town or village), has provided another level of difficulty in assessing the boundaries of the Historic Métis Nation Homeland. The irony is that while the Powley case clearly established the Métis as a rights-bearing collective, the Supreme Court tied the expression of these rights to a specific site, a determinate piece of land. This reflects the Court's assumption that the Métis lived in stable, continuous communities and hunted primarily in the immediate environs of that community. Hence, in order to exercise their harvesting rights, the Powley test requires that Métis must first prove their membership in a historical and continuous Métis community that can be geographically specified.[134] However, "it is a peculiar and most unwelcome twist of logic that a highly mobile hunter/gatherer/trader society that never lived in small, stable, continuous, localized communities is now required to provide the existence of just such an entity in order to exercise harvesting rights in the near vicinity."[135]

The differentiated patterns of social and cultural organization that define the Métis, along with the usage of the term "community" in *R. v. Powley*, not only has implications for Métis harvesting rights in Canada, but directly bears on the larger issue of the Métis right to self-government. As Fred Caron queries, if self-government is a right held by the Nation as a collectivity, what does this indicate for smaller groupings (or communities) that make up the Nation? If, on the other hand, the right to self-government is held at the community level, what precisely constitutes a Métis community, where do such communities exist in Canada, and what is the makeup of their citizenship? Unlike Métis harvesting rights, which pertain to activities that can be undertaken individually or in tandem with others, "a right of self-government involves the collective exercise of significant power over the lives of individual citizens. It is all the more important, then, to be sure of where that power vests before attributing an inherent right to a specific polity."[136] Caron further explains that the inherent right of self-government involves jurisdiction: the power to govern through the making and enforcement of laws. Jurisdiction can take two forms: personal and territorial. In the latter case, jurisdiction applies to individuals that are located within a known territory or land base, while the former applies to individuals "independently of their location."[137] Given that Métis self-governance will continue to evolve without a land base equivalent to an Indian reserve, at least in the foreseeable future, then Métis jurisdiction would be personal, rather than territorial. This necessitates a clear and easily recognizable determination of Métis citizenship in order to determine those individuals who would fall under the jurisdiction of Métis governing bodies.

While the precise boundaries that constitute the Historic Métis Nation Homeland may be fluid, so too is Métis cultural identity. As a mixed-race people, the early Métis often moved among European, First Nation, and distinctly Métis communities. Indeed, some see this as an inherent marker of Métis culture, reflecting their emergence as the "people in between."[138] Many Métis today, while culturally identifying themselves as Métis, nonetheless carry strong attachments to their First Nations relations as well.[139] As Jean Teillet explains, the Métis have never fit comfortably into the North American cultural landscape; "the very concept of Métis, as a people, challenged the established boundaries of culture in Canada."[140] It is not surprising then that historically there has not been one uniform definition of the Métis; indeed, as discussed earlier, many Métis organizations began as a combination of Métis and Non-Status Indian entities. As each provincial organization evolved, it determined its own rules of membership and application requirements. As a result, many provincial Métis organizations undoubtedly contain generations of families that are no longer eligible for membership on the basis of the more restrictive 2002 MNC definition. Contemporary Métis governments face a stark choice: dealing with the deeply emotional and traumatic issues involved in forcibly removing these individuals from their provincial Métis registries—people who may have identified as Métis their entire lives—or, alternately, allowing these individuals to remain members despite the fact that they do not fit the new criteria (thereby creating a two-tier system of Métis). Given this difficult scenario, it is not surprising that a consensus has yet to emerge among the governing members regarding how to logistically proceed with implementation of the 2002 definition.

While these aspects of identity and homeland are related, unfortunately little clarity is provided by the MNC definition and the test of a Métis rights-bearing community contained in *R. v. Powley*. As Paul Chartrand notes, if the definition of the Historic Métis Nation Homeland is not clear, then it is impossible to determine what contemporary communities descend from it today. And in turn, "the Homeland cannot be defined more specifically without deciding more specifically who the Métis are."[141]

The issue has been further complicated by the Canadian government's imposed definitions of Aboriginality on Canada's Native peoples, the implications of which have been articulated by scholars such as Joe Sawchuk and Sébastien Grammond. Changing state definitions over Aboriginal identity, as reflected in Bill C-31 and Bill C-3, has resulted in situations in which individuals who culturally identified as Métis subsequently chose to also register as Status Indians when Bill C-31 came into effect in 1985. For those "C-31s" who either wish to maintain their Métis and First Nations status simultaneously, or, alternatively, wish to return to their previous Métis organizations, there are no options available to them. Under the MNC's 2002 definition of "Métis," in order to be a member of a provincial Métis organization an individual cannot also be on another Aboriginal registry, such as the *Indian Act* registry.

The right of the Métis to limit membership to Métis only, and to determine for themselves what this consists of, was recently upheld by the Supreme Court in *Alberta (Aboriginal Affairs and Northern Development) v. Cunningham*. This case involved members of the Cunningham family, who had previously been members of the Peavine Métis Settlement in Alberta. When the Cunninghams chose to register as Indians under the *Indian Act*, their membership in the Métis Settlement was revoked under section 75 of the *Métis Settlements Act*. The Court, in a unanimous decision, upheld the constitutionality of the membership requirements outlined in the act and spoke specifically to the right of the Métis to determine their own membership and identity requirements. As the judgment read, "the Métis have a right to their own culture and drawing distinctions on this basis reflects the Constitution and serves the legitimate expectations of the Métis people. The exclusion (of Status Indians from the Settlements) corresponds to the historic and social distinction between the Métis and Indians and respects the role of the Métis in defining themselves as a people."[142]

Despite the Court's ruling this remains a deeply divisive issue, one for which there is no easy resolution. On the one hand, some argue that "C-31s" made a choice, and just because the anticipated benefits of Indian status may have failed to materialize, this does not mean they should be able to return to the Métis fold now that the latter have been gaining momentum with having their rights recognized and affirmed.[143] On the other hand, however, the fact remains that individuals currently registered as Status Indians under C-31 cannot legally remove themselves from the *Indian Act* registry, even if they wish to return to their former Métis roots: "Registered Indians who culturally identify as Métis argue that if Métis identity is based on a common culture, why should a racist and external piece of legislation such as the *Indian Act* define Métis citizenship."[144]

A further problem rests with the fact that the identification and registration of Métis citizens continues to occur at the provincial level. In *R. v. Powley*, the Supreme Court instructed provinces to work with Métis organizations to develop objective and verifiable mechanisms to identify Métis rights-holders. While the MNC continues to lobby the federal government for the necessary funding in order to create and maintain a national registry, in the interim it has fallen to the provinces to develop their own means of identifying and registering members. While all of the provincial Métis governments accepted in principle the 2002 MNC definition, given that one aspect of this definition involves community acceptance (a subjective evaluation), there has been little consistency in how each provincial government has interpreted and applied this definition. In the absence of a national clearinghouse on membership, with credible and objectively verifiable identification systems, what has emerged is a patchwork of programs and services that varies across the provinces. Certainly, the Métis leadership in Canada recognizes the need for clarity and consistency in determining which people are Métis. However working through the practicalities of these issues, and the highly charged emotions that lie at the heart of discussions of cultural identity in Canada, will not be an easy task.

Enhancing Accountability

A second key challenge facing the Métis Nation as it advances its self-government agenda concerns the need for greater capacity building, and the implementation of effective and transparent systems of checks and balances within Métis organizations. Despite such innovative features as elders councils, senates and judiciary councils, Métis politics remains a highly personalized, familial and clan-based mode of governance. Certainly, opposition factions do exist in every province to offset the powers exercised by provincial presidents. While there are no political parties per se, the fact that regional representatives are elected separately from the provincial president inevitably leads to counter-balances within the system. Nonetheless, there fails to exist any fully independent dispute settlement or grievance mechanisms for Métis citizens to express their concerns and seek redress against their political organizations. Unfortunately, situations like those that occurred in Saskatchewan in 2004 not only speak to the need for some kind of independent electoral tribunal, they also feed into stereotypes regarding the questionable accountability of Aboriginal politics and the right to self-government. In the 2004 MN-S election, questions arose almost immediately regarding the validity of the voting process in parts of the province. Amid allegations of ballot box tampering and other electoral illegalities, provincial and federal funding to the organization was suspended, and an investigation into the election was launched by the Province of Saskatchewan. In the absence of any Métis-specific redress mechanisms it fell to the state to oversee new elections, in the form of a joint Saskatchewan–Government of Canada Independent Oversight Committee.[145] While no government is automatically impervious to scandal or questionable practices (witness the Sponsorship Scandal that contributed to the downfall of Paul Martin's Liberal government), questions related to accountability and corruption become particularly magnified when they pertain to Aboriginal politics and governance. In this, the Métis are not immune.

There is also a need for greater clarification of the roles and responsibilities of the provincial presidents and their boards, on the one hand, and the provincial executives and the Métis National Council on the other. Currently, most Métis governance functions are carried out at the provincial level. Provincial organizations deliver programs and services, co-ordinate and manage the Métis right to harvest, oversee the membership process, and manage most cultural, historical, linguistic and educational facilities.[146] The current structure of the MNC and the provincial Métis governments is based on a confederal model, with the balance of power tilted toward the provinces at the expense of the national structure (and within this, largely contained in the three prairie provinces).[147] The president of the MNC is elected by the leadership of the provincial Métis organizations, rather than by a national vote of the entire Métis population. As such, the national president has no direct base of support of his or her own to use as leverage over the provincial presidents.[148] Certainly, this model has its benefits. Most obviously, the emergence of powerful provincial organizations reflected the realities of Canadian federalism as well as the federal government's refusal to accept fiduciary responsibility for the Métis, hence necessitating the creation of strong entities that could negotiate more effectively with provincial governments. Nonetheless, there is general recognition among the governing members that better co-ordination and consistency at the national level with respect to issues of citizenship, elections and rights policy would allow the Métis Nation to speak more effectively and with a unified voice in its dealings with the Crown. Recognition of the need for a more equitable balance of power between the provincial organizations and the national body, along with the greater legitimacy that a directly elected national president would provide, has not escaped past and current presidents of the MNC.[149] However, the steps necessary to achieve such electoral reform are many. This would involve the harmonization of Métis elections at the provincial level; a national enumeration process; and, to come full circle, clarification of Métis identity and citizenship. Fundamentally, these measures would also entail the provincial Métis governments ceding some of their influence and power to the national body, a scenario that has met with resistance, particularly within the stronger prairie organizations.

Despite these challenges, in 2003 the MNC, along with its governing members, began work on building a stronger and more effective national governance structure and creating a national Métis constitution.[150] In the intervening years progress on this front stalled as other issues related to limited resources and the fears of some provincial governments over the potential shift of some of their power to the national level came to the fore. However, at the annual general assembly in December 2010, MNC President Clément Chartier unveiled a three-year plan to kickstart the process toward constitutional development. As proposed, this plan involves the standardization of provincial registration and identity processes, the separation of the MNC's governing activities from its business affairs (similar to that undertaken by MN-S and MNBC, discussed earlier), and the passage of a National Métis constitution. While the specific contours of this constitutional process will be guided by extensive community consultations within each of the provinces and at the national level, it is anticipated that the national constitution would form the basis of negotiations with the federal government on a Canada–Métis Nation Relations Act and "signal our declaration of self-government within the Canadian state."[151]

Conclusion

This chapter has explored the evolution of Métis self-governing institutions and processes in Canada. It began by noting how the Métis have historically been a self-governing people who have not only organized the internal affairs of their own communities but have also engaged in political action as the most effective way to protect their unique identity and way of life. Métis organization continued even in the face of repeated challenges by the state that sought to undermine the survival of the Métis as a distinct Aboriginal people. Indeed, it was through the organization of the biannual buffalo hunts that a nascent political consciousness among the Métis began to flourish. At the same time, the democratic principles upon which these hunts were based served as the model for community governance among the Métis.[152] By the early 1800s the Métis were already beginning to organize politically to protest the usurpation of Métis lands by settlers arriving in Red River, a practice that continued throughout the century as the Métis sought out new economic opportunities in the changing fur trade. From the establishment of provisional governments to the negotiation of the *Manitoba Act, 1870*, and the numerous rights and land petitions initiated in Métis communities scattered throughout the Métis homeland, "the Métis were consistently a force to be reckoned with in Canada's nation-building exercise."[153]

Against this historical backdrop, contemporary Métis governing structures existing in provinces from British Columbia to Ontario were examined, along with the national umbrella organization, the MNC. Excluded from the *Indian Act* and denied by federal and provincial governments for decades, the Métis were left to devise their own forms of political representation. As I argue, while these organizations fall short of providing the Métis with the necessary tools to fully implement their section 35 rights, even within these limitations the Métis have continually sought out opportunities to push beyond the constraints that have been imposed upon them. Blending European models of governance with such traditional Métis political values as community, kinship, inclusiveness and consensus-building, these entities have steadily evolved from advocacy and lobby organizations into truer expressions of Métis self-government. Today, these Métis governments are responsible for the design, delivery and implementation of a wide range of programs and services to Métis citizens located throughout the Homeland, including those in areas such as justice, health, education and training, housing, child and family services and economic development.

At the same time, however, Métis governance in Canada faces some significant challenges. Questions related to citizenship and identity, improving accountability and checks and balances, clarifying the relationship between the provincial bodies and the national organization, and developing a national Métis constitution—these and other issues represent a daunting to-do list for the Métis Nation in Canada. Nonetheless, if history is any guide, the Métis have proven themselves to be nothing if not adaptable, creative and, above all, resolute in their desire to remain the people that own themselves.

Author's Note

My thanks to Christopher Adams and the anonymous reviewers for their helpful comments on earlier versions of this chapter.

Notes

1. Quoted in Murray Dobbin, *The One-And-A-Half-Men: The Story of Jim Brady and Malcolm Norris, Métis Patriots of the 20th Century* (Regina: Gabriel Dumont Institute, 1987), 67.

2. There is an extensive body of academic work supporting the inherent right of the Métis to self-government. While discussion of this literature is beyond the scope of this chapter, for some examples see Bradford Morse and John Giokas, "Do the Métis Fall Within Section 91(24) of the Constitution Act, 1867?" in *Aboriginal Self-Government: Legal and Constitutional Issues, Royal Commission on Aboriginal Peoples* (Ottawa: Supply and Services Canada, 1995); Royal Commission on Aboriginal Peoples (RCAP), *Restructuring the Relationship*, vol. 2, pt. 1 (Ottawa: Supply and Services Canada, 1996); Clément Chartier, "Aboriginal Self-Government and the Métis Nation," in *Aboriginal Self-Government in Canada*, ed. John Hylton (Saskatoon: Purich Publishing, 1999); Paul Chartrand, *Who Are Canada's Aboriginal Peoples?* (Saskatoon: Purich Publishing, 2002); Larry Chartrand, "'We Rise Again': Métis Traditional Governance and the Claim to Métis Self-Government," in *Aboriginal Self-Government in Canada: Current Trends and Issues*, 3rd ed., ed. Yale Belanger (Saskatoon: Purich Publishing, 2008); Jason Madden, "The Métis Nation's Self-Government Agenda: Issues and Options for the Future," in *Métis–Crown Relations: Rights, Identity, Jurisdiction, and Governance*, ed. Frederica Wilson and Melanie Mallet (Toronto: Irwin Law, 2008); and Jean Teillet, *Métis Law Summary*, 2009, available at www.pstlaw.ca.

3. John Weinstein, *Quiet Revolution West: The Rebirth of Métis Nationalism* (Calgary: Fifth House, 2007), 209.

4. Chartier, "Aboriginal Self-Government and the Métis Nation"; Paul Chartrand, "Defining the 'Métis' of Canada: A Principled Approach to Crown–Aboriginal Relations," in Wilson and Mallet, *Métis-Crown Relations*; L. Chartrand, "'We Rise Again.'"

5. Paul Chartrand, "All My Relations," 6.

6. D. Bruce Sealey and Antoine S. Lussier, *The Métis: Canada's Forgotten People* (Winnipeg: Pemmican Publications, 1975); Ute Lischke and David T. McNab, *The Long Journey of a Forgotten People: Métis Identities and Family Histories* (Waterloo, ON: Wilfrid Laurier University Press, 2007).

7. Mark Stevenson, "Section 91(24) and Canada's Legislative Jurisdiction with Respect to the Métis," *Indigenous Law Journal* 1, no. 1 (Spring 2002); Larry Chartrand, "The Definition of Métis Peoples in Section 35(2) of the *Constitution Act, 1982*," *Saskatchewan Law Review* 67 (2004); Joseph Magnet, "Who Are the Aboriginal People of Canada?," in *Aboriginal Rights Litigation*, ed. Joseph E. Magnet and Dwight Dorey (Markham, ON: LexisNexis Canada, 2003); and Thomas Isaac, *Aboriginal Case Law: Commentary, Cases and Materials*, 3rd ed. (Saskatoon: Purich Publishing, 2004).

8. MNC, "*R. v. Powley*: A Case Summary and Frequently Asked Questions," 2004, 1, available at www.metisnation.ca; Clément Chartier, President, Métis National Council, personal interview, 2009.

9. Jean Teillet, "The Winds of Change: Métis Rights after Powley, Taku and Haida," in Lischke and McNab, *The Long Journey of a Forgotten People*, 63.

10. Jean Teillet, "Federal and Provincial Crown Obligations to the Métis," in Wilson and Mallet, *Métis-Crown Relations*.

11. Robert Groves and Bradford Morse, "Constituting Aboriginal Collectivities: Avoiding new Peoples 'In Between,'" *Saskatchewan Law Review* 67, no. 1 (2004).

12. Robert Nichols, "Prospects for Justice: Resolving the Paradoxes of Métis Constitutional Rights," *The Canadian Journal of Native Studies* 23, no. 1 (2003).

13. Morse and Giokas, "Do the Métis Fall Within Section 91(24) of the Constitution Act, 1867?" 144.

14. By this I refer to the band council system that the federal government imposed on First Nations reserves through the *Indian Act*. Certainly, First Nations peoples also established their own political organizations at the provincial, regional and national levels, outside of Crown dictates.

15. RCAP, vol. 4, 1996, 4.

16. L. Chartrand, "'We Rise Again,'" 150.

17. Belanger and Newhouse make a compelling argument against the canon of literature on Aboriginal–non-Aboriginal relations in Canada that rejects the possibility of Indigenous agency in challenging colonial norms through political activity. As they argue, "by accepting this impoverished interpretation of events is to present Aboriginal people as powerless to effect change, standing helplessly by as the forces of colonialism swept them into the political abyss." See Yale Belanger and David Newhouse, "Emerging from the Shadows: the Pursuit of Aboriginal Self-Government to Promote Aboriginal Well-being," *The Canadian Journal of Native Studies* 24, no. 1 (2004): 185.

18. John E. Foster, "Wintering, the Outsider Adult Male and the Ethnogenesis of the Western Plains Métis," in *From Rupert's Land to Canada*, ed. Theodore Binnema, Gerhard J. Ens and R.C. Macleod (Edmonton: University of Alberta Press, 2001); Gerhard Ens, *Homeland to Hinterland: The Changing Worlds of the Red River Métis in the Nineteenth Century* (Toronto: University of Toronto Press, 1996).

19. L. Chartrand, "'We Rise Again,'" 150.

20. Samuel Corrigan, "Some Implications of the Current Métis Case," in *The Struggle for Recognition: Canadian Justice and the Métis Nation*, ed. Samuel Corrigan and Lawrence Barkwell (Winnipeg: Pemmican Publications, 1991), 197.

21. Quoted in RCAP, 1996, vol. 2, pt. 1, 114.

22. In particular was the "pemmican proclamation," issued by Governor Miles Macdonnell in 1814. Issued without the consultation or prior knowledge of the Métis, this proclamation forbade the export of pemmican, a necessary staple of the fur trade. This was soon followed by another proclamation forbidding the running of buffalo. See J.M. Bumsted, *Trials and Tribulations: The Red River Settlement and the Emergence of Manitoba 1811–1879* (Winnipeg: Great Plains Publications, 2003).

23. Marcel Giraud, *The Métis in the Canadian West*, trans. George Woodcock, 2 vols. (Edmonton and Lincoln: University of Alberta Press and University of Nebraska Press, 1986) (Original title: *Le Métis canadien: son role dans l'histoire des provinces de l'Ouest*. Paris: Institut d'ethnologie, 1945); Teillet, *Métis Law Summary*.

24. Lawrence Barkwell, "Early Law and Social Control among the Métis," in *The Struggle for Recognition: Canadian Justice and the Métis Nation*, ed. Samuel Corrigan and Lawrence Barkwell (Winnipeg: Pemmican Publications, 1991), 10.

25. L. Chartrand, "The Definition of Métis Peoples"; Thomas Berger, *Fragile Freedoms: Human Rights and Dissent in Canada* (Toronto: Irwin Publishing, 1982).

26. Sealey and Lussier, *The Métis: Canada's Forgotten People*; George Goulet and Terry Goulet, *The Métis: Memorable Events and Memorable Personalities* (Calgary: FabJob, 2006). Historians such as W.L. Morton and G.F.G. Stanley have suggested that it was the North West Company in their power struggles with the HBC for control of the fur trade in the Northwest that fomented the idea among the Métis that they constituted a New Nation. In this way the Métis are presented as "loyal dupes" of the Nor'Westers in their struggle with the HBC, with the Battle of Seven Oaks the result of these machinations. Yet, as Thomas Berger points out, "if the Nor'Westers had called forth the New Nation only as a counter in their struggle with Hudson's Bay Company it should have disintegrated when the two companies amalgamated in 1821 under the name and charter of the older company" (*Fragile Freedoms: Human Rights and Dissent in Canada*, 30–31). In other words, if the New Nation was an artificial creation, it should have vanished in the absence of the HBC monopoly that followed. Yet not only did the Métis consciousness of themselves as a distinct people continue, it in fact flourished in the following decades. Fred Shore, noting that such ethnocentric interpretations of history are common when describing events on the periphery of the British Empire, concludes that "the fact remains that Métis nationalism had more to do with the dynamics of Métis cultural, economic and political evolution than it ever had to do with the war plans of a few NWC bourgeois." Fred Shore, "The Emergence of the Métis Nation in Manitoba," in *Métis Legacy: A Métis Historiography and Annotated Bibliography*, ed. Lawrence Barkwell, Leah Dorion and Darren R. Préfontaine (Winnipeg: Pemmican Publications, 2001), 73.

27. Julia Harrison, *Métis: People Between Two Worlds* (Vancouver: Douglas & McIntyre, 1985); Irene Spry, "The Métis and Mixed-Bloods of Rupert's Land before 1870," in *The New Peoples: Being and Becoming Métis in North America*, ed. Jacqueline Peterson and Jennifer S.H. Brown (Winnipeg: University of Manitoba Press, 1985); Diane Payment, *The Free People—Li Gens Libres: a History of the Métis Community of Batoche, Saskatchewan* (Calgary: University of Calgary Press, 2009). Payment provides specific examples of several of these petitions in the Batoche area, largely involving issues related to Métis representation on state governing bodies and the surveying of land in river lots (129ff).

28. Quoted in J.M. Bumsted, *Louis Riel v. Canada: The Making of a Rebel* (Winnipeg: Great Plains Publications, 2001), 43–44; and Bumsted, *Trials and Tribulations*, 193. Gerhard Ens (1994) argues that the Red River Resistance was primarily motivated by the desire of Riel and his supporters to protect their French and Catholic

rights, rather than any Aboriginal title to the land. In particular, Ens draws attention to the pivotal role played by the Catholic Church in establishing and legitimizing Riel's political credentials. See Gerhard Ens, "Prologue to the Red River Resistance: Pre-liminal Politics and the Triumph of Riel," *Journal of the Canadian Historical Association* 5, no. 1 (1994).

29. Norma Hall, "A History of the Legislative Assembly of Assiniboia." Paper jointly commissioned by Indian and Northern Affairs Canada, MMF and the Province of Manitoba, 2010.

30. Hall, "A History of the Legislative Assembly of Assiniboia"; J.M. Bumsted, *The Red River Rebellion* (Winnipeg: Watson & Dwyer, 1996).

31. Hall, "A History of the Legislative Assembly of Assiniboia," 1.

32. Weinstein, *Quiet Revolution West.*

33. Bumsted, *Louis Riel v. Canada*; Bumsted, *The Red River Rebellion.*

34. Weinstein, *Quiet Revolution West*, 11.

35. Gerhard Ens, "Dispossession or Adaptation? Migration and Persistence of the Red River Métis, 1835–1890," *Historical Papers* 23, no. 1 (1988).

36. Payment, *The Free People—Li Gens Libres*, 125; Berger, *Fragile Freedoms*; Don McLean, *50 Historical Vignettes: Views of the Common People* (Regina: Gabriel Dumont Institute, 1987).

37. Irene Gordon, *A People on the Move: The Métis of the Western Plains* (Vancouver: Heritage House, 2009); Yale Belanger, *Ways of Knowing: An Introduction to Native Studies in Canada* (Toronto: Nelson Education, 2010); Joseph Sawchuk, *The Métis of Manitoba: Reformulation of an Ethnic Identity* (Toronto: Peter Martin Associates, 1978).

38. Barkwell, "Early Law and Social Control among the Métis," in *The Struggle for Recognition: Canadian Justice and the Métis Nation*, ed. Samuel Corrigan and Lawrence Barkwell (Winnipeg: Pemmican Publications, 1991), 12.

39. George Woodcock, *Gabriel Dumont: The Métis Chief and his Lost World* (Edmonton: Hurtig Publishers, 1976).

40. Payment, *The Free People—Li Gens Libres.* Jack Bumsted points out that it was not only the Métis of Batoche that were frustrated with the Canadian government at the time (*Louis Riel v. Canada: The Making of a Rebel*, 248). While their grievances concerned the failure of the government to properly fulfill its promises of scrip under the *Manitoba Act*, First Nations in the area were also disturbed by their treatment by Indian Affairs. In addition, the European settlers in Batoche were becoming restive in their demands for responsible government. While led into

the Resistance by Riel and the Métis, together "all of these interest groups had in common an abiding anger with the government of Canada." Gerald Friesen also makes a similar point in *The Canadian Prairies: A History* (Toronto: University of Toronto Press, 1987).

41. Payment, *The Free People—Li Gens Libres*.

42. Berger, *Fragile Freedoms*. The account presented here over-simplifies the complexity and fluidity that marked the Northwest region during this time. Despite the significant grievances that existed among First Nations, white settlers, and French and English Métis against the policies of the federal government, not all groups unanimously supported Riel's leadership and tactics. At the same time, the federal government was also complicit in actively seeking to create divisions among these groups in an effort to quell opposition. Indeed, in the 1880s Northwest it was difficult to create systematic co-operation between and among the various Métis communities. See Payment, *The Free People—Li Gens Libres*; Bumsted, *Louis Riel v. Canada: The Making of a Rebel*; and Friesen, *The Canadian Prairies*, for a fuller discussion of these events.

43. L. Chartrand, "The Definition of Métis Peoples," 217.

44. Joe Sawchuk, *Métis Land Rights in Alberta: A Political History* (Edmonton: The Métis Association of Alberta, 1981); George Goulet and Terry Goulet, *The Métis: Memorable Events and Memorable Personalities* (Calgary: FabJob, 2006); Weinstein, *Quiet Revolution West*.

45. Donald Purich, *The Métis* (Toronto: James Lorimer & Company, 1988); Goulet and Goulet, *The Métis: Memorable Events and Memorable Personalities*; and Barkwell, "Early Law and Social Control among the Métis."

46. Alexander Ross, *The Red River Settlement: Its Rise, Progress and Present State* (Edmonton: Hurtig Publishers, 1972).

47. Giraud, *The Métis in the Canadian West*.

48. Tim Chodan and Dan Asfar, *Gabriel Dumont: War Leader of the Métis* (Calgary: Folklore Publishing, 2003), 27.

49. P. Chartrand, "Defining the 'Métis' of Canada," 152.

50. Thomas Pocklington, *The Government and Politics of the Alberta Métis Settlements* (Regina: Canadian Plains Research Center, 1991), 4.

51. Pocklington, *The Government and Politics*, 5.

52. RCAP, vol. 4, 227.

53. Weinstein, *Quiet Revolution West*.

54. Jason Madden, John Graham and Jake Wilson, *Exploring Options for Métis Governance in the 21st Century* (Ottawa: Institute on Governance, 2005). Some specific examples of this included gathering documents and interviewing witnesses who were involved in the Red River Resistance and the Battle of Batoche in order to "present the Métis point of view [on these events] whenever the historical role of the Métis was denigrated" (Goulet and Goulet, *The Métis*, 144). The Union also engaged the services of a non-Métis, but sympathetic, newspaper editor named Auguste-Henri de Trémaudan to write a history of the Métis people on the basis of these accounts. Originally published by the Union in French in 1936, an English translation was published in 1982 under the title *Hold High Your Heads: History of the Metis Nation in Western Canada*. John Friesen and Virginia Lyons Friesen, *We are Included! The Métis People of Canada Realize Riel's Vision* (Calgary: Detselig Enterprises, 2004); John Friesen, *The Riel/Real Story: An Interpretive History of the Métis People of Canada* (Ottawa: Borealis Press, 1996); Jennifer Brown, "The Métis: Genesis and Rebirth," in *Native People, Native Lands: Canadian Indians, Inuit and Métis*, ed. Bruce Alden Cox (Montreal: McGill-Queen's University Press, 2002).

55. Brown, "The Métis: Genesis and Rebirth"; Patrick Douaud, *The Western Métis: Profile of a People* (Regina: Canadian Plains Research Center, 2007).

56. Howard Adams, *Tortured People: The Politics of Colonization*, rev. ed. (Penticton, BC: Theytus Books, 1999).

57. Pocklington, *The Government and Politics*; Friesen, *The Riel/Real Story*.

58. For a discussion of scrip see Sawchuk, *Métis Land Rights in Alberta*.

59. That the Métis population as a whole continues to face the challenges of poverty and lower socio-economic outcomes compared with other Canadians is evidenced by numerous empirical studies. Statistics Canada reports lower median incomes for Métis compared with the non-Aboriginal population in Canada, as well as poorer and more over-crowded housing conditions, lower educational completion rates and lower participation rates in post-secondary education (Statistics Canada, "Métis in Canada: Selected Findings of the 2006 Census," www.stat.can.gc.ca). A study released in June 2010 by the Manitoba Centre for Health Policy at the University of Manitoba found that compared with all Manitobans, Métis in the province suffer from higher premature mortality rates (21%), higher rates of substance abuse (47%), a suicide rate 38% higher than that of other Manitobans, and poorer education and social service outcomes. The study also found that Métis children in the province were 24% more likely to be under the care of Child and Family Services, and twice as likely to be living in

families receiving provincial income assistance. See Manitoba Centre for Health Policy, "Profile of Métis Health Status and Healthcare Utilization in Manitoba: A Population-Based Study," June 2010, www.umanitoba.ca.

60. Leah Dorion and Darren R. Préfontaine, "Métis Land Rights and Self-Government," (Regina: Gabriel Dumont Institute, 2003), 17; Dobbin, *The One-And-A-Half Men*.

61. MMF, "Snapshot of the Nation," 2002, 1, available at www.metisnation.ca.

62. Sawchuk, *The Métis of Manitoba*, 13.

63. Sawchuk, *The Métis of Manitoba*, 12. Gerhard Ens highlights the importance of economic factors in his analysis of Métis ethnogenesis. As he writes, "Métis identity was not defined by biology, blood, or religion, but rather by the economic and social niche they carved out for themselves within the fur trade" (Ens, *Homeland to Hinterland*, 4).

64. Joe Sawchuk, *The Dynamics of Native Politics: The Alberta Métis Experience* (Saskatoon: Purich Publishing, 1998); Dobbin, *The One-And-A-Half Men*; Siomonn P. Pulla, "Regional Nationalism or National Mobilization? A Brief Social History of the Development of Métis Political Organization in Canada, 1815-2011," in this volume.

65. Métis Nation of Alberta, "Snapshot of the Nation," 2002, available at www.metisnation.ca; Pocklington, *The Government and Politics of the Alberta Métis Settlements*; Friesen, *The Riel/Real Story*; Catherine Bell, *Alberta's Métis Settlements Legislation: An Overview of Ownership and Management of Settlement Lands* (Regina: Canadian Plains Research Center, 1994); Catherine Bell, "Métis Self-Government: The Alberta Settlements Model," in *Aboriginal Self-Government in Canada*, ed. John Hylton (Saskatoon: Purich Publishing, 1999). While an in-depth discussion of the Métis Settlements is beyond the scope of this chapter, see also Sawchuk, *Métis Land Rights in Alberta*; Sawchuk, *The Dynamics of Native Politics: The Alberta Métis Experience* (Saskatoon: Purich Publishing, 1998); and John Graham, "Advancing Governance of the Métis Settlements of Alberta: Selected Working Papers," Ottawa: Institute on Governance, 2007, available at www.iog.ca.

66. Joe Sawchuk, *The Dynamics of Native Politics*; Dobbin, *The One-And-A-Half Men*.

67. RCAP, 1996, vol. 4.

68. Sawchuk, *The Métis of Manitoba*; Harrison, *Métis: People Between Two Worlds*.

69. Sealey and Lussier, *The Métis: Canada's Forgotten People*.

70. Weinstein, *Quiet Revolution West*; Brown, "The Métis: Genesis and Rebirth";
    Jennifer Reid, *Louis Riel and the Creation of Modern Canada* (Albuquerque:
    University of New Mexico Press, 2008).

71. Brown, "The Métis: Genesis and Rebirth."

72. Weinstein, *Quiet Revolution West*.

73. Joe Sawchuk, "The Métis, Non-Status Indians and the New Aboriginality:
    Government Influence on Native Political Alliances and Identity," in *Readings in
    Aboriginal Studies*, vol. 2, *Identities and State Structures*, ed. Joe Sawchuk (Brandon,
    MB: Bearpaw Publishing, 1992), 72; MNC, "Snapshot of the Nation," 2002, 2,
    available at www.metisnation.ca.

74. Weinstein, *Quiet Revolution West*, 32.

75. Sawchuk, "The Métis, Non-Status Indians and the New Aboriginality."

76. Weinstein, *Quiet Revolution West*, 45.

77. Weinstein, *Quiet Revolution West*; Sawchuk, "The Métis, Non-Status Indians and
    the New Aboriginality"; Sawchuk, *The Dynamics of Native Politics*.

78. These events resulted in more than just the formation of the Métis National
    Council. It also marked a turning point in operational strategy for Métis lead-
    ers. In the wake of four such conferences (between 1983 and 1987), in addition
    to the Meech Lake and Charlottetown Accords—all of which resulted in fail-
    ure—the goal of a political settlement with provincial and federal governments
    recognizing and affirming Métis rights became an increasingly distant option.
    Particularly disappointing for the Métis was the failure of the Charlottetown
    Accord, which contained within it a specific Métis Nation Accord. This Accord
    would have committed the federal government to the negotiation of self-gov-
    ernment agreements, lands and resources with the Métis, and would also have
    clarified that the reference to Indians in section 94 of the *Constitution Act, 1867*
    included the Métis. With the death of the Charlottetown Accord, what had rep-
    resented the "most significant breakthrough at the bargaining table for the
    Métis people since Riel's provisional government negotiated provincehood for
    Manitoba" (Weinstein, *Quiet Revolution West*, 132), also died as well. In the wake
    of this defeat, in the words of Clément Chartier, president of the Métis National
    Council (MNC), "it was clear that the political process had failed us" (Chartier,
    personal interview).

79. MNC, *Consolidated By-Laws*, 2003.

80. MNC, "Snapshot of the Nation"; Madden et al., *Exploring Options*.

81. MNC, "Snapshot of the Nation: Executive Summary," 2002, 4, available at www. metisnation.ca.

82. Madden, "The Métis Nation's Self-Government Agenda," 327.

83. Weinstein, *Quiet Revolution West*, 208.

84. Weinstein, *Quiet Revolution West*, 208.

85. An exception to this is the Treaty No. 3 adhesion of 1874, which included the Métis of Rainy River, as well as several land claims negotiations involving the Métis in the NWT. See Teillet, *Métis Law Summary*, for a discussion of these various land claim negotiations. The MMF, in *MMF v. Attorney General of Canada and Attorney General of Manitoba*, is pursuing a land claim outside of the federal government's land claim resolution process, from which the Métis are excluded. This case is currently before the Supreme Court of Canada.

86. As explained by Murray Trachtenberg, legal counsel to the MMF, provincial law allows for the incorporation of a non-share corporation (often referred to as a not-for-profit corporation) which provides its members with the protection of limited liability. Banks and other financial institutions as well as governments are familiar with and comfortable with this form of legal entity and will insist that there be a corporation to hold assets and represent its members. The creation of a non-share corporation allows for its members to participate in the affairs of the organization and for its directors to govern, all without individual liability being incurred or putting individual assets at risk. Ownership of assets (buildings, vehicles, equipment) belongs to the corporation and not to any individual member. (Personal correspondence from Murray Trachtenberg, January 2011).

87. RCAP, 1996, 2, 116.

88. MNO, "Snapshot of the Nation," 2002, 1, available at www.metisnation.ca.

89. An excellent example of this involves the institutional and legal frameworks that Métis governments in each of the provinces have enacted to implement Métis harvesting rights. In Alberta, for example, the MNA established hunting regulations for its membership, overseen by Captains of the Hunt appointed in Métis communities throughout the province. In commenting on the appointment of these individuals, the MNA minister responsible for harvesting drew on oral traditions concerning Métis hunting practices. As he stated, "similar to the role Captains of the Hunt have historically played within the Métis Nation, these Métis harvesters will play the important role of communicating with our harvesters and working to ensure a safe and successful Métis harvest." MNA, "Métis Nation of Alberta Moves Forward on Harvesting Action Plan," press

release, 26 September 2007, available at www.albertametis.com. See also Kelly L. Saunders, "The Hunt for Justice: Métis Harvesting Rights and the Pursuit of Self-Government," *The Canadian Journal of Native Studies* 31, no. 1 (2011) for an examination of Métis harvesting rights in Manitoba.

90. L. Chartrand, "'We Rise Again.'"

91. Will Goodon, Special Advisor to MMF President David Chartrand, personal interview, 2010. All major policy decisions of the provincial Métis governments must be approved and ratified by the membership at the annual general assemblies. An example of this in Manitoba is Resolution no. 8, which was brought to the floor at the MMF's 39th annual general assembly in September 2007. Concerns had been raised in some communities over the manner in which the Province of Manitoba had been fulfilling its duty to consult obligations with the Métis. As a result, the membership passed a resolution requiring the MMF Home Office to take the lead on all present and future negotiations with the province, and empowering the MMF board of directors to pursue "legal and other actions" if this consultation did not occur. This resolution provides the executive of the MMF with the necessary direction, authority and legitimacy to carry forward its negotiations with the Government of Manitoba. See also the MMF Constitution, 34–35, available at www.mmf.mb.ca.

92. Madden, "The Métis Nation's Self-Government Agenda," 326.

93. RCAP, 1996, 2.

94. MNA, *By-laws of the Métis Nation of Alberta Association*, 2010, 2–3, available at www.albertametis.com.

95. Joe Sawchuk, "Negotiating an Identity: Métis Political Organizations, the Canadian Government, and Competing Concepts of Aboriginality," *American Indian Quarterly* 25, no. 1 (Winter 2001); Sawchuk, *The Dynamics of Native Politics*.

96. Sawchuk, *The Dynamics of Native Politics*, 48.

97. MNC, "Snapshot of the Nation," 22.

98. MNC, "*R. v. Powley*: A Case Summary and Frequently Asked Questions."

99. MMF, Constitution, 2–5.

100. MNC, "Snapshot of the Nation: Executive Summary."

101. Sawchuk, *The Dynamics of Native Politics*.

102. MMF, "Government Structure," www.mmf.mb.ca.

103. MMF, "Vision, Integrity, Pride: A New Era for Metis," *MMF Annual General Report*, 2009, 42.

104. Chartier, personal interview.

105. MMF, "Honouring the Past, Celebrating the Present, Embracing the Future," *MMF Annual General Report*, 2003, 4. The consolidated by-laws of the MNC mandate that all of its provincial members hold province-wide, ballot box elections. Prior to the establishment of direct elections, the chairs of each local were responsible for electing all executive positions (regional directors, vice-presidents and the president).

106. MNC, *Consolidated By-laws*, 2003.

107. In Manitoba, any female that is a member of the MMF can join the Métis Women of Manitoba. The spokesperson is elected by the Métis Women of Manitoba membership at their annual general meetings, which are held separately from the MMF's annual general assemblies. The spokesperson is elected to a three-year term (personal interview with Anita Campbell, spokesperson of the Métis Women of Manitoba, April 2010).

108. MNC, "Snapshot of the Nation: Executive Summary," 6.

109. See the MNA and MMF websites for a list of current executive members.

110. Since ballot box elections began in 1984, a total of 223 elected representatives have been elected to the MMF board of directors, 103 of whom have been women. Data compiled by author based on MMF electoral returns.

111. A. Campbell, personal interview, 2010.

112. The number of people that attend these annual general assemblies varies from province to province. In the case of the MMF, the last assembly held in Brandon, Manitoba, was attended by over 3,000 delegates (Goodon, personal interview).

113. Local elections can be held at any time of the year, pending notification to the MMF Head Office.

114. Prior to constitutional changes brought in after the 2006 election, terms of office for the MMF president and board of directors consisted of three years.

115. MMF, Office of the Chief Electoral Commissioner, Report on the 2010 Manitoba Metis Federation General Election, 2010; MMF, Office of the Chief Electoral Commissioner, Chief Electoral Officer Report on the 2003 Election, 2004.

116. MMF, Constitution, 13.

117. MMF, Report on the 2010 Manitoba Metis Federation General Election, 9.

118. MMF, Chief Electoral Officer Report on the 2003 Election; MMF, Office of the Chief Electoral Officer, Report on the 2000 Manitoba Metis Federation Provincial Election, 2000.

119. Goodon, personal interview.

120. Madden et al., *Exploring Options*.

121. Helen Johnson, Regional Director, Métis Nation-Saskatchewan, personal interview, July 2010.

122. MN-S, "Snapshot of the Nation," 2002, 1, available at www.metisnation.ca.

123. MNBC, Constitution, 2010, available at www.mnbc.ca.

124. Government of Saskatchewan, *The Métis Act, 2002*, available at http://www.qp.gov.sk.ca/documents/English/Statutes/Statutes/M14-01.pdf.

125. Teillet, *Métis Law Summary*.

126. MNBC, *Senate Act*, revised September 2009, 5, available at www.mnbc.ca.

127. MNA, *By-laws of the Métis Nation of Alberta Association*.

128. MN-S, "Snapshot of the Nation," 4.

129. This section draws on work undertaken by Métis legal scholar Jason Madden (*Exploring Options for Métis Governance in the 21st Century* and "The Métis Nation's Self-Government Agenda: Issues and Options for the Future"), who has written cogently on the numerous governance challenges facing the Métis Nation as it continues to advance its rights agenda.

130. Nichols, "Prospects for Justice," 97.

131. L. Chartrand, "The Definition of Métis Peoples"; Isaac, *Aboriginal Case Law*; Sawchuk, "Negotiating an Identity."

132. That this remains a point of contention among the Métis was evident at the MNC annual general assembly in December 2010, when delegates engaged in a spirited discussion of this very issue.

133. Sawchuk, *Métis Land Rights in Alberta*; Herman Sprenger, "The Métis Nation: Buffalo Hunting versus Agriculture in the Red River Settlement, 1810–1870," in Cox, *Native People, Native Lands*.

134. R. v. Powley, SCC 43 [2003], 2 SCR 207, 19 September 2003.

135. Teillet, *Métis Law Summary*, 21.

136. Fred Caron, "Métis Self-Government: Reflections on the Way Forward," in Wilson and Mallet, *Métis-Crown Relations*, 399.

137. Caron, "Métis Self-Government," 401.

138. Jacqueline Peterson, "The People In-Between: Indian–White Marriage and the Genesis of a Métis Society and Culture in the Great Lakes Region, 1680–1830" (PHD diss., University of Illinois at Chicago, 1981).

139. P. Chartrand, "All My Relations."

140. Teillet, *Métis Law Summary*, 4.

141. P. Chartrand, "Defining the 'Métis' of Canada," 64.

142. Alberta (Aboriginal Affairs and Northern Development) v. Cunningham [2011], SCC 37, 2 SCR 670, 3.

143. Goodon, personal interview.

144. Madden et al., *Exploring Options*, 35.

145. Saskatchewan, "Canada and Saskatchewan Announce Oversight Committee for Métis Nation-Saskatchewan Election," press release, 30 June 2006, available at www.gov.sk.ca; Keith Lampard, *A Study to Answer the Question: Was the Métis Election of 2004 run in a fair and democratic manner such that its results can be relied upon by Métis people and the Government of Saskatchewan?* (Lampard Report), 7 October 2004.

146. Madden, "The Métis Nation's Self-Government Agenda."

147. The consolidated by-laws of the MNC give greater decision-making powers to the three prairie organizations (the MMF, the MNA and the MN-S) over the MNO and MNBC. For example, in the determination of voting delegates for the election of MNC president, the three prairie members each have five votes, while the MNO and MNBC only have one vote each. This differentiation reflects the prairie organizations' status as "founding members" of the MNC, and the western prairies as the birthplace of the Historic Métis Nation Homeland in Canada. However, it does remain a contentious issue within the MNC.

148. Madden et al., *Exploring Options*.

149. Weinstein, *Quiet Revolution West*; Chartier, personal interview.

150. MNC, *Consolidated By-Laws*, 2003.

151. MNC, "President's Newsletter," 2012.

152. Weinstein, *Quiet Revolution West*; P. Chartrand, 2008; Goulet and Goulet, *The Métis*; L. Chartrand, 2008; Fred Shore and Lawrence Barkwell, *Past Reflects the Present: The Métis Elders' Conference* (Winnipeg: Manitoba Metis Federation, 1997); Corrigan and Barkwell, 1991.

153. Madden et al., *Exploring Options*, 13.

Bibliography

Adams, Howard. *Tortured People: The Politics of Colonization*, Revised Edition. Penticton, BC: Theytus Books: 1999.

Alberta (Aboriginal Affairs and Northern Development) v. Cunningham [2011], SCC 37, 2 SCR 670.

Barkwell, Lawrence. "Early Law and Social Control among the Métis." In *The Struggle for Recognition: Canadian Justice and the Métis Nation*, edited by Samuel Corrigan and Lawrence Barkwell, 7–37. Winnipeg: Pemmican Publications, 1991.

Belanger, Yale. *Ways of Knowing: An Introduction to Native Studies in Canada*. Toronto: Nelson Education, 2010.

Belanger, Yale, and David Newhouse, 2004. "Emerging from the Shadows: the Pursuit of Aboriginal Self-Government to Promote Aboriginal Well-being." *The Canadian Journal of Native Studies* 24, no. 1 (2004): 129–22.

Bell, Catherine. *Alberta's Métis Settlements Legislation: An Overview of Ownership and Management of Settlement Lands*. Regina: Canadian Plains Research Center, 1994.

———. "Métis Self-Government: the Alberta Settlements Model." In *Aboriginal Self-Government in Canada*, edited by John Hylton, 329–50. Saskatoon: Purich Publishing, 1999.

Berger, Thomas. *Fragile Freedoms: Human Rights and Dissent in Canada*. Toronto: Irwin Publishing, 1982.

Brown, Jennifer. "The Métis: Genesis and Rebirth." In Cox, *Native People, Native Lands*, 136–47.

Bumsted, J.M. *Louis Riel v. Canada: The Making of a Rebel*. Winnipeg: Great Plains Publications, 2001.

———. *The Red River Rebellion*. Winnipeg: Watson & Dwyer, 1996.

———. *Trials and Tribulations: The Red River Settlement and the Emergence of Manitoba 1811–1879*. Winnipeg: Great Plains Publications, 2003.

Campbell, Anita. Spokesperson, Métis Women of Manitoba. Personal interview, April 2010.

Caron, Fred. "Métis Self-Government: Reflections on the Way Forward." In Wilson and Mallet, *Métis-Crown Relations*, 391–410.

Chartier, Clément. President, Métis National Council. Personal interview, September 2009.

———. "Aboriginal Self-Government and the Métis Nation." In *Aboriginal Self-Government in Canada*, edited by John Hylton, 112–28. Saskatoon: Purich Publishing, 1999.

Chartrand, Larry. "The Definition of Métis Peoples in Section 35(2) of the *Constitution Act, 1982*," *Saskatchewan Law Review* 67 (2004): 209–33.

———. "'We Rise Again': Métis Traditional Governance and the Claim to Métis Self-Government." In *Aboriginal Self-Government in Canada: Current Trends and Issues*, 3rd ed., edited by Yale Belanger, 145–57. Saskatoon: Purich Publishing, 2008.

Chartrand, Paul. "All My Relations: Métis–First Nations Relations." Paper prepared for the National Centre for First Nations Governance, June 2007.

———. "Defining the 'Métis' of Canada: A Principled Approach to Crown–Aboriginal Relations." In Wilson and Mallet, *Métis-Crown Relations*, 27–70.

———. *Who Are Canada's Aboriginal Peoples?* Saskatoon: Purich Publishing, 2002.

Chodan, Tim, and Dan Asfar. *Gabriel Dumont: War Leader of the Métis*. Calgary: Folklore Publishing, 2003.

Corrigan, Samuel. "Some Implications of the Current Métis Case." In *The Struggle for Recognition: Canadian Justice and the Métis Nation*, edited by Samuel Corrigan and Lawrence Barkwell, 195–206. Winnipeg: Pemmican Publications, 1991.

Cox, Bruce Alden, ed. *Native People, Native Lands: Canadian Indians, Inuit and Métis*. Montreal: McGill-Queens University Press, 2002.

Devine, Heather. *The People Who Own Themselves: Aboriginal Genesis in a Canadian Family, 1660–1900*. Calgary: University of Calgary Press, 2004.

Dobbin, Murray. *The One-And-A-Half Men: The Story of Jim Brady and Malcolm Norris, Métis Patriots of the 20th Century*. Regina: Gabriel Dumont Institute, 1987.

Dorion, Leah, and Darren R. Préfontaine. "Métis Land Rights and Self-Government." Regina: Gabriel Dumont Institute, 2003.

Douaud, Patrick. *The Western Métis: Profile of a People*. Regina: Canadian Plains Research Center, 2007.

Ens, Gerhard. "Dispossession or Adaptation? Migration and Persistence of the Red River Métis, 1835–1890," *Historical Papers* 23, no. 1 (1988): 120–44.

———. *Homeland to Hinterland: The Changing Worlds of the Red River Métis in the Nineteenth Century*. Toronto: University of Toronto Press, 1996.

———. "Prologue to the Red River Resistance: Pre-liminal Politics and the Triumph of Riel," *Journal of the Canadian Historical Association* 5, no. 1 (1994): 111–23.

Foster, John E. "Wintering, the Outsider Adult Male and the Ethnogenesis of the Western Plains Métis." In *From Rupert's Land to Canada*, edited by Theodore Binnema, Gerhard J. Ens and R.C. Macleod, 179–92. Edmonton: University of Alberta Press, 2001.

Friesen, Gerald. *The Canadian Prairies: A History*. Toronto: University of Toronto Press, 1987.

Friesen, John. *The Riel/Real Story: An Interpretive History of the Métis People of Canada*. Ottawa: Borealis Press, 1996.

Friesen, John, and Virginia Lyons Friesen. *We are Included! The Métis People of Canada Realize Riel's Vision*. Calgary: Detselig Enterprises, 2004.

Giraud, Marcel. *The Métis in the Canadian West*. Translated by George Woodcock. 2 vols. Edmonton and Lincoln: University of Alberta Press and University of Nebraska Press, 1986. (Original title: *Le Métis canadien: son role dans l'histoire des provinces de l'Ouest*. Paris: Institut d'ethnologie, 1945).

Goodon, Will. Special Advisor to MMF President David Chartrand. Personal interview, August 2010.

Gordon, Irene. *A People on the Move: The Métis of the Western Plains*. Vancouver: Heritage House, 2009.

Goulet, George, and Terry Goulet. *The Métis: Memorable Events and Memorable Personalities*. Calgary: FabJob, 2006.

Graham, John. "Advancing Governance of the Métis Settlements of Alberta: Selected Working Papers." Ottawa: Institute on Governance, 2007.

Grammond, Sébastien. "Finding Métis Communities." *The Canadian Journal of Native Studies* 32, no. 1 (2012): 33–48.

Groves, Robert, and Bradford Morse. "Constituting Aboriginal Collectivities: Avoiding new Peoples 'In Between.'" *Saskatchewan Law Review* 67, no. 1 (2004): 257–99.

Hall, Norma. "A History of the Legislative Assembly of Assiniboia." Paper jointly commissioned by Indian and Northern Affairs Canada, MMF and the Province of Manitoba, 2010.

Harrison, Julia. *Métis: People Between Two Worlds*. Vancouver: Douglas & McIntyre, 1985.

Isaac, Thomas. *Aboriginal Case Law: Commentary, Cases and Materials*, 3rd ed., Saskatoon: Purich Publishing, 2004.

Johnson, Helen. Regional Director, Métis Nation-Saskatchewan. Personal interview, July 2010.

Lampard, Keith. 2004. *A Study to Answer the Question: Was the Métis Election of 2004 run in a fair and democratic manner such that its results can be relied upon by Métis people and the Government of Saskatchewan?* (Lampard Report), 7 October 2004.

Lischke, Ute, and David T. McNab, eds. *The Long Journey of a Forgotten People: Métis Identities and Family Histories*. Waterloo, ON: Wilfrid Laurier University Press, 2007.

Madden, Jason. "The Métis Nation's Self-Government Agenda: Issues and Options for the Future." In Wilson and Mallet, *Métis-Crown Relations*, 323–89.

Madden, Jason, John Graham and Jake Wilson. *Exploring Options for Métis Governance in the 21st Century*, Ottawa: Institute on Governance, 2005.

Magnet, Joseph E. "Who Are the Aboriginal People of Canada?" In *Aboriginal Rights Litigation*, edited by Joseph Magnet and Dwight Dorey, 23–91. Markham, ON: LexisNexis Canada, 2003.

Manitoba Metis Federation. Office of the Chief Electoral Commissioner. *Chief Electoral Officer Report on the 2003 Election*. Winnipeg: M M F, 2004.

———. *Constitution*, 2008. www.mmf.mb.ca.

———. "Honouring the Past, Celebrating the Present, Embracing the Future," M M F *Annual General Report: 2003*, Winnipeg: M M F, 2003.

———. Office of the Chief Electoral Officer. *Report on the 2000 Manitoba Metis Federation Provincial Election*. Winnipeg: M M F, 2000.

———. Office of the Chief Electoral Commissioner. *Report on the 2010 Manitoba Metis Federation General Election*, Winnipeg: M M F, 2010.

———. "Snapshot of the Nation," 2002. www.metisnation.ca.

———. "Vision, Integrity, Pride: A New Era for Metis," M M F *Annual General Report*, 2009. 2009.

McLean, Don. *50 Historical Vignettes: Views of the Common People*. Regina: Gabriel Dumont Institute, 1987.

Métis Nation of Alberta. 2010. *By-laws of the Métis Nation of Alberta Association*. www.albertametis.com.

———. "Métis Nation of Alberta Moves Forward on Harvesting Action Plan." Press release, 26 September 2007. www.albertametis.com.

———. "Snapshot of the Nation," 2002. www.metisnation.ca.

Métis Nation British Columbia. *Constitution*, 2010. www.mnbc.ca.

———. *Senate Act*, revised September 2009. www.mnbc.ca.

———. "Snapshot of the Nation," 2002. www.metisnation.ca.

Métis Nation of Ontario. "Annual Report, 2008–2009," 2009. www.metisnation.org.

———. "Snapshot of the Nation," 2002. www.metisnation.ca.

Métis Nation-Saskatchewan. "Snapshot of the Nation," 2002. www.metisnation.ca.

Métis National Council. *Consolidated By-Laws*. 2003.

———. "President's Newsletter," 2012. www.metisnation.ca.

———. 2004. "R. v. Powley: A Case Summary and Frequently Asked Questions." www.metisnation.ca.

———. "Snapshot of the Nation," 2002. www.metisnation.ca.

———. "Snapshot of the Nation: Executive Summary," 2002. www.metisnation.ca.

Morse, Bradford, and John Giokas. "Do the Métis Fall Within Section 91(24) of the Constitution Act, 1867?" In *Aboriginal Self-Government: Legal and Constitutional*

Issues, Royal Commission on Aboriginal Peoples, 140–276. Ottawa: Supply and
Services Canada, 1995.

Nichols, Robert. "Prospects for Justice: Resolving the Paradoxes of Métis
Constitutional Rights." *The Canadian Journal of Native Studies* 23, no. 1 (2003):
91–111.

Payment, Diane. *The Free People—Li Gens Libres: a History of the Métis Community of
Batoche, Saskatchewan*. Calgary: University of Calgary Press, 2009.

Peterson, Jacqueline. "The People In-Between: Indian-White Marriage and the Genesis
of a Métis Society and Culture in the Great Lakes Region, 1680–1830," PHD diss.,
University of Illinois at Chicago, 1981.

Peterson, Jacqueline, and Jennifer S.H. Brown. *The New Peoples: Being and Becoming
Métis in North America*. Winnipeg: University of Manitoba Press, 1985.

Pocklington, Thomas. *The Government and Politics of the Alberta Métis Settlements*.
Regina: Canadian Plains Research Center, 1991.

Purich, Donald. *The Métis*. Toronto: James Lorimer & Company, 1988.

R. v. Powley. SCC 43 [2003], 2 SCR 207, 19 September 2003.

Reid, Jennifer. *Louis Riel and the Creation of Modern Canada*. Albuquerque: University of
New Mexico Press, 2008.

Ross, Alexander. *The Red River Settlement: Its Rise, Progress and Present State*. Edmonton:
Hurtig Publishers, 1972.

Royal Commission on Aboriginal Peoples. *Perspectives and Realities*, vol. 4. Ottawa:
Supply and Services Canada, 1996.

———. *Restructuring the Relationship*, vol. 2, pt. 1. Ottawa: Supply and Services Canada,
1996.

Saskatchewan, Government of. "Canada and Saskatchewan Announce Oversight
Committee for Métis Nation-Saskatchewan Election." Press release, 30 June
2006.

———. *The Métis Act*, 2002. http://www.qp.gov.sk.ca/documents/English/Statutes/
Statutes/M14-01.pdf.

Saunders, Kelly L. "The Hunt for Justice: Métis Harvesting Rights and the Pursuit of
Self-Government." *The Canadian Journal of Native Studies* 21, no. 1 (2011): 161–85.

Sawchuk, Joe. *The Dynamics of Native Politics: The Alberta Métis Experience*. Saskatoon:
Purich Publishing, 1998.

———. *Métis Land Rights in Alberta: A Political History*. Edmonton: The Métis
Association of Alberta, 1981.

————. *The Métis of Manitoba: Reformulation of an Ethnic Identity*. Toronto: Peter Martin Associates, 1978.

————. "The Métis, Non-Status Indians and the New Aboriginality: Government Influence on Native Political Alliances and Identity." In *Readings in Aboriginal Studies: Identities and State Structures*, vol. 2, edited by Joe Sawchuk, 70–86. Brandon, MB: Bearpaw Publishing, 1992.

————. "Negotiating an Identity: Métis Political Organizations, the Canadian Government, and Competing Concepts of Aboriginality." *American Indian Quarterly* 25, no. 1 (Winter 2001): 73–92.

Sealey, D. Bruce, and Antoine S. Lussier. *The Métis: Canada's Forgotten People*. Winnipeg: Pemmican Publications, 1975.

Shore, Fred. "The Emergence of the Métis Nation in Manitoba" in Lawrence Barkwell, Leah Dorion and Darren R. Préfontaine, eds., *Métis Legacy: A Métis Historiography and Annotated Bibliography*. Winnipeg: Pemmican Publications, 2001.

Shore, Fred, and Lawrence Barkwell. *Past Reflects the Present: The Métis Elders' Conference*. Winnipeg: Manitoba Metis Federation, 1997.

Sprenger, Herman. "The Métis Nation: Buffalo Hunting versus Agriculture in the Red River Settlement, 1810–1870." In Cox, *Native People, Native Lands*, 120–35.

Spry, Irene. "The Métis and Mixed-Bloods of Rupert's Land before 1870." In *The New Peoples: Being and Becoming Métis in North America*, edited by Jacqueline Peterson and Jennifer S.H. Brown, 95–118 Winnipeg: University of Manitoba Press, 1985.

Stevenson, Mark. "Section 91(24) and Canada's Legislative Jurisdiction with Respect to the Métis." *Indigenous Law Journal* 1, no. 1 (Spring 2002): 237–73.

Teillet, Jean. "Federal and Provincial Crown Obligations to the Métis." In Wilson and Mallet, *Métis-Crown Relations*, 71–93.

————. *Métis Law Summary*. 2009. www.pstlaw.ca.

————. "The Winds of Change: Métis Rights after Powley, Taku and Haida" in *The Long Journey of a Forgotten People: Métis Identities and Family Histories*, edited by Ute Lischke and David T. McNab, 55–78. Waterloo, ON: Wilfrid Laurier University Press, 2007.

Weinstein, John. *Quiet Revolution West: The Rebirth of Métis Nationalism*. Calgary: Fifth House, 2007.

Wilson, Frederica, and Melanie Mallet, eds. *Métis-Crown Relations: Rights, Identity, Jurisdiction, and Governance*. Toronto: Irwin Law, 2008.

Woodcock, George. *Gabriel Dumont: The Métis Chief and his Lost World*. Edmonton: Hurtig Publishers, 1976.

Regional Nationalism or | 10
National Mobilization?

A Brief Social History of the Development of
Métis Political Organization in Canada, 1815–2011

SIOMONN P. PULLA

BUILDING ON Joe Sawchuk's substantial contributions to the field of
Métis studies[1] and John Weinstein's more current examination of Métis
nationalism,[2] this chapter examines the relationship between the historic
establishment and contemporary organization of Métis associations and
their intensification during the late nineteenth and early twentieth centuries. I explore the development of Métis organizations in response to
historical circumstances, cultural survival and political necessity. The shift
from early pre-confederation Nation-to-Nation Métis relations[3] to relationships based on the framework of the *Indian Act* ultimately begin to
emerge during the mid-1800s as the jurisdictional framework of Indian
policy in Upper and Lower Canada. While early commissions and resulting legislation in Upper and Lower Canada differentiating the colonial
government's fiduciary obligations toward Métis and First Nations were
not necessarily tangible in the Northwest, they provided the foundation
for an emerging national Indian policy and "civilizing program" that, for
the most part, excluded the recognition of Métis rights.

The resulting political and social mobilization of Métis peoples in
regions across Canada during the mid-1800s cannot therefore be

examined completely in isolation from coexisting Indigenous political organizations and the development of a national Canadian Indian policy. Unrestrained from the confines of the *Indian Act* and Canada's historic policies of aggressive civilization, the Métis developed their own political organizations and processes, building their local and regional associations and lobby groups into a cohesive voice for Métis across Canada.[4] This chapter focusses specifically on a socio-historical context associated with the establishment and operation of these regional and national Métis political organizations. This includes an examination of the relationship between Métis political organizations and the growth of a national pan-Aboriginal organizational movement during the mid-1960s; and the resulting tensions between regional Métis, Non-Status and First Nation organizations during this period. I conclude with some reflections on the complex current relationships between Métis organizations and issues surrounding land claims, constitutional participation and ongoing dialogues surrounding Aboriginal governance, economic development and cultural sustainability.

The Establishment of Local and Regional Métis Organizations during the Nineteenth Century

Early Aboriginal–European relations primarily focussed on the maintenance of alliances for military and trade purposes; post-1812, however, the increased demand by Europeans for Indigenous lands to facilitate colonial settlement shifted the focus of these Nation-to-Nation relationships.[5] In particular, by the mid-nineteenth century, the Crown's emphasis on how to best protect Aboriginal peoples and their land was largely replaced by questions of how best to "civilize" Aboriginal peoples and prepare them for what was assumed to be their inevitable assimilation into Canadian-settler society. The resulting "Indian Civilization program" revolved around three philosophical principles: Indian protection, based on the *Royal Proclamation of 1763*; the improvement of Indian living conditions; and Indian assimilation into the dominant society.[6] This new policy of civilization also had three main and overlapping branches: the first was a system of land cession treaties based largely on the tenets of the *Royal Proclamation of 1763*; the second was the establishment of a system of Indian reserves and supervisory Indian agents; and the final branch was the development of a system of schools—first day and industrial schools, and later residential schools—to educate Indians[7] in the ways and manners of mainstream Canadian society.[8] The philosophy and pragmatic structure associated with this new program provided the basis upon which the new Dominion government would form its own Indian policy, and from which many Aboriginal organizations would form in response to this policy during the late nineteenth century.

During the early nineteenth century, Métis in the northwest increasingly identified themselves in relation to a lifestyle that was connected to but distinct from that of the Indians of the area. This is best illustrated in the events leading up to the 1816 Battle of Seven Oaks and the escalating tensions between Métis inhabitants and the Selkirk settlers. After the resignation of the colony's governor, Miles Macdonell, during the summer of 1815, the HBC appointed Peter Fidler, Chief Surveyor of the Selkirk Settlement, as temporarily in command. Fidler was authorized to offer a proposal of peace to the Métis of the Red River region, led by Cuthbert Grant. Fidler assured these Métis that the establishment of the Selkirk colony would not interfere with their lifestyle and promised them that they would "enjoy the full liberty of running buffalo and living according to the custom in which they have been brought up."[9] He also stressed that Métis would not be subject to the local laws of the colony unless they so desired and that they would receive an equal share of the annuities distributed to the local Indians.[10] These Métis at Red River rejected Fidler's proposals. In response they issued their own list of demands requesting the HBC disband the settlement of the Selkirk colony and remain in the area for trade purposes only.[11]

The escalation of these tensions eventually culminated in the 1816 Battle at Seven Oaks, in which Cuthbert Grant and his Métis followers defeated a contingent of Red River settlers and HBC men led by Robert Semple, the new Governor of the Selkirk settlement. On June 19, 1816, the Métis killed Semple and 20 of his men and the HBC subsequently abandoned the Selkirk settlement. Two years later, in 1818, colonial officials convened a commission of inquiry to determine the causes of the conflict and to apportion blame.[12] The records of this investigation indicate that while the officers of the HBC recognized the Métis as a distinct group, they asserted that the Métis acted as a military outfit on behalf of the rival North West Company.[13] Officers of the North West Company, however, represented the Métis as a new and independent tribe of Indians over whom the North West Company had little control.[14] In a statement to the commission dated 14 March 1818, the head of the North West Company, William McGillivray stated: "The assemblage of half-breeds requires a little further comment; we need not dwell here upon the organization of that class of men. You are yourself, Sir, personally aware, that although many of them, from the ties of consanguinity and interest, are more or less connected with the North-West company's people, and either as clerks or servants, or as free hunters, are dependent on them; yet they one and all look upon themselves as members of an independent tribe of natives, entitled to a property in the soil, to a flag of their own, and to protection from the British Government."[15] McGillivray further stated that the Métis should be given the same recognition under British law as that enjoyed by the Indians. He argued that because the Métis could not gain any recognition as British subjects by paternal right, they should not lose their rights as Indians gained through the matriline. He concluded that, under Indian law, the Métis exercised their right to form a new group on any unoccupied or any conquered territory and that, subsequently, "the half-breeds under the denomination of bois brulés and metifs have formed a separate and distinct tribe of Indians for a considerable time back, [which] has been proved to you by various depositions."[16]

In his final report on the Battle of Seven Oaks, dated 30 June 1818, W.B. Coltman, the officer in charge of the investigation, acknowledged the

Métis as maintaining a separate social and political identity. In particular, Coltman attributed the hostilities at the Selkirk Settlement as the Métis' response to an attempt by officials of the HBC to confiscate their horses and provisions. The HBC intended the confiscation as a punishment for the Métis' refusal to follow an order to cease hunting buffalo on horseback. Coltman stressed that the Métis at Red River maintained connections with their Indian relations and, as a result, continued to exercise their hunting and fishing rights, noting that the Métis were very concerned about the effects of increased settlement on their rights. He stated: "[the] half-breeds are very jealous, as were their ancestors of their rights, and that they often complained of the occupation of their lands by the settlers, especially when they found them acting with so much injustice in other respects."[17]

In an additional report dated 5 June 1824 regarding the population of the Red River Settlement, Governor George Simpson further pointed out that the Half-breeds maintained the largest population in the settlement and a significant amount of pride and independence in their unique lifestyle. Simpson warned that if the government did not work toward the permanent settlement of the Métis, they would "become worse and more destitute than Indians being unaccustomed to the privations and hardships to which the latter are frequently exposed and ignorant of the mode of hunting fur bearing animals."[18] The problem was that while the Métis considered themselves to be unique from both their Indian and European cousins, the colonial government in the Northwest did not feel legally responsible to address Métis concerns regarding land settlement issues.

This increasing division of jurisdiction over Indians and Métis is further illustrated in Upper Canada by the recommendations of the 1844 Bagot Commission regarding the government's practice of issuing annual presents to Indians. Because this practice was becoming more costly and cumbersome, Bagot recommended that presents be limited in the immediate future and eventually abolished. This process entailed the enumeration of all resident Indians and the construction of specific band lists.

According to Bagot, only Indians on band lists would receive presents, a practice that ultimately affected the Métis. With regard to the question of "half breeds" and their status, Bagot recommended that neither "half breeds" nor their descendants receive presents unless they "be adopted by the Tribe with which they are connected, and live, as Indians among them."[19] He stressed that this rule should be applied particularly to the Indians of Upper Canada, who frequently married Canadians, and noted that the Governor General of the province recently sanctioned the principle that no Indian woman living, married, or otherwise, with a white man, would receive presents.[20]

In response to the colonial government's increasing distinction between Indian and Métis rights throughout its colonies, on August 29, 1845, prominent leader of the Red River settlement, James Sinclair, and 23 Métis signatories, requested the Governor of Assiniboia, Alexander Christie, to clarify whether the colonial government recognized the Métis' rights to hunting, trapping and the trade of furs in the area. Sinclair stressed that as natives of the country and as half-breeds, the Métis maintained the rights "to hunt furs in the Hudson's Bay Company's Territories, wherever we think proper, and again, sell those furs to the highest bidder—likewise having a doubt, that, natives of this Country can be prevented from trading and trafficking with one another."[21] While Christie ultimately denied that the Métis maintained any special rights, he clearly regarded the Métis as a distinct group, suggesting that they maintained the same rights as British subjects as well as persons born in Canada of European parentage.[22]

By the mid-1800s the colonial government began implementing some of Bagot's recommendations in Upper Canada, and in 1850 two separate bills were passed that defined the term "Indian": *An Act for the protection of the Indians in Upper Canada from imposition, and the property occupied or enjoyed by them from trespass and injury,* and the *Act for the Better Protection of the Lands and Property of the Indians in Lower Canada.* Designed to protect Indian reserve lands, the legislation made a clear distinction between

Indian and Métis. Following Bagot's distinction, the bills stated that Half-breeds were only considered Indians if they lived with an Indian band and were accepted as members.[23]

While the colonial government's new legislation did not apply to its jurisdiction of the Northwest and Rupert's Land, the underpinning philosophy of distinct rights for Indians set the framework that would be used nationally after 1868. In 1858, the colonial government in Upper Canada further refined their distinction between Métis and Indian. In his report on Indian Affairs in Canada, Special Commissioner Pennefather noted that only Half-breeds who claimed Indian descent on the father's side could claim rights to Indian land and moneys. He stated: "The word 'Indian' in Western Canada [Canada West], is held, more perhaps from usage than from any legal authority, to comprise not only all persons of pure Indian blood, but also those of mixed race, who are recognized members of a tribe or band resident in Canada, and who claim Indian descent on the father's side. An Indian woman marrying a white loses her rights as a member of the tribe and her children have no claim on the lands or moneys belonging to their mother's nation."[24] This legal definition of Indian did not change until 1869, when Canada passed the *Act for the gradual enfranchisement of Indians, the better management of Indian Affairs, and to extend the provisions of the Act 31st Victoria, Chapter 42*. While the amended definition still maintained recognition of Indian status through the patriline, it now included a clause that stated that "any Indian woman marrying any other than an Indian, shall cease to be an Indian within the meaning of this Act, nor shall the children issue of such marriage be considered as Indians within the meaning of this Act."[25] Subsequently, Canada did not consider Métis who assumed an identity separate from Indians and who lived separate from Indian bands as "Indian," but, rather, ordinary citizens with no special privileges.

During the 1870s, in response to the assertion of these increasing policies of aggressive civilization, Aboriginal peoples across the country began to organize themselves into political associations. These predominantly regional associations focussed on addressing specific issues relevant to their immediate membership, and usually revolved around access to lands and resources. Under the organized leadership of Louis Riel and his provisional government during the period between November 1869 and the spring of 1870, the Métis in the Northwest were anxious to have their outstanding concerns related to continued access to lands and resources addressed.[26] The HBC's transfer of Rupert's Land and the North-Western Territory to Canada in 1868 officially opened up the western part of the country for settlement and caused a significant ripple effect among the Métis and First Nations populations in this region. To address these rising tensions, Canada passed the *Manitoba Act* in 1870, establishing the province of Manitoba and providing for the distribution of land to Métis.[27] In particular, sections 31 and 32 of the legislation set aside 1.4 million acres of land for distribution among the children of Métis heads of families while also recognizing the rights of Métis and non-Aboriginal settlers to land on the Red River settlement.[28]

In 1874, however, Canada revised the *Dominion Lands Act* to provide all Métis heads of families with $160 in scrip, redeemable in Dominion lands.[29] Distribution of this scrip did not begin to occur until 1876. By this time, many of these Métis had already moved from Manitoba to the Northwest, where they established small settlements south of Prince Albert at St. Laurent, Batoche, Duck Lake and St. Louis. The lands in these settlements were divided based on the Red River land allotment system. Instead of parceling out squares of land with an emphasis on agricultural activities, lots were organized on the waterfront, measuring ten chains in width by two miles in depth, with wood lots and hayfields at the back of the lot to accommodate the Métis lifestyle of lumbering, hay production, small farming, fishing and water transport.[30]

By the mid-1870s, the successful negotiation of four distinct treaties[31] with First Nations of present-day Manitoba, Saskatchewan and Alberta provided the land needed for the establishment of the railway and the colonial settlement of the Northwest. During the early 1880s, Canada further surveyed and parceled approximately 16 million acres of this land in the Northwest into farms.[32] And by 1881, settlement in the Prince Albert region began to increase.

Stipulations under the *Dominion Lands Act* regarding the procedure for officially registering a parcel of land proved difficult for Métis settlers. According to the legislation, land patent claims could only be processed once a Dominion Land Surveyor (DLS) officially surveyed the land. Métis settlers, however, maintained their distinct form of land holding based on the Red River system of allotment. The Métis argued that their system of land holding was a representation of their Aboriginal title and that their rights should not be subjected to homestead regulations applied to European settlers in the Northwest. The federal government, however, did not recognize Métis rights to land, stressing that settlers had as much right to the unoccupied land as the Métis.[33]

During the early 1880s, Métis in Prince Albert increasingly raised concerns over the federal government's policy of setting aside large areas of land around Prince Albert for non-Aboriginal settlement and development. In numerous petitions submitted to the federal government, the Métis requested that Canada recognize their Aboriginal right to lands, stressing that they should not be bound to the same requirements under the *Dominion Lands Act* as immigrants or homesteaders. This included waiving the $2 per acre fee for people living on odd-numbered sections of land within the CPR tract, as well as exclusion from the standardized system of surveying employed by the DLS. The Métis maintained that their lands be surveyed following their traditional system of land allotment into river lots.[34] Métis settlers at St. Louis, for example, refused to submit their lands to the township survey system and requested that the government resurvey their lands into river lots based on their traditional system of land holding. In response, the government proposed dividing the Métis lands into legal subdivisions, enabling the Métis to register their claims at the land patent office in Prince Albert.

Fueled by their increasing distrust of the government, Métis settlers continually refused to register their lands as legal subdivisions, preferring their traditional system of land holding as a representation of their Aboriginal title.[35] Canada's refusal to acknowledge this distinct pattern of land holdings in the Northwest ultimately contributed to the escalation in tensions in the region.[36] In response to these tensions, on September 24, 1884, Louis Riel and Gabriel Dumont organized themselves into the Union métisse Saint-Joseph (UMSJ). Riel and Dumont built the UMSJ around the highly organized provisional government established 11 years earlier by the Métis in St. Laurent, a Métis winter camp built around Duck Lake. This included the establishment of a council, the election of a president and the enforcement of regulations overseeing the day-to-day functioning of the community. The enforcement of a formalized list of rules and regulations included the collection of taxes, and regulations to settle disputes over boundaries and land ownership issues.[37] By the spring of 1885, however, the UMSJ's frustration with the delays and unfulfilled promises of the federal government led to violent conflict. UMSJ leaders, Dumont and Riel, believed that armed resistance against the government's settlement policy would force Canada to address Métis claims and acknowledge their Aboriginal rights.[38] The result of the conflict, however, led to the eventual execution of Riel on November 16, 1885, and the disbanding of the UMSJ in 1887.

An immediate result of the 1885 conflict was the establishment of the Northwest Scrip Commission in 1885. The commission was modelled after the earlier 1870 Manitoba Scrip Commission and, during the late nineteenth and early twentieth centuries, worked to include Métis in the Treaty process.[39] On an organizational level, the 1885 conflict also led to the establishment of specific regional Métis populations in the Northwest. Many of the Métis in St. Laurent returned to Manitoba and the increasing urban development of Winnipeg, while others joined the thriving settlements of Métis further west. A result of this increasing Métis regionalism was the establishment of specific organizations to address the needs of the local Métis populations.

On March 1, 1888, the Union nationale métisse Saint-Joseph du Manitoba was established in the St. Vital[40] district of Winnipeg. The organization's main purpose was to counter the negative image of the Métis in Canada and to help restore Métis pride in their identity by preserving the memory of the contributions of Louis Riel to Métis ethnogenesis. During the early twentieth century, the organization worked to further a unique political status for the Métis. This included the development of a Métis national flag and the establishment of a Métis historical committee to ensure that the Métis perspective on the history of Canada was included in textbooks and other media.[41]

In 1897 the Métis in present-day Alberta established their own regional association, the St. Albert Métis Association, also known as the Alberta Half-Breed Association and the Half-Breed Association of St. Albert. The organization expressed concern about the way in which the federal government was addressing Métis land claims. It sent various petitions to Ottawa, either requesting scrip for children or recommending changes to the existing scrip programs.[42] The group was organized formally, with an elected president, and meetings were based around parliamentary procedure—motions proposed and seconded, committees formed to take on specific tasks, and minutes of meetings recorded.[43]

The Early Twentieth Century: Moving toward National Representation
During the mid-nineteenth century, the federal government's focus on Indian Affairs began to shift significantly. In response, the Aboriginal political consciousness across the country began to grow and become more organized, both regionally and nationally.[44] The assumption by nineteenth-century scholars, missionaries and government officials that Aboriginal peoples across Canada were vanishing due to a combination of disease, assimilation and low birth rates proved misleading. By the early 1930s, the Aboriginal population in Canada was, in fact, on the rise. The increasing strains over Aboriginal land and resource use, the lack of funding for Indian Affairs, the increasingly crowded and poor living

conditions on Indian reserves and misunderstandings related to federal-provincial jurisdictional issues, all contributed to growing frustration among Aboriginal peoples. In many instances, this frustration was the impetus from which Aboriginal peoples strengthened pre-existing associations, established new ones, and developed liaisons between regional and national memberships.[45]

The western region of Canada, in particular, saw a considerable amount of Aboriginal political mobilization during this period. A significant contributing factor to this regional mobilization was the federal government's transfer of jurisdiction over Crown lands and natural resources to the provinces of Alberta, Saskatchewan and Manitoba in 1930. The Alberta, Saskatchewan and Manitoba Natural Resources Transfer Agreements (NRTAS) recognized the rights of First Nations with respect to hunting, trapping and fishing for food in all seasons of the year on all unoccupied Crown lands and on any other lands to which the First Nations may have had a right of access. A clause in the agreements, however, stipulated that the provinces could apply their own fish and game laws, including the enforcement of closed seasons, overriding the traditional land-use practices of First Nations in the provinces.

With respect to the Métis, the general understanding among provincial and federal officials was that, since the Métis did not fall under the federal jurisdiction of section 91(24) of *The British North America (BNA) Act*, the provinces maintained the discretionary power to deal with Métis land-use practices as they saw fit. A result of this jurisdictional shift was the establishment of distinct Métis and First Nation regional organizations. Although the Métis had established an organizational presence in the prairies as early as 1884, Status and Treaty Indians in the region only began to organize themselves into specific regional and provincial associations during the mid-1920s.

While the tensions associated with the recognition of Métis land claims in the Northwest during the late nineteenth century and the subsequent lack of official surveys of lands occupied by Métis largely resulted in

Métis "squatting" on Crown lands, the passage of the 1930 NRTAS opened up a large portion of these Crown lands for homesteading. This increased pressure of non-Aboriginal settlement in the region necessitated an organized Métis response to clarify their legal access to lands.[46] From the early 1930s through the mid-1960s, Métis regional organizations were largely focussed on the Prairie provinces, with associations in British Columbia and Ontario forming in the late 1960s and early 1970s.

In an effort to have their rights recognized and claims addressed, the Métis realized that they needed to organize themselves more cohesively. In 1928, two years prior to the establishment of the NRTAS, Métis in Alberta and northern Saskatchewan established the Association des Métis Alberta et les Territoires du Nord-Ouest. Led by Charles Delorme, the association eventually incorporated and changed its name to the Métis Association of Alberta (MAA) in December 1932. With a membership consisting of 31 locals throughout Alberta, the MAA sought to promote the claims of Alberta's Métis population and obtain a reasonable settlement that included a secure land base and access to resources.[47]

In response to the MAA's lobbying efforts, in 1933, the Government of Alberta adopted a resolution to investigate the condition of the Métis in the province. One year later, the provincial government established the provincial Ewing Commission. This special commission was mandated to investigate Métis complaints and address the issue of creating Métis "reserves" or settlements in the province. After two years of investigation, the commission tabled its 14-page final report to the provincial government, advising that a "band-aid" solution to Métis claims was not an adequate response. As part of a comprehensive scheme to provide a lasting solution, the commission recommended that the Métis be allotted a secure land base and that the provincial government provide adequate services to ensure the successful development of these Métis settlements. The commission further recommended that these settlements be established in areas where Métis would have access to resources for farming, lumbering, fishing and hunting and where they would be free from the interference of non-Aboriginal settlers. The commission stressed, however, that the proposed scheme was part of a larger social-welfare program provided to other Albertans, and not a recognition of the Métis' Aboriginal rights.[48]

As a result of the MAA's political movement and the recommendations of the Ewing Commission, the Government of Alberta established the *Métis Population Betterment Act* on November 22, 1938. The legislation ultimately recognized that the organized efforts of Métis peoples could gain lasting and substantial results from government. In fact, in its introduction, the provincial government indicated that the legislation was the result of negotiations between government officials and Métis representatives. Under the legislation, the provincial government sought to develop further its relationship with Métis associations through the establishment of specific settlement associations. These Métis settlement associations were to act together with the provincial government in establishing programs for bettering the lives of the Métis in the province and settling them on the specific lands set aside for this purpose. Each settlement association was responsible for establishing a constitution, setting the conditions for membership and electing a board to oversee these activities.[49]

The success of the MAA's efforts led to the establishment of two similar organizations in Saskatchewan: the Saskatchewan Métis Association (SMA), which represented the large Métis population in the northern areas of the province; and the Métis Society of Saskatchewan (MSS), which represented the Métis population in the southern region of the province. Unlike the MAA, however, the Métis associations in Saskatchewan sought the provincial government's assistance in their quest for federal recognition of their claims. In particular, the MSS requested the federal government provide Métis with assistance in pursuing their livelihoods in exchange for the extinguishment of Métis Aboriginal title to portions of Saskatchewan.[50] While it is unclear whether the government of Saskatchewan supported these claims, during the

1940s it worked to establish Métis settlements in the north and south of the province. Following the Alberta model, these settlements were to be set up for the exclusive use of Métis as a means of bettering their livelihoods. In northern Saskatchewan, a settlement was established at Green Lake for 125 Métis families that maintained a traditional association with the area. In order to establish the settlement, non-Aboriginal peoples were relocated and Métis families were leased 40-acre plots for a 99-year period. Each family also received assistance from the provincial government to establish farming operations. In southern Saskatchewan, a similar settlement was established at Lebret in the Qu'appelle valley during the early 1940s. By the early 1950s, the government established seven more Métis settlements at Crooked Lake, Lestock, Crescent Lake, Baljennie, Willow Bunch, Duck Lake and Glen Mary. By the mid-1950s, these nine Métis settlements maintained a total population of 2,500 Métis.[51]

Unlike the Alberta settlements, however, the Saskatchewan settlements were not protected under legislation and were not managed by Métis settlement associations. Instead, these settlements relied on the direct relationship maintained by church organizations with the provincial government.[52] Unfortunately, it is unclear from my research what the roles of the SMA and SMS were in the establishment and functioning of these settlements. While the MAA played a major role in the establishment of the Métis settlements in Alberta, the SMA and SMS may have played a similar role in Saskatchewan.

During the late 1930s, the Métis in Manitoba also began to organize themselves in order to press the federal government to settle their claims. The first of these associations was a small regional organization, the Northern Halfbreed Association, that represented the Métis and Non-Status Indians of the Métis settlements near The Pas, Moose Lake and Cedar Lake. These settlements included the Thomas settlement, Wooden Tent (*Metikewap*), Pine Bluff, Moose Lake, Big Eddy, Young Point, Rall's Island and Umphreville. This association focussed specifically on Métis land issues; its activities included protesting provincial land-use practices and working toward gaining official title to the settlement lands through formal land surveys.[53]

Throughout the 1950s and 1960s, the primary channel by which Métis in Manitoba were able to voice their concerns and mobilize social action was through the annual Indian and Métis Conference hosted by the Community Welfare Planning Council of Winnipeg. Métis who attended the annual conference, however, consistently complained that the conference focussed too much on First Nations' issues and not enough on the distinct needs of the Métis.[54] As a result, at the annual meeting of the Indian and Métis Conference in 1967, a number of Métis delegates decided that the only means for Métis concerns to be addressed was to establish an independent organization. Subsequently, on October 1, 1967, the Manitoba Metis Federation (MMF) was established and incorporated as a non-profit association. The following year, in 1968, the MMF held its own meetings, separate from those of First Nations, at the annual Indian and Métis Conference in Winnipeg.[55] These events mirrored the split occurring at the national level between Status Indians and Métis during this period.

Métis in Ontario and British Columbia began to organize formally during the mid to late 1960s. In Ontario, two organizations were established in 1965: the Ontario Métis and Non-Status Indian Association (OMNSIA) and the Lake Nipigon Métis Association (LNMA). While the LNMA maintained a regional focus on the Métis population of northwestern Ontario, the vision of the OMNSIA was to represent Métis and Non-Status Indians across the province. Its early activities focussed on Métis issues in northern Ontario and, by the early 1970s, OMNSIA had established itself as a provincial organization.[56]

Similar to developments in Ontario, Métis and Non-Status Indians in British Columbia began organizing themselves during the late 1960s and early 1970s. In response to the increasing political mobilization of First Nations in British Columbia during this period, in 1969 the British Columbia Association of Non-Status Indians was established.[57] While it is unclear, it seems likely that this organization was established to represent the unique interests of Aboriginal peoples who fell outside of the membership of organizations such as the Confederacy of Native Indians of British Columbia (1966), the British Columbia Land Claims Committee (1968) and the Union of British Columbia Indian Chiefs (1969).

The period between the mid-1940s and 1969 can best be characterized as one in which the predominant focus of Aboriginal organizations was on addressing federal Indian policy as reflected through amendments to the *Indian Act*. National and regional Métis representation at discussions revolving around Indian policy, however, was limited. This was most likely due to the fact that the federal government considered the resolution of Métis issues predominantly a provincial jurisdiction. While the Supreme Court of Canada's 1939 decision in *Re: Eskimos* recognized that Inuit were considered "Indians" under section 91(24) of the *British North America Act*, and hence were a federal and not a provincial responsibility, provincial governments did not test the Supreme Court's interpretation of whether the Métis were also considered "Indians" under section 91(24). During the same period as *Re: Eskimos*, provincial governments in Alberta and Saskatchewan were busy addressing Métis social and economic issues with the establishment of Métis settlements and provincial programming for education and access to resources for hunting, trapping and fishing. Métis did, however, participate in the activities of the National Indian Council (NIC), which was established during the early 1960s, and was perhaps the largest Aboriginal organization with national representation during this period.

The mandate of the NIC was to promote Aboriginal cultural and political issues in Canada, and to network with and assist in the development of regional and provincial Aboriginal organizations. While the NIC represented treaty and Status Indians, as well as Non-Status Indians and Métis, Inuit were not represented by the organization.[58] As a largely urban-based organization, however, the NIC had difficulties acquiring funding from the federal government and support from the large on-reserve population of Status Indians. Status Indians, as well as the Department of Indian Affairs, felt that the organization did not and could not represent the complex and diverse needs of the national Aboriginal population regarding amendments to the *Indian Act* and establishment of federal programming.[59] This led to the formal separation of national Métis/Non-Status and Status Indian organizations during the period leading up the rejection of Department of Indian Affairs and Northern Development's (DIAND) 1969 White Paper.[60]

In 1968, under increasing internal pressure, the NIC split into two separate associations, the National Indian Brotherhood (NIB) and the Canadian Métis Society, later incorporated as the Native Council of Canada (NCC). The split was spearheaded by three First Nations provincial organizations, the Federation of Saskatchewan Indians (FSI), the Indian Association of Alberta (IAA) and the Manitoba Indian Brotherhood (MIB), which played a significant role in the establishment of the NIB in 1969. As a national representative organization, the NIB sought to assist its affiliated provincial and territorial organizations (PTOs) in the settlement of outstanding land claims and the resolution of ongoing social issues. This included developing and implementing research projects to study the specific issues facing Status Indians across the country and acting as a national voice on issues of concern for the affiliated PTOs and regional membership. High on the agenda of the NIB were the enforcement and fulfillment of treaty promises and the recognition of Aboriginal rights by the federal, provincial and territorial governments.[61]

While the NIB was established to represent Status and treaty Indians, the NCC, officially established in 1971, was organized to represent the combined needs of Métis and Non-Status Indians at the national level.[62] This "alliance" between Métis and Non-Status Indians was a direct result of the federal government's "core-funding" policy, which encouraged the establishment of links between regional associations and a national representative body. As a result, during the early 1970s, regional Métis associations began forming links with regional Non-Status Indian associations in an effort to forge a stronger, unified national voice via the NCC.[63]

Interestingly, the increasing division of national Aboriginal organizations founded specifically on the basis of status under the *Indian Act* foreshadowed the eventual internal split between Métis and Non-Status Indian organizations a decade later. This was a direct result of the increasing disconnection between the rebirth of Métis nationalism in the prairies and western Canada and the specific concerns of Non-Status Indians regarding their history of discrimination based on the *Indian Act*.[64]

The Mid-twentieth Century: A "Unified" National Métis response to Land Claims, Self-Government and the *Indian Act*

During the same period of Jean Chrétien's infamous 1969 *Statement of the Government of Canada on Indian policy* (The 1969 White Paper),[65] the federal government supported a proposal tabled by North American oil companies to build a pipeline to channel oil and gas north from the Yukon, extending from Prudhoe Bay to the Mackenzie Delta, and running south for use in Canadian and American consumer markets. Before the project could move forward, however, the federal government had to investigate the impact of the proposed mega-project on Aboriginal peoples, the economy and environment of the region. While Aboriginal peoples' rejection of DIAND's White Paper was the catalyst for the increased formation of regional and national organizations, the Mackenzie Valley Pipeline proposal and the resulting Berger Commission provided an important forum in which these regional and national organizations could unite to raise awareness and promote the settlement of Aboriginal claims in Canada.[66] The prospect of development in Canada's North also led to the establishment of specific Inuit organizations. Up until the late 1960s, Inuit largely kept to themselves. By the early 1970s, however, they presented a cohesive, organized presence in the North, working with the federal, provincial and territorial governments to settle their four outstanding claims and to address regional social issues.

During the early 1970s, Aboriginal issues became a growing national concern in Canada and, by the mid-1970s, DIAND was increasingly faced with a mandate to resolve outstanding Aboriginal issues. The Supreme Court of Canada's (scc) 1973 decision in *Calder et al. v. Attorney-General of British Columbia* was the first step in the initiation of a new land claims process in Canada. While DIAND had assumed the question of Aboriginal title in British Columbia had been settled during the 1920s, the scc's judgment in *Calder* questioned the validity of the extinguishment of Aboriginal interests to land in British Columbia. A direct result of the *Calder* decision was the creation of the Indian Claims Commission in 1974, and the establishment of the first modern-day treaty signed in 1975 between Canada, Quebec, the James Bay Cree and the Inuit of northern Quebec. Additionally, the scc's decision in the Laval-Bedard case in 1973, as well the establishment of the federally appointed Berger Commission and the Joint Cabinet-National Indian Brotherhood Committee in 1974, ushered in a new period of Aboriginal–government relations. Unlike the preceding periods of Aboriginal–government relations, this new contemporary period was marked by the increased participation and influence of Aboriginal organizations in setting DIAND's policy agenda, largely facilitated by the Aboriginal Representative Organizations Program (AROP).[67]

By the early 1980s, AROP had achieved its initial goal of addressing issues related to health, economic involvement and housing, and had raised public awareness regarding land claims and constitutional reform.[68] This included the increasing devolution of social control to First Nations peoples by DIAND through the transfer of responsibility for programs, such as education, to Status Indian organizations and communities. Initial AROP programming had also branched out, resulting in the establishment of key national Aboriginal programming initiatives such as the Aboriginal Friendship Centre Program, the Aboriginal Women's Program, the Native Social and Cultural Development Program, and the Aboriginal Communications programs.[69] A direct result of this programming was the establishment of regional and national First Nations organizations to manage the various aspects of these programs. AROP, however, failed to provide funds to organizations representing Métis and Non-Status Indians, whom the Federal government recognized as "minority Aboriginal peoples" with "special problems rather than special rights."[70]

During this period, the activism and distrust that characterized the previous decades of Aboriginal political mobilization also gave way to serious attempts at meaningful discussions and interactions. This included the participation of Inuit, Status Indians, Métis and Non-Status Indians in discussions resulting in the inclusion of sections 35 and 37 in the *Constitution Act, 1982*, participation in the federal government's Parliamentary Task Force on Indian Self-Government in the mid-1980s, and the significant revisions of the *Indian Act* in 1985 with the passage of the federal government's Bill C-31.[71]

The organizational split between Status Indians and Métis/Non-Status Indians during the late 1960s, however, contributed to growing tensions between the agendas of these distinct groups; Status and treaty Indians wanted to focus on influencing government policies to strengthen their special status and develop stronger regional bodies to protect treaty rights; the Métis sought the development of all-inclusive equality legislation and recognition of their unique Aboriginal rights; and Non-Status Indians—women in particular—were concerned about the discriminatory provisions of the *Indian Act*. These tensions were also a driving force in the negotiations resulting in the inclusion of sections 35 and 37 in the *Constitution Act, 1982*. While the NCC sought a united Aboriginal front, the NIB made it clear to the federal government that it would have to deal separately with the three national Aboriginal organizations.[72]

In 1980, difficulties with gaining participant status at the constitution table briefly led the NIB, NCC and the Inuit Committee on National Issues (ICNI) to join forces. Together they drafted a common position on constitutional provisions and presented a unified front to the British Foreign Affairs Committee in England to gain support. Their common position stated that any changes to the Constitution would have to include provisions recognizing treaty and Aboriginal rights, Aboriginal self-government, and Aboriginal consent in any further constitutional amendments affecting Aboriginal rights. In January 1981, the federal government agreed to include these provisions in the new constitution. Two new sections were inserted into the draft, sections 25 and 34: section 25 protected Aboriginal rights from the egalitarian provision of the Charter of Rights, a request made by the Union of British Columbia Indians; and section 34, which recognized and affirmed Aboriginal and treaty rights and defined Aboriginal peoples as Indian, Métis and Inuit. The federal government, however, insisted on providing the provincial and territorial governments with the power to amend section 34 as they required. This was considered unacceptable by many member organizations in the NIB, who refused to ratify the draft. The Indian Association of Alberta (IAA) and Four Nations Confederacy of Manitoba (FNCM), in fact, withdrew completely from the NIB. The IAA, in particular, proved to be the most vocal in its rejection of the NIB's position. It was displeased at what it considered to be NIB collusion with the federal government, the NCC and ICNI. The president of the NCC, Harry Daniels, eventually withdrew NCC support for the draft sections, arguing that the Métis and Non-Status Indians could only support the draft if the governments agreed to include a "consent clause" for potential amendments to section 34.[73]

The NIB's failure to gain full support from its membership for the proposed sections 25 and 34 eventually led it back to Britain to lobby for support of its position in the British Parliament. While the NIB was focussed on gaining support in Europe, the NCC gained increasing momentum in Canada, building on the support of the ICNI, Native Women's Association of Canada (NWAC), the Dene Nation and the Council of Yukon Indians to continue negotiating with the federal government on the constitution. The result of these efforts led to the formation of the Aboriginal Rights Coalition (ARC), and concessions by the Trudeau government to revisit the inclusion of section 34, with specific application to the northern territories where the federal government maintained full jurisdiction. The ICNI rejected this proposal, arguing that it would be unfair to Aboriginal peoples in the rest of the country. By the fall of 1981, however, the federal, provincial and territorial governments renewed their efforts to address Aboriginal rights. After intense consultations with the Métis Association of Alberta, the Premiere of Alberta, Peter Lougheed, tabled an amendment to section 34, recommending that the wording be changed to recognize and affirm "existing" Aboriginal and treaty rights. While the nine provinces and the MAA agreed to the new wording, the ICNI and the NIB rejected the proposal. At this same time, provincial Status-Indian organizations in British Columbia, Alberta and Saskatchewan could not agree on whether or not treaties provided an adequate safeguard to their Aboriginal rights, or whether or not constitutional protection was necessary. Although the Status-Indian organizations could not agree on a unified position, by April 1982 the Canada Bill gained Royal Ascent as the *Constitution Act*, with Lougheed's proposal maintained in the newly numbered section 35.[74]

The resulting inclusion of section 35 in the *Constitution Act, 1982*, was an important step forward for the Métis in Canada, who were now recognized as one of the three distinct Aboriginal peoples in Canada. The intense politics of the constitution debates, however, took their toll on the NCC. In March 1983, the Métis organizations in Ontario, Manitoba, Saskatchewan, Alberta and British Columbia separated from the NCC to form their own Métis national representative body, the Métis National Council (MNC). Established on March 8, 1983, the MNC sought to provide a more representative voice for the "historic" Métis people on the key issues of a Métis land claims and Métis self-government in western Canada. The charter members of the new national organization were the Métis Association of Alberta, the Association of Métis and Non-Status Indians of Saskatchewan and the Manitoba Metis Federation.[75]

Over the next five years, as John Weinstein[76] has so well documented, the MNC and the NCC sought further clarification of and action on the constitutionally protected Métis Aboriginal rights at the four First Ministers Conferences (FMCS) with the Prime Minister, provincial leaders and, now, four national representative Aboriginal organizations. While the MNC pushed specifically for recognition of their historic Métis land claim for a homeland in western Canada, the NCC was focussed on challenging the validity of section 91(24) of the *British North America Act* and the resulting exclusion of Métis and Non-Status peoples as a federal responsibility. After a long, hard fight, however, neither the MNC nor the NCC were able to make any significant strides at the FMCs in clarifying Métis rights and the jurisdictional responsibility toward these rights.[77]

As a result of this lack of progress, in the early 1990s the NCC restructured itself under the veteran leadership of Métis grassroots politician Jim Sinclair. The new national umbrella organization, the Congress of Aboriginal Peoples (CAP), cultivated regional representation across the country. Each regional association was responsible for maintaining its own constitution, membership, and elected executive officers with its own administrative staff and program officers. As a reorganization of the NCC, CAP continues to represent the interests of off-reserve and Non-Status First Nations people as well as Métis and mixed-ancestry peoples throughout Canada.

Conclusions: Moving forward into the Twenty-first Century

Métis organizations maintained a measured level of success in the constitutional discussions of the early 1980s. By the early 1990s, however, cuts in federal funding to AROP, combined with the dissatisfaction of Métis organizations with the Mulroney government's attempts at constitutional reform, limited the growth of national and provincial Métis organizations. The MNC, however, continued to push their Métis rights agenda forward with their proposed Métis Nation Accord in 1992. The Accord provided a framework for transforming Métis organizations into governments, clarifying the criteria for Métis citizenship and identification within the new Métis Nation, and setting up a relationship with the federal, provincial and territorial governments for negotiating self-government agreements and land and resource-sharing protocols. The Accord was to be supported by a significant amendment to section 91(24) of the BNA *Act* to ensure that it applied to all Aboriginal peoples in Canada.[78] The Accord, however, was never realized, due in large part to the failure of the referendum on the Charlottetown Accord, which proposed a series of constitutional amendments regarding the division of federal and provincial powers that would have supported the framework set out in the Métis Nation Accord.

The significant contribution of Métis organizations and leaders to the Royal Commission on Aboriginal Peoples' (RCAP) extensive analysis of Aboriginal–Canadian relations reinforced the understanding that the general goals of Métis people were not very different from those of other Aboriginal peoples in Canada. The Métis sought to reinforce their culture and practices, as well as assume greater political responsibility for themselves. This required obtaining a viable land base for economic and cultural development, and ensuring that Métis children were healthy, well-educated and ready to lead the Métis Nation in their turn.[79]

The federal government's official response to RCAP's final report, *Gathering Strength*, stressed the need for mutual respect, recognition, responsibility and sharing in the continued development of Aboriginal–government relations. This included strengthening Aboriginal governance, affirming treaty relationships, and working toward the fair settlement of outstanding Aboriginal land claims. As a means to facilitate self-governance, *Gathering Strength* recommended the establishment of financial arrangements with Aboriginal governments and organizations to foster self-reliance, in addition to improving health and public safety and strengthening Aboriginal economic development.[80]

In November 2005, these basic principles were reiterated to Aboriginal and non-Aboriginal leaders by former Prime Minister Paul Martin at the roundtable discussions held in Kelowna, British Columbia. The resulting "Kelowna Accord" mapped out a ten-year strategic plan, with five-year targets, to address social and economic issues facing First Nations, Métis and Inuit in Canada. The Accord proposed working with National Métis organizations, such as the MNC and CAP, to strengthen Métis institutions in an effort to support Métis socio-economic development, and the implementation of a Métis-Federal government bilateral agreement to ensure the further clarification and recognition of Métis rights.

Current and ongoing discussions and litigation revolving around the questions of Métis Aboriginal rights and title, Métis identity and Métis status are all indicative of this continuing and evolving relationship between the Métis and the federal, provincial and territorial governments. Ongoing efforts of Métis organizations, such as MNC and CAP, to develop further clarification regarding the distinction between the "historic Métis" and those who maintain a mixed Aboriginal–non-Aboriginal ancestry, reflect the continuing impact of these organizations in moving Métis issues forward.

Notes

1. Joe Sawchuk, "The Métis of Manitoba: Reformulation of an Ethnic Identity" (master's thesis, University of Manitoba, 1973); Joe Sawchuk, "Métis Politics and Métis Politicians: A New Political Arena in Canada" (PHD diss., University of Toronto, 1983); Métis Association of Alberta, Joe Sawchuk, Patricia Sawchuk and Theresa Ferguson, *Métis Land Rights in Alberta: A Political History* (Edmonton: Métis Association of Alberta, 1981); Manitoba Metis Federation, *Metis Political Organizations and Political Terms*, www.mmf.mb.ca/pages/educational/edu-pages/metispolitical.php; Joe Sawchuk, *The Dynamics of Native Politics: The Alberta Métis Experience* (Saskatoon: Purich Publishing, 1998); Joe Sawchuk, "Negotiating an Identity: Métis Political Organizations, the Canadian Government, and Competing Concepts of Aboriginality," *American Indian Quarterly* 25, no. 1 (Winter 2001): 73–92.

2. John Weinstein, *Quiet Revolution West: The Rebirth of Métis Nationalism* (Calgary: Fifth House, 2007).

3. In this chapter I use the term "Aboriginal peoples" when discussing more general historical relationships. Whenever possible I will distinguish between Métis, First Nations and Inuit in Canada.

4. Kelly Saunders, "No Other Weapon: Métis Political Organization and Governance in Canada," in this volume.

5. See John Borrows, "Wampum at Niagara: The Royal Proclamation, Canadian Legal History, and Self-Government," in *Aboriginal and Treaty Rights in Canada*, ed. M. Asch (Vancouver: University of British Columbia Press, 1997); John Tobias, "Protection, Civilization, Assimilation: An Outline History of Canada's Indian Policy," in *As Long as the Sun Shines and the Water Flows*, ed. I.L. Getty and A.S. Lussier (Vancouver: University of British Columbia Press, 1983), 40.

6. Tobias, "Protection, Civilization, Assimilation," 39; See also Joan Holmes, "The Original Intentions of the Indian Act," paper presented at the Pacific Business and Law Institute's conference *Beyond the Indian Act*, Ottawa, April 2002, 38; John Leslie, "The *Indian Act*: An Historical Perspective," *Canadian Parliamentary Review* 25, no. 2 (2002): 24; and John Leslie and R. Maguire, *The Historical Development of the Indian Act* (Ottawa: Department of Indian Affairs, 1978).

7. I use the term "Indian" to reflect the specific distinction between First Nation and Métis during this period.

8. Leslie, "The *Indian Act*: An Historical Perspective," 24.

9. Peter Fidler's Red River Journal, 24 June to 16 July 1815, Library and Archives Canada, *Selkirk Papers Transcripts*: 18,430–18,536.

10. Fidler's Red River Journal.

11. Fidler's Red River Journal.

12. *Papers Relating to the Red River Settlement: viz Return to an Address from the Honourable House of Commons to His Royal Highness The Prince Regent, dated 24th June 1819.* British Parliamentary Papers, 1819.

13. "Observations respecting the employment of illegal Force by the North-West company, the causes which have rendered an Appeal to the Law for redress impracticable on the part of the Hudson's Bay Company," in *Papers Relating to the Red River Settlement*, 314.

14. Weinstein, *Quiet Revolution West*, 2–4.

15. "W. McGillivray to W.B. Coltman, 14 March 1818," in *Papers Relating to the Red River Settlement*, 318.

16. "W. McGillivray to W.B. Coltman," 318.

17. "W.B. Coltman, 30 June 1818: A general Statement and Report relative to the Disturbance in the Indian Territories of British North America, by the undersigned Special Commissioner for inquiring into the Offences committed in the said Indian Territories, and the Circumstances attending to the Same," in *Papers Relating to the Red River Settlement*, 350–51.

18. Simpson's Report of 5 June 1824. Library and Archives Canada, Hudson's Bay Company Archives, D4/8, folios 3-17d.

19. "Report on the Affairs of the Indians of Canada," Journals of the Legislative Assembly, 8 Vic. 1844-45, Appendix EEE; "Report on the Affairs of the Indians in Canada; submitted to the Honorable the Legislative Assembly, for their information." Province of Canada. Journals of the Legislative Assembly, 11 Victoria A.1847, Sessional Papers. Appendix T.

20. "Report on the Affairs of the Indians of Canada," Journals of the Legislative Assembly, 8 Vic. 1844-45, Appendix EEE; "Report on the Affairs of the Indians in Canada; submitted to the Honorable the Legislative Assembly, for their information." Province of Canada. Journals of the Legislative Assembly, 11 Victoria A.1847, Sessional Papers. Appendix T.

21. J. Sinclair et al. to A. Christie, 29 August 1845. Library and Archives Canada, Hudson's Bay Company Archives, D5/15, folio 139a.

22. A. Christie to J. Sinclair, B. Larocque, T. Logan and others, 5 September 1845. Library and Archives Canada, Hudson's Bay Company Archives, D5/15, folio. 139a–139b.

23. "An Act for the protection of the Indians in Upper Canada from imposition, and the property occupied or enjoyed by them from trespass and injury," Statutes of the Province of Canada, 13 & 14 Vict. Chap 74; "An Act for the Better Protection of the Lands and Property of the Indians in Lower Canada," Statutes of the Province of Canada, 13 & 14 Vict. Chap 42.

24. "Report of the Special Commissioners appointed to investigate Indian Affairs in Canada (Messrs. Pennefather, Talfourd, and Worthington) to Sir Edmund Head, April 1858, Province of Canada," Journals of the Legislative Assembly, Sessional Papers 1858, Appendix 21.

25. Statutes of Canada 1869, c. 6 [32–33 Vict.].

26. Saunders, "No Other Weapon."

27. Sawchuk, The Métis of Manitoba, 27.

28. During this same period, the federal government began the formalized treaty process with First Nations in the western regions of the country. The first of the "numbered treaties," Treaty No. 1 and Treaty No. 2 were signed with First Nations in the southern portion of Manitoba in 1871 and 1872.

29. B. Milne, "The Historiography of Métis Land Dispersal, 1870–1890," Manitoba History 30 (Autumn 1995): 30; Diane Payment, The Free People Otipemisiwak:

Batoche, Saskatchewan 1870–1930 (Ottawa: National Historic Parks and Sites, Parks Canada, 1990), 260.

30. Payment, *The Free People Otipemisiwak*, 261.

31. Treaty No. 4 in 1874 covered much of present-day southern Saskatchewan; Treaty No. 5 in 1875 covered the northern region of present-day Manitoba; Treaty No. 6 in 1875 covered a large portion of the middle part of present-day Saskatchewan and Alberta; and Treaty No. 7 in 1877 covered a large portion of present-day southern Alberta.

32. D. McLean, *Home from the Hill: The Métis in Western Canada* (Regina: Gabriel Dumont Institute, 1987), 138.

33. Payment, *The Free People Otipemisiwak*, 267–68.

34. McLean, *Home from the Hill*, 146–48; Payment, *The Free People Otipemisiwak*, 265–69.

35. Payment, *The Free People Otipemisiwak*, 265–66.

36. McLean, *Home from the Hill*, 148–51.

37. Sawchuk, "The Métis of Manitoba," 28–29.

38. McLean, *Home from the Hill*, 187; Payment, *The Free People Otipemisiwak*, 268–69.

39. The commission travelled with treaty commissioners in 1899 for the signing of Treaty No. 8. Metis were also awarded scrip in 1906 at the signing of Treaty No. 10 and in 1908 at the signing of Treaty No. 5.

40. While important connections exist between historic Metis organizations and the Catholic Church, a detailed analysis of these elements is beyond the scope of this chapter.

41. Manitoba Metis Federation, *Metis Political Organizations and Political Terms*, www.mmf.mb.ca/pages/educational/edupages/metispolitical.php.

42. Sawchuk, "Métis Politics and Métis Politicians," 52.

43. Sawchuk, "Métis Politics and Métis Politicians," 53–54.

44. A starting point for this national movement was the establishment of the League of Indians of Canada (LIC) in 1919 by Mohawk Leader F.O. Loft. In 1920, regional associations, such as the Allied Tribes of British Columbia (ATBC) and the Six Nations Confederacy Council (SNCC), joined with the LIC to protest against the inclusion of a provision in the new *Indian Act* to provide for the compulsory enfranchisement of Indians. While the proposed amendment eventually passed into law as section 107 of the 1920 *Indian Act*, it was dropped in 1922 after further protests and pressure by the SNCC. See Peter Kulchyski, "'A Considerable Unrest': F.O. Loft and the League of Indians," *Native Studies Review* 4, nos. 1–2 (1988); and

Richard Lueger, "A History of Indian Associations in Canada" (master's thesis, Carleton University, 1977), 97–99.

45. J.R. Miller, *Skyscrapers Hide the Heavens: A History of Indian–White Relations in Canada* (Toronto: University of Toronto Press, 2000), 311.

46. Métis Association of Alberta, *Métis Land Rights in Alberta: A Political History* (Edmonton: Métis Association of Alberta, 1981), 187.

47. Métis Association of Alberta, *Métis Land Rights in Alberta*, 187–89; Sawchuk, "Métis Politics and Métis Politicians," 59–60.

48. Métis Association of Alberta, *Métis Land Rights in Alberta*, 59–60.

49. Métis Association of Alberta, *Métis Land Rights in Alberta*, 196–99; Sawchuk, "Métis Politics and Métis Politicians," 63–65.

50. Doug Sanders, "Métis Rights in the Prairie Provinces and the Northwest Territories: A Legal Interpretation," in *The Forgotten People: Métis and Non-Status Indian Land Claims*, ed. H. Daniels (Ottawa: Native Council of Canada, 1979), 16–17.

51. Laurie Barron, "The CCF and the Development of Métis Colonies in Southern Saskatchewan during the Premiership of T.C. Douglas, 1944–1961," *The Canadian Journal of Native Studies* 10, no. 2 (1990): 249–53; Sanders, "Métis Rights in the Prairie Provinces and the Northwest Territories," 16–17.

52. Barron, "The CCF and the Development of Métis Colonies," 253–54.

53. Manitoba Metis Federation, *Metis Political Organizations and Political Terms*, www.mmf.mb.ca/pages/educational/edupages/metispolitical.php.

54. Sawchuk, "The Métis of Manitoba," 47.

55. Sawchuk, "The Métis of Manitoba," 48–49.

56. Manitoba Metis Federation, "Métis Political Organizations and Political Terms."

57. Manitoba Metis Federation, "Métis Political Organizations and Political Terms."

58. Assembly of First Nations, *Assembly of First Nations—The Story*, www.afn.ca/index.php/en/about-afn/our-story.

59. In the early 1960s, the federal government initiated a series of national programs for Status Indians that inadvertently helped to facilitate the increased regional and national organization of First Nation associations. These initiatives included the community development program, the establishment of Indian advisory bodies and increased consultations with First Nation organizations in an attempt to finally solve the "Indian problem." Subsequently, these programs also facilitated a more significant split between regional and national First Nation associations and Métis organizations. P. Tennant, *Aboriginal Peoples and Politics: The Indian Land Question in British Columbia, 1849–1989* (Vancouver: University of British

Columbia Press, 1990), 141–42; Sally Weaver, *Making Canadian Indian Policy: The Hidden Agenda* (Toronto: University of Toronto Press, 1981), 27–31; J.S. Frideres, *Canada's Indians: Contemporary Conflicts* (Toronto: Prentice Hall Canada, 1974).

60. Weaver, *Making Canadian Indian Policy*, 42–43.

61. J. Ponting and Roger Gibbins, *Out of Irrelevance: A Socio-Political Introduction to Indian Affairs in Canada* (Toronto: Butterworth and Company, 1980), 195–97.

62. Assembly of First Nations, *Assembly of First Nations—The Story*, www.afn.ca/index.php/en/about-afn/our-story.

63. Weinstein, *Quiet Revolution West*, 32–33.

64. Weinstein, *Quiet Revolution West*, 35.

65. Department of Indian Affairs and Northern Development, *Statement of the Government of Canada on Indian Policy*, Ottawa: DIAND, 1969.

66. See Siomonn Pulla, *Striking a Balance: The Impacts of Major Projects in the North* (Conference Board of Canada, 2011); Thomas Berger, "Keep it Up: Land Use Planning—Land Claims and Canada's North," in *Canada's North: What's the Plan?* by Thomas Berger, Steven A. Kennett and Hayden King (Ottawa: The Conference Board of Canada, 2010), 5–35; Thomas Berger, *Northern Frontier, Northern Homeland: The Report of the Mackenzie Valley Pipeline Inquiry*, vol. 1. (Ottawa: Government of Canada, 1977).

67. Yale Belanger, David Newhouse and Kevin Fitzgerald, "Creating a Seat at the Table: Aboriginal Programming at Canadian Heritage, A Retrospective Study for Canadian Heritage," *The Canadian Journal of Native Studies* 28, no. 1 (2009): 33–70.

68. Belanger et al., "Creating a Seat at the Table," 33–38.

69. Belanger et al., "Creating a Seat at the Table," 39.

70. This approach was changed in 2003. Current AROP guidelines state that organizations "seeking eligibility under this program as representatives of Métis and/or Non-Status Indians *must demonstrate that they are democratically controlled and that they have the support and are representative of the majority of potential constituents within their geographic area* to ensure that the views being put forward to Government are supported (mandated) by the majority of the defined population that the organization is claiming to represent." Indian and Northern Affairs Canada, *Policy On Funding To Aboriginal Representative Organizations*, www.ainc-inac.gc.ca/ap/fnd/pfaro-eng.asp [emphasis added]; Weinstein, *Quiet Revolution West*, 31–32.

71. Belanger et al., "Creating a Seat at the Table," 40–41.

72. Doug Sanders, "The Indian Lobby," in *And No One Cheered: Federalism, Democracy and the Constitution Act*, ed. Keith Banting and Richard Simeon (Toronto: Methuen Press, 1984), 308–09.

73. Sanders, "The Indian Lobby," 316.

74. Ponting and Gibbins, *Out of Irrelevance*, 213–14; Sanders, "The Indian Lobby," 303–24.

75. Weinstein, *Quiet Revolution West*, 60–85.

76. Weinstein, *Quiet Revolution West*, 88–117.

77. Weinstein, *Quiet Revolution West*, 112–17.

78. Weinstein, *Quiet Revolution West*, 133–35.

79. Royal Commission on Aboriginal Peoples, *Voices of Métis People* (1996). www.ainc-inac.gc.ca/ap/pubs/rpt/rpt-eng.asp.

80. Department of Indian Affairs and Northern Development, *Gathering Strength: Canada's Aboriginal Action Plan* (Ottawa: DIAND, 1997). www.ainc-inac.gc.ca/gs/chg_e.html#reconciliation.

Bibliography

Archival Sources

Peter Fidler's Red River Journal, 24 June to 16 July 1815, Library and Archives Canada, *Selkirk Papers Transcripts*: 18,430–18,536.

Papers Relating to the Red River Settlement: viz Return to an Address from the Honourable House of Commons to His Royal Highness The Prince Regent, dated 24th June 1819. British Parliamentary Papers, 1819.

Library and Archives Canada, Hudson's Bay Company Archives, D4/8, folios 3–17d.

Library and Archives Canada, Hudson's Bay Company Archives, D5/15, folio 139a.

"Report on the Affairs of the Indians of Canada." *Province of Canada, Journals of the Legislative Assembly*, 8 Vict. 1844–45, Appendix EEE.

"Report on the Affairs of the Indians in Canada; submitted to the Honorable the Legislative Assembly, for their information." *Province of Canada, Journals of the Legislative Assembly*, 11 Vict. A.1847, Sessional Papers. Appendix T.

"An Act for the protection of the Indians in Upper Canada from imposition, and the property occupied or enjoyed by them from trespass and injury." *Statutes of the Province of Canada*, 1850 13 & 14 Vict. Chap 74.

"An Act for the Better Protection of the Lands and Property of the Indians in Lower
Canada." *Statutes of the Province of Canada*, 1850, 13 & 14 Vict. Chap 42.

"Report of the Special Commissioners appointed to investigate Indian Affairs in
Canada (Messrs. Pennefather, Talfourd, and Worthington) to Sir Edmund Head,
April 1858, Province of Canada." *Journals of the Legislative Assembly, Sessional Papers*
1858, Appendix 21.

Secondary Sources

Assembly of First Nations, *Assembly of First Nations—The Story*. www.afn.ca/index.php/
en/about-afn/our-story.

Barron, Laurie. "The CCF and the Development of Métis Colonies in Southern
Saskatchewan during the Premiership of T.C. Douglas, 1944-1961." *The Canadian
Journal of Native Studies* 10, no. 2 (1990): 243-70.

Belanger, Yale, David Newhouse and Kevin Fitzgerald. "Creating a Seat at the Table:
Aboriginal Programming at Canadian Heritage, A Retrospective Study for
Canadian Heritage. *The Canadian Journal of Native Studies* 28, no. 1 (2009): 33-70.

Berger, Thomas. "Keep it Up: Land Use Planning—Land Claims and Canada's North." In
Canada's North: What's the Plan? Ottawa: The Conference Board of Canada, 2010.

————. *Northern Frontier, Northern Homeland: The Report of the Mackenzie Valley Pipeline
Inquiry*. Vol. 1. Ottawa: Government of Canada, 1977.

Borrows, John. "Wampum at Niagara: The Royal Proclamation, Canadian Legal History,
and Self-Government." In *Aboriginal and Treaty Rights in Canada*, edited by M.
Asch, 155-72. Vancouver: University of British Columbia Press, 1997.

Department of Indian and Northern Affairs. *Métis and Non-Status Indians: An
Historical Outline of their Origins, Interests and Organizations*. A staff paper
for the Consultative Group on Métis and Non-Status Indian Socioeconomic
Development, n.d.

Department of Indian Affairs and Northern Development. *Statement of the Government
of Canada on Indian Policy*. Ottawa: DIAND, 1969.

————. *Gathering Strength: Canada's Aboriginal Action Plan*. Ottawa: DIAND, 1997.

Fidler, Peter. "*Red River Journal*." *The Selkirk Papers*. Library and Archives Canada,
Ottawa: 18,430-18,536.

Frideres, J.S. *Canada's Indians: Contemporary Conflicts*. Toronto: Prentice Hall Canada,
1974.

Holmes, Joan. "The Original Intentions of the Indian Act." Paper presented at the Pacific Business and Law Institute's conference *Beyond the Indian Act*, Ottawa, April 2002.

Kulchyski, Peter. "'A Considerable Unrest': F.O. Loft and the League of Indians." *Native Studies Review* 4, nos. 1-2 (1988): 95-117.

Leslie, John. "The *Indian Act*: An Historical Perspective." *Canadian Parliamentary Review* 25, no. 2 (2002): 23-27.

Leslie, John, and R. Maguire. *The Historical Development of the Indian Act*. Ottawa: Department of Indian Affairs, 1978.

Lueger, Richard. "A History of Indian Associations in Canada, 1870-1977." Master's thesis, Carleton University, 1977.

Manitoba Metis Federation. *Metis Political Organizations and Political Terms*. www.mmf. mb.ca/pages/educational/edupages/metispolitical.php.

McLean, D. *Home from the Hill: The Métis in Western Canada*. Regina: Gabriel Dumont Institute, 1987.

Métis Association of Alberta, Joe Sawchuk, Patricia Sawchuk and Theresa Ferguson. *Métis Land Rights in Alberta: A Political History*. Edmonton: Métis Association of Alberta, 1981.

Miller, J.R. *Skyscrapers Hide the Heavens: A History of Indian-White Relations in Canada*. Toronto: University of Toronto Press, 2000.

Milne, B. "The Historiography of Métis Land Dispersal, 1870-1890." *Manitoba History* 30 (Autumn 1995): 30-41.

Payment, Diane. *The Free People Otipemisiwak: Batoche, Saskatchewan 1870-1930*. Ottawa: National Historic Parks and Sites, Parks Canada, 1990.

Ponting, J. Rick, and Roger Gibbins. *Out of Irrelevance: A Socio-Political Introduction to Indian Affairs in Canada*. Toronto: Butterworth and Company, 1980.

Pulla, Siomonn. *Striking a Balance: The Impacts of Major Projects in the North*. Ottawa: The Conference Board of Canada, 2011.

Sanders, Doug. "The Indian Lobby." In *And No One Cheered: Federalism, Democracy and the Constitution Act*, edited by Keith Banting and Richard Simeon, 301-32. Toronto: Methuen Press, 1984.

———. "Métis Rights in the Prairie Provinces and the Northwest Territories: A Legal Interpretation." In *The Forgotten People: Métis and Non-Status Indian Land Claims*, edited by H. Daniels, 5-22. Ottawa: Native Council of Canada, 1979.

Sawchuk, Joe. *The Dynamics of Native Politics: The Alberta Métis Experience*. Saskatoon: Purich Publishing, 1998

————. "The Métis of Manitoba: Reformulation of an Ethnic Identity." Master's thesis, University of Manitoba, 1973.

————. "Métis Politics and Métis Politicians: A New Political Arena in Canada." PHD diss., University of Toronto, 1983.

————. "Negotiating an Identity: Métis Political Organizations, the Canadian Government, and Competing Concepts of Aboriginality." *American Indian Quarterly* 25, no. 1 (Winter 2001): 73–92.

Tennant, Paul. *Aboriginal Peoples and Politics: The Indian Land Question in British Columbia, 1849–1989*. Vancouver: University of British Columbia Press, 1990.

Tobias, John. "Protection, Civilization, Assimilation: An Outline History of Canada's Indian Policy." In *As Long as the Sun Shines and the Water Flows*, edited by I.L. Getty and A.S. Lussier, 29–38. Vancouver: University of British Columbia Press, 1983.

Weaver, Sally. *Making Canadian Indian Policy: The Hidden Agenda*. Toronto: University of Toronto Press, 1981.

Weinstein, John. *Quiet Revolution West: The Rebirth of Métis Nationalism*. Calgary: Fifth House, 2007.

From Service Providers | 11
to Decision Makers

Building a Métis Government in Saskatchewan

JANIQUE DUBOIS

Having experienced physical and political conflict and dispossession in the late 1800's, we [the Métis Nation and People] are still engaged in a continuing struggle to rebuild our social case and revive our cultural heritage and pride. As such, we are striving for the political, legal and constitutional recognition and guarantees of the rights of our People, including the right to a land and resource base, self-government and self-government institutions.

—Constitution of the Métis Nation-Saskatchewan, 1993

At the Métis National Council's Annual General Assembly in 2010, President Clément Chartier called for the development of a Métis Nation Constitution to better define the Métis' political existence within Canada.[1] President Chartier emphasized that the Métis cannot engage in a government-to-government relationship and advocate for the recognition of Métis rights without first giving themselves the tools to work as a government and to speak as a nation. "Before we can realistically press for this stronger relationship, we must strengthen our internal governance. We can't demand recognition of our constitution when we don't have one."[2]

The development of a constitution is at the centre of the Métis National Council's current self-government agenda: "Within a Métis Nation Constitution, we can effectively recognize our unique existence and political history, as well as set out our beliefs as to who we are as an Aboriginal people and how we choose to exercise our self-government. A Métis Nation Constitution can serve to bind our people together so we can move forward as a united Aboriginal nation exercising its inherent right of self-government."[3] As the Métis National Council and several of its members prepare to develop their own constitutions, it is pertinent to look back at the successes and challenges of the country's first Métis constitution, developed in Saskatchewan.[4]

Building on a commitment to self-government, the Métis in Saskatchewan adopted a new constitution in 1993 that establishes the Métis Nation-Saskatchewan (MN-S) as a self-governing entity. Most notably, the constitution distinguishes the MN-S's corporate character as a not-for-profit program and service delivery organization from its political existence as a Métis government. Recognizing the political aspirations of the Métis, the Government of Saskatchewan passed *The Métis Act* in 2002. This legislation furthers the division of administrative duties from governance functions by establishing a regulatory framework under which the MN-S's corporate secretariat can operate, as well as a bilateral process through which the MN-S's elected leadership can negotiate as an equal partner with the Government of Saskatchewan on matters related to capacity building, land, harvesting and governance. Through a closer examination of the MN-S Constitution and *The Métis Act*, this chapter argues that, in principle and on paper, these legislative tools provide an unprecedented recognition of Métis organizations as governance institutions, and thus lay the foundation for the realization of Métis self-government in Saskatchewan. Although not without challenges, the Saskatchewan experience bears lessons worth sharing and represents an achievement that all governments—Aboriginal and non-Aboriginal—can build upon.

This chapter is divided into three parts. The first part provides an overview of the evolution of Métis political organizations in Saskatchewan and illustrates how Métis citizens of this province have historically pursued self-government. Focussing on the recent political history of Métis governance in Saskatchewan, the second part discusses symbolic and substantive changes that have resulted from the adoption of the MN-S Constitution and *The Métis Act*. While these changes constitute important steps toward realizing Métis self-government, the third part identifies challenges that continue to hinder this goal. It is still too soon to assess the full impact and breadth of these developments—only time will tell whether the MN-S Constitution and *The Métis Act* will have a lasting impact on the Métis' pursuit of self-government.

Part One: Historical Overview of Métis Mobilization

The Métis' history of political mobilization in present-day Saskatchewan can be traced back to the nineteenth century. Beginning with the emergence of governance structures along the South Saskatchewan River in the 1870s, this section describes the evolution of political organizations in Saskatchewan and illustrates the way in which the Métis have formalized their governance structures and developed legislative tools to pursue their self-government agenda.

The South Saskatchewan Settlements

After the creation of the province of Manitoba in 1870, many of the Red River Métis who had been dispossessed of their land settled on the South Saskatchewan River, founding the communities of St. Laurent, Duck Lake, Batoche and St. Louis. This area forms the core of what Donald Purich calls "Saskatchewan's Métis belt."[5] On 10 December 1872, the Métis of the South Saskatchewan settlements gathered for a meeting outside the church doors at St. Laurent to form the St. Laurent Council.[6] With Gabriel Dumont as president, the Council served as the administrative, military and judicial body for the settlement.

The St. Laurent Council has been described as "a formally constituted local self-government...based on the natural right of Aboriginal peoples to govern themselves and initiate any form of civil authority."[7] Relying on the decades-old Laws of the Buffalo Hunt, which provide the foundation of Métis governance, the St. Laurent Council adopted a constitution and codified 28 laws in its first two years of existence.[8] These laws addressed a range of concerns, such as Sunday observance, respect for private property, and the prevention and control of prairie fires. By formalizing governance practices with a constitution, laws and regulations, the South Saskatchewan settlements would set a precedent for future Métis political mobilization.

The "Little" Provisional Government

In the early 1880s, non-Aboriginal settlers arrived in the St. Laurent region. Given the prominence of Métis ways and the number of Métis individuals, most settlers integrated into Métis society, filling gaps among professionals and workers.[9] Wanting to secure title to the lands in which they were living, the Métis and white settlers petitioned the government in Ottawa to settle land claims. In her autobiography, acclaimed Métis author Maria Campbell captures this historical moment: "[The Halfbreeds] were squatters with no title to the land they lived on. They wanted assurance from Ottawa of their right to keep the land before the incoming white settlers encroached on them by using homestead laws. Our people believed the lands acts discriminated against them, stating that they had to live on the land and wait three years before filing a claim. They had lived on the lands for years before the lands acts had ever been thought of, and didn't believe they should be treated like newcomers."[10] The federal government, preoccupied with the expansion of the railway and the exploitation of the west, ignored petition after petition.[11] As Murray Dobbin writes, "by the spring of 1885 the settlers had exhausted all hope in petitions and they looked to the leader who had once before inspired the Métis."[12] During a secret meeting in March 1885, Louis Riel and a group of prominent Métis signed an oath to "save our country from a wicked government by taking up arms if necessary."[13] A few weeks later, the "little" Provisional Government of Saskatchewan was declared.[14]

Preceded by years of political activism, the creation of the Provisional Government on 19 March 1885 marked a momentous development in Métis political history. Through this government, the Métis demanded parliamentary representation, responsible government, and local control of public lands. The federal government at the time responded to Métis demands with military force, which culminated in the Battle of Batoche and ended in Riel's eventual arrest, trial and execution on the charge of high treason.[15] The hostile political environment that followed the events in Batoche led to the dissolution of Métis governance structures in the mid-1880s.

Formalizing Emergent Political Structures

In the land from which they came, in the land they helped to build.
They found themselves the alien, found their vision unfulfilled.
And despite their valiant effort, to defend what they believe.
When at last the battle ended, they were only left to grieve.

—Métis National Anthem, 1991[16]

The political marginalization of the Métis after the Battle of Batoche was compounded by decades of economic hardship. Following the events of 1885, some of the Métis abandoned hunting to seek new opportunities in farming, but the drought and the Great Depression of the 1930s contributed to the destitution of numerous Métis families. As Maria Campbell describes, "That generation of my people was completely beaten. Their fathers had failed during the Rebellion to make a dream come true; they failed as farmers; now there was nothing left. Their way of life was a part of Canada's past and they saw no place in the world around them, for they believed they had nothing to offer. They felt shame, and with shame the loss of pride and the strength to live each day. I hurt inside when I think of those people."[17] Faced with difficult conditions, some of the Métis started mobilizing politically to improve their situation. Led by leaders such as Joseph Ross, Joe McKenzie, J.Z. LaRocque, Thomas Major and Fred DeLaronde, Métis community councils emerged in the 1930s. These councils were organized as "locals," a representative structure modelled on those of labour organizations, which was also being adopted by the Métis in neighbouring Alberta.[18] The first locals in Saskatchewan were created in Regina and Lebret to demand the recognition of Métis rights to land. As the sense of political awareness and social activism among the Métis grew, locals emerged throughout the province in rural and urban centres like Estevan, Yorkton, North Battleford, Saskatoon, Prince Albert, Baljennie, Swift Current, Maple Creek, Fort Qu'Appelle, Torquay, Indian Head, Lestock and Rocanville.[19]

In these early years of political activism, the Métis learned their demands would only be taken seriously if they developed formal governance bodies with constitutions and bylaws through which to voice their demands. To formalize their governance structures, a group of Métis individuals formed a committee and adopted a constitution in Regina under the name Saskatchewan Métis Society (SMS) in 1937.[20] Echoing, and in many ways rivaling, efforts in the south, the Saskatchewan Métis Association was created in 1943 to represent the Métis in the north of the province.[21] One aim of these newly created governance bodies was to develop relationships and affiliate with local Métis organizations. The newly chosen president of the SMS, J.Z. LaRocque, travelled throughout the province to find and create such organizations. Despite the political and economic challenges that marked the late 1930s, the number of locals soared to 38 by 1940, and represented over 2,500 members. However, division and turmoil over political party affiliation, combined with general paralysis in the context of the war, led to the slow dissolution of Métis political organizations in the 1940s.[22]

It was not until the 1960s that the Métis political movement was revived in Saskatchewan. Maria Campbell contends that the return of the Métis to the political scene was inevitable, but that strong leaders were needed to lead the way: "My people have always been very political. They get involved in political campaigns for local white politicians. As a child I remember listening to them talk and argue far into the night about why this party or that was the best. They talked about better education, a better way of life, but mostly about land for our people. However, when one of our own people said to hell with white politicians—let's get our own men in, that was something else. Uncle Miles used to say often that we had to do it ourselves, because no one would do it for us, and then he'd explain why, but no one really listened until Jim Brady and Malcolm Norris came to our country."[23] Among the most vocal leaders at the time, Norris and Brady, who had played a significant role in organizing the Métis in Alberta, helped revive the Métis Association of Saskatchewan in the north by advocating for the economic independence of the Métis.[24] In the south and centre of the province, the Métis Society of Saskatchewan (MSS) was established with Joe Amyotte as its leader. These organizations later amalgamated in 1967 and adopted the MSS's name.[25] The political developments of the 1960s set the stage for the creation of a province-wide governance structure for the Métis in Saskatchewan.

Once again widening the scope of membership, the Métis political movement underwent a further restructuring under Jim Sinclair in the 1970s. He oversaw the replacement of the MSS with the Association of Métis and Non-Status Indians of Saskatchewan (AMNSIS). Non-Status Indians, many of whom were First Nation women who had married outside of their community or were children of First Nation women and non-First Nation men, were not afforded the same rights as individuals who met the criteria for status under the *Indian Act*. They therefore faced similar challenges to the Métis in light of their ambiguous position in the country's political and legal landscape. As Canada prepared to patriate the constitution in the early 1980s, AMNSIS played a key role in lobbying for the rights of all Aboriginal peoples and demanded the inclusion of the Métis as an Aboriginal people in the *Constitution Act, 1982*. The changes brought about during the constitutional discussions and the adoption of Bill C-31 in 1985, which allowed many individuals to obtain status under the *Indian Act*, led the Métis in Saskatchewan to opt for a Métis-only membership. Wanting to strengthen their political organization in order to actively pursue their Métis-specific rights, the MSS was resuscitated in 1988.

Contemporary Métis Organizations

By the early 1990s, the Métis in Saskatchewan had renewed their commitment to aggressively pursue self-government. Consultations and conferences that addressed the creation of a province-wide governance body for Métis people were organized in various communities throughout the province. The objective was to determine how to restructure the MSS to better address the needs and aspirations of the Métis people in Saskatchewan. One of the key leaders of this process, Gerald Morin, maintained that "it was the people who were driving the agenda,...they had their input, and...they were driving the organization."[26] During a general assembly in 1993 attended by Métis from across the province, a constitution was adopted with three principal objectives: to "bring more power to presidents of MSS locals, remove the society from the jurisdiction of the Non-Profit Corporations Act, and set up a Métis Legislature."[27] The newly created Métis Nation-Saskatchewan (MN-S), which replaced the MSS, has achieved these three goals.

The constitution adopted in 1993 allowed the Métis to take government into their own hands by creating an organization with an explicitly political mandate, the MN-S, and developing a governance structure built around an elected Métis legislature and a Senate of Elders. Foremost, the constitution established the Métis Nation Legislative Assembly, which has the authority to enact legislation, regulations, rules and resolutions

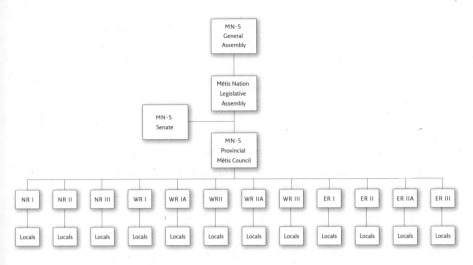

FIGURE 11.1 *Overview of* MN-S *Governance Structure*

governing the affairs and conduct of the Métis in Saskatchewan.[28] At its
first sitting in 1994, the Assembly adopted the *Métis Wildlife and Conservation
Act* and has since passed other legislation including the *Citizenship Act* and
the *Senate Act*. According to the MN-S Constitution, the laws and legislation adopted by the Assembly now govern the MN-S and its citizens.[29] The
Assembly includes representation from Métis communities through their
local presidents, who sit alongside representatives from the Métis Women
of Saskatchewan, the Provincial Métis Youth Council and the Provincial
Métis Council.

As evidenced in the MN-S's organizational chart, the grassroots interests of Métis individuals are primarily represented through locals. Today,
there are more than 130 locals in Saskatchewan that vary in size, capacity and level of activity.[30] Locals are grouped into 12 regions, each of
which is governed by a regional council. The elected presidents of the 12
regional councils sit on the Provincial Métis Council with an executive of
four members elected province-wide and a representative from the Métis
women association and the youth association. Whereas the Assembly has
the supreme authority within the MN-S to pass legislation, the 18-member

Provincial Métis Council is responsible for the administration of programs and ministries.[31] It therefore acts as the executive body for Métis citizens.

The elected leadership is guided by the Senate of Elders. Originally established in 1991 to provide elders with greater opportunities to guide Métis activities, the Constitution provides the Senate with "the quasi-judicial role of dispute resolution at the regional and local levels."[32] In addition to honouring the central role of elders in traditional Métis communities, the creation of the Senate is consistent with attempts to improve Métis accountability structures as discussed by Kelly Saunders in this volume.[33]

The brief overview of the development of Métis political organizations in Saskatchewan reveals that Métis political activism has waxed and waned over the last three centuries. Despite the changing political circumstances that range from colonial expansion to the repatriation of the Canadian Constitution, the Métis have remained committed to creating and strengthening political organizations to represent and serve their communities. The next section discusses the ways that the tools developed by Métis citizens through their political organizations have helped to further the Métis' self-government agenda.

Part Two: Pursuing Métis Self-Government through Substantive and Symbolic Changes

The Report of the Royal Commission on Aboriginal Peoples affirms the right of self-government for all Aboriginal peoples, including the Métis.[34] In 2003, the Supreme Court's *Powley* decision confirmed that the Métis hold section 35 rights under the Canadian Constitution.[35] Despite the recognition of this right in legal documents and proceedings, federal and provincial governments have been slow to acknowledge Métis self-government. As Jean Teillet argues, "The lack of recognition for Métis organizations affects almost every aspect of Métis life. The Crowns—both federal and provincial—seem willing to recognize Métis organizations for the purposes of program and service delivery; however, for the purposes of rights recognition, protection, or litigation, the Crown has consistently denied recognition for Métis organizations south of the 60th parallel."[36] Without the formal recognition by provincial and federal governments, the Métis have incorporated their political organizations under not-for-profit legislation.[37] Had they not done so, Métis organizations would not be eligible to apply for funding from government agencies, and they would not be able to hold title to land.[38] This situation changed with the adoption of the 1993 MN-S Constitution and the subsequent passing of *The Métis Act* in 2002, which acknowledge the MN-S's role as the governance body for the Métis people in Saskatchewan. In principle and on paper, these legislative documents provide a new framework for fulfilling the Métis' inherent right to self-government. Below, two of the most significant changes that were made possible by the adoption of the MN-S Constitution and of *The Métis Act* are discussed: the first is symbolic, the second is substantive.

Making Symbolic Change Possible: From Service Provider to Decision Maker
The Métis National Council contends that the foreign corporate structures that govern Métis communities were never intended for self-government and fundamentally limit their political aspirations.[39] As Saunders remarks, "On a symbolic level...the issue of having to resort to provincially dictated corporations or societies law in order to have their inherent right to self-government formally recognized by the state remains an untenable situation for the Métis."[40] Capturing this sentiment, one Métis leader remarked, "One of the things that really annoyed me, [was that when a] Métis organization was incorporated, [it was] incorporated the same as a non-profit corporation. In a non-profit corporation act, which made you the same as a golf club or a curling club, you had a similar constitution and if you had the two or three dollars you could buy a membership [*sic*] and I always spoke against that. I said, 'No we need something more than that.'"[41] In 1993, the MN-S distanced itself from the requirements of not-for-profit corporations by adopting a political constitution that guided

its transformation from a service delivery agent to a decision-making body. Most notably, the MN-S Constitution divides administrative duties from governance functions. Accordingly, it establishes the MN-S as a self-governing body outside the Saskatchewan *Non-Profit Corporations Act* to legitimize its status as a Métis government rather than as a not-for-profit society. Instead of answering to a corporate body and corporate bylaws, the MN-S now answers to its citizens through the governance institutions that have been established pursuant to the MN-S Constitution (see discussion above). As the political representative of Métis citizens, the MN-S now makes governance decisions through its Assembly and Senate whereas administrative duties related to program and service delivery are carried out through a separate corporate secretariat.[42] For decades, predecessors to the MN-S performed functions similar to those of governments, but their authority to make decisions as governments was not formally established.

The adoption of the MN-S Constitution brought about a symbolic shift that compelled recognition of the MN-S as a decision-making body, rather than as a mere service provider. The passing of *The Métis Act* by Saskatchewan's Legislative Assembly in 2002 furthered this shift. The only legislation of its kind in Canada, *The Métis Act* builds on the MN-S's self-government agenda in three important ways.[43] First, the act recognizes "the important contribution of the Métis Nation-Saskatchewan in representing the needs and aspirations of the Métis people."[44] Second, it outlines the general terms for a bilateral relationship between the MN-S and the provincial government: "The Act commits the province and the Métis Nation to collaborate on practical non-rights based issues including: working toward developing a framework for devolution of provincial programs and service delivery; discussion of access to land and opportunities for economic development; harvesting opportunities (for example fishing, mushroom and berry picking); and enhanced governance and accountability for Métis communities and institutions."[45] Third, the act recognizes the MN-S's secretariat outside the legislation destined for not-for-profits.

Consistent with the MN-S Constitution, *The Métis Act* therefore acknowledges the division of the MN-S's governance body, cited in the act as "the Métis Nation-Saskatchewan," from its administrative entity, "the Métis Nation-Saskatchewan Secretariat Inc."

Although *The Métis Act* does not explicitly recognize the MN-S as self-governing, its content and language nevertheless acknowledge its governance role. For instance, the MN-S's authority to act on behalf of the Métis people of Saskatchewan as a governance body is recognized in Part III of the act, which deals with the bilateral relationship. In addition, Part IV alludes to aspects of the MN-S Constitution and mentions the Provincial Métis Council, further acknowledging the governance structures Métis citizens have created through their constitution. Although *The Métis Act* falls short of recognizing the MN-S as a government, it includes a de facto acknowledgement of the MN-S as the governance institution for the Métis of Saskatchewan. In the words of then Justice Minister Chris Axworthy, "[the adoption of *The Métis Act*] is a symbolic gesture, but it is one under which lies a great deal of respect and commitment to moving forward."[46] Coupled with the adoption of the MN-S Constitution, the passing of *The Métis Act* provides a legislative framework under which the Métis can pursue their self-government agenda.

Making Substantive Change Possible: Moving Beyond Not-for-Profit Legislation
In addition to the symbolic change brought about by the MN-S Constitution and *The Métis Act*, these legislative documents also lay the ground for substantive changes with respect to Métis self-government. Prior to the adoption of the MN-S Constitution, Métis leaders objected that self-government initiatives at the local level were handcuffed by not-for-profit legislation.[47] Rooted in business legislation, not-for-profit legislation set parameters through which groups can establish themselves and operate as non-profit organizations. While the Métis have been successful in pushing the limits of this legislation to shape their own approach to governance, the fact remains that this legislation constrains

the Métis' self-government objectives.[48] This is evidenced by the fact that any constitution or bylaw adopted by a corporation is subject to approval by the province: the ratification by members is secondary to provincial or federal approval.[49]

An additional challenge the Métis face under not-for-profit legislation stems from the fact that every Métis organization is incorporated independently, which puts considerable administrative strain on Métis organizations. For instance, political, fiscal and statutory accountability mechanisms, which are linked to the bylaws and constitution of each corporate body, must be upheld by each corporate body's board of directors, composed of three to twenty members.[50] As Madden, Graham and Wilson note, the multiplication of corporate bodies that contain their own boards of directors "makes it difficult to have direction or decisions in one corporation uniformly implemented in all associated corporations."[51] This is particularly true for Métis locals and affiliates that act as partners with the MN-S to deliver various services and programs. Affiliates that develop and deliver Métis-specific programs are relatively independent insofar as they determine their relationship with the MN-S through their own corporate bylaws.[52] Similarly, each of the approximately 130 Métis locals throughout Saskatchewan has the authority under its own bylaws to make wide-ranging decisions affecting Métis governance.[53] If the board of directors of a local were to misappropriate the Métis community's assets, the MN-S would not have any jurisdiction to intervene on behalf of Métis citizens according to the rules of not-for-profit legislation.[54]

In its constitution, the MN-S formalized its relationship with affiliates to increase its role and authority to act on behalf of Métis citizens. For example, Article 14 of the MN-S Constitution states that "the Métis Nation Legislative Assembly, on behalf of the Métis Nation-Saskatchewan, shall exercise all voting rights, powers, and duties of ownership in relation to the affiliates, based upon the recommendations of the Provincial Métis Council." In addition, the constitution mandates that a Provincial Métis Council member automatically sit as the chairperson of the affiliate(s) that falls under his or her portfolio.[55] These constitutional provisions challenge the requirements of not-for-profit legislation, which identify affiliates as independent corporate entities that autonomously determine their relationship with the MN-S through their bylaws. According to the MN-S Constitution and legislation adopted by the MN-S Legislative Assembly, affiliates are accountable to Métis citizens. The *Legislative Assembly Act* adopted by the Assembly in 1999 states that "any decision ratified by the Métis Nation Legislative Assembly shall be binding on all Métis Nation-Saskatchewan citizens, subsidiary bodies and Affiliates."[56] Moreover, this act mandates that affiliates be held accountable to the Assembly through annual reports submitted via their minister.[57] The MN-S Constitution and the legislation passed by the Métis Nation Legislative Assembly opens the door to the possibility of enhancing the MN-S's role as a governance body by substantively changing its relationship with affiliates.

Part Three: Has Anything Changed in Practice?
The adoption of the MN-S Constitution and the subsequent acknowledgement of the MN-S as a Métis governance body through *The Métis Act* have brought Métis citizens closer to self-government in two significant ways. Symbolically, these changes recognize the status of the MN-S outside not-for-profit legislation as a decision-making body, rather than as a service provider, thereby formally acknowledging its jurisdiction and authority over the decisions that affect Métis citizens. Substantively, these changes allow the MN-S to expand its jurisdiction and its capacity to act as a government. Yet, the impact of these changes is limited by a number of challenges discussed below.

Capacity and Legitimacy: Prerequisites for Substantive Change
The most significant challenge faced by the MN-S in bringing about substantive changes to Métis governance is the fact that it does not currently have the capacity nor the legitimacy to take on the responsibilities laid out in its constitution. One of the means by which the constitution proposes

to increase the MN-S's role as a Métis government is by treating affiliates as subsidiaries, which in legal terms means that Métis organizations would be partially controlled by the MN-S. As a result, the MN-S would be in a position to control the allocation of funding, which is currently distributed directly by the provincial government to affiliates, and would therefore be able to hold the leaders of locals accountable should any funds be misappropriated.

In response to attempts to more firmly establish the MN-S as a Métis government, some affiliates have chosen to integrate the MN-S into their governance structure. For instance, the Gabriel Dumont Institute (GDI), a Métis post-secondary education institution, has the 12 regions of the MN-S represented on its board of governors, which is chaired by the Minister of Education for the MN-S in concordance with Article 14.2 of the MN-S Constitution.[58] Although the GDI has chosen to respect the constitution and the laws adopted by Métis citizens, it remains independent of the MN-S insofar as it constitutes an autonomous corporate body registered under the Saskatchewan *Non-Profit Corporations Act*. Despite the provisions of the MN-S Constitution, Métis organizations like the GDI have been hesitant to move away entirely from the legal protections afforded by not-for-profit legislation and become a subsidiary of the MN-S. Consultations with the GDI faculty and staff attributed this reluctance to concerns related to timing and principle: "This is an issue of *timing* (the current [Métis] government [is] viewed as lacking an entrenched and effective governance model, experience and stability, and thus a discussion of a change in the relationship [is] premature) and *principle* (training and education institutions [need] to have governance that is autonomous from political bodies)."[59] Fundamentally, Métis organizations fear that the MN-S has neither the capacity nor the legitimacy to sustain more robust governance responsibilities.

Still an evolving governance body, the MN-S is struggling to establish itself as a legitimate Métis government. Controversial elections paired with recent internal squabbling over leadership have undermined its legitimacy within and outside the Métis community. In a 2005 report that looked at irregularities of the 2004 MN-S election, the Métis Electoral Consultation Panel put forward a series of recommendations to strengthen democratic legitimacy.[60] Métis citizens who participated in the electoral consultation process voiced serious concerns about the MN-S's governance structures and processes, and these have yet to be adequately addressed. Despite the public support that led the MN-S to establish itself as a governance body for Métis citizens in the 1990s, allegations of corruption and stories of internal power struggles have dampened efforts to increase the political profile of the MN-S.

The former director of the GDI, Murray Hamilton, acknowledges the recent instability of the MN-S, but nevertheless argues that it is the only institution available to ensure that affiliates are accountable to Métis citizens. He acknowledges, "sure, there are problems...but it's what we have to work with."[61] Many Métis agree that the MN-S has an important role to play as an advocate for Métis services such as education, economic development and health at the political level, but affiliates are hesitant to surrender their autonomy to a political body that is undergoing tumultuous transitions.[62] Until the MN-S becomes more politically stable and its legitimacy more firmly established, affiliates will continue to be reluctant to work with the MN-S within a different type of relationship. For the moment, the relationship between the MN-S and its affiliates remains unchanged, despite the fact that the framework is in place for the MN-S to take on a more substantive governance role in Métis affairs. Without demonstrable capacity and legitimacy to carry out the responsibilities outlined in its constitution, the MN-S's ability to make substantive changes to effect self-government will continue to be limited.

Building a New Symbolic Relationship?
In principle and on paper, Métis citizens—through their democratically elected representative government[63]—have the authority to negotiate as equal partners with the Province of Saskatchewan on matters

related to economic, political and social development. Despite the symbolic acknowledgement of the MN-S as a governance institution for Métis citizens in the MN-S Constitution and *The Métis Act*, this recognition is limited by the narrow scope of both these documents. Although the MN-S is the first Métis political body to have its existence recognized outside not-for-profit legislation through *The Métis Act*, establishing the MN-S as a Métis government in practice will require revising the act and amending the MN-S Constitution to more thoroughly clarify governance roles and responsibilities.[64]

The adoption of *The Métis Act* was the culmination of a process that began in 1991.[65] Put in motion with the signing of a bilateral process agreement by the Government of Saskatchewan and the Métis Society of Saskatchewan (now the MN-S) in 1993, a series of community consultations were undertaken to inform negotiations.[66] In a 1996 discussion paper jointly prepared by the MN-S and the provincial government, the parties agreed that the act should recognize "the right of Métis to govern themselves..., the Métis right to determine their membership,...[and recognize] a process to resolve the outstanding land rights of Métis people."[67] While the act met some of the objectives outlined in this discussion paper, it offers a watered-down recognition of the Métis' right to govern themselves, and only provides a narrow and limited framework to sustain this right. Fundamentally, *The Métis Act* falls short of fulfilling its original intent. One of the most significant shortcomings of the act is its lack of a clear statement of the provincial government's responsibility for the Métis. In fact, the preamble of *The Métis Act* explicitly rejects provincial responsibility for the Métis people: "nothing in this Act is to be construed as altering or affecting the position of the Government of Saskatchewan that legislative authority in relation to Métis people rests with the Government of Canada." As a result, the weight, and to some extent the legitimacy, of any agreement reached under *The Métis Act* is limited.

Members of the Métis community flagged many of the shortcomings of the act during community consultations that preceded its adoption, arguing that the act did not have "enough substance" or "go far enough."[68] During a consultation process following the MN-S's 2004 elections, Métis citizens identified two major problems with *The Métis Act*: "The first problem is that many Métis people are unaware of its existence and/or relevance for either the operation of the Métis Nation-Saskatchewan Secretariat Inc. or the legal rights of bona fide MN-S members. The second problem identified by those who were aware of its existence is that it is not sufficiently detailed. More specifically, it does not contain sufficient provisions to ensure that the board and members of the Métis Nations Secretariat Inc. (i.e., the members of the Provincial Métis Council) operate under adequate checks and balances."[69] The shortcomings of *The Métis Act* are compounded by the fact that the MN-S Constitution has not yet evolved to fill governance gaps. As it now stands, the constitution includes some of the principles according to which the MN-S will be governed. However, it also includes specific provisions and appendices outlining procedural and organizational details. As the constitution evolves, some of its principles of governance will need to be supported and more thoroughly developed in statutes as well as rules and regulations. In particular, the adoption of statutes and regulations would help clarify the respective responsibilities of the MN-S's political and corporate bodies and their relationship with provincial and federal governments. Building a more comprehensive body of laws and rules that complement the MN-S Constitution is necessary to ensure adequate checks and balances exist within the Métis governance structure to strengthen and clarify the mechanisms of accountability that govern Métis citizens.[70]

Despite their lacunae, *The Métis Act* and the MN-S Constitution are nevertheless tools that can be amended and reformed to fully establish the MN-S as a governance institution and to advance the Métis' self-government agenda. Made possible by the awakening of political consciousness and the development of governance structures by Métis leaders, these contemporary documents provide a political and legislative foundation that will secure the Métis' continued pursuit of self-government. In the words of the late Métis rights activist Jim Sinclair, all of these efforts have enabled the Métis to get a "foot in the door." To move to the next level and become self-governing, Sinclair had warned, "it's going to take not just one leader, it's going to take many leaders."[71] By using the MN-S Constitution in its internal affairs and by sitting at the constitutional and negotiation table alongside other government representatives, Métis leaders have already altered the political and legislative landscape in Canada. To keep up with these developments, Madden, Graham and Wilson argue that federal and provincial policies that deny Métis rights and only recognize Métis governance structures as "organizations" in lieu of "governments" will have to be revisited.[72] Likewise, *The Métis Act* and the MN-S Constitution will require revision. In the meantime, the Métis are moving forward with their self-government agenda but will have to intensify their efforts to achieve their end goals.

Conclusion

In a presentation at the 2010 Annual General Assembly of the Métis National Council's discussion of the feasibility of a national Métis Constitution, John Weinstein and Marc LeClair identified three steps required to achieve Métis self-government:

1. *Separate Métis self-government (Constitution) from business affairs (Secretariat bylaws)*
2. *Adopt federal and provincial legislation recognizing the Constitution as a source of authority for Métis government*
3. *Negotiate the authority of the Constitution and Métis governments (jurisdiction and transfer payments)*

In Saskatchewan, the first step has been achieved by the adoption of the MN-S Constitution and the subsequent recognition of the MN-S's corporate secretariat in *The Métis Act*. This chapter has suggested that the second step has also been successful insofar as *The Métis Act* offers a de facto acknowledgement of the MN-S's governance role. As for the third step, the MN-S and the provincial government are in the early stages of negotiating jurisdiction with respect to harvesting.[73] The signing of a memorandum of understanding by the provincial and MN-S governments signals that initial progress is being made. While negotiating the scope and authority of Métis governments will be a long and contentious process, history indicates the Métis will continue to pursue their inherent right to self-government regardless of the challenges that emerge.

From the humble beginnings of political organizations in St. Laurent, the Métis in Saskatchewan have developed legislative tools and formal governance structures to seek the recognition and develop the capacity necessary to exercise their inherent right of self-government. Although Métis political bodies need to solidify their legitimacy as governments in the eyes of both Métis citizens and non-Métis society, the experience of the MN-S suggests that developing laws and institutions that support the Métis' political aspirations is a necessary first step. Recognizing the challenges ahead, the Métis National Anthem reminds Métis citizens that they can rely on a long history of political mobilization and leadership to help sustain their self-government agenda: "As we build the Métis nation, as we watch it rise again, our past lost is motivation, to inspire our future gain."[74]

Author's Note

This chapter is based on a paper presented at the National Research Conference on Urban Aboriginal Peoples in February 2011. The author would like to thank Kelly Saunders and Jason Madden for their helpful suggestions, as well as the editors and anonymous peer reviewers of this volume for their comments. Whatever errors remain are solely the author's.

Notes

1. CBC News, December 12, 2010, "Chartier Reelected MNC President," accessed 5 March 2011, www.cbc.ca/news/canada/saskatchewan/story/2010/12/12/sask-mnc-chartier-metis-nation.html.

2. Clément Chartier, cited in Darla Read, "Chartier Re-elected President," *Eagle Feather News* 14, no. 1 (January 2011): 2.

3. Métis National Council, "Towards a Métis Nation Constitution" (Ottawa: MNC, 2003), 15.

4. The MN-S is the first Governing Member of the MNC to adopt a Constitution. Other Governing Members are at various stages of their own constitutional reform processes. Métis National Council, "Métis Rights" (2011), accessed 4 February 2011, www.metisnation.ca/rights/governance.html.

5. Donald Purich, *The Métis* (Toronto: James Lorimer & Company, 1988), 7.

6. See D.N. Sprague, *Canada and the Métis, 1869–1885* (Waterloo, ON: Wilfrid Laurier University Press, 1988), and Diane Payment, *The Free People—Li Gens Libres: A History of the Métis Community of Batoche, Saskatchewan* (Calgary: University of Calgary Press, 2009).

7. Payment, *The Free People*, 342 note 8.

8. George Woodcock, *Gabriel Dumont: The Metis Chief and his Lost World* (Edmonton: Hurtig Publishers, 2003 [1976]), 110–12. See the discussion of the Laws of the Buffalo Hunt in Kelly Saunders, "No Other Weapon: Métis Political Organization and Governance in Canada," in this volume; and Laws of St. Laurent, "Copy of the Laws and Regulations Established for the Colony of St. Laurent on the Saskatchewan," *Archives of the Virtual Museum of Métis History and Culture*, 1873, accessed 10 November 2011, www.metismuseum.ca/resource.php/12631.

9. Diane Payment, *The Free People*, 41.

10. Maria Campbell, *Halfbreed* (Toronto: McClelland & Stewart, 1973), 4.

11. Howard Adams, *Prison of Grass* (Saskatoon, Fifth House, 1989), 77.

12. Murray Dobbin, *The One-And-A-Half Men: The Story of Jim Brady and Malcolm Norris, Metis Patriots of the Twentieth Century* (Vancouver: New Star Books, 1981), 24.

13. Cited in Woodcock, *Gabriel Dumont*, 169.

14. It was also called *le petit Provisoire* by many Métis to distinguish it from Riel's Red River Provisional Government in 1869. See Woodcock, *Gabriel Dumont*, 175.

15. John Weinstein, *Quiet Revolution West: The Rebirth of Métis Nationalism* (Calgary: Fifth House, 2007), 21.

16. "Métis Anthem" is a popular song written by Clint Buehler (music by Dennis Charney) in 1991. A new version of the song was written by Andrea Menard, Karen Shmon and Clint Buehler in 2010 as part of the 125th anniversary of the 1885 Resistance.

17. M. Campbell, *Halfbreed*, 8.

18. For a discussion of the relationship between the Métis and labour organization, more specifically the Co-operative Commonwealth Federation (CCF), see Laurie Barron, *Walking in Indian Moccasins: The Native Policies of Tommy Douglas and the CCF* (Vancouver: University of British Columbia Press, 2005).

19. Métis Electoral Consultation Panel, "Métis Governance in Saskatchewan for the 21st Century: Views and Visions of the Métis People," report submitted to the Saskatchewan Minister of First Nations and Métis Relations, 2005, accessed 4 February 2011, www.publications.gov.sk.ca/details.cfm?p=10180.

20. The SMS was mostly a south central Métis organization. In 1947, Norris and Brady organized various meetings to activate locals in northern communities. See Dobbin, *The One-And-A-Half Men*, 176.

21. Barron, *Walking in Indian Moccasins*, 37.

22. Murray Dobbin, "Métis Struggles of the Twentieth Century, Part Three: Political Interference and Internal Divisions," *New Breed* (October 1978): 10. See discussion in Barron, *Walking in Indian Moccasins*, 35–38; Weinstein, *Quiet Revolution West*, 27.

23. M. Campbell, *Halfbreed*, 72.

24. Prior to becoming active in Saskatchewan, Norris and Brady played an important role in furthering Métis rights in Alberta. Norris believed that economic and political autonomy should be achieved through a provincial organization that "would start in the north and base its independence among north Metis." See Dobbin, *The One-And-A-Half Men*, 215–21.

25. Dobbin, *The One-And-A-Half Men*, 241.

26. Métis Society of Saskatchewan, "Restructuring Committee Meeting Minutes, April 26," *Saskatchewan Archives Board*, 1993, Doucette fonds, file 476.

27. Jeff Campbell, "A New Constitution in Place," *New Breed* (Spring 1994): 13.

28. Métis Nation-Saskatchewan, *Constitution of the Métis Nation-Saskatchewan*, Saskatchewan, MN-S, 1993, Article 2, accessed 24 January 2012, www.mn-s.ca/main/governance/legislation/.

29. Métis Nation-Saskatchewan, *Constitution of the Métis Nation-Saskatchewan*, MN-S, 1993, Article 2.

30. There is ongoing debate regarding the role of locals in Métis governance. Some are only "paper locals" that have been inactive for a long time, and others have been unilaterally created or dissolved by a regional or provincial body, often without ratification of the Assembly as required in the MN-S's constitution. See Marilyn Poitras, "Electoral Reform Study: A Review of the Election Issues for the Métis Nation of Saskatchewan," prepared for the Métis Nation-Saskatchewan, 2001, 34. Also, a study conducted in 1998 showed that the vast majority of locals did not have a constitution or membership list and did not keep minutes of their meetings. This was confirmed by the Lampard Report. See Métis Nation-Saskatchewan, "Secretary Report: Provincial Métis Council Meeting," 20 August 1998, in author's possession, and Keith Lampard, "A Study to Answer the Question: Was the Métis Election of 2004 run in a fair and democratic manner such that its result can be relied upon by Métis people and the Government of Saskatchewan?" 2004, 59, accessed 18 January 2012, www.publications.gov.sk.ca/details.cfm?p=10179.

31. Métis Nation-Saskatchewan, *Constitution*, Article 3.

32. Métis Nation-Saskatchewan, "Constitution/Legislation," accessed 5 February 2011, www.mn-s.ca/index.php?id=84. Although the Senate is supposed to perform an independent and impartial judicial function, it has become politicized. For a discussion, see Métis Electoral Consultation Panel, "Métis Governance," 42.

33. Saunders, "No Other Weapon."

34. Royal Commission on Aboriginal Peoples. *Perspectives and Realities*, vol. 4, Ottawa: Supply and Services Canada, 1996.

35. R. v. Powley, [2003] SCR 207, 2003 SCC 43.

36. Jean Teillet, "Federal and Provincial Crown Obligations to the Métis," in *Métis-Crown Relations: Rights, Identity, Jurisdiction, and Governance*, ed. F. Wilson and M. Mallet (Toronto: Irwin Law, 2008), 92.

37. Jason Madden, John Graham and Jake Wilson note that Métis differ from First Nations in this respect. First Nation bands are recognized as legal entities under the *Indian Act*, whereas the Métis are incorporated under not-for-profit legislation. In *Exploring Options for Métis Governance in the 21st Century* (Ottawa: Institute on Governance, 2005).

38. Provincial legislation states that title to land can only be held by natural persons or corporate bodies. Other reasons that lead to the incorporation of organizations include formalizing a governance structure and protecting members from

personal liability. Government of Saskatchewan, "The Non-Profit Corporations Act: How to Incorporate?" (Regina: Government of Saskatchewan, 1995).

39. Métis National Council, "Métis Rights."

40. Saunders, "No Other Weapon."

41. Interview with Mike Mercredi, January 2004.

42. Métis Nation-Saskatchewan, *Constitution*, Article 14.

43. Jason Madden, "The Métis Nation's Self-Government Agenda: Issues and Options for the Future," in Wilson and Mallet, *Métis–Crown Relations*, 348.

44. Government of Saskatchewan, *The Métis Act*, 2002, II.2i, accessed 4 February 2011, www.qp.gov.sk.ca/documents/English/Statutes/Statutes/M14-01.pdf.

45. Government of Saskatchewan, "The Métis Act," accessed 24 January 2012, www.fnmr.gov.sk.ca/community/metis-history5.

46. Cited in Anne Kyle, "Province Gives Métis Recognition," Regina *Leader-Post*, 29 January 2002.

47. J. Campbell, "A New Constitution in Place," 13.

48. See Saunders, "No Other Weapon."

49. Institute on Governance, "Ethnic Minorities in Canada: A Governance Perspective," Ottawa, Institute on Governance, 2000, 24–25.

50. Institute on Governance, "Ethnic Minorities in Canada: A Governance Perspective," 26.

51. Madden, Graham and Wilson, *Exploring Options*, 23.

52. The M N - S affiliates include Métis Addictions Council of Saskatchewan Incorporated; The Gabriel Dumont Institute of Native Studies and Applied Research; Métis Family and Community Justice Services Incorporated; Clarence Campeau Development Fund; Saskatchewan Native Economic Development Corporation; Métis Employment and Training of Saskatchewan Incorporated; The Provincial Métis Housing Corporation; and Metis Sports, Culture, Recreation and Youth.

53. Métis Nation-Saskatchewan, "Snapshot of the Nation."

54. Madden, Graham and Wilson, *Exploring Options*, 23.

55. Métis Nation-Saskatchewan, *Constitution*, Article 14.2.

56. Métis Nation-Saskatchewan, "Métis Nation of Saskatchewan Legislative Assembly Act," 1999, Article 4.4, accessed 18 January 2012, www.mn-s.ca/main/governance/legislation/.

57. Métis Nation-Saskatchewan, "Métis Nation of Saskatchewan Legislative Assembly Act," 1999, Article 15.2.

58. Gabriel Dumont Institute, "Governance," accessed 24 January 2012, www.gdins. org/node/129.

59. EKOS Research Associates, "Evaluation of the Gabriel Dumont Institute of Native Studies and Applied Research, Final Report," submitted to Saskatchewan Advanced Education, Employment and Labour and Gabriel Dumont Institute of Native Studies and Applied Research (Ottawa: EKOS Research Associates, 6 May 2008), vi, emphasis added, accessed 7 February 2011, www.gdins.org/ documents/1217-final.pdf.

60. Métis Electoral Consultation Panel, "Métis Governance."

61. Interview with Murray Hamilton, 4 January 2011.

62. Interview with Murray Hamilton.

63. The MN-S has faced serious challenges with respect to elections that threaten its legitimacy as a democratically elected representative government. One notable example were the MN-S elections held in 2004; complaints about electoral irregularities led the Government of Saskatchewan to commission a report that confirmed elections were not conducted in a fair and democratic manner. See Lampard, "A Study to Answer the Question."

64. While the MN-S is the first Métis provincial organization to be recognized outside not-for-profit legislation, the Metis Settlements in Alberta are also a legally recognized Metis government, as indicated in Alberta's *Métis population Betterment Act*. See Catherine Bell and Harold Robinson, "Government on the Métis Settlements: Foundations and Future Directions," in Wilson and Mallet, *Métis–Crown Relations*.

65. Métis Nation-Saskatchewan and Province of Saskatchewan, "Towards a New Legal Foundation—A Metis Recognition Act. Draft," Doucette fonds, file 1090. *Saskatchewan Archives Board* (Saskatoon, 1996).

66. Métis Nation-Saskatchewan and Province of Saskatchewan, "Bilateral Process Agreement," Doucette fonds, file 178, *Saskatchewan Archives Board* (Saskatoon, 1993).

67. Métis Nation-Saskatchewan and Province of Saskatchewan, "Towards a New Legal Foundation," Doucette fonds, file 1090, *Saskatchewan Archives Board* (Saskatoon, 1996).

68. Métis Nation-Saskatchewan, "Summary of Round 1 of the Metis Act Consultations," Doucette fonds, file 1690, *Saskatchewan Archives Board* (Saskatoon, 1997).

69. Métis Electoral Consultation Panel, "Métis Governance," 49.

70. Métis Electoral Consultation Panel, "Métis Governance," 49.

71. Interview with Jim Sinclair, March 2007.

72. Madden, Graham and Wilson, *Exploring Options*, 28.

73. In November 2010, the MN-S signed a Memorandum of Understanding with the Government of Saskatchewan on Metis Food Harvesting Rights, which establishes the terms for negotiating harvesting rights as provided for in *The Métis Act*. For a discussion of harvesting rights, see Jean Teillet, "Metis Law Summary," 2010, accessed 6 February 2011, www.pstlaw.ca.

74. Clint Buehler, "Proud to be Métis," The Métis Nation Anthem (Saskatoon, Gabriel Dumont Institute, 1991), *Archives of the Virtual Museum of Métis History and Culture*, www.metismuseum.ca/resource.php/05174.

Bibliography

Adams, Howard. *Prison of Grass*. Saskatoon: Fifth House, 1989.

Adams, Howard, Donna Heimbecker, Hartmut Lutz and Murray Hamilton. *Howard Adams: Otapawy! The Life of a Metis Leader in His Own Words and in Those of His Contemporaries*. Saskatoon: Gabriel Dumont Institute, 2005.

Barron, Laurie. *Walking in Indian Moccasins: The Native Policies of Tommy Douglas and the CCF*. Vancouver: University of British Columbia Press, 2005.

Bell, Catherine, and Harold Robinson. "Government on the Métis Settlements: Foundations and Future Directions." In *Métis–Crown Relations: Rights, Identity, Jurisdiction, and Governance*, edited by F. Wilson and M. Mallet, 437–74. Toronto: Irwin Law, 2008.

Buehler, Clint. "Proud to be Métis." The Métis Nation Anthem. Saskatoon: Gabriel Dumont Institute, 2001. *Archives of the Virtual Museum of Métis History and Culture*. www.metismuseum.ca/resource.php/05174.

Campbell, Jeff. "A New Constitution in Place." *New Breed* (Spring 1994): 13.

Campbell, Maria. *Halfbreed*. Toronto: McClelland & Stewart, 1973.

CBC News. December 12, 2010. "Chartier Reelected MNC President." Accessed 5 March 2011, www.cbc.ca/news/canada/saskatchewan/story/2010/12/12/sask-mnc-chartier-metis-nation.html.

Dobbin, Murray. *The One-And-A-Half Men: The Story of Jim Brady and Malcolm Norris, Metis Patriots of the Twentieth Century*. Vancouver: New Star Books, 1981.

———. "Métis Struggles of the Twentieth Century: Saskatchewan Metis Society 1935–1950. Part One: Early Beginnings." *New Breed* (August 1978): 16–19.

———. "Métis Struggles of the Twentieth Century. Part Two: The Land Issue: Whitemen's Advice and Government Deceit." *New Breed* (September 1978): 10–13.

———. "Métis Struggles of the Twentieth Century. Part Three: Political Interference and Internal Divisions." *New Breed* (October 1978): 10–15.

———. "Métis Struggles of the Twentieth Century. Part Four: The Saskatchewan Métis Society—The Final Chapters, 1944–1949." *New Breed* (November–December 1978): 10–15.

EKOS Research Associates. "Evaluation of the Gabriel Dumont Institute of Native Studies and Applied Research, Final Report." Submitted to Saskatchewan Advanced Education, Employment and Labour and Gabriel Dumont Institute of Native Studies and Applied Research, Ottawa: EKOS Research Associates, 6 May 2008. Accessed 7 February 2011, www.gdins.org/documents/1217-final.pdf.

Gabriel Dumont Institute. "Governance." Accessed 24 January 2012, www.gdins.org/node/129.

Hamilton, Murray. Personal interview with the author, 4 January 2011.

Institute on Governance. "Ethnic Minorities in Canada: A Governance Perspective." Ottawa: Institute on Governance, 2000.

Kyle, Anne. "Province Gives Métis Recognition." *Leader-Post* (Regina), 29 January 2002.

Lampard, Keith. "A Study to Answer the Question: Was the Métis Election of 2004 run in a fair and democratic manner such that its result can be relied upon by Métis people and the Government of Saskatchewan?" 2004. Accessed 18 January 2012, www.publications.gov.sk.ca/details.cfm?p=10179.

Laws of St. Laurent. "Copy of the Laws and Regulations Established for the Colony of St. Laurent on the Saskatchewan." Archives of the Virtual Museum of Métis History and Culture, 1873. Accessed 10 November 2011, www.metismuseum.ca/resource.php/12631.

LeClair, Marc, and John Weinstein. "The Métis National Council: 27 Years in Pursuit of Self-Determination for the Métis Nation." Presentation at the Annual General Assembly of the Métis National Council, Saskatoon, 12 December 2010.

Madden, Jason. "The Métis Nation's Self-Government Agenda: Issues and Options for the Future." In *Métis-Crown Relations: Rights, Identity, Jurisdiction, and Governance*, edited by F. Wilson and M. Mallet, 233–90. Toronto: Irwin Law, 2008.

Madden, Jason, John Graham and Jake Wilson. *Exploring Options for Métis Governance in the 21st Century*. Ottawa: Institute on Governance, 2005. Accessed 4 February 2011, www.iog.ca.

Mercredi, Mike. Interview. *Archives of the Virtual Museum of Métis History and Culture,* 2004, accessed December 10, 2011, www.metismuseum.ca/resource.php/06162.

Métis Electoral Consultation Panel. 2005. "Métis Governance in Saskatchewan for the 21st Century: Views and Visions of the Métis People." Report submitted to the Saskatchewan Minister of First Nations and Métis Relations, 2005. Accessed 4 February 2011, www.publications.gov.sk.ca/details.cfm?p=10180.

Métis National Council. "Métis Rights." 2011. Accessed 4 February 2011, www.metisnation.ca/rights/governance.html.

———. "Towards a Métis Nation Constitution," Ottawa, MNC, 2003.

Métis Nation-Saskatchewan. *Constitution of the Métis Nation-Saskatchewan.* Saskatchewan: MN-S, 1993. Accessed 24 January 2012, www.mn-s.ca/main/governance/legislation/.

———. "Constitution/Legislation." 2009. Accessed 5 February 2011, www.mn-s.ca/index.php?id=84.

———. "History of the Métis: 1930–1945." 2009. Accessed 3 March 2011, www.mn-s.ca/index.php?id=74.

———. "Secretary Report: Provincial Métis Council Meeting." 20 August 1998. In author's possession.

———. "Snapshot of the Nation: Executive Summary." 2002. Accessed 4 February 2011, www.metisnation.ca/mnc/snapshot.html.

———. "Summary of Round 1 of the Metis Act Consultations." Doucette fonds, file 1690. *Saskatchewan Archives Board*, Saskatoon, 1997.

Métis Nation-Saskatchewan and Province of Saskatchewan. "Bilateral Process Agreement." Doucette fonds, file 178. *Saskatchewan Archives Board*, Saskatoon, 1993.

———. "Towards a New Legal Foundation—A Metis Recognition Act. Draft." Doucette fonds, file 1090. *Saskatchewan Archives Board*, Saskatoon, 1996.

Métis Society of Saskatchewan, "Restructuring Committee Meeting Minutes, April 26." *Saskatchewan Archives Board*. Doucette fonds, file 476, 1993.

Payment, Diane. *The Free People—Li Gens Libres: A History of the Métis Community of Batoche, Saskatchewan.* Calgary: University of Calgary Press, 2009.

Pocklington, Thomas. *The Government and Politics of the Alberta Métis Settlements.* Regina: Canadian Plains Research Center, 1991.

Poitras, Marilyn. "Electoral Reform Study: A Review of the Election Issues for the Métis Nation of Saskatchewan." Prepared for the Métis Nation-Saskatchewan, 2001.

Purich, Donald. *The Métis*. Toronto: James Lorimer & Company, 1988.

R. v. Powley, [2003] 2 SCR 2007, 2003 SCC 43.

Read, Darla. "Chartier Re-elected President." *Eagle Feather News* 14, no. 1 (January 2011): 2.

Royal Commission on Aboriginal Peoples. *Perspectives and Realities*. Vol. 4. Ottawa: Supply and Services Canada, 1996.

Saskatchewan, Government of. "The Métis Act." Accessed 5 February 2011, www.fnmr. gov.sk.ca/community/metis-history5.

————. *The Métis Act*. 2002. Accessed 4 February 2011, www.qp.gov.sk.ca/documents/ English/Statutes/Statutes/M14-01.pdf.

————. "The Non-Profit Corporations Act: How to Incorporate?" Regina: Government of Saskatchewan, 1995.

Sawchuk, Joe. *The Dynamics of Native Politics: The Alberta Métis Experience*. Saskatoon: Purich Publishing, 1998.

————. "The Métis, Non-Status Indians and the New Aboriginality: Government Influence on Native Political Alliances and Identity." In *Readings in Aboriginal Studies: Identities and State Structures*, vol. 2, edited by Joe Sawchuk, 70–86. Brandon, MB: Bearpaw Publishing, 1992.

————. "Negotiating an Identity: Metis Political Organizations, the Canadian Government, and Competing Concepts of Aboriginality." *American Indian Quarterly* 24, no. 3 (Summer 2000): 73–92.

Sinclair, Jim. 2007 Interview. *Archives of the Virtual Museum of Métis History and Culture*. Accessed December 14, 2011, www.metismuseum.ca/browse/index.php?id=796.

Sprague, D.N. *Canada and the Métis, 1869–1885*. Waterloo, ON: Wilfrid Laurier University Press, 1988.

Teillet, Jean. "Federal and Provincial Crown Obligations to the Métis." In *Métis–Crown Relations: Rights, Identity, Jurisdiction, and Governance*, edited by F. Wilson and M. Mallet, 71–93. Toronto: Irwin Law, 2008.

————. "Metis Law Summary." 2010. Accessed 6 February 2011, www.pstlaw.ca.

Weinstein, John. *Quiet Revolution West: The Rebirth of Métis Nationalism*. Calgary: Fifth House, 2007.

Woodcock, George. *Gabriel Dumont: The Metis Chief and his Lost World*. Edmonton: Hurtig Publishers, 2003 [1976].

Government Relations and Métis People | 12

Using Interest Group Strategies

CHRISTOPHER ADAMS

THIS CHAPTER provides an overview of how organizations representing Métis people seek to influence their provincial government
counterparts on rights-related issues, such as land and harvesting rights,
as well as to promote social and economic policies and programs of benefit
to Métis people. It does this by focussing on the notion of lobbying, which
may be defined as "the practice of communicating...with government officials to try to influence a government decision"[1] and, as this chapter
demonstrates, sometimes these communications are supported by public
awareness campaigns, demonstrations and even court action. In Ontario
and western Canada, Métis people are represented by entities that are formally titled "Métis Nations," while in Quebec and further east they are
represented by a number of other organizations, some of which focus on
Métis issues while others advocate on behalf of non-status indigenous
peoples, including Métis.

Because the leaders of all of these entities state that they speak on
behalf of Métis people when interacting with their provincial and territorial government counterparts, organizations representing Métis people in

Canada will be studied here from an interest group perspective. "Interest groups" are defined by Canadian political scientist A. Paul Pross as "organizations whose members act together to influence public policy in order to promote their common interest."[2] By showing how the activity of Métis organizations sometimes resemble other interest groups such as the Canadian Federation of Agriculture, the Chambers of Commerce, or Greenpeace, my purpose is not to argue that this is the *only* characteristic of these entities. The aim here is to demonstrate what political scientist Kiera Ladner refers to as the "organizational capacity" of Aboriginal people when interacting with non-Aboriginal governments,[3] and to explore the means by which organizations achieve their ends by using tools and strategies that are used regularly by non-Aboriginal interest groups.[4]

Discussing Aboriginal issues in terms of interest group politics and organizational capacity may rankle some readers in light of the fact that Métis people and their leaders, especially those in western Canada, assert that they represent a Métis "nation" through Métis "governments." For example, the Métis Nation British Columbia (MNBC) operates with a vision statement that asserts that the MNBC "will build a proud, self-governing, sustainable Nation in recognition of Inherent Rights for our Métis citizens."[5] As such, Métis groups are comparable to major organizations representing other Aboriginal peoples, including the Assembly of First Nations (AFN) and the Inuit Tapiriit Kanatami (ITK), whose leaders are known to interact with government leaders by means of government-to-government relations rather than mere lobbying. This is especially demonstrated by their occasional attendance at "First Ministers" meetings.[6] Examples include special consultation sessions involving constitutional matters and the signing of formal agreements and accords such as the Charlottetown Accord in 1992, which included provisions for a "third order of government"; and the 2005 Kelowna Accord, which was to provide $5.085 billion over five years to improve the socio-economic living conditions of Aboriginal people across Canada. Although agreed to by Aboriginal and non-Aboriginal political leaders, both agreements failed, the former due to a lack of support in a national referendum and the latter due to a change in government.[7]

One means by which Métis organizations enter into government-to-government negotiations in their dealings with the provincial or federal government is to develop labour market agreements with the federal government. Across many parts of Canada, including Ontario and the western provinces, Human Resources and Skills Development Canada (HRSDC) has negotiated such agreements with Métis representatives to provide labour market development services through the organizations themselves.[8] In the case of Manitoba, for example, the Manitoba Metis Federation (MMF) signed the Métis Human Resources Development Agreement (MHRDA) with the Federal Government, which involves annual federal transfers to the MMF of $12.3 million.[9]

Another aspect that distinguishes Métis organizations from other interest groups such as professional societies, business associations, and labour unions, is that the major Métis groups tend to shape their internal organization in the form of government structures and often use government-like titles for their senior personnel. In Manitoba, for example, the MMF's directors are identified as "ministers" or "deputy ministers" and they oversee what are called "portfolios," such as "Natural Resources" or "Agriculture."[10] So too in British Columbia where the MNBC's board of directors are identified as ministers with specific cabinet-like titles and portfolios such as "Minister Responsible for Veterans and Child and Family Services."[11] It is not hard to see that this terminology aims to instil the idea that when these ministers advocate on behalf of Métis people, they do so in the form of government-to-government relations which are similar to those that exist between provinces and the federal government, or between two nation-states.

Based on the above discussion, one can see that many Métis organizations are not simply organizations that represent the interests of an industry, ethnic group, or occupational sector. They represent something more: a distinct people with specific rights. However, the reader will soon see that Métis organizations are often more similar to interest groups than they are to governments. In the Canadian federal system the reality is that the provincial and federal governments hold most of the country's constitutionally defined powers, such as defence, education and finance. This is not to say that Métis organizations will always lack major government-related powers, but currently Métis organizations more closely resemble interest groups with regard to three of the following four defining characteristics put forward by Pross and other political scientists:

1. *They operate with a formal structure that allows them to determine their objectives and strategies for achieving these objectives;*
2. *They are able to aggregate the interests of their members, and articulate these interests;*
3. *They operate within the political system in order to influence policy making; and*
4. *They seek to influence power without exercising government responsibility themselves.*[12]

While the fourth characteristic does not fit well with the Métis organizations we are studying here, the first three points do fit well in light of the earlier discussion. Métis groups operate with formal structures (characteristic #1), they aggregate the interests of their members and articulate their concerns (characteristic #2), and they operate within the political system to influence policy making (characteristic #3). One has only to look at their websites, annual reports (including annual budgets), member activities and their lobbying activities to see how the above listed characteristics are apparent. Because Métis organizations differ from interest groups in that they do seek to exercise government responsibilities, this chapter will focus on the first three characteristics of interest groups as they apply to the representative organizations of Métis people in Canada.

Before proceeding further, we can also look at Métis organizations from another group-related angle, that is, from a membership benefits approach. The American political scientist Robert Salisbury, in his influential article "An Exchange Theory of Interest Groups," categorizes membership benefits as follows: "material benefits," "solidary benefits"[13] and "expressive benefits."[14] "Material benefits" include goods and services that are offered to members by the organization itself (such as discounts or access to an organization's facilities). "Solidary benefits" are those that provide members with a sense of belonging or shared interests (such as social events and conventions). And, finally, "expressive benefits" occur when the organization advocates on behalf of its members. This might include public awareness campaigns, government lobbying, and court action. The importance of this third type of benefit leads political scientists Lisa Young and Joanna Everitt to simply label these organizations "advocacy groups."[15]

It is clear that Métis organizations across Canada offer their members benefits that belong to all three of the above-discussed categories, especially by the larger Métis Nation organizations located west of the Ontario–Quebec border.[16] This includes developing social programs and services for Métis people, such as employment-related assistance and housing programs, as is the case for the Métis in Alberta through the activities of the Métis Nation of Alberta (MNA).[17] Likewise, solidary benefits obtained for their members by Métis organizations include membership newsletters, promoting Friendship Centres, and hosting community gatherings, with a particular emphasis on those that help promote Métis history and identity. For example, the Métis Nation-Saskatchewan (MN-S) sponsors "Back to Batoche Days," which is a major annual event at the site where the Métis led an armed resistance to defend their land rights.[18] In 2010, Métis people from across Canada attended the festival in order to commemorate the 125th year of the battle.[19] While both material and solidary benefits are clearly important for the Métis communities at large, and of course for those who are direct recipients, of particular interest here is how Métis organizations are able to advocate on behalf of Métis people and influence public policy. Therefore, the focus

TABLE 12.1 *Métis population in Canada, by region*

Provinces in which MNC-*affiliated organizations operate*					Regions in which there are no MNC-*affiliated organizations*		
Ontario	Manitoba	Sask.	Alberta	B.C.	Territories	Atlantic	Quebec
73,605	71,805	48,115	85,500	59,445	4,515	18,805	27,980

Source: Statistics Canada, 2006 Census Data.

of the research as presented in this chapter will be on the expressive benefits of Métis organizations. That is, how the Métis organizations seek to articulate the interests of their members and advocate on their members' behalf when pressuring their provincial and territorial government counterparts on issues of importance.

The findings presented in this chapter are based on in-depth interviews conducted by the author with senior representatives of Métis organizations across all major regions in Canada. These include four of the five organizations that fall within the Métis National Council (MNC) umbrella, all of which are located in provinces west of the Ontario–Quebec boundary.[20] The MNC itself is not included in this study because its role is to serve as a national umbrella organization representing these provincial organizations and thus serves the interests of Métis people through these regional organizations, rather than doing so directly. Alongside the western organizations, representative organizations located in the Northwest Territories, as well as central and eastern Canada, are included in this study. While none of the latter groups are affiliated with the MNC, they are generally perceived to be legitimate representatives of Métis people by their federal or provincial government counterparts.[21] These include the Native Alliance of Quebec (Alliance Autochtone du Québec), NunatuKavut (previously titled the Labrador Métis Nation), Sou'West Nova Métis Council (which serves the Métis people of Nova Scotia), and the Northwest Territory Métis Nation.

In the 2006 Census, there were over 389,000 individuals who identified themselves as Métis. Table 12.1 reveals how the population numbers vary considerably across the different regions of Canada. The provinces in which MNC-affiliated organizations operate have the largest numbers of Métis people.

Results from the interviews that were conducted for this study, in addition to information derived through secondary sources, including annual reports and press releases, provide answers to the following questions:

- *What are the specific tools that Métis leaders use to articulate their concerns and influence government policy makers?*
- *To what extent do Métis leaders describe their relationship with their provincial or territorial government counterparts as "collaborative" rather than "confrontational"?*
- *Are there links between the types of lobbying tools used by Métis organizations and whether or not their government relations are marked by collaboration or confrontation?*

Before describing the tools and strategies that the leaders of Métis people use to influence government policy, it is important to identify the major issues that are raised by Métis leaders when interacting with their provincial government counterparts. In most parts of the country, Métis leaders report that these usually pertain to at least one of the following issue areas: the recognition of Métis people as a distinct Aboriginal people with specific rights, including harvesting rights; the right to self-government; the negotiation and recognition of treaties and land entitlement; and access to improved social services, including education, health, employment and family services.

Organizational Capacity

Discussions about "capacity development" often surround the study of organizations operating in the developing world where their services are desperately needed, but they arise also when studying organizations serving people living in urban centres where poverty is prevalent, as well as in underserviced rural and remote regions of Western developed societies. This includes Aboriginal organizations seeking to improve the socio-economic conditions of Canada's First Nations, Métis and Inuit people, either within traditional communities and reserves or in larger urban centres such as Saskatoon or Winnipeg.[22] The extent to which an organization has access to funds and other resources, such as skilled leaders and committed volunteers, influences which tactics or tools are available to influence government decision making. For example—and here we use examples independent of the specific topic of Aboriginal issues—it is doubtful that a small neighbourhood environmental group whose members are concerned about a local river's condition would be able to launch a major advertising campaign. In contrast, a major manufacturer that is seeking government incentives before relocating to a specific province would probably have the resources to launch a public awareness campaign. To paraphrase George Orwell, some interest groups are more equal than others—an assertion effectively proven by the economist Mancur Olson in his critique of those who believe that the prevalence of interest groups will reflect a healthy liberal democracy.[23] Small and well financed groups can often outperform the lobbying efforts of organizations with large membership numbers. Or, as Canadian political scientist Stephen Brooks asserts, "a successful influence strategy is usually quite expensive [and] business groups tend to be better able to pay for...expensive strategies than other groups."[24]

This brings us to ask: Why is "organizational capacity" important to Métis people? The term refers to elements within an organization that support its potential to successfully manage the various aspects of its existence[25] while "capacity development" refers to how organizations are able to "unleash, strengthen, create, adapt and maintain capacity over time."[26] In this context, building organizational capacity pertains to improving an organization's ability to serve the needs of its members or those it represents. This includes the three previously discussed benefit categories put forward by Robert Salisbury. Furthermore, organizations that have developed their capacity are able to withstand stressful conditions, including the departure of key individuals and funding crises.[27] Developing an organization's capacity also involves pursuits relating to financial stability, strategic planning, board leadership, management skills, human resources, voluntarism, office-related resources, accountability, stakeholder engagement and, of particular importance to the discussion in this chapter, government relations and influence.

Paul Pross describes organizations with well-developed capacity as "mature," "institutionalized" groups, and these tend to be treated by government and media as legitimate organizations whose leaders can speak on behalf of their members.[28] Examples include the Canadian Labour Congress for workers, the Canadian Bankers Association for the chartered banks, the Canadian Federation of Small Businesses for small business owners, and the Canadian Federation of Agriculture for farm producers. For our purposes here, what can be labelled the "capacity continuum" in interest groups politics (that is, the range spanning small fledgling groups and the well-established institutional groups), also appears to apply to the study of Aboriginal people and their organizations. For example, James Frideres, in his book regarding Aboriginal politics in Canada, asserts that "institutional groups...can bring extensive financial and human resources to bear on a variety of issues. Clearly, the Native organizations that are more institutional in nature have a greater chance of achieving their goals. Institutional organizations can choose from a variety of persuasive techniques, such as advertising, and can cultivate long-term formal and informal relations with government and senior civil servants."[29]

In many ways, and especially with regard to the Métis Nations in western Canada, the provincial Métis organizations exhibit the characteristics of well-institutionalized entities that participate in collaborative arrangements with their provincial government counterparts. They are also generally perceived to be the legitimate representatives of Métis people in their respective provinces. However, as will be discussed later regarding their need to use the courts to resolve some of their disputes, their government relations are often fraught with friction.

A focus of this chapter is to show whether or not Métis leaders are using the same tools typically identified by Canadian political scientists, such as Paul Pross, and by American researchers who have contributed to the group literature. Here we draw from published studies conducted in the United States by well-established writers in this field: Jeffrey Berry, Kay Schlozman and John Tierney, and Jack Walker,[30] all of whom used surveys to study how groups use different tools and tactics to influence government decision making. Collectively, these authors measured the extent to which each of the following tools are used: attending meetings with government personnel, making presentations to government boards and hearings, conducting public awareness campaigns, participating in marches and public demonstrations, using the court system and endorsing a particular candidate or party during an election.[31] Using results arising from in-depth interviews conducted with Métis leaders across Canada, we now turn to an examination of how the tools described by those who write about interest groups are used by the leading Métis organizations when seeking to influence government decision making in Canada.

Meetings with Government Officials and Presentations

Having some form of access to those who make government decisions is a basic necessity for any effective interest group. This includes access to those who set the direction for policy making, such as government ministers or the premier, as well as those who are responsible for implementing new programs and policies, such as deputy ministers and other senior officials.[32]

It is clear that leaders of each of the Métis organizations in all parts of the country see a positive value in working through the established mechanisms of government consultations, including attending meetings with government personnel and making use of government-sponsored forums by which they can advocate on behalf of Métis people. As shown in Table 12.2, all of the representatives of the eight leading organizations who were interviewed for this study reported they attend meetings with government officials, either with government ministers or senior bureaucrats. At the same time, all of the Métis organizations were reported to have put forward presentations to government boards and hearings.[33] As also shown in Table 12.2, there are many other tools used to varying degrees by the Métis organizations. These include advertising campaigns, contacting the media, participating in marches and demonstrations, endorsing candidates or political parties during an election and using the court system. Each of these is discussed in turn.

TABLE 12.2 *Tools used to influence government*

Government relations tools employed	Leading Metis Nation (MN) organizations (and MNC affiliation)		
	Total (N=8)	MNC-MNS (N=4)	Non-MNC-MNS (N=4)
Presentations to boards and hearings	100%	100%	100%
Meetings with government personnel	100%	100%	100%
Advertising campaigns	38%	50%	25%
Marches/Demonstrations	50%	50%	50%
Endorsing candidates or parties	38%	25%	50%
Using the courts	87%	100%	75%
Contacting journalists and media	63%	75%	50%

General Elections

Because elections inevitably produce changes in government, with some who were previously in government eventually retiring or finding themselves sitting on the opposition benches, and others not being elected at all, many well-established interest groups such as the Canadian

Federation of Agriculture and the Canadian Manufacturers Association are careful to convey a non-partisan image, or they hedge their bets by supporting *all* of the mainstream parties, as was once a tradition among business groups in their simultaneous support of both the Liberals and the Progressive Conservatives.[34] Robert Jackson and Doreen Jackson observe that with the exception of labour unions, which often support the NDP, most groups fear that being attached to a specific party "might close their routes of access to other parties, [and therefore] many groups declare non-partisanship."[35]

For this study, each senior Métis leader was asked whether or not his or her organization had recently endorsed a candidate or political party during a federal, provincial or territorial election. Most responded that they limit their electoral involvement to expressing Métis-related concerns to candidates and parties, and will sometimes circulate information among their members about the policies of candidates or parties on issues of importance to Métis people. Only three of the eight reported having formally endorsed a candidate or party in recent years. Various reasons are given for this practice: one representative reported that they supported the federal Liberals in a previous election due to the fate of the Kelowna Accord after the Conservatives gained power in 2006, two reported that their endorsements were tied to the records of their provincial governments on dealing with Métis issues, while one provincial group had endorsed a well-recognized figure from the Métis community who was running in the federal election. Worth noting is that one representative reported that the organization became involved in a provincial party leadership campaign when one of the contenders articulated views that were anathema to the interests of Métis people. While not endorsing any of the other leadership candidates, the organization disseminated information about each candidate's position on Métis issues to its members.

Using the Courts

Many political scientists have observed, some with alarm, that the Canadian court system has expanded its role within the Canadian polity, especially since the signing of the *Constitution Act, 1982*.[36] In regards to this phenomenon, or what some have called the "judicialization of Canadian politics"[37] many social issues regarding minority rights, as well those relating to Aboriginal treaty rights, land entitlement and harvesting rights, have since worked their way out of cabinet and legislative decision making and into the court system.[38] While the courts are a very powerful tool for resolving persistent and difficult problems, this option is usually seen by interest group leaders as something to use only when there is no other recourse—due largely to the costs and time involved with court processes. In particular, this has been the case with the MMF's land claims case, which was heard in provincial courts and then appealed to the Supreme Court.[39] Another major example is the assertion of Métis harvesting rights: although the Supreme Court's decision on *Powley* affirmed Métis harvesting rights (as discussed by authors Ian Peach and Jeremy Patzer in two other chapters in this volume), having these rights effectively recognized in many provinces continues to be very challenging and has resulted in what Métis spokespersons say is the waste of "millions of dollars" on court action.[40]

With the exception of only one organization's representative interviewed for this study, all of the senior Métis representatives affirmed their organization's recent involvement in court action to resolve disputes with their provincial or territorial governments.

Public Awareness Campaigns

Another way that interest groups can influence public policy—with fewer difficulties when compared with resorting to court action—is through promoting public awareness about issues of concern. William Stanbury, in his book on business–government relations in Canada, calls this strategy "transforming private interests into the public interest"; this strategy

seeks to justify a specific policy to the general public.[41] This involves
achieving any of the following objectives: getting an issue onto the public agenda, "setting the record straight" when the media are ill-informed
about the subject of discussion, competing for the public's attention when
facing an organized and opposing interest group (or groups), or when
seeking to shape the "language" on a contentious issue.[42] In many ways,
promoting public awareness, or shaping the way in which an issue is
framed, involves media relations. In their book *Business and Government in
Canada*, Wayne Taylor, Allan Warrack and Mark Baetz, explain why and
how this occurs: "Acting as an intermediary between government and its
public is the media, which channels public opinion to government decision makers and sells (whether wittingly or unwittingly) government
programs to the electorate. This has a profound effect on public policy....
Not only can the media report public opinion—it also has the potential to
filter, shape, and distort public opinion and government policy."[43]

Here we focus on three tools used by groups when they seek to influence issues on the public agenda. Specifically, we look at the extent to
which Métis organizations use any of the following: 1) communication
with journalists and the local media, 2) participation in public protests
and peaceful demonstrations, and 3) conducting advertising campaigns
on issues of importance. The results that are provided in Table 12.2 reveal
that not all of the Métis organizations surveyed here use these three tools.
Only five of the eight organizations have representatives who seek out
journalists to make their position known. However, those who do not
reported that they did not trust the local media to properly understand
the group's position or they had had experiences in which their concerns
were previously conveyed to the public in a non-positive manner. Only
four of eight organizations had been involved in a protest march or peaceful demonstration; the reason given for not participating in such activities
was that the organization preferred to work with government personnel
in ways they perceived to be more "positive" and collaborative in nature.
Finally, only three of the eight reported using advertising to promote

issues of importance to Métis people, with cost-related factors being the primary reason cited by those that did not use this avenue.

Communications Personnel

It is one thing to understand the value of having the general public on one's side, it is another thing to have the capacity to work toward this goal. Therefore, here we ask: To what extent do Métis organizations have the capacity raise the public's awareness of issues of importance, and thereby influence public policy makers? While there are many ways to measure capacity in this regard, here we focus on whether or not Métis organizations employ dedicated staff whose role it is to communicate the organization's message to members and the public at large. Of the representatives of the eight organizations interviewed for this study, one-half reported having at least one employee whose main responsibilities revolved around communications and public affairs,: three reported that this person was a full-time employee and one reported that the employee filled a two-thirds full-time position.

There were differences between the two major categories of Métis groups encompassed in this study. Three of the four Métis Nation organizations operating under the MNC umbrella reported that they employed a full-time communications person; the fourth organization's representative stated that this activity was shared by senior leaders in the organization according to the issue of concern(for example, education, housing, harvesting rights). In contrast, three of the four non-MNC affiliated organizations reported that they do not have an employee who is devoted to communications and public affairs and that they rely on other personnel to perform this role, including senior representatives, office assistants and, in one case, volunteers.

Collaboration vs. Confrontation

So far this chapter has examined the tools typically used by interest groups that seek to influence government decision making, and the extent to which these are used by Métis organizations in Canada. As a final part of the discussion, we explore the extent to which representatives of the Métis organizations report that their organization's relationship with their provincial or territorial government counterparts can be characterized as either mainly "collaborative" or "confrontational." Collaborative relations would be those that usually involve low-key activities such as meetings between group leaders and government representatives wherein the group leaders are recognized as the legitimate voice of their members. Under such conditions, the objectives of the group leaders and government personnel are often shared.

With regard to Métis people in particular, meetings between Métis and government representatives occur in which agreements are reached that improve Métis employment and housing conditions. Examples include the aforementioned agreements between the MNA and the provincial government of Alberta that addressed housing and employment services, and, in Manitoba, there has been a longstanding relationship between the MMF and the Manitoba Housing and Renewal Corporation (MHRC), with agreements reaching back to the 1970s to promote access to affordable housing for Métis people.[44]

At the other end of the government relations spectrum are those relationships that tend to be marked by court action or confrontational activities designed to force a resistant government to redirect existing policies.[45] For example, President Chris Montague of NunatuKavut in Newfoundland and Labrador, led in December 2010 a Métis demonstration to stop the development of the Muskrat Falls hydroelectric dam project. In his address to the group of approximately 100 protestors, President Montague declared that the "premier of Newfoundland has said that she will not deal with us until we have a land claim. Well, what I say to her is that she won't have a project until she deals with us."[46] As already discussed in this chapter, many Métis organizations continue to participate in a wide range of activities, and almost all of the groups are involved in court action.

Many of the Métis representatives interviewed characterized their relationship with government as being collaborative, while others reported that the nature of their relations is dependent on the policy area being discussed. Where confrontations exist, it was reported that these usually revolve around ongoing activities that aim to force governments to recognize Métis harvesting rights (even after the *Powley* decision). Animosity between Metis and specific premiers and cabinet ministers was cited in Newfoundland and Labrador and in Quebec, while some leaders reported refusals by provincial government representatives to meet with Métis representatives to resolve a particular issue.

There appears to be a distinct difference in how government relations are described by Métis representatives among the MNC-affiliated groups and by those representing the non-MNC-affiliated groups included in this study. Representatives among all the MNC-affiliated Métis Nations in this study reported their relations as being either collaborative (2 of 4) or at least partly collaborative (2 of 4), especially when dealing with challenges related to the provision of social services and housing. At the same time, only one of the four groups outside the MNC's orbit reported having collaborative dealings with its provincial government counterpart.

As discussed previously, well-established interest groups can usually be expected to enjoy good government relations. Such groups tend to assert their influence by presenting their concerns at board meetings and hearings and in meetings with government personnel. In other words, they lobby governments in a non-disruptive fashion and seek to communicate their message to the government without causing the decision makers to feel they are, to use a colloquialism, "losing face." Stephen Brooks writes that at the other end of the spectrum "groups that are not well-established within a policy community are more likely to rely on confrontation, media campaigns, and other public strategies to get policy makers to pay attention and respond to the interests they represent."[47] In contrast to what one would expect if referring to the interest group literature, there is no clear pattern of this nature when examining Métis organizations. As shown in Table 12.3, representatives of seven of the eight organizations reported being involved in court actions, regardless of having collaborative or confrontational relations with their government, and one of the three organizations that reported having collaborative relations with their government also reported being involved in marches or demonstrations.

The only difference that appears to differentiate the groups according to the reported character of their government relations is that all of those who reported having confrontational relations with their government had also become directly involved in the electoral process by endorsing a candidate or party, while at the same time none of these groups was involved in conducting advertising campaigns on issues of importance to their members. This leads to the finding that Métis organizations tend to use the electoral process when lacking resources and access to consultative channels within government. On this point, there is agreement between the findings presented here and the interest group literature.

TABLE 12.3 *Government relations and strategies*

Government relations tools employed	Nature of relations between Métis and provincial/territorial government counterparts (8 organizations)		
	Confrontational (N=3)	*Mixed (N=2)*	*Collaborative (N=3)*
Presentations to boards and hearings	100%	100%	100%
Meetings with government personnel	100%	100%	100%
Advertising campaigns	0%	100%	33%
Marches/Demonstrations	66%	50%	33%
Endorsing candidates or parties	100%	0%	33%
Using the courts	100%	100%	66%
Contacting journalists and media	33%	100%	66%

Conclusion

Using an interest group approach for studying Métis organizations helps to provide insights into how leaders in Métis communities across Canada seek to influence public policy and government decision making. Indeed, the findings shown here reveal that each of the tools typically identified by those who study interest groups is used to varying degrees by Métis organizations. With regard to how Métis leaders characterize their relations with their provincial or territorial government counterparts, these are said to be collaborative or at least partly collaborative (depending on which issue is being dealt with at the time) by those Métis groups that are affiliated with the MNC. However, representatives of Métis people who live outside the MNC's orbit tend to characterize their government relations as being confrontational.

There is no single strategy that works for all of the organizations or is effective for all issues. As one representative said, the tools the organization selects to lobby on issues of importance to Métis people and the nature of the organization's relations with their provincial government counterparts are "dependent on the issue at hand." This echoes the response of a Washington-based lobbyist who, when asked what he thought was the most effective way to lobby government, reported, "Well, it depends on what the issue is."[48]

Author's Note

The author would like to thank Grant Anderson and Lynn Berthelette of the Louis Riel Institute for their initial sponsorship of this study. This chapter's findings are those of the author's and do not necessarily reflect those of the Louis Riel Institute. Thanks are also due to Shannon Sampert, who is with the Department of Politics at University of Winnipeg, and Ed Bruning, at the I.H. Asper School of Business at the University of Manitoba, for their insightful comments on earlier drafts of this chapter. Also, thanks are due to my colleague Curtis Brown who assisted with the research and writing on capacity building. Brendan Wild was very helpful in cleaning up errors in style, while all errors in this chapter remain the author's.

Notes

1. Lisa Young and Joanna Everitt, *Advocacy Groups* (Vancouver: University of British Columbia Press, 2004).

2. The terms "interest group" and "pressure group" can be used interchangeably. See, for example, Stephen Brooks, *Canadian Democracy: An Introduction* (Don Mills, ON: Oxford University Press, 2007), 317; Jacquetta Newman and A. Brian Tanguay, "Crashing the Party: The Politics of Interest Groups and Social Movements," in *Citizen Politics: Research and Theory in Canadian Political Behaviour*, ed. Joanna Everitt and Brenda O'Neill (Toronto: Oxford University Press, 2002), 388.

3. Kiera L. Ladner, "*Aysaka'paykinit:* Contesting the Rope Around the Nations' Neck," in *Group Politics and Social Movements in Canada*, ed. Miriam Smith (Peterborough, ON: Broadview Press, 2008), 233.

4. Joe Sawchuk, "Anthropology and Canadian Native Political Organizations," in *Anthropology, Public Policy and Native Peoples in Canada*, ed. Noel Dyck and James Waldram (Montreal: McGill-Queen's University Press, 1995).·

5. Métis Nation British Columbia, "MNBC Overview,"2009, accessed 20 July 2010, http://mnbc.ca/overview.asp.

6. Assembly of First Nations, "AFN National Chief Phil Fontaine Meets with Federal-Provincial-Territorial Ministers to Discuss First Ministers Meeting," press release, 27 June 2005, accessed 28 August 2010, www.afn.ca/article.asp?id=1546; Inuit Tapiriit Kanatami, "National Inuit Leader Rallies Support for First Ministers' Meeting," press release, 5 August 2010, accessed 27 August 2010, www.itk.ca/media-centre/media-releases/national-inuit-leader-rallies-support-first-ministers%E2%80%99-meeting.

7. Eric Mintz, Livianna Tossutti and Christopher Dunn, *Democracy, Diversity, and Good Government: An Introduction to Politics in Canada* (Toronto: Pearson Canada, 2011), 327–28, 341.

8. Human Resources and Skills Development Canada, "Agreement Details," 2009, accessed 12 February 2011, www8.hrsdc.gc.ca/edrha-ahrda/Ententes-Agreements-eng.asp?SORT=0&Region=7&AgreementType=4.

9. Manitoba Metis Federation. 2010. "Community Housing Managers of Manitoba," accessed 30 September 2010, www.mmf.mb.ca/index.php?option=com_content&view=article&id=77&Itemid=2.

10. Manitoba Metis Federation. 2010. "Metis Human Resource Development and Training," accessed 12 February 2011, www.mmf.mb.ca/index. php?option=com_content&view=article&id=78&Itemid=41.

11. Métis Nation British Columbia. 2009. "MNBC Overview," accessed 20 July 2010, http://mnbc.ca/overview.asp.

12. A. Paul Pross, "Pressure Groups: Adaptive Instruments of Political Communication," in *Pressure Group Behaviour in Canadian Politics*, ed. Paul Pross (Toronto: McGraw-Hill Ryerson, 1975), 2–3; Robert J. Jackson and Doreen Jackson, *Politics in Canada*, 7th ed. (Toronto: Pearson Canada, 2009), 469.

13. The term in its original is used here. Since this article was published, many now use the term "solidarity" in place of "solidary." See for example, Newman and Tanguay, "Crashing the Party: The Politics of Interest Groups and Social Movements," 393.

14. Robert H. Salisbury, "An Exchange Theory of Interest Groups," *Midwest Journal of Political Science* 13, no. 1 (February 1969): 1–32.

15. Young and Everitt, *Advocacy Groups*.

16. This chapter focusses only on Métis organizations that represent Métis people within defined regions, provinces or territories.

17. Métis Nation of Alberta, "Métis Nation of Alberta," 2007, accessed 12 July 2010, www.albertametis.com/MNAHome/MNA2.aspx.

18. Métis Nation-Saskatchewan, "Back to Batoche: History," accessed 29 January 2012, www.backtobatoche.org/history.php.

19. Bob Weber, "Tears of Past Turn to Hope for Future, Events Mark Anniversary of 1885 Métis Resistance," *Winnipeg Free Press*, 24 July 2010, accessed 15 August 2010, www.winnipegfreepress.com/canada/tears-of-past-turn-to-hope-for-future-99162749.html.

20. Métis Nation Council, "Métis Governments," 2010, accessed 12 July 2010, www.metisnation.ca/gov/index.html.

21. Government of Canada, "Métis Card," 2010, accessed 12 July 2010, www.aboriginalcanada.gc.ca/acp/site.nsf/eng/ao35055.html.

22. John Loxley and Fred Wien, "Urban Aboriginal Economic Development," in *Not Strangers in These Parts: Urban Aboriginal Peoples*, ed. David Newhouse and Evelyn Peters (Ottawa: Policy Research Initiative, 2003); David Newhouse, "The Invisible Infrastructure: Urban Aboriginal Institutions and Organizations" in the same volume.

23. Mancur Olson, *The Logic of Collective Action: Public Goods and the Theory of Groups* (Cambridge, MA: Harvard University Press, 1965).

24. Brooks, *Canadian Democracy*, 336.

25. Gary Craig, "Community Capacity Building: Something Old, Something New...?" *Critical Social Policy* 27, no. 3 (2007): 335–59; Ismet Fanany, Rebecca Fanany and Sue Kenny, "The Meaning of Capacity Building in Indonesia," *Community Development Journal* 46, no. 1 (2009): 1, accessed 12 February 2011, http://cdj. oxfordjournals.org/content/early/2009/08/12/cdj.bsp044.full.

26. Organisation for Economic Co-operation and Development, *The Challenge of Capacity Development: Working Towards Good Practice* (Paris: OECD, 2006).

27. Organisation for Economic Co-operation and Development, *The Challenge of Capacity Development*; J.D. Straussman, "An Essay on the Meaning(s) of 'Capacity Building'—With an Application to Serbia," *International Journal of Public Administration* 30, no. 10 (2007): 1103–20.

28. A. Paul Pross, "Pressure Groups: Talking Chameleons," in *Canadian Politics in the 1990s*, ed. Michael Whittington and Glen Williams (Toronto: Methuen, 1995), 261–63.

29. James S. Frideres. *Native People in Canada: Contemporary Conflicts*, 2nd ed., (Scarborough, ON: Prentice Hall Canada, 1983), 254.

30. Jeffrey M. Berry, *Lobbying for the People: The Political Behavior of Public Interest Groups* (Princeton, NJ: Princeton University Press, 1977); Kay Lehman Schlozman and John T. Tierney, *Organized Interests and American Democracy* (New York: Harper and Row, 1986); Jack L. Walker, *Mobilizing Interest Groups in America* (Ann Arbor: University of Michigan Press, 1991).

31. Frank Baumgartner and Beth Leech, *Basic Interests: The Importance of Groups in Politics and in Political Science* (Princeton, NJ: Princeton University Press, 1998), 152.

32. William T. Stanbury, *Business-Government Relations in Canada: Influencing Public Policy* (Scarborough, ON: Nelson Canada, 1993), 143.

33. The question is as follows: "When seeking to influence government decisions and public policy that pertain to issues of importance to your people, in the past two years has your organization done any of the following...."

34. Stephen Brooks and Andrew Stritch, *Business and Government in Canada* (Scarborough, ON: Prentice Hall Canada, 1991), 274–80; Reginald Whitaker, *The Government Party: Organizing and Financing the Liberal Party of Canada 1930–58* (Toronto: University of Toronto Press, 1977).

35. Jackson and Jackson, *Politics in Canada*, 484.

36. F.L. Morton and Rainer Knopff, *The Charter Revolution and the Court Party* (Peterborough, ON: Broadview Press, 2000).

37. Raymond Bazowski, "The Judicialization of Canadian Politics," in *Canadian Politics*, 4th ed., ed. James Bickerton and Alain-G. Gagnon (Peterborough, ON: Broadview Press, 2004).

38. Radha Jhappan, "Charter Politics and the Judiciary," in *Canadian Politics in the 21st Century*, ed. Michael Whittington and Glen Williams (Scarborough, ON: Nelson Thompson Learning, 2000); Miriam Smith, "Ghosts of the Judicial Committee of the Privy Council: Group Politics and Charter Litigation in Canadian Political Science," *Canadian Journal of Political Science* 35, no. 1 (March 2002).

39. *Grassroots News* [Staff], "Supreme Court of Canada Agrees to Hear M M F Land Claims Case," 15 February 2011, 1–3; Mia Rabson, "Top Court to Hear Historic Land-Claim Appeal," *Ottawa Citizen*, 11 February 2011, accessed 19 February 2011, www.ottawacitizen.com/news/court+hear+historic+Metis+land+claim+app eal/4258416/story.html.

40. *Edmonton Journal*, "Alberta Government Cowardly for Forcing Metis to Court: Lawyer," 24 June 2010.

41. Stanbury, *Business–Government Relations*, 427.

42. Robert Bragg, "Encountering Spin: The Evolution of Message Control," in *Mediating Canadian Politics*, ed. Shannon Sampert and Linda Trimble (Toronto: Pearson Canada, 2010); A. Paul Pross and Iain S. Stewart, "Breaking the Habit: Attentive Publics and Tobacco Regulation," in *How Ottawa Spends 1994–1995: Making Change*, ed. Susan Phillips (Ottawa: Carleton University Press, 1994); Stuart N. Soroka, *Agenda-Setting Dynamics in Canada* (Vancouver: University of British Columbia Press, 2002).

43. D. Wayne Taylor, Allan A. Warrack and Mark C. Baetz, *Business and Government in Canada: Partners for the Future* (Scarborough, ON: Prentice Hall Canada, 1999), 177.

44. Manitoba Metis Federation, "Community Housing Managers of Manitoba," accessed 30 September 2010, www.mmf.mb.ca/index.php?option=com_content& view=article&id=77&Itemid=2.

45. Hugh Faulkner, "Pressuring the Executive," in *Governing Under Pressure: The Special Interest Groups*, ed. Paul Pross (Toronto: Institute of Public Administration of Canada, 1982).

46. Newfoundland Broadcasting Company, "Labrador Métis Protest Muskrat Falls Project," 10 December 2010, accessed 19 February 2011, http://ntv.ca/video/?p=9417.

47. Brooks, *Canadian Democracy*, 336.

48. Baumgartner and Leech, *Basic Interests*, 147.

Bibliography

Assembly of First Nations. "AFN National Chief Phil Fontaine Meets with Federal-Provincial-Territorial Ministers to Discuss First Ministers Meeting." Press release, 27 June 2005. Accessed 28 August 2010. www.afn.ca/article.asp?id=1546.

Bazowski, Raymond. "The Judicialization of Canadian Politics." In *Canadian Politics*, 4th ed., edited by James Bickerton and Alain-G. Gagnon, 203-22. Peterborough, ON: Broadview Press, 2004.

Baumgartner, Frank, and Beth Leech. *Basic Interests: The Importance of Groups in Politics and in Political Science*. Princeton, NJ: Princeton University Press, 1998.

Berry, Jeffrey M. *Lobbying for the People: The Political Behavior of Public Interest Groups*. Princeton, NJ: Princeton University Press, 1977.

Bragg, Robert. "Encountering Spin: The Evolution of Message Control." In *Mediating Canadian Politics*, edited by Shannon Sampert and Linda Trimble, 243-55. Toronto: Pearson Canada, 2010.

Brooks, Stephen. *Canadian Democracy: An Introduction*. Don Mills, ON: Oxford University Press, 2007.

Brooks, Stephen, and Andrew Stritch. *Business and Government in Canada*. Scarborough, ON: Prentice Hall Canada, 1991.

Clatworthy, Stewart. "Indian Registration, Membership, and Population Change in First Nations Communities." In *Aboriginal Policy Research: Moving Forward, Making a Difference*. Vol. 5, edited by Jerry P. White, Susan Wingert and Dan Beavon, 99-120. Toronto: Thompson Educational Publishing, 2007.

Comeau, Pauline, and Aldo Santin. *The First Canadians: A Profile of Canada's Native People Today*. Toronto: James Lorimer & Company, 1990.

Craig, Gary. "Community Capacity Building: Something Old, Something New...?" *Critical Social Policy* 27, no. 3 (2007): 335-59.

Edmonton Journal. "Alberta Government Cowardly for Forcing Metis to Court: Lawyer," 24 June 2010.

Fanany, Ismet, Rebecca Fanany and Sue Kenny. "The Meaning of Capacity Building in Indonesia." *Community Development Journal* 46, no. 1 (2009): 89–103. http://cdj. oxfordjournals.org/content/early/2009/08/12/cdj.bsp044.full.

Faulkner, Hugh J. "Pressuring the Executive." In *Pressure Group Behaviour in Canadian Politics*, edited by Paul Pross, 240–53. Toronto: McGraw-Hill Ryerson, 1975.

Frideres, James S. *Native People in Canada: Contemporary Conflicts*, 2nd ed. Scarborough, ON: Prentice Hall Canada, 1983.

Government of Canada. "Métis Card," 2010. www.aboriginalcanada.gc.ca/acp/site.nsf/eng/a035055.html.

Grassroots News [Staff]. "Supreme Court of Canada Agrees to Hear M M F Land Claims Case," 15 February 2011.

Human Resources and Skills Development Canada. "Agreement Details," 2009. www8. hrsdc.gc.ca/edrha-ahrda/Ententes-Agreements-eng.asp?SORT=0&Region=7&Ag reementType=4.

Inuit Tapiriit Kanatami. "National Inuit Leader Rallies Support for First Ministers' Meeting." Press release, 5 August 2010. Accessed 27 August 2010. www.itk.ca/media-centre/media-releases/national-inuit-leader-rallies-support-first-ministers%E2%80%99-meeting.

Jackson, Robert J., and Doreen Jackson. *Politics in Canada*, 7th ed. Toronto: Pearson Canada, 2009.

Jhappan, Radha. "Charter Politics and the Judiciary." In *Canadian Politics in the 21st Century*, edited by Michael Whittington and Glen Williams, 255–90. Scarborough, ON: Nelson Thompson Learning, 2002.

Ladner, Kiera L. "*Aysaka'paykinit:* Contesting the Rope Around the Nations' Neck." In *Group Politics and Social Movements in Canada*, edited by Miriam Smith, 227–49. Peterborough, ON: Broadview Press, 2008.

Loxley, John, and Fred Wien. "Urban Aboriginal Economic Development." In *Not Strangers in These Parts: Urban Aboriginal Peoples*, edited by David Newhouse and Evelyn Peters, 217–42. Ottawa: Policy Research Initiative, 2003.

Manitoba Association of Friendship Centres. "Manitoba Association of Friendship Centres: History," n.d. Accessed 15 August 2010. www.mac.mb.ca/online/index. php?option=com_content&task=view&id=26&Itemid=40.

Manitoba Metis Federation. "Community Housing Managers of Manitoba," 2010. Accessed 30 September 2010. www.mmf.mb.ca/index.php?option=com_content& view=article&id=77&Itemid=2.

Manitoba Metis Federation. "Metis Human Resource Development and Training,"
2010. Accessed 12 February 2011. www.mmf.mb.ca/index.php?option=com_
content&view=article&id=78&Itemid=41.

Métis Nation British Columbia. "MNBC Overview," 2009. Accessed 20 July 2010. http://
mnbc.ca/overview.asp.

Métis Nation of Alberta. "Métis Nation of Alberta," 2007. Accessed 12 July 2010,
www.albertametis.com/MNAHome/MNA2.aspx.

Métis Nation Council. "Métis Governments," 2010. Accessed 12 July 2010, www.metis-
nation.ca/gov/index.html.

Métis Nation-Saskatchewan. "Back to Batoche: History," n.d. Accessed 29 January
2012. www.backtobatoche.org/history.php.

Mintz, Eric, Livianna Tossutti and Christopher Dunn. *Democracy, Diversity, and Good
Government: An Introduction to Politics in Canada.* Toronto: Pearson Canada, 2011.

Morton, F.L., and Rainer Knopff. *The Charter Revolution and the Court Party.*
Peterborough, ON: Broadview Press, 2000.

Newman, Jacquetta, and A. Brian Tanguay. "Crashing the Party: The Politics of Interest
Groups and Social Movements." In *Citizen Politics: Research and Theory in Canadian
Political Behaviour*, edited by Joanna Everitt and Brenda O'Neill, 387-412. Toronto:
Oxford University Press, 2002.

Newfoundland Broadcasting Company. "Labrador Métis Protest Muskrat Falls
Project," December 10, 2010. Accessed 19 February 2011. http://ntv.ca/
video/?p=9417.

Newhouse, David. "The Invisible Infrastructure: Urban Aboriginal Institutions and
Organizations." In *Not Strangers in These Parts: Urban Aboriginal Peoples*, edited by
David Newhouse and Evelyn Peters, 243-54. Ottawa: Policy Research Initiative,
2003.

Olson, Mancur. *The Logic of Collective Action: Public Goods and the Theory of Groups.*
Cambridge, MA: Harvard University Press, 1965.

Organisation for Economic Co-operation and Development. *The Challenge of Capacity
Development: Working Towards Good Practice.* Paris: OECD, 2006.

Pross, A. Paul. "Pressure Groups: Adaptive Instruments of Political Communication."
In *Pressure Group Behaviour in Canadian Politics*, edited by Paul Pross, 1-28.
Toronto: McGraw-Hill Ryerson, 1975.

———. "Pressure Groups: Talking Chameleons." In *Canadian Politics in the 1990s*,
edited by Michael Whittington and Glen Williams, 252-75. Toronto: Methuen,
1995.

Pross, A. Paul, and Iain S. Stewart. "Breaking the Habit: Attentive Publics and Tobacco Regulation." In *How Ottawa Spends 1994-1995: Making Change*, edited by Susan Phillips, 129-64. Ottawa: Carleton University Press, 1994.

Rabson, Mia. "Top Court to Hear Historic Land-Claim Appeal," *Ottawa Citizen*, 11 February 2011. Accessed 19 February 2011. www.ottawacitizen.com/news/court +hear+historic+Metis+land+claim+appeal/4258416/story.html.

Royal Commission on Aboriginal Peoples. *Final Report*. Vol. 4, *Perspectives and Realities*. Ottawa: Government of Canada, 2006. www.ainc-inac.gc.ca/ap/rrc-eng.asp.

Salisbury, Robert H. "An Exchange Theory of Interest Groups." *Midwest Journal of Political Science* 13, no. 1 (February 1969): 1-32.

Sawchuk, Joe. "Anthropology and Canadian Native Political Organizations." In *Anthropology, Public Policy and Native Peoples in Canada*, edited by Noel Dyck and James Waldram, 271-92. Montreal: McGill-Queen's University Press, 1995.

Schlozman, Kay Lehman, and John T. Tierney. *Organized Interests and American Democracy*. New York: Harper and Row, 1986.

Smith, Miriam. "Ghosts of the Judicial Committee of the Privy Council: Group Politics and Charter Litigation in Canadian Political Science." *Canadian Journal of Political Science* 35, no. 1 (March 2002): 3-29.

Soroka, Stuart N. *Agenda-Setting Dynamics in Canada*. Vancouver: University of British Columbia Press, 2002.

Stanbury, William. *Business-Government Relations in Canada: Influencing Public Policy*. Scarborough, ON: Nelson Canada, 1993.

Statistics Canada. "Aboriginal Peoples Survey (APS): Detailed Information for 2006," 2008. www.statcan.gc.ca/cgi-bin/imdb/p2SV.pl?Function=getSurvey&SDDS=325 0&lang=en&db=imdb&adm=8&dis=2.

Straussman, J.D. "An Essay on the Meaning(s) of 'Capacity Building'—With an Application to Serbia." *International Journal of Public Administration* 30, no. 10 (July 2010): 1103-20.

Taylor, D. Wayne, Allan A. Warrack and Mark C. Baetz. *Business and Government in Canada: Partners for the Future*. Scarborough, ON: Prentice Hall Canada, 1999.

Walker, Jack. *Mobilizing Interest Groups in America*. Ann Arbor: University of Michigan Press, 1991.

Weber, Bob. "Tears of Past Turn to Hope for Future, Events Mark Anniversary of 1885 Métis Resistance," *Winnipeg Free Press*, 24 July 2010. Accessed 15 August 2010. www.winnipegfreepress.com/canada/tears-of-past-turn-to-hope-for-future-99162749.html.

Whitaker, Reginald. *The Government Party: Organizing and Financing the Liberal Party of Canada 1930–58*. Toronto: University of Toronto Press, 1977.

Young, Lisa, and Joanna Everitt. *Advocacy Groups*. Vancouver: University of British Columbia Press, 2004.

Conclusion

"Métis" as a Unique, Diverse, Complex and
Contingent Concept in Canada

IAN PEACH, GREGG DAHL &
CHRISTOPHER ADAMS

IF EDITING THIS BOOK has taught us anything, it is that the group
of communities in Canada subsumed by the term "Métis" is remarkably
diverse. As peoples, the Métis presence predates the Canada of today with
its modern boundaries, and they developed communities on both sides
of today's Canada–United States border because that border was effectively meaningless, particularly to those who lived in the Prairie West.
We have focussed on the Métis in Canada because it is a rich reality to
explore: the Métis are unique within Canada and can, depending on the
definition one chooses, constitute a number of communities right across
the country, each with its own history of ethnogenesis, its own sense of
collective identity, its own relationship with settler society and its representative, the Crown, and its own arrangements (both historically and
in the modern era) for engaging in the processes of democratic discourse
as a community. Indeed, the very definition of "Métis," and even the use
of the term "Métis" as a collective label for these diverse communities,
is disputed in some quarters, as Gregg Dahl's chapter clearly indicates.
About the only elements that tie this diversity together are the facts of
the Métis peoples' distinctiveness—from other Indigenous peoples and

from the settlers—and their constitutional recognition as rights-bearing, Indigenous peoples in Canada.

As we noted in the introduction to this volume, the conceptual change that resulted in this blossoming of different conceptions of what it means to be "Métis" followed the Supreme Court of Canada's decision in *R. v. Powley*. As a consequence of the Court's careful defining of "Métis" in that decision, being Métis was no longer tied to a historical connection to the Red River colony, or even Rupert's Land; now, the miscegenation of Inuit and European peoples in Atlantic Canada could, at least potentially, be understood to be Métis. As we have noted, while earlier generations of Métis scholars tried to find Métis community within Indigenous diversity, the Supreme Court of Canada provided encouragement for exploring the diversity that exists within the Indigenous community legally labelled "Métis." Today, courts and governments, as well as Métis persons and their own political organizations, are reflecting on this new understanding of what it means to be Métis and adapting the law, public policy, and the processes of governance to take account of this newly articulated reality of diversity.

Yet, even in this process of adapting to diversity, the law and democratic politics still seek to establish unity, tangibility and certainty within the diverse set of identities known collectively as Métis. This effort results in further essentializing an understanding of what makes Métis people Métis and wipes away some of the diversity of the Métis reality, which Jeremy Patzer addresses in his chapter. As we noted in the introduction, the Manitoba Metis Federation's legal claims are a prime example of this wiping away of the diversity of the Métis. While the Federation claims that it should be the interlocutor or agent of the Manitoba Métis in negotiations with the federal and provincial governments to fulfill the constitutional obligations of the Crown toward Métis, the class of beneficiaries of these alleged obligations would not be congruent with the membership in the Manitoba Metis Federation: it is necessary neither that all members of the Federation be beneficiaries, nor that all beneficiaries be members of the Federation. The effort to assign rights to a class of persons called Métis essentializes what it means to be Métis in one way— as rights-bearers—while the need to create certainty and finality in negotiations essentializes what it means to be Métis in yet another way—as members of the Manitoba Metis Federation.

In contrast, the scholars in this collection have taken on the challenge of recognizing and revealing the diversity that exists within the category of peoples captured by the term "Métis" and were once presumed to be a uniform community. Indeed, within this collection are varied, and occasionally conflicting, understandings of what it is to be Métis, historically, sociologically, legally and politically. That different scholars have conflicting understandings is revealing of the complexity and diversity of the Métis reality and the imperfections of the social constructions of identity we use to situate individuals within communities.

In the end, it may be that all we can, or even should, say is that being Métis in Canada is the result of a confluence of factors that the individual and the community determine are relevant to creating a sense of community and giving the individual a feeling of belonging within that community. This condition, of course, is no different from that of any identity we choose to declare for ourselves. Self-identification is certainly at the root of identity. If the individuals themselves do not feel they are part of a community, or do not consider their identity as members of a community to be relevant to how they seek to be recognized by the world at large, they cannot be forced to define themselves as community members—at least not in a democratic society that believes in the fundamental right of individual self-determination.

Self-identification, however, cannot be the entirety of our understanding of identity. For one thing, history matters too. Métis communities and the concept of Métis identity arose out of particular sets of historical circumstances that led to the ethnogenesis of distinctive Métis communities. Admittedly, historical circumstances were different in different locations, and even now members of some Métis communities may not recognize members of other Métis communities as matching their understanding of what it means to be Métis. This, however, does not alter the fact that a sense of shared history, experienced as a community that is distinct from, and yet is in some ways in between, First Nations and settler communities, is a central component of what gives meaning to an individual's identity as a Métis person.

Of course, for an individual to be part of a community in a meaningful sense, the community, too, has to see the individual as a member; thus, community acceptance is the third essential element of identity, at least insofar as Métis identity has been imported into our legal order by the Supreme Court of Canada. This qualification, however, raises important questions: What is the community? And who has the right to speak for it—to accept or challenge an individual's claim to be a community member (and thus to share in the richness and benefits of community life). These questions are the stuff of politics and political representation, matters that several of our authors address. In this, too, diversity is a key theme of our collection. The political organizations that have grown up to represent Métis communities and assert claims on their behalf have, like the communities themselves, developed in and adapted to the particular historical circumstances and political necessities they have confronted. Métis political organizations, with the strategies they have deployed to advance their communities' interests, have had to meet the twin challenges of making space for the exercise of self-determination on behalf of these communities and ensuring effective participation in the democratic politics of the wider Canadian community. These are challenges that Pulla, Saunders, Dubois and Adams explore in Part Four of this volume. The ability of Métis communities to function cohesively, to be heard in the processes of democratic politics and to have their claims recognized by the broader society can be understood as a consequence of their political organizations' efficacy in meeting these twin challenges. Their effectiveness is also, however, a consequence of the degree of legitimacy and acceptance granted by the members of the Métis communities to the organizations claiming to represent them. Saunders and Dubois provide examples of how these processes of representation have played themselves out in different Métis political organizations and communities, while Adams looks specifically at how modern Métis organizations are participating in democratic politics today by situating their interests and claims in the broader political agenda of provincial and federal governments.

If identity, for both the individual and the community, arises out of the interaction, over time, of self-identification, a shared history and community acceptance, we are left to end where we began, with the emerging recognition of the diversity of identities that have been subsumed in the term "Métis" by law, politics and public policy. Creating a more complete and nuanced understanding of what is meant by the term "Métis," while acknowledging the contingency of all attempts to define the term, is a process that is arguably just beginning. We are grateful to our contributors for helping us explore and reveal the diversity and complexity that exists within the reality (or is that realities?) of the Métis in Canada as we seek to make our own contribution to this journey toward understanding. Perhaps, as further conceptual changes occur in the future, another collection of essays will be needed to provide another snapshot of the evolving reality of being Métis in Canada.

Contributors

CHRISTOPHER ADAMS serves as the rector of St. Paul's College at the University of Manitoba and was previously a vice president at Probe Research in Winnipeg and director of the firm's annual study titled *Indigenous Voices: The Probe Research Survey on Aboriginal People in Manitoba*. He holds a PHD from Carleton University and is the author of *Politics in Manitoba: Parties, Leaders and Voters*.

GLORIA JANE BELL conducts research on Native arts in Canada and the USA and is currently the web editor for the Aboriginal Curatorial Collective. During 2010–2011, she completed an internship at the Indian Arts Research Center (IARC) at the School for Advanced Research in Santa Fe, New Mexico, conducting collections management, registration and curatorial activities. She holds an MA from Carleton University in Native Studies and Art History. Gloria works with Aboriginal communities in Ontario and researches storytelling, self-determination and colonial art. She is Métis with ancestral ties to the Red River Settlement and James Bay. She writes about Aboriginal cultural heritage issues on her blog: http://metisramblings.blogspot.com.

GLEN CAMPBELL is professor emeritus of French at the University of Calgary. He has published various articles on the poetry of Louis Riel, was a volume editor of *The Collected Writings of Louis Riel/Les Écrits complets de Louis Riel* and has co-edited two other books of Riel's poems.

GREGG DAHL is a former senior policy analyst with the Office of the Federal Interlocutor for Métis and Non-Status Indians in the federal department of Indian Affairs and Northern Development. He holds an MA from the University of Ottawa in philosophy, an undergraduate degree in math and economics, and is a proud descendant of a Half-breed family that lived in St. Paul's parish in the Red River Settlement.

JANIQUE DUBOIS is a PHD candidate in Political Science at the University of Toronto. Originally from Saskatchewan, her current research investigates the way in which territorial dispersion and cultural diversity affect the ability of minorities to pursue self-government. Bridging empirical and theoretical approaches, her research examines the boundaries of political communities.

TOM FLANAGAN is professor of political science at the University of Calgary. He has published several books on Louis Riel and the Métis, and was deputy editor of the five-volume *The Collected Writings of Louis Riel/Les Écrits complets de Louis Riel*.

LIAM J. HAGGARTY is an assistant professor in the Department of Humanities at Mount Royal University in Calgary, where he teaches Indigenous Studies and Canadian History. His work on the Métis history of Northwest Saskatchewan is based on doctoral research conducted at the University of Saskatchewan supervised by Dr. Keith Carlson.

LAURA-LEE KEARNS is a proud member of the Métis Nation of Ontario, a mother of two and an assistant professor at the Faculty of Education at Saint Francis Xavier University. Dr. Kearns holds a PHD and a Bachelor of Education from the University of Toronto, an MA from the University of Western Ontario in philosophy, as well as an Honours BA from Trent University.

DARREN O'TOOLE is a descendant of the Métis of the White Horse Plains. He currently holds a SSHRC post-doctoral fellowship and is pursuing his research on the territorial dispossession of the Métis of Manitoba with the Canada Research Chair on the Aboriginal Land Question at the Université du Québec à Montréal. He recently completed his PHD dissertation in Political Science at the University of Ottawa on the political discourse of the Métis during the Resistance of 1869–1870 and holds an LLB from the Université de Moncton.

JEREMY PATZER is a PHD candidate in the Department of Sociology and Anthropology at Carleton University. With both Métis and German roots in rural Manitoba, his substantive research interest in Aboriginal rights has been driven by a theoretical interest in examining the concrete practices that we marry to idealized notions such as justice.

IAN PEACH has had an extensive career with federal, provincial and territorial governments, as well as in academia and the private sector. Mr. Peach has been involved in policy development and numerous intergovernmental negotiations on a broad range of issues and has published on Aboriginal law, Aboriginal policy issues, constitutional law and Canadian federalism.

SIOMONN P. PULLA is an expert in the field of Indigenous issues and participatory research methods. He is a university instructor and applied researcher with numerous publications, reviews and reports regarding various aspects of Aboriginal–settler relations, postcolonialism and collaborative anthropology. Dr. Pulla holds a PHD from Carleton University and is currently working as a Senior Research Associate for the Conference Board of Canada's Centre for the North.

KELLY L. SAUNDERS is an assistant professor and chair in the Department of Political Science at Brandon University where she teaches courses in Canadian Politics, Public Administration, and Public Policy. Her current research interests involve Métis politics and governance in Canada; she has written on Métis harvesting rights in

Manitoba, the imagery of Louis Riel in the shaping of Métis political identity, and the role of women in Métis governments.

Index

Page numbers in italics refer to photographs. Page numbers with a "t" refer to tables and diagrams.

Because the spelling and capitalization of "Métis," "Half-breed" and related terms vary across the essays, only "Métis" and "Half-breed" are used for consistency in the index. Information on spelling variations in specific essays is found under the subentry *terms*. For more information on the use of "Métis" in this collection, see page xv in the Introduction. For more information on terminology generally, see the main entries "Métis terminology and identity" and "Half-breed terminology and identity."

increase in late 20th c., xii

NWC promotion of, 112–13, 119, 162–66, 171–72, 379n26

Powley decision and, xiii–xiv

Red River region, 9, 94–95, 143–44, 153, 162–66, 379n26

See also historiography of Métis/ Half-breed identity

Native Alliance of Quebec, 468, 472–73t, 476–77, 479, 480t, 481

Native Council of Canada, 105, 352–53, 414, 417, 418–20

Natural Resources Transfer Agreements

Blais decision, 285–86, 296

case law before *Powley*, 281–85, 298–99

First Nations subsistence rights, 281–86, 298–99, 408

Métis not Indians under, 281–86, 298–99, 408

political organizations and advocacy, 350–51, 408–09

Powley decision, 285–86

provincial powers, 408–09

NCC. *See* Native Council of Canada

New Brunswick and Métis rights

case law after *Powley*, 296, 302n45

R. v. Acker, 302n45

R. v. Bernard, 302n45

R. v. Lavigne, 302n45

The New Peoples (Peterson and Brown), xi–xii, xxviin2, 147–48

Newfoundland and Labrador

duty to consult Aboriginal peoples, 290–91, 303n62, 322–23

government relations, 478–79

See also Labrador Métis Nation; *Labrador Métis Nation v. Newfoundland and Labrador*; NunatuKavut

NIB. *See* National Indian Brotherhood

Nichols, Robert, 366

Nicks, Trudy, 147

Niezen, Ronald, 317

Nisga'a people. See *Calder et al. v. Attorney-General of British Columbia*

Noah-Quet, Known as Rice the Interpreter (Winter), 31–32, 33

Nolin, Joseph, 250

Non-Profit Corporations Act (Saskatchewan), 434, 443–48

Non-Status Indians and Métis political organizations, 352–53, 357, 369–71, 412–15, 420, 439–40

Norquay, John, 134n52

Norris, Malcolm, 439, 455n24

North West Company

horizontal homogeneity, 168–69

Métis alignment with, 164–67, 171

nationalism promotion by, 112–13, 119, 143–44, 162–66, 171, 379n26

religion and, 170–71

social class and identity, 150, 151–52

social mobility, 168–69

term: *half-breed*, 51n32

wintering and intermarriage, 168

See also fur trade; voyageurs

North West Mounted Police

Métis sharing system and, 226–27

Riel's English poetry to, 268–72

Peterson, Jacqueline, xi–xii, xiii–xiv,
     xxviin2, 5–7, 46, 145–51, 153–55,
     163, 165–68, 176–77
  terms: *metis* and *Métis*, xiv–xv
Phillips, Ruth, 16
Pocklington, Thomas, 348–49
Pocock, John, 172, 175
political organizations, 355–97
  accountability, 371–74
  community-based structures, 357–
     60, 363–64
  co-operation of Non-Status and
     Métis, 352–53, 357, 369–71, 412–15,
     439–40
  elders councils, 364–65, 440, 442,
     456n32
  future challenges, 365–66, 442–43
  identity, citizenship, and
     membership, xviii–xix, 88n16,
     366–71
  identity formation and, 350
  membership benefits, 466–67
  Métis/Half-breed as terms, 126–27
  non-profit or societies status, 355,
     385n86
  overview, xxvi–xxviii, 339–42,
     353–57, 374–76
  preference for *Métis* as term, 136n61
  separation of Status Indians and
     Métis, 413–14, 426n59, 440
  traditional culture and, 348–49,
     354–56, 372, 374–75
  values, 355–56, 375
  women's roles, 360–61

  See also interest group politics;
     Métis National Council; self-
     government
political organizations, history, 397–431
  history (before 1870s), 347–49,
     374–75, 399–403, 435–36
  history (1870s–1880s), 257, 274n25,
     344–45, 346, 403–07, 436–37
  history (1890s–1930s), 349–56, 407–
     10
  history (1940s–1960s), 352–53, 409–
     13
  history (1970s–1990s), 352–53, 415–20
  overview, xxvi–xxviii, 397–98
  See also political organizations
population. *See* demographics
Potawatomis, 13, 24, 27, 31–32, 36, 38
Povinelli, Elizabeth, 321
Powley decision, 279–306
  ancestral connections, 357, 367, 369
  "authenticity" tests, 308–09, 321–22
  "common way of life," xiii, 286
  "community," xiii, 367–68
  "community" as regional, xiii,
     289–91, 292, 296–97
  cultural rights approach, 308–09,
     316–18, 326, 327–29
  definition of *Métis* by MNC, 357,
     366–68, 369–71
  "distinctive collective identity," xiii,
     286, 287–88
  diversity of identities and, xv, 492–
     95
  "effective European control," 109,
     286–87, 293, 315
  ethnogenesis and, xiii, 109

R. v. Powley. See Powley decision
R. v. Sparrow, 313, 316, 320
R. v. Van der Peet (distinctive culture
    test), 313-14, 315-16, 318
R. v. Willison, 288-89
racism and racial theories
    blood quantum and, 122-23, 127
    civilization markers, 27, 48
    golden age paradigm, 10-12, 15
    interracial marriages, 19, 22-23
    noble savage theory, 26, 28-29
    racial hierarchies (19th c.), 19, 21-23,
        26-27
    racial prejudice in Alberta, 126
    racial prejudice in Red River, 124-25
    as social constructs, 126, 127, 136n60,
        159-60
    See also colonialism; stigma and
        prejudice
Ray, Arthur, xiv, 171, 218
RCAP. See Royal Commission on
    Aboriginal Peoples
Re: Eskimos, 413
Rebellion of 1885, 120, 176
The Red River Expedition at Kakabeka
    Falls (Hopkins), 45
"Red River Redux" (Peterson), xiv
Red River Settlement and identity,
    143-203
    beadwork and floral embroidery,
        10-11
    clothing and, 13, 18-19
    community recognition and Powley,
        282, 293-94

comparison of Indian and Métis/
    Half-breed communities, 293-95,
    324-25, 400
comparison of Métis and Half-breed
    communities, 95-97, 111-13,
    156-61, 167-71, 175, 324-25
dispersal and dispossession after
    1870, 320
early history, 143-44
genealogical research, 178-79,
    188n133
geographic area of "community"
    after Powley, 296-97, 318-19
Great Lakes identity and, 6, 13, 145-
    46, 152-53, 155, 162-64, 167, 174
identity as fluid and multiple, 152,
    324-25
immigrants from Ontario, 124-25
kinship networks and, 178-79
land allotments, 404-05
languages and, 161, 162
location of Métis/Half-breed
    communities, 96
maternal ancestry, 97, 121, 156
nationalism and, xiv, 9, 94-95,
    111-13, 119-21, 143-44, 153, 162-66,
    175, 379n26
nationalism in late 20th c., xii
occupational niches and, xxiii, 148-
    49, 154-56, 167-68, 171-72, 174-75
"ordinary" Métis as political forces,
    348-49
organizational capacity, 146, 162-63
overview, xxiii-xxiv, 156-61
political connections to Sault Ste.
    Marie, 177

Tiedema, Olivine Bousquet, 60–61, 75–83

title, First Nations. *See* First Nations and Aboriginal rights

title, Métis. *See* Aboriginal rights of Métis

Tlingit tribal courts, 323–24

Tough, Frank, 172

traditional culture, indigenous
political organizations and, 348–49, 354–56, 372, 374–75
values (RCAP), 355–56
worldview and, 231–32
See also Cree (Rock/Woodland); Dene (Chipewyan); elders; kinship relations; Laws of the Buffalo Hunt; sharing systems, Métis/Cree/Dene, north Saskatchewan; subsistence

travel literature and identity, 14, 15–19, 21–27, 155

Travers, Karen J., 5–6

treaties
indigenous sharing systems and, 226
land titles and Aboriginal groups not under, 312–13, 315–16
modern-day treaties, 416
Robinson Treaty, xiv
scrip and, 425n39
terms: *Aboriginal rights* and *treaty rights*, 330n15

Treaty No. 3, 177, 385n85

Treaty No. 10, 226

Trent University, elders conferences, 62

Trigger, Bruce, 175–76

Union métisse Saint-Joseph, 406

Union nationale métisse Saint-Joseph du Manitoba, 187n113, 349, 382n54, 407

Van Kirk, Sylvia, 14–15, 97, 124–25

voyageurs
canoes, 39–40, 42, 44–46
clothing, 39–40, 41
as symbol, 55n89
travel literature representations, 14–27, 155
visual images (19th c.), 15–16, 38, 39–40, 41–48
See also fur trade; Hopkins, Frances Anne

Waldram, James, 235

Weinstein, John, 339, 345, 397, 419, 452

White Paper (1969), 414–15

"The Will" (Scofield), 93–94

Wilson, Jake, 452

Winter, George, xxi, 13, 28, 31–32, 33–35, 36, *37*, 38, 43

women
artists, restrictions on, 41
fur trade roles, 14–15, 97
Indian Act and discrimination, 61–62, 88n16, 370–71, 403, 417, 439–40
political organizations, 360–61, 418
values and political organizations, 355, 356
See also storytelling and female identity

Women of the Métis Nation, 360–61

Woodland Cree. *See* Cree (Rock/
Woodland)

Other Titles from The University of Alberta Press

From Rupert's Land to Canada

Essays in Honour of John E. Foster

THEODORE BINNEMA, GERHARD J. ENS AND

R.C. MACLEOD, *Editors*

294 pages | Maps, notes, index

978-0-88864-363-6 | $34.95 (X) paper

History/Native Studies

A Son of the Fur Trade

The Memoirs of Johnny Grant

JOHN FRANCIS GRANT

GERHARD J. ENS, *Editor*

468 pages | B&W photographs, maps, introduction, notes,

genealogical appendices, bibliography, index

978-0-88864-491-6 | $34.95 (S) paper

Native History/North American History/Postcolonial Studies

Massacre Street

PAUL ZITS

128 pages

Robert Kroetsch Series

978-0-88864-675-0 | $19.95 (T) paper

978-0-88864-714-6 | $15.99 (T) PDF

Poetry/Canadian Literature/Historiography